INTRODUCTION TO
COMPUTER SCIENCE
WITH APPLICATIONS IN PASCAL

INTRODUCTION TO
COMPUTER SCIENCE

WITH APPLICATIONS IN PASCAL

STEPHEN J. GARLAND

DARTMOUTH COLLEGE

THE SOUTHEAST BOOK COMPANY
ADDISON-WESLEY PUBLISHING COMPANY
Reading, Massachusetts ▪ Menlo Park, California
Don Mills, Ontario ▪ Wokingham, England ▪ Amsterdam
Sydney ▪ Singapore ▪ Tokyo ▪ Madrid ▪ Bogotá
Santiago ▪ San Juan

James T. DeWolf ■ Sponsoring Editor
Laura Skinger ■ Production Supervisor
Jerrold Moore ■ Production Editor
Vanessa Pineiro-Robbins ■ Text Designer
Joseph Vetere ■ Art Coordinator
George Nichols ■ Artist
Marshall Henrichs ■ Cover Designer
Hugh Crawford ■ Manufacturing Supervisor

臺內著字第　　　　　號

發 行 人：卓　　　鑫　　　淼
發 行 所：東　南　書　報　社
地　　址：台 北 市 博 愛 路 1 0 5 號
登 記 證：局 版 臺 業 字 第 0 7 2 5 號
總 經 銷：新 月 圖 書 股 份 有 限 公 司
地　　址：台北市重慶南路一段143號3樓
電　　話：三 三 一 七 八 五 六 號
郵政劃撥：0005981-1號卓劉慶弟帳號
印 刷 所：合 興 彩 色 印 刷 有 限 公 司
地　　址：西 園 路 2 段 261 巷 34 弄 44號
中 華 民 國 七 十 五 年　　月　　日 第　　版

Library of Congress Cataloging in Publication Data

Garland, Stephen J.
  Introduction to computing and computer science with
applications in Pascal.

  Includes index.
  1. Electronic data processing.   2. Electronic digital
computers—Programming.   3. Data structures (Computer
science)   5. Algorithms.   5. PASCAL (Computer program
language)   I. Title.
QA76.G315   1986   001.64   86-15879
ISBN 0-201-04398-X

ABCDEFGHIJ-DO-89876

To Ardie,

... for her price is far above rubies ...

PREFACE

A title does not always express accurately the contents of a book. Yet the title of this book, *Introduction to Computer Science with Applications in Pascal,* was chosen to describe clearly its coverage and to distinguish it from other books intended for use in a first course on computing.

COMPUTER SCIENCE

The key words in the title are *computer science.* They indicate a more disciplined approach to a more broadly conceived subject than do titles such as *Introduction to Computer Programming* or *Programming in Pascal.* Although many readers will become expert programmers, our purpose is not just to teach the use of a particular programming language. Computer science, or computer programming in its broadest sense, encompasses a collection of technical skills and scientific methodologies with which we can create high-quality computer-based solutions to real problems. Hence this book emphasizes three important aspects of computer science: programming methodology, algorithms, and data structures.

The words *with applications* in the title suggest that students can learn computer science best by doing it, that is, by tackling real problems in a disciplined manner. Applications of computing provide a context within which to develop and apply computing techniques. And a particular programming language, namely Pascal, serves as a tool for implementing computer-based solutions to particular problems.

This book is designed for use in a year-long introductory course in computer science. Its coverage is consistent with the curriculum recommendations of the Association for Computing Machinery, as described for the courses CS1 and CS2 in *Curriculum '78* and updated in the October 1984 and August 1985 issues of *Com-*

munications of the ACM. It is also suitable for use in a high school Advanced Placement course in computer science, as defined by The College Board.

GENERAL COVERAGE

Good programming methodology provides the means for writing high-quality programs economically and rapidly, whether those programs are for a programmer's own use or for use in a commercial application. Modern programming languages such as Pascal aid programmers by making a systematic approach to program construction easier through the use of modular programming, structured programming, and top-down design. Hence our aim is to teach not just how to program, but how to program well, by conveying a concern for structure, style, and discipline.

There is more to programming well, however, than just the disciplined use of a modern programming language. It also involves several other important skills: the selection of appropriate data structures to represent information processed by a program; the selection of understandable, verifiable, and flexible algorithms for processing information in preference to algorithms that simply minimize length of code or execution time; and the ability to analyze algorithms and data structures for speed, space, and clarity, and then to make reasonable trade-offs among these factors. In short, to program well requires being well versed in computer science.

In this book we develop particular algorithms and data structures, both to provide a set of general purpose tools for program construction and also to illustrate the general process of program and tool construction. We analyze these tools to determine which are appropriate in which contexts and to emphasize that good methodology involves choosing appropriate tools. And we use semiformal assertions of program correctness to establish and document the fact that these tools do what they should do.

Use of the programming language Pascal clarifies these topics and enables students to practice what they learn in a laboratory setting. Although *language-free* books attempt to deemphasize the details of programming, and thereby place greater emphasis on computer science itself, we have found that such books generally are confusing and force students to learn not one, but two languages: an informal language ("pidjin Pascal") used in the book to describe algorithms, and a real language (Pascal itself) that is covered in detail in a supplement to the textbook. Instead, we integrate the use of Pascal with coverage of computer science. Our aim, however, is no more limited to teaching Pascal than the aim of a mathematics instructor is limited to teaching algebraic notation.

Details of how a computer system actually executes a program, or of how a computer system is organized, are covered briefly at the end of the first few chapters. The intent of including this material in these chapters is to provide a working vocabulary with respect to the components of a computer system without dwelling on the subject. A more detailed discussion of topics such as assembly language or computer architecture is left to later courses and more advanced books.

COVERAGE BY CHAPTERS

This book is divided into two parts, corresponding roughly to the division of a year into semesters. The first part places greater emphasis on programming and programming methodology, the second on algorithms and data structures. But both parts address all these topics, the first raising issues that will be addressed in the second, and the second extending the techniques developed in the first.

Part I **Chapter 1** is a general introduction to the topics covered in the book. It serves primarily to set the tone for the detailed treatment that follows.

Chapters 2 and 3 cover the elementary details of programming in Pascal. They set a general pattern for approaching problems later in the book by presenting applications of computing, the types of data used in those applications, algorithms for manipulating data, and basic programming methodology intermixed with the details of programming in Pascal. In these two chapters, we demonstrate that even simple problems have many solutions, that some solutions are easier to communicate than others, and that it pays to analyze the merits of alternative solutions before choosing a particular solution.

These chapters also introduce important concepts such as programming style, program correctness, and the analysis of algorithms. Our purpose here is to recognize that students come into an introductory course with widely varying amounts of prior experience and backgrounds, and that almost all students need to fill in some gaps in their background. Instructors should encourage students to move through these chapters as rapidly as possible lest a year-long course degenerate into an all-too-typical course in programming followed by a let's-do-it-all-over-again, but-do-it-right-this-time course in computer science. Some of the material in these chapters can be deferred for use as a reference later in the course. These chapters also provide an opportunity for students to reflect on their prior experience and to consolidate their knowledge of programming.

Chapter 4 is concerned with the use of procedures and defined functions to structure solutions to problems. Students with some prior experience in Pascal may well start with this chapter. This chapter also introduces at an early stage the important concept of recursion, both to stress its importance and to avoid the impression that recursion is such an advanced topic that it can be approached only after much preparation. Students are not expected to master recursion completely by the end of the chapter, however. Later chapters lead to mastery through repeated exposure, so that students are comfortable with recursion when it finally plays an important role in the last two chapters.

Chapters 3 and 4 also address the issue of program correctness more extensively than do most introductory books, but without resorting to intimidating notations or formalisms. They stress the importance of documenting the action of loops using invariant assertions and the action of procedures using preconditions and postconditions. Such assertions appear in sample programs throughout the book.

Chapters 5 and 6 approach data structures from the standpoint of developing useful ways to represent information and useful packages of tools. Chapter 5 introduces nonnumeric applications of computing, which serve as a primary source of examples in the rest of the book. Chapter 6 introduces the composite data structures (array, record, and file) most commonly provided by programming languages.

Chapter 7 rounds out the first part of the book by showing how to define and apply new data types in a way that emphasizes how to use them rather than how to represent their objects. In particular, Chapter 7 develops variable-length strings as an abstract data type to remedy a particular defect in standard Pascal.

Part II   Chapter 8 begins the second part of the book with an in-depth study of the design and analysis of algorithms for searching and sorting. Many of the concerns raised in this chapter lead to the introduction of more advanced material in later chapters.

Chapter 9 returns briefly to the subject of programming methodology. It develops a large program using the algorithms and data structures presented in Chapter 8, providing a case study in the design and development of large programs.

Chapter 10 takes the book beyond its predominant emphasis on nonnumeric algorithms. It illustrates the special nature of numeric computations by developing and analyzing several algorithms to approximate zeroes of functions. It also shows how to apply numeric techniques to simulate deterministic and nondeterministic systems. Typical applications include simulating the motion of a space vehicle, the outcome of a game of chance, and lines of customers waiting for service. Some of the material in this chapter is appropriate only for students with a more advanced knowledge of mathematics.

Chapter 11 introduces linked data structures (and the pointer data type in Pascal). Here and later, data structures are treated as abstract data types; that is, their implementation emphasizes the operations available to manipulate data rather than its physical representation. Two particular data structures, the stack and the queue, are applied to problems from earlier in the book, namely, to translating recursive algorithms into iterative algorithms and to simulating a waiting line.

Chapter 12 covers binary trees and their application to searching and sorting. This chapter reveals the true power of recursion by using it to implement algorithms more clearly than is possible with iteration alone. The chapter concludes with a brief introduction to sets as a data type.

The final chapter, **Chapter 13,** applies the algorithms and data structures developed in the preceding two chapters to a variety of interesting problems. First it improves the treatment of multiple-precision arithmetic carried out with more primitive data structures in Chapter 7. Then it shows how to parse arithmetic expressions using recursion. This approach to parsing avoids the undue emphasis that many books place on notational devices such as postfix or Polish notation. Finally, it uses trees to solve some simple problems in artificial intelligence.

The entire book contains numerous sample programs, both to make its approach to algorithms and data structures more concrete and also to provide models of good programs.

SUPPLEMENTARY MATERIAL

The sample programs in this book are available on magnetic tape and floppy disks from the publisher. Where appropriate, these programs have been modified slightly to conform to the conventions of different implementations of Pascal.

A separate instructor's manual contains sample syllabi for courses based on this textbook. It also contains suggestions on how to teach each chapter and complete solutions to selected problems.

ACKNOWLEDGMENTS

I am indebted to the many students and colleagues at Dartmouth College whose reactions to preliminary versions of the material in this book helped me refine my ideas of how best to teach programming and computer science. Special thanks go to William Y. Arms, Larry R. Harris, and Thomas E. Kurtz, who taught the introductory computer science course with me in the days before there was a book. Robert L. (Scot) Drysdale, John G. Kemeny, Donald L. Kreider, J. Laurie Snell, and Sue H. Whitesides also offered valuable advice and criticism based upon classroom experience.

Sara Baase at San Diego State University and Zsuzsi Makkai helped greatly by their careful and critical reading of early versions of this material. Sara Baase, Gerard J. Berry of the Fairfax County Public Schools, Taylor Booth at the University of Connecticut, Frank Burke at Middlesex Community College, John Gannon at the University of Maryland, and Suzanne Golomb at the National Cathedral School provided useful comments regarding later versions.

Dartmouth College, The Hebrew University of Jerusalem, and Harvard University made writing a computer science text of this length possible by providing access to ample computer resources, both for word processing and for developing the programs in the book. I am indebted to Emily Bryant, Danny Braniss, and Nicholas Horton, the systems administrators at those three institutions, for making things work better when they were working well and for making them work at all when they weren't.

Finally, I would like to express my appreciation to the many people I worked with at Addison-Wesley: to William B. Gruener and Peter S. Gordon, who encouraged me to undertake a project of this magnitude; to James T. DeWolf, who encouraged me to finish it; to Jerry Moore, who shared my concern for details and strove to improve them; to Laura Skinger, who kept the production schedule moving; and to Carolyn Berry, Mark Dalton, Mary Dyer, Katherine Harutunian, Herb Nolan, Vanessa Piñeiro-Robbins, Marilee Sorotskin, Martha Stearns, Joe Vetere, Hugh Crawford, Marshall Henrichs, and George Nichols for their interest and help.

Cambridge, Mass.   S.J.G.

CONTENTS

INTRODUCTION TO
COMPUTER SCIENCE
WITH APPLICATIONS IN PASCAL

P   A   R   T

I

PECTS OF COMPUTING INTRODUC
PUTING INTRODUCTION: ASPECTS
ECTS OF COMPUTING INTRODUCTI
DUCTION: ASPECTS OF COMPUTIN
TS OF COMPUTING INTRODUCTION
PUTING INTRODUCTION: ASPECTS
DUCTION: ASPECTS OF COMPUTING
PECTS OF COMPUTING INTRODUCT

INTRODUCTION: ASPECTS OF COMPUTING

C H A P T E R

1

Computers are powerful tools that extend our mental abilities just as mechanical and other electrical tools extend our physical abilities. Hammers, automobiles, and telephones enhance the use of hands for construction, of feet for transportation, and of mouths and ears for communication. Likewise, computers enhance the use of minds to solve problems, to keep track of information, and to control complex phenomena.

Properly instructed, computers can be used to find a move in a game of chess, to transfer funds from one bank to another, to predict tomorrow's weather, or to guide a spacecraft. If we are to instruct computers properly, we must understand both how computers function and what we wish to do with them. Computers by themselves know nothing about games, accounting, meteorology, or orbital motion. Only when we understand these subjects well enough to delegate some specific, well-formulated task to a computer can it aid us in our efforts.

While our primary emphasis in this book is on learning how to use computers to solve problems, we must also learn something about several other fields (such as games, accounting, meteorology, and orbital motion) in order to understand what we wish to do before we set about using a computer to do it. We therefore begin each new topic with an analysis of a particular problem. Only then do we proceed to the development of a computer *program*, that is, of a set of instructions for a computer, to solve the problem.

As we proceed from the statement of each problem to its solution, we will encounter an increasingly familiar sequence of activities, all of which give shape to that solution. First, we analyze the problem, organizing our thoughts and specifying exactly what we wish to do. Next, we design an attack on the problem, that is, we formulate ways to represent information pertinent to the problem together with explicit actions to take in order to solve the problem. Then we construct a computer program and use it to produce a solution to the problem. However, before accepting any such "solution" as a real solution to the problem, we must analyze how well it accomplishes our aims. Thus the process of using a computer begins and ends with analysis, first of the problem and finally of its solution.

The development of a computer-based solution to a problem is actually an iterative task. Each of the activities just described may cause us to return to an earlier activity in order to correct a mistake or to make a significant improvement. Easy problems may require only a single pass through these activities; more complex problems may require many passes. But all problems, to be solved well, require us to perform all activities. Hence we begin our study by examining these activities in somewhat greater detail.

APPLICATIONS: STRUCTURING PROBLEMS

When faced with a potential application of computing, we must first decide exactly what we want to compute. Initial descriptions of applications tend to be vague and incomplete. Hence we must specify precisely what we wish to do before considering how to do it with a computer.

Once we have a specific task in mind, we may or may not decide to design a computer program to perform that task. For example, we may decide to design a program to solve an equation, to correct spelling mistakes in a text, or to display a graph. Alternatively, our analysis may lead us to decide to perform the task by hand rather than by computer.

At times our needs may warrant the design of a number of interrelated programs, together called a *system*, in order to perform several related tasks. For example, we may decide to design a text processing system to help us store, edit, reformat, and display textual information. Other examples of computer systems are database systems (used to manage information in businesses and other organizations), process control systems (used to monitor and regulate operations in a factory), spacecraft guidance systems, and election forecasting systems.

Having decided what we wish to compute, we must next determine what we can compute it from. Computers can process information, but they cannot create it. Hence, in order to design a computer program to solve a particular problem, we must identify relevant information available as *input* to that program together with a method that will produce *output* indicating a solution to the problem. (See Fig. 1.1.) It is important that we not equate the input supplied to a program with real information, or the output from a program with the final solution to a problem. Input and output are merely representations of information, and one of our jobs in designing a program is to specify the relation of that program's input and output to real information.

Suppose, for example, that we wish to write a program to compute the final grades for students enrolled in a computer science course. We must specify which grades are to be supplied as input to the program and in which order (for example,

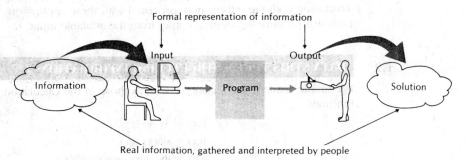

FIGURE 1.1 ■ Processing information with a computer program

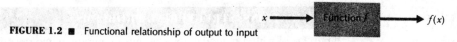

FIGURE 1.2 ■ Functional relationship of output to input

student by student or test by test); in this process, information is abstracted or simplified (for example, by using letter grades for tests as opposed to numeric grades for individual items on the tests). Likewise, we must specify what form the output of that program is to take (for example, a listing of all grades or of final grades alone, with students arranged in alphabetical order or in order of increasing final grades) and how that output is to be interpreted (for example, as the actual final grades or as tentative final grades that must be adjusted by the instructor's subjective evaluation of student performance).

In addition to specifying the information that is supplied to and produced by a program, we must specify a precise relation between the program's input and output. For example, we must specify the rules by which a final grade is to be computed as a weighted average of test scores. In mathematical terms, we describe a program's output as a *function* of its input, that is, as a quantity that varies as the input varies, but in a way that for each value of the input there is a corresponding unique value of the output. (See Fig. 1.2.) Using this terminology, we may describe many computer applications in terms of computing the values of particular functions, such as:

$$f(x) = 3x + 7,$$
$$f(x) = \sin(x),$$
$$f(n) = \text{the } n\text{th prime number,}$$
$$f(n) = \text{a list of the first } n \text{ primes,}$$
$$f(w) = \text{the first letter in the word } w,$$
$$f(L) = \text{the list } L \text{ of words arranged in alphabetic order,}$$
$$f(g, a, b) = \text{the graph of the function } g \text{ on the interval } (a, b),$$
$$f(t) = \text{the position of a rocket at time } t,$$
$$f(T) = \text{formatted version of text } T, \text{ and}$$
$$f(P, i) = \text{the output of computer program } P, \text{ given input } i.$$

In order to construct programs that will compute these and other functions, we must proceed from structuring our thoughts about proposed computer applications to structuring both the information associated with these applications and also the actions that produce the desired output from the available input.

1.2   DATA STRUCTURES: STRUCTURING INFORMATION

For simple numeric computations, such as those in the calculation of values of the functions

$$f(x) = 3x + 7,$$
$$f(x) = \sin(x), \text{ and}$$
$$f(n) = \text{the } n\text{th prime number,}$$

we must manipulate information that consists of single numeric quantities. For symbolic computations, such as those in the calculation of values of the function

$$f(w) = \text{the first letter in the word } w,$$

we must manipulate information consisting of characters, that is, of letters, digits, and other special symbols. These two types of data—numbers and characters—are *primitive data types* that can be manipulated directly by most computer systems and upon which we can base other, more elaborate structures.

When we need to manipulate more complex information, we can combine items from primitive data types to form structures belonging to a *composite data type*. For example, in programs that calculate the values of the functions

$$f(n) = \text{a list of the first } n \text{ prime numbers, and}$$

$$f(L) = \text{the list } L \text{ of words arranged in alphabetic order,}$$

we manipulate *lists* or *sequences* of numeric or character data. A word, in fact, is itself a sequence of characters, so that a list of words is a list of lists of characters.

Such a hierarchical organization is typical of the way we structure information for processing by a computer program. When we wish to process some particular information (such as a text T or a computer program P), we must decide how to represent that information using composite structures built up from primitive data types (such as a sequence of lines that are themselves sequences of characters). Though most computer systems cannot manipulate such composite structures directly, we can build programs that manipulate these structures by manipulating their elements.

In general, both primitive and composite data types have three components: (1) a collection of similar objects (such as numbers or words) that we call the elements of the data type; (2) a collection of operations (such as addition or capitalization) that we can use to manipulate these objects; and (3) a collection of relations (such as numeric or alphabetic order) that we can use to compare these objects.

1.3   ALGORITHMS: STRUCTURING ACTIONS

Just as we must structure the information to be processed by a computer program, we must also structure the actions used to process that information. What we need is something like a recipe for a meal or a blueprint for a building; recipes, blueprints, and plans for computer programs specify systematic methods for producing a desired result. An explicit method for carrying out a computation is known as an *algorithm*.

Algorithms constitute a primary topic in this book. We will examine many different algorithms for solving many different kinds of problems. Generally speaking, we can classify algorithms as direct, search, approximation, and problem-reduction algorithms.

DIRECT ALGORITHMS

Many problems have a straightforward, though often lengthy, solution. We can attack such problems head on by algorithms that proceed directly through a sequence of explicit steps toward a solution. For example, we can solve a quadratic equation by evaluating the quadratic formula, or we can compute the final grades in a course by computing weighted averages of exam and homework scores and then scaling the results. In such applications, what has to be done is often clear, and we might as well get on with it.

Direct algorithms are not necessarily simple algorithms because we may have to devote considerable thought to devising a direct attack on a problem. Although direct algorithms may proceed by brute force alone, we generally prefer to apply cleverness rather than force even in the most direct of computations.

SEARCH ALGORITHMS

When we cannot solve a problem directly, we often can search for a solution to that problem. Finding a number in a telephone book involves a search through a list of names; finding the prime factors of an integer involves a search for divisors of that integer. Search algorithms, like direct algorithms, may employ brute force by searching exhaustively for a solution (as if we begin on the first page of the telephone book and proceed serially to find a name). Or they may capitalize upon the nature of the information involved to search in a less time-consuming fashion (as if we open the telephone book to the approximate location for a name and proceed from there to find it). When all else fails, we may have to resort to a trial-and-error search for a solution to a problem. But even in this case, we prefer to search intelligently rather than haphazardly.

APPROXIMATION ALGORITHMS

Numeric problems in particular may be solved by *approximation*, that is, by algorithms that produce solutions as close as we desire to an exact solution to a problem. For example, it is impossible to compute an exact value of π, the ratio of the circumference of a circle to its diameter, since there are an infinite number of digits in the decimal representation for π. Nevertheless, we can compute π by generating as many of these digits as we desire. One technique for computing such an approximation to π is to inscribe a regular polygon inside a circle, with diameter $D = 1$, and then measure the perimeter P of this polygon; if the polygon has a large number of sides, P will be close to the circumference $C = \pi D = \pi$ of the circle.

PROBLEM-REDUCTION ALGORITHMS

As an alternative to searching for a solution to a problem, we can try to break the problem down into a number of simpler subproblems, solve each of these subproblems, and then assemble a solution to the original problem. Algorithms that reduce the solution of a problem to the solution of subproblems are often said to involve a *divide and conquer* approach.

For example, to arrange a list of names in alphabetical order, we can divide the list into two sublists, one containing the names that begin with the letters A through M and the other containing the names that begin with the letters N through Z. If we then arrange these two sublists in alphabetical order (possibly dividing them into still shorter sublists as we go), we can simply append the second list to the first to create an alphabetical list of all the names. Thus we have conquered the problem of alphabetizing a long list by dividing it into shorter lists that are easier to alphabetize and then combining the shorter lists.

1.4 PROGRAMMING: IMPLEMENTING SOLUTIONS TO PROBLEMS

After we have designed an algorithm and a representation for the information it manipulates, we are ready to produce a computer program that carries out, or *implements*, the algorithm. The activity that produces a working computer program is known as *programming* and consists of coding, testing, debugging, verification, optimization, and documentation subactivities.

CODING

Coding is the process of writing a computer program. It involves translating an English-language description of an algorithm into a particular computer language, such as Basic, Cobol, Fortran, Pascal, or PL/I. We must learn the details of one of these languages in order to perform this subactivity.

TESTING

All computer programs, once they have been coded, must be tested to determine whether they contain errors. Errors may occur for a variety of reasons: we may have prepared a faulty specification for the problem originally; we may have made errors in logic in the design of the algorithm; or we may have made a mistake in coding. A well-planned series of tests is needed to uncover these types of errors.

DEBUGGING

Debugging is the popular term for the process of removing errors from a program. The metaphor suggested is appealing to many programmers: tests are administered to a program to determine whether it is in good health (whether or not it works properly); if a test uncovers the symptom of a disease (if it uncovers an error), we must diagnose the *bug* responsible and treat the symptom (by removing the bug from program). Unfortunately, programmers too often use this metaphor to avoid or minimize their own responsibility. Bugs are not some sinister viruses that infect an otherwise healthy program. Rather they are the result of our own mistakes, and the process of debugging a program is actually the process of getting it to work the way we meant it to work in the first place.

VERIFICATION

Edsger Dijkstra has noted aptly that "testing can be used to show the presence of bugs, but never to show their absence." To assure ourselves that a program works in all cases we must examine what it does and how it does it, not just hunt for what it fails to do. The process of reasoning about a program and proving that it works is known as *verification*. Ideally, we should verify programs as we construct them, convincing ourselves along the way that the parts of a computer program do what they are supposed to do and that they fit together properly to accomplish the entire task.

OPTIMIZATION

Once a program is working, we may wish to make it work better. For example, we may want to speed it up or make it cost less to use. The efficiency of a program is of concern if we intend to use that program many times or if the algorithm it employs cannot succeed unless coded in an efficient fashion. When we plan to use a program only once or to solve a routine problem, it may not pay to invest a great deal of time and energy just to make the program more efficient. We need to optimize our use of the program, not the program itself, and that includes the time it takes us to develop the program.

Optimizing a computer program is somewhat like tuning the engine of an automobile. It can make the automobile run more efficiently, but only when the engine is running. Nor is it of much use if our transportation needs are for a train or an airplane instead of an automobile. Efficiency in programming, as in transportation, is best addressed first in the design stage, only minimally during construction, and once again when a working product can be measured and tuned.

DOCUMENTATION

Documentation describes what a program does, how it is to be used, how it was constructed, and why certain choices were made. It serves as a record of the programming process, reminding us at later stages in the development and use of a program of what we did earlier and what we still need to do. Good documentation helps us to develop, use, improve, and modify our programs. Good documentation also allows several people to cooperate in developing and using a single program. Consequently, effort spent on writing documentation is as important as effort spent coding a program.

1.5 ANALYSIS: EVALUATING SOLUTIONS

Analysis is necessary throughout the programming process. At first, analysis is aimed at producing a set of specifications and a design for a program. Analysis during program construction keeps that effort on track and aids in verifying the correctness of the program. Finally, analysis after the program has been completed helps in assessing the worth of the program.

Among the aspects of a program worth analyzing are the following:

- Generality. How broadly applicable is the program?
- Robustness. How well does it handle unexpected special cases?
- Maintainability. How easy is it to change or improve?
- Efficiency. How economically does it use computer resources?
- Practicality. Is the program worth using at all?

In general there are many ways to perform any given task. Finding a good way, or the best way, involves thinking about what we are doing and expending some effort along the way to identify and evaluate alternative ways of proceeding. Such thought pays off not only in the quality of the immediate product, but also in the development of good habits that enhance our ability to undertake more ambitious projects in the future.

1.6 SYSTEMS: HOW COMPUTERS WORK

Much of this book is devoted to the methodology of writing programs that instruct computers to perform a variety of useful tasks. What we must learn is similar to what someone traveling to a foreign country must learn in order to converse with its inhabitants. Language plays a central role in our preparation. But just as knowing something about a country, its language, and its customs helps us to speak intelligently when there, so knowing something about computers helps us to instruct them well. Hence, from time to time, we will consider briefly the ways that computer systems handle the programs we are learning to write.

COMPONENTS OF COMPUTER SYSTEMS

Computer systems contain two complementary types of components. The *hardware* in a computer system is a raw machine consisting of a variety of electromechanical devices. The *software* in a computer system is a collection of programs that enable the machine to perform useful work.

Most systems have at least the following hardware components:

- a *memory* in which programs or data may be stored;

■ a *processor* that is capable of interpreting the programs stored in the memory and performing the indicated computations;

■ an *input–output controller* that controls transmission of information to and from the memory; and

■ *peripherals* or *input–output devices* that enable the system to communicate with users and with other systems.

Some computer systems have little else. For example, the least expensive personal microcomputers have a memory, a processor that doubles as an input–output controller, a keyboard for input, and a video screen for output—all assembled in a single cabinet. (See Fig. 1.3.) The limitations of such systems are instructive to our understanding the purpose of the additional components in more sophisticated systems.

The processing power of a small personal computer is slowed severely by the slow speed of its keyboard. Even skilled typists can key in only ten or so characters per second, whereas computers can process thousands or millions of characters per second. In many personal computers the processor must stand idle while programs or data are entered from or sent to slow input–output devices. This idle time may be of little concern on personal computers, which are relatively inexpensive. For larger and more expensive systems idle time is wasted time and money.

More efficient use of processors is achieved by sophisticated computer systems in a variety of ways. Faster input–output devices, such as magnetic tapes and disks, speed program and data entry. Tapes and disks also save time for their users by providing permanent storage for data and programs, which then do not need to be retyped each time they are to be used. Small personal computers use flexible or *floppy* disks for such storage; larger computers use *hard* disks, which have a greater capacity and which transfer information at a higher rate.

Even high speed input–output devices are much slower than processors, so sophisticated systems keep their processors going while input–output is in progress. For example, in a *multiprogrammed* system processor time is allocated among several programs so that, whenever one of the programs is stalled (waiting for input–output), the processor can run another program. Special hardware in these systems allows

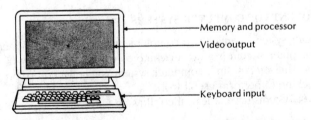

—Memory and processor

—Video output

—Keyboard input

FIGURE 1.3 ■ Typical configuration for personal computer

the processor to continue while input–output is in progress; when input–output terminates, this hardware *interrupts* the processor to notify it of that event. A control program then tells the computer system which action to take next.

When several operations can occur simultaneously in a computer system, special software is required to keep everything in order. This software is known as an *operating system*; it· manages the computer system, directing input and output and scheduling use of the processor. Operating systems for personal computers are fairly simple since only a few things can happen at once. Operating systems for larger computers are generally more ambitious. *Batch processing* systems accept programs and data from many users and schedule execution of those programs to make maximal use of the system. They generally service programs on a first-come first-served basis, and they acquire their input from, or direct it to, high-speed input–output devices such as magnetic tape; separate and cheaper facilities are used to transfer information back and forth between magnetic tape and slower, humanly accessible peripherals. *Time-sharing* systems service many users simultaneously; they speed input–output by transferring information to and from many input–output devices at once, and they generally apportion processing time among the users on a round-robin basis.

The memories of microcomputers are limited in size, so they can accommodate only small programs or small amounts of data. Larger computers have much larger memories but still must trade off the speed of memory against its size. In order to balance requirements for quick access and bulk storage, most computers have a moderately sized *primary memory*, which permits fast access to data (on the order of a microsecond or less per datum), together with several larger, slower (and hence less expensive) *secondary* memories, such as magnetic disks, which enable users to save long-term information in a directly accessible medium.

Larger primary and secondary memories allow time-sharing operating systems to serve many users. Programs can be moved back and forth between primary and secondary memory, enabling the system to devote processor time to more programs than can reside in primary memory simultaneously. By sharing a computer's time and memory, a time-sharing system gives each user the illusion of direct access to a smaller, slower computer that is under the complete control of that user.

Figure 1.4 shows a simplified configuration for a large computer facility. Users access the facility through a large number of terminals. Several communications computers accumulate messages from and distribute messages to these terminals, interrupting the main computer periodically to relay batches of messages. The main system has two processors that can access primary memory.

COMPUTER LANGUAGES

The hardware in most computer systems understands programs written in a very primitive language known as *machine language*. Unfortunately, trying to write a complicated program in machine language is about as easy as trying to express a

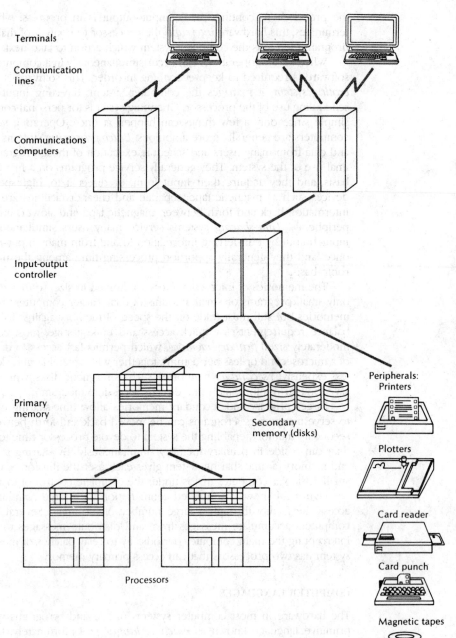

Terminals

Communication lines

Communications computers

Input-output controller

Primary memory

Secondary memory (disks)

Peripherals: Printers

Plotters

Card reader

Card punch

Processors

Magnetic tapes

FIGURE 1.4 ■ Typical configuration for a multiple-user computer system

complex idea in writing but using words with no more than two syllables—we can do it, but only laboriously, and few would care to read the result. Hence we prefer to write programs in *high-level* languages such as Pascal that have richer vocabularies than machine language.

A computer can understand a program written in Pascal only after it has been translated into machine language. Fortunately, computers can help us with that translation. A *compiler* is a piece of computer software that translates programs written in a high-level language into machine language. Alternatively, an *interpreter* is a piece of software that carries out the computations specified by programs written in a high-level language without bothering to translate those programs into machine language. Most computers come equipped with compilers or interpreters for languages such as Pascal, and we can simply use this software without ever learning how to communicate directly with the hardware of the computer.

Generally speaking, interpreters are more convenient to use during program development, when we do not wish to incur the overhead of retranslating a program into machine language each time we make a change. Compilers, on the other hand, are more useful when we have a working program because we do not then wish to incur the overhead of reinterpreting the program each time we use it. The efficiency gained by compiling a program can be particularly important when an algorithm calls for repetition of a certain computation many times.

High-level languages are the languages of choice for most applications of computing. By suppressing the details of how a particular machine operates, these languages allow us to express ourselves in terms related to the problems we wish to solve rather than in terms tied to the machine we intend to use. In this book we concentrate on learning to use high-level languages well. However, knowing whether we are using a language well sometimes involves an understanding of how a computer reacts to what we say.

HARDWARE VERSUS SOFTWARE

The boundary between what computers do through hardware and what they do through software is constantly shifting, owing to changes in technology. Many early computers required elaborate software simply to divide two decimal numbers. Today, pocket calculators evaluate complicated mathematical functions using hardware alone. In the future, compilers and interpreters may well move from software to hardware.

In an oversimplified and, perhaps, misleading view of computing, electrical engineers produce hardware and programmers produce software. In a more realistic view, people with a variety of backgrounds combine efforts to produce integrated systems. For this reason alone it is important for us to pay attention to what goes on inside a computer as we learn to program. Furthermore, our understanding of how a computer works complements our understanding of what we want a computer to do, and these two understandings together enable us to construct useful computer programs.

SUMMARY

Computer programs are sets of instructions designed to solve specific problems. The development of a computer program involves a sequence of activities:

- analysis of a potential application of computing;
- specification of a task or set of tasks to be carried out by a computer;
- design of a computer program that accomplishes these tasks, which involves
  1. designing data structures to represent information and
  2. designing algorithms to process information;
- implementation of the design, which involves
  1. coding a program in a particular programming language,
  2. debugging the program to correct mistakes,
  3. testing and verifying that the program is correct, and
  4. documenting the actions taken by the program and the ideas underlying its construction;
- analysis of the resulting computer program to determine
  1. how well it carries out its intended tasks and
  2. how easily it can be maintained or adapted to solve related problems.

Computer systems carry out the instructions in computer programs. They have the following components:

- hardware, which includes
  1. a processor for performing the computations specified by a program,
  2. a primary memory to hold programs and data for the processor,
  3. a secondary memory, consisting of disks or other bulk storage devices, for long-term storage of programs and data, and
  4. input–output devices for communicating with users and with other computer systems;
- software, which includes
  1. an operating system that manages the resources provided by the hardware,
  2. editors that enable users to enter programs and data,
  3. compilers and interpreters that process programs written in programming languages such as Pascal, and
  4. application programs that carry out specific tasks for users.

E ACTIONS PRIMITIVE ACTIONS
TIONS PRIMITIVE ACTIONS PRIM
PRIMITIVE ACTIONS PRIMITIVE
E ACTIONS PRIMITIVE ACTIONS P
ACTIONS PRIMITIVE ACTIONS PRIM
PRIMITIVE ACTIONS PRIMITIVE
E ACTIONS PRIMITIVE ACTIONS P
TIONS

PRIMITIVE ACTIONS

C H A P T E R

*O*ur primary aim in the next few chapters is to begin acquiring the skill in programming needed for our study of computer science. Hence we will be occupied initially with the details of programming rather more than in subsequent chapters, where we place greater emphasis on algorithms and data structures. But, even from the beginning, we are concerned with more than the details of programming in a particular language. We are also concerned with what we can accomplish through programming and how we can accomplish it easily and well.

In this chapter we concentrate on the most primitive actions that a computer can take. These actions enable a computer to receive information, to perform a simple calculation, and to display the result of that calculation. The art of programming is the art of organizing such simple actions so that they will perform a complicated task.

To get started, we will write several short programs that perform simple calculations. Since we can perform these computations easily with a pocket calculator, the practical significance of the programs in this chapter is limited to increasing our understanding of how calculators work. Yet, by learning how to write programs as simple as these, we prepare ourselves to write much more elaborate programs in the following chapters.

APPLICATIONS: POCKET CALCULATORS

A pocket calculator is a small-scale computer that is able to perform many of the same computations as its larger relatives, although more slowly and with a greater degree of assistance from its operator. Its chief advantages over a larger computer are its inexpensive price, portability, and ease of operation. Calculators also provide an excellent way to get acquainted with computers and programming. By writing programs to mimic the operation of various pocket calculators, we can learn how to use computer systems and programming languages to perform simple calculations, setting the stage for learning how to perform much more sophisticated computations.

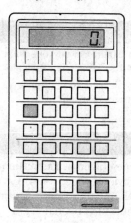

A typical pocket calculator has ten digit keys, function or operation keys, and a display for results. In order to mimic the operation of such a calculator we must specify explicitly both its design and an analogous design for a computer program. In particular we must specify the numbers that can be entered into the calculator and how we enter them into our program, the functions that can be performed by the calculator and how we specify them in our program, and the results that are to be displayed, both by the calculator and by our program.

In this chapter and Chapter 3, we concentrate on calculators that are designed to accomplish a single, fixed task. Our first program *add* will mimic the operation of a pocket calculator that performs a particularly simple task: it allows us to enter two numbers, whereupon it calculates and displays their sum. Such a program is admittedly of limited practical use, but then we are interested not so much in using it as we are in the details of its construction.

A calculator that adds two numbers is conceptually similar to a variety of special-purpose calculators, each of which accepts one or two numbers as input and then calculates a specific quantity such as a reciprocal, product, or difference. Not surprisingly, we can easily modify a program that mimics one calculator of this type in order to mimic others of the same type. We will write a program *circle* that prints interesting information about a circle with a given radius to demonstrate this.

Someone who is more interested in performing calculations than learning how to write programs would prefer to use a more elaborate calculator. At the very least, a calculator that can perform several different operations is better than a collection of special purpose calculators, each of which can perform only a single operation. In Chapters 5 and 7 we will write programs that mimic a multipurpose calculator. And, in Chapter 13, we will mimic an even more elaborate calculator, one that recognizes parentheses and begins to approach a small computer in its capabilities. Thus we will experience a phenomenon common in computing: even the simplest of applications suggests a host of questions and problems worthy of further study and consideration.

EXERCISES

1. Examine a small pocket calculator. Can it perform any operation other than addition, subtraction, multiplication, and division? If so, what other operations can it perform?
2. List several advantages of using a pocket calculator to perform a computation rather than doing it by hand. Are there any disadvantages? Explain.

2.2 DATA STRUCTURES: NUMBERS

Computers process two fundamental types of information: numbers and symbols. Programs that mimic pocket calculators obviously need to process numbers. Programs such as those in Chapter 5, which mimic multipurpose calculators, must also recognize and process symbols to determine which operations to perform.

In the first few chapters we concentrate on applications of computing that involve numeric data. Later, in Chapter 5, we address the use of symbolic data. We begin now by considering general aspects of numeric data, leaving specific details of how the programming language Pascal treats numbers until later in this chapter.

THE INTEGER DATA TYPE

Integers are the simplest type of numeric data. The objects in the integer data type are those signed whole numbers

$$\ldots, -3, -2, -1, 0, 1, 2, 3, \ldots$$

that fall within a *range* handled by a particular computer system. For example, some systems might handle integers that can be represented with ten or fewer decimal digits, while others might handle integers that fall within the range from -2^{31} to $+2^{31}$.

The usual arithmetic operations of addition, subtraction, and multiplication, when applied to integers, yield integer results. If the result of such an operation should lie outside the range handled by a given computer system, then an *overflow* is said to occur. Some systems report overflows as errors; others ignore overflows, using that integer within the computer's range closest to the true result as the value of the operation. When we develop programs to manipulate small enough integers we do not need to worry about overflows. However, when we develop programs to manipulate large integers, we should watch for overflows in order to guard against erroneous results.

The operation of division, unlike the other arithmetic operations, may yield a nonintegral result even when applied to integers. Hence many programming languages make a distinction between two operations of division: the normal one, which may yield a nonintegral result, and a special operation of integer division, which yields the greatest integer in a quotient.

The principal relations involving integers are equality and the natural order "less than." This order is a *discrete order* in which each integer n has an immediate successor $n + 1$ and an immediate predecessor $n - 1$. Other relations, such as "greater than or equal to," can be defined in terms of these two relations; for example, $m \geq n$ precisely when either $n < m$ or $n = m$.

THE REAL DATA TYPE

In mathematics there are several number systems that extend and encompass the integers. *Rational numbers*, of which $1/2$, $-2/3$, and $37/22$ are examples, can be represented as fractions whose numerators and denominators are integers. Rational numbers can also be represented in decimal notation, although an infinite number of digits may be required beyond the decimal point to represent some rational numbers exactly; for example,

$$1/2 = 0.5$$
$$-2/3 = -0.6666666\ldots$$
$$37/22 = 1.6818181\ldots$$

are decimal representations of rational numbers. In all cases, infinite decimal representations for rational numbers contain repetitive patterns of digits such as those shown.

Real numbers include the integers and rational numbers as well as such numbers as the square root of 2 and π. Real numbers are those numbers that can be represented in decimal notation, possibly with an infinite number of digits beyond the decimal point and possibly with no repetitive pattern among those digits; for example,

$$1/2 = 0.50000000\ldots$$
$$\sqrt{2} = 1.41421356\ldots$$
$$\pi = 3.14159265\ldots$$

are decimal representations of real numbers.

Complex numbers, of which $3 + \sqrt{-4}$ is an example, can be represented as a sum $x + iy$, where x and y are real numbers and i is the imaginary square root of -1; for example, $3 + \sqrt{-4} = 3 + 2i$. Complex numbers have important applications in mathematics, physics, and engineering, but real numbers suffice for most of our purposes in this book, and we will be primarily concerned with them.

Few computer systems treat rational and complex numbers as primitive data types. However, most do treat real numbers as a primitive data type, but define that type in a way that reflects the realities of those systems. Since computers are finite devices, it is impossible for them to represent all real numbers exactly. Hence the objects in the real data type are finite representations of real numbers, namely those real numbers that fall within a fixed *range* and that can be represented with a fixed *precision* or number of significant digits. Both the range and precision of the real data type are determined by the particular computer system being used.

The range of the real data type is typically quite large, enabling us to perform computations involving such diverse quantities as the number of seconds in a century, which is approximately $60 \times 60 \times 24 \times 365 \times 100$ or 3,153,600,000, or the diameter of a hydrogen molecule, which is approximately 0.00000000028 meters. When dealing with numbers that are extremely large or extremely small, it is convenient to employ scientific notations such as

$$3.1536 \times 10^9 \quad \text{or} \quad 2.8 \times 10^{-10}$$

that use a scaling factor, expressed as a power of 10, to dispense with leading and trailing zeroes. The permissible values for this scaling factor determine the range of the real data type. For example, some computer systems handle scaling factors of $10^{\pm 100}$, while others handle scaling factors of only $10^{\pm 38}$. In general, the range of the real data type consists of three subranges: a positive subrange, extending, for example, from 10^{-100} to 10^{+100}; the number zero by itself; and a negative subrange, extending, for example, from -10^{-100} to -10^{+100}.

As with integers, if the result of an arithmetic operation is so large as to lie outside the range of the real data type, then an *overflow* is said to occur. If the result of an arithmetic operation is very close to zero, say, 10^{-200}, then an *underflow* is said to occur. Some systems report underflows as errors; others ignore underflows, using zero as the value of the operation that produced the underflow.

The precision of the real data type measures the number of digits, exclusive of leading and trailing zeroes, that are available for decimal representations of real numbers. For example, some computer systems handle real numbers with a precision of ten decimal digits, while others handle more.

The usual arithmetic operations, when applied to real numbers, yield real numbers as results. The accuracy of these results is necessarily limited by the precision of the real data type. For example, the result of dividing 1 by 3 on a system with ten-digit precision will be 0.3333333333, which is not exactly $1/3$. In simple numeric calculations this loss of accuracy poses no problem. In other calculations particularly those in which the results of many minor inaccuracies can accumulate, some care must be taken to ensure the accuracy of the final result.

As for the integers, the principal relations involving real numbers are equality and the natural order "less than." But, unlike the natural order of the integers, that of the real numbers is not discrete. Between any two real numbers x and y lie many others [for example, $(x + y)/2$].

EXERCISES

1. Suppose that a computer system can handle integers whose decimal representations contain ten or fewer digits, and suppose that n is a 6-digit integer. How many digits can another integer m contain so that we can

   (a) add it to n,

   (b) subtract it from n,

   (c) multiply it by n, or

   (d) divide it into n,

   and be assured that the result will contain at most ten digits, that is, that no overflow will occur?

2. Suppose that a computer system can handle real numbers that can be represented as an integer with eight or fewer decimal digits times a scaling factor of $10^{\pm n}$, where n is a two-digit integer.

   (a) What is the largest positive real number that the system can handle?

   (b) What is the smallest nonzero positive real number that the system can handle?

   (c) How would that system represent the real numbers $1/2$, $\sqrt{2}$, and π?

3. Addition of ordinary real numbers is both commutative and associative; that is,

   $$x + y = y + x \quad \text{and} \quad x + (y + z) = (x + y) + z$$

   for any x, y, and z. Is addition of objects in the real data type commutative? Associative?

4. Multiplication of ordinary real numbers is also commutative and associative. Is multiplication of objects in the real data type commutative? Associative?

5. The ordering of the real numbers is not a discrete order. Is the ordering of the objects in the real data type a discrete order?

2.3   ALGORITHMS: SEQUENTIAL COMPUTATIONS

We need to use only the simplest of algorithms to instruct a general-purpose computer to perform the tasks of simple pocket calculators. These calculators produce their results by direct computation, and we can imitate them by a direct algorithm that takes three simple actions: obtain some input, perform a calculation, and display a result.

In general, we can perform any computation by taking some number of simple actions in a particular order. Although the total number of actions taken in any particular computation may be very large, most of these actions bear a strong resemblance to each other, and the number of different types of simple actions is relatively small. Likewise, the number of ways to compose simple actions is relatively small. When we seek to perform even the most elaborate computation, we find that we need only three ways of composing actions: we must be able to perform a sequence of actions one after the other, to choose from among several alternative actions, and to repeat an action many times. Hence, by learning a few fundamental actions and a few ways to compose them, we lay a foundation for all programming.

This section introduces us to programming by describing what we can do with sequences of simple actions. Chapter 3 addresses the issues of choice and repetition. As in Section 2.2, we concentrate first on features common to many programming languages, leaving specific details of how the programming language Pascal treats these features until later in the chapter.

TYPES OF PRIMITIVE ACTIONS

Most programming languages provide only three types of primitive or indivisible actions: obtaining a value as input, performing an operation (such as addition) to produce a new value, and displaying a value as output. Different languages may provide different means for obtaining input and displaying output, and they may differ as to exactly which operations are primitive (for example, some languages treat raising a number to a power as a primitive action and some do not). But they all start with essentially the same small stock of primitive actions, and they all provide us with enough ways to compose their primitive actions to undertake any computation that we may want to perform.

SEQUENTIAL COMPUTATIONS

On a single-function calculator a single operation produces the desired result. For slightly more complicated applications, such as computing the number of seconds in a year, we can evaluate an arithmetic expression:

$$\text{seconds in a year} = 60 \times 60 \times 24 \times 365 \quad \text{or} \quad 31{,}536{,}000.$$

Or we can perform a sequence of computations:

$$\text{seconds in a minute} = 60;$$
$$\text{seconds in an hour} = 60 \times \text{seconds in a minute} \quad \text{or} \quad 3{,}600;$$
$$\text{seconds in a day} = 24 \times \text{seconds in an hour} \quad \text{or} \quad 86{,}400;$$
$$\text{seconds in a year} = 365 \times \text{seconds in a day} \quad \text{or} \quad 31{,}536{,}000.$$

Computations of this sort are *sequential* in nature; their execution consists of a single, fixed sequence of primitive actions (in this case, multiplication).

FIGURE 2.1 ■ A step in a computation as a "black box"

In order to visualize the structure of an entire computation it is sometimes helpful to depict a single step in that computation as being performed by a *black box* that accomplishes some well-defined task. (See Fig. 2.1.) The size of the task, or the details of how it is performed by the black box, are unimportant so long as the job gets done—hence the name "black box," which suggests an opaque container, the inner workings of which are invisible to us.

With this convention, we can depict a sequential computation as a sequence of black boxes, each taking up the computation where the previous one leaves off. (See Fig. 2.2.)

Alternatively, we can describe a sequential computation by a list of the steps in that computation.

first step
second step
.
.
.
last step

PROBLEM DECOMPOSITION

To solve a wide variety of problems using a computer, it helps to vary the size of what we regard as a single step in a computation. At one extreme, we can regard the entire computation as a single, giant step. At the other extreme, we can force each step to consist of a single primitive action. Between these extremes we can regard certain intermediate actions as single steps, examining both their role in solving the entire problem and their reduction to even simpler actions. In this way we can decompose the solution of a difficult problem into the solution of a manageable number of simpler problems.

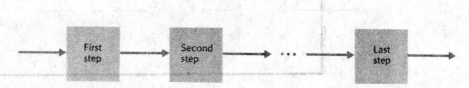

FIGURE 2.2 ■ Sequential computation as sequence of black boxes

Suppose, for example, that we want to raise a number x to the fourth power. If raising a number to a power is a primitive action, we can do this in a single step:

set result to x^4.

Otherwise, we can compute x^4 by a sequence of four steps:

set result to x,
multiply result by x,
multiply result by x, and
multiply result by x.

Or we can compute it by a sequence of three steps:

set result to x,
square result, and
square result,

in which we first square x to compute x^2 and then square x^2 to compute x^4. However we compute x^4, we can regard its computation as a new action available for use in other computations. For example, to compute x^5, we do not need to use a sequence of five primitive actions; instead, we can compute it using a sequence of two actions, one a primitive action and one defined in terms of simpler actions:

set result to x^4, and
multiply result by x.

Pictorially, we can depict an entire sequential computation as a single black box in order to suppress the details of how the computation is structured and to view the computation itself as a single action. (See Fig. 2.3.) This ability to vary the size of what we regard as a single step in a computation aids us considerably as we develop large programs. At each stage in the development of a program, we can concentrate on a particular task to be performed by breaking that task down into a number of smaller tasks, without getting bogged down prematurely in the details of how to perform those smaller tasks.

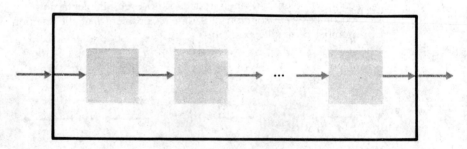

FIGURE 2.3 ■ Black box containing a sequential computation

Answer the questions in Exercises 1–3 for each of the following tasks:

(a) baking a cake;

(b) building a house;

(c) traveling to Yosemite National Park;

(d) converting a temperature from Fahrenheit to Celsius; and

(e) turning the minute hand on a clock ten minutes ahead.

1. How would you break the task down into a sequence of steps?

2. How could the individual steps in your answer to Exercise 1 be subdivided into smaller steps?

3. What larger tasks might contain this task as a single step?

2.4 PROGRAMMING: PROGRAMS AND STATEMENTS

Having considered data structures and algorithms in the abstract, we now apply them concretely by constructing programs to mimic the operations of pocket calculators. At this point we must come to grips with the details of a particular programming language, in our case the programming language Pascal. We will become familiar with the details of Pascal by writing several programs in that language and examining their construction. The first of these programs is *add*, which asks its user to enter two integers and which then calculates and displays their sum. In outline, this program consists of a sequence of three actions:

request that user enter two integers,
get two integers as input, and
display their sum.

When translated into Pascal, this outline takes the form of Pascal Sample 2.1.

This Pascal sample—and the others that follow—exhibits the text of a program and an illustration of its use. Within the illustration, input supplied by the user is shaded to distinguish it from output produced by the program. The actual format of the output may vary somewhat from one computer system to another. (See the discussion of output in Section 2.6.) The sample output in this book was produced using Berkeley Pascal and the UNIX operating system.†

Even before learning the details of Pascal, we can read the program *add* and get a general impression of how it works. The lines between the words **begin** and **end** appear to do the outlined work of getting two integers and displaying their sum, while other lines appear to provide descriptive information about the program. To

†UNIX is a trademark of Bell Laboratories.

■ **PASCAL SAMPLE 2.1**   The program *add*

{ calculates the sum of two integers }
program *add*(*input*, *output*);
var *a*, *b* : *integer*;
begin
    writeln('Enter two integers.');
    read(*a*, *b*);
    writeln;
    writeln('Their sum is ', *a+b*)
end.

SAMPLE USE OF *add*:

Enter two integers.
3 4

Their sum is   7

be able to write programs, rather than just skim them, we need to examine in detail just why *add* is constructed as it is; we need to learn what is required and what is optional in a program as well as how to spell and punctuate program components. This we now proceed to do.

THE GENERAL FORM OF A PROGRAM

All Pascal programs have a form similar to that of *add*. This form consists of four parts:

■   an optional *comment* describing the nature of the program;
■   a *header* naming the program and describing its environment;
■   a *declaration section* identifying the objects used by the program; and
■   a *program body* specifying what actions to take.

Additional comments may be inserted throughout the program.

Boldface words such as **program**, **var**, **begin**, and **end** are known as *keywords* and have fixed meanings in Pascal that determine the structure of a program. Italicized words such as *add*, *input*, and *output* are known as *identifiers*, since they identify objects used in a program or actions taken by the program. In this book and some computer systems special typefaces are used to distinguish keywords and identifiers from other words occurring in a program, but we need not worry about different typefaces when we enter a program into a computer. We can type a program using the ordinary characters on our keyboard and leave it to the computer system to determine which characters belong to which types of words.

COMMENTS

Programs convey information not only to computer systems, which must execute them, but also to people, who must read them. Thus most elements in a program do double duty, being addressed both to computer systems and to human readers. However, *comments* are addressed solely to the reader of a program. The first line

{ calculates the sum of two integers }

of *add* is such a comment. It describes the purpose of the program, but has no effect on the execution of the program.

If the execution of a program is unaffected by the presence or absence of comments, why do we include them? We do so to make a program more comprehensible to its readers, to provide an overview of a program or of one of its components, or to supply extra information about why a program was constructed as it was. We discuss the appropriate uses of comments more fully when we present the important topic of programming style in Section 2.8.

Comments in Pascal consist of characters enclosed by braces { and }; any character other than the right brace (}) may occur within a comment. For computer systems that do not provide braces, the symbol pairs (* and *) may be used instead to enclose comments. A comment may appear in a Pascal program anywhere that a space may occur (other than within a string constant, as described in Section 2.5, where it would be interpreted as part of that constant). As a matter of style we will place a comment only at the end of a line in a program or on a line by itself, never in the middle of a line.

HEADERS

Headers serve to identify programs. The second line

program *add*(*input, output*);

in *add* is the header for that program. It consists of the keyword **program**, the name of the program, and a specification of how this particular program interacts with external data. The header is terminated by a semicolon.

Until Chapter 6, all of our programs will interact with external data in a single fashion: they will obtain input from a standard source of input (such as from the user at a terminal), and they will display their output on a standard destination for output (such as on the same terminal). The identifiers *input* and *output* enclosed by parentheses in the header of a Pascal program indicate that the program obtains its input and generates its output in the standard fashion.

DECLARATIONS

Declarations identify and describe objects used by a program. The declarations in the program *add* consist of a single line

var *a*, *b* : *integer*;

which identifies *a* and *b* as variables capable of taking on integer values. Declarations can be quite extensive in programs that are larger or more sophisticated than *add*. Not only can they specify variables for use by a program (as in *add*), but they can also specify symbolic constants, data types, and computational procedures. Section 2.5 treats numeric variables and their declarations in greater detail; Chapters 5 and 6 treat declarations for other types of variables, while Chapter 4 treats declarations for computational procedures.

THE BODY OF A PROGRAM

The body of a program specifies the actions to be taken when the program is executed. It consists of a sequence of *statements*, separated by semicolons, between the keywords **begin** and **end**. These statements specify the individual steps in a computation. A period following the keyword **end** marks the physical end of a program.

In Pascal, statements may be either atomic statements (such as input or output statements) or composite statements, which are composed of other Pascal statements and mirror computational structures for sequence, choice, and repetition. The body of a Pascal program is a composite statement known as a *compound statement*; later we shall encounter other types of composite statements. When a compound statement is executed, its component statements are executed one by one in the order in which they occur. As we will see, a compound statement may be used in a Pascal program anywhere that a single statement can be used. Thus it serves to define a single composite action as a sequence of simpler actions.

SYNTAX AND SYNTAX DIAGRAMS

Although we can describe the form, or *syntax*, of Pascal programs using ordinary English, the resulting descriptions often suffer from wordiness, ambiguity, or both. We can minimize these undesirable characteristics by using precise graphic notations, known as *syntax diagrams*, to describe the rules governing the formation of elements in a Pascal program.

We will illustrate the use and utility of syntax diagrams with several examples. Consider first the syntax diagram shown in Fig. 2.4, which governs the construction of a comment in Pascal. To construct a legal comment, we may follow any sequence

comment

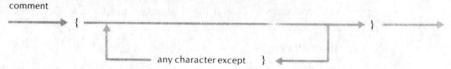

FIGURE 2.4 ■ Syntax diagram, comment

program

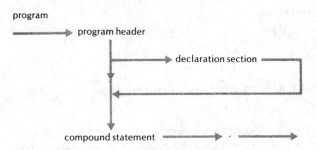

FIGURE 2.5 ■ Syntax diagram, program

of arrows from the entry on the left to the exit on the right, copying down the symbols described or encountered along the way. At any point where arrows go off in two or more directions, we may follow whichever arrow we wish to follow.

In the syntax diagram for a comment, it is impossible to avoid encountering the left brace ({) upon entry to the diagram; hence any legal comment must begin with that symbol. Likewise, since it is impossible to avoid encountering the right brace (}) upon exit from the diagram, any legal comment must end with that symbol. In between may come no characters at all (if we follow the arrow directly from the left brace to the right brace), or any number of characters, except a right brace (one for each time we choose to follow an arrow down and to the left).

The syntax diagram governing the construction of a Pascal program utilizes the same conventions to provide a more succinct description of a program than is possible in English. (See Fig. 2.5.) Phrases such as "program header," "declaration section," and "compound statement" refer to constructs, the formation of which is governed by other syntax diagrams. We present syntax diagrams for declaration sections in later chapters; those for program headers and compound statements are shown in Figs. 2.6 and 2.7.

In these diagrams and others that follow, special symbols (such as parentheses, commas, and semicolons) and boldface or italicized words (such as **begin**, **end**, and *read*) indicate symbols and words that are to be incorporated directly into the text of a Pascal program. Other words (such as "identifier" and "statement") refer to constructs the formation of which is governed by other syntax diagrams.

program header

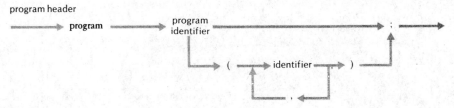

FIGURE 2.6 ■ Syntax diagram, program header

compound statement

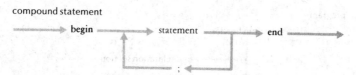

FIGURE 2.7 ■ Syntax diagram, compound statement

Our syntax diagrams say nothing about blank space in a Pascal program. In general, we can use spaces and carriage returns anywhere in the program in order to improve its readability. However, we must follow two rules:

■ Spaces and carriage returns must not appear inside keywords, identifiers, or numbers.

■ At least one space or carriage return must separate adjacent keywords and identifiers. Comments may occur anywhere that blank space may occur.

IDENTIFIERS AND KEYWORDS

Identifiers in Pascal programs serve to name various objects. In the syntax diagram for a program header, the identifier following the keyword **program** names the program, and the identifiers enclosed by parentheses (for now limited to the two special identifiers *input* and *output*) describe how the program interacts with external data.

All identifiers in a Pascal program, whether they are program identifiers, variable identifiers, or some other kind, consist of a sequence of letters and digits, the first character in the sequence being a letter. Thus the single syntax diagram in Fig. 2.8 serves to govern the formation of all identifiers. However, for the sake of clarity in syntax diagrams such as Fig. 2.6, we will describe the use of a particular identifier by referring, for example, to a "program identifier" rather than simply to an identifier. According to Fig. 2.8,

a	*x1*	*sum*	*lengthOfLongestWord*
b	*y2*	*distance*	*xtimes2plus3timesy*

identifier

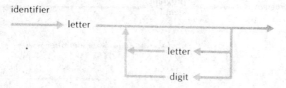

FIGURE 2.8 ■ Syntax diagram, identifier

TABLE 2.1 Predefined Identifiers in Pascal

abs	arctan	boolean	char	chr	cos
dispose	eof	eoln	exp	false	get
input	integer	ln	maxint	new	odd
ord	output	pack	page	pred	put
read	readln	real	reset	rewrite	round
sin	sqr	sqrt	succ	text	true
trunc	unpack	write	writeln		

are all legitimate identifiers, whereas

    2a   big# $total   minimum-size

are not. There is no limit on the length of an identifier, although some Pascal systems treat two identifiers with the same first eight characters as denoting the same object.

In general, we must declare the meaning of each identifier we use in a Pascal program. (See Section 2.5.) However, Pascal recognizes the identifiers listed in Table 2.1 without our having to declare them. We will discuss each of these special identifiers as needed. Some implementations of Pascal may predefine further identifiers.

Keywords such as **program**, **begin**, and **end** have a special meaning in Pascal and may not be used as identifiers. Table 2.2 contains a list of Pascal keywords. Some implementations of Pascal may define further keywords and prohibit their use as identifiers.

Uppercase and lowercase letters may be used interchangeably in identifiers and keywords without affecting the interpretation of those words. Thus

    sum   SUM   Sum   sUm

are equivalent identifiers, and

    begin   BEGIN   Begin   beGIn

are variant spellings of the same keyword. (Some implementations of Pascal do not follow this convention and regard *Sum* as a different identifier than *sum*.)

TABLE 2.2 Pascal Keywords

and	array	begin	case	const	div
do	downto	else	end	file	for
function	goto	if	in	label	mod
nil	not	of	or	packed	procedure
program	record	repeat	set	then	to
type	until	var	while	with	

statement

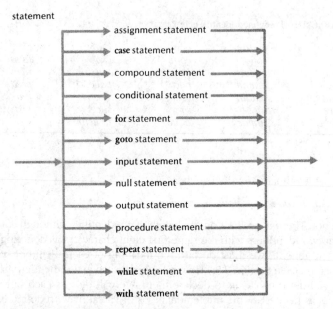

FIGURE 2.9 ■ Syntax diagram, statement

STATEMENTS

We conclude this section with a syntax diagram (Fig. 2.9) that describes the different statements provided by Pascal. In later sections and chapters we will consider each of these statements in detail.

EXERCISES

1. Execute the program *add* on your computer system.
2. What changes must be made to *add* in order to have it subtract one integer from another? To multiply them? To divide them? Try to make these changes and execute the resulting programs.
3. Using the following syntax diagram, which of the words in (a)–(k) can we construct?

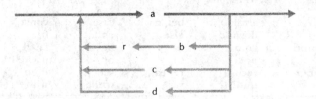

(a) a	(d) d	(g) adda	(j) acada
(b) aa	(e) ad	(h) abra	(k) acacaca
(c) aaa	(f) ada	(i) arba	(l) abracadabra

4. Modify the syntax diagrams in this section (Figs. 2.4–2.9) to

  (a) require that comments contain at least one character;

  (b) require the presence of the identifiers *input* and *output* in all program headers; and

  (c) require that all programs have a declaration section.

2.5 PROGRAMMING: CONSTANTS AND VARIABLES

In order for a program to manipulate data, it must have some means for referring to individual items of data. Constants and variables provide such means.

CONSTANTS

Constants in a program denote fixed items of data. Pascal provides constants that denote numbers and strings. (See Fig. 2.10.)

  Constants that denote integers are simply sequences of digits which may be preceded by a plus or minus sign. (See Figs. 2.11 and 2.12.) For example,

$$2 \qquad 4096 \qquad -32 \qquad +123456$$

are integer constants. Commas and spaces may not be used to separate groups of digits in constants in Pascal; thus a constant for the number of seconds in a year must

constant

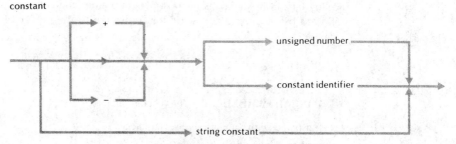

FIGURE 2.10 ■ Syntax diagram, constant (preliminary version)

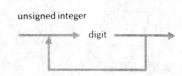

FIGURE 2.11 ■ Syntax diagram, unsigned integer

digit

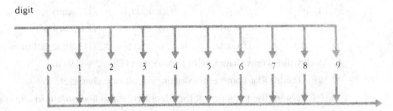

FIGURE 2.12 ■ Syntax diagram, digit

be written as 31536000, not as 31,536,000. The text of *add* contains no integer constants, although *add* expects integers as input and produces one as part of its output.

Pascal also provides a symbolic integer constant *maxint*, which denotes the largest integer that can be manipulated by the computer system being used. To find the value of this constant for a particular system, execute the program *intmax* in Pascal Sample 2.2.

Constants that denote real numbers may be expressed in *fixed-point* notation as a sequence of digits containing a decimal point; the digits may be preceded by a plus or minus sign. For example,

$$3.14159265 \qquad 0.00000000028 \qquad -1234.567$$

are fixed-point real constants. In Pascal, at least one digit must occur both before and after the decimal point in a real constant; thus neither .5 nor 5. are legal constants in Pascal.

Constants that denote real numbers may also be expressed in *floating-point* notation as an integer, or as a fixed-point real constant, followed by a scaling factor. Scaling factors in Pascal, as in most programming languages, consist of the letter **e** followed by an integer and stand for "times ten to the power of that integer." For example,

$$0.31459265e+1 \qquad 2.8e-10 \qquad -12.34567e2$$

PASCAL SAMPLE 2.2   The program *intmax*

{ displays the maximum value for an integer }

program *intmax*(*input, output*);
begin
    writeln(*maxint*)
end.

SAMPLE USE OF *intmax*:

2147483647

unsigned number

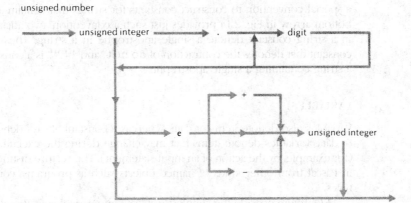

FIGURE 2.13 ■ Syntax diagram, unsigned number

are floating-point real constants with the same values as the fixed-point constants displayed above. As for integer constants, commas and spaces may not be used in real constants in Pascal. (See Fig. 2.13.)

The text of *add* contains no numeric constants, but it does contain two symbolic constants

```
'Enter two integers.'
```

and

```
'Their sum is '
```

that denote *strings* or sequences of characters. For the moment, we use strings solely to generate output from a program. Later, in Chapters 5 and 6, we will learn how to supply strings as input to a program and how to process those strings. As in *add*, string constants consist of sequences of characters surrounded by apostrophes. (See Fig. 2.14.) Since an apostrophe ordinarily marks the end of a string constant, we need

string constant

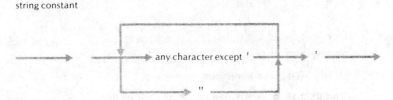

FIGURE 2.14 ■ Syntax diagram, string constant

a special convention to construct constants for strings that contain apostrophes. The bottom arrow in Fig. 2.14 provides just such a convention: two adjacent apostrophes in a string constant denote a single apostrophe in a string. Thus 'don''t' is a constant that denotes the contraction of do not, and '''' is a constant that denotes a string containing a single apostrophe.

VARIABLES

Variables also denote items of data. Whereas a constant always denotes a fixed item of data, variables denote items that may change during the execution of a program (for example, by the action of an input statement). This feature distinguishes variables in Pascal from other kinds of named objects such as programs, constants, and data types.

Identifiers provide the simplest way to name variables in Pascal. (See Fig. 2.15.) We will discuss other naming conventions for variables in Chapter 6, when we consider composite data types.

DECLARATIONS

Declarations describe the way in which we intend to use individual identifiers in a program. With one exception, Pascal requires us to declare all the identifiers we use in a program, that is, to describe them in the declaration section of that program. The only exception to this rule concerns the predefined identifiers in Table 2.1: if we are content with the meaning that Pascal assigns to these identifiers, we do not need to declare them ourselves. In a Pascal program we can declare both symbolic constants and variables. As shown in Fig. 2.16, declarations for symbolic constants precede those for variables.

Some programming languages do not require us to declare all identifiers; they determine the meaning of undeclared identifiers from their spelling or from the context in which they are used. While beginning or casual programmers may find it burdensome to declare all identifiers, experienced programmers find that declarations make their programs more reliable and more readable; at the very least, misspellings and other programming oversights are less likely to lead to undetected errors. Hence Pascal encourages good programming habits by requiring us to state our intentions.

variable

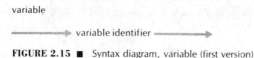

FIGURE 2.15 ■ Syntax diagram, variable (first version)

declaration section

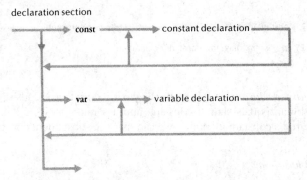

FIGURE 2.16 ■ Syntax diagram, declaration section (first version)

CONSTANT DECLARATIONS

In Pascal, as opposed to many other programming languages, we can declare identifiers to be symbolic constants. For example, in the program *circle* presented as Pascal Sample 2.3, we use a symbolic constant *pi* for π to avoid writing its decimal expansion twice. Unlike a variable named *pi*, a constant named *pi* cannot have its value changed in the course of executing a program.

PASCAL SAMPLE 2.3   The program *circle*

{ calculates circumference and area of a circle given its radius }

```
program circle(input, output);
const pi = 3.14159265;
var radius : real;
begin
    write('radius: ');
    read(radius);
    writeln;
    writeln('circumference = ', 2*pi*radius);
    writeln('area = ', pi*radius*radius)
end.
```

SAMPLE USE OF *circle*:

```
radius: 10

circumference =   6.28318530000000e+01
area =   3.14159265000000e+02
```

constant declaration

FIGURE 2.17 ■ Syntax diagram, constant declaration

Constant declarations follow the keyword **const** and consist of an identifier followed by an equals sign, a constant, and a semicolon. (See Fig. 2.17.) After we have declared a constant identifier, we can use it in subsequent constant declarations. For example,

>   **const** *largenumber* = 10000;
>   *smallnumber* = −*largenumber*;

declares *smallnumber* to be − 10000.

VARIABLE DECLARATIONS

We declare variables in Pascal programs in *variable declarations* following the keyword **var** in the declaration section. As shown by Fig. 2.18, a variable declaration consists of a list of variable names, separated by commas, followed by a colon and the name of a data type; a variable declaration is terminated by a semicolon. Among the types available in Pascal are the numeric types denoted by the predefined identifiers *real* and *integer*. We introduce other types in Chapters 5 and 6.

We can use as many variable declarations as we please to declare our variables. We can replace the single variable declaration

>   **var** *a*, *b* : *integer*;

in *add* by two separate declarations

>   **var** *a* : *integer*;
>   *b* : *integer*;

without changing the meaning of the program.

We can also transform the program *add*, which adds two integers, into a program that adds two real numbers simply by changing its declarations to

>   **var** *a*, *b* : *real*;

variable declaration

FIGURE 2.18 ■ Syntax diagram, variable declaration

Of course, we should also change the comment and the message printed to reflect the revised purpose of the program, but it is a simple matter to change the type of a variable from *integer* to *real*. As we introduce more data types, we will be able to declare variables to range over data of these types in the same manner.

Variable declarations provide natural locations in a Pascal program for comments that describe the use of variables. For example,

> **var** *a*, *b* : *integer*;   { numbers to add }

and

> **var** *a* : *integer*;   { first operand   }
>   *b* : *integer*;   { second operand }

are both more informative than declarations that are not accompanied by comments. Commented declarations are similar to a list of the cast for a play: they tell not only who will be involved in the action that follows, but also what roles they will play.

EXERCISES

1. Investigate the range of the integer data type on your computer system.
   - (a) Execute *intmax* to find the largest integer that can be handled by your system.
   - (b) What happens if you try to output *maxint* + 1?
   - (c) What is the smallest integer that can be handled by your system? Is it −*maxint*?
2. Investigate the range and precision of the real data type on your computer system.
   - (a) Modify *add* to add two real numbers instead of two integers. How many digits does your system display in the output from this program?
   - (b) What is the largest real number that your system will display? What happens if you try to display a larger real number?
   - (c) What is the smallest real number greater than zero that your system will display? What happens if you try to display a smaller real number?
   - (d) What is the smallest positive real number x such that *write*$(1 + x)$ will display a number other than 1 on your system?

2.6   PROGRAMMING: INPUT AND OUTPUT

Programs must communicate with their users. Users must incorporate data required for a computation in the text of a program or supply that data as input. Programs must display the results of their computations as output.

The program *add* requires two integers as input and produces a single line of output. For the input

> 3   4

the program will produce the output

```
Their sum is            7
```

when Berkeley Pascal is used. (The output produced by other systems may differ slightly.) We will explain exactly how a program obtains its input and produces its output by examining the input and output statements in Pascal.

INPUT STATEMENTS

Input statements enable a program to obtain data from an external source (a terminal, a file on a disk, or punched cards) and to assign the values of the data to specified variables. The statement

   read(a, b)

in *add* causes that program to obtain two integers and to assign them to the integer variables *a* and *b*.

An input statement consists of the word *read* or *readln* (for "read line") followed by a list of variables enclosed by parentheses and separated by commas. (See Fig. 2.19.) We can omit this list and its enclosing parentheses from the *readln* variant of an input statement, but not from the *read* variant. When executed, an input statement assigns values to the variables, in the order in which they are listed, from input data we supply to the program.

We must supply appropriate types of data for the variables in an input statement: integer variables require integer constants, and real variables require either integer or real constants. Pascal skips spaces when looking for a numeric constant, so we can use spaces to separate constants.

The way that we supply data to a program varies for different computer systems. When we use an *interactive* (terminal-oriented) system, we are present when our program is being executed, and the program can prompt us to enter data. Some Pascal systems automatically prompt a user to supply input by blinking a cursor or by typing a question mark; others simply pause, leaving it to the program to provide prompting (such as the message Enter two integers. printed by *add*). For *batch* (noninteractive) systems, a user is not present when a program is being exe-

input statement

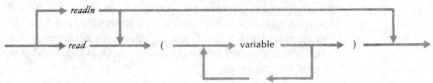

FIGURE 2.19 ■ Syntax diagram, input statement (preliminary version)

cuted, and data must be obtained from a previously prepared source, such as a file on a disk or a deck of punched cards, that accompanies a program submitted for execution.

In general, data for a program are supplied in the form of sequences of characters called *lines*. Lines of input from a terminal have varying lengths and are terminated by carriage returns; lines of input from cards have fixed lengths and are terminated by the ends of the cards. Pascal treats the end of a line of input as a space; hence we can use the end of a line to separate numbers we supply as input, but we cannot type the first digits in a number on one line and the rest on the next.

When an input statement is executed, as many lines of input as necessary will be requested in order to assign values to all the variables listed in that statement. For example, we can supply input to the program *add* on a single line, as in

```
Enter two integers.
3 4

Their sum is          7
```

or on several lines, as in

```
Enter two integers.
3
4

Their sum is          7
```

or in

```
Enter two integers.
3

4

Their sum is          7
```

In each of these cases, execution of the input statement terminates only after we have supplied two integers as input.

The *read* and *readln* variants of the input statement differ only as to how they treat the end of a line of input. The *readln* discards the remainder, if any, of the final line of input it considers, so that the next input statement executed obtains its data starting at the beginning of the next line of input. Execution of an input statement that consists only of the word *readln* simply discards the remainder of the data on the current line of input. The *read* variant does not discard any data, so that the next input statement executed obtains its data starting where the last left off. For example, for the input

```
1 2 3
4 5 6
```

the statements

> *read(a);*
> *read(b);*
> *write(a, b)*

produce the output

> 1   2

whereas the statements

> *readln(a);*
> *readln(b);*
> *write(a, b)*

or the statements

> *read(a);*
> *readln;*
> *read(b);*
> *write(a, b)*

produce the output

> 1   4

since the *readln* variant discards the remainder of the first line of input before *b* is read. The *readln* variant is used most commonly to ensure the separation of data supplied in response to distinct requests for input, whereas the *read* variant is used to input an entire stream of data without regard to line boundaries.

OUTPUT STATEMENTS

Output statements generate output for an external destination, typically a terminal or a printer. An output statement consists of the word *write* or *writeln* (for "write line") followed by a list of items enclosed by parentheses and separated by commas. (See Fig. 2.20.) These items may be constants, variables, or expressions (Section 2.7), which may be followed by information to control the format used to display their values.

The actions induced by the *write* and *writeln* variants of the output statement differ with respect to how output is divided into lines. The *writeln* variant ends a line of output after the value of the last item has been displayed; output from the next executed output statement begins on a new line. The *write* variant does not end a line of output, so that output from the next executed output statement continues on the same line. The output produced by the single statement

> *writeln('Their sum is ', a+b)*

in *add* could equally well be produced by the sequences

output statement

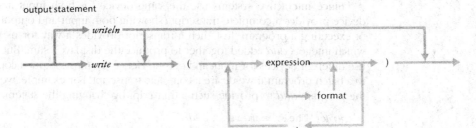

FIGURE 2.20 ■ Syntax diagram, output statement (preliminary version)

> *write*('Their sum is ');
> *writeln*(*a*+*b*)

or

> *write*('Their sum is ');
> *write*(*a*+*b*);

of statements. A statement consisting of the word *writeln* alone terminates the current line of output, producing a blank line in the output if there were no characters on that line.

The value of a string constant is displayed as is by the action of an output statement. Thus the statement

> *writeln*('Enter two integers.')

in *add* generates the line

> Enter two integers.

of output. When we execute *add* interactively, this statement reminds us of what we must supply to satisfy the next input statement; its sole purpose is to make the program *add* easier to use and the record of its use easier to understand. Since this statement uses the word *writeln*, the input that we supply will appear on the line following the one containing the message Enter two integers.; if we had wanted the input to appear on the same line as the message, we could have used the word *write* instead, and we would have included spaces in the message following the period to separate the input from the message. These considerations illustrate how attention to detail creates a program that interacts nicely with its users.

We must attend to details somewhat differently if we execute *add* using a batch system. Since we will not be present when *add* requests its input, there is no need to print the message Enter two integers.—no one will be around to read it. A considerable amount of time may elapse between submission of our input and receipt of the output, so we should take care to clarify which input generates what output.

Since interactive systems use the same device for both input and output, that device provides a complete transcript (showing both input and output) of the result of executing a program. Just such a transcript provides a way for us to reconstruct which integers *add* added together to produce the displayed sum. But batch systems use different devices for input and output. Hence we must output a copy of the input to a batch program if we desire a complete transcript. For example, we could modify the program *add* to provide such a transcript by changing the statement

write('Their sum is ', $a+b$)

to

write('The sum of ', a, ' and ', b, ' is ', $a+b$, '.')

Numeric values are displayed either as integers or as floating-point real numbers, according to the type of the constant, variable, or expression being written. In the program *circle*, for example, the value of *pi*radius*radius* is a real number; hence *circle* displays the floating-point number 3.14159265000000e+02 as the area of a circle with radius 1 and not the fixed-point number 3.14159265.

OUTPUT FORMAT

Pascal permits us to control output spacing and format. Unless we request otherwise, Pascal uses fixed-width output fields to display various types of values. If a value does not fill such a field completely, it is preceded by enough spaces to fill that field. Pascal generally displays integers in fields that are sufficiently large (say, ten characters) to display the integer $-maxint$. Fields for real numbers may be larger (say, 20 characters) to accommodate floating-point representations.

Fixed-width output fields make it easy to generate tabular output. For example, if the width of the output field for integers is 10, then the sequence

writeln('A', 23, −128);
writeln('B', 100000, 7)

of statements produces the output

```
A        23      -128
B    100000         7
```

However, fixed-width output fields make it more difficult to generate normally punctuated sentences as output. For example, the statement

writeln('The sum of ', a, ' and ', b, ' is ', $a+b$, '.')

produces the output

```
The sum of          3 and          4 is          7.
```

format

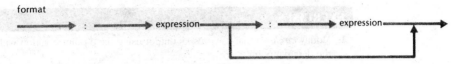

FIGURE 2.21 ■ Syntax diagram, format

when $a = 3$, $b = 4$, and the length of the output field for integers is 10. Fortunately, Pascal enables us to control the length of the output field and thereby eliminate undesired spaces. If we follow an expression in an output statement by a *format* (described in Fig. 2.21) that consists of a colon and an expression with an integer value, that value is taken as the width of the field in which to display the item. Spaces are used to fill the left-hand part of a field that is larger than needed, whereas a field that is too small is extended until it is large enough to display the item. Thus the statement

writeln('The sum of ', a:1,' and ', b:1,' is ', $a+b$:1,'.')

will attempt to display the values of the integers in fields of width 1, extending those fields if necessary. This statement can be used to generate the following lines of output:

```
The sum of 3 and 4 is 7.
The sum of -2 and 1001 is 999.
```

Note that careful use of spaces in string constants in this statement prevents output such as

```
The sum of3and4is7.
```

We can cause the values of real expressions to be displayed in fixed-point, as opposed to floating-point, notation by following a field-width specification with a second colon and another expression that yields an integer value. This value is taken as the number of digits to display following the decimal point. (See Fig. 2.21.) For example, the statement

writeln('The final balance is $', *amount*:1:2,'.')

can be used to generate the following lines of output:

```
The final balance is $1000.00.
The final balance is $-23.14.
```

Generation of output that is easy to read requires care. The flexibility provided by output statements in Pascal enables us to exercise this care.

EXERCISES

1. Modify *circle* so that it writes its output using fixed-point notation with eight digits after the decimal point.

2. Modify *add* so that, given appropriate input, it produces output in the following format:

        2 + 2 = 4
        13 + -1 = 12

3. Modify *add* so that the input entered by the user appears on the same line as the message that prompts the input.

4. Write programs to print
   (a) your name;
   (b) the following picture.

            *
           ***
            *

5. Some Pascal systems accept input character by character rather than line by line. To see what your system does, try supplying three integers that are separated by spaces and followed by a carriage return as input to *add*. If your system prints the sum of the first two integers only after you have typed the carriage return, then it is accepting input line by line. If it prints the sum before you have a chance to type the third integer, then it is accepting input character by character. The sample programs in this book were written for a system that accepts input line by line. If your system accepts input character by character, you may have to modify some of the programs slightly to produce exactly the output shown in this book.

6. What is the minimum width output field your system uses for printing
   (a) strings?
   (b) integers?
   (c) real numbers?

2.7   PROGRAMMING: EXPRESSIONS AND ASSIGNMENTS

We can manipulate data, and thereby obtain new values, by evaluating *expressions*. Furthermore, we can display these new values directly, as in the last output statement of *add*, or we can assign them to variables for later use in a computation.

EXPRESSIONS

Arithmetic expressions in Pascal, of which $a+b$ in *add* is an example, may be constructed in the usual manner from variables, unsigned constants, and function values using parentheses and the operation symbols listed in Table 2.3. More precisely, the

TABLE 2.3	Arithmetic Operations in Pascal	
+	addition	(7 + 2 = 9)
−	subtraction	(7 − 2 = 5)
*	multiplication	(7 * 2 = 14)
/	division	(7 / 2 = 3.5)
div	integer division	(7 **div** 2 = 3)
mod	integer modulus	(7 **mod** 2 = 1)

formation of arithmetic expressions is governed by the syntax diagram in Fig. 2.22. As can be seen from the diagram, two operation symbols may not occur adjacent to one another; thus $a/-b$ is illegal in Pascal and must be written as $a/(-b)$. Furthermore, multiplication in Pascal, as in other programming languages, must be indicated explicitly, as in $a*b$, rather than implicitly, as in ab (which is a single Pascal identifier).

As the list of operations indicates, Pascal makes the distinction noted in Section 2.2 between two operations of division: that denoted by the symbol / is the usual operation and yields a real value even when applied to integers; and that denoted by **div** may be applied only to integers and yields the integer of greatest magnitude in their quotient. The remainder resulting from the division of one integer by another

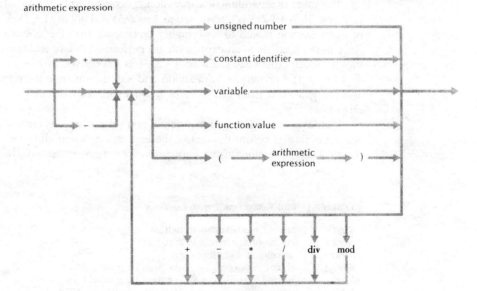

FIGURE 2.22 ■ Syntax diagram, arithmetic expression (simplified version)

TABLE 2.4	Numeric-Valued Functions in Pascal	
$abs(x)$	absolute value of x	$(abs(2) = abs(-2) = 2)$
$sqr(x)$	square of x	$(sqr(2) = 4)$

is given by the operator **mod**, which satisfies the relationship

$$a = b \times (a \ \mathbf{div} \ b) + a \ \mathbf{mod} \ b,$$

when a and b are both positive.

Pascal also provides a number of standard mathematical functions. The two functions in Table 2.4 yield integer values, when applied to integers, and real values, when applied to reals. The functions in Table 2.5 always yield real values, even when applied to integers.

Pascal does not provide an operation symbol for raising a number to a power. Some languages use the symbols ↑ or ** for this purpose, so that $a \uparrow 2$ or $a**2$ represents the square of the number a. If we wish to raise a number to a power in Pascal, we must use repeated multiplications or the logarithm and exponential functions; for example,

$$x^3 = x \times x \times x, \text{ and}$$
$$x^y = (e^{\ln(x)})^y \quad \text{or} \quad \exp(y \ln(x)), \qquad \text{if } x > 0.$$

The value of an arithmetic expression is determined by the usual algebraic conventions. Thus $1 + 2*3$ is interpreted as $1 + (2*3)$ and not as $(1 + 2)*3$. The operation of multiplication is said to have higher *precedence* than the operation of addition, since multiplications in an expression are performed before additions unless parentheses dictate otherwise. Likewise $4 - 2 + 1$ is interpreted as $(4 - 2) + 1$ and not as $4 - (2 + 1)$. The operations of addition and subtraction have the same precedence and are evaluated from left to right in an expression unless parentheses dictate otherwise.

Within an expression, function values and subexpressions enclosed by parentheses are evaluated before the rest of the expression. When all functions and parenthesized subexpressions in an expression have been evaluated, the multiplicative

TABLE 2.5	Real-Valued Functions in Pascal	
$sin(x)$	sine of x, where x is in radians	
$cos(x)$	cosine of x, where x is in radians	
$arctan(x)$	arctangent, in radians, of x	
$sqrt(x)$	square root of x	(x must be nonnegative)
$ln(x)$	natural logarithm of x	(x must be positive)
$exp(x)$	exponential of x	(i.e., e^x, where $e = 2.718...$)

operations *, /, **div**, and **mod** receive higher precedence than (are evaluated before) the additive operations + and −. Operations of the same precedence are evaluated from left to right, so that $a/b/c$ is interpreted as $(a/b)/c$ and not as $a/(b/c)$.

The precedence of arithmetic operators is shown in the more detailed syntax diagrams, Fig. 2.23–2.25, that govern the construction of arithmetic expressions. Although syntax diagrams generally govern only the form of Pascal programs—not their meaning—these diagrams do suggest that "factors" in arithmetic expressions are evaluated first, then "terms," and finally entire expressions.

arithmetic expression

FIGURE 2.23 ■ Syntax diagram, arithmetic expression

arithmetic term

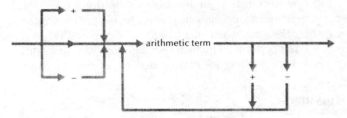

FIGURE 2.24 ■ Syntax diagram, arithmetic term

arithmetic factor

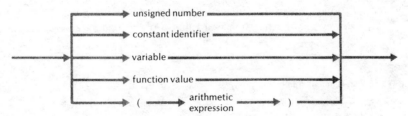

FIGURE 2.25 ■ Syntax diagram, arithmetic factor

TABLE 2.6	Integer-Valued Functions in Pascal
trunc(x)	the truncated value of x (*trunc*(1.6) = 1, *trunc*(−1.2) = −1)
round(x)	the rounded value of x (*round*(1.6) = 2, *round*(−1.2) = −1)

When real and integer values are intermixed in the same arithmetic expression, the value of that expression is forced, or *coerced*, to be real. Thus (3/2)*2 has the real value 3.0 and not the integer value 3. As a result, such an expression cannot be used in contexts (such as an argument to the **div** function) that require integers. Some programming languages also coerce real values to be integers, either by rounding or by truncating, when such coercion is required (as in 3.2 **div** 2). However, Pascal will not perform an implicit coercion from reals to integers; instead, programmers must explicitly use one of the functions listed in Table 2.6.

ASSIGNMENTS

We can assign the value of an expression to a variable in a Pascal program by an *assignment* statement. As shown in Fig. 2.26, such a statement consists of a variable followed by the assignment operator := followed by an expression (which may be nothing more than a constant or a variable). For example, the statement

  sum := a + b

assigns the value of the expression a + b to the variable *sum*. It is important to note that the assignment statement is an instruction to be followed, not a statement of fact. Thus the statement

  sum := *sum* + a

instructs the computer to add the values of the variables *sum* and a and then to assign the resulting value as the new value of the variable *sum*. It is a mistake to interpret this statement as asserting that *sum* and *sum* + a have the same value (that a = 0).

We can assign integer values either to integer variables or to real variables. However, we can assign real values only to real variables; we must use either the

assignment statement

FIGURE 2.26 ■ Syntax diagram, assignment statement (preliminary version)

PASCAL SAMPLE 2.4   The program *add1*

{ calculates the sum of two integers }

```
program add1(input, output);
var a, b, sum : integer;
begin
    writeln('Enter two integers.');
    read(a, b);
    sum := a + b;
    writeln;
    writeln('Their sum is ', sum)
end.
```

SAMPLE USE OF *add1*:

```
Enter two integers.
3 4

Their sum is            7
```

---

round or *trunc* function to convert a real value to an integer if we want to assign it to an integer variable.

Assignment statements permit us to use values later in a computation without having to recompute them each time we need them. A variant *add1* of the program *add* illustrates the use of an assignment statement. (See Pascal Sample 2.4.)

Often in programming we find ourselves faced with the need to interchange the values of two variables. If we attempt to do this with two assignment statements

```
a := b;
b := a
```

we lose the original value of the variable *a* when we assign the value of *b* to it. The proper way to interchange the values is to use an auxiliary variable and a third assignment statement

```
spare := a;
a := b;
b := spare
```

to save the value of *a* while assigning *b* to it.

We have now finished our examination of simple programs and the program *add*. In Chapter 3, we will go on to more powerful means of structuring programs.

EXERCISES

1. Write Pascal programs to compute the following quantities:

(a) the temperature in Celsius, given the temperature in Fahrenheit;

(b) the temperature in Fahrenheit, given the temperature in Celsius;

(c) the distance between two points in the plane with coordinates $<x1, y1>$ and $<x2, y2>$;

(d) the number of radians in a given number of degrees;

(e) the tangent of an angle expressed in radians;

(f) the tangent of an angle expressed in degrees.

2. Which of the following errors does your computer system detect?

(a) integer overflow (Try to output *maxint* + 1.)

(b) real overflow (Try to output *exp*(100).)

(c) real underflow (Try to output *exp*(− 100).)

(d) division by zero

(e) square root of a negative number

(f) logarithm of zero or a negative number

If your system does not report these errors automatically, try to find some special feature that you can invoke to have them reported. If there is one, use that feature each time you execute a program. Don't take chances with unreported errors!

3. What properties does *a* **mod** *b* satisfy when

(a) $a < 0$ (Pascal specifies what should happen here),

(b) $b < 0$ (Pascal doesn't specify what happens here), and

(c) $b = 0$ (this should be an error).

4. What are the values of *round*(1.5) and *round*(− 1.5)? Should a good program depend on these values being rounded exactly as they are? Why?

5. Modify the program *add* or *add1* so that it prints

(a) the average of *a* and *b*,

(b) $a + 1$ raised to the power *b*, and

(c) the logarithm of *a* to the base *b*.

6. Write a series of assignment statements to rotate the values of three variables *a*, *b*, and *c*, that is, to give the value of *a* to *b*, the value of *b* to *c*, and the value of *c* to *a*.

2.8   ANALYSIS: PROGRAMMING STYLE

The few programs that we have written so far are short and simple. Nonetheless, it is instructive to examine them further before going on to write longer and more complicated ones. They provide excellent guidance for programming efforts—guidance that will help us to keep our more ambitious undertakings as short and simple as possible.

The single most important measure of the quality of a computer program is whether it works. A program may be a work of art, embody the most modern techniques, and consume practically no resources, but if it doesn't work, it is of little use. This seems to imply that other considerations, such as structure, style, simplicity, or even neatness, are of lesser importance. Yet, experience has shown just the opposite: these considerations are crucial if we are to produce working, high-quality programs. Some of the reasons for this are as follows:

- Almost all programs contain errors initially. Well-written programs excel in two ways. They are less likely to contain errors in the first place, and those errors they do contain are easier to locate and correct than errors hidden in poorly written programs.

- For a program to be used with confidence, not only must it work, but potential users must be convinced that it works. While evidence that a program worked in the past is sometimes convincing, it does not guarantee that the program will work in untried circumstances. Nothing builds confidence like a well-organized, coherent, and easy-to-understand program.

- Programs are rarely used only once. Future users of a program (including the original programmer) must be able to read the program in order to understand what it is supposed to do and how it does it.

- Few programs are never changed. It is far easier and safer to modify a well-written program than a poorly written one.

- A well-written program reflects a well-conceived design; such a program is almost always simpler and more efficient than a hastily written or jumbled one.

For these reasons, the task of writing a computer program should be taken as seriously as the task of writing English prose. Programs and prose are both means of communication. Authors must think first about what they wish to communicate; then they must think about how to organize and express ideas clearly and logically. Good programs, like good prose, should be a pleasure to read.

As with English style, programming style is subjective. Nonetheless, there are rules you can follow that almost always lead to better style and that are a good foundation for developing your own personal style. Following are some of these rules for documentation, program display, and coding. Additional rules aimed at enhancing your programming style are presented in Section 3.6.

DOCUMENTATION

Document your program well. Use one or more lines of comments to introduce your program. The programs in this book all begin with short descriptions of what they do. Comments at the beginning of your programs should also include such other information as your name, the date on which you wrote the program, the date and reasons for any modifications you made to the program, directions for using the program, and so on. These are all things that you or someone else may wish to know when reading the program. Don't trust them to memory!

Insert comments in your program as you go. If you change your program, change your comments, too. Nothing destroys comprehensibility so much as a lack of comments or inaccurate comments. Try writing your comments first; then write your program to do what the comments say.

Express your comments in concise, coherent English. Spell properly and correct typing mistakes. Do not think that typing mistakes in comments are unimportant and can be ignored or corrected later. All too often, later turns out to be never, and misspelled comments unnecessarily irritate a reader who is trying to understand the program.

Do not use too many comments or comments that ramble on forever. A few well-chosen comments convey more information than a rambling dissertation. Consider what your reader needs to know, not just what you want to say.

DISPLAYING THE PROGRAM

Display your program in a way that accurately reflects its structure and makes that structure pleasing to the eye. Indent variable declarations, the bodies of programs, and other structures in a consistent fashion, such as the one used in this book. Use a utility program, sometimes known as a *pretty printer*, which indents your programs automatically, if you have one available. Indentation makes it easier for a reader to visualize the structure of your program and to focus attention on a particular section of that structure. In longer programs, use blank lines to separate sections of the program and to avoid straining the reader's eyes.

Use adequate blank space within program lines and use it consistently. Use spaces around keywords, around the assignment operator, and in long expressions. Use a blank space at the beginning and end of each comment. Choose a convention that improves readability and stick to it.

CODING STYLE

Hold lines in your program to a reasonable length. Break up an expression or a line that is too complicated; if it is too long to write compactly, it is also too long to be understood at a glance.

Choose meaningful, but succinct, names for your variables and other identifiers. If you use a variable for an obvious purpose in several adjoining statements, then give it a single-character name; if you use it to communicate information among distant parts of a program, give it a longer name that describes its use.

Assign names to constants that may change when you modify the program. Use these symbolic constants instead of the constants themselves in program statements.

SYSTEMS: HOW COMPUTERS REPRESENT NUMBERS AND INSTRUCTIONS

By learning a programming language, we learn to communicate with computer systems that can execute our programs. In programming, as in all forms of communication, we can communicate most effectively if we understand the nature of our audience. Hence this section provides a brief introduction to how computer systems handle information. For now we concentrate on information that consists of numeric data and simple programs. In later chapters we will discuss how computer systems handle other types of data and programs.

UNITS OF INFORMATION

The unit of information in most computer systems is the *word*. A word consists of a sequence of *bits*, or *binary digits*. Each bit is either a zero or a one, the digits in the binary number system. The value of a bit in a word is determined by the state of some physical device (for example, by the presence or absence of a voltage drop in a circuit or by the orientation of a magnet).

Many microcomputers have words that consist of 8 or 16 bits; larger computers are based on word sizes of 16, 32, 36, or 40 bits. Although word sizes vary from one computer to another, most computer systems identify a sequence of 8 bits as a *byte* and decompose a word into several bytes. (However, not all systems follow this convention; some define a byte as 7 or 9 bits.) Because most computer systems are organized around the binary number system, we measure the capacity of storage devices (such as disks) in multiples of $1K = 1024 = 2^{10}$ bytes or words, rather than in multiples of 1000 (base 10) bytes or words.

The size of a word determines how much information it can hold. Some of the types of information that can be stored in a word are unsigned binary integers, signed binary integers, floating-point numbers, and instructions.

UNSIGNED BINARY INTEGERS

Each n-bit word can hold the binary representation of a nonnegative integer less than 2^n. For example, with 8-bit words we can represent any integer from 0 to 255, which equals $2^8 - 1$. With 16-bit words, we can represent any integer from 0 to 65,535, which equals $2^{16} - 1$. And with 32-bit words, we can represent those integers with decimal representations that contain nine or fewer digits since 2^{32} equals $(2^{10})^{3.2}$, which is approximately $(10^3)^{3.2}$ or $10^{9.6}$. Figure 2.27 shows how the decimal number 100, which

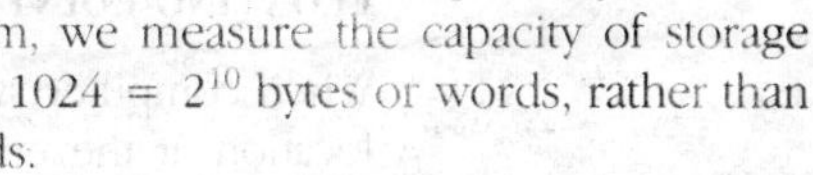

Word 00000000000000000000000001100100

FIGURE 2.27 ■ Representation of 100 as 32-bit unsigned integer

Bits 1   32

equals $64 + 32 + 4$ or $2^6 + 2^5 + 2^2$, is represented as an unsigned binary integer in a 32-bit word.

SIGNED BINARY INTEGERS

In order to distinguish positive from negative integers, computers regard the first bit of a word as a *sign bit* that indicates whether the integer is positive (sign bit = 0) or negative (sign bit = 1). The rest of the bits in the word represent the magnitude of the integer. For positive integers, this representation is the same as for unsigned binary integers; for negative integers, the representation may be somewhat different.

With 8-bit words, only 7 bits are available to represent the magnitude of an integer, thereby enabling us to represent integers lying between -128 and 128, that is, between -2^7 and $+2^7$. Since this range is not very large, systems with 8-bit words generally utilize several words to represent a single integer, thereby extending the range of the integer data type.

With 16-bit words, 15 bits are available to represent the magnitude of an integer, thereby enabling us to represent integers lying between $-32,768$ and $32,768$, that is, between -2^{15} and $+2^{15}$. Systems with 16-bit words may also utilize several words to represent a single integer. With 32-bit words, we can represent signed integers with decimal representations that contain nine or fewer digits since $2^{31} > 10^9$.

FLOATING-POINT NUMBERS

When computer systems store an integer in a word, the decimal point is in a fixed location at the end of the word. Hence integers are a special case of *fixed-point* numbers. On the other hand, computer systems store approximations of real numbers as *floating-point* numbers, where the location of the decimal point is not fixed. They generally represent floating-point numbers by two signed binary integers stored within a single word: a *significand s* (typically 24 bits in a 32-bit word) and an *exponent e* (the other 8 bits in a 32-bit word). Usually the decimal point is presumed to be to the right of the sign in the significand, so that together the two integers s and e represent the number $s \times 2^{e-23}$. Figure 2.28 shows how the decimal number 3.25 is represented in this fashion.

We lose precision if a computation (such as a multiplication) results in more significant digits than the significand will hold. In this case, the result is generally *rounded* to as many digits as the significand will hold. An *overflow* occurs if a computation results in an exponent that is too large. An *underflow* occurs if a computation results in an exponent that is too small.

INSTRUCTIONS

The processor in a computer system is capable of interpreting *machine language instructions* stored one per word in the memory of the computer. Each instruction

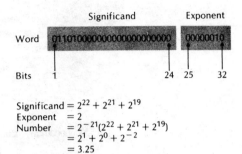

$$Significand = 2^{22} + 2^{21} + 2^{19}$$
$$Exponent = 2$$
$$Number = 2^{-21}(2^{22} + 2^{21} + 2^{19})$$
$$= 2^1 + 2^0 + 2^{-2}$$
$$= 3.25$$

FIGURE 2.28 ■ Floating-point representation of 3.25

consists of an *operation code* telling the processor what to do and an *address* telling the processor where to do it. Addresses specify words in the computer's memory, which are numbered by integers starting with 0. The processor has a few additional words of working storage in which it can perform arithmetic; these words are called *registers*.

Table 2.7 lists some typical operation codes for a fictitious computer with 64K ($64 \times 2^{10} = 2^{16}$) 32-bit words. Each operation code occupies 8 bits (enabling us to perform 256 separate operations) and is accompanied by a 16-bit address (enabling us to name any word in the computer's memory); the remaining 8 bits in a word that contains an instruction are unused.

Operation codes that are written directly as binary numbers in machine language are hard to read and remember, so programmers who must work with machine language specify these codes by mnemonics such as LDA (for "load A register") or ADA (for "add to A register"). Furthermore, they specify memory addresses symbolically by names, such as x and y. Software *assemblers* translate *assembly language* programs written in this shorthand into machine language. Assemblers are similar to, but simpler than compilers. Writing programs in assembly language is still some-

TABLE 2.7 Operations for Hypothetical Computer

Operation Code	Assembly Language Mnemonic	Interpretation
00010000	LDA x	load A register from location x
00100000	STA x	store A register in location x
01010000	ADA x	add integer in location x to A register
01100000	SBA x	subtract integer in location x from A register
01110000	MUL x	multiply A register by integer in location x
10000000	DIV x	divide A register by integer in location x (retain quotient and discard remainder)

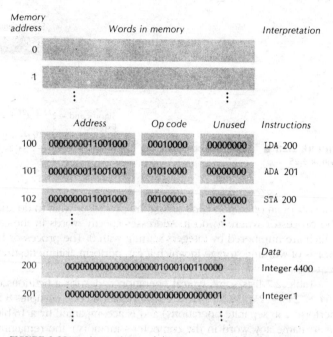

FIGURE 2.29 ■ Instructions and data in memory of simple computer

thing of a chore, and most programmers write their programs in *high-level* languages, such as Pascal, that permit them to use more natural and concise notations.

Figure 2.29 displays a segment of a machine language program that uses the operation codes from Table 2.7. The instruction in memory location 100 instructs the processor to transfer the word in location 200 (location 11001000 in binary) to the *arithmetic* or *A register*. The next instruction in memory location 101 instructs the processor to add the word in memory location 201 (location 11001001 in binary) to the *A* register, interpreting both this word and the contents of the *A* register as signed integers. The third instruction in memory location 102 instructs the processor to store the contents of the *A* register back in memory location 200. Thus this sequence of three instructions performs the action required by the Pascal statement

   sum := *sum* + *number*

when the integer value of *sum* is stored in memory location 200 and the integer value of *number* is stored in memory location 201.

Operation codes such as those illustrated in Table 2.7 form the basis for the arithmetic capabilities of a typical computer. In Section 3.9 we will learn how other operation codes govern the flow of control in a program.

1. What are the largest signed and unsigned integers that can be stored in words with 8, 16, 36, or 40 bits?

2. What is the largest floating-point number that can be represented with a 24-bit significand and an 8-bit exponent?

3. What is the smallest nonzero positive floating-point number that can be represented with a 24-bit significand and an 8-bit exponent?

4. Consider the hypothetical computer for which operation codes are listed in Table 2.7.

    (a) Which operations can cause overflows?

    (b) Write a series of instructions that compute the value of the $b^2 - 4ac$, where the values of a, b, and c are stored in memory locations 200, 201, and 202. (*Hint:* Use additional memory locations to store useful constants and intermediate results.)

    (c) Write a series of instructions that interchange the contents of memory locations 200 and 201.

SUMMARY

Computer programs manipulate numeric and symbolic information using the following primitive actions:

- input (obtaining values from an external source);

- output (displaying values); and

- assignment (evaluating expressions to produce values).

A program specifies the order in which primitive actions are performed.

A programming language provides a precise vocabulary and format for describing data and actions. In Pascal,

- a program consists of

    1. a header naming the program,

    2. declarations, or definitions, of the objects used in a program (in particular, of constants and variables),

    3. a sequence of statements forming the body of the program and specifying the actions taken by the program, and

    4. comments interspersed throughout the program;

- numeric data can be either *integer* or *real*;

- the *read* statement acquires input;

- the *write* statement produces output; and

- the assignment operator := assigns the value of an expression to a variable.

Computer programs communicate ideas to humans as well as instructions to computers. Hence their form is as important as their content. Programs are more readable and more reliable if they

- contain accurate, informative comments;
- are displayed neatly in a fashion that reflects their structure; and
- use meaningful names for variables and constants.

Computer systems generally encode data and instructions using the binary number system.

- A bit encodes a single binary digit, that is, a 0 or a 1.
- A byte encodes a single symbol and typically consists of eight bits.
- A word typically encodes a single number or instruction and consists of several bytes.

Programming languages such as Pascal enable programmers to think about how they want to use data and instructions, not about how computers represent them. Compilers translate a programmer's intentions, expressed in a programming language such as Pascal, into the codes understood by a computer.

POSITE ACTIONS COMPOSITE ACT

TE ACTIONS COMPOSITE ACTION

MPOSITE ACTIONS COMPOSITE AC

ONS COMPOSITE ACTIONS COMP

POSITE ACTIONS COMPOSITE ACT

ITE ACTIONS COMPOSITE ACTION

MPOSITE ACTIONS COMPOSITE A

IONS **COMPOSITE ACTIONS** COMP

C · H · A · P · T · E · R

3

*T*aken alone or in a single sequence, primitive actions accomplish only primitive tasks. In order to accomplish more ambitious tasks, we must combine primitive actions in imaginative ways. We can create such combinations in two ways: by composition or by decomposition. For a given problem we can work from the ground up, composing primitive actions into increasingly larger actions until we arrive at a solution to the problem. Alternatively, we can work with the problem itself, decomposing it into simpler subproblems until we can solve these subproblems by sequences of simple actions and assemble these partial solutions into a solution of the entire problem. Whether we proceed by composition or by decomposition, we need to master three fundamental methods—sequence, choice, and repetition—for composing smaller actions into larger actions. Armed with these methods, we can tackle the most ambitious tasks.

As we learn how to compose actions, we will begin to recognize the importance of writing programs in a disciplined or structured manner. On the one hand, if we recognize the composite structure that is appropriate for a given task, we can expedite the design of a program to accomplish that task. On the other hand, if we understand and use the three fundamental composite structures, we can expedite the process of convincing ourselves and others that our programs do what we want them to do. In short, if we proceed systematically, we can write programs that are correct by design, not programs that need to be corrected.

APPLICATIONS: MORE POCKET CALCULATORS

The primitive actions that we studied in Chapter 2 enabled us to imitate some particularly simple pocket calculators. In this chapter we will use composite actions to imitate more interesting calculators: calculators that compute useful mathematical, statistical, and financial values.

MATHEMATICAL CALCULATORS

In order to mimic mathematical calculators, we will write two programs. The first, *intPower*, raises a real number x to an integer power n, enabling us to compute values of x^n such as 2^{20} or π^{-4}. The second, *powerOf2*, does approximately the opposite: for a real number x, it finds the smallest integer n such that $2^n \geq x$. This n is an approximation to $\log_2(x)$, the logarithm to the base 2 of x, that is, to a real number p such that $2^p = x$. Being able to compute this n helps us, for example, to determine how many bits we need for the binary representation of a particular integer. With n bits, we can represent integers from 0 to $2^n - 1$; hence to represent an integer m, we must use n bits where $2^n - 1 \geq m$ or, equivalently, $2^n \geq m + 1$. The program *powerOf2* enables us to find the smallest such n.

STATISTICAL CALCULATORS

Statistical calculators enable us to analyze collections of numbers, measuring both the *central tendency* and the *dispersion* of those numbers. There are various measures of central tendency: the *mean* of a collection of numbers is the arithmetic average of those numbers; the *mode* is the number that occurs most frequently in the collection; and the *median* is a number that splits the collection into two equal-sized pieces, one consisting of the numbers at least as large as the median and the other consisting of the numbers no larger than the median. For example, given the collection 3, 7, 6, 2, 3, 6, 4, 5, 6 of nine numbers, the mean is $4\frac{2}{3}$ (which equals 42/9), the mode is 6 (which occurs three times), and the median is 5 (which is larger than four numbers in the collection and smaller than four).

Statistical measures of dispersion indicate the variability of a collection of numbers by showing how close those numbers are to the mean. For example, the *maximum* and *minimum* of the collection are the extreme values in the collection; the *variance* of a collection $x_1, x_2, \ldots, x_n$ of n numbers is

$$\frac{1}{n} \sum_{i=1}^{n} (x_i - m)^2,$$

where m is the mean of the collection; and the *standard deviation* of a collection is the square root of its variance. The greater the variation of the numbers in a collection, the larger the variance and the standard deviation. Generally, in *normally distributed* collections of numbers (such as scores on College Board examinations, which have a mean of 500), approximately two-thirds of the numbers lie within one standard deviation of the mean (that is, lie between College Board scores of 400 and 600), and approximately 95% lie within two standard deviations of the mean.

In this chapter, we will write programs that compute the mean, maximum, and minimum. In later chapters we will learn how to compute and use the other statistical measures.

FINANCIAL CALCULATORS

Financial calculators help us to solve problems concerning the value of investments or the repayment of loans. Not only do these calculators have a certain fascination (given the frequency with which people invest or borrow money), but they also illustrate how the nature of a problem influences the structure of a program that solves the problem.

When we borrow money to finance the purchase of a new car or a home, several factors determine the exact terms of the loan. The first of these is the *principal* or the amount of money borrowed. The next two govern the repayment of the loan: the *life* of the loan specifies the number and timing of payments that must be made, while the *installment size* specifies the amount of each payment. Finally, the fee charged by the lender for the use of the borrowed money is expressed in terms of an annual *interest rate*, to be applied against the portion of the loan not yet repaid.

If we know values for all these factors, it is a relatively straightforward task to produce a repayment schedule for the loan. Such a schedule shows when each payment is due, the amount of interest covered by that payment, the amount of principal repaid by that payment, and the *balance* of the loan, that is, the amount of money still owed, both before and after that payment. Banks and other lending institutions typically provide such schedules for their customers to indicate how much interest has been paid up to a certain date and how much money is still owed as of that date.

The repayment schedule in Table 3.1, for example, shows the effect of monthly payments of $90.26 on a one-year loan of $1000 at 15% interest. Note that the last payment is $90.24 so as to leave a final balance of $0.00 and not to overpay the loan by two cents.

If we know values for any three of the four factors for a loan, we can determine the value of the fourth. Indeed, we often know the value of only three of the factors when we begin to consider borrowing money; at such times we need to determine the value of the remaining factor in order to understand the exact terms of a loan.

For example, we may know how much money we need to borrow, the current interest rate being charged by a bank, and the amount we can afford to repay each month. Given these factors, we might want to determine how long it would take to repay the loan; if that period were very long, then the loan might not be practical because of the total amount of interest we would end up paying.

Another example would be a sales promotion that involves a particular way of financing the purchase of some item: all we have to do is make a certain number of

TABLE 3.1. Typical Loan Repayment Schedule

Principal borrowed: $1000.00
Installment amount: $90.26   monthly
Interest rate: 15%   per year
Life of loan: 12   months

Payment number	Payment amount	Interest paid	Principal paid	Previous balance	New balance
1	90.26	12.50	77.76	1000.00	922.24
2	90.26	11.53	78.73	922.24	843.51
3	90.26	10.54	79.72	843.51	763.79
4	90.26	9.55	80.71	763.79	683.08
5	90.26	8.54	81.72	683.08	601.36
6	90.26	7.52	82.74	601.36	518.62*
7	90.26	6.48	83.78	518.62	434.84
8	90.26	5.44	84.82	434.84	350.02
9	90.26	4.38	85.88	350.02	264.14
10	90.26	3.30	86.96	264.14	177.18
11	90.26	2.21	88.05	177.18	89.13
12	90.24	1.11	89.13	89.13	0.00

small monthly payments. We know the price of the item and the number and amount of the payments, but we might want to determine the hidden factor, namely the effective rate of interest being charged. If this rate is high, then it might be cheaper to borrow money from a bank to make the purchase.

Inexpensive pocket calculators can perform financial computations such as those just described. In this chapter we will write two programs, *loan1* and *loan2*, that illustrate how to perform such financial computations. The first will compute the balance left after a certain number of payments, and the second will compute the life of a loan. In Chapter 4, we will tackle the more difficult problem of calculating the effective interest rate. As we write these programs, we will see how programs that solve related problems are themselves related to one another and how, if we structure these programs properly, we can transform one into another with a minimum of effort.

EXERCISES

1. Write a program that computes x^n directly for a real number x and an integer n. (*Hint:* Use the *exp* and *ln* functions.)

2. Write a program that, for real numbers x and y, computes directly the largest integer n such that $x^n \leq y$. (*Hint:* Use the *ln* and *trunc* functions.)

3. Examine a scientific pocket calculator to see what mathematical functions it can compute. Which of these functions can you compute using pencil and paper?

ALGORITHMS: CHOICE AND REPETITION

Not all computations proceed in a direct line from beginning to end; most require us to make decisions along the way. For instance, to mimic a pocket calculator that displays the minimum of two numbers, we need to decide which of the numbers is smaller and to display that number. Likewise, to mimic a pocket calculator that computes the average of a list of numbers, we need to decide when to stop accumulating a running total of those numbers and to divide that total by the number of items in the list.

Decisions such as these fall into two categories: those that choose from among several alternative courses of action (as in the first example, where we decide which number to display), and those that govern how long to repeat a certain action (as in the second example, where we decide how many times we add numbers to a running total). In Chapter 2, we learned how to compose actions into a single sequence, the execution of which required no decisions along the way. In this chapter we will compose actions into structures involving choice and repetition, the execution of which permits us to make decisions along the way. Taken together, these three ways of composing actions form the basis of all programming.

This section provides a general introduction to choice and repetition. We concentrate on features that are common to many programming languages and leave the specific details of how these features are treated in Pascal until later in the chapter.

CHOICE

The simplest choice that we can make in a computation involves deciding whether we must perform a given step in that computation. For example, a program that interacts with a user may give the user an opportunity to request instructions concerning the use of the program. It can do so through the following sequence of steps.

> ask whether user wants instructions
> get response
> if response is yes, then print instructions

Whether the third step in this sequence results in the printing of instructions depends on how the user responds to the question. Implicit in this step is a structure, depicted in Fig. 3.1, in which the outcome of a decision determines whether a particular action is taken or passed over. If the outcome of the decision in this structure is positive, then the action is taken; otherwise, it is not. Since the decision governs only a single action, we call the structure a *single-alternative structure*. We view the action itself as a black box because the contents of that box do not affect the rest of the structure.

Decisions in alternative structures typically involve comparisons between objects of data. For example, we can base a decision on the answer to the question

> Is the response equal to yes?

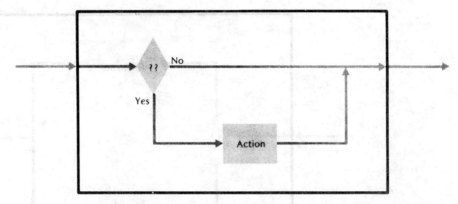

FIGURE 3.1 ■ Single-alternative structure for yes–no decision

or on the answer to the question

Is the second letter of the response a vowel; that is, is it an a, e, i, o, or u?

We can also use comparisons of magnitude or order, as in

Is the average greater than 50?

or

Does her name come between Harris and Jones?

as the basis for a decision.

The next simplest alternative structure involves a binary decision, that is, a choice between two courses of action. For example, to display the minimum of two numbers, we might proceed as follows:

ask user to enter two numbers
get two numbers, a and b
if $a \leq b$, then display a; otherwise display b

Implicit in the third step of this computation is a *double-alternative structure*, depicted in Fig. 3.2, which contains a pair of black boxes, one of which is selected for execution by the outcome of a decision. Note that a single-alternative structure is but a special case of a double-alternative structure in which one of the alternatives is to do nothing.

Most modern programming languages provide explicit program structures for specifying a choice between two alternative courses of action. Generally, we can recognize these structures by the appearance of words such as **if**, **then**, and **else** (which is how most programming languages spell "otherwise").

Many programming languages also provide explicit program structures, called *case structures*, that allow us to choose among an arbitrary number of alternative

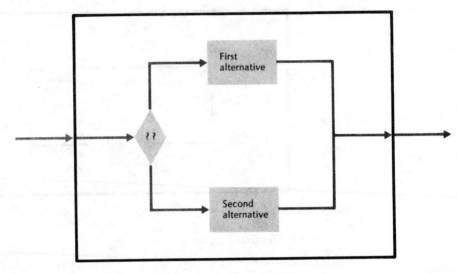

FIGURE 3.2 ■ Double-alternative structure for binary decision

courses of action. Such a structure is well-suited to the task of imitating a multiple-function pocket calculator, where the cases we must handle correspond to the different operations that the calculator can perform. Figure 3.3 depicts a case structure as containing several black boxes, one of which is selected for execution by the outcome of a decision that permits many answers. In languages that do not provide an explicit case structure, we can use a sequence of single- or double-alternative structures to provide for a choice from among many alternatives. (See Exercises 2 and 3 at the end of this section.)

REPETITION

The true power of computers does not come into play if we compose actions solely into sequences and alternatives. It takes us as long to describe such composite actions as it does to perform them. But, if we can instruct a computer to "repeat the following steps one million times," then we can describe computations that are utterly beyond our ability to perform without the aid of a computer. Hence it is not surprising that most computer programs contain instructions that cause them to repeat some steps many times.

To perform an action repeatedly is to *iterate* that action: to mimic a pocket calculator that raises a number to an integer power, we need to iterate the multiplication of that number by itself; to simulate the motion of a rocket, we need to iterate the computation of its position at successive moments in time. Consequently program structures for repetitive tasks such as these are called *iterative* structures.

Iterative structures have two components: an action to be performed repeatedly, and a means of deciding when to stop performing that action. Our view of an iterative

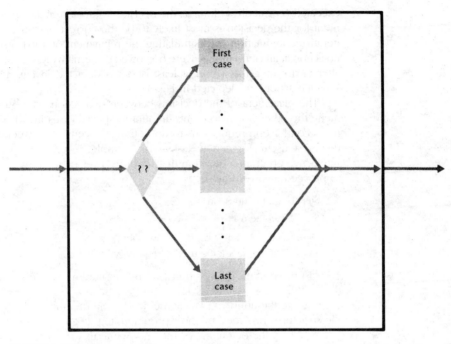

FIGURE 3.3 ■ Case structure for multiple-outcome decision

structure depends on the point at which we make this decision with respect to performing the action. If we make the decision before performing the action, we can depict the iterative structure as shown in Fig. 3.4, which contains a black box that is

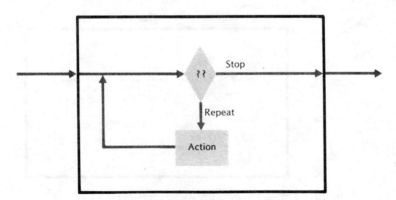

FIGURE 3.4 ■ Iterative structure with decision before action

executed repeatedly so long as the decision to do so remains positive. Such a placement for the decision is most likely to be the correct one since the objective of an iterative computation (say, simulating the repayment of a loan) sometimes requires no action at all (if no money were borrowed). Alternatively, we can make the decision after performing the action at least once, as depicted in Fig. 3.5, or between two separate actions, as depicted in Fig. 3.6.

The placement of the decision between two actions is the most general placement; the other two placements amount to special cases in which either the first or the second action requires us to do nothing. Placement between two actions is also the most useful for certain tasks. For example, if we wish to ask the user of an interactive program a question that requires a yes or no answer, then a natural way to proceed involves four steps.

Step 1: Ask the question.

Step 2: Get the user's response.

Step 3: If the response is yes or no, then proceed.

Step 4: Otherwise ask the user to respond yes or no and go back to step 2.

The last three of these steps translate into an iterative structure with the decision in the middle.

Despite the utility of placing the decision in the middle of an iterative structure, the structures provided by most programming languages allow us to place the decision only at the beginning or the end. While this restriction may be inconvenient, it is not impossible to live with. We can always move the decision to the beginning of an iterative structure by minor surgery: we move the first action outside the structure and place a cloned copy of that action after the second action inside the structure. (See Fig. 3.7.)

The diagrams that depict iterative structures differ from those that depict sequential or alternative structures in that we can, by following the arrows in the

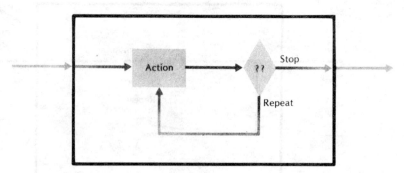

FIGURE 3.5 ■ Iterative structure with decision after action

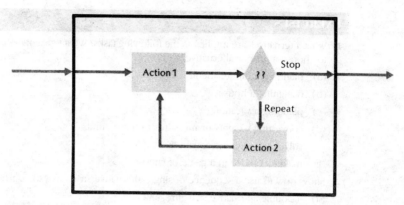

FIGURE 3.6 ■ Iterative structure with decision between two actions

diagram, arrive back at the same point in the diagram many times. For this reason iterative structures are commonly known as *loops*. The decision that stops the iteration is said to *terminate*, or cause an *exit* from, the loop.

Loops are both powerful and dangerous: powerful because we can use the great speed of a computer to iterate a computation many times; dangerous because we may cause a computation to be iterated forever, in what is known as an *infinite loop*, or for an excessively large number of times, requiring several centuries of computing before the loop terminates. Hence a major concern in programming and in computer science is to analyze and control the looping behavior of programs.

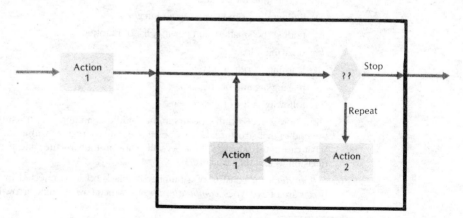

FIGURE 3.7 ■ Moving a decision to the beginning of an iterative structure

EXERCISES

1. What alternatives are implicit in the following tasks? What types of decisions must be made to choose a proper alternative?

 (a) planning a dinner menu

 (b) designing a house

 (c) planning a vacation

 (d) converting weights or measures to metric units

 (e) solving a quadratic equation

 (f) making a move in a game of chess

2. Show how to use a sequence of single-alternative structures to construct

 (a) a double-alternative structure, and

 (b) a case structure with n cases.

 In your constructions does the order of the alternatives matter? In particular, can the outcome of the decision governing an early alternative affect the outcome of later decisions? If so, what trouble might this cause and how can the defect be remedied?

3. Explore the construction of case structures as follows.

 (a) Show how to construct a case structure with n cases as a double-alternative structure that has a second alternative consisting of another double-alternative structure that has a second alternative . . .

 (b) In what ways is this construction preferable to the construction used for Exercise 2?

 (c) How many double-alternative structures did you use for the construction?

 (d) Can you construct a case structure with n cases using fewer double-alternative structures? If so, what is the fewest number required?

4. What kinds of iterations are implicit in the following tasks? What decisions govern how long to continue the iteration?

 (a) finding the prime factors of an integer

 (b) finding the smallest number in a list of numbers

 (c) repaying a loan

 (d) learning to ride a bicycle

 (e) playing a game of chess

 (f) following a list of instructions

5. Show how a decision that occurs in the middle of an iterative structure can be moved to the end of that structure. (*Hint:* Use an alternative structure within the iterative structure. What care must be taken if the second action in the structure affects the outcome of the decision to exit the structure?)

*6. A *flow diagram* consists of a number of black boxes connected by arrows. The black boxes are of two types: *computation boxes*, which have a single arrow leading from them;

---

*An asterisk denotes an exercise that is more challenging than the others.

and *decision boxes,* which have two arrows leading from them. Boxes may have any number of arrows leading into them. With two exceptions, all arrows in a flow diagram lead from one box to another; the *start arrow* leads to a box, but does not start from one, and the *stop arrow* begins at a box, but does not lead to one. A flow diagram is executed by following the arrows (starting with the start arrow and ending with the stop arrow), performing the computations specified by the computation boxes and making the decisions specified by the decision boxes along the way.

A *structured flow diagram* is a flow diagram that is built up by using sequential, alternative, and iterative structures. Show that the execution of any flow diagram at all can be simulated by the execution of a corresponding structured flow diagram. (*Hint:* Number the boxes in the flow diagram, introduce a variable *nextbox,* and add computation and decision boxes to the flow diagram that manipulate this variable and allow the computation to be structured as a simple loop.)

3.3 PROGRAMMING: CONDITIONALS FOR CHOICE

To illustrate how we can choose from among several alternative courses of action, we will now construct a program *minOf2* to mimic a pocket calculator that displays the minimum of two integers. This program will have the same overall form as *add* and *add1,* since it will allow us to enter two integers and it will display a single integer as the result. However, two steps in the program will be different: the output statement will display the minimum rather than the sum of the two integers; the message accompanying the display will reflect the revised function of the calculator. Furthermore, new comments will explain what the program does.

As we noted in Section 3.2, a program structure for alternative computations is appropriate for this task. There we proposed the following strategy:

> ask user to enter two numbers
> get two numbers, *a* and *b*
> **if** $a \le b$ **then** display *a* **else** display *b*

A straightforward translation of this strategy into Pascal produces the program *minOf2* (Pascal Sample 3.1), which is based on *add* and employs a *conditional statement* to specify the alternatives implicit in the third step.

In this program, the sequence <= of symbols stands for the relation $\le$ ("less than or equal to"); the format :1 in the output statement causes the minimum to be displayed with no preceding spaces. Alternatively, we could perform the same task using the variant *minOf2a* of *minOf2* (Pascal Sample 3.2), which is more like *add1* than *add.*

Despite the differences in the way we display the conditional statements in *minOf2* and *minOf2a,* these statements have the same general form. They, as well as all conditional statements in Pascal, consist of the keyword **if** followed by a logical expression (such as $a \le b$), a statement introduced by the keyword **then,** and another statement introduced by the keyword **else.** As shown by the syntax diagram

PASCAL SAMPLE 3.1   The program *minOf2*

{ displays the minimum of two integers }

```pascal
program minOf2(input, output);
var a, b : integer;
begin
    writeln('Enter two integers.');
    read(a, b);
    writeln;
    if a <= b then
        writeln('Their minimum is ', a:1)
    else
        writeln('Their minimum is ', b:1)
end.
```

SAMPLE USE OF *minOf2*:

```
Enter two integers.
8 3

Their minimum is 3
```

in Fig. 3.8, we can omit the keyword **else** and its following statement (we simply follow the arrow to the right rather than the arrow to the left after the statement introduced by the keyword **then**).

PASCAL SAMPLE 3.2   The program *minOf2a*

{ displays the minimum of two integers }

```pascal
program minOf2a(input, output);
var a, b, minimum : integer;
begin
    writeln('Enter two integers.');
    read(a, b);
    if a <= b then minimum := a else minimum := b;
    writeln;
    writeln('Their minimum is ', minimum:1)
end.
```

SAMPLE USE OF *minOf2a*:

```
Enter two integers.
8 3

Their minimum is 3
```

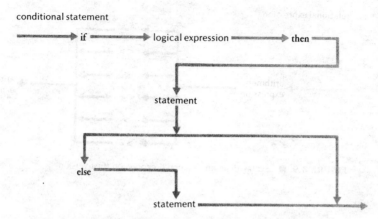

conditional statement

FIGURE 3.8 ■ Syntax diagram, conditional statement

When a conditional statement is executed, the value of its logical expression is used to select either the statement following the keyword **then** or the statement following the keyword **else** for execution; if this value is true, the statement following the keyword **then** is executed; if it is false and the keyword **else** is present, the following statement is executed; if it is false and the keyword **else** is absent, no action is taken.

A second variant *minOf2b* of *minOf2* (Pascal Sample 3.3) illustrates how to use a conditional statement that lacks the keyword **else** to construct a single-alternative

---

PASCAL SAMPLE 3.3 The program *minOf2b*

{ displays the minimum of two integers }
program *minOf2b*(*input, output*);
var *a, b, minimum* : *integer*;
begin
    writeln('Enter two integers.');
    read(*a, b*);
    minimum := *a*;
    if *b* < *minimum* **then** *minimum* := *b*;
    writeln;
    writeln('Their minimum is ', *minimum*:1)
end.

SAMPLE USE OF *minOf2b*:

```
Enter two integers.
8 3

Their minimum is 3
```

relational expression

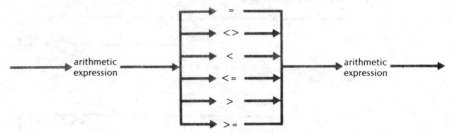

FIGURE 3.9 ■ Syntax diagram, relational expression (first version)

decision structure. In *minOf2b* we make a preliminary guess that the first integer entered is the minimum and then revise that guess if it turns out to be wrong.

LOGICAL AND RELATIONAL EXPRESSIONS

The logical expressions used in conditional statements are expressions that have logical values of either truth or falsity. In Chapter 5 we will learn how to assign the value of a logical expression to a variable that belongs to the *logical* or *boolean* data type, as well as how to use such variables in constructing logical expressions. However, our first examples do not need such generality; we can use a special case of a logical expression, known as a *relational expression*, that consists of two arithmetic expressions separated by a symbol that denotes a relational operator. (See Fig. 3.9.)

There are six relational operators that produce a logical value of true or false when applied to arithmetic values. The symbols for and meanings of these operators are listed in Table 3.2. Pascal, as opposed to some other programming languages, uses distinct symbols for the relational operator of equality ($=$) and the assignment operator ($:=$). Thus Pascal does not invite confusion about whether $a=b$ is a statement of fact, which can be either true or false, or an imperative statement, which

TABLE 3.2	Relational Operators in Pascal
$=$	equal to
$<>$	not equal to
$<$	less than
$<=$	less than or equal to
$>$	greater than
$>=$	greater than or equal to

logical expression

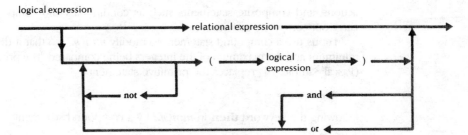

FIGURE 3.10 ■ Syntax diagram, logical expression (simplified version)

dictates that the value of *b* be given to *a*; in Pascal, as opposed to Fortran and PL/I, it can only be the former.

We can combine relational expressions themselves into more complex logical expressions by using the logical operators **and**, **or**, and **not**. For example, the statement

    if $(a <= b)$ **and** $(a <= c)$ **then** . . .

checks whether *a* is the minimum of the three numbers *a*, *b*, and *c*. Because of the way Pascal treats logical operators we cannot dispense with parentheses in logical expressions such as this. Figure 3.10 provides a simplified diagram for the syntax of logical expressions; a more detailed diagram and discussion appears in Chapter 5.

NESTED STRUCTURES AND COMPOUND STATEMENTS

Pascal requires that single statements follow the keywords **then** and **else** in a conditional statement. Hence we need a way to handle alternative structures in which we must perform more than one action in one or the other of the alternatives. For example, suppose we wish to display two numbers *a* and *b* in increasing order on two separate lines. Ideally, we would like to modify *minOf2* somewhat as follows:

    if $a <= b$ **then**
        { write *a* first; then write *b* on a new line }
    else
        { write *b* first; then write *a* on a new line }

In Pascal, our problem is how to accomplish the two actions required by each of the comments in a single statement.

The compound statement, introduced in Section 2.4, provides a solution to our problem. So far we have used compound statements—sequences of statements separated by semicolons and bounded by the keywords **begin** and **end**—to form the bodies of programs. But compound statements can also occur in the body of a program anywhere that a single statement can occur. In Pascal, statements carry out actions, and composite statements such as conditionals and compound statements carry out composite actions.

Let us use a compound statement to modify *minOf2*, so that it displays both the minimum and the maximum of the integers being compared. The program *arrange2* (Pascal Sample 3.4) replaces the primitive statement

   minimum := *a*

following the keyword **then** in *minOf2* by a compound statement

   begin
      minimum := *a*;
      maximum := *b*
   end

and similarly replaces the primitive statement following the keyword **else** by another compound statement. Here the indented display greatly enhances the readability of the program, showing which statements are contained, or *nested*, in which.

PASCAL SAMPLE 3.4   The program *arrange2*

{ arranges two integers in increasing order }

program *arrange2*(*input, output*);
var *a, b, minimum, maximum* : *integer*;
begin
    writeln('Enter two integers.');
    read(*a, b*);
    if *a* <= *b* **then**
        begin
            minimum := *a*;
            maximum := *b*
        end
    else
        begin
            minimum := *b*;
            maximum := *a*
        end;
    writeln;
    writeln(*minimum*:1, ' <= ', *maximum*:1)
end.

SAMPLE USE OF *arrange2*:

```
Enter two integers
2 4

2 <= 4
```

THE SEMICOLON AS A STATEMENT SEPARATOR

It is worth focusing our attention briefly on the role of the semicolon in Pascal as a *separator* for the component statements of a compound statement. Other languages, most notably PL/I, use the semicolon as a statement *terminator*. In order to program in either language, we must learn where to place the semicolons. The body of *arrange2* contains five statements: an output statement, an input statement, the conditional statement

```
if a <= b then
    begin
        minimum := a;
        maximum := b
    end
else
    begin
        minimum := b;
        maximum := a
    end
```

and two more output statements. The semicolon after the conditional statement in *arrange2* separates it from the following output statement. The statements nested in this conditional statement are themselves compound statements in which a single semicolon separates their two component statements. A PL/I programmer would punctuate the conditional statement as

```
if a <= b then
    begin;
        minimum := a;
        maximum := b;
    end;
else
    begin;
        minimum := b;
        maximum := a;
    end;
```

since, in PL/I, **begin** and **end** are statements themselves which, like all other PL/I statements, must be terminated by a semicolon. However, in Pascal **begin** and **end** are not statements, but rather delimiters (somewhat like parentheses) that mark the boundaries of compound statements. Extra semicolons following **begin** and preceding **end** do no harm. Pascal simply interprets the revised compound statements as containing two additional component statements that have no effect when executed; such *null statements* are invisible. (See Fig. 3.11.) On the other hand, the extra semicolon before the keyword **else** is illegal in Pascal, which would treat it as separating a single-alternative conditional statement from an illegal statement beginning with the keyword **else**.

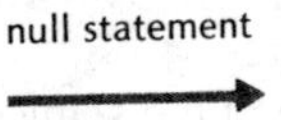

null statement

⟶

FIGURE 3.11 ■ Syntax diagram, null statement

NESTED CONDITIONAL STATEMENTS

We can nest other conditional statements (as well as compound statements) in conditional statements. For example, to display the minimum of three integers a, b, and c, we might utilize the following strategy:

> **if** $a <= b$ **then**
>   { display minimum of a and c }
> **else**
>   { display minimum of b and c }

In order to transform this strategy into a Pascal program, we take conditional statements, similar to the one in *minOf2* that displays the minimum of two integers, and nest them inside another conditional statement. The resulting program *minOf3* is displayed as Pascal Sample 3.5. Here again the form of the display greatly enhances the readability of the program, showing which statements are nested in which.

It is important to recognize that the definition of Pascal, and not the way we display a program, dictates how that program is interpreted. For example, execution of

> **if** $a <= b$ **then**
>   **if** $a <= c$ **then**
>   *write*(a);
>   *write*(b);
>   *write*(c)

always results in writing the values of both b and c. The display tempts us to believe that the statement *write*(b) should be grouped with the statement *write*(a), but the semicolon preceding *write*(b) dictates that it follows, and is not part of, the conditional statement.

One particular use of nested conditional statements requires a special interpretation. If we want to interpret the statement

> **if** $a < b$ **then if** $b < c$ **then** *write*(a) **else** *write*(b)

we need to know whether Pascal treats the keyword **else** as matching the first **if**, as suggested by the display

> **if** $a < b$ **then**
>   **if** $b < c$ **then** *write*(a)
> **else**
>   *write*(b)

PASCAL SAMPLE 3.5   The program *minOf3*

{ displays the minimum of three integers }

```
program minOf3(input, output);
var a, b, c, minimum : integer;
begin
    writeln('Enter three integers.');
    read(a, b, c);
    if a <= b then
        if a <= c then
            minimum := a
        else
            minimum := c
    else
        if b <= c then
            minimum := b
        else
            minimum := c;
    writeln;
    writeln('Their minimum is ', minimum : 1)
end.
```

SAMPLE USE OF *minOf3*:

```
Enter three integers.
3 1 2

Their minimum is 1
```

or the second **if**, as suggested by the display

```
if a < b then
    if b < c then
        write(a)
    else
        write(b)
```

The rule in Pascal is that such a "dangling **else**" always belongs to the nested conditional statement. Thus, if we want the interpretation that is incorrectly suggested by the first display, we must embed the nested conditional statement in a compound statement, as in

```
if a < b then
    begin if b < c then write(a) end
else
    write(b)
```

or we must transform it into a conditional statement with a null statement following the keyword **else**, as in

> **if** $a < b$ **then**
>   **if** $b < c$ **then** *write(a)* **else** { do nothing }
> **else**
>   *write(b)*

EXERCISES

1. How would you modify *minOf2* to display the maximum, rather than the minimum, of two numbers?

2. Write a Pascal program, without using nested conditional structures, to display the minimum of three numbers. (*Hint*: Generalize *minOf2b*.)

3. Write a Pascal program *arrange2a* that arranges two numbers in increasing order using a single-alternative decision structure. (*Hint*: Modify *minOf2b*.)

4. Write a Pascal program to arrange three numbers in increasing order. (*Hint*: Modify *arrange2* or your solution to Exercise 3.)

5. Write a Pascal program to input four numbers and print the second largest.

6. The XYZ Shipping Company charges $10 per ton for the first 20 tons of a shipment, $8 per ton for the next 30 tons, and $6 per ton for the remainder of the shipment. Write a Pascal program to input the weight of a shipment and print the shipping cost.

7. Write a Pascal program to determine whether a particular year is a leap year (a year is a leap year if it is divisible by 400 or if it is divisible by 4 but not by 100).

8. Write a Pascal program to input an employee's gross medical expenses for a calendar year and compute the amount of reimbursement from his or her group medical insurance. The insurance does not cover the first $100 of medical expenses, pays 90% of the first $2000 of covered expenses, and 100% of any additional expenses. Test your program with gross expenses of $10, $100, $200, $2000, $2100, and $3000.

9. Write a Pascal program to determine the fee a lawyer charges her client in a suit for damages. The lawyer works either on a fixed fee amounting to 1/3 of the damages recovered or on a sliding fee amounting to 50% of the first $4000 recovered, 40% of the next $6000, 35% of the next $20,000, and 25% of any recovery over $30,000. Your program should accept the amount recovered as input, determine whether the fixed or sliding fee is less expensive, and display that fee together with an indication of how it was computed. Test your program for amounts of $2000, $8000, $20,000, and $36,000.

10. Write a Pascal program to determine the winner in a variant of the game of paper—scissors—stone. In that game, each of two players picks one of the words scissors, paper, or stone. If each player chooses the same word, the game is a draw. Otherwise, paper loses to scissors (which can cut it), scissors lose to stone (which can smash them), and stone loses to paper (which can wrap it). Your program should accept one number from each player as input (1 for paper, 2 for scissors, and 3 for stone) and print one of four messages: illegal move, draw, first player wins, or second player wins.

11. Write a Pascal program to display the roots of the quadratic equation $ax^2 + bx + c = 0$, with a, b, and c as input. Your program should determine the number of roots and whether these roots are real or complex. (*Hint:* By the quadratic formula, the equation has roots at

$$\frac{-b \pm \sqrt{b^2 - 4ac}}{2a},$$

if $a <> 0$. What happens if $a = 0$?)

*12. How well does the program you wrote for Exercise 10 work if $b^2 - 4ac$ is close to 0 or to b^2?

13. Write a Pascal program to compute x^y, where x and y are real numbers, whenever that quantity is defined and to print a message when it is not.

3.4 PROGRAMMING: LOOPS FOR REPETITION

We continue our imitation of pocket calculators by writing several programs to perform mathematical and financial calculations. Each of these programs will involve repeating some task several times. Hence they will illustrate iterative program structures, otherwise known as loops, such as those we discussed in Section 3.2.

LOOPS WITH COUNTERS

Consider the problem of calculating the value x^n of a real number x raised to the power n, where n is a positive integer. One way to proceed is to multiply x by itself n times, that is, to execute the statement $y := y*x$ repeatedly n times after giving y an initial value of 1. This is accomplished by the **for** statement in the program *intPower* in Pascal Sample 3.6 on p. 86. By careful use of the absolute-value function *abs*, *intPower* can handle negative as well as positive values for n.

The general format of the **for** statement in Pascal is the same as in *intPower*. As shown by the syntax diagram in Fig. 3.12, a **for** statement begins with the keyword

for statement

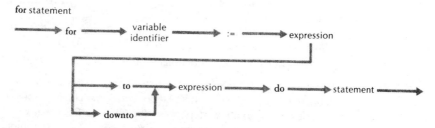

FIGURE 3.12 ■ Syntax diagram, **for** statement

PASCAL SAMPLE 3.6 The program *intPower*

{ raises a real number to an integer power }

program *intPower(input, output)*;

```
var x      : real;                              { base      }
    n      : integer;                           { exponent }
    y      : real;                              { result    }
    count  : integer;

begin
    write('Enter base, exponent: ');
    read(x, n);
    y := 1;                                     { y = x**0      }
    for count := 1 to abs(n) do y := y*x;       { y = x**count }
    if n < 0 then y := 1/y;                      { y = x**n      }
    writeln;
    writeln(x:7:5, ' ** ', n:1, ' = ', y:7:5)
end.
```

SAMPLE USE OF *intPower*:

```
Enter base, exponent: 2 10

2.00000 ** 10 = 1024.00000
```

for followed by an integer variable serving as the *control variable* for the loop, the assignment operator :=, and an expression giving the initial value for the control variable. Next comes the keyword **to** followed by an expression giving the final value for the control variable. Finally comes the keyword **do** followed by the *body* of the loop, which is a (possibly compound) statement to be executed once for each integer value of the control variable, in increasing order, from the initial value to the final value. If the final value is less than the initial one (for example, if $n = 0$ in *intPower*), the body of the loop is not executed.

A variant of the **for** statement in Pascal uses the keyword **downto** instead of the keyword **to**. In this variant, the loop is also executed once for each integer value of the control variable, but in decreasing order, from the initial value to the final value; if the final value is greater than the initial one, the body of the loop is not executed.

Pascal imposes several restrictions on the control variable in a **for** statement:

- The control variable must be of type *integer* (or some other ordinal type, as defined in Section 5.5) and not of type *real*. Some languages allow reals as control variables and also allow step sizes other than ±1 for that variable. Pascal does not allow this because the approximate nature of real arithmetic often leads to problems. (See Exercise 16 at the end of this section.)

■ The control variable must not occur in a context within the body of the loop where it can be modified (such as in an input statement). This restriction prevents abuses of the language, such as setting the value of the control variable to *maxint* in order to terminate a loop; Pascal provides other, more appropriate looping mechanisms for this purpose.

■ The value of the control variable becomes undefined when execution of the loop terminates. Some programming languages specify that the control variable retains the last value used in the loop; some specify that it has the first value not used. Pascal avoids confusion by assigning meaning to the control variable only within the loop.

LOOPS WITH GENERAL EXITS

Loops that are constructed using the **for** statement are appropriate when we know in advance how many times we want to execute the body of the loop. Often we do not know how many times this should be. For example, if the purpose of the loop is to search for a value having a certain property, we may not know in advance how many values must be examined before one with that property is found. Consider how we might go about finding the smallest integer n such that $2^n > x$ for some real number x. We could find n by executing *intPower* repeatedly, raising 2 to the first power, then to the second, and so on, until the displayed result exceeds x. Alternatively, we could automate this procedure by the program *powerOf2*, displayed as Pascal Sample 3.7 on p. 88.

Here we use a **while** statement in Pascal to execute the statement $y := y*2$ repeatedly until y is greater than x. As shown by the syntax diagram in Fig. 3.13, a **while** statement consists of the keyword **while** followed by a logical expression, the keyword **do**, and a (possibly compound) statement that forms the body of the loop. A **while** statement is executed by evaluating its logical expression; if it is true, then the body of the loop is executed and the logical expression is evaluated again; if and when evaluation of the logical expression produces the value false, execution of the loop terminates. The body of the loop will not be executed at all if the logical expression is false initially. Indeed, this is just what we wish to happen in the program *powerOf2* when x is 0.

A third variety of loops in Pascal is provided by the **repeat** statement, which differs from the **while** statement in that the body of the loop is always executed at least once. For example, if n is an integer variable, the following loop echoes integers

while statement

FIGURE 3.13 ■ Syntax diagram, **while** statement

■ **PASCAL SAMPLE 3.7**   The program *powerOf2*

{ finds smallest power of two exceeding an integer }

program *powerOf2*(*input, output*);

var *x* : *integer*;	{ number to exceed }
n : *integer*;	{ exponent }
y : *integer*;	{ power of 2 }

begin

    write('Enter number to exceed: ');

    read(*x*);

    y := 1;   { $y = 2**0$ }

    n := 0;   { $y = 2**n$ }

    while *y* <= *x* **do**

        begin

            n := *n* + 1;   { $y = 2**(n-1)$ }

            y := 2*y   { $y = 2**n$ }

        end;

    writeln;

    writeln(*x*:1, ' < ', *y*:1, ' = 2**', *n*:1)

end.

SAMPLE USE OF *powerOf2*:

```
Enter number to exceed: 2000

2000 < 2048 = 2**11
```

that are supplied as input until a zero is supplied:

repeat

    read(*n*);

    write(*n*)

until *n* = 0

As shown by this example and by the syntax diagram in Fig. 3.14, a **repeat** statement consists of the keyword **repeat** followed by a list of statements separated by semi-colons, the keyword **until**, and a logical expression. When executed, the preceding **repeat** statement produces exactly the same result as the following sequence of statements:

    read(*n*);

    write(*n*);

    while *n* <> 0 **do**

        begin

            read(*n*);

            write(*n*)

        end

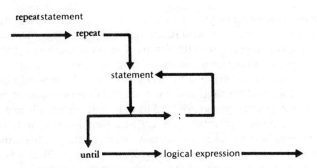

repeat statement

FIGURE 3.14 ■ Syntax diagram, **repeat** statement

In general, we use **repeat** statements less frequently than **while** statements; most loops, if properly constructed, must allow for the possibility that their bodies are executed zero times.

TWO FURTHER EXAMPLES: FINANCIAL CALCULATORS

The repayment of an installment loan is an iterative process, and thus it is not surprising that programs performing loan repayment calculations utilize iterative program structures. As we will see, the nature of these iterative structures is determined by the nature of the calculations that they must perform.

The fundamental quantity that we must compute for repayment of a loan is the amount of interest due at the time of each payment. We compute this interest by prorating the annual interest rate—usually expressed as a percentage—over the time since the last payment and applying that prorated rate to the current balance; thus, for repayment of a loan in monthly installments, we compute the interest due at the end of a month by the formula

$$interest \ = \ balance \ \times \ \frac{annual \ interest \ rate}{12 \ \times \ 100},$$

where *balance* is the balance at the beginning of the month, the factor of 12 converts the yearly interest rate into a monthly rate, and the factor of 100 converts the percentage interest rate (say, 15%) into a fraction (0.15).

Knowing the interest on the unpaid balance, we can compute the balance remaining after the next payment by setting

$$new \ balance \ = \ old \ balance \ + \ interest \ - \ payment.$$

If we iterate this computation once for each payment that is made, then we mimic or *simulate* the actual repayment of the loan.

Simulation is a powerful tool that we can use in more complex situations to answer questions such as: "What happens if . . . ?" If an experiment designed to answer such a question is expensive, dangerous, time-consuming, or otherwise undesirable, we do not need to perform that experiment ourselves. Instead, we can have a computer conduct the experiment for us by simulating what would happen in real life. Thus, in order to determine how much we still owe on a loan after making a certain number of payments, we do not have to wait until we actually make those payments. Rather, we can use a program such as Pascal Sample 3.8, *loan1*, to simulate making the payments and to calculate the new balance after each payment. The iterative structure of *loan1* clearly mimics the structure of the problem it is designed to solve: to simulate a specified number of monthly payments, the **for** loop in *loan1* calculates the new balance precisely the required number of times.

Our use of simulation in loan repayment calculations anticipates a more extensive study of simulation in Chapter 10; it also enables us to make several general obser-

---

█ **PASCAL SAMPLE 3.8**   The program *loan1*

{ finds the final balance of a loan given the amount borrowed, }
{ the annual interest rate, the number of monthly payments,   }
{ and the amount of each payment   }

program *loan1*(*input, output*);

var *amount* : *real*;   { initial amount of loan   }
　　rate   : *real*;   { annual interest rate in % }
　　months   : *integer*;   { length of loan   }
　　payment : *real*;   { monthly payment   }
　　m   : *integer*;   { counter for months   }

begin

　　write('Amount, rate, months, payment: ');
　　read(*amount, rate, months, payment*);

　　rate := *rate*/1200;   { monthly rate as a fraction }

　　{ find amount still owed after each payment }

　　for *m* := 1 **to** *months* **do**
　　　　amount := *amount* + *amount*∗*rate* − *payment*;

　　writeln;
　　writeln('The final balance is $', *amount*)

end.

SAMPLE USE OF *loan1*:

Amount, rate, months, payment: 1000 15 11 90.26

The final balance is $ 8.9124241e+01

vations about the nature of simulations at this time. A simulation depends on the existence of a *model* of the process being simulated. In the case of loan repayments, this process itself is a computational one, and hence a simulation model is easy to develop. In other cases, such as the prediction of tomorrow's weather, a considerable amount of scientific research is needed to develop an adequate model. The accuracy of a simulation depends on the extent to which the model used represents reality. Everyone who has planned a picnic knows that models used to forecast the weather fail to approximate reality exactly. Perhaps less obviously, the model used in *loan1* also fails to approximate reality exactly.

The output in Pascal claims that the final balance on a loan of $1000 at 15-percent interest after 11 monthly payments of $90.26 is $89.124241. But this output cannot be the true final balance, as shown in Table 3.1, since banks measure loans in dollars and cents, not in fractions of a cent.

The problem with *loan1* lies in the fact that it does not simulate the repayment of a loan quite closely enough: when interest is paid, the amount of that interest must be rounded to the nearest cent. In order to improve the accuracy of the simulation in *loan1* we must build rounding into the program. Doing this requires two programming decisions: (1) where rounding should occur in *loan1*; and (2) how it should be accomplished. Neither decision is terribly difficult.

Banking practice dictates that rounding occur each time we compute a new balance; simply rounding the final balance will not suffice since the true final balance is $89.13 and not $89.12. The *round* function in Pascal provides a way to accomplish the rounding: *round*(x) rounds x to the nearest integer, and *round*($100*x$)/100 rounds x to the nearest hundredth. Hence we can replace the statement

amount := *amount* + *amount*∗*rate* − *payment*

that computes the new balance each month by a compound statement

```
begin
    amount := amount + amount*rate − payment;
    amount := round(100*amount)/100
end
```

that computes and rounds this balance, or by a single statement

amount := *round*($100*(amount + amount*rate − payment)$)/100

that rolls both computations into one. By modifying *loan1* in either of these two ways, and by formatting how we print the final balance in the form

writeln('The final balance is $', *balance*:4:2)

we enable *loan1* to display the true final balance $89.13 on a loan of $1000 at 15-percent annual interest after 11 monthly payments of $90.26.

One of the primary benefits of using simulation models in well-structured programs is the ease with which we can make improvements such as this in the simulation. If a minor change in the model improves the accuracy of the simulation, we can make a minor change in the program to reflect the change in the model. Although these modifications do the job, they lengthen and obscure the computation of the balance by the details of how rounding is accomplished. If Pascal provided a function *roundToCents* that rounded to the nearest hundredth, then it would be clearer to use a statement

$$amount := roundToCents(amount + amount*rate - payment)$$

to compute the new balance. In Chapter 4, we will see that, even though Pascal does not provide this function, it does enable us to define that function ourselves.

As a second example of the use of simulation in loan repayment computations, we will construct a program *loan2* that computes the life of a loan given the amount of money borrowed, the annual interest rate, and the size of the monthly payments. (See Pascal Sample 3.9.) The iterative structure of *loan2* resembles that of *loan1*, differing only in that it uses a **while** loop in place of a **for** loop. Since we do not know the required number of monthly payments in advance, we describe the termination condition for the loop in *loan2* in terms of the balance becoming zero (or negative) rather than in terms of the number of payments. Hence the structure of the problem (what we wish to compute) is reflected directly in the structure of the program. Note that the sample output produced by *loan2* confirms the amount of the final payment for the loan illustrated in Table 3.1.

Simulation is not the only tool we can use to draw conclusions from a model. For example, we can apply a simple mathematical analysis to the model for loan repayment, provided we do not complicate that model by rounding. This analysis enables us to derive a formula for the balance of a loan that has an initial balance of b after a certain number of payments of size p, with interest at the rate r being applied at the time of each payment. After one payment, the new balance is

$$b + br - p \quad \text{or} \quad b(1+r) - p.$$

After two payments, it is

$$(b(1+r) - p)(1+r) - p \quad \text{or} \quad b(1+r)^2 - p(1+r) - p.$$

After m payments, the balance is

$$b(1+r)^m - p(1+r)^{m-1} - \cdots - p(1+r) - p,$$

which equals

$$b(1+r)^m - p((1+r)^{m-1} + \cdots + (1+r) + 1),$$

$$b(1+r)^m - p\frac{(1+r)^m - 1}{r},$$

and finally

$$\left(b - \frac{p}{r}\right)(1+r)^m + \frac{p}{r}.$$

■ **PASCAL SAMPLE 3.9**   The program *loan2*

{ finds the life in months of a loan given the amount borrowed, the   }
{ annual interest rate, and the amount of each monthly payment   }

program *loan2*(*input, output*);

var *amount*   : *real*;   { initial amount of loan   }
    rate   : *real*;   { annual interest rate in % }
    payment : *real*;   { monthly payment   }
    months   : *integer*;   { months into loan   }

begin
    write('Amount, rate, payment: ');
    read(*amount, rate, payment*);

    rate := *rate*/1200;   { monthly rate as a fraction }

    { simulate payments until loan is repaid }

    months := 0;
    while *amount* > 0 **do**
        begin
            months := *months* + 1;
            amount := *amount* + *amount*∗*rate* − *payment*;
            amount := *round*(100∗*amount*)/100
        end;

    writeln;
    write('The loan ends in ', *months*:1, ' months ');
    writeln('with a final payment of $', *payment*+*amount*:4:2)
end.

SAMPLE USE OF *loan2*:

```
Amount, rate, payment: 1000  15  90.26

The loan ends in 12 months with a final payment of $90.24
```

In making this derivation we use the standard technique for summing a finite geometric series

$$1 + x + x^2 + \cdots + x^{m-1} ;$$

we set

$$s = 1 + x + x^2 + \cdots + x^{m-1}$$

and observe that

$$sx = x + x^2 + \cdots + x^{m-1} + x^m;$$

subtracting the first equation from the second, we find that

$$sx - s = x^m - 1, \quad \text{and} \quad s = \frac{x^m - 1}{x - 1}.$$

The virtues of mathematical analysis in this application are twofold: it provides a formula that we can use to compute final balances, without iteration, on any pocket calculator that has an exponential operator; and it makes explicit the ways in which the final balance of a loan depends on the factors b, r, m, and p. The virtues of simulation are also twofold: it circumvents the need for mathematical analysis; and it enables us to draw conclusions from models (such as that for loan repayment with rounding) that do not submit readily to mathematical analysis. Mathematical analysis and simulation actually go hand in hand. Analysis aids in the development of a simulation model and improves the efficiency of a computational process based upon that model.

EXERCISES

1. Write programs to print
   - (a) your name 10 times,
   - (b) a block of asterisks 10 characters wide and 10 characters high,
   - (c) a triangle of asterisks 10 characters high, 10 characters wide at the base, and 1 character wide at the top, and
   - (d) a table of the square roots of the integers from 1 to 10.

2. Recode the program *powerOf2* without using a loop. (*Hint:* Use the *trunc*, *ln*, and *exp* functions.)

3. How many multiplications does the program *intPower* perform when raising the real number x to the integer power n? Can you devise a way to do this with fewer multiplications (but still without using *ln* or *exp*)?

4. Modify *loan1* to produce a loan repayment schedule like the one in Table 3.1.

5. What would be the difference, if any, if we round only the interest in *loan1*, rather than the resulting balance, at the time of each payment, that is, by using

   amount + *round*(100*amount*rate)/100 − *payment*

   rather than

   round(100*(amount + amount*rate − payment*))/100

   to compute the balance after each payment? (*Hint:* Try to print as many decimal places as possible for the final balance after 12 monthly payments of $90.26 on a loan of $1000 at 15%.)

6. Derive a formula that gives the life of a loan in months, using the initial balance b of the loan, the size p of the monthly payments, and the interest rate r applied each time a

payment is made. (*Hint:* Set the formula for the final balance of a loan equal to zero and solve for *m*.)

7. Write a program that computes the balance in a savings account for a given initial balance, annual interest rate, and number of years that interest has been accumulated. Assume that interest is compounded (computed and credited) once a year.

8. Write a program to compute how many years it takes for an amount of money deposited in a savings account at a specified annual interest rate to double in value.

9. Modify your compound-interest program to allow interest to be compounded several times per year. Experiment with the effect of compounding the interest quarterly, monthly, daily, and every minute. Where in this program should the balance be rounded to the nearest cent?

10. Write programs to input a positive integer *n* and then print

    (a) a list of all integers that divide *n*,

    (b) a list of the prime numbers that divide *n*, and

    (c) a complete factorization of *n* into primes.

    Identify the similarities among these programs.

11. Write a program to read a positive integer *n* and then print all integers between 1 and *n* that can be expressed as the sum of the squares of two integers.

12. Write a program to make change for a specified amount of money, that is, to determine the smallest number of bills and coins worth that amount of money.

13. Write a program that enables two users to play the following game. There are 100 chips in a pile. The first player removes any number of chips from the pile, leaving at least one. From then on the players alternate removing chips from the pile until it is empty, each player removing at least one chip at each turn, but not more than double the number of chips last removed by the other player. The player to remove the last chip wins.

14. Show how to recode a **while** statement using a conditional statement and a **repeat** statement.

15. Show how to recode a **for** statement using a **while** statement.

16. Some programming languages provide **for** statements of the form

    for *v* := *a* **to** *b* **step** *c* **do** . . .

    where *v* is a numeric variable and *a*, *b*, *c* are numeric expressions. If *c* is positive, then the effect is the same as that of the statement

    for *v* := *a* **to** *b* **do** . . .

    except that the control variable *v* is incremented by *c*, rather than by 1, each time through the loop; the loop terminates as soon as *v* exceeds *b*. If *c* is negative, then the effect is the same as that of the statement

    for *v* := *b* **downto** *a* **do** . . .

    except that the control variable is changed by *c* each time through the loop, with the loop terminating as soon as *v* is less than *b*.

(a) Show how to code this variant of the **for** statement using a **while** statement.

(b) How many times is the body of the loop likely to be performed in the statement

for $v := 0$ **to** 1 **step** c **do** ...

when c is $\pm 1/3$, $\pm 1/6$, or $\pm 1/1000$? Why?

(c) Suggest how to code the statement

for $v := 0$ **to** 1 **step** $1/1000$ **do** ...

in Pascal so as to avoid the effects noted in (b).

3.5 PROGRAMMING: LOOPS FOR PROCESSING INPUT

Let us now determine how we can use the three varieties of loops in Pascal to read variable amounts of data as input. Here we will see how the care we take writing a program makes that program reliable and easy to use.

Consider how we might mimic a calculator that computes the average of a list of numbers. The key decision to be made, both by the designer of the calculator and by the programmer who mimics it, concerns how to specify the end of the list. Several approaches are possible.

The first approach, which is the simplest to program, is to ask the user how many numbers there are. If we know how long the list is, we can use a **for** statement to

---

PASCAL SAMPLE 3.10   The program *average1*

{ averages a list of numbers with a given length }

program *average1*(*input, output*);

```
var  n       : integer;              { length of list    }
     number  : real;                 { number from list }
     sum     : real;                 { sum of numbers   }
     count   : integer;

begin
    write('How many numbers? ');
    readln(n);
    writeln('Enter ', n:1, ' numbers.');
    sum := 0;
    for count := 1 to n do
        begin
            read(number);
            sum := sum + number
        end;
    writeln;
    writeln('Average = ', sum/n:7:5)
end.
```

SAMPLE USE OF *average1*:

```
How many numbers? 4
Enter 4 numbers.
23 100 85 41

Average = 62.25000
```

read exactly as many numbers as we need and to accumulate their sum. (See Pascal Sample 3.10, *average1*.) Unfortunately, this approach results in a program that is awkward to use: we must count (correctly!) how many numbers there are in what may be a long list before beginning to enter that list.

A second approach, which is also easy to program, is to have the user mark the end of the list of numbers by a special value, say zero, and to use a **repeat** statement to read numbers until this special value is detected. (See Pascal Sample 3.11, *average2*.)

■ **PASCAL SAMPLE 3.11**   The program *average2*

```
{ averages a list of numbers whose end is marked by a 0  }
{ (an example of a poorly designed and written program) }
program average2(input, output);
var count    : integer;          { length of list       }
    number : real;               { number from list }
    sum      : real;             { sum of numbers   }
begin
    writeln('Enter list of numbers ending with 0.');
    sum := 0;
    count := 0;                  { no numbers yet }
    repeat
        read(number);
        sum := sum + number;
        count := count + 1
    until number = 0;
    writeln;
    writeln('Average = ', sum/(count−1):7:5)
end.
```

SAMPLE USE OF *average2*:

```
Enter list of numbers ending with 0.
23 100 85 41 0

Average = 62.25000
```

Here the variable *count* counts the numbers in the list as we enter them; since the zero that marks the end of the list should not be counted, we use $count - 1$ to compute the average. However, there are several problems with this program and with this approach. The most severe is the heavy dependence of *average2* on the particular value used to mark the end of the input. If the nature of our data changes slightly, then we must fiddle with *average2* to make it work properly with a different value for the marker.

This problem is compounded by the nature of loops in Pascal. Ideally, on each pass through the loop, we would like to read a number, exit from the loop if it is zero, and process it only if it is not zero. That way *count* and *sum* would be correct, even if we chose to mark the end of the list with a nonzero value. If Pascal permitted an exit from the middle of a loop, we could write something like

```
do
    read(number)
when number = 0 exit
    sum := sum + number;
    count := count + 1
loop
```

for our loop. Unfortunately, few programming languages at present provide such a looping mechanism. In Pascal, we have a choice of two looping mechanisms. The **repeat** statement in *average2* allows us to read a number and then process it on each pass through the loop, but it tempts us to process one number too many. A better way to code the loop is to use a **while** statement instead of a **repeat** statement:

```
read(number);
while number <> 0 do
    begin
        sum := sum + number;
        count := count + 1;
        read(number)
    end
```

However, this construction requires two *read* statements instead of one, and it reads a number inside the loop only after it has processed the previous number. But it is typical of the way in which we move the exit from the middle of a loop to the beginning.

In order to avoid the problems with *average1* and *average2*, how else could we construct a program to detect the end of the list? A possible third approach is to ask the user after each number is entered whether that number is the last. But this approach would make data entry exceedingly tedious, and we will not bother to code it. Many existing computer programs, through poor design or programming laziness, are as awkward or tedious to use as those resulting from the approaches we have considered so far. Although they are convenient to program, we need to find an approach that is convenient for the user as well.

As is usually the case, we find the key to a successful design by examining the proposed application of computing more carefully. A pocket calculator that averages a list of numbers must itself have some way of knowing when to display the average. Hence we look to the design of such a calculator for guidance in designing our program. Most typically such a calculator has a particular key—for example, one labeled *average*—that the user depresses to display the average of the numbers just entered. This suggests using a special key on the terminal, say the carriage return, to terminate a list.

DETECTING THE END OF A LINE OF INPUT

As we noted in Section 2.6, Pascal ordinarily treats a carriage return like a space, enabling us to use either spaces or carriage returns to separate numbers that we supply as input to *average2*. But Pascal also enables us to distinguish a carriage return from spaces occurring earlier in a line by providing a logical function *eoln* (for "end of line"). This function has the value true if no characters remain on the current line of input (that is, if the next character is the space marking the end of the line), and it has the value false otherwise. Thus changing the exit condition

until *number* = 0

for the loop in *average2* to

until *eoln*

stops the loop when it reaches the carriage return and saves us from having to type a 0 to end the list.

However, a word of caution is necessary. For the modified loop to stop, we must type a carriage return immediately after the last number in the list, with no intervening spaces. The *eoln* function is false as long as any characters, including spaces, remain on the line; an input statement skips spaces only before reading a number, not after. This quirk actually allows us to supply numbers on several lines if we modify *average2* as described: by typing extra spaces at the end of all lines of input except the last, we cause the loop to terminate only at the end of the last line. Pascal Sample 3.12, *average3*, incorporates these changes into *average2*.

The program *average3*, while better than *average1* or *average2*, still is not the ideal solution to our problem. It relies much too heavily on exactly how the input statement in Pascal treats carriage returns and spaces, making the program somewhat dangerous to use and susceptible to error. For example, batch systems with card input generally add spaces to the ends of lines having fewer than 80 characters, so that it is difficult to arrange for a line to end immediately following the last number in the list. The presence or absence of spaces at the end of a line of input is difficult, if not impossible, for a human to detect when reading that input; a more visible symbol would leave a better record of what we typed than an invisible symbol such as a space.

PASCAL SAMPLE 3.12   The program *average3*

{ averages a list of numbers ending with a carriage return }

program *average3*(*input, output*);

var *count*   : *integer*;   { length of list   }
      number : *real*;   { number from list }
      sum   : *real*;   { sum of numbers }

begin
    writeln('Enter list of numbers.');
    writeln('Follow last number immediately by a carriage return.');
    sum := 0;
    count := 0;   { no numbers yet }
    repeat
        read(*number*);
        sum := *sum* + *number*;
        count := *count* + 1
    until *eoln*;
    writeln;
    writeln('Average = ', *sum*/*count*:7:5)
end.

SAMPLE USE OF *average3*:

```
Enter list of numbers.
Follow last number immediately by a carriage return.
23 100 85 41

Average = 62.25000
```

DETECTING THE END OF THE INPUT

For a final approach to our problem, we use the physical end of the input itself to mark the end of the list. This is possible on batch systems, where we supply the entire input when we submit a program for execution. In general, this approach is not possible on interactive systems where we can always supply more input at a terminal. However, some interactive systems employ terminals with a special key that we can use to designate the end of the input. On such systems, the logical function *eof* (for "end of file") becomes true when no characters remain in the input and is false before that. If we change the **repeat** statement in *average3* to

    repeat
        readln(*number*);
        sum := *sum* + *number*;
        count := *count* + 1
    until *eof*

the program will read a list of numbers, one per line, from the input and average them when it reaches the end of the input.

As we did with the *eoln* function, we must exercise caution when using the *eof* function. The problem is that *eof* becomes true only when no characters remain in the input; if the input contains no further numbers, but still contains spaces or carriage returns, then *eof* will be false and the modified loop will expect to find another number in the input.

We have addressed this problem here by changing the keyword *read* to *readln*. The *readln* variant of the input statement reads the carriage return at the end of a line after reading the number on that line, causing *eof* to become true when no more lines of input remain. The *read* variant does not read the carriage return until it attempts to read another number on the next line, causing the loop to expect more numbers than are present. In Chapter 5 we will learn how to skip over spaces and carriage returns that follow a number in the input, thereby enabling us to enter several numbers per line, using the *read* variant of the input statement, and still detect the end of the input with the *eof* function.

If we try to read a number when *eof* is true, or when only spaces or carriage returns remain in the input, an error will result. As a safeguard against such errors, it is better to test *eof* before attempting to read a number rather than after. That way, if we try to average a list containing no numbers, our program will not generate an error by attempting to read a nonexistent first number in the list. As shown in Pascal Sample 3.13, *average4*, the best way to process input uses a *while* statement and not a *repeat* statement. The symbol ■ in the sample input for that program represents the key that we must depress on our terminal to designate the end of the input.

PASCAL SAMPLE 3.13   The program *average4*

{ averages a list of numbers ending with an end-of-file mark }

program *average4*(*input, output*);

```
var count    : integer;        { length of list    }
    number  : real;           { number from list }
    sum     : real;           { sum of numbers  }
begin
    writeln('Enter list of numbers, one per line.');
    writeln('Follow last line by end-of-file mark.');
    sum := 0;
    count := 0;                { no numbers yet }
    while not eof do
       begin
          readln(number);
          sum := sum + number;
          count := count + 1
       end;
```

PASCAL SAMPLE 3.13   The program *average4* (continued)

> *writeln*;
> **if** *count* = 0 **then**
>   *writeln*('No numbers in list.')
> **else**
>   *writeln*('Average = ', *sum/count*:7:5)
> **end**.

SAMPLE USE OF *average4*:

```
Enter list of numbers, one per line.
Follow last line by end-of-file mark.
23
100
85
41
```

```
Average = 62.25000
```

We can summarize the properties of the Pascal *eoln* and *eof* functions as follows:

> *eof*   *true* when all characters in input have been read
>
> *eoln*   *true* when next character in input marks end of line
>   (it is an error to invoke *eoln* when *eof* is *true*)

We will have more to say about these functions in Chapter 5, when we discuss character and text processing. For now, four ways to solve one problem are enough. What we should gather from these examples is that there are many ways to approach a problem, even a seemingly simple one, and that it pays to think about the alternatives before plunging into any particular approach.

EXERCISES

1. Which of the programs *average1* through *average3* allow us to enter a list with no numbers in it? How should these programs be modified to avoid dividing by zero when computing the average?

2. Write a program to read a list of numbers and print the smallest number in the list.

3. Write a program to read a list of numbers and print the second largest number in the list.

3.6   ANALYSIS: PROGRAM DESIGN AND PROGRAMMING STYLE

Composite actions enable us to write programs that are longer and more ambitious than those constructed as a single sequence of primitive actions. In longer programs style is even more important than in shorter ones. Good style makes long programs comprehensible; poor style makes them unintelligible. Thus it is appropriate to extend our earlier observations concerning both program design and programming style.

PROGRAM DESIGN

When faced with the task of writing a program, particularly a short one, there is always the temptation to begin coding right away in order to get the job done as soon as possible. After all, why spend more time writing a program than you will spend using it? There are several reasons for investing time and thought in designing a program before beginning to code it. In fact, it may not be necessary to write a program at all. A little investigation into a problem might uncover a solution that does not require the use of a computer, a program that already solves the problem, or a program that can be modified easily to solve it.

If a program must be written, one that is designed well is more likely to produce the correct results than one that is designed hastily. Time spent designing a program—which need not be much for short programs—is more than repaid by time saved getting it to work. Also, programs are rarely used only once. A well-designed program can be used over and over, both by the original programmer and by others. It can be modified easily to adapt it to changed circumstances, either by the original programmer or by others.

Programs intended for use by others demand extra care in their design. They must communicate clearly and intelligibly with their users, who may not understand exactly what a program does. Furthermore, programs must contain safeguards to ensure that they do what users intend, not what a programmer assumes users intend.

Finally, time spent writing a program produces more than just that program. It also produces code and experience that can be applied when writing other programs. For this reason it pays to think about a program as you write it. How does this program differ from others you have written? How is it like them? Can you use programs or techniques previously developed in coding this one? Are the techniques needed for this program likely to be useful in the future? All too often programmers treat the writing of each program as an isolated experience, reinventing the wheel over and over. Properly done, programming results in an ever-expanding stock of general purpose tools and experience.

We will have much to say about the design of programs in later chapters, where we will construct programs that are considerably longer than those in this chapter. However, we can draw several important conclusions about design from the way we wrote the sample programs in this chapter.

First, from among the many ways of solving a problem, the most useful are often those that generalize to the solution of related problems. In Chapter 5 we will observe that minor modifications to *minOf2*, *minOf2a*, or *minOf2b*—all of which display the minimum of two integers—enable them to display the first (alphabetically) of two characters. Then in Chapter 8 we will see that we need to take only small steps to progress from finding the minimum of two integers to finding the minimum of a whole list of integers to arranging that list in increasing order; similarly we can take small steps to progress from finding the first (alphabetically) of two characters to arranging a list of strings of characters (such as a list of names) in alphabetic order.

Second, from among the many programs that solve a problem, the shortest or the cleverest is not always the best. For example, the program *minOf2c* displayed as Pascal Sample 3.14 is shorter than *minOf2* and makes do without a conditional statement. But is *minOf2c* in any sense better than *minOf2*? Probably not, because we cannot immediately see why it works, and it cannot be modified as easily as *minOf2* to handle characters instead of integers.

Third, from among the many programming languages that may be used to solve a problem, the best are those that encourage programmers to construct general solutions rather than to rely on tricks. Pascal does this by treating data types in a more consistent fashion than most programming languages and by avoiding a host of special features that are present in many languages but that encourage *ad hoc* rather than general purpose solutions.

And fourth, it takes little effort to have a program communicate with its users in an intelligible and attractive fashion. The programs in this chapter all prompt their users for input, and they display their output the way we might write it by hand.

These observations lead to the following suggestions.

Approaching the problem   Approach the problem to be solved in a systematic fashion and let your design reflect that systematic approach. Think first and code later!

■ PASCAL SAMPLE 3.14   The program *minOf2c*

{ displays the minimum of two integers }

program *minOf2c*(*input, output*);
var *a, b, minimum* : *integer*;
begin
    writeln('Enter two integers.');
    read(*a, b*);
    minimum := *round*(($a+b$)/2 $-$ *abs*(($a-b$)/2));
    writeln;
    writeln('Their minimum is ', *minimum*:1)
end.

SAMPLE USE OF *minOf2c*:

Enter two integers.
8 3

Their minimum is 3

Look for a short, straightforward solution to your problem. Short, well-conceived solutions are always better than lengthy, brute-force solutions.

Avoid tricky coding. Trying to be too clever wastes time and invites disaster. If you must show how clever you are, do it by writing a program that works spectacularly well, not one that works in a spectacular fashion.

Communicating with the user   Precede all requests for input from the user of an interactive program by clear, succinct printed messages. Echo input from the user of a noninteractive program so that the output of that program provides a complete transcript of its use.

Check all input carefully for errors. If two responses to a request are possible (yes and no), do not assume that the second is meant if the first is not given (don't interpret yep as no). If the input is erroneous or unintelligible, request that it be resupplied.

Generate the right amount of output—neither too much nor too little. Too much output must be searched manually to extract an answer that the program should have found. Too little output leaves some doubt about the question that was being answered.

PROGRAMMING STYLE

Good programming style enhances good program design. Following are some ways to make your programs readable and to convey your design.

Documentation   Use one or more lines of comments to explain major sections of your program. The comment

{ simulate payments until loan is repaid }

in *loan2* explains the purpose of the loop that follows. Do not force the reader to reconstruct your train of thought from your code. Tell what you are about to do, then do it.

Put comments at the end of lines where further explanation would help. Do not repeat what can be understood from the code itself. Comments such as

$y := 1;$ { set y to 1 }

do not help at all, whereas

$y := 1;$ { $y = x**0$ }

conveys the intent and effect of the statement. In the next section we have more to say about using comments such as these to describe what we have done, rather than what we are trying to do.

When you declare constants or variables, use comments to explain their intended use or meaning. Then follow your stated intentions.

Don't be cute. Programs are read many times, and cute identifiers or comments, as in

```
begin              { Away we go!!      }
    speed := lots;  { Give 'er the juice!!! }
    .
    .
    .
```

convey little information and get stale rather quickly. Good programs do not have to be dull, but a light touch should be just that—light!

Do not clutter up your code by using a commenting style that is too dense. Use blank space between comment and code so that the reader's eye can separate the two easily. Be consistent about your placement of comments; align comments that occur on successive lines.

Program display and indentation   Pascal permits us to be somewhat flexible about displaying the text of a program. For example, we can display conditional statements on a single line, as in *minOf2a* and *minOf2b*, or on several lines, as in *minOf2* and *arrange2*. Properly used, this flexibility enhances the readability of a program, making its display reflect its structure and design.

Display a short conditional statement on a single line. Display longer ones on multiple lines, with the keywords **if** and **else** aligned and with the nested statements indented (say, three spaces), as follows:

```
if logical expression then
    { statement to execute if expression is true }
else
    { statement to execute if expression is false }
```

Here systematic indentation helps us to spot the components of the conditional statement at a glance.

Display compound statements with the keywords **begin** and **end** aligned and with the nested statements indented (say, three spaces), as follows:

```
begin
    { statement 1 };
    .
    .
    .
    { statement n }
end
```

Here indentation helps us to spot the end of the compound statement and each of its components.

When the body of a loop consists of a single short statement (a simple assignment, input, or output statement), display the loop on a single line. When the body of the loop is longer, display it on several lines. Indent the first line of the body of a **for** or **while** statement more than the first line of the loop (say, three spaces), as follows:

for variable := expression **to** expression **do**
{ body of loop }
while logical expression **do**
{ body of loop }

Indent the statements in the body of a **repeat** statement (say, three spaces) and align them between the keywords **repeat** and **until**, as follows:

repeat
{ statement 1 };

.
.

{ statement n }
until logical expression

If your system provides a program (known as a pretty printer) that generates the proper indentation automatically, use it.

Coding style Let form reflect function. Whether you program in Pascal or in some other well-structured programming language, choose structures that are appropriate to the task at hand.

Put statements where they belong. Statements to be executed before a loop belong before that loop, not buried inside the loop and protected by a conditional statement that checks for the first pass through the loop. Similarly, statements to be executed after a loop terminates belong after the loop, not buried in the body of the loop.

Make your statements and expressions read naturally from left to right. For example, to test whether x lies inside the interval $(0, 1)$ use

if $(0 <> x)$ **and** $(x < 1)$

rather than

if $(x < 1)$ **and** $(x > 0)$

3.7 ANALYSIS: PROGRAM CORRECTNESS

A program is correct if it performs in accordance with its specifications. To determine whether a program works, we must first know with some degree of precision what it is supposed to do. Without a complete specification it is impossible for us to determine whether some particular, and possibly peculiar, behavior exhibited by a program is a bug or a feature.

There are several ways to demonstrate, or at least provide evidence, that a program is correct. We can *test* a program to demonstrate that it works in a representative set of circumstances. We can *verify* a program to prove certain properties about its behavior. And we can *walk through* a program, trying to convince a devil's advocate that the program is correct. These activities provide complementary evidence in support of the correctness of a program; taken together they can substantially increase our confidence that a program works.

TESTING

Testing, like programming, should be a systematic activity, not a haphazard one. The goal of programming is to produce a working program. The goal of testing is to provide convincing evidence that a program works.

Design a comprehensive test plan, not just a series of random test cases. Decide which aspects of the program need to be tested; then find test data that check each of those aspects. Organize your tests so that anyone who reads your test plan will be convinced that a program passing all of the tests must be correct.

Determine the output you expect your program to produce in each test case. Only by knowing what you expect in advance can you test your program rather than merely observe its behavior.

Pay particular attention to boundary conditions. Programs are most likely to fail for data at the extremes of the expected values. For example, when testing a program that prints a table with column headings that are repeated every 20 lines, try producing tables that have 0, 19, 20, and 21 lines; such cases are more likely to cause difficulties than tables that have 5 or 10 lines.

Do not overtest. It is the quality of your test cases that counts, not the quantity. Do not search for a needle in a haystack without even knowing what the needle looks like.

Design test cases on the basis of what your program should do, not on the basis of how you wrote it. Better yet, design test cases before you begin writing a program. This will ensure that your tests are not biased in favor of the way that you wrote the program. Furthermore, it will help you to understand the problem that you are trying to solve, thereby making it easier for you to develop a complete specification and to write the program.

To test the program *minOf3*, for example, you should design at least three test cases to determine that the program properly detects the minimum of the three numbers regardless of whether the minimum comes first, second, or third. Such test cases demonstrate that the program exhibits the desired range of output behavior. To test a program further, you can select further test data to determine that it handles expected variations in the input. For example, to test how *minOf3* handles input, you could supply it with three distinct numbers arranged in all six possible orders. Such *functional tests* check whether the program meets its specifications without regard to how the program was written.

After you have written a program, you should make sure that your test cases exercise every part of that program. If they do not, you should then design further *structural tests* that exercise every statement nested inside every structure in the program. For example, at least four test cases are required to exercise each of the statements nested in the conditionals in *minOf3*.

When you have a test plan and a program, apply that test plan systematically. As you discover errors in your program, track them down and correct them. Whenever you correct an error in a program, retest the program with the entire set of test cases. Do not assume that an error is fixed until you have tested the correction. And do not assume that tests that succeeded before a correction was made will succeed afterwards. Hastily made corrections can introduce more errors into a program than they eliminate. Only when you are satisfied that your program works at least as well as it did before the correction should you proceed further with the test plan.

DEBUGGING

The process of tracking down and repairing the cause of an error is known as *debugging*. It may involve the design and application of additional tests in order to pinpoint the location and exact nature of an error. And it may involve inserting additional statements in your program so that you can monitor its behavior more closely. Debugging calls for the skills of a detective: if you have evidence that an error exists, you must find the guilty party and establish its guilt. Errors can enter a program in a number of ways:

- The program's design may be faulty. You may have to modify that design or rework it completely.

- A program may use a faulty algorithm, one that is either incorrect or does not apply to the situation at hand. You must correct the algorithm or find a better one.

- A program may be coded incorrectly. *Syntactic errors*, or errors in your use of a programming language, are generally called to your attention when you attempt to use a program. Sometimes a single syntactic error, such as omitting or misspelling a crucial keyword like **do** or **if**, can trigger a multitude of error reports; in such cases it pays to correct the first error reported and try the program again to find out whether any errors remain. *Semantic* or *logical errors* are errors in carrying out your design; you must detect them yourself.

- Sometimes a computer system may not execute a program correctly. Resist the temptation to blame aberrant behavior on a *hardware* or *system error*, trying to shift the blame from yourself to the machine. Such errors are rare. Most likely you need to look further for the source of an error; or you need to learn more about what the computer system actually does, as opposed to what you think it should do.

- A program may be applied in unanticipated situations with incorrect results. In this case you need to revise the program, its specification, or both.

Whatever the cause of an error, you must find and correct it. Sometimes an error is so striking that you realize immediately which part of your program must be at fault, and rereading that part indeed discloses the source of the error. At other times you may need to insert additional output statements in your program, either to serve as *checkpoints* indicating that execution of the program successfully reached a certain stage or to *trace* changes in the values of certain key variables; the additional evidence provided by such output statements helps you to determine exactly when something goes wrong.

Use all available evidence when tracking down a bug. If you think that you have found the source of an error, make sure that you can explain the observed behavior of your program completely in terms of what you have found. If you can, fixing what you found will probably eliminate the error. If you cannot, another bug may be lurking nearby.

If you discover two errors simultaneously, first fix the one that occurs later in the program; otherwise you may make it difficult to reproduce and correct the other error. Do not presume that an error has disappeared when it may have simply gone into hiding.

Long programs are rarely fully debugged. Some errors remain undetected for long periods of time. Others are introduced or reintroduced when a program is modified. Therefore you may wish to retain code for checkpoints and traces in your program even after you have removed the error they were designed to detect. So that this code does not interfere with the normal operation of your program, you can embed it within conditional structures of the form

> **if** *debugLevel* > *levelHere* **then** . . .

that enable you to select the amount of debugging information to generate each time you execute the program; supplying a high value for *debugLevel* generates a lot of information; supplying a low value generates none.

WALKTHROUGHS

Programming does not need to be a solitary activity. Indeed, for many large programming projects, it cannot be a solitary activity: the talents of many programmers may be needed to construct a large program in a reasonable period of time. Even on small projects you can benefit from trying out your ideas for a program on someone else or from reviewing or *walking through* a program that you have already written in front of an audience.

Simply reading your program to someone else provides an excellent way to detect errors in that program. A second person will not share your preconceptions about how the program ought to work; by having a disinterested view of how it really works, that person is more likely to discover errors or omissions.

When you cannot track down an elusive bug, try to prove to someone else that the bug cannot exist. Often you will spot the bug yourself in midsentence; the mere act of verbalizing your beliefs can expose those that are not quite sound. If you cannot spot the bug, perhaps the other person can.

A well-structured program, being easier to read, enhances your ability to conduct walkthroughs and to involve others in your programming activities. The structure of your program imposes a structure on your interactions with others; a good structure leads to productive interactions, a poor one to disorganized and frustrating interactions.

VERIFICATION

When you test a program, you observe and analyze its behavior. On the basis of your analysis, you may be willing to make certain *assertions* about the program: if it is supplied with certain data, then it will produce certain results. Assertions that describe the data a program is equipped to handle are known as *preconditions*; no claim is made about the behavior of the program if its preconditions are not satisfied. Assertions that describe the results of a program are known as *postconditions*; if the preconditions are satisfied when execution of a program begins, then the postconditions will be satisfied when execution finishes.

Consider, for example, the program *intPower* that raises a number x to an integer power n. (See Section 3.4.) When *intPower* terminates we want the postcondition $y = x^n$ to be true. For this to happen, n must be an integer; that is, the precondition $n = trunc(n)$ must be true when execution is begun. If we had not equipped *intPower* to handle negative exponents, the postcondition would be attained only if a stronger precondition, namely, $n = trunc(n)$ **and** $n \geq 0$, were true initially.

Consider, also, the program *minOf3* that finds the minimum of three numbers a, b, and c. (See Section 3.3.) When *minOf3* terminates we want the postcondition

$$(minimum = a \textbf{ or } minimum = b \textbf{ or } minimum = c) \textbf{ and } minimum \leq a, b, c$$

to be true. For this to happen we need to know nothing about the nature of a, b, and c; that is, the precondition for *minOf3* is automatically true.

When we test *intPower* or *minOf3* we supply those programs with sample data that satisfy their preconditions and check that their output satisfies their postconditions. In order to test *intPower* we would supply it with various values—positive, negative, and zero—for both x and n; we might even supply it with values that did not satisfy the precondition just to see how the program handled erroneous data (not very well in this case). In order to test *minOf3* we would supply it with values for a, b, and c, arranged in various orders.

However, such tests do not establish conclusively that *intPower* and *minOf3* will always perform as expected. For some unanticipated reason they may fail in untested cases: *intPower* may work perfectly well for exponents up to 100 but fail thereafter; *minOf3* may work perfectly well for positive numbers but fail for negative numbers. We could, of course, test these cases also; but, regardless of the number of cases that we test, there will always be more that we do not.

When we verify—as opposed to test—a program, we attempt to prove that the program always performs in accordance with its preconditions and postconditions. We do this by inspecting the program itself and by reasoning about the actions it performs. To aid in this process, we can embed assertions in the form of comments directly in the text of the program. Such assertions help to focus our attention on what a program achieves, rather than on how it does it. For example, the comment

$$\{ y = x**n \}$$

in *intPower* makes explicit exactly what has been achieved when execution reaches the line containing that comment. This comment stands in sharp contrast to the comment

{ simulate payments until loan is repaid }

in *loan2*, which describes what the following lines in the program are supposed to achieve.

How can we prove that assertions embedded within a program are true? Here the systematic and intelligent use of control structures in a programming language makes it possible for us to determine the effect that each statement in a program has on whatever assertion is true before that statement is executed; hence·we can determine a new assertion that is true after execution of that statement. We will examine the principal statement types one at a time to learn how this can be done.

The first statement we consider is the assignment statement. Whatever was true of the expression in the statement

variable := *expression*

before the assignment is performed must be true of the variable receiving the value of that expression after the assignment. Thus, in order to verify the effect of the assignment statements in the program *powerOf2* (see Section 3.4), we need to check the truth of the accompanying assertions:

```
y := 1;                  { y = 2**0      }
n := 0;                  { y = 2**n      }
while y <= x do
    begin
        n := n + 1;      { y = 2**(n-1) }
        y := 2*y         { y = 2**n      }
    end
```

The first assertion is true regardless of what was true before since $1 = 2^0$. The next assertion is true, since $y = 2^0$ before and n receives the value 0. The third assertion is true on the first pass through the loop, since $y = 2^n$ before and n is increased by one. And the last assertion is true, since $y = 2^{n-1}$ before and y is multiplied by 2.

To continue our verification of the correctness of *powerOf2* we must consider the interaction between assertions and loops. Since the last two assertions occur inside a loop, we must verify that they are true each time the body of the loop is executed. But this presents no problem because the truth of the second of these assertions is precisely what we need to know in order to establish the truth of the first on the next pass through the loop.

Assertions that occur within a loop are known as *invariants* of that loop, as their truth is invariant under repeated execution of the loop. Constructing loop invariants can aid us tremendously in understanding what a loop accomplishes. Many programmers lose track of what is true after a loop has been executed several times because they view loops as making repeated changes; by using loop invariants to concentrate on what remains the same, as opposed to what changes, we can eliminate much of the mystery surrounding what a loop does.

Loop invariants describe what is true during execution of a loop. But what happens when a loop terminates? Here the condition that causes the loop to terminate supplies further information. For example, after the loop in *powerOf2* terminates, we know that the assertion

$$y = 2^n > x$$

must be true: $y = 2^n$ is true because it was true at the end of every pass through the loop and, in those cases where the body of the loop was not executed, because it was true before the loop was encountered; $y > x$ is true because the loop did terminate. Hence the loop in *powerOf2* does indeed produce a power of 2 that is greater than x.

But how do we know that this is the smallest power of 2 with that property? We have succeeded in verifying part, but not all, of the intended behavior of *powerOf2*. To establish that y is the smallest power of 2 exceeding x, we need to go back and strengthen our assertions. Such a strengthening is possible because we have not used all the information available to us: the exit condition for the loop also provides information about what is true each time the body of the loop is executed. In this case, it establishes that $y \leq x$ is true at the beginning of each pass through the loop. Thus we can strengthen the assertions within the loop as follows:

```
while y < = x do
    begin
        n := n + 1;      { y = 2**(n-1) < = x             }
        y := 2*y         { y = 2**n and 2**(n-1) < = x }
    end
```

Now, when the loop terminates, we know that the assertion

$$y = 2^n > x \quad \textbf{and} \quad 2^{n-1} \leq x$$

is true provided that it is true in those cases when the body of the loop is never executed. Those cases occur when the original value 1 of y is already greater than x; hence, we also need to strengthen the assertions preceding the loop:

```
y := 1;      { y = 2**0 and 2**(-1) < = x  }
n := 0;      { y = 2**n and 2**(n-1) < = x }
```

These assertions fail for numbers less than $\frac{1}{2}$, so we have discovered an unstated precondition for the program *powerOf2*, namely that $x \geq \frac{1}{2}$. Thus the process of verifying the behavior of *powerOf2*, which is almost complete, not only establishes the correctness of *powerOf2* in untested cases, but it also helps us discover in which cases *powerOf2* does work as intended.

To complete our verification of the correctness of *powerOf2*, we must show that its loop does indeed terminate. Assertions only describe what is true when a loop terminates; something more is needed to establish that it does terminate. In *powerOf2* the loop terminates because, by repeatedly doubling the positive number y, we will eventually produce a number greater than x.

In general, to verify that a loop will terminate, we must show that its exit condition eventually will be true. There is no automatic procedure for producing such demonstrations. In fact, the mathematician Alan Turing proved in 1937 that it is impossible to write a computer program to examine other computer programs and determine whether they will terminate. (See Exercise 6 at the end of this section.) Hence we usually need to use some ingenuity to verify that a given loop must terminate.

To illustrate the interaction between assertions and conditional structures, let us verify the correctness of the program *minOf3*. Just as the exit condition from a loop provides information about what is true when execution of the body of the loop begins, the logical expression in a conditional structure provides information about what is true at the beginning of each of the clauses in that structure. For example, we could annotate each keyword **then** and **else** in *minOf3* with what we know to be true when we reach that keyword:

```
if a <= b then          { a <= b       }
    if a <= c then       { a <= b, c    }
        minimum := a
    else                 { c < a <= b }
        minimum := c
else                     { b < a        }
    if b <= c then       { b <= a, c    }
        minimum := b
    else                 { c < b <= a }
        minimum := c
```

With these assertions in place, we can easily add further assertions, documenting what happens in each of the cases:

```
if a <= b then          { a <= b                          }
    if a <= c then       { a <= b, c                       }
        minimum := a     { minimum = a <= b, c    }
    else                 { c < a <= b                      }
        minimum := c     { minimum = c < a <= b }
else                     { b < a                           }
    if b <= c then       { b <= a, c                       }
        minimum := b     { minimum = b <= a, c    }
    else                 { c < b <= a                      }
        minimum := c     { minimum = c < b < a    }
```

Finally, we can draw the desired conclusion that

$$(minimum = a \textbf{ or } minimum = b \textbf{ or } minimum = c) \textbf{ and } minimum \leq a, b, c$$

upon completion of *minOf3* since this assertion is true at the end of each case in the conditional statement.

It is tempting to believe at this point that we have verified everything about *powerOf2* and *minOf3*. But, in fact, we can still do more. For example, if we want only to make the postcondition $2^{n-1} \leq x < 2^n$ for *powerOf2* true, we could do so simply by setting $x = 1$ and $n = 1$. Similarly, if we want only to make the postcondition for *minOf3* true, we could do so by setting a, b, c, and *minimum* all equal to 0. Of course this would be cheating, but it does illustrate other properties of *powerOf2* and *minOf3* that we may wish to verify (for example, that the final values of key variables are the same as their initial values). We can easily verify this property of *powerOf2* and *minOf3* by observing that we never change the values of these variables.

Specifications play an even more important role in verification than they do in testing. We do not prove that a program is correct in the abstract. Rather we verify that it meets the specifications imposed by stated preconditions and postconditions.

Despite its utility, program verification is not yet as common or well-understood an activity as program testing. Since the early 1970s computer scientists have put a great deal of effort into developing verification techniques, and these techniques enable us to verify the behavior of many small or medium-sized programs. However, long programs are still difficult to verify completely: it can be difficult to specify exactly what long programs should do; the amount of detail in a formal proof of correctness can be overwhelming; and people can make mistakes in proofs as well as in programs.

Even if we do not attempt to prove that each program we write is correct, the methodology of program verification still teaches us how to reason about programs and how to document programs in a way that increases our confidence in their correctness. We use assertions in programs throughout this book to state preconditions and postconditions, to state invariant properties of loops, and to state other important facts about the operation of these programs. Such assertions form an important component of the documentation that accompanies our programs and that should accompany any computer program.

EXERCISES

1. Design a test plan for a program such as *loan2* that computes the life of an installment loan, given the amount borrowed, the annual interest rate, and the size of the monthly payments. (*Hint:* Which values for the inputs lead to results that are easy to check by hand? Which values lead to results that are representative of the output we expect from *loan2?*)

2. Design a test plan for programs such as *average1* through *average4* that compute the average of a list of numbers. What properties of those programs are worth testing?

3. Consider the task of arranging three numbers a, b, and c in increasing order.

   (a) How many sets of test data do we need to demonstrate that a program for this task works correctly? (*Hint:* How many ways are there to order three distinct numbers? How many ways are there to order the input if duplicates are present?)

   (b) Write a program to perform this task. (See Exercise 4, Section 3.3.)

   (c) Test your program with the sets of test data you determined were necessary in part (a).

   (d) Write a postcondition for your program to assert that the final values of a, b, and c are in increasing order.

   (e) Verify that this postcondition is true when your program terminates.

   (f) Verify furthermore that the final values of the variables a, b, and c are a rearrangement of their initial values.

4. Consider the problem of finding the smallest prime factor of a positive integer.

   (a) Write a precondition and a postcondition that describe the behavior of a program that solves this problem.

   (b) Write a program to solve the problem. (*Hint:* Write a loop that checks candidate factors of the integer.)

   (c) Write an assertion that is an invariant of the loop in this program.

   (d) Use this assertion to verify the correctness of your program.

   (e) Prove that your program always terminates.

5. Consider the problem of finding the second largest of four numbers.

   (a) Design a test plan for a program that solves this problem.

   (b) Specify the behavior of such a program precisely by constructing appropriate preconditions and postconditions.

   (c) Does either of these activities reveal any ambiguity in the statement of the problem? If so, what is that ambiguity and how can it be removed?

6. Show that it is impossible to write a Pascal program *haltTest* that examines an arbitrary Pascal program, printing `halts` if that program terminates regardless of the input we give it and printing `loops` if that program runs forever for some specific input. (*Hint:* Suppose such a program *haltTest* exists. Consider another program *doesItStop* that examines an arbitrary Pascal program, stopping with no output if *haltTest* prints `loops` and running forever if *haltTest* prints `halts`. What happens if you ask *doesItStop* to examine itself?)

3.8	ANALYSIS: EFFICIENCY

Some programs are better than others. Some are easier to use. Some produce better or more accurate results. Some are easier to read, modify, and maintain. Some require smaller amounts of computer time and memory.

Of these measures of program quality, that of program efficiency too easily preoccupies a programmer at the wrong time and to the detriment of other measures of program quality. Little is to be gained from resorting to obscure coding techniques in an attempt to speed up a program if its overall design is fundamentally inefficient. And there is little use for a program that quickly produces the wrong results.

We do not need to be concerned with efficiency if a program must solve a particularly simple problem or if it will be used only a few times; in such instances it hardly pays to invest large amounts of time and energy in making a program efficient. On the other hand, if a program must solve a particularly difficult problem, or if it will be used many times, it may pay or even be necessary to invest the time and energy required to make it efficient.

When efficiency is a concern, how can we best achieve it? First, we specify exact efficiency requirements; for example, an airline reservation system may be required to process each reservation within a certain time limit and to process a certain number of reservations per day; a disaster warning system must detect a disaster before it occurs. Then, we design an approach that promises to be efficient enough to meet these requirements. Finally, we construct and fine-tune a program to embody that approach.

ALGORITHMIC EFFICIENCY

The choice of algorithms and data structures has by far the greatest impact on the efficiency of an approach to a problem. Indeed, one of the primary motivations for studying algorithms and data structures is to develop an arsenal of weapons that can be used to attack difficult problems. In order to know which algorithms can meet various efficiency requirements, we must analyze the efficiency of those algorithms we develop.

There are two ways to analyze algorithms: empirically and theoretically. To conduct an empirical analysis, we embody the algorithm in a program and measure the resources consumed by that program in actual use. However, such an analysis has severe limitations: it may provide little indication of the resources consumed when the program is applied to untried cases or is transported to a different computer system. To conduct a theoretical analysis, we seek to establish an intrinsic measure of the amount of work done by an algorithm; this measure enables us to compare one algorithm with another and to select the most promising for implementation.

In Chapter 8 we will gain experience in the analysis of algorithms by studying methods for searching and sorting. As a preview, we analyze here the efficiency of several methods for solving a particularly simple problem, which we discussed previously in this chapter.

Consider the task of computing the minimum m of three numbers a, b, and c. Despite the simplicity of this problem, there are many ways to approach it. Here are four:

```
{ Method 1 }

m := a;
if b < m then m := b;
if c < m then m := c
```

{ Method 2 }
if $a <= b$ **then**
    if $a <= c$ **then**
        $m := a$
    else
        $m := c$
else
    if $b <= c$ **then**
        $m := b$
    else
        $m := c$

{ Method 3 }
if $(a <= b)$ **and** $(a <= c)$ **then** $m := a$;
if $(b <= a)$ **and** $(b <= c)$ **then** $m := b$;
if $(c <= a)$ **and** $(c <= b)$ **then** $m := c$

{ Method 4 }
if $(a <= b)$ **and** $(a <= c)$ **then**
    $m := a$
else if $b <= c$ **then**
    $m := b$
else
    $m := c$

What can we say about the relative efficiency of these four methods? Method 1 requires two comparisons and from one to three assignments. The first assignment sets m equal to a candidate for the minimum of the three numbers, namely a. Then a comparison of b with m determines whether another assignment is needed to replace this candidate by a better one. Finally, a comparison of c with m determines whether yet another replacement is needed.

Method 2, which we used in *minOf3*, also requires two comparisons: one between a and b, and either one between a and c or one between b and c. As opposed to Method 1, it requires but a single assignment. Note that the efficiency of an algorithm is measured by the amount of work it performs (two comparisons in the case of Method 2), not by the length of the program that implements the algorithm (which contains three conditionals, only two of which are ever executed, in the case of Method 2). In particular, programs containing loops may be very short, yet still perform a lot of work.

Method 3, despite its straightforward nature, requires much more work: six comparisons and from one to three assignments. Even if the two comparisons in the first statement establish that a is the minimum, four more comparisons are made and two more assignments can be performed (such as the case in which $a = b = c$).

Method 4 suffers similarly. Although it requires only a single assignment, it can require three comparisons.

It may seem that the difference between two comparisons and three or six comparisons is of little consequence, yet the impact of seemingly small differences is easily magnified. Suppose, for example, that we want to find the first (alphabetically) of three strings rather than the minimum of three numbers. If those strings contained several thousand characters each, we would breathe a sigh of relief if we had to perform only two comparisons. Suppose, further, that we want to find the minimum of n numbers, when n is much larger than three. Generalizing from Method 3, we would have to compare each of the n numbers with each of the others, for a total of $n(n - 1)$ comparisons, whereas generalizing from Method 1, we would have to compare a candidate minimum m with each number other than the first, for a total of only $n - 1$ comparisons; thus Method 3 requires n times more work than Method 1.

As a result of this analysis, Method 1 emerges as a method that is simultaneously efficient and easy to generalize. By identifying the intrinsic unit of work performed by each of the four methods (namely, performing a comparison between two numbers), we are able to determine which methods perform superfluous work and which perform the minimum work necessary to accomplish the task. No amount of fancy coding will make a method that performs superfluous work more efficient than one that does not. Thus a theoretical analysis of algorithms, applied before coding begins, helps us to select the algorithm that is most worthy of further development.

Method 4 is not a particularly good method, but it does serve to illustrate an important point concerning the analysis of algorithms. Each of the other methods results in the same number of comparisons regardless of the values of a, b, and c. Method 4 exhibits more typical behavior in that the number of comparisons it performs may vary for different values of a, b, and c.

We describe this difference by saying that Method 4 requires two comparisons in its *best case* and three comparisons in its *worst case*. Generally, we are more interested in the worst-case behavior of an algorithm than in its best-case behavior. We do not care how speedily an algorithm may perform if we present it with just the right data. But we often care very much about how slowly it performs if we present it with troublesome data. Stringent response-time requirements, such as those for disaster-detection applications, often apply to all cases, particularly the worst; hence it is important for us to determine whether an algorithm in its worst case can meet those requirements.

We may also be interested in the *average-case* behavior of an algorithm, for example, when we wish to predict how long we must wait for an algorithm to accomplish its task or to estimate how many times we can repeat the use of that algorithm in a fixed period of time. In general, it is harder to estimate the average-case behavior of an algorithm than its worst-case behavior, as we must enumerate and analyze all cases rather than identify and analyze only the worst case. For example, when we wish to find the minimum of three distinct numbers, a total of six different cases correspond to the six different orderings of the three numbers; in the two cases where a is least, Method 4 makes two comparisons; and in the other four cases, it makes three comparisons. Hence, if all cases are equally likely, Method 4 makes $2\frac{2}{3}$ comparisons on the average.

PROGRAM EFFICIENCY

Efficient programs are based on efficient algorithms. We can enhance the efficiency of such programs further by observing some simple guidelines concerning efficient coding.

Do not repeat computations unnecessarily. Writing

```
t := x*x*x;
y := 1/(t-1) + 1/(t-2) + 1/(t-3) + 1/(t-4)
```

instead of

```
y := 1/(x*x*x-1) + 1/(x*x*x-2) + 1/(x*x*x-3) + 1/(x*x*x-4)
```

not only saves typing, but also avoids recomputing the value of $x*x*x$ four times. (Some computer systems recognize that the recomputation can be avoided, but many do not.)

Move computations that remain the same on each iteration of a loop outside that loop. Writing

```
t := x*x*x;
y := 0;
for n := 1 to 20 do y := y + 1/(t-n)
```

instead of

```
y := 0;
for n := 1 to 20 do y := y + 1/(x*x*x-n)
```

again saves recomputing the value of $x*x*x$.

Save intermediate results to make later computations more efficient. Writing

```
t := -x*x/2;
p := 1;
y := 1;
for n := 1 to 20 do
    begin
        p := p*t;        {p = (-x*x/2)**n }
        y := y + p       {y = 1 + t + ··· + t**n }
    end
```

requires but a single multiplication within the loop to raise $-x*x/2$ to higher and higher powers.

Do not equate efficiency with brevity of code. As the above examples illustrate, the most compact code is not always the most efficient.

EXERCISES

1. Can the minimum of three numbers be found by a program that makes fewer than two comparisons in its worst case? If so, how? If not, why not?

2. Consider the task of arranging three numbers in increasing order.

   (a) What is the worst-case behavior of the program you wrote to perform this task for Exercise 4 in Section 3.3? If your program makes more than three comparisons in its worst case, rewrite it so that it makes no more than three.

   *(b) Is it possible to arrange three numbers in increasing order by making only two comparisons in the worst case? If so, how? If not, why not?

3. Consider the task of finding the second largest of four numbers. Show that an algorithm can perform this task by making only four comparisons in the worst case.

4. Consider the task of determining how many of three items supplied as input are distinct.

   (a) Write a program to perform this task.

   (b) How many comparisons does your program perform in the worst case?

   (c) How many comparisons does your program perform in the average case? (*Hint:* Assume that there are 27 cases based on the numbers 1, 2, and 3.)

3.9   SYSTEMS: HOW COMPUTERS CONTROL THE FLOW OF CONTROL

When a compiler translates a Pascal program into machine language, the instructions in the resulting machine-language program occupy consecutive locations in memory. Ordinarily these instructions are executed in sequence, starting with the first and continuing until a special halt instruction stops execution of the program. *Transfer* instructions override the normal sequential execution of instructions, making it possible for machine-language programs to select alternative courses of action and to execute loops. These instructions specify circumstances in which the next instruction to execute is not the next one in sequence.

Table 3.3 illustrates some typical transfer instructions for the hypothetical computer discussed in Section 2.9. The *unconditional transfer* TRA instructs the computer

TABLE 3.3   Transfer Instructions for Hypothetical Computer

Operation code	Assembly language mnemonic	Interpretation
00000000	HLT	halt (i.e., terminate execution of program)
00001000	TRA x	transfer to location x
00001001	TZE x	transfer to location x if A register is zero
00001010	TPL x	transfer to location x if A register is positive
00001011	TMI x	transfer to location x if A register is negative
00001100	TOF x	transfer to location x if an overflow has occurred since the last TOF was executed

to take its next instruction from the memory location with the specified address. The *conditional transfers* TZE, TPL, and TMI instruct the computer to take its next instruction from the memory location with the specified address only if the contents of the *A* register are zero, positive, or negative. Finally, the conditional transfer TOF enables machine-language programs to detect an overflow resulting from an arithmetic operation.

Figure 3.15 shows how transfer instructions can be used to construct the loop required by the Pascal statements

$a := 1;$
while $a < b$ **do** $a := a*2$

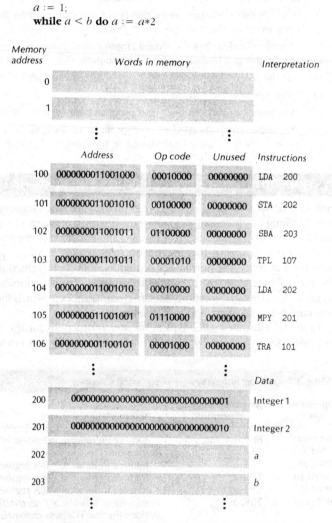

FIGURE 3.15 ■ Machine language instructions for simple loop

The instructions in locations 100 and 101 assign the initial value 1 to a, storing that value in location 202. Then the instructions in locations 102 and 103 test whether $a < b$ by subtracting b from a; if the result is negative, then $a < b$ and execution continues in sequence; if the result is positive, the loop terminates and execution continues with the instruction in location 107. The instructions in locations 104–106 load the value of a into the A register, multiply it by 2, and transfer back to location 101; there the value in the A register is stored back in location 202 as the new value of a and once again compared with the value of b.

Operation codes such as those illustrated in Table 3.3 and used in Fig. 3.15 give machine-language programs the ability to execute arbitrary composite actions.

EXERCISES

1. Suppose that the hypothetical computer described in this section and in Section 2.9 contains the integers 1 and 2 in locations 200 and 201, as well as the values of the variables a and b in locations 202 and 203. Write sequences of machine-language instructions to execute the following Pascal statements:

   (a) $a := abs(a)$

   (b) **if** $a = 0$ **then** $b := 1$ **else** $b := 2$

   (c) **if** $(0 <= a)$ **and** $(a <= 2)$ **then** $a := a + 1$

   (d) **if** $(a < 0)$ **or** $(2 < a)$ **then** $a := a + 1$

   (e) **repeat**
          $a := a*2$
        until $a >= b$

   (f) **while** $n <> 1$ **do**
          if n **mod** $2 = 0$ **then**
              $n := n$ **div** 2
        else
              $n := 3*n + 1$

2. Can you think of any situations in which it would be helpful to load an instruction into the A register and alter its address using an arithmetic operation? Explain.

3. Can you think of other ways to handle the situations you described in Exercise 2? What are the potential advantages and disadvantages of the various alternatives?

SUMMARY

Programs impose an order or structure on the primitive actions required to solve a problem. Most programming languages provide three mechanisms for assembling primitive actions into larger, composite actions:

- sequence (serial structures);
- choice (conditional structures); and
- repetition (iterative structures, or loops).

Composite actions can themselves be assembled into, or nested within, still larger actions. In Pascal, these mechanisms produce composite statements from simpler constituents.

- Compound statements are sequences of statements, surrounded by the keywords **begin** and **end**, that are executed in order.

- Conditional statements are distinguished by the keywords **if**, **then**, and **else** and provide a choice of executing one statement or another.

- Loops take one of three forms:

  1. the **for** statement, which provides a counter-controlled loop;

  2. the **while** statement, which provides an exit before the body of a loop; and

  3. the **repeat** statement, which provides an exit after the body of a loop.

Proper indentation and display clarify the composition of a program in terms of primitive actions.

Good programs are both correct and efficient. A program is correct if it performs in accordance with its specifications. In order to demonstrate that a program is correct, we can

- test its behavior by supplying carefully chosen sets of data as input and observing its output; and

- verify, by formal reasoning, that its actions accomplish what is intended.

Verification of a program is facilitated by comments containing

- assertions that describe the results a program produces, as opposed to the actions it takes; and

- loop invariants that describe what is the same, as opposed to what is different, on each pass through a loop.

Efficient algorithms and programs make economical use of resources. Worst-case analyses estimate the maximum amount of time or space that can be used; they are appropriate when there are strict limits on the resources available for individual actions. Average-case analyses estimate the expected amount of time or space that will be used; they are appropriate when there is a concern only about the resources required by a group of actions.

PROGRAM STRUCTURES PROGRAM
ES PROGRAM STRUCTURES PRO
UCTURES PROGRAM STRUCTURE
ROGRAM STRUCTURES PROGRAM
ES PROGRAM STRUCTURES PRO
UCTURES PROGRAM STRUCTURE
ROGRAM STRUCTURES PROGRAM
ES **PROGRAM STRUCTURES** PRO

C   H   A   P   T   E   R

4

*T*he programs that we wrote in Chapters 2 and 3 were short and their organization was straightforward. As we proceed to write longer programs, organizational issues will become increasingly important. If we construct programs in a logical and comprehensible fashion, then we can exercise control over the processes of program development and maintenance. If we allow the organization of our programs to become haphazard or indiscernible, then we are no longer in control. Therefore, in this chapter, we focus our attention on how to structure programs in ways that keep them under our control.

When writing a program to solve a problem, we will design and write that program in stages. A good design will enable us to break our program into a number of manageable pieces, called *subprograms*, each of which accomplishes some well-defined action and all of which fit together smoothly to create the desired program. We will find uses for some subprograms in more than one program, using them as computational tools that expand the power of our programming language and that ease the task of writing new programs. Other subprograms will be more specific to the problem at hand. But in any case, subprograms will help us to structure the task of writing a program and will enable us to incorporate well-chosen tools in a well-chosen design.

APPLICATIONS: COMPUTATIONAL TOOL KITS

Most programming languages provide a small kit of specialized tools for performing common computations. The most primitive of these tools appear as operators in the language, and we can invoke them by typing just a few symbols. For example, we can add or multiply two numbers by typing a short arithmetic expression. More powerful, but less frequently used, tools appear as functions in the language, and we can invoke them by typing a few more symbols. For example, we can compute the absolute value or sine of a number by typing an arithmetic expression involving the *abs* or *sin* functions in Pascal. Still other tools, known as *procedures*, help us accomplish useful actions instead of helping us compute useful values. For example, we can enter data into and obtain output from a Pascal program by using the *read* and *write* procedures.

No programming language provides a specific tool for every task. Some provide more tools than others, but generally we have to create, through programming, new tools for new tasks. So far we have concentrated on constructing tools for our own use, that is, on writing programs that we can use to carry out interesting computations. However, such tools are not as flexible as functions and procedures. We must use programs manually, whereas we can turn the task of using functions and procedures over to the programs we write. Hence we need to learn how to package new tools as conveniently as the *abs* and *sin* functions or the *read* and *write* procedures in Pascal.

One benefit of packaging is that it gives us the ability to enlarge the kit of useful tools provided by our programming language. For example, a function to compute the minimum of two numbers, or to raise a number to a specified power, is at least as useful as the *abs* and *sin* functions. Since Pascal does not provide these functions, we may wish to provide them ourselves and have them ready when the need arises. Fortunately, we have already written programs to carry out these computations, and it is not difficult to transform these programs into functions for inclusion in our tool kit.

Another benefit of packaging is that it provides us with the ability to construct special-purpose tool kits for particular applications. In the next few chapters, we will develop tools to help us manipulate symbolic as well as numeric data. Armed with these tools, we will be able to write sophisticated programs that maintain and analyze such diverse textual information as computer programs, English prose, and census data.

Whatever their utility, the specific tools that we create will not be as important as our ability to create new tools when we need them. Good tools do lead to good programs. But what constitutes a good tool is best determined by what we want to do, not by what we have done already. True programming power comes from being able to shape tools to the task at hand, not from being able to fall back on a stock of tools—however large—that we or the designers of Pascal had the foresight to provide.

To illustrate how good tools help us to design good programs, we continue the consideration of financial calculators begun in Chapter 3. When we computed the final balance of an installment loan, we saw the need for one specialized tool, namely, a function *roundToCents* that rounded a real number to the nearest hundredth. In this chapter we will learn how to create that tool. Furthermore, we will perform more complicated financial computations by constructing other new tools.

Consider, for example, the problem of determining the rate of interest being charged on a loan of $3000 that we must repay in 36 monthly installments of $100 each. Unfortunately, there is no way to compute the effective rate of interest directly, either by a simple program like *loan1* or *loan2* or by a formula like the one we derived in Section 3.4. If we are willing to spend the time, we can determine the effective interest rate by using *loan1* to perform a manual trial-and-error search for an interest rate that leaves a final balance of $0.00 after 36 payments. If we choose to spend our time more productively, we can write a program that calculates effective interest rates rather than search ourselves for one particular effective rate with the aid of *loan1*.

In order to compute the effective interest rate for a loan, we must replace a trial-and-error search for the rate by a more systematic search. Although writing a program to conduct a systematic search requires an extra investment in thought and programming, that investment has a high payoff. The time we spend using *loan1* for a trial-and-error search produces no further benefits once we have found the effective interest rate for a single loan. On the other hand, the time we spend modifying *loan1* to conduct a systematic search results in a tool that we can use, without trial-and-error, to compute the effective interest rate for many loans.

A good way to begin is by converting the program *loan1* into a function *finalBalance* such that *finalBalance*(*amount, months, payment, rate*) is the final balance of a loan of *amount* dollars at *rate*% annual interest after *months* monthly payments of *payment* dollars each. (See Fig. 4.1.) With such a function, and with fixed values for *amount, months,* and *payment,* we can try to automate a search for a value of *rate* such that *finalBalance*(*amount, months, payment, rate*) = 0.

Put somewhat more abstractly, finding the effective interest rate for a particular loan means finding a zero of the function *f* defined by

$$f(rate) = finalBalance(3000, 36, 100, rate).$$

[A *zero* of a function *f* is a value *x* such that *f*(*x*) = 0.] If *f*(*rate*) = 0, then a loan at *rate*% interest is repaid exactly by the fixed repayment schedule. Thus we should not tinker with *loan1*, or even focus our attention on interest rates, in writing our

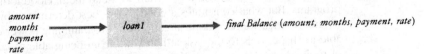

FIGURE 4.1 ■ Computation of final balance viewed as a function

desired program. Rather we should create a tool that finds a zero of a function, and we should use this tool in conjunction with *finalBalance* to calculate the effective interest rate.

In the next section we will design this tool and use it to solve the problem. In later sections we will learn how to code *roundToCents*, *finalBalance*, and this new tool in Pascal. Our plan is to learn first how to use tools, design them, and design programs that use them. Then, when we know how we wish to use tools, we will concentrate on how to create them in Pascal.

EXERCISES

1. Describe some other functions, not present in Pascal, that would be handy to have in a kit of computational tools.

2. Consider the problem of determining the size of the monthly payments required to repay an installment loan with a fixed amount, number of payments, and interest rate.

   (a) Describe a way to solve this problem using a tool that finds the zero of a function.
   (b) Derive a formula for the size of the monthly payments required to repay the loan. (*Hint:* Set the formula derived in Section 3.4 equal to zero and solve for p.)

4.2 ALGORITHMS: PROBLEM DECOMPOSITION

All but the simplest of programming tasks require us to assemble a number of pieces into a coherent, working program. For example, to calculate the effective interest rate for a loan, we must assemble pieces that compute the final balance of a loan, that round a number to the nearest hundredth, that calculate a zero of a function, and that interact with the user of the program. (See Fig. 4.2.) How should we assemble such pieces?

For small tasks we may be tempted simply to throw the pieces together, much as we could build a shanty quickly by grabbing a hammer, some nails, and whatever boards happen to be at hand. But for larger tasks we need to exercise care in selecting pieces and fitting them together, much as we would exercise care in planning and building a house or a factory. Since it is sometimes hard to tell whether a proposed project will turn out to be small or large, it pays to develop good habits and to use them in the assembly of all programs.

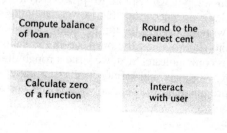

FIGURE 4.2 ■ Separate tasks in calculating effective interest rates

A good design for a program identifies the pieces of that program and organizes these pieces in a logical and workable manner. When building a program, we can construct it a piece at a time. When trying to understand an existing program, we can tackle it a piece at a time. And when trying to fix a program, we can identify and fix the faulty piece. In addition, a good design helps to eliminate repetitious code: a single piece (say, to round a number to the nearest hundredth) can, without duplication, be used many times in a program (say, to round various quantities to the nearest cent).

However, we cannot simply chop a program into pieces of arbitrary sizes and shapes; that is how buildings are demolished, not put together. Each piece, or subprogram, should have a well-defined purpose and be of reasonable size. In short, they should be good tools. Subsidiary computations should be isolated in separate subprograms; we should not confuse the finished product with the tools we use to build that product. Subprograms should be reasonably independent but should fit together neatly; our tools should not get in each other's way.

TOP-DOWN PROGRAM DEVELOPMENT

When we begin to write a long program, we have two choices: (1) we can first assemble a collection of tools that we think will be useful in solving our problem, thereby gaining confidence that we can handle a large task by completing some easy preliminary tasks; or (2) we can take the bull by the horns and grapple with the problem itself, first clarifying exactly which tools will be most useful in solving the problem.

In general, we will use the second approach and write programs in a *top-down* fashion, proceeding from high levels of generality to successively greater amounts of detail through a process known as *stepwise refinement*. Top-down programming stands in sharp contrast to *bottom-up* programming, in which we focus our attention on low-level details first and then attempt to build a program from a collection of previously written pieces.

Although top-down and bottom-up programming represent opposite approaches to program construction, they actually go hand in hand. In top-down programming, the process of stepwise refinement must stop somewhere. Properly used, bottom-up programming creates a collection of general-purpose tools, thereby providing a good place for the process of stepwise refinement to stop.

To write a program in a top-down fashion, we proceed as if we were writing an essay. We first decide what we want to say; that is, we clarify the specifications for our program. Then we write an outline for the program, describing the decomposition of that program into subprograms, the purposes of the subprograms, and the way that the subprograms communicate. Next, we write a rough draft of the program from the outline. Finally, we fill in and refine details, starting at the top with the overall skeleton of the program and working downward one step at a time through its subprograms.

During the entire process of program construction, we try to employ previously written subprograms wherever possible. In this way, we avoid the wasted effort of reinventing the wheel every time we begin to program.

AN EXAMPLE OF PROGRAM DEVELOPMENT

We illustrate how a top-down approach works by designing a program *loan3* to compute effective interest rates. In sequence, we develop a specification, outline, rough draft, and final version for that program.

Specification The specification for our problem seems straightforward: we want to find the effective interest rate for a loan, knowing the amount of the loan, the number of monthly payments, and the size of each payment. Giving this specification some thought, we realize that we may be asking too much of a program. Do we really need to know the rate exactly, or would we be happy knowing it to within 1 percent or 0.1 percent?

Computing the rate exactly seems the most natural thing to do. But we may waste a lot of time computing the rate exactly if we need to know it only within a tenth of a percent and it turns out to be a number like 12.0000000003. Worse yet, the rate may be an irrational number, which we will never be able to compute exactly. Hence, for reasons of economy or mathematical expediency, we may be willing to settle for an *approximation* to the rate, that is, for an interest rate that is as close as we desire to the actual rate. We modify our specifications for *loan3*, then, by requiring only that it approximate to within 0.001 percent the interest rate being charged for a loan with a specified amount, number of payments, and installment size.

Outline In Section 4.1 we saw that we could compute effective interest rates if we had a tool that helped us find a zero of a function f, that is, a value x such that $f(x) = 0$. In *loan3*, the effective interest rate is a zero of the function f defined by

$$f(x) = finalBalance(amount, months, payment, x)$$

and we want to apply such a tool to finding this zero. With our revised specification for *loan3*, we are content to approximate a zero of f to within 0.001 percent. A natural outline for our program consists of the following three steps:

get values for *amount*, *months*, and *payment*
approximate a zero of f to within 0.001%
display this zero

This outline suggests dividing the program *loan3* into several pieces. The *main program*, that is, the body of *loan3*, will accomplish the tasks listed in the outline. But it will farm out the task of computing f to a subprogram that computes *finalBalance*; that subprogram, in turn, will farm out the task of keeping the balance of the loan rounded to the nearest cent to a subprogram defining the function *roundToCents*. These three pieces of *loan3* will communicate by means of the arguments supplied to the two functions and the values they return.

The advantage of dividing *loan3* into these three pieces is that we can avoid getting bogged down in irrelevant details as we write each of the pieces. Since the main program is concerned with approximating a zero of a function, we do not want to spend much time thinking about the mechanics of repaying loans when we write that portion of the program. And since rounding a number to the nearest hundredth is a minor detail, we do not want to waste time worrying about that detail when concentrating on how to repay the loan. By properly dividing our program into pieces, we can focus our attention on those pieces one at a time.

Rough draft   The next step in a top-down approach to program development is to refine our outline and produce a rough draft for *loan3*. Part of this task is routine. We simply create a skeleton Pascal program directly from the outline, adding declarations for key variables, coding those parts of the outline that translate directly into Pascal, and writing comments to remind us of the harder work yet to be done. This refinement produces Pascal Sample 4.1, a rough draft of the program *loan3*.

In order to make this rough draft somewhat more complete, we need to figure out how we intend to approximate a zero of the function *f*. Since we have no way

---

PASCAL SAMPLE 4.1   The program *loan3* (rough draft)

{ finds the effective interest rate of a loan to within 0.001% given }
{ the amount borrowed, the number of monthly payments, and   }
{ the amount of each payment   }

program *loan3*(*input, output*);

const *tolerance* = 0.001;   { accuracy desired for rate   }

var *amount*   : *real*;   { initial amount of loan   }
    months   : *integer*;   { length of loan   }
    payment : *real*;   { monthly payment   }
    x   : *real*;   { unknown rate in %   }
    low, high : *real*;   { bounds on approximation }

{ definitions for *roundToCents* and *finalBalance* go here }

begin
    write('Amount, months, payment: ');
    read(*amount, months, payment*);

    { approximate to within *tolerance*% a zero of $f(x)$ = }
    { *finalBalance*(*amount, months, payment, rate, x*)   }

    writeln;
    writeln('The effective interest rate is ', *x*:6:3, '%.')
end.

of finding a zero directly, we must search for it using a loop such as

{ loop to approximate a zero x of f }
repeat
    generate trial value for x
    compute $f(x)$
until satisfied with x

Again, we have avoided the difficult details. But by now we have refined our thoughts to the point where we know exactly what those details must accomplish, and we are finally ready to tackle them.

Filling in the details   The crucial step in refining our rough draft involves a decision about how to generate trial values for x. For guidance, we consider how we might find a zero of a function f by hand. Most likely, we would draw the graph of f and see where it crossed the horizontal x-axis. (See Exercise 1 at the end of this section.) We can automate this process by computing the point at which the graph of f crosses the x-axis, without actually drawing the graph.

This is not as hard as it may seem, particularly since the graph of our function f is simple. Since $f(x)$ gives the final balance of a loan at x percent interest, small values of x will lead to small values of f: the lower the interest rate, the less we still owe after making a fixed number of payments. Hence f is an increasing function; that is, its graph rises steadily. To find where this graph crosses the horizontal x-axis, we can compute successive values of f until we find a positive value using a loop such as:

    rate := 0;
    while $f(x) < 0$ **do** $x := x + $ *tolerance*

We know that, upon exit from this loop, the graph of f crosses the x-axis somewhere between $x - $ *tolerance* and x. Therefore we know a zero of f to within *tolerance*.

Unfortunately, this method is rather slow, particularly when the zero of f is large and *tolerance* is small. Hence we reject this refinement of our rough draft and seek a more efficient way to proceed.

For a second attempt at refining our rough draft, we try to systematize a trial-and-error search for a zero of an increasing function f. Suppose we start with two values *low* and *high* such that a zero of f lies between *low* and *high*; for example, *low* = 0 and *high* = 100. Then we can try to "trap" a zero of f between systematically revised values of *low* and *high* that get progressively closer together. Since f is increasing and a zero of f lies between *low* and *high*, $f(low)$ will be less than zero and $f(high)$ will be greater than zero. We preserve these properties while moving *low* and *high* closer together.

At each stage in our search for a zero of f, we let x be the value halfway between *low* and *high*, that is, $(low + high)/2$, or the value that *bisects* the distance between *low* and *high*. If $f(x) < 0$, then f must have a zero between x and *high*. If $f(x) \geq 0$,

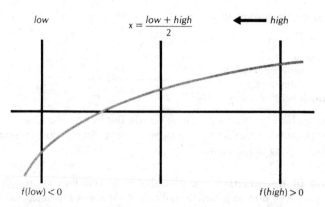

FIGURE 4.3 ■ Bisecting an interval containing a zero of a function *f*

then *f* must have a zero between *low* and *x*. In either case we can narrow by a factor of two the range of possible values for a zero of *f* by changing the value of either *low* or *high*, as appropriate, to the value of *x*. (See Fig. 4.3.) Having done this, we repeat the process of bisection with the new values for *low* and *high*. In fact, we continue bisecting the interval from the original *low* to the original *high* until we have trapped a zero of *f* inside an interval of size *tolerance*.

This method is known as the *bisection algorithm* for approximating a zero of an increasing function *f*. With it, we can refine our rough draft for *loan3* into Pascal Sample 4.2, which is now complete except for the definitions of the two functions *finalBalance* and *roundToCents*.

In the next section we proceed to define these functions and thereby complete the construction of *loan3*. Later—most notably in Chapter 9—we will work through much longer examples of top-down program development.

PASCAL SAMPLE 4.2   The program *loan3* (main program)

```
{ finds the effective interest rate of a loan to within 0.001% given }
{ the amount borrowed, the number of monthly payments, and   }
{ the amount of each payment                                  }

program loan3(input, output);

const tolerance = 0.001;          { accuracy desired for rate   }

var amount   : real;              { initial amount of loan      }
    months   : integer;           { length of loan              }
    payment  : real;              { monthly payment             }
    x        : real;              { unknown rate in %           }
    low, high : real;             { bounds on approximation     }

{ definitions for roundToCents and finalBalance go here }
```

begin

    write('Amount, months, payment: ');
    read(*amount, months, payment*);

    { bisection algorithm to find, within the specified *tolerance*, }
    { a value $0 < x < 100$ such that the final balance of the loan }
    { is \$0.00 when the annual interest rate is x%   }

    low := 0;   { initial range for x }
    high := 100;

    repeat
        $x := (low + high)/2$;
        if *finalBalance*(*amount, months, payment, x*) < 0 **then**
            low := x
        else
            high := x
    until *high* $-$ *low* $<$ *tolerance*;

    writeln;
    writeln('The effective interest rate is ', *x*:6:3, '%.')

end.

SAMPLE USE OF *loan3*:

Amount, months, payment: 3000 36 100

The effective interest rate is 12.249%.

EXERCISES

1. Write a program to plot (or aid you in plotting) the graph of the function f giving the final balance $f(x)$ of a loan of \$3000 at x% annual interest after 36 monthly payments of \$100. Use the graph to estimate the effective interest rate for this loan.

2. Modify *loan3* to check that its input is reasonable (for example, that the interest rate is indeed between 0 and 100%).

3. Modify *loan3* to compute the size of the monthly payment for a loan with a known amount, number of payments, and interest rate. (*Hint:* See Exercise 2, Section 4.1.)

4. Design programs to solve the problems in parts (a) and (b). Describe functions that will help you solve the problems, but do not attempt to define those functions just yet. Instead, write main programs that employ still-to-be-written functions to solve the problems.

    (a) Print a list of the prime numbers that divide a positive integer.

    (b) Find the smallest perfect number larger than a given integer. (A perfect number is an integer equal to the sum of all smaller integers that divide it. For example, $6 = 1 + 2 + 3$ is perfect.)

5. Modify *loan3* to approximate a zero of a function f on an interval (a, b) to within a specified tolerance, given only that $f(a)$ and $f(b)$ have different signs. Use your program to approximate a zero of the *sin* function.

6. What happens to the bisection algorithm if

   (a) the function f is zero at the midpoint of an interval being bisected?

   (b) it is applied to a function f on an interval (a, b) such that $f(a)$ and $f(b)$ have the same sign?

7. Suppose that f is a function such that $f(a) < 0$ and $f(b) > 0$. Which of the following additional properties of f will guarantee that the bisection algorithm locates a zero of f?

   (a) f is increasing.

   (b) f takes on every value between $f(a)$ and $f(b)$.

   (c) f has at least one zero between a and b.

   (d) f is continuous.

   (e) f has no additional properties.

8. Suppose that f is a function that possesses the properties you identified in Exercise 7 and such that $f(0.1) < 0$ and $f(0.15) > 0$.

   (a) What can you say about the number of values between 0.1 and 0.15 for which f is zero?

   (b) How many times must we evaluate f to approximate a zero to within 0.01?

4.3   PROGRAMMING: FUNCTIONS

Our goal in this section is twofold: (1) to finish writing the program *loan3* by learning how to define the functions *finalBalance* and *roundToCents*; and (2) to learn how to define other such subprograms for use in writing additional programs.

Most programming languages provide two methods for creating subprograms. The first is by means of *function definitions*, which we will use to complete *loan3*. Function definitions specify computations that produce values needed to evaluate expressions. The second method is by means of *procedure definitions*, which specify computations that perform actions instead of producing values.

Functions and procedures are known as *subprograms* since their definitions specify computations subsidiary to a program, that is, computations that produce some required value or action. In order to handle subprograms properly, we need to understand the following aspects of how they operate.

▪ *How subprograms are defined*   Just as specific rules govern the construction of programs, so specific rules govern the construction of function and procedure definitions. We treat Pascal's rules for functions in this section and for procedures in Section 4.4.

▪ *When subprograms are executed*   Execution of a subprogram begins only when that subprogram is *invoked* during the execution of a program. A function is invoked whenever it must be evaluated. A procedure in Pascal is invoked whenever a *procedure statement* naming that procedure is executed. (See Section 4.4.)

■ *How information is supplied to subprograms* Figure 4.4 illustrates the transmission of information to and from a subprogram. In general, subprograms receive information through *formal parameters* (or *dummy variables,* such as x and n in Fig. 4.4). Each invocation of a subprogram supplies information by means of *actual parameters* (or *arguments,* such as 2.5 and -3 in Fig. 4.4). Actual parameters specify the actual values to be used for formal parameters in the subprogram definition. We examine the precise relation between actual and formal parameters, known as the *parameter passing* mechanism, in this section and Section 4.4.

■ *How information is returned from subprograms* A function returns information in the form of a value (such as 0.064 in Fig. 4.4) to be used in the evaluation of an expression. A procedure returns values through its parameters, as explained in Section 4.4.

■ *How variables in separate subprograms interact* A variable employed in a subprogram may be *local* to that subprogram, in the sense that it is declared within that subprogram and is distinct from variables with the same name declared elsewhere in the program. Alternatively, it may be more *global* in nature, in the sense that it is not declared within that subprogram and inherits an identity from some exterior declaration. In some programming languages, though not in Pascal, variables declared in a subprogram may retain their values between successive invocations of that subprogram. In Pascal, they cease to exist between invocations. The extent to which a variable has an identity, both in the definition of a program and during its execution, is known as the *scope* of that variable.

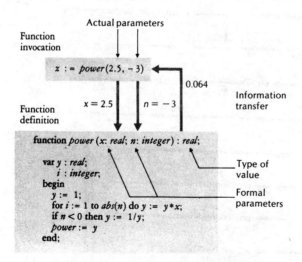

FIGURE 4.4 ■ Definition and invocation of a function to compute x^n

FUNCTION DEFINITIONS

Function definitions enable us to expand the stock of functions provided by a programming language. We may define functions ourselves within a program and use them to construct expressions in the same way that we use those functions (such as *abs*, *round*, *int*, or *sin*) provided by the language.

The definitions for functions and procedures belong in the declaration section of a program, following constant and variable declarations, as shown in Fig. 4.5. Since we declare functions and procedures along with other identifiers, we sometimes refer to their definitions as subprogram declarations.

Function definitions themselves, as illustrated in Fig. 4.4 and described by the syntax diagram in Fig. 4.6, have the same general form as programs. These definitions consist of a header, a declaration section, and a body.

Header   The header in a function definition names the function and describes how information is communicated to and from the definition. Information is communicated to a function definition through *formal parameters* declared within the function header, and information is communicated from a function definition through a *function value*, with its type also declared within the function header.

A function header begins with the keyword **function** followed by the name of the function. Next is a list of declarations, separated by semicolons and enclosed

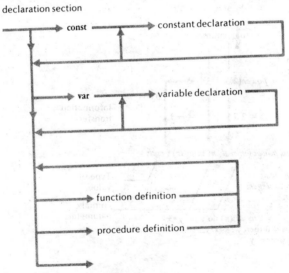

FIGURE 4.5 ■ Syntax diagram, declaration section (second version)

function definition

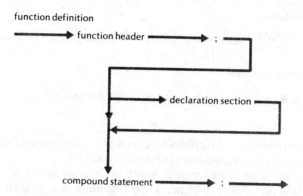

FIGURE 4.6 ■ Syntax diagram, function definition

within parentheses, of the formal parameters for the function; we can omit this list and its enclosing parentheses if the function has no parameters. The header ends with a colon and the type of the value returned by the function. (See Fig. 4.7.)

For now, our formal parameters are simply variables, and their declarations conform to the syntax diagram in Fig. 4.8. For example, the header

    function *power*(*x* : *real*; *n* : *integer*) : *real*;

in Fig. 4.4 declares *power* to be a function with two formal parameters, *x* of type *real* and *n* of type *integer*, that returns a result of type *real*.

Declarations The declaration section in a function definition, and in subprogram definitions in general, identifies objects (other than parameters) that will be used in a subprogram, but not elsewhere within a program containing that subprogram. We

function header

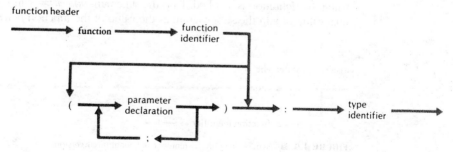

FIGURE 4.7 ■ Syntax diagram, function header

parameter declaration

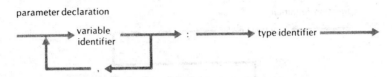

FIGURE 4.8 ■ Syntax diagram, parameter declaration (first version)

can declare constants and variables here, as well as in a program following its header. In fact, we can also declare other subprograms here.

The point of declaring variables within subprogram definitions, rather than simply declaring all variables together at the beginning of a program, is to make subprogram definitions self-contained. Self-containment has at least two important advantages. We can incorporate a previously written subprogram into a program more easily if we can insert its entire definition as a single textual unit; if we had to insert the declarations required by the definition separately from the definition itself, the extra effort involved might dissuade us from modularizing our programs. We can also achieve a large measure of safety by localizing the declaration of a variable to the subprogram in which it is used. Localization permits us to choose a name for a variable without having to worry about whether that name has already been, or will be, used elsewhere in the program; and it prevents execution of the subprogram from having unintended side effects.

Body   The body of a function definition specifies the actions to be taken when a value for that function is required. It consists of a compound statement delimited by the keywords **begin** and **end**. A semicolon, rather than a period, follows the keyword **end** to mark the end of the function definition.

Within the body of a function definition, the name of the function being defined must appear at least once as the target of an assignment statement, that is, on the left-hand side of the assignment operator, $:=$. (See Fig. 4.9.) The value returned by the function definition is determined by the last such assignment statement executed when the definition is invoked. Thus the statement *power* $:= y$ in Fig. 4.4 assigns the final value of *y* in the subprogram as the value of the function *power*.

assignment statement

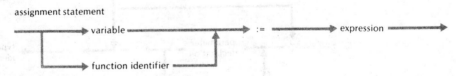

FIGURE 4.9 ■ Syntax diagram, assignment statement (final version)

function value

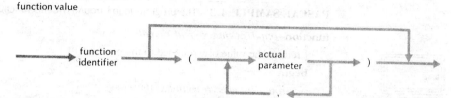

FIGURE 4.10 ■ Syntax diagram, function value

INVOCATION OF FUNCTIONS

A function definition is invoked whenever an expression involving the defined function is evaluated. The number and types of actual parameters supplied for the function in the expression must match the number and types of formal parameters in the definition of the function; for example, the function *power* in Fig. 4.4 must be supplied with two parameters, the first of type *real* and the second of type *integer*. Actual parameters may be arbitrary expressions of the appropriate types. They follow the name of the function, are enclosed by parentheses, and are separated by commas. (See Figs. 4.10 and 4.11.)

When a function is invoked, the values of the actual parameters become the initial values of the formal parameters, and the body of its definition is executed. Variables declared within the function definition have undefined values when execution of the body begins. Variables not declared within the definition retain their current values when execution of the body begins; they also retain their (possibly new) current values when execution of the body terminates.

The value last assigned within the body of a function definition to the identifier for that function becomes the value of the function. This value is used in evaluating the invoking expression, just as the values of the standard functions *abs, sin, cos,* … are used in evaluating expressions that involve these functions.

ORDER OF FUNCTION DEFINITIONS

In programs such as *loan3* that require several function definitions, we must be careful to define those functions in the proper order. Pascal requires us to declare identifiers before we use them. Since the definition of *finalBalance* in *loan3* will invoke *roundToCents*, we must declare *roundToCents* before *finalBalance*. This declaration, displayed as Pascal Sample 4.3, requires only a single statement in its body.

The declaration of *finalBalance* is not much harder to create, particularly since we have already written a program *loan1* that computes the final balance of a loan.

actual parameter

expression

FIGURE 4.11 ■ Syntax diagram, actual parameter (first version)

PASCAL SAMPLE 4.3   The program *loan3* (*roundToCents* function)

function *roundToCents*(*x* : *real*) : *real*;
    { returns the value of *x* rounded to the nearest 0.01 }
    begin
        roundToCents := *round*(*x**100)/100
    end;   { of *roundToCents* }

To convert that program into a function definition, we simply turn the variables *amount*, *months*, *payment*, and *rate* into parameters, strip out all input and output statements, and add a statement that assigns the value of the function. The result is shown as Pascal Sample 4.4.

LOCALITY OF PARAMETERS

The variable *x* plays two quite different roles in the completed program *loan3*. On the one hand, it is a formal parameter in the definition of the function *roundToCents*. On the other hand, it is a variable in the main program that records the midpoint of the interval from *low* to *high* and occurs as an actual parameter in the invocation of *finalBalance*.

Although the parameter *x* and the variable *x* have the same name, these two identifiers have nothing to do with each other; the identity of a formal parameter in a function definition is *local* to that definition. A formal parameter serves as a dummy variable and has no value of its own until it receives one from an actual parameter during an invocation of the function; it has no relation to any other variable in the

PASCAL SAMPLE 4.4   The program *loan3* (*finalBalance* function)

function *finalBalance*(*amount* : *real*;   { amount of loan }
                   months : *integer*;   { life of loan   }
                   payment : *real*;   { installment size }
                   rate   : *real*) : *real*;   { interest rate   }
    { returns final balance of loan when annual interest rate is *rate*%   }
    var *m* : *integer*;   { counter for months }
    begin
        rate := *rate*/1200;   { monthly rate as a fraction }
        for *m* := 1 **to** *months* **do**
            amount := *roundToCents*(*amount* + *amount**rate − *payment*);
        finalBalance := *amount*
    end;   { of *finalBalance* }

PASCAL SAMPLE 4.5   The program *loan3* (alternate definition of *roundToCents*)

function *roundToCents*(*y* : *real*) : *real*;
    { returns the value of *y* rounded to the nearest 0.01 }
    begin
        roundToCents := *round*(*y*∗100)/100
    end;   { of *roundToCents* }

---

program, not even to a variable with a similarly spelled name. Since the formal parameter *x* is a dummy variable, we can call it anything, and *roundToCents* will behave in exactly the same way. In Pascal Sample 4.5, we call it *y*, thereby avoiding the double use of *x* in *loan3*.

Likewise, the parameter *amount* in *finalBalance* is distinct from the variable *amount* in the main program. Thus changing the value of this parameter *amount* as we compute the final balance of a loan does not affect the value of the variable *amount* in the main program. This is fortunate because, otherwise, *loan3* would lose the original amount of the loan after one invocation of *finalBalance*.

The program *loan3* might invite less confusion if it did not contain two declarations each for *amount*, *months*, *payment*, and *x*. But then the world might also be less subject to confusion if there were but one person named John or one person named Mary. The trouble is that there are few enough good names to go around. The price we pay for using (or having the freedom to use) whatever names we choose is that of having to recognize from the context which *x*, John, or Mary we mean. If we had not wanted to make this point about names now, we could certainly have avoided the double identities in *loan3*. But fairly soon we will want the freedom to name variables as we choose in function definitions, without regard to how they might be used elsewhere in a program; hence we allow variables like *x* to get a good workout in a small program.

BLOCK STRUCTURE

The fact that the identity of a formal parameter is local to the subprogram in which it occurs follows from general rules concerning programs and identifiers in Pascal. A Pascal program is composed of a number of building *blocks*: the program itself is a block, and each function or procedure defined within that program is a block. Since we can declare subprograms at the beginning of any block, we can nest blocks within other blocks, as illustrated in Fig. 4.12.

We must declare each identifier in a Pascal program at the beginning of some block within that program, that is, at the beginning of the program itself or at the beginning of a subprogram contained within the program. An identifier has an identity and may be used only within a block in which it is declared, or within a block

```
program A (input, output);
var x : real;

  function f ( y : integer ) : real;
    var z : integer;
    begin
       .
       .
       .
    end;



  function g (z : real ) : real;
  var y : real;

    function h (w : real) : real;
      begin
         .
         .
         .
      end;

  begin

  end;

begin       { main program }
   .
   .
   .
end.
```

FIGURE 4.12 ■ Nesting of blocks in a Pascal program

contained in that block. Because of this restriction, an identifier is said to be *local* to the block that contains its declaration. Since we declare formal parameters in the header for a subprogram, they are automatically local to that subprogram.

Consider, for example, the use of identifiers in Fig. 4.12. The identifiers x, f, and g are declared at the beginning of the program and may be used throughout that program, that is, in the main program itself and in all blocks contained within it. For this reason they are said to be *global* identifiers. The identifiers y and z, on the other hand, are local to the blocks defining f and g; they may be used only in these blocks and not in the main program. Furthermore, they have different identities in these two blocks, being integer variables in the first and real variables in the second. Finally, the function h is local to the block defining g, and the variable w is local to the block defining h; these identifiers may not be used outside those blocks.

When we declare identifiers more than once in a program, they have several separate identities—one for each declaration. This freedom to *redeclare* identifiers and to localize their identity to particular subprograms allows us to construct several independent subprograms and then combine them into a single program. If we could not redeclare identifiers, we would have to be exceedingly careful about which identifiers we used in which subprograms.

To illustrate the effect of redeclaring identifiers several times within a program, let us consider Fig. 4.13: the structure of program B is similar to that of program A in Fig. 4.12, but the use of identifiers in program B is somewhat more involved. In program B, the function f has two separate identities: one as a function of two arguments in the main program and one as a function of a single argument in the block defining g. This second identity supersedes the first in the block that defines g since f is redeclared within that block. We describe this situation by saying that the

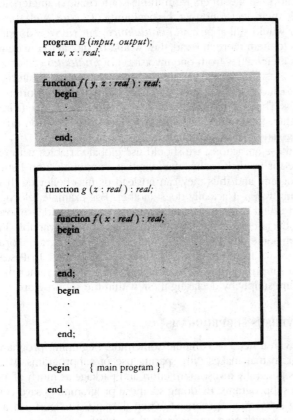

FIGURE 4.13 ■ Redeclaration of identifiers in a Pascal program

scope of an identifier is all of the block in which it is declared, except for any interior blocks in which it is redeclared. Thus, in program *B*, the scope of the variable *w* is the entire program, but the scope of the variable *x* declared along with *w* is the entire program minus the block that defines *f* as a function with one parameter, in which *x* is redeclared.

Let us reexamine the program *loan3* in the light of these conventions. The scope of the variable *m* is the block in which it is declared, namely, that which defines the function *finalBalance*. The parameters *amount*, *months*, *payment*, and *rate* are also local to this block. The function *roundToCents*, which is declared at the beginning of the program, is global to the entire program. If we had declared it inside the definition of *finalBalance*, *loan3* would still work as before, but the definition of *roundToCents* would now be inaccessible to the main program.

In *loan3*, once we assign values to the identifiers *months* and *payment*, those values never change. Hence we could take a shortcut in writing *loan3*. In particular, we could omit these identifiers from the list of formal parameters for *finalBalance*, retaining only their declarations at the beginning of *loan3*. With this change, *months* and *payment* would still appear in *finalBalance*, but we would neither declare nor assign values to them there. Instead, they would be global to the entire program and would retain their values from one invocation of *finalBalance* to the next.

In some situations, global variables provide a convenient alternative for passing information to and from a subprogram. They can help us to shorten impossibly long parameter lists. They can also hide quantities that do not change from one invocation of a subprogram to another, enabling us to focus our attention on those quantities that do change and that are distinguished as parameters.

Despite these attractions, we should use global variables with extreme caution. They provide for implicit, rather than explicit, communication between a program and a subprogram, and thus they can mislead us into believing that a subprogram does one thing when it actually does another. For example, global variables often result in inadvertent communication between a program and a subprogram, as when we forget to declare a variable in a subprogram and that variable inherits an interpretation from some other declaration outside the subprogram. For this reason it is generally safest to avoid using global variables altogether. In Pascal we can force variables in a subprogram to be local to that subprogram, rather than global to the entire program, simply by declaring them within the subprogram.

PROGRAMS VERSUS SUBPROGRAMS

When faced with a need to compute something, beginning programmers generally write a program that makes only sparing use of subprograms. More experienced programmers generally invest more effort and package as much of a computation as possible into subprograms. By doing so, these programmers save considerable time when writing subsequent programs. When they need to perform a task for which they have already written a subprogram, they simply write a program to invoke that subprogram. Less experienced programmers, by contrast, find themselves spending considerable time modifying existing programs to meet new needs. Having modified *loan1* to produce *finalBalance* and *loan3*, we will count ourselves as experienced and seek to use subprograms as a matter of course.

EXERCISES

1. Define a function f such that $f(a, b, c)$ is the number of distinct values x for which $ax^2 + bx + c = 0$.

2. Define a function f such that $f(x, y) = 1$ if the point with coordinates (x, y) lies within a circle of radius 1 about the origin and $f(x, y) = 0$ otherwise.

3. Define a function *posInt* with a single real parameter that has a value of 1 if the value of its parameter is a positive integer, 0 if it is zero or a negative integer, and -1 if it is not an integer.

4. Following is a fragment of a Pascal program to input two numbers and print the maximum of their absolute values, using a defined function *maxabs* to compute this maximum.

```
       .
       .
       .
       a := abs(a);
       b := abs(b);
       if a < b then maxabs := b else maxabs := a
       .
       .
       .
   begin { main program }
       read(x, y);
       z := maxabs(x, y);
       writeln(z)
   end.
```

What must be added to this fragment to complete the program, presuming that *maxabs* is to be defined as a function with two parameters a and b?

5. Consider a program A with a structure as depicted in Fig. 4.12.

   (a) Name two ways in which the main program can pass information to the function f.

   (b) Name two ways in which the function f can return information to the main program.

   (c) Which of the functions defined in A can be invoked from within the definition of f? From within the definition of g? From within the definition of b?

   (d) Suppose that a new variable v is declared in the header for the function g. Where in the program may we use this variable?

   (e) Where else in the program, if anywhere, may we declare the variable w without affecting the operation of any of the existing subprograms?

    (f) Where else in the program, if anywhere, may we declare the variable *x* without affecting the operation of any of the existing subprograms?

  6. Consider the following program.

```
program demo(input, output);

var a, b : integer;

function addone( x : integer ) : integer;
   begin
       x := x + 1;
       addone := x
   end;

begin
   a := 10;
   b := addone(a);
   writeln( a, ' + 1 = ', b)
end.
```

    (a) What output is produced by this program?

    (b) What output would be produced if the statement $x := x + 1$ were replaced by $a := a + 1$? Why?

    (c) What output would be produced if the statement *addone* := *x* were replaced by the statement *addone* := *a*? Why?

    (d) What output would be produced if both the changes suggested in (b) and (c) were made?

    (e) How would your answers to (a) through (d) be affected if the declaration **var** *a* : *integer*; were added to the definition of *addone*? Why?

4.4   PROGRAMMING: PROCEDURES

Procedure definitions enable us to expand the stock of actions that can be performed by a single statement in a program. We may define procedures within a program and invoke them in the same way that we invoke the procedures *read*, *readln*, *write*, and *writeln* provided by Pascal.

Procedures complement functions. We use them to encapsulate a computation that does not produce a single value, but that takes some other action. We may prefer such an encapsulation when we find ourselves repeating certain sequences of statements within a program or when we cannot package a needed subprogram as a function.

Consider, for example, the task of arranging three numbers (say, 5, 4, and 2) in increasing order. (See Exercise 4, Section 3.3.) Among the many ways of performing this task, we could decide to arrange the first two numbers in order (to give 4, 5, 2) and then arrange the second two numbers in the resulting list in order (to give 4, 2,

5); at this point, the number now third in the list is guaranteed to be the largest, but we may still need to place the other two in order. In any event, we may place the entire list of three numbers in order by performing at most three interchanges of numbers in that list. Pascal Sample 4.6, *arrange3*, illustrates the use of this method to arrange three numbers in order.

 PASCAL SAMPLE 4.6   The program *arrange3*

{ arranges three integers in increasing order }

program *arrange3*(*input, output*);

var *a, b, c : integer*;   { integers to arrange   }
    t   : *integer*;   { temporary copy   }

begin

   write('Enter three integers: ');
   read(*a, b, c*);

      if *a > b* **then**   { order *a* and *b*   }
         begin
            t := a;
            a := b;
            b := t
         end;   { now *a* <= *b*   }
      if *b > c* **then**   { order *b* and *c*   }
         begin
            t := b;
            b := c;
            c := t
         end;   { now *a, b* <= *c*   }
      if *a > b* **then**   { reorder *a* and *b*   }
         begin
            t := a;
            a := b;
            b := t
         end;   { now *a* <= *b* <= *c* }

   writeln;
   writeln(*a*:1, ' <= ', *b*:1, ' <= ', *c*:1)

end.

SAMPLE USE OF *arrange3*:

Enter three integers: 7 1 5

1 <= 5 <= 7

Note that essentially the same sequence of statements is repeated three times within *arrange3*. That sequence interchanges the values of two variables when those values are found to be out of order. To shorten the length of *arrange3*, and to shift emphasis from the details of how interchanges are performed to when they are needed, we can rewrite *arrange3* as a program *arrange3a*, which employs a procedure to perform the interchanges. (See Pascal Sample 4.7.)

In *arrange3a* we have packaged three statements that interchange the values of two variables as a *procedure*, that is, as a subprogram that performs a specified action. The definition of a procedure is similar to that of a function, differing only in the construction of its header. This header consists of the keyword **procedure** (rather than **function**), the name of the procedure (which is an identifier), and a list of declarations for formal parameters enclosed by parentheses; since a procedure does not return a value, the colon and type specification that are present in a function header do not occur in a procedure header. (See Figs. 4.14 and 4.15.)

■ **PASCAL SAMPLE 4.7**   The program *arrange3a*

```
{ arranges three integers in increasing order }
program arrange3a(input, output);
var a, b, c : integer;      { integers to arrange }
procedure swap( var x, y : integer );
    { interchanges the values of x and y }
    var t : integer;
    begin
        t := x;
        x := y;
        y := t
    end;   { of swap }
begin { main program }
    write('Enter three integers: ');
    read(a, b, c);
    if a > b then swap(a, b);      { now a <= b        }
    if b > c then swap(b, c);      { now a, b <= c     }
    if a > b then swap(a, b);      { now a <= b <= c }
    writeln;
    writeln(a:1, ' <= ', b:1, ' <= ', c:1)
end.
```

SAMPLE USE OF *arrange3a*:

```
Enter three integers: 7 1 5

1 <= 5 <= 7
```

procedure definition

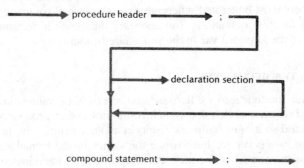

FIGURE 4.14 ■ Syntax diagram, procedure definition

procedure header

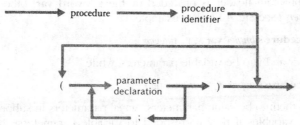

FIGURE 4.15 ■ Syntax diagram, procedure header

A procedure is invoked by execution of a procedure statement such as

swap(a, b)

which consists of the name of the procedure followed by a list of actual parameters enclosed by parentheses. (See Fig. 4.16.)

procedure statement

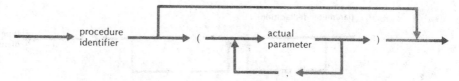

FIGURE 4.16 ■ Syntax diagram, procedure statement

In order for an invocation of *swap* to achieve its intended purpose, its formal parameters must be treated differently from the formal parameters that we encountered in function definitions. The necessary difference in treatment is achieved by the use of the keyword **var** in the procedure header.

PARAMETER MECHANISMS

Recall that the functions we have defined receive their values through their parameters and return a single value as their result. However, a procedure does not possess a value, and so it must return its results in another manner. In the case of *swap* it is clear that, whenever we interchange the values of the formal parameters x and y during an invocation of the procedure, we intend to interchange the values of the actual parameters supplied in the procedure statement; in *arrange3a*, we intend to interchange the values of a and b or of b and c. Such a result is achieved by declaring the formal parameters in *swap* to be *variable*, rather than *value* parameters.

A formal parameter in a subprogram is a *variable parameter* if its declaration in the subprogram header is preceded by the keyword **var**; otherwise it is a *value parameter*. (See Fig. 4.17.) For example,

> **procedure** *sample*(**var** *x, y* : *integer*);

declares x and y to be variable parameters, while

> **procedure** *sample*(*x, y* : *integer*);

declares them to be value parameters. Actual parameters in subprogram invocations must be variables if they correspond to variable parameters; they may be either variables or expressions if they correspond to value parameters. (See Fig. 4.18.)

When a subprogram is invoked, actual parameters that correspond to value parameters are evaluated, and their values are assigned to the corresponding formal parameters. However, actual parameters that correspond to variable parameters are not evaluated upon invocation of the subprogram. Instead, every occurrence of a variable parameter within a subprogram definition is treated as a reference to, or a synonym for, the variable used as the corresponding actual parameter; when a variable parameter is used in an expression, its value is the current value of the corresponding actual parameter; and when a variable parameter is assigned a value, that value is assigned to the corresponding actual parameter.

parameter declaration

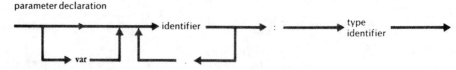

FIGURE 4.17 ■ Syntax diagram, parameter declaration (second version)

actual parameter

FIGURE 4.18 ■ Syntax diagram, actual parameter (second version)

These two different parameter mechanisms are characterized by the information that is passed from an invocation of a subprogram to the definition of that subprogram. In the case of value parameters, an actual value is passed from invocation to definition. In the case of variable parameters, only a reference to a value is passed. Therefore we say that information is *passed by value* to value parameters and *passed by reference* to variable parameters. The existence of two types of parameter mechanisms enables procedures to return results by changing the values of selected variables, while at the same time lessening the chance that functions and procedures will inadvertently change the values of other variables.

In *loan3*, for example, we do not want to pass the actual parameters *amount* and x by reference to the formal parameters *amount* and *rate* in *finalBalance*, because then changing the values of *amount* and *rate* within the function definition would have the side effects of changing the values of the variables *amount* and x in the main program. Such side effects would have disastrous consequences: changing the value of x would cause the bisection algorithm to lose track completely of where it was, and changing the value of the variable *amount* would cause *loan3* to lose track of the initial amount of the loan. In *roundToCents*, as in all functions, we use only parameters passed by value to ward off such side effects.

PROCEDURES VERSUS FUNCTIONS

With minor modifications, we can use procedures and functions interchangeably. To recast a function as a procedure, we simply supply an extra parameter to return a value from its definition. For example, we could repackage *finalBalance* as a procedure rather than a function by making a few simple changes. We could replace the function header

```
function finalBalance( amount  : real;
                       months  : integer;
                       payment : real;
                       rate    : real ) : real;
```

by the procedure header

```
procedure finalBalance(   amount  : real;
                          months  : integer;
                          payment : real;
                          rate    : real;
                      var result  : real );
```

and the final statement

>   *finalBalance* := *amount*

in the body of the definition by

>   *result* := *amount*

in order to transform the definition into that of a procedure. If we did this, then we would need to change the statement

>   **if** *finalBalance*(*amount, months, payment, x*) < 0 **then** ...

which invokes *finalBalance* to a sequence of statements

>   *finalBalance*(*amount, months, payment, x, y*);
>   **if** *y* < 0 **then** ...

which, in turn, invoke the procedure. Note that only the variable *result* needs to be, or should be, declared as a variable parameter when *finalBalance* is transformed into a procedure; *amount* and *rate,* in particular, should remain value parameters to avoid having changes in their values affect the values of the actual parameters *amount* and *x*.

   Although we can use procedures and functions interchangeably, it is more natural to use functions in those applications that require a subprogram to return a single value. For example, it is more natural to compute the maximum of four numbers by a single statement

>   *m* := *max*(*max*(*a, b*), *max*(*c, d*))

that employs a function *max* to find the maximum of two numbers than by several statements

>   *maximum*(*a, b, m1*);
>   *maximum*(*c, d, m2*);
>   *maximum*(*m1, m2, m*)

that employ a procedure *maximum* to set the value of the third parameter equal to the maximum of the first two.

EXERCISES

1. Define a procedure *arrange2* such that the statement *arrange2*(*a, b*) arranges the values of *a* and *b* in increasing order.

2. Define a procedure *arrange3* such that the statement *arrange3*(*a, b, c*) arranges the values of *a, b,* and *c* in increasing order. (*Hint:* Have *arrange3* call *arrange2*.)

3. Following is a fragment of a Pascal program to input two numbers and print the maximum of their absolute values, using a procedure *maxabs* to compute this maximum.

$a := abs(a)$;
$b := abs(b)$;
if $a < b$ **then** $m := b$ **else** $m := a$

begin { main program }
    $read(x, y)$;
    $maxabs(x, y, z)$;
    $writeln(z)$
end.

(a) What must be added to this fragment to complete the program, presuming that *maxabs* is to be defined as a procedure with the three parameters a, b, and m?

(b) Which of a, b, and m should be value parameters and which should be variable parameters?

4. Consider the following program.

```
program demo(input, output);

var a : integer;

procedure addtwo( var x : integer );
    begin
        x := x + 1;
        x := x + 1
    end;

begin
    a := 10;
    addtwo(a);
    writeln(a)
end.
```

(a) What output is produced by this program?

(b) What output would be produced if the first of the two statements $x := x + 1$ is replaced by $a := a + 1$? Why?

(c) How would your answers to (a) and (b) be affected if the formal parameter x to *addtwo* were a value parameter and not a variable parameter?

4.5   PROGRAMMING: SUBPROGRAM LIBRARIES

As we have just learned, subprogram definitions enable us to expand the stock of procedures and functions provided by programming languages such as Pascal. Many of the subprograms that we define are specific to the task at hand: we design them in an effort to structure a solution to a particular problem, and we use them only in the solution of that problem. But other subprograms have a far greater utility: although we may design them with a particular problem in mind, we can use them in the solution of many related problems. Hence it pays to package these subprograms in order to have them at hand when we need them.

Some programming languages make it easy for us to write and employ general-purpose subprograms. These languages distinguish *internal* subprograms, which we define and use within a single program, from *external* subprograms, which we define independently of any program and use whenever they are needed. Some dialects of Pascal (such as UCSD Pascal) provide a facility for external subprograms, but standard Pascal does not. However, with a minimum of effort, we can emulate this important and powerful feature even in standard Pascal.

Just as we can write a program and file it away for future use, so we can write a collection of subprograms and file them away, creating a *library* of procedures and functions for use whenever the need arises. A subprogram library is nothing more than a collection of procedure and function definitions that are suitable for inclusion in the declaration section of a program.

As an example, we assemble a library *maxmin* of four useful functions that are not provided by Pascal. (See Pascal Sample 4.8.) These functions allow us to compute

---

PASCAL SAMPLE 4.8   The library *maxmin*

{ *maxmin*: library of functions to compute maxima and minima }

```
{ Function              Value                         }
{ --------------        ---------                     }
{ intmax(m, n)          maximum of the integers m, n  }
{ intmin(m, n)          minimum of the integers m, n  }
{ max(x, y)             maximum of the reals x, y     }
{ min(x, y)             minimum of the reals x, y     }

function intmax( m, n : integer ) : integer;
    { returns the maximum of m and n }
    begin
        if m >= n then intmax := m else intmax := n
    end;   { of intmax }

function intmin( m, n : integer ) : integer;
    { returns the minimum of m and n }
    begin
        if m <= n then intmin := m else intmin := n
    end;   { of intmin }
```

```
function max( x, y : real ) : real;
    { returns the maximum of x and y }
    begin
        if x >= y then max := x else max := y
    end;   { of max }
function min( x, y : real ) : real;
    { returns the minimum of x and y }
    begin
        if x <= y then min := x else min := y
    end;   { of min }
```

the minimum and maximum of two integers or of two reals. Just as we use comments at the beginning of a program to describe its purpose, so we use comments at the beginning of a library to describe its contents. Definitions of the functions themselves follow these comments.

To use any of the functions in *maxmin* in a particular program, we simply insert the entire library in the declaration section of that program. We can do this either manually, using the editing facilities of our computer system, or automatically, using an additional statement provided by some dialects of Pascal. In Berkeley Pascal, for example, the **#include** statement

#include `'maxmin'`;

directs the Pascal compiler or interpreter to insert the library *maxmin* at the indicated point in a program. Pascal Sample 4.9, *minOf4*, employs such a **#include** statement to gain access to the *intmin* function in *maxmin*.

PASCAL SAMPLE 4.9   The program *minOf4*

```
{ displays the minimum of four integers }
program minOf4(input, output);
var a, b, c, d : integer;
#include 'maxmin';
begin
    writeln('Enter four integers.');
    read(a, b, c, d);
    writeln;
    writeln('Their minimum is ', intmin(intmin(a, b), intmin(c, d)):1)
end.
```

■ **PASCAL SAMPLE 4.9**   The program *minOf4* (continued)

SAMPLE USE OF *minOf4*:

```
Enter four integers.
3 2 1 4

Their minimum is 1
```

When using a dialect of Pascal other than Berkeley Pascal, we can use a text editor to replace the **#include** statement by the contents of the library *maxmin*. Alternatively, we can write a program to make the replacement for us. (See Exercises 6 and 7, Section 6.6).

AN IMPROVED BISECTION ALGORITHM

To further illustrate the utility of subprogram libraries, we modify the program *loan3* to create a subprogram *zero* that approximates a zero of a continuous function f, that is, of a function that has a continuous curve for its graph. While modifying *loan3*, we take the opportunity to improve the bisection algorithm. Most importantly, we cease to require that the function f be increasing. It is necessary only that f have different signs at the endpoints of a specified interval (the *sign* of a value y is $+1$ if y is positive, -1 if y is negative, and 0 if y is zero). Thus we can use the improved

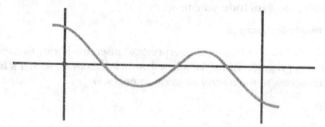

FIGURE 4.19 ■ Function with multiple zeroes in an interval

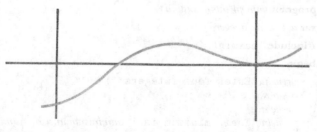

FIGURE 4.20 ■ Function vanishing on a subinterval

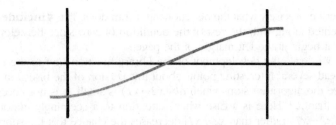

FIGURE 4.21 ■ Function appropriate for bisection algorithm in *loan3*

algorithm to approximate zeroes of functions with graphs that look like those in Figs. 4.19 and 4.20, as well as functions with graphs that look like that in Fig. 4.21.

The bisection strategy works in each of these cases because the graph of a continuous function f with different signs at the endpoints of an interval must intersect the horizontal axis somewhere in that interval. When bisecting such an interval, we can decide which half to retain by comparing the sign of f at the midpoint of the interval with its sign at the left-hand endpoint and then choosing the left or right subinterval, as appropriate, to ensure that f still has different signs at the endpoints of the subinterval (and hence a zero somewhere in that subinterval).

Pascal Sample 4.10, *bisect1*, is a library containing a subprogram *zero* that corresponds to this version of the bisection algorithm. The initial comment in the library describes its contents. More detailed comments within the function definition itself

PASCAL SAMPLE 4.10   The library *bisect1*

{ *bisect1*: bisection algorithm to approximate a zero of the function f }

function *zero*(*x1, x2, epsilon* : *real*) : *real*;

    { assumes: f is continuous and $sign(f(x1)) <> sign(f(x2))$}
    { returns: a value in $(x1, x2)$ within *epsilon* of a zero of f }

    var *x* : *real*;   { the approximation }
        s : *integer*;   { sign of f at *x1*   }

#include 'sign';   { definition of *sign* }

    begin
        s := *sign*(*f*(*x1*));
        repeat
            x := (*x1* +*x2*)/2;
            if *s* = *sign*(*f*(*x*)) **then** *x1* := *x* **else** *x2* := *x*
        until *abs*(*x2* − *x1*) < 2∗*epsilon*;
        zero := (*x1* +*x2*)/2
    end; { of *zero* }

describe precisely what the bisection algorithm does. The **#include** statement is not indented along with the rest of the definition of *zero* since Berkeley Pascal requires that it begin at the left margin of the page.

We leave the development of the library function *sign* to the exercises, noting instead several interesting points about this version of the bisection algorithm. First, since the algorithm stops when $abs(x2 - x1)$ is small, it is not necessary that $x1$ be less than $x2$. Here is a case where attention to a seemingly minor matter [testing $abs(x2 - x1)$ rather than $x2 - x1$] decreases the chance that the subprogram will fail if it is supplied with unexpected arguments.

Second, even though the value of $x1$ may change inside the loop, the sign of $f(x1)$ never changes. Hence it is more efficient to compute this quantity only once by the statement $s := sign(f(x1))$ outside the loop rather than repeatedly within the loop, as would be done if we had used

    if $sign(f(x1)) = sign(f(x))$ . . .

rather than

    if $s = sign(f(x))$ . . .

there. Optimizations of this sort are an easy way to make a program more efficient.

Finally, *zero* will work even if it encounters a value of zero when evaluating $f(x1)$ or $f(x)$ for the midpoint x of some interval being bisected. These values are unlikely to be zero (no need to use *zero* if they were), so it makes little sense to complicate *zero* by treating a function value of zero as a special case. However, it is important that *zero* work in all cases, no matter how unlikely they may be. Our use of the *sign* function guarantees that this will happen. Less careful implementations of the bisection algorithm can lead to subtle errors. (See Exercise 5, Section 4.7.)

In order to test the subprogram *zero* in *bisect1*, we write a program *zeroDemo1* that invokes *zero*. (See Pascal Sample 4.11.) Such a program is known as a *subprogram driver* since it puts a subprogram through its paces. To make the results of *zeroDemo1* easy to check, we have it find the zero of a particularly simple function; to test *zero* more thoroughly, we can modify the definition of f in *zeroDemo1* to have it compute other interesting functions such as $f(x) = sin(x)$ or $f(x) = x^3 - 5x^2 + 2x + 7$.

We can use *zeroDemo1* again in Chapter 10, when we construct other algorithms for approximating zeroes of functions. There we will need to change only a single **#include** statement to make *zeroDemo1* work with those algorithms.

FUNCTIONS AS PARAMETERS (OPTIONAL)*

Numeric variables are not the only objects that can serve as parameters in subprogram definitions. In Chapters 5 and 6 we will introduce other types of variables that can

---

*Sections identified as optional may be skipped without loss of continuity.

■ **PASCAL SAMPLE 4.11** The program *zeroDemo1*

{ subprogram driver for algorithms that approximate zeroes of a function f }

program *zeroDemo1(input, output)*;

const a = 1.0;   { interval containing a zero }
     b = 10.0;
     tolerance = 1**e** − 6;   { accuracy desired for zero }

var z : *real*;   { the approximation }

function $f($ x : *real* $)$: *real*;   { sample function }
   begin
      $f := x*x − 4$
   end; { of f }

#include 'bisect1';   { subprogram to approximate zero }

begin
   $z := zero(a, b, tolerance)$;
   writeln('sqr(', z, ') − 4 = ', $f(z)$)
end.

SAMPLE USE OF *zeroDemo1*:

sqr(1.99999994039536e+00) − 4 = −2.38418575548849e−07

serve equally well as parameters. In connection with our examples in this chapter, we note that even function identifiers can serve as parameters.

Consider the library *bisect1*. The defined function *zero* approximates a zero of the function f. But what if we want to approximate a zero of a function g or to approximate zeroes of two different functions in the same program? We could certainly write several variants of *zero*, one for each function that has zero we want to approximate. However, this would be exceedingly tedious and would result in much longer programs than necessary.

A better solution, which we employ to create the library *bisect2* (Pascal Sample 4.12), is to make the function f a formal parameter to *zero*. Then we can supply names of functions, such as g and h, which have zeroes we want to find, as actual parameters in separate invocations of *zero*. In this way we convert *zero* into a truly general purpose subprogram.

The header for *zero* in *bisect2* declares f to be a function parameter by incorporating a complete header for f. We can use any identifiers to describe the formal parameters of f in this header: we could have used y in place of x, for example. What does matter is that the number and types of formal parameters for f and the type of the value of f all match the corresponding attributes of the actual parameters supplied

---

■ **PASCAL SAMPLE 4.12**   The library *bisect2*

{ *bisect2*: bisection algorithm to approximate a zero of a continuous function }

function *zero*(**function** $f(x : real) : real$;

                                    $x1, x2, epsilon : real) : real$;

    { assumes: f is continuous and $sign(f(x1)) <> sign(f(x2))$ }
    { returns: a value in $(x1, x2)$ within *epsilon* of a zero of f }

  var $x : real$ { the approximation }
      $s : integer$;   { sign of f at $x1$ }

#include `'sign'`;

  begin
      $s := sign(f(x1))$;
      repeat
          $x := (x1+x2)/2$;
          if $s = sign(f(x))$ **then** $x1 := x$ **else** $x2 := x$
      until $abs(x2-x1) < 2*epsilon$;
      $zero := (x1+x2)/2$
  end; { of *zero* }

---

for f in each invocation of *zero*. The syntax diagram in Fig. 4.22 governs declarations for function parameters.

Actual parameters that correspond to formal function parameters must themselves be function identifiers, as shown by the syntax diagram in Fig. 4.23. In the subprogram driver *zeroDemo2*, displayed as Pascal Sample 4.13, the formal parameter f in *zero* receives a specific value either from the actual parameter g or from the actual parameter h.

As with variables that serve as parameters, the use of f as a formal parameter in the definition of *zero* in *bisect2* is local to that definition. If we had named this parameter g instead of f, *zeroDemo2* would be unaffected by the change: the use of g as a formal parameter would be local to the definition of *zero* and have nothing to do with the use of g elsewhere in *zeroDemo2*.

parameter declaration

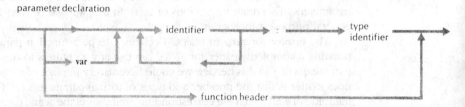

FIGURE 4.22 ■   Syntax diagram, parameter declaration (third version)

actual parameter

FIGURE 4.23 ■ Syntax diagram, actual parameter (third version)

PROCEDURES AS PARAMETERS (OPTIONAL)

We can employ procedures as parameters to other subprograms in Pascal in the same manner that we can employ functions as parameters. We will rarely have occasion to use this feature of Pascal; we note here only that we declare a procedure parameter

---

PASCAL SAMPLE 4.13   The program *zeroDemo2*

{ subprogram driver for algorithms that approximate zeroes of functions }

```
program zeroDemo2(input, output);
const a        = 1.0;                          { interval containing zeroes }
      b        = 10.0;
      tolerance = 1e−6;                        { accuracy desired for zeros }
var z : real;                                  { the approximation }
function g( x : real ) : real;                 { sample function }
    begin
        g := x*x − 4
    end;  { of g }
function h( x : real ) : real;                 { another sample function }
    begin
        h := sin(x)
    end;  { of h }
#include 'bisect2';                            { subprogram to approximate zeroes }
begin
    z := zero( g, a, b, tolerance );
    writeln('sqr(', z, ') − 4 = ', g(z));
    z := zero(h, a, b, tolerance);
    writeln('sin(', z, ')      = ', h(z))
end.
```

SAMPLE USE OF *zeroDemo2*:

```
sqr( 1.99999994039536e+00) − 4 = −2.38418575548849e−07
sin( 3.14159315824509e+00)     = −5.04655293379524e−07
```

parameter declaration

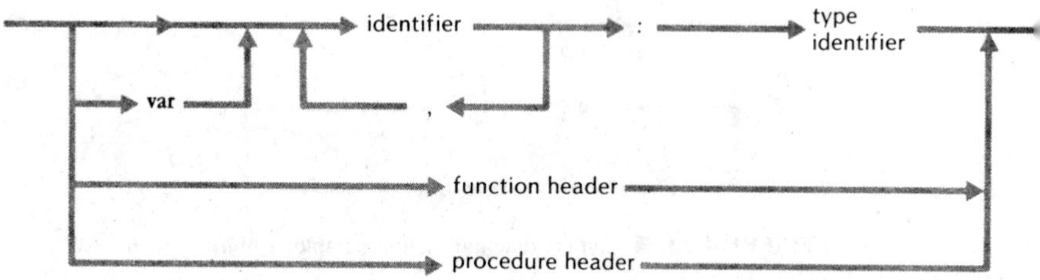

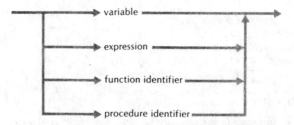

FIGURE 4.24 ■ Syntax diagram, parameter declaration (final version)

to a subprogram in the same manner that we declare a function parameter, name
by including a header for the procedure among the declarations for formal parar
eters in the subprogram header. For example, we can use the header

> **procedure** *apply*(**var**   *object* : *real*;
>   **procedure** *process*(**var** *x* : *real*));

to declare a procedure that applies a specified process to a specified object.

    With this observation, our treatment of parameters in Pascal is complete. Hen
we can present the final versions of the syntax diagrams that govern the declaratio
of formal parameters and the kinds of actual parameters. (See Figs. 4.24 and 4.25.)

LIBRARIES AND PROGRAM DEVELOPMENT

The simple process of developing general-purpose subprograms and filing them i
libraries helps us tremendously in the task of writing programs. With a good set o
libraries at hand, we do need not to reinvent the wheel—or search for one in a scra
heap—whenever we are faced with a task we have accomplished before. Furthermore
whenever we discover a way to improve the subprograms in one of our libraries, a
the programs that use that library benefit immediately. A good filing system helps u
to get the most out of our handiwork.

actual parameter

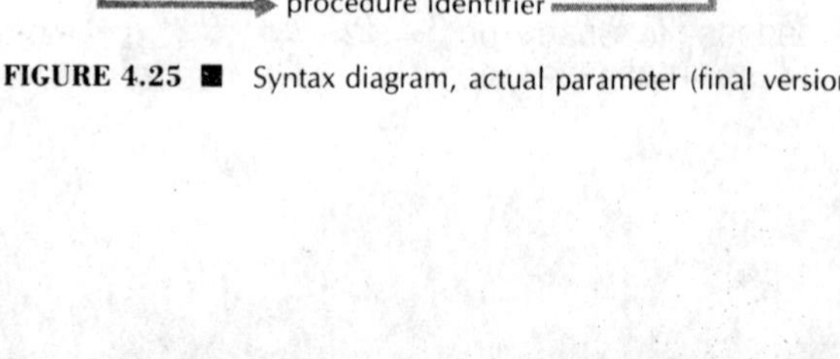

FIGURE 4.25 ■ Syntax diagram, actual parameter (final version)

In the next few chapters we will develop several libraries of general-purpose procedures. Then, in Chapters 7 and 9, we will return to the general issue of program design and development.

EXERCISES

1. Rewrite the program *arrange3a* to utilize a subprogram library containing the *swap* procedure.

2. Create a library containing a definition of the *sign* function required by *bisect1* and *bisect2*. Write that definition to begin with the header

   function *sign*(*x* : *real*) : *integer*;
   { returns −1 if $x < 0$, 0 if $x = 0$, +1 if $x > 0$ }

3. Create a library *mathfcts* containing definitions for
   (a) the logarithm *log2(x)* to the base 2 of *x*;
   (b) the logarithm *log10(x)* to the base 10 of *x*;
   (c) the tangent *tan(x)* of *x*, where *x* is in radians; and
   (d) the *n*th power *power(x, n)* of a real number *x*, where *n* is an integer.

4. What advantage, in *bisect1* and *bisect2*, is there in coding the bisection algorithm as

   ```
   s := sign(f(x1));
   repeat
       x := (x1+x2)/2;
       if s = sign(f(x1)) then x1 := x else x2 := x
   until abs(x2−x1) < 2*epsilon;
   zero := (x1+x2)/2
   ```

   rather than coding it more simply as

   ```
   s := sign(f(x1));
   repeat
       x := (x1+x2)/2;
       if s = sign(f(x1)) then x1 := x else x2 := x
   until abs(x2−x1) < epsilon;
   zero := x
   ```

5. Define a function *sum* with two parameters, one a function and one an integer, such that $sum(f, n) = f(1) + f(2) + \cdots + f(n)$. Use this definition in a program that inputs a number *k* and then prints the sum of the first *k* integers, the sum of their squares, and the sum of their cubes.

4.6 ALGORITHMS: RECURSION

Subprograms help us solve complicated problems by enabling us to divide their solution into manageable pieces. If we can break a problem down into a number of simpler subproblems, we can write subprograms to solve the subproblems and then assemble those subprograms into a program that solves the entire problem. Moreover, if any of the subproblems are themselves complicated, we can write subprograms to solve them by having these subprograms invoke yet other subprograms. In this way we can produce a hierarchy of subprograms to solve a problem, with "higher-level" subprograms assigning well-defined tasks to "lower-level" subprograms in order to complete a job.

Sometimes, when breaking a problem down into subproblems, we find that one or more of the subproblems bears a striking resemblance to the original problem. For example, the bisection algorithm reduces the problem of finding a zero of a function in a given interval to the problem of finding a zero of that function in one-half the interval. In such situations we can use a loop to handle increasingly simpler subproblems iteratively, as we did with the bisection algorithm. Alternatively, we can recognize that the subprogram we are writing solves these increasingly simpler subproblems as well as the original problem, and we can have that subprogram invoke itself to handle these subproblems. Subprograms that invoke themselves are called *recursive* subprograms.

A RECURSIVE VERSION OF THE BISECTION ALGORITHM

The library *bisect3*, displayed as Pascal Sample 4.14, contains a recursive definition of the bisection algorithm in contrast to the iterative definition in *bisect1*. To locate a zero of f to within *epsilon*, the subprogram *zero* in *bisect3* simply decides whether to look for that zero in the left- or right-half interval (by invoking itself recursively)

■ PASCAL SAMPLE 4.14   The library *bisect3*

```
{ bisect3: recursive variant of bisect1 }

function zero( x1, x2, epsilon : real ) : real;
        { assumes: f is continuous and sign(f(x1)) <> sign(f(x2)) }
        { returns: a value in (x1, x2) within epsilon of a zero of f }

    var midpoint : real;

#include 'sign';

    begin
        midpoint := (x1 + x2)/2;
        if abs(midpoint − x1) < epsilon then
            zero := midpoint
        else if sign(f(x1)) = sign(f(midpoint)) then
            zero := zero(midpoint, x2, epsilon)
        else
            zero := zero(x1, midpoint, epsilon)
    end;   { of zero }
```

or to quit when the interval is sufficiently small. The apparent circularity in the new definition disappears if we reason as follows. Suppose that we have the subprogram *zero* in *bisect3* invoke not itself, but rather the subprogram *zero* defined in *bisect1*. Then the two versions of *zero*—that in *bisect1* and the modified version in *bisect3*— would produce exactly the same results. Hence we may as well have *zero* in *bisect3* invoke itself rather than a separate subprogram that does the same thing.

REQUIREMENTS FOR RECURSIVE SOLUTIONS

A recursive subprogram must meet two requirements if it is to solve a problem successfully. If it meets these requirements, successive invocations cause it to reduce a problem to successively simpler problems, until these can be solved outright, and then to assemble solutions to the simpler problems into a solution of the original problem. If the subprogram does not meet these requirements, then it will invoke itself endlessly in a futile attempt to solve the problem.

First, any invocation of a recursive subprogram from within its own definition must solve a problem simpler than the one we first invoked the subprogram to solve. If this is not the case, then the subprogram will invoke itself endlessly trying to solve harder and harder problems. The function *zero* in *bisect3*, for example, reduces the size of the interval by a factor of two before it invokes itself recursively.

Second, there must be some instances in which a recursive subprogram does not invoke itself recursively. If this is not the case, then there is no way for the recursion to stop. The function *zero* in *bisect3*, for example, does not invoke itself recursively when the interval is small enough. Exercise 1 at the end of this section illustrates what can go wrong if these two requirements are not met.

When we invoke a subprogram recursively, it is as if we invoke a carbon copy of that subprogram. Just as libraries can provide duplicate copies of frequently used books, computer systems can provide duplicate copies of frequently used subprograms. And just as we can borrow a second copy of a book from a library when we have one on loan already, a program can invoke a second copy of a subprogram when it has invoked one copy already. Each copy or invocation of a subprogram is supplied with its own parameters and is executed independently of all other copies. Furthermore, variables local to a subprogram are local to each invocation of that subprogram, as they would be if different subprograms, rather than copies of the same subprogram, were invoked.

RECURSION AND ITERATION

We illustrate recursion further by writing two programs that compute the factorial

$$n! = n \times (n - 1) \times (n - 2) \times \cdots \times 2 \times 1$$

of an integer n. The first of these is Pascal Sample 4.15, *fact1*, which operates iteratively, multiplying together the integers from 1 to n.

■ **PASCAL SAMPLE 4.15**   The program *fact1*

{ computes factorials by iteration }

program *fact1*(*input, output*);

var *m* : *integer*;

function *fact*(*n* : *integer*) : *integer*;
    { returns *n*! assuming *n* >= 0 }
    var *i, product* : *integer*;
    begin
        product := 1;
        for *i* := 2 **to** *n* **do** *product* := *product**i;
        fact := *product*
    end;   { of *fact* }

begin
    write('Enter a nonnegative integer: ');
    read(*m*);
    writeln;
    writeln(*m*:1, ' ! = ', *fact*(*m*):1)

end.

SAMPLE USE OF *fact1*:

```
Enter a nonnegative integer: 10

10! = 3628800
```

The second program to compute factorials operates recursively and is based on the observation that

$$n! = \begin{cases} 1 & \text{if } n \leq 1 \\ n(n-1)! & \text{if } n > 1. \end{cases}$$

This observation prompts us to reduce the problem of computing *n*! when *n* > 1 to the simpler problem of computing (*n* − 1)!, as in Pascal Sample 4.16, *fact2*.

When computing factorials, there is little advantage in proceeding recursively rather than iteratively. However, for some problems, recursive solutions are much simpler to develop than are iterative solutions.

Consider, for example, the problem of computing the number of different ways to represent an integer *n* as the sum of a nonincreasing sequence of positive integers. There are five such ways to represent the integer *n* = 4:

$$4 = 4;$$
$$4 = 3 + 1; \qquad 4 = 2 + 1 + 1; \text{ and}$$
$$4 = 2 + 2; \qquad 4 = 1 + 1 + 1 + 1.$$

Analyzing the problem does not suggest any obvious way to proceed iteratively, but it does suggest how to proceed recursively. If we define a function *sums* such that

$$sums(n, m) = \text{number of ways to represent } n \text{ as the}$$
$$\text{sum of a nonincreasing sequence of}$$
$$\text{positive integers no larger than } m,$$

then we can reduce the problem of computing *sums*(*n, m*) to simpler problems by noting that

$$sums(n, m) = sums(n - m, m) + sums(n, m - 1)$$

when $n, m \geq 1$. This identity is true since we can partition the number of ways to represent *n* into two nonoverlapping subsets: *sums*(*n* − *m, m*) ways that include the integer *m* (together with further integers ranging from 1 to *m*, the sum of which is *n* − *m*), and *sums*(*n, m* − 1) ways that do not include the integer *m* (and hence consist of integers ranging from 1 to *m* − 1, the sum of which is *n*).

The identity helps us compute *sums*(*n, m*) recursively; both *sums*(*n* − *m, m*) and *sums*(*n, m* − 1) are easier to compute than *sums*(*n, m*) itself, the value of one or the other actual parameter being reduced in size. Hence we meet the first requirement for a recursive definition. To meet the second, we note that we can com-

---

■ **PASCAL SAMPLE 4.16** The program *fact2*

{ computes factorials by recursion }

program *fact2*(*input, output*);

var *m* : *integer*;

function *fact*(*n* : *integer*) : *integer*;
  { returns *n*! assuming *n* >= 0 }
  begin
    if *n* <= 1 **then** *fact* := 1 **else** *fact* := *n**fact(*n* − 1)
  end; { of *fact* }

begin
  write('Enter a nonnegative integer: ');
  read(*m*);
  writeln;
  writeln(*m*:1, '! = ', *fact*(*m*):1)
end.

SAMPLE USE OF *fact2*:

Enter a nonnegative integer: 10

10! = 3628800

pute the value of *sums*(*n, m*) outright when either *n* or *m* is small enough. When *n* = 0,

$$sums(0, m) = 1,$$

because there is only one way to represent 0 as a sum of positive integers, namely, as a sum containing no terms. Furthermore,

$$sums(n, m) = 0, \quad \text{when } n < 0 \text{ or when } n > 0 \text{ and } m < 1,$$

because there is no way to represent a negative integer as a sum of positive integers or a positive integer as a sum of integers smaller than 1.

These three identities constitute a *recurrence relation* defining the value of *sums*(*n, m*) for all values of *m* and *n*. This recurrence relation serves as the basis for Pascal Sample 4.17, *sums1*, which solves our original problem.

■ **PASCAL SAMPLE 4.17**   The program *sums1*

```
{ computes the number of different ways to represent an }
{ integer n as the sum of a nonincreasing sequence of    }
{ positive integers                                       }

program sums1(input, output);

var n : integer;

function sums( n, m : integer ) : integer;
    { returns the number of different ways to represent  }
    { n as the sum of a nonincreasing sequence of         }
    { positive integers ranging from 1 to m               }
    begin
        if n = 0 then sums := 1
        else if (n < 0) or (m < 1) then sums := 0
        else sums := sums(n, m - 1) + sums(n - m, m)
    end;  { of sums }

begin
    write('Enter a nonnegative integer: ');
    read(n);
    writeln;
    write('There are ', sums(n, n):1);
    writeln(' representations for ', n:1, '.')
end.
```

SAMPLE USE OF *sums1*:

```
Enter an integer: 4

There are 5 representations for 4.
```

This solution emerges naturally from an analysis of the problem, but it is not the most efficient solution. If we were to display the values of n and m each time we invoked *sums*, we would see that certain values of *sums* are recomputed many times. A more efficient solution would compute the value of *sums* just once for each pair of values for n and m, for example, by using a nested loop. Such an iterative solution needs a way to record the computed values of *sums* for small n and m for later use in computing values of *sums* for larger n and m. The array data structure (to be introduced in Section 6.2) provides an appropriate mechanism for recording these values; Exercise 15 at the end of Section 6.2 calls for using an array to convert the recursive definition of *sums* into an iterative one.

An iterative definition of the function *sums* is not without defects of its own. For example, if we want to display all the representations of n as a sum of positive integers, rather than just count the number of such representations, we would find an iterative definition of *sums* much more difficult to modify than the recursive one. (See Section 7.2 for a variant *sums2* of *sums1* that displays all representations of n.) Hence, whether we prefer a recursive or an iterative definition for *sums* depends on whether we are more interested in the efficiency of, or in the ease of extending, the solution to our problem.

As these examples illustrate, recursion and iteration provide alternative and complementary means of formulating an attack on a problem. It turns out that whatever can be programmed using recursion can be reprogrammed using iteration, and whatever can be programmed using iteration can be reprogrammed using recursion. (See Section 11.4.) The great advantage of recursion, and the reason for mastering this important technique, is that we can often gain considerable clarity—and in so doing, solve problems more easily—by proceeding recursively rather than iteratively. The technique of reducing a problem to simpler instances of the same problem is a powerful technique indeed, and we will use it frequently.

EXERCISES

1. Which of the following correctly defines a function *fact* such that $fact(n) = n!$ for all $n > 0$?

(a) **function** *fact*(n : *integer*) : *integer*;
    begin
        fact := $n*fact(n-1)$
    end;

(b) **function** *fact*(n : *integer*) : *integer*;
    begin
        if $n <= 1$ **then**
            fact := 1
        else
            fact := $fact(n+1)/(n+1)$
    end;

(c) **function** *fact*(*n* : *integer*) : *integer*;
    begin
        if $n <= 2$ **then**
            fact := *n*
        else
            fact := $n*(n-1)*fact(n-2)$
    end;

(d) **function** *fact*(*n* : *integer*) : *integer*;
    var *f* : *integer*;
    begin
        $f := fact(n-1)$;
        if $n <= 1$ **then** *fact* := 1 **else** *fact* := $f*n$
    end;

2. An integer is a *Fibonacci number* if it occurs in the sequence

$$1, 1, 2, 3, 5, 8, 13, 21, \ldots$$

of integers each of which (beyond the second) is the sum of the two preceding integers. Let *fib* be a function such that *fib*(*n*) is the *n*th Fibonacci number.

(a) Provide a recursive definition for *fib*.

(b) Provide an iterative definition for *fib*.

(c) How efficient is the recursive definition compared to the iterative definition? (*Hint:* When computing *fib*(*n*) recursively, how many times do we compute *fib*(*m*) for each $m < n$?)

3. The *greatest common divisor* of two integers *m* and *n* is the largest integer that divides both *m* and *n* without leaving a remainder.

(a) Define a function *gcd* such that *gcd*(*m*, *n*) is the greatest common divisor of *m* and *n*. [*Hint:* Use a recursive definition based on the fact that *gcd*(*m*, *n*) equals *m* if $n = 0$ and equals *gcd*(*n*, *m* **mod** *n*) otherwise.]

(b) Mathematically, *gcd*(*m*, *n*) = *gcd*(*n*, *m*). However, something goes wrong with a recursive definition of *gcd* if it is based on the fact that

$$gcd(m, n) = gcd(m \bmod n, n) \qquad \text{if } n \neq 0.$$

Explain why.

(c) Construct a definition for *gcd* using iteration rather than recursion.

4. Write a variant of the program *sums1* based on a recurrence relation involving a function *f* such that *f*(*n*, *m*) is the number of ways to represent *n* as the sum of *m* positive integers arranged in nonincreasing order.

5. Write a program to determine the number of ways that a positive integer *n* can be represented as a sum of distinct positive integers.

6. Define a function *power* with two parameters, *x* and *n*, where *n* is an integer, that produces the value x^n. Use a recursive algorithm based on the observation that

$$x^n = \begin{cases} x^{n/2} \times x^{n/2} & \text{if } n \text{ is even} \\ x^{(n-1)/2} \times x^{(n-1)/2} \times x & \text{if } n \text{ is odd.} \end{cases}$$

Do not use the *ln* or *exp* functions, or a loop of any kind in your program. Be careful to treat negative values for n properly.

7. How many multiplications are performed by the program in Exercise 6 to compute x^{512}? (*Hint*: Many fewer than 100 are needed.)

8. The Tower of Hanoi puzzle consists of n discs with decreasing diameters stacked on one of three needles. The object of the puzzle is to move the discs to the second of the three needles, using the third needle as a temporary resting place for the discs and observing the following rules:

   (a) only one disc may be moved at a time; and

   (b) no disc may be placed on top of a smaller disc.

   Write a program to input a number n and solve the Tower of Hanoi puzzle for n discs, printing the moves that must be made to transfer the discs.

4.7   ANALYSIS: SUBPROGRAM STYLE AND CORRECTNESS

Throughout this chapter we have paid particular attention to issues of programming style and methodology. Indeed, our purpose in studying program structures and subprograms was to find systematic, logical, and comprehensible ways of organizing both our programs and our development of those programs. In this section we reflect briefly on what we have learned, expanding on previous advice and observations concerning programming style and program correctness.

PROGRAM DESIGN AND DEVELOPMENT

Organize your program systematically in a top-down manner to make it easy to read. Have the main program provide an introduction to the entire program, conveying its overall design. (Unfortunately, Pascal requires that the main program occur at the end of the program rather than at the beginning, but this placement should not prevent it from playing an introductory role.) As in a well-written newspaper article, have subprograms that are invoked by the main program reveal more and more detail, covering major ideas first before plunging into detail. Relegate inessential details to lower-level subprograms. (Again, Pascal requires that low-level subprograms occur at the beginning of the program rather than at the end, but it still permits us to arrange subprograms so that the details and an overview occur at opposite ends of the program.) Make it possible to understand any aspect of a program by identifying and reading only a few relevant subprograms.

Always work with a prototype of your final program. Aim to have your prototype work relatively soon. Such a working prototype should be a complete program: one that may lack much of the functionality and refinement of a finished product, but one that you can use, test, and improve. Add subprograms to this prototype one at a time; the design and construction of each subprogram will be more manageable than the design and construction of the entire program. As you add and refine subprograms, your prototype should become a better and better approximation to the final program. Test subprograms as you add them to the prototype, thereby assuring yourself that your design is sound and that the prototype still works before proceeding further.

A major benefit of top-down programming appears if you discover, as often happens, that a feasible-looking approach does not work. It is better to discover this early in the process rather than after you have spent extensive time generating code. Top-down programming, by focusing your attention first on important issues such as communication between subprograms and only later on details, helps you to identify major difficulties before you head down blind alleys. It encourages you to go back and produce a correct design that is accompanied by clean code rather than push forward with a program patched together from pieces of existing code in a disorganized way.

Finally, top-down programming helps you avoid last minute all-or-nothing efforts. With bottom-up programming, it is hard to determine the amount of time you will need to assemble the pieces of a program, whether the pieces will work when you put them together, or what went wrong when you combine several pieces and discover something does not work. With top-down programming, you always possess a working prototype. As deadlines approach, you can use that prototype, improve its behavior by adding or replacing subprograms one at a time, and test your improvements one at a time rather than all together. In short, top-down programming is a well-structured activity designed to help you produce a well-structured program.

DOCUMENTATION

Use comments at the beginning of a subprogram to state what it does. Describe the roles of all parameters, stating any assumptions that you make about their initial values and describing any new values that you assign to the parameters. Do the same for all global variables you use or modify in the subprogram.

Provide enough information for yourself or another person to use a subprogram safely. Be complete, but concise. Defer comments about how the subprogram works until later in the subprogram; it is less important to convey how a subprogram works than what it does. Use comments at the beginning of a subprogram library to provide a table of contents for that library.

PROGRAM DISPLAY AND INDENTATION

Follow the format used in this book to display subprograms. Make it easy to identify where a subprogram begins and ends. Indent the declaration section and body of a subprogram more than its header (say, three spaces). Follow the keyword **end** at the end of the body with a comment containing the name of the subprogram.

Make subprograms stand out as separate units. Use more blank lines between subprograms than within them. Or use a comment such as

```
{ ************************************************************ }
```

stretching across the page to separate one subprogram from the next.

CODING STYLE

Divide your program into reasonably sized pieces, each accomplishing a well-defined task. Don't duplicate code unnecessarily. Isolate often-used sequences of statements into subprograms.

Write subprograms that are easy to read and comprehend one at a time. Keep the size of each subprogram small enough, say, to fit on a single page.

Minimize the connections between the different segments of your program. Avoid global variables wherever possible and keep parameter lists as short as possible. The more independent your subprograms are, the easier they are to comprehend and the less there is that can go wrong with them.

PROGRAM CORRECTNESS

When we use them well, subprograms ease the process of program development and also the task of demonstrating that programs are correct. By enabling us to conceptualize the solution to a problem in terms of component actions leading to that solution, subprograms lend clarity to program design, helping us see the forest and not just the trees. At the very least, well conceptualized programs are more likely to be correct—and easier to correct when they aren't—than disorganized programs. More importantly, by structuring programs, subprograms help us structure demonstrations of program correctness.

When we decompose a program into subprograms, we can decompose the task of showing that the program is correct, as follows.

1. Assuming that all subprograms are correct, show that the entire program is correct.

2. Show that each subprogram is correct.

For this approach to work, we need to formulate precise specifications for each subprogram. Such specifications tell us what we can assume about subprograms when we try to demonstrate that the program itself is correct, and they tell us what we must establish when we try to demonstrate that the subprograms are correct.

A good way to specify what a subprogram does is to state both a precondition and a postcondition for that subprogram. The precondition asserts the conditions under which the subprogram will operate correctly, and the postcondition asserts what will be true when the subprogram terminates. For example, the comments

{ assumes: f is continuous and $sign(f(x1)) <> sign(f(x2))$ }
{ returns: a value in $(x1, x2)$ within *epsilon* of a zero of f }

in *bisect1* specify the assumptions we made in writing the function *zero* and the nature of the value returned by that function. Recall also that we annotated the definition of the function *fact* in *fact1* and *fact2* with the comment

{ returns $n!$ assuming $n >= 0$ }

which states a precondition and a postcondition for that function.

Such explicit statements of preconditions and postconditions for subprograms make clear what we must establish to show that those subprograms are indeed correct. On the one hand, we can construct subprogram drivers like *zeroDemo1* to test that a subprogram satisfies its postcondition when its precondition is true: the value of *z* printed by *zeroDemo1* is indeed within 10^{-6} of a zero of the function *f*. On the other hand, we can verify or prove that the truth of the precondition for a subprogram leads to the truth of its postcondition.

Furthermore, such explicit statements of preconditions and postconditions for subprograms make clear what we can assume when we use those programs. On the one hand, we can test a program even in the absence of its subprograms by simulating what those programs are required to do. On the other hand, we can verify the effect of invoking a subprogram by proving that its precondition is true when it is invoked; once we have done this, we know that the subprogram's postcondition must be true when it terminates.

This technique for program verification is particularly useful for establishing the correctness of recursive subprograms. For example, the recursive definition of *zero* in *bisect3* is correct since *midpoint* is within *epsilon* of a zero of *f* when *abs(midpoint − x1) < epsilon*, there being a zero of *f* somewhere in the interval (*x1, x2*), and since the precondition for the recursive invocation of *zero* is true in the other two cases.

In this way, we can build up a proof of the correctness of a large program from proofs of the correctness of the subprograms comprising that program. The better structured and decomposed into subprograms a large program is, the easier it is for us to verify its behavior. By dividing a large program into subprograms with clear and precise specifications, we can break a correctness proof into a manageable collection of subproofs. And by keeping the size of our subprograms small, we can make each of those subproofs easy to construct.

EXERCISES

1. Design a test plan for a subprogram such as *zero* in *bisect1* or *bisect3*. How many different functions and intervals should be used in such a test plan?

2. Design a test plan for a program, such as *fact1* or *fact2*, that computes factorials. How many different factorials should be computed in such a test plan?

3. Construct an assertion that is an invariant of the loop in *bisect1* (that is true at the beginning of each pass through this loop). Use this assertion to verify the correctness of *bisect1*.

4. What change would be needed in the precondition for the function *zero* in *bisect1* if the condition controlling the exit from the loop in *zero* were changed from *abs(x2 − x1) < 2*epsilon* to *x2 − x1 < 2*epsilon*?

5. Determine which of the following variants of the bisection algorithm produce an *x* within *epsilon* of a zero of *f* when *f(x1)* and *f(x2)* have different signs. For those that do not produce the correct result, describe the circumstances in which they fail. For those that produce the correct result, construct an invariant assertion that is true at the beginning

of each pass through the loop.

(a) $s := sign(f(x2))$;
$x := (x1+x2)/2$;
while $abs(x-x1) >= epsilon$ **do**
  begin
    if $s = sign(f(x))$ **then** $x2 := x$ **else** $x1 := x$;
    $x := (x1+x2)/2$
  end

(b) $s := sign(f(x1))$;
$x := (x1+x2)/2$;
while $abs(x-x1) >= epsilon$ **do**
  begin
    if $s*f(x1) > 0$ **then** $x1 := x$ **else** $x2 := x$;
    $x := (x1+x2)/2$
  end

(c) $s := sign(f(x2))$;
$x := (x1+x2)/2$;
while $abs(x-x1) >= epsilon$ **do**
  begin
    if $s*f(x1) >= 0$ **then** $x1 := x$ **else** $x2 := x$;
    $x := (x1+x2)/2$
  end

6. Verify that the computation of factorials in *fact1* and *fact2* is correct.

4.8   SYSTEMS: HOW SUBPROGRAMS WORK AND COMMUNICATE

When we execute a program, it resides in the primary memory of a computer together with the data it manipulates. Other programs and their data may reside in memory at the same time. For example, the Pascal compiler, the operating system, and several users' programs may all share the memory of a large computer. As illustrated in Fig. 4.26, the portion of a computer's memory that is occupied by a particular program and its data is known as the *address space* of that program.

The area in a program's address space that is devoted to the program itself contains either the text of the program (if we are using an interpreter to execute the program) or a machine-language program produced by a compiler. The area devoted to data contains the values of the constants and variables employed by that program; it may also contain additional information that records intermediate results in a computation or otherwise keeps track of the computation. Although program and data reside in the same address space, the only changes that occur in the address space during a computation occur in the area devoted to data; the area devoted to the program serves solely to direct the course of the computation.

To understand how a program with subsidiary procedures keeps track of where it is during a computation, let us examine how it utilizes its address space. Consider,

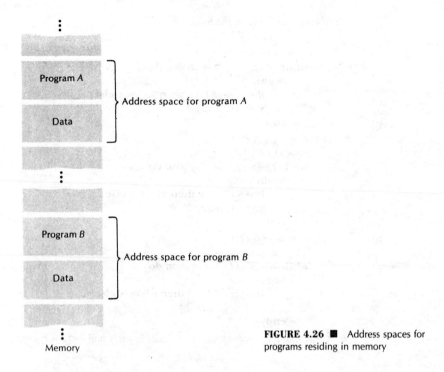

FIGURE 4.26 ■ Address spaces for programs residing in memory

for example, the operation of the program *zeroDemo1*. That program contains a main program (which uses the variable *z* and three constants *a, b,* and *tolerance*), two functions *sign* and *f* (each of which has a single parameter *x*), and the function *zero* (which uses the variables *x* and *s* together with the parameters *x1, x2,* and *epsilon*). Figure 4.27 shows how a simple scheme uses the address space to keep track of the execution of *zeroDemo*.

In this scheme, the data area in the address space for *zeroDemo1* is divided into four parts, one for the main program and one each for the three subsidiary functions. Each part contains locations for recording the values of constants, variables, and parameters. In addition, each of the parts associated with *zero, sign,* and *f* contains a location for recording the address of the instruction that last invoked these functions. Since two of them—*sign* and *f*—are invoked at several points, we must know where to resume execution when we finish evaluating these functions.

The identifier *x* is declared three times in *zeroDemo1*, once as a variable in *zero* and once each as a parameter for *sign* and *f*. Hence three separate locations are assigned to record the value of this identifier. In this way, separate local identities for *x* are maintained in three subareas of the address space.

The values displayed in Fig. 4.27 describe the state of the computation of *zeroDemo1* just prior to the first pass through the **repeat** loop in *zero*. The locations assigned

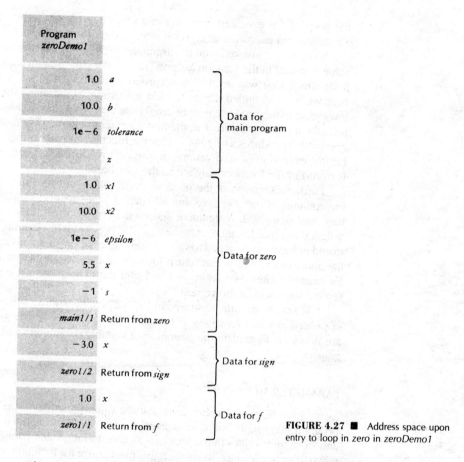

FIGURE 4.27 ■ Address space upon entry to loop in *zero* in *zeroDemo1*

to the const?...s *a*, *b*, and *tolerance* contain the values of those constants. The locations assigned to the parameters *x1*, *x2*, and *epsilon* contain the values of *a*, *b*, and *tolerance*, which we supplied as actual parameters when invoking *zero*. The location assigned to the variable *x* in *zero* contains the average 5.5 of the values of *x1* and *x2*. And the location assigned to the variable *s* in *zero* contains the value -1, which equals $sign(f(x1))$.

How did this value get into the location assigned to *s*? Let us examine what happens when we execute the statement $s := sign(f(x1))$. First, *f* is invoked with the argument *x1*, and the value of *x1* is stored in the location assigned to the parameter *x* in the data area for *f*. Also, so that we can resume the computation of *zero* upon termination of *f*, the address from which *f* was invoked is recorded in the return location in the data area for *f*; here we have identified that return address simply as following the first function invocation in the first statement of *zero*. Now the body of f is executed, resulting in a real value of -3.0. This value is placed in a register, and execution of *zero* resumes at the return address for f.

Next, *sign* is invoked with the argument -3.0, the value just returned by f. This value is stored in the location assigned to x in the data area for *sign,* and the address from which *sign* was invoked is recorded in the return location in that data area here we have identified the return address simply as following the second function invocation in the first statement of *zero* (note that *sign* is invoked after f, even though textually it appears before f in the first statement of *zero*). When the body of *sign* is executed, it produces a value of -1 for the function and places this value in a register. Finally, execution of *zero* resumes at the return address for *sign,* and the value $-$ is stored in the location assigned to the variable s.

Further execution of the program *zeroDemo1* will result in further changes the contents of the data area, but all such changes will be similar to those that we have just described. Assignment statements change the values stored in location assigned to variables; these statements and subprogram invocations change the value stored in locations assigned to value parameters. Subprogram invocations also change the addresses stored in the return locations for those subprograms; in *zeroDemo* for example, later invocations of f and *sign* must record return addresses inside the second statement of the **repeat** loop.

The simple scheme illustrated in Fig. 4.27 explains most aspects of the operation of procedures and functions in Pascal. However, two modifications to this scheme are necessary to explain the operation of variable parameters and recursive subprograms.

PARAMETER MECHANISMS

As we have learned, we can easily handle value parameters. Upon invoking a subprogram, we simply evaluate all actual parameters associated with value parameter and store their values in the locations assigned to the value parameters. Since values move from one location to another, this mechanism for handling parameters is known as a *pass-by-value.*

Variable parameters require a more elaborate treatment since the final values these parameters must be transmitted back to the program that invokes a subprogram. Actual parameters associated with variable parameters must themselves be variable (not expressions) in order to receive these transmitted values.

We can handle variable parameters upon invoking a subprogram by copying values of the actual parameters into the locations assigned to the variable parameter. Then, upon exit from the subprogram, we copy the values currently stored in the locations back into the locations associated with the actual parameters. Such a parameter mechanism, which moves values in two directions, is know as a *pass-by-value-result.*

Passing parameters by value/result can be very costly, as will become apparent in Chapter 6 when we consider data types that are more elaborate than *real integer.* Some of these data types require many locations to store the value of a single variable, and copying the contents of all these locations twice each time we invoke a subprogram is much too expensive. Therefore variable parameters are passed by a different mechanism.

When we invoke a subprogram that has a variable parameter, we do not record the value of the corresponding actual parameter in the location assigned to the variable parameter. Instead, we record the address of the actual parameter. Hence this parameter mechanism is known as a *pass-by-address.* When the body of the subprogram is executed, a special addressing mode, known as *indirect addressing,* is used to manipulate variable parameters. Let us illustrate the way in which this addressing mode works, and the treatment of variable parameters, by examining the program *arrange3a.*

Figure 4.28 shows successive states of the data area for *arrange3a* during the first invocation of the procedure *swap* to interchange the values of the variables *a* and *b.* The procedure *swap* has two variable parameters, *x* and *y,* and a single local variable, *t,* all of type *integer.* When *swap* is invoked with *a* and *b* as actual parameters, the addresses (not the values) of those variables are stored in the locations assigned to *x* and *y.*

Consider now what happens when the assignment $t := x$ is executed. If t and x were both ordinary variables, this assignment would be accomplished by two machine-language instructions such as

```
LDA 203
STA 205
```

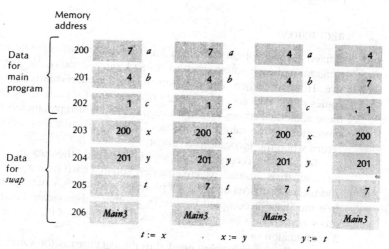

FIGURE 4.28 ■ Data area during invocation of *swap* in *arrange3a*

which load the A register with the contents of location 203 and then store those contents in location 205. But x is not an ordinary variable, and we want to load the A register, not with the contents of location 203, but with the contents of the location having its address stored in location 203. This is exactly what happens when we use a modification LDAI of the LDA operation that employs indirect addressing. The instructions

    LDAI 203
    STA 205

copy the value 7 of the actual parameter a from location 200—the address stored in location 203—into location 205, which is assigned to t. The next assignment, x := y, uses indirect modifications

    LDAI 204
    STAI 203

of both the LDA and STA operations to copy the contents of the location having its address stored in location 204 into the location having its address stored in location 203, that is, to copy the value 4 of the actual parameter b into the location assigned to the actual parameter a. Finally, the assignment y := t uses indirect addressing for the STA operation alone to copy the value of t into the location assigned to the actual parameter b.

Thus, when all operations that involve a variable parameter employ indirect addressing instead of direct addressing, any reference to a variable parameter in a subprogram results in a reference to the location containing the corresponding actual parameter. For this reason, a pass-by-address is also known as a *pass-by-reference*.

RECURSION

A fixed division of the data area for a program into separate areas for the main program and each subprogram works so long as none of the subprograms is recursive. However, when a subprogram invokes itself recursively, we need additional copies of the data area for that subprogram, one for each active invocation. Without these additional copies we cannot keep track of which parameters belong with which invocation, of the values of variables local to particular invocations, or of where to return when the invocations terminate.

To allow for recursion, then, we do not divide the data area for a program into fixed subareas. Instead, we create a new subarea each time a subprogram is invoked and use that subarea until the subprogram terminates, whereupon we discard it and free the space it occupied for use by another subprogram. Figure 4.29 shows how this scheme works by depicting the successive states of the data area for *fact2* during a computation of 3!.

Initially, the only value needed in the data area is the value 3 of the variable m in the main program; the rest of the data area is unused. When the main program

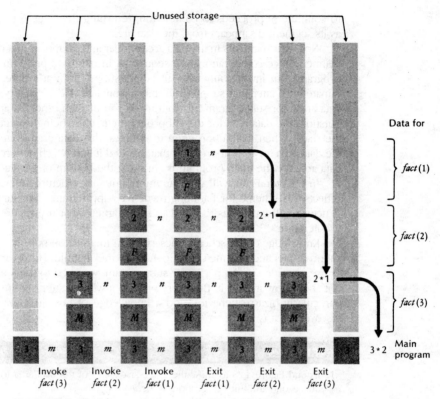

FIGURE 4.29 ■ Data area during computation of 3! by fact2

invokes *fact* to compute 3!, a new segment appears in the data area to record the value 3 of the parameter *n* of *fact* together with the address for the return when *fact* terminates (here *M* designates a return to the main program). Now, for *fact* to compute 3!, it must invoke itself recursively to compute 2!. Hence another segment appears in the data area to record the value 2 of the parameter *n* for this invocation of *fact* as well as the address for the return (here *F* indicates a return to the previous invocation of *fact*). When *fact* attempts to compute 2!, it invokes itself recursively one more time to compute 1!. A final segment appears in the data area to record the value 1 of the parameter *n* for the third invocation of *fact* together with the return address.

At this point, the value of 1! is computed without any further calls to *fact*. Upon completion of this computation, the segment in the data area created for the last invocation of *fact* disappears, and the value 1 is returned to the previous invocation. This invocation can now complete the computation of 2!, returning the value 2 as the segment of the data area created for it disappears. Finally, the invocation of *fact* to compute 3! proceeds to completion, returning the value 6 to the main program as its segment disappears from the data area.

Note that segments in the data area appear and disappear in a particularly orderly manner. Since computations are sequential in nature, a program or one of its subprograms can invoke only one subsidiary subprogram at a time, and it cannot terminate until after that subprogram has terminated. Hence it is possible to stack the data areas for subprogram invocations on top of each other. At any point in a computation, the data area for the subprogram currently being executed is at the top of the stack. When that subprogram terminates, this data area disappears, uncovering the data area for the subprogram that invoked it and which now regains control. The data area for the main program is always at the bottom of the stack.

In Chapter 11 we will study an important data structure known as a *stack,* which reflects this scheme for handling recursive subprograms. Not surprisingly, this data structure will enable us to translate subprograms that use recursion into ones that use iteration.

Knowledge of the schemes described in this section bolster our confidence that subprograms and parameters do behave as they should. However, when attempting to use or understand a particular subprogram, we need to think about what it does, not about how it does it. But every once in a while a subprogram will exhibit some particularly bizarre behavior, and a knowledge of how it operates can lead us to discover what is going on.

EXERCISES

1. Extend Figure 4.28 to show the successive states of the data area for *arrange3a* during the second and third invocations of *swap.*

2. Draw diagrams similar to Figure 4.29 to depict the successive states of the data area for

   (a) *zeroDemo1* used in conjunction with *bisect3*; and

   (b) *sums1* given input 4.

   (*Hint:* The data areas for the recursive procedures in those programs must contain an auxiliary location to record an intermediate value in the evaluation of an expression.)

3. Consider the following program.

   ```
   program demo(input, output);
   var a : integer;
   procedure increment( var x, y : integer );
      begin
         x := x + 1;
         y := y + 2
      end; { of increment }
   begin
      a := 10;
      increment(a, a);
      writeln(a)
   end.
   ```

(a) What output is produced by this program?

(b) Show how this output is produced by drawing a diagram depicting the successive states of the data area during the computation.

(c) Suppose that the parameters x and y were passed by value/result instead of by reference. What output would be produced? Why?

(d) If we change the procedure header to

    procedure *increment*(x : *integer*; **var** y : *integer*);

what output will the program produce?

(e) If we change the procedure header to

    procedure *increment*(**var** x : *integer*; y : *integer*);

what output will the program produce?

SUMMARY

Large programs require systematic construction. Two types of subprograms help decompose a large program into manageable pieces:

- functions define computations that produce values for use in expressions; and
- procedures define composite actions that can be performed by a single statement.

In Pascal, subprogram definitions are similar to programs and consist of

- a header naming the subprogram and the parameters it uses for explicit communication with the main program and with other subprograms;
- declarations of objects local to that subprogram;
- a sequence of statements forming the body of the subprogram; and
- comments describing the subprogram.

Parameters provide a mechanism for passing information to and from a subprogram.

- Formal parameters are dummy variables appearing in the definition of a subprogram.
- Actual parameters are arguments supplied when a subprogram is invoked.
- Value parameters are formal parameters that receive values from actual parameters but do not affect the values of those actual parameters.
- Variable parameters are formal parameters that serve as synonyms for actual parameters and that can affect the values of those actual parameters.

Global variables (used in a subprogram but not declared there) provide a less reliable mechanism for passing information to and from a subprogram. They inherit their definitions from outside the subprogram.

Careful use of subprograms plays an important role in good programming methodology.

- Libraries of subprograms provide collections of general-purpose tools.
- Stepwise refinement, or top-down programming, provides a systematic approach to program construction.

Proper documentation makes the specifications for a subprogram explicit:

1. preconditions describe the circumstances in which a subprogram is expected to operate;

2. postconditions describe what will be true when a subprogram terminates; and

3. a subprogram is correct if the truth of its preconditions implies the truth of its postconditions.

Recursive subprograms, which invoke themselves, provide an alternative to iteration and a natural means for implementing divide-and-conquer, or problem-reduction, algorithms. Such algorithms reduce the solution of a complicated problem to simpler instances of the same problem. The bisection algorithm, for example, approximates a zero of a continuous function in an interval on which the function changes sign by dividing that interval in half and then approximating a zero in one of the subintervals.

PRIMITIVE DATA PRIMITIVE DATA
MITIVE DATA PRIMITIVE DATA PI
TA PRIMITIVE DATA PRIMITIVE D
E DATA PRIMITIVE DATA PRIMIT
PRIMITIVE DATA PRIMITIVE DA
MITIVE DATA PRIMITIVE DATA PI
TA PRIMITIVE DATA PRIMITIVE D
E DATA PRIMITIVE DATA PRIMIT

*P*rograms process information. In the last few chapters we learned how to create programs by composing primitive actions, and we saw how the structure of good programs reflects the structure of the problems they were designed to solve. Yet the problems and programs we have considered so far all deal with relatively primitive and unstructured information.

In order to solve many problems, we must structure information as well as actions. Just as we cannot accomplish much with primitive actions alone, we cannot accomplish much with primitive data alone. There are only a few types of primitive actions (input, output, assignment, and subprogram invocation), and there are only a few types of primitive information. Among these are the by-now-familiar integers and real numbers and several primitive symbolic data types, which we introduce in this chapter.

In Chapter 6 we will learn how to compose primitive data types in ways that reflect the structure of real information. But, just as mastering primitive actions in Chapter 2 prepared us to tackle composite actions in Chapter 3, so mastering primitive data in this chapter will prepare us to tackle composite data in Chapter 6.

APPLICATIONS: SYMBOLIC COMPUTATIONS

The earliest applications of computing were largely numeric in nature. The first electronic computers appeared during the 1940s, with World War II hastening their development. Mathematicians and physicists in the United States applied these machines to compute trajectories for ballistic missiles and to solve other similar numeric problems.

At that time a few scientists realized that computers could be applied to symbolic as well as numeric problems. In Great Britain, at least, computers played a major role in breaking German diplomatic and military codes during World War II.

However, it was not until modern computing reached its second and third decades of use that symbolic applications received as much emphasis as numeric applications. First, in the 1950s, came an interest in programming aids: assemblers, compilers, program editors, and other symbolic tools designed to increase productivity in solving numeric problems. Later, in the 1960s, came an interest in word processing: text editors and formatters, typesetters, and other tools designed to increase productivity in handling written information.

Today symbolic applications, if anything, outweigh numeric applications. Computers process large amounts of information, and the techniques they utilize only occasionally rely upon the numeric nature of information. Numbers, when written in decimal or binary notation, are just one type of symbolic information. Thus, at their very core, computers manipulate symbols, not numbers.

In this chapter we begin to acquaint ourselves with symbolic applications of computing by continuing our development of programs to imitate pocket calculators. In Chapter 2 we imitated some particularly simple special-purpose calculators, and in Chapter 3 we imitated special-purpose calculators that carried out somewhat more sophisticated computations. Now we turn our attention to imitating general-purpose calculators, shifting our interest from how these calculators compute their results to how they interpret a sequence of symbols that describe the results we want. In particular, we write two programs, *calc1* and *calc2*, that imitate multiple-function pocket calculators capable of performing a number of arithmetic operations in a row and displaying the result.

From imitating calculators to processing computer programs is not a very large step, and our work with *calc1* and *calc2* will prepare us to interpret and manipulate sequences of symbols that constitute computer programs. The techniques involved here are not very different from those needed to process much simpler symbolic information. For example, good interactive programs allow their users to respond to questions in ordinary English, typing words like yes or no in either upper or lower case. Hence the mechanisms we study for processing sequences of characters will apply to a wide variety of problems.

In Chapters 6 and 7, we will extend the simple programs written in this chapter to much more sophisticated programs, which also process symbolic information. But even sophisticated applications have simple beginnings, and they lose much of their mystery when we see how simple their origins really are.

EXERCISES

1. In what sense is adding two numbers a symbolic computation?
2. Examine a typical pocket calculator. How do you indicate which operations you want to perform? In what order must you specify those operations? What happens if you specify them in some other order? In what sense does the calculator consider that its keys represent numbers, and in what sense does it consider that they represent symbols?
3. Make a list of the ways in which you use a computer. Which of these ways involve numeric computations and which involve symbolic computations?

5.2   DATA STRUCTURES: SYMBOLIC AND LOGICAL DATA

When we studied numeric data, we identified three components in each data type: (1) a collection of similar objects (integers or real numbers); (2) a collection of operations for manipulating those objects (addition, subtraction, multiplication, division, and various mathematical functions); and (3) a collection of relations for comparing those objects (equality and order relations). We follow the same approach as we shift our attention to nonnumeric data.

THE CHARACTER DATA TYPE

To mimic a multiple-function pocket calculator we need a means of specifying the operation we want to perform. We can code operations numerically (using, say, 1 for addition, 2 for subtraction, 3 for multiplication, and so on) and have our calculator accept three numbers, two to be used in the calculation and one to serve as a code telling the calculator what to do. However, it would be more natural to use common symbols (+ for addition, − for subtraction, * for multiplication, and so on) for arithmetic operations. The character data type enables us to do this.

The objects in the character data type are the symbols or characters that a particular computer system or programming language can handle. In general, these characters include the uppercase letters of the alphabet, possibly the lowercase letters as well, the ten digits, and various special characters such as punctuation marks and symbols denoting arithmetic operations.

Few computer systems provide primitive operations that manipulate characters directly. However, they do provide relations that enable us to examine characters and to manipulate them ourselves.

Each computer system imposes a discrete ordering, called the *collating sequence*, on the set of all characters. In practice, the ordering of the characters is determined by the order of integer codes assigned to those characters: if the code assigned to character c is less than that assigned to another character d, then c comes before in the collating sequence, and we say that c *collates* before d.

For the most part, the collating sequence arranges characters in alphabetic order. Yet different computer systems assign different codes to characters, and collating sequences do vary from system to system. Two common codes are ASCII (American Standard Code for Information Interchange) and EBCDIC (Extended Binary Coded Decimal Interchange Code). The more common ASCII code consists of 128 characters, 95 of which are printable and the remainder of which are special *control characters* (such as backspace, carriage return, and line feed) that cannot be printed. Most IBM computers use EBCDIC instead of ASCII; it consists of 256 characters, 95 of which again are printable. Appendix B contains a complete list of the characters in each of these character sets.

Whichever character set is used, the lowercase letters always collate in alphabetic order, as do the uppercase letters; the digits collate in increasing numeric order, with consecutive digits receiving consecutive codes. These properties of all collating sequences allow us to arrange textual information in alphabetic order. However, collating sequences differ as to whether the uppercase letters come before the lowercase letters or whether consecutive letters have consecutive codes. (They do in ASCII, but not in EBCDIC.) Collating sequences also differ with regard to the order of punctuation marks and other special symbols.

THE LOGICAL, OR BOOLEAN, DATA TYPE

Sometimes in the course of a computation it is useful to record the result of a decision. For example, we may wish to remember whether the value of some function was positive, or whether some combination of circumstances caused us to take a certain action. By keeping a record of what happened, we do not need to recompute the value of a function, or reexamine previous circumstances, if we need to recall certain facts later in a computation.

The logical data type allows us to record these facts. It consists of two objects—the logical values *true* and *false*—that signify whether something was or was not the case. In the 1850s George Boole studied the properties of various logical operators that help us draw valid conclusions from given facts. Because of his work, we often refer to the logical data type as the *boolean data type*.

Among the logical operators studied by Boole are the operators **and**, **or**, and **not**, which we introduced in Section 3.5 to construct composite logical expressions. Table 5.1 specifies the values of these operators in terms of the values of their operands.

TABLE 5.1   Truth Tables for Logical Operators

p	not p		p	q	p and q	p or q
true	false		true	true	true	true
false	true		true	false	false	true
			false	true	false	true
			false	false	false	false

TABLE 5.2   Truth Table for Composite Logical Expression

p	q	r	p and q	(p and q) or r
true	true	true	true	true
true	true	false	true	true
true	false	true	false	true
true	false	false	false	false
false	true	true	false	true
false	true	false	false	false
false	false	true	false	true
false	false	false	false	false

Tables such as Table 5.1 are known as *truth tables* because they enumerate the cases in which a logical expression is true and the cases in which it is false. As Table 5.2 shows, we can use truth tables to determine the truth or falsity of much more complicated logical expressions in a systematic fashion. To construct that table, we apply the definitions of the logical operators given by Table 5.1 first to parenthesized subexpressions and then to expressions involving these subexpressions.

We can also compare boolean values using expressions such as $p = q$. When we do, the result is itself a boolean value: *true* if p and q have the same value, *false* otherwise. Hence, for the boolean data type, relations and operations amount to the same thing: when applied to boolean values, they both produce a result that is a boolean value.

EXERCISES

1. How many characters are there on the keyboard you use? Can you tell from the keyboard whether your computer uses ASCII or EBCDIC?

2. Construct truth tables that show the values of the logical operators = and ≠ for all values of their operands.

3. Find the values of the following logical expressions for all values of p and q.

   (a) p **and** (p **or** q)

   (b) **not** (p **and** q)

   (c) p **or** (p **and** q)

4. Table 5.2 defines the operator **or** to be an "inclusive or": p **or** q is true if p is true, q is true, or both. Another logical operator is the "exclusive or" **xor**, which makes p **xor** q true if either p or q is true, but not both.

   (a) Construct a truth table for the operator **xor**.

   (b) Find a logical expression using **and**, **or**, and **not** that has the same truth table as **xor**.

PROGRAMMING: THE CHARACTER DATA TYPE

In the last section we discussed the character data type in general terms. In this section, we see how to manipulate characters and put them to work in Pascal.

CONSTANTS AND VARIABLES

A character constant in Pascal consists of a single symbol surrounded by apostrophes. For example, `'a'` is a constant denoting the lowercase letter a. One special character constant, `''''` denotes the apostrophe character. Thus character constants are special cases of string constants, which we introduced in Section 2.5 to label the output produced by the *write* procedure.

If we want to use a variable with characters as values, we declare that variable to have the predefined type *char*, as in the declaration:

> **var** *c* : *char*;

We can also supply a character as a parameter to a subprogram by declaring a formal parameter to have the type *char*, and we can return a character as a value of a function by declaring the type of that function to be *char*. Thus a function to translate a character from uppercase to lowercase might begin with the header

> **function** *lcase*(*c* : *char*) : *char*;

INPUT AND OUTPUT

We can read characters using the *read* procedure and write them using the *write* procedure. With these procedures we can write a program *calc1* to simulate a simple multiple-function pocket calculator, the input for which consists of two integers separated by one of the characters +, −, *, or /. Upon reading its input, the calculator performs the indicated operation and displays the result, as in Pascal Sample 5.1, printing an error message if the user specifies an unknown arithmetic operation.

■ **PASCAL SAMPLE 5.1**   The program *calc1*

```
{ simulates a pocket calculator that evaluates an  }
{ expression of the form: integer operator integer }
{ where the operator is one of +, −, *, /          }

program calc1(input, output);

var a, b      : integer;
    operator  : char;

begin
    write('Expression:  ');
    read(a, operator, b);
```

■ **PASCAL SAMPLE 5.1**   The program *calc1* (continued)

```
writeln;
if operator = '+' then
    writeln(a + b)
else if operator = '-' then
    writeln(a - b)
else if operator = '*' then
    writeln(a*b)
else if operator = '/' then
    writeln(a/b)
else
    writeln('"', operator, '" is not a legal operator.')
end.
```

SAMPLE USE OF *calc1*:

```
Expression: 3*5
            15
```

The program *calc1* is somewhat sensitive to spaces in its input. Though the *read* procedure skips leading spaces when asked to read a number, it does not skip leading spaces when asked to read a character. As a result, *calc1* skips over spaces given input like 3− 5 to find the value of *b*, but it assigns a space as the value of *operator* given input like 3 −5 and reports that " " is not a legal operator. Fortunately, it is easy to make *calc1* skip over spaces before reading the value of *operator* as well: all we need to do is replace the statement *read(a, operator, b)* by the sequence

```
read(a);
repeat
    read(operator)
until operator <> ' ';
read(b)
```

of statements that read the characters following the value of *a* until something other than a blank appears. With this improvement, *calc1* can handle input such as 3   +5.

By treating a space like any other character, Pascal enables us to write programs that read their entire input a character at a time. We will use this ability later in this section and even more extensively in later chapters.

EXPRESSIONS AND ASSIGNMENTS

Expressions produce values that we can assign to variables, compare with other values, or supply as arguments to subprograms. Just as Pascal permits us to form numeric-valued expressions, so it permits us to form character-valued expressions. However, since Pascal provides no operators that apply to characters, there are only three kinds of character-valued expressions: character constants; variables of type *char*; and functions that return a value of type *char*. (See Fig. 5.1.)

character expression

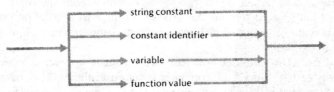

FIGURE 5.1 ■ Syntax diagram, character expression

THE ORDERING OF CHARACTERS

We can compare characters as well as numbers using the relational operators =, <>, <, <=, >, and >= to form relational expressions. (See Section 3.3.) When comparing characters, "less than" means "earlier in the collating sequence than." (See Section 5.2.) This ordering coincides with the usual alphabetical order when the characters involved are both uppercase characters or both lowercase characters.

We can easily modify the program *minOf2a*, which displays the minimum of two integers, to produce a program *minChar*, which displays the first (alphabetically) of two characters. All we need to do is redeclare its variables to be of type *char*, rather than of type *integer*, and change the messages printed to reflect the revised function of the program. (See Pascal Sample 5.2.)

PREDEFINED FUNCTIONS FOR PROCESSING CHARACTERS AND INPUT

We can illustrate more ways to process characters in Pascal by constructing a program *lowercase* that converts uppercase letters in its input into lowercase. As we construct

---

PASCAL SAMPLE 5.2   The program *minChar*

{ displays the alphabetically first of two characters }

```
program minChar(input, output);
var a, b, first : char;
begin
    writeln('Enter two characters.');
    read(a, b);
    if a <= b then first := a else first := b;
    writeln;
    writeln('The character "', first, '" comes first.')
end.
```

SAMPLE USE OF *minChar*:

```
Enter two characters.
to

The character "o" comes first.
```

lowercase, we introduce two new character-related functions, *ord* and *chr*, provided by Pascal, and reexamine the two logical functions, *eoln* and *eof*, that we introduced in Section 3.5 to determine the structure of input to a Pascal program. We will also see how the structure of such input influences the structure of programs to process that input.

First, let us consider how to convert a single uppercase letter into lowercase. This is easiest to do if the computer system uses the ASCII character set. Since the uppercase letters have consecutive ASCII codes, we can use a statement such as

if ('A' <= c) **and** (c <= 'Z') **then** . . .

to determine whether the character *c* is in fact an uppercase letter. To convert an uppercase letter to lowercase, we obtain its ASCII code as the value of the *ord* function in Pascal: *ord(c)* is the code assigned to *c* or the *order* of *c* in the collating sequence. Since the lowercase letters have consecutive ASCII codes, we can compute the code of the lowercase equivalent of an uppercase letter *c* by evaluating the expression

$ord(c) - ord('A') + ord('a')$

which adjusts the code for *c* by an appropriate offset. (This code conversion also works in EBCDIC even though the uppercase and lowercase letters do not have consecutive codes.) Finally, we can use the *chr* function provided by Pascal to convert the code for a character back into the character itself. The *chr* function has the property that

$c = chr(ord(c))$.

Hence the statement

if ('A' <= c) **and** (c <= 'Z') **then** c := chr(ord(c) - ord('A') + ord('a'))

converts uppercase characters *c* to lowercase and leaves other characters alone. We can summarize these properties of the *ord* and *chr* functions as follows:

ord(c)	code assigned to *c* by collating sequence
chr(n)	the character whose code is *n*

To embed this statement for converting characters in a program that processes all its input, we must make a decision about the overall structure of that program. A first attempt at such a structure regards the input as a sequence of characters and processes them as follows:

while more characters remain in input **do**
    read next character
    translate it to lowercase
    display translation

As we noted in Section 3.5, the major problem in refining this design concerns the detection of whether any characters remain in the input. On some systems there is a special marker, called an *end of file* marker, that marks the end of the input. (On batch systems this marker is simply the physical end of the input; on some interactive systems, depressing a particular key generates an end of file marker.) If we are using one of these systems, we can use the *eof* function in Pascal to detect the end of the input: *eof* is true when we reach the end-of-file marker and is false as long as unread characters remain in the input. Using *eof* we can refine the design for our program as follows:

```
while not eof do
    begin
        read(c);
        if ('A' <= c) and (c <= 'Z') then
            c := chr( ord(c) − ord('A') + ord('a') );
        write(c)
    end
```

If we are using a system that does not provide an end-of-file marker for interactive input, we must detect the end of the input in some other way, for example, by looking for a special character. (See Exercise 6 at the end of this section.)

Unfortunately, such a simple structure for our program does not quite work. At best, it will generate only a single line of output, regardless of the number of lines the input contains. The reason for this is that our design takes too simple a view of the structure of textual input. In Pascal, textual input is not just a sequence of characters, but rather a sequence of lines of characters. The end of each line is marked by a special *end-of-line* marker, which is similar to the end-of-file marker. On some systems the end-of-line marker consists of a sequence of control characters (such as a carriage return and line feed); on others, it is the physical end of the line.

For the sake of uniformity, Pascal treats the end-of-line marker as a single character. When read, that character is a space. But we can distinguish it from an ordinary space, and we can detect the end of a line of input in Pascal, using the *eoln* function: *eoln* is true when we reach the end of a line (when the next character in the input is the end-of-line marker) and is false as long as unread characters (other than the end-of-line marker) remain on the line.

Pictorially, textual input to a Pascal program has the structure shown in Fig. 5.2. A correct design for processing textual input in Pascal proceeds line by line, and character by character within each line, as shown in Fig. 5.3. The *readln* procedure in this design advances us past the end-of-line marker, which we must skip when *eoln* becomes true (*read(c)* would work just as well here, but *readln* is more descriptive). When applied to our problem of translating uppercase letters into lowercase, this design results in the program *lowercase*, displayed as Pascal Sample 5.3. The symbol ■ in the sample input for that program represents the key on the terminal that we must depress to generate an end-of-file marker.

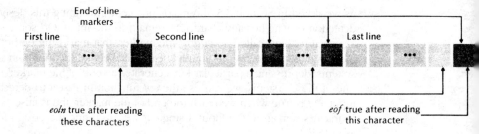

FIGURE 5.2 ■ Structure of textual input in Pascal

```
while not eof do
    begin
        while not eoln do
            begin
                read(c);
                { process c }
            end;
        readln;
        { process end of line }
    end
```

FIGURE 5.3 ■ Skeleton program for processing textual input

PASCAL SAMPLE 5.3   The program *lowercase*

{ converts uppercase letters in input to lowercase }

program *lowercase*(*input, output*);

var *offset* : *integer*;   { uc/lc conversion factor }
        c   :   *char*;   { character from input   }
begin
        offset := *ord*('a') − *ord*('A');
        while not *eof* **do**
            begin
                while not *eoln* **do**
                    begin
                        read(c);
                        if ('A' <= c) **and** (c <= 'Z') **then** c := *chr*(*ord*(c)+*offset*);
                        write(c)
                    end;
                readln;
                writeln
            end
end. { of *lowercase* }

SAMPLE USE OF *lowercase*:

```
This program converts uppercase ASCII letters to lowercase.
this program converts uppercase ascii letters to lowercase.
ABCDEFGHIJKLMNOPQRSTUVWXYZabcdefghijklmnopqrstuvwxy
abcdefghijklmnopqrstuvwxyzabcdefghijklmnopqrstuvwxy
1234567890!@#$%^&*()_+~-='{}[]:;,."'<>?/
1234567890!@#$%^&*()_+~-='{}[]:;,."'<>?/
```

■

LOOKING AHEAD IN THE INPUT

Many times, what we do next in a program depends on what comes next in its input. For example, suppose we want to enhance *calc1* to accept a line of input like 2*3 + 4 − 5 , perform the indicated operations left to right, and display the result when it reaches the end of the line. Then not only must *calc1* skip any spaces following a number to reach the next operation symbol in the line, but it must also skip any spaces following the last number on the line to detect the end of that line. (See Exercise 2 at the end of this section.)

Sometimes the situation is even more complicated because how we read the input depends on what comes next in that input. For example, suppose we want to modify *average3* so that it averages the numbers supplied on a single line of input, ignoring any spaces that occur on that line. Then we must skip over any spaces following a number to see whether another number or the end of the line comes next. But here we are faced with a dilemma: if we skip spaces by reading numbers as in *average3*, we will miss the end of the line, which looks like a space to Pascal; and if we skip spaces by reading characters, as we proposed to do in *calc1*, we will read the first digit in a number as a character and lose the ability to read the entire number as a number.

What we really need is the ability to look ahead in the input before deciding how to read what comes next. Pascal gives us this ability by means of the variable *input*↑, its value being the next character in the input. We will discuss this special *buffer variable* more throughly in Section 6.6. For now, we use it to write a library procedure *skipSpaces* (Pascal Sample 5.4) that skips over spaces in a line of input, stopping either at the end of the line (when *eoln* is true) or when the next character is not a space (when *input*↑ <> ' '). With this procedure we can modify *average3* so that it is no longer sensitive to invisible spaces at the end of a line. The resulting program, *average3a*, is displayed as Pascal Sample 5.5.

In Section 5.4 we will write a procedure *skipBlanks* that skips both spaces and end-of-lines in the input. Simply changing the body of *skipSpaces* to

while not *eof* **and** (*input*↑ = ' ') **do** *read(c)*

does not quite do it: *input*↑ is undefined when *eof* is true, and many Pascal systems will report an error when trying to evaluate *input*↑ at the end of a file.

PASCAL SAMPLE 5.4   The procedure *skipSpaces*

{ *skipSpaces*: skips spaces in a line of input }
procedure *skipSpaces*;
    { assumes: **not** *eof*   }
    { returns: *eoln* **or** (*input*↑ <> ' ') }
    var *c* : *char*;
    begin
        while not *eoln* **and** (*input*↑ = ' ') **do** *read*(*c*)
    end;   { of *skipSpaces* }

PASCAL SAMPLE 5.5   The program *average3a*

{ averages a list of numbers supplied on a single line of input }
program *average3a*(*input, output*);
var *count*   : *integer*;   { length of list   }
      number : *real*;   { number from list }
      sum   : *real*;   { sum of numbers }
#include 'skipSpaces':
begin
    writeln('Enter list of numbers on a single line.');
    sum := 0;
    count := 0;   { no numbers yet   }
    repeat
        read(*number*);
        sum := *sum* + *number*;
        count := *count* + 1;
        skipSpaces
    until *eoln*;
    writeln;
    writeln('Average = ', *sum*/*count*:7:5)
end.

SAMPLE USE OF *average3a*:

```
Enter list of numbers on a single line.
    23    100 85    41

Average = 62.25000
```

EXERCISES

1. Modify *calc1* to print the message `Division by zero not allowed` if the user attempts such a division.

2. Modify *calc1* to accept a single line of input consisting of integers separated by arithmetic operators, perform the indicated operations from left to right, and display the result. Allow spaces anywhere in the line except within the integers.

3. Write a program that counts the number of characters on each line of input, stopping when it reaches

   (a) the end of the input,

   (b) a line of input containing no characters at all, or

   (c) a line of input beginning with a #.

4. Write a program that counts the number of uppercase letters, lowercase letters, and digits on each line of input.

5. The program *lowercase* may not work as shown in Pascal Sample 5.3 on all interactive computer systems. Some systems may not provide any way to signal the end of the input, so we need some other way to stop the program. Some systems may read the input character by character rather than line by line, so that *lowercase* will echo the lowercase equivalent of each character as soon as we type it. And some systems may discard all pending input each time new output is generated. If *lowercase* works poorly on your system, modify it so that it works better.

6. Modify *lowercase* so that it

   (a) converts lowercase letters to uppercase,

   (b) works for the EBCDIC character set as well as ASCII, and

   (c) uses one of the conventions in Exercise 3 to detect the end of the input.

7. How does *average3a* behave if given a blank line of input?

PROGRAMMING: THE BOOLEAN DATA TYPE

In Pascal we can assign the value of any expression to a variable of the appropriate type. Thus we can assign the value of an arithmetic expression to a numeric variable or the value of a character expression to a character variable. But what about the values of relational and logical expressions? We can assign these, too, to variables of the boolean data type.

CONSTANTS AND VARIABLES

In Pascal the identifiers *true* and *false* serve as constants that denote the two objects in the boolean data type. Furthermore, if we declare a variable to be of type *boolean*, we can assign the value of a relational or logical expression to that variable. Thus, the declaration

>**var** *isDigit*, *identical* : *boolean*;

enables us to perform assignments such as

>*identical* := (*x* = *y*);
>*isDigit* := ('0' <= *character*) **and** (*character* <= '9');

and to use the variables *identical* and *isDigit* subsequently in statements such as

>**if** *identical* **then** . . .
>**while** *isDigit* **do** . . .

INPUT AND OUTPUT

In standard Pascal, we can display boolean values using the *write* procedure, but we cannot read them using the *read* procedure. Instead, we must read and translate numeric or character representations for the value of a boolean variable *b*, as in

>*writeln*('Type "t" for true, "f" for false.');
>*read*(*c*);
>**if** *c* = 't' **then**
>   *b* := *true*
>**else if** *c* = 'f' **then**
>   *b* := *false*

However, we rarely seek to read boolean values. More typically, we use boolean variables to record the values of logical expressions for reference later in a computation.

EXPRESSIONS

Logical expressions, which we glimpsed in Chapter 3, are constructed from boolean constants, variables, and relational expressions using a variety of logical operators. Among these are the operators **not**, **and**, and **or**, introduced in Section 3.3 and defined precisely in Section 5.2. The relational operators =, <>, <, <=, >, and >= also double as logical operators. When applied to boolean values, the operator = corresponds to the logical operator of *equivalence*, which is true if its operands have identical logical values, and the operator <> corresponds to the logical operator of *exclusive or*, which is true if only one of its operands is true. For example, the logical expression

>($f(a) < 0$) <> ($f(b) < 0$)

expresses the fact that either $f(a)$ or $f(b)$ is negative, but not both.

Pascal assigns meanings to the other relational operators by the convention that *false* < *true*. With this interpretation, <= corresponds to the logical operator of implication: if $p \leq q$, then the truth of p implies that of q. We will rarely apply these other operators to logical values, preferring instead to use the more familiar operators **and**, **or**, and **not**. However, their presence in Pascal explains why we must use parentheses in logical expressions such as

$(x < y)$ **and** $(y < z)$

instead of writing

$x < y$ **and** $y < z$

as we can in other languages. If x and y were boolean variables, Pascal would have little idea of what we meant if we omitted the parentheses. (In the author's view, it is unfortunate that flexibility in sophisticated uses of logical expressions comes at the expense of economy in common uses. But so be it.)

EVALUATION OF LOGICAL EXPRESSIONS

Like the arithmetic operators, the logical operators have a well-defined precedence in Pascal that, in the absence of parentheses, governs the order of evaluation of an expression. The operator **not** has the highest precedence (is evaluated first), followed by **and**, **or**, and the relational operators, in that order. The detailed syntax diagrams for logical expressions in Figs. 5.4–5.6 reflect this precedence.

There are two strategies for determining the truth or falsity of a logical expression. Many languages, including Pascal, provide for *full evaluation* of logical expressions, that is, the evaluation of each factor and term in that expression. Some languages provide for *partial* or *short-circuit evaluation* instead, that is, the evaluation of only as many factors or terms as needed to determine the truth or falsity of the entire

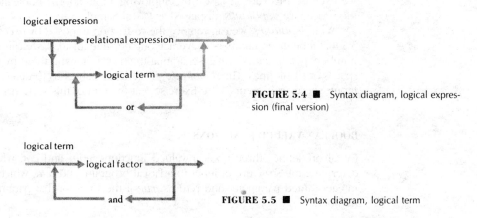

FIGURE 5.4 ■ Syntax diagram, logical expression (final version)

FIGURE 5.5 ■ Syntax diagram, logical term

logical factor

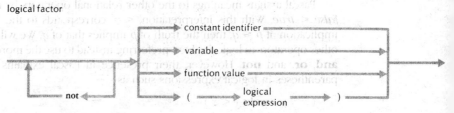

FIGURE 5.6 ■ Syntax diagram, logical factor

expression. Consider, for example, the logical expression

$(n = 0)$ **or** $(m/n > 1)$.

Full evaluation of this expression results in a division-by-zero error when $n = 0$. By contrast, partial evaluation decides that the entire expression must be true as soon as it establishes that $n = 0$, thereby circumventing the need to evaluate m/n and cause an error. For another example, full evaluation of the expression

not *eof* **and** $(input\uparrow = ' ')$

results in an error when *eof* is true (since $input\uparrow$ is undefined then), whereas partial evaluation decides that the entire expression must be false if *eof* is true.

Partial evaluation would simplify many looping constructs. With it we could skip over blanks in a file by a simple statement

while not *eof* **and** $(input\uparrow = ' ')$ **do** *read(c)*

without having to worry about whether an error occurs at the end of the file. With full evaluation, we must be careful not to evaluate $input\uparrow$ when *eof* is true. Typically we exercise this care in Pascal by employing an additional boolean variable, as in the procedure *skipBlanks*, displayed as Pascal Sample 5.6.

With *skipBlanks*, we can remove the restriction imposed by *average4* in Section 3.5 that it be given numbers to average one per line. Instead, we can supply as many numbers per line as we like, separating them or following them by any number of spaces or blank lines. The *skipBlanks* procedure enables us to detect the end of the input wherever it occurs. (See Exercise 3 at the end of this section.)

BOOLEAN-VALUED FUNCTIONS

Pascal predefines three boolean-valued functions: *eoln* and *eof*, which we use to determine the structure of input to a Pascal program, and *odd*, which takes a single integer-valued parameter and returns *true* if the value of that parameter is an odd number.

■ **PASCAL SAMPLE 5.6**   The procedure *skipBlanks*

{ *skipBlanks*: library procedure to skip over blanks in the input }

procedure *skipBlanks*;

　　{ returns: *eof* **or** (*input*↑ <> ' ') }

　　var *done* : *boolean*;

　　　　c　　: *char*;

　　begin

　　　　done := *false*;

　　　　repeat

　　　　　　if *eof* **then**

　　　　　　　　done := *true*

　　　　　　else if *input*↑ = ' ' **then**

　　　　　　　　read(*c*)

　　　　　　else .

　　　　　　　　done := *true*

　　　　until *done*

　　end;　{ of *skipBlanks* }

We can define boolean-valued functions of our own simply by declaring the type of their values to be *boolean*. For example, the function defined by

function *isDigit*(*c* : *char*) : *boolean*;

　　begin

　　　　isDigit := ('0' <= *c*) **and** (*c* <= '9')

　　end; { of *isDigit* }

has the value *true* if its argument is a digit.

BOOLEAN VARIABLES AS STATE VARIABLES

In order to illustrate a typical application of boolean variables, we construct a program that counts the number of times the addition symbol + occurs as an operator in a Pascal program. This would be an easy task if we could just count the total number of times that the symbol + occurred in the text of a program. But symbols can occur in comments and in string constants as well as in expressions. Hence we need to distinguish one type of occurrence from another; that is, we need to keep track of the state we are in—in a comment, in a string, or outside of both—as we read through a program.

Pascal Sample 5.7, *plusCount1*, is a first approximation to our desired program. It reads input a character at a time, processing each character as it goes and using a boolean variable *inComment* to keep track of whether it is in a comment. Rather

PASCAL SAMPLE 5.7   The program *plusCount1*

{ counts addition operators occurring in Pascal program }

{ preliminary version }

program *plusCount1*(*input, output*);

const *symbol* = '+';

var *inComment* : *boolean*;
    count   : *integer*;
    c   : *char*;

begin
    inComment := *false*;
    count := 0;
    while not *eof* **do**
        begin
            read(*c*);
            if *inComment* **then**
                inComment := (*c* <> '}')
            else if *c* = '{' **then**
                inComment := *true*
            else if *c* = *symbol* **then**
                count := *count* + 1
        end;
    writeln;
    writeln(*symbol*, ' occurs ', *count*:1, ' times outside of comments.
end.

SAMPLE USE OF *plusCount1*:

```
program junk (input, output);
begin
    writeln ('1+2+3=', 1+2+3);    { ++++ output ++++ }
end. { of junk }
```

```
+ occurs 4 times outside of comments.
```

than use a second boolean variable *inString* to keep track of when *plusCount*
reading a string, we wait until Section 5.5, where we can employ a better strat
one that lets us define three states instead of the four we would get with two boo
variables.

EXERCISES

1. Each of the logical expressions in the first column, (a)–(e), is equivalent to one of
logical expressions in the second column, (f)–(j). Write a program to determine w

expressions are equivalent. (*Hint:* Tabulate the values of the logical expressions for all possible values of the boolean variables *p* and *q*.)

(a) **not** (*p* **and** *q*)

(b) **not** (*p* **or** *q*)

(c) *p* <= *q*

(d) *p* <> *q*

(e) **not** *p* **and** *q*

(f) **not** *p* **and not** *q*

(g) (*p* **and not** *q*) **or** (**not** *p* **and** *q*)

(h) **not** *p* **or not** *q*

(i) **not** (*q* <= *p*)

(j) **not** *p* **or** *q*

2. Write a program to determine which of the following logical expressions are equivalent. (*Hint:* Tabulate the values of the logical expressions for all possible values of the boolean variables *p*, *q*, and *r*.)

(a) *p* **and** (*q* **or** *r*)

(b) (*p* **and** *q*) **or** (*p* **and** *r*)

(c) *p* **or** (*q* **and** *r*)

(d) (*p* **or** *q*) **and** (*p* **or** *r*)

(e) *p* <= (*q* <= *r*)

(f) (*p* **and** *q*) <= *r*

(g) (*p* <= *q*) <= *r*

3. Enhance the program *average4* so that it will accept more than one number per line. (*Hint:* Replace *readln* by *read* and invoke *skipBlanks* before testing *eof.*)

4. Define a subprogram to get a yes/no response from the user in response to a previously asked question. Have the subprogram return *true* if the user types yes and *false* if the user types no. Have it ask the user to retype any other response.

5. Define a boolean-valued function *numberNext* that is *true* if the next nonblank symbol in the input is a digit and is false otherwise. (*Hint:* Use *skipBlanks* to reach the next nonblank symbol and use *input*↑ to examine that symbol.)

6. Enhance *calc1* to detect and report all errors occurring in its input. (*Hint:* Use *numberNext* from Exercise 5 to check whether numbers occur where expected.)

5.5   PROGRAMMING: DISCRETELY ORDERED TYPES

Three of the four data types that we have studied so far arrange their objects in a discrete order, that is, in an order where a well-defined next object follows each object other than the last and a well-defined previous object precedes each object other than the first. For this reason, the *integer, char,* and *boolean* data types, but not the *real* data type, are known as *ordinal types.* In this section we examine those features of Pascal that are shared by all ordinal types, and we introduce two additional ordinal types: enumerated and subrange types.

Three functions in Pascal supply information about the order of objects in an ordinal type. For any object *x* other than the last in an ordinal type, *succ(x)* is the *successor* of *x*, that is, the next object after *x*. And for any object *x* other than the first in an ordinal type, *pred(x)* is the *predecessor* of *x*, that is, the object immediately preceding *x*. Thus for the *integer* data type, $succ(n) = n + 1$ unless $n = maxint$ and $pred(n) = n - 1$ unless $n = -maxint$. And for the *boolean* data type, $succ(false) = true$ and $pred(true) = false$.

The third function, *ord*, gives the *ordinal position* or order of an object *x* among all objects belonging to an ordinal type. We have already encountered the *ord* function in conjunction with the *char* data type, where *ord*(*c*) is a numeric code assigned to the character *c*. But Pascal defines *ord* for any ordinal type. For the *integer* data type, *ord*(*n*) = *n*. For any other ordinal type, *ord*(*x*) counts the number of objects *y* in that type such that *y* < *x*; thus *ord*(*x*) = 0 if *x* is the first object in an ordinal type. We can summarize the properties of these three ordinal functions in Pascal as follows:

ord(*d*)	ordinal position of *d* in ordinal data type
pred(*d*)	datum before *d* in ordinal data type
	(evaluating *pred*(*d*) when *ord*(*d*) = 0 is an error)
succ(*d*)	datum after *d* in ordinal data type
	(evaluating *succ*(*d*) when undefined is an error)

Ordinal types enjoy several privileges not shared by other types in Pascal. The control variable in a **for** statement can belong to any ordinal type, but not to any other type. Thus we can construct loops such as:

```
for p := false to true do . . .
for c := '9' downto '0' do . . .
```

Objects in an ordinal type can be used to index elements in an array (Section 6.3), as members of sets (Section 12.4), and to select among the alternatives distinguished by the **case** statement to be introduced later in this section.

ENUMERATED DATA TYPES

The two values in the boolean data type, which correspond to the two clauses in an **if** statement, enable us to distinguish between two alternatives. Often, however, we must distinguish among a larger number of alternatives, though not as many as provided by the *integer* or *char* data types. In such cases it is handy to tailor a data type with more than two values specifically to the situation.

Pascal enables us to do this by using the mechanism of an *enumerated* type. To declare a variable with an enumerated type, we simply list, or *enumerate*, the possible values for that variable, as in the following declarations.

```
var color : (red, white, blue);
    state : (normal, inComment, inString);
    day   : (Sunday, Monday, Tuesday, Wednesday, Thursday, Friday, Saturday);
```

The identifiers listed in parentheses are symbolic constants that denote the possible values for the declared variables. These identifiers must be distinct from other identifiers declared in the same declaration section. For example, the declaration sections

```
var fruit : (apple, lemon, orange, peach, pear);
    car   : (new, used, lemon);
```

and

> **var** *stripe1* : (*red, white, blue*);
> *stripe2* : (*red, white, blue*);

are illegal because each mentions a constant identifier more than once. To declare *stripe1* and *stripe2* to belong to the same enumerated type, we must use a single declaration

> **var** *stripe1*, *stripe2* : (*red, white, blue*);

or we must assign a name to the enumerated type. (See Section 5.6.) The syntax diagram in Fig. 5.7 specifies how to construct the description for an enumerated type.

We can use variables and constants that belong to an enumerated type in statements such as

> *color* := *white*
> **if** (*state* = *normal*) **and** (*c* = ' { ') **then** *state* := *inComment*
> **for** *day* := *Monday* **to** *Friday* **do** . . .

The last of these statements makes sense because an enumerated type is an ordinal type, with the declaration for that type specifying the order of its objects (*ord*(*Sunday*) = 0, *ord*(*Monday*) = 1, . . .).

Values in an enumerated type serve primarily to identify a fixed list of possibilities in a program. There is little we can or need to do with these values other than assign or compare them. In particular, we cannot read or write them directly: neither *read*(*day*) nor *write*(*color*) is legal in standard Pascal. Instead, we must use a conditional statement such as

> **if** *color* = *red* **then**
>   *write*('red')
> **else if** *color* = *white* **then**
>   *write*('white')
> **else**
>   *write*('blue')

to display the value of the variable *color*. The **case** statement, which we discuss next, provides a more compact way to distinguish these values.

enumerated type

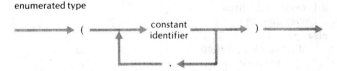

FIGURE 5.7 ■ Syntax diagram, enumerated type

THE CASE STATEMENT

Conditional statements provide for a choice between two alternative courses of action. By following the keyword **else** in one conditional statement with another conditional, as in Fig. 5.8, we can provide for a choice from among as many alternatives as we wish. When we nest conditionals in this manner, we display them as in Fig. 5.8 with the alternatives neatly aligned and not indented relentlessly to the right, as our usual rules for indenting conditional statements would require. (See Fig. 5.9.)

Although the **else if** construct is sufficient for many applications that require a choice from among several alternatives, the **case** statement in Pascal often provides an even more natural and readable way of performing such a choice. For example, the following **case** statement displays the values of the variable *color* belonging to the enumerated type (*red, white, blue*).

```
case color of
    red   : write('red');
    white : write('white');
    blue  : write('blue')
end
```

The **case** statement here, as elsewhere, begins with the keyword **case**, which is followed by an expression with a value that belongs to some ordinal type. This value selects for execution one of the statements, separated as usual by semicolons, that

```
if { condition 1 } then
   { alternative 1 }
else if { condition 2 } then
   { alternative 2 }

        .
        .
        .

else if { condition n − 1 } then
   { alternative n − 1 }
else
   { alternative n }
```

FIGURE 5.8 ■ Multiple alternatives using **else if** construction

```
if { condition 1 } then
   { alternative 1 }
else
   if { condition 2 } then
      { alternative 2 }
   else
      if { condition 3 } then
         { alternative 3 }
      else
         { alternative 4 }
```

FIGURE 5.9 ■ Awkward display of **else if** construction

follow the keyword **of** and precede the keyword **end**, which marks the end of the **case** statement. Each of these statements is labeled by a constant of the same data type as the selecting expression; a colon separates the label from the statement itself. (See Fig. 5.10.) The statement with a label that matches the value of the selecting expression is the one executed. An error results if no label matches the value of the selecting expression.

We choose to display **case** statements with the keyword **end** aligned under the keyword **case**, the labels for the subsidiary statements indented (say, three spaces) and aligned under each other, and the subsidiary statements themselves aligned to the right of the labels (or indented underneath the labels if they occupy too much room). Such a display makes it easy to distinguish the entire **case** statement and each of its parts.

The labels attached to subsidiary statements in a **case** statement must be constants that denote objects in an ordinal type, that is, in an enumerated type or in one of the types *integer*, *char*, or *boolean*. They cannot be variables or expressions, and they cannot come from a type such as *real*. Furthermore, these labels must be distinct. Two or more labels, separated by commas, can identify a single case, as in

```
case operator of
   '+', '-' : write('additive operator');
   '*', '/' : write('multiplicative operator')
end
```

A given label can occur at most once, so the order in which the cases in a **case** statement are listed does not matter.

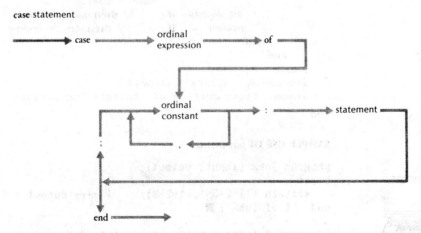

case statement

FIGURE 5.10 ■ Syntax diagram, **case** statement

ENUMERATED TYPES AND STATE VARIABLES

Enumerated types provide a convenient means for keeping the logic of a program under control. As an illustration, we improve the program *plusCount1* by enabling it to distinguish when the symbol + occurs as an operator in a Pascal program from when it occurs in a string constant, as well as from when it occurs in a comment.

PASCAL SAMPLE 5.8   The program *plusCount2*

```
{ counts addition operators occurring in Pascal program }
program plusCount2(input, output);
const symbol = '+';
var state  : (normal, inComment, inString);
    count : integer;
    c     : char;
begin
    state := normal;
    count := 0;
    while not eof do
        begin
            read(c);
            case state of
                normal     : if c = symbol then
                                    count := count + 1
                             else if c = '{' then
                                 state := inComment
                             else if c = '''' then
                                 state := inString;
                inComment : if c = '}' then state := normal;
                inString  : if c = '''' then state := normal
            end
        end;
    writeln;
    write(symbol, ' occurs ', count:1);
    writeln(' times outside of comments and strings.')
end.
```

SAMPLE USE OF *plusCount2*:

```
program junk (input, output);
begin
    writeln ('1+2+3=', 1+2+3);      { ++++ output ++++ }
end. { of junk } ■
```

```
+ occurs 2 times outside of comments and strings.
```

Like *plusCount1*, the improved program *plusCount2* reads the text of a Pascal program character by character. As it reads that program, it can be in one of three states: within normal program text; within a comment; or within a string constant. Hence we find it natural to define these possibilities as an enumerated type and to keep track of the state we are in by using a variable of this type. Pascal Sample 5.8, *plusCount2*, does just that.

Programs such as *plusCount2* are known as *state-driven* programs. By enumerating the possible states that we can encounter, and by using a **case** statement to take the appropriate action in each state, we can often produce a much clearer program than by using nested **if** statements or by using several boolean variables to keep track of where we are.

AN IMPROVED POCKET CALCULATOR

In order to illustrate further the utility of the **case** statement, we modify the program *calc1* to use this statement instead of an **else if** construct. At the same time, we enhance *calc1* so that it can perform a sequence of arithmetic operations, thereby having it imitate a typical multiple-function pocket calculator. The resulting program *calc2* is displayed as Pascal Sample 5.9.

Here *calc2* invokes the procedure *skipSpaces* developed in Section 5.3, so that we can surround operation symbols (rather than just follow them) by spaces in the input. If we have a clean program design, we can easily add such niceties. With a poor design, our attempts to add niceties usually result in a program that is either incorrect or unreadable.

The program *calc2* is not the ultimate program we can write to evaluate arithmetic expressions, but it is not a bad beginning. In later chapters we will return to this program several times, enhancing it to handle assignments to variables, errors in its input, parentheses, and the usual precedence for arithmetic operators.

PASCAL SAMPLE 5.9   The program calc2

```
{ simulates a pocket calculator that evaluates, from left to right, an  }
{ expression on a single line consisting of numbers separated by        }
{ the operators +, -, *, /                                              }

program calc2(input, output);

var result    : real;        { result so far                }
    operator  : char;        { next operation to perform }
    operand   : real;        { operand for that operation}

#include 'skipSpaces';

begin
    write('Expression: ');
    read(result);
    skipSpaces;
```

PASCAL SAMPLE 5.9   The program *calc2* (continued)

```
    while not eoln do
        begin
            read(operator, operand);
            case operator of
                '+' : result := result + operand;
                '-' : result := result - operand;
                '*' : result := result * operand;
                '/' : result := result / operand
            end;
            skipSpaces
        end;
    writeln;
    writeln('Result = ', result:7:5)
end.
```

SAMPLE USE OF *calc2*:

```
Expression: 3*5 - 4

Result = 11.00000
```

SUBRANGES AND SETS

In many applications we don't want to use all the values provided by an ordinal type such as *integer* or *char*. For example, we may want to work with the positive integers alone or with the lowercase ASCII letters alone. For documentation and safety, we can declare in Pascal exactly the range of values we want to use.

A *subrange* data type is an ordinal type that consists of a contiguous sequence of values from some other ordinal type. As shown in Fig. 5.11, we describe a subrange type by specifying the first and last values in this sequence, separating those values by a symbol consisting of two periods.

The following examples illustrate some possibilities for a subrange type.

```
var month : 1..12;        { subrange of integer }
    n     : 0..maxint;    { subrange of integer }
    letter : 'a'..'z';    { subrange of char }
```

subrange type

```
  ───────────────►  ┌──────────┐  ──────►  ..  ──────►  ┌──────────┐  ──────►
                    │ ordinal  │                        │ ordinal  │
                    │ constant │                        │ constant │
                    └──────────┘                        └──────────┘
```

FIGURE 5.11 ■ Syntax diagram, subrange type

However, the main application of subrange types occurs in conjunction with the array data type, which we present in Section 6.3.

In many applications, we also want to determine whether the value of a particular variable belongs to a certain set or range of values in an ordinal type. For example, to determine whether a symbol is an arithmetic operator, we want to know if it is among the symbols +, −, *, and /; to determine whether a symbol is a letter, we want to know if it is in one of the ASCII ranges a–z or A–Z.

We can determine whether a variable has one of several particular values using conditional statements such as

> **if** $(c = $ '+'$)$ **or** $(c = $ '−'$)$ **or** $(c = $ '*'$)$ **or** $(c = $ '/'$)$ **then** . . .
>
> **if** $(($ 'a' $<= c)$ **and** $(c <= $ 'z'$))$ **or** $(($ 'A' $<= c)$ **and** $(c <= $ 'Z'$))$ **then** . . .

But such statements become cumbersome very quickly, and Pascal enables us to express ourselves more succinctly by providing a notation for a set of values from an ordinal type. In ordinary mathematics, we describe a set by listing its members inside braces; thus {1, 3, 5, 7, 9} is the set of positive odd numbers less than 10. Since we use braces to bound comments in Pascal, we describe sets by listing their members within square brackets. As the syntax diagram in Fig. 5.12 shows, we can describe sets as lists ['+', '−', '*', '/'] or ['a'..'z', 'A'..'Z'] of objects or subranges from an ordinal type.

To determine whether a value belongs to one of these sets, we can form a new kind of relational expression using the relational operator **in**. The expression

> n **in** [1, 3, 5, 7, 9]

is true if the value of n belongs to the set and is false otherwise. With such descriptions for sets, we can write compact conditional statements such as

> **if** c **in** ['+', '−', '*', '/'] **then** . . .
>
> **if** c **in** ['a'..'z', 'A'..'Z'] **then** . . .

which are equivalent to the more cumbersome conditionals presented before.

For the moment we leave applications of set descriptors to the exercises. In Section 7.4 we will use them to simplify an improved version of *calc2*. And in Chapter 12 we will treat sets as a data type in much greater detail.

set descriptor

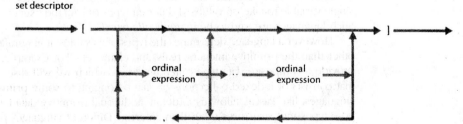

FIGURE 5.12 ■ Syntax diagram, set descriptor

EXERCISES

1. Write a program that allows the user to input a date in the format 7/4/80 and then prints the date in the format July 4, 1980. Use a **case** statement to print the month. How difficult is it to handle errors in the input?

2. How does the use of an enumerated type improve the clarity of programs like *plusCount2*? (*Hint:* Rewrite *plusCount2* to use boolean variables instead of an enumerated type.)

3. Some Pascal systems allow us to begin comments with (* and to end them with *) in addition to { and }. Modify *plusCount2* to work properly when these symbols are used. (*Hint:* Introduce more states in the enumerated type.)

4. Modify *plusCount2* to count the number of times one of the symbols +, −, *, and / occurs in the text of a program. (*Hint:* Use the notation for a set of characters.)

5. In what cases will *calc2* accept more than a single line of input? How can you fix *calc2* to require that its input occur on a single line?

6. Modify *calc2* to make the following changes:

   (a) print an error message division by zero if the user attempts to divide by zero;

   (b) recognize ** as the exponentiation operator;

   (c) display the result of the computation in fixed-point notation if that can be done by using six or fewer decimal digits with no loss of accuracy; and

   (d) have the symbol =, not the end of a line, mark the end of an expression (thereby allowing one expression to stretch over several lines or several expressions to occur on a single line).

5.6   PROGRAMMING: TYPE DECLARATIONS

Almost all programming languages allow us to manipulate several types of data; among these types are one or more primitive types such as integers, reals, and characters. Some languages, such as Pascal, require us both to declare the types of all variables and to ensure that all values assigned to a variable have the appropriate type. Such languages are said to be *strongly typed*. Some strongly typed languages, such as Basic, determine the type of a variable from its spelling rather than from a declaration. Such languages are said to be *self typing*. Still other languages allow a single variable to take on values of different types during the execution of a program. Such languages are said to be *dynamically typed*.

However a language determines the types of variables, it generally provides types other than the primitive integers, reals, and characters. For example, most languages provide a composite data type called an *array*, which we will discuss in Chapter 6, that consists of indexed collections of data belonging to some primitive type. Some languages, like Pascal, allow us to define additional primitive data types and to compose types into structures other than an array. Different languages provide different types in different ways, but they all allow us to define variables with a variety of types.

TYPE DECLARATIONS

Pascal goes even further than most languages by allowing us to assign names to types and to use these names in subsequent declarations. For example, we can replace the declaration

var *a, b* : (*red, white, blue*);

for two variables in an enumerated type by the declarations

type *color* = (*red, white, blue*);
var *a* : *color*;
    b : *color*;

which assign a specific name, *color*, to the type of the variables *a* and *b*. Few other languages permit us to name types so explicitly.

But why should we bother to write more declarations when fewer would do? We will soon see that Pascal compels us to do so in certain circumstances. More importantly, separate type declarations share the following advantages with constant and variable declarations.

■ *Flexibility*. We can change the way we represent information by changing a single type declaration rather than many variable declarations. For example, we can add a new element to an enumerated type, or we can change the size of several related arrays, without having to locate and change all the relevant variable declarations. By providing a central place for making such changes, type declarations allow us to modify a program easily.

■ *Documentation*. We can assign names to types that describe how they will be used rather than how they are constructed. Furthermore, we can assign different names (such as *additiveNumbers* and *multiplicativeNumbers*) to types we intend to manipulate in different ways, even though the objects in those types may be identical (that is, *additiveNumbers* and *multiplicativeNumbers* may both be integers). Hence type declarations help make programs easier to read and understand.

■ *Safety*. We can reduce the chance of making mistakes when we write or modify a program by declaring how we intend to use all variables. Furthermore, we can make it easier for Pascal to detect mistakes when they do occur. Hence type declarations help make programs reliable.

As shown in Fig. 5.13, type declarations belong in the declaration section of a Pascal program, after the constant declarations and before the variable declarations.

Each type declaration defines a *type identifier* for use in subsequent type, variable, procedure, and function declarations. As shown in Fig. 5.14, a type declaration also contains a description of the type named by the type identifier. That description may be as simple as the name of a previously defined type, or it may describe the construction of an entirely new type.

declaration section

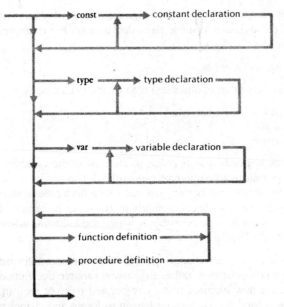

FIGURE 5.13 ■ Syntax diagram, declaration section (third version)

RENAMING TYPES

The simplest type declarations enable us to rename Pascal's predefined types. Declarations such as

    type *numericType* = *integer*;

or

    type *numericType* = *real*;

introduce no new types, but still serve a useful purpose. They allow us to write general-purpose procedures such as

    function *min*(*a*, *b* : *numericType*) : *numericType*;
      { returns the minimum of *a* and *b* }
      begin
        if *a* < *b* **then** *min* := *a* **else** *min* := *b*
      end; { of *min* }

type declaration

FIGURE 5.14 ■ Syntax diagram, type declaration

without having to commit ourselves in advance to the type of data they handle. By deferring the decision about the specific type of data manipulated by *min* until we incorporate it into a program, we can write a single procedure that will work in a variety of settings.

Type declarations that rename types also enable us to consolidate the work of several programmers, each of whom may have employed slightly different naming conventions. For example, if one programmer had declared a function *min* as above, but another had declared a function *max* using

> **function** *max*(*a, b* : *numberType*) : *numberType*;
>   { returns the maximum of *a* and *b* }
>   **begin**
>   **if** *a* > *b* **then** *max* := *a* **else** *max* := *b*
>   **end**; { of *max* }

we can straighten out the discrepancy in names by a single declaration

> **type** *numericType* = *numberType*;

that identifies the two types.

SPECIFYING TYPES

The true power of type declarations comes into play when we use them to create new types. The syntax diagram in Fig. 5.15 enumerates the possibilities for specifying types in Pascal, which may be *simple*, *structured*, or *pointer* types. So far, we have considered the simple types: the predefined types *integer*, *real*, *char*, and *boolean*,

type

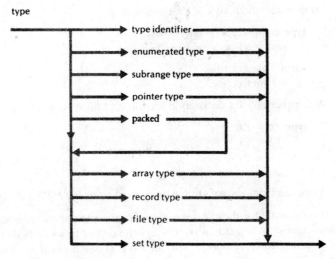

FIGURE 5.15 ■ Syntax diagram, type

together with enumerated and subrange types. In Chapter 6 we will consider three composite types (arrays, records, and files) and the effect of the keyword **packed**. Later, we will introduce a new primitive type (pointers) in Chapter 11 and a final composite type (sets) in Chapter 12.

Pascal is a strongly typed language in that it forces us to abide by our declared intentions for using a variable. For example, if we declare a variable to be of type *real*, then we cannot assign to it a value of type *char*. What we can do with variables of various types is governed by three sets of rules; one governing assignments of values; one governing comparisons of values; and one governing passing parameters to subprograms.

TYPES AND SUBPROGRAMS

The strictest rules apply to parameters passed by reference to subprograms: the type of an actual parameter must be the same as the type of a **var** parameter for which it is supplied. Two variables have the *same* type if they are declared in one of the following ways.

▪ In the same declaration, as in

   var *a, b* : (*red, white, blue*);

▪ Using the same type identifier, as in

   type *color* = (*red, white, blue*);

   var *c* : *color*;
     d : *color*;

▪ Using synonymous type identifiers, as in

   type *numericType* = *integer*;
     numberType = *integer*;

   var *m* : *numericType*;
     n : *numberType*;

More precisely, if a declaration section contains a sequence

   type *T1* = *T2*;
     T2 = *T3*;
        .
        .

of type declarations, we say that the type identifiers *T1, T2, T3*, ... are *synonymous*.

The rationale for these rules is that a formal **var** parameter is simply a synonym for the corresponding actual parameter. Hence the types of both parameters must be the same. However, Pascal will not expend much effort to detect whether two types are the same; it will go so far as to recognize synonymous types, but not so far as to recognize that the variables *a*, *b*, *c*, and *d* in the preceding list all have equivalent types. In particular, the type of *a* and *b* is an *anonymous* type since it possesses no type identifier as a name. We cannot supply variables with anonymous types as arguments to subprograms.

In Pascal we can declare functions that have values belonging to any simple type, that is, to the type *real* or to any ordinal type. We can also declare functions that have values belonging to the pointer data type, but we cannot declare functions that have values belonging to a composite data type.

TYPES AND ASSIGNMENTS

The rules that govern assignments in Pascal are slightly less stringent than those for **var** parameters. For the sake of completeness, we list all these rules now, even though some apply only to types introduced in later chapters. We can assign a value of type *T1* to a variable of type *T2* in any one of the following cases.

▪ *T1* is the same type as *T2* (but see Section 6.6 for a restriction regarding file types).

▪ *T1* is the type *integer* and *T2* is the type *real*.

▪ *T1* is a subrange of *T2*, or vice versa, and the value of type *T1* is in the subrange *T2*.

▪ *T1* and *T2* are subranges of the same ordinal type *T3*, and the value of type *T1* is in the subrange *T2*.

▪ *T1* and *T2* are string types (Section 6.4) having the same length.

▪ *T1* and *T2* are set types (Section 12.4), both are packed or both are unpacked, and all members of the value of type *T1* are also members of the base type of *T2*.

The same rules apply to passing a value of type *T1* to a value parameter of type *T2*.

TYPES AND COMPARISONS

Finally, the rules that govern comparisons are the least stringent. We can compare a value of type *T1* to a value of type *T2* using one of the relational operators =, <>, <, <=, >, >= in any of the following cases.

▪ *T1* and *T2* are the same simple type.

▪ *T1* is the type *integer* and *T2* is the type *real*, or vice versa.

▪ *T1* is a subrange of *T2*, or vice versa, or both are subranges of an ordinal type *T3*.

▪ *T1* and *T2* are string types with the same length (Section 6.4).

■ *T1* and *T2* are set types with comparable base types (Section 12.4), both are packed or both are unpacked, and the relational operator is one of =, <>, <=, or >=.

■ *T1* and *T2* are the same pointer type (Chapter 11) and the relational operator is one of = or <>.

The essence of these formidable-looking rules is really quite simple: anything that makes sense according to our declared intentions for using variables is legal, and anything else is illegal.

EXERCISES

1. Suppose that a program contains the declarations

> **type** *posInt* = 0..*maxint*;
>
> **var** *x, y* : *real*;
> *i, j* : *integer*;
> *p, q* : *boolean*;
> *c, d* : *char*;
> *m*   : *posInt*;
> *n*   : 0..*maxint*;
>
> **procedure** *a*(**var** *r* : *real*; *k* : *posInt*);
> . . .
>
> **procedure** *b*(*r* : *real*; **var** *k* : *posInt*);
> . . .

Which of the following expressions and statements are legal?

(a) *x* := *i*	(k) *x* < *y* **or** *p* < *q*
(b) *i* := *x*	(l) (*x* < *y*) **or** *p* < *q*
(c) *m* := *n* + 1	(m) *x* < *y* **or** (*p* < *q*)
(d) *n* := *ord*(*c*)	(n) (*x* < *y*) **or** (*p* < *q*)
(e) *n* := *ord*(*i*)	(o) *a*(*x, m*)
(f) *n* := *ord*(*p*)	(p) *a*(*x, n*)
(g) *n* := *ord*(*x*)	(q) *a*(*i,* 3)
(h) **not** *x* < *y*	(r) *b*(*x, m*)
(i) **not** *p* < *q*	(s) *b*(*x, n*)
(j) **not not** *p*	(t) *b*(*i,* 3)

2. Suppose that a program contains the declarations exhibited in Exercise 1. Which of the following headers can appear in subprogram declarations within that program?

(a) **procedure** *increment*(**var** *n* : *posInt*);

(b) **procedure** *increment*(**var** *n* : 0..*maxint*);

(c) **function** *predecessor*(*n* : *posInt*) : −1..*maxint*;

5.7 SYSTEMS: HOW COMPUTERS REPRESENT NONNUMERIC DATA

At the end of Chapter 2 we saw how computer systems represent numeric data. Now that we are familiar with other types of data, we need to consider how computer systems handle them as well.

Recall that the basic units of information in a computer system are the bit, byte, and word. A single bit can hold two values: zero or one. Hence it provides a representation for boolean data, with a zero corresponding to the value *false* and a one corresponding to the value *true*.

A byte generally consists of eight bits, although some computers utilize bytes that contain, for example, six or nine bits. Whatever the size of a byte, it provides a representation for character data. The moderate number of different values that a byte can hold—256 or 2^8 in the case of an 8-bit byte—are sufficient to encode the characters in a typical character set. For example, Fig. 5.16 shows how the characters e f g h can be stored in four bytes in a 32-bit word using the ASCII encoding. Appendix B describes both the ASCII and EBCDIC codes.

A byte suffices to encode the values in most enumerated types in Pascal. If x is an element of an enumerated type with at most 2^8 objects, then $ord(x)$ is a numeric encoding of x that can be stored within a single 8-bit byte. If x is an element of an enumerated type with more objects, its representation will occupy several bytes.

Words vary in size from computer to computer. On a small microcomputer, a word may contain a single 8-bit byte. On a larger computer, a word may contain four or five bytes, for a total of 32 or 40 bits. As we saw in Chapter 2, 32-bit words can hold integers having decimal representations that contain up to nine digits, and they can hold floating-point representations with several fewer decimal digits in the significand. Hence *single precision*, or one number per word, is the practice on computers having words of 32 bits or more. Machines with fewer bits per word generally employ *multiple-precision* representations for numbers; that is, they use two or more words to represent a single numeric value.

Thus the simple data types all possess representations ranging in size from a single bit (for boolean data) to one word (for numbers on computers with large words) to several words (for numbers on computers with small words). As we will see, the composite data types also possess representations that range in size from a few bits (for a packed array of several boolean values) to many words (for an array containing many records).

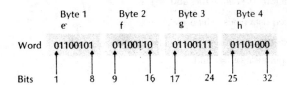

FIGURE 5.16 ■ Representation of character data in 32-bit word

EXERCISES

1. Not all languages provide a predefined boolean data type. Yet we can manipulate logical data even in the absence of this data type: we represent the values *true* and *false* by the integers 1 and 0, and we define numeric-valued functions corresponding to the various logical operations. Provide such an alternate representation for the logical data type in Pascal by declaring *logical* to be the subrange type 0..1 and by writing definitions for

   (a) **function** *logicalNot(p : logical) : logical;*

   (b) **function** *logicalAnd(p, q : logical) : logical;*

   (c) **function** *logicalOr(p, q : logical) : logical;*

2. Not all languages provide enumerated types. Yet we can generally imitate such types by declaring symbolic constants for the objects in an enumerated type and by defining our own versions of the *ord, pred,* and *succ* functions. Provide such an alternate representation for the enumerated type (*Sunday, Monday, Tuesday, Wednesday, Thursday, Friday, Saturday*).

SUMMARY

Computers process various types of numeric and symbolic information. Each type is characterized by a collection of similar objects together with a collection of operations for manipulating those objects. The primitive data types in Pascal include

▨ the real data type, which has

   1. objects that are finite representations of real numbers and

   2. operations of *read, write,* :=, +, −, *, /, and functions such as *sin* or *sqrt;*

▨ the integer data type, which has

   1. objects that are integers between −*maxint* and +*maxint* and

   2. operations of *read, write,* :=, +, −, *, **div, mod**, and functions such as *abs;*

▨ the boolean data type, which has

   1. objects that are the logical values *true* and *false* and

   2. operations of *write,* :=, **and, or**, and **not;**

▨ the character data type, which has

   1. objects that are symbols such as letters, digits, and punctuation marks and

   2. operations of *read, write,* and :=;

▨ enumerated data types, which have

   1. objects that are programmer-defined constants and

   2. the operation of := ; and

■ subrange data types, which have

   1. objects that are a range of objects from some primitive data type other than the *real* data type and

   2. operations that are the operations of that primitive data type.

Objects in a primitive data type can also be compared by means of the relations $<$, $<=$, $>$, $>=$, $=$, and $<>$. These relations are themselves operations with values in the *boolean* data type. Appendix A contains a complete list of the operations available in each of the primitive data types.

Pascal is a strongly typed language. It requires declarations for the types of all variables. Furthermore, it requires that all values assigned to variables or passed as parameters have the appropriate types. Pascal also permits programmer-defined data types, of which enumerated types are an example.

ATA COMPOSITE DATA COMPOSIT
COMPOSITE DATA COMPOSITE DA
SITE DATA COMPOSITE DATA COM
COMPOSITE DATA COMPOSITE D
ATA COMPOSITE DATA COMPOSIT
COMPOSITE DATA COMPOSITE DA
SITE DATA COMPOSITE DATA COM
DATA **COMPOSITE DATA** COMPOS

C H A P T E R

6

*J*ust as structuring a program enables us to exercise control over that program, so structuring the information processed by a program enables us to exercise control over that information. And just as three fundamental program structures—for sequence, choice, and repetition—enabled us to compose primitive actions into sophisticated programs, so three fundamental data structures—the array, record, and file—will enable us to compose primitive data into sophisticated data structures.

One of the particular strengths of the programming language Pascal is the ability it gives us to define data types beyond those provided by the language. In Chapter 5, we considered not only the primitive data types (integers, reals, booleans, and characters) predefined by Pascal, but also two means (enumerated and subrange types) for defining new primitive types. In this chapter, we consider the three fundamental means (arrays, records, and files) for defining composite data types. Later, in Chapter 11, we will consider a final primitive type (pointers) provided by Pascal; in Chapter 12 we will consider a final composite type (sets).

For each of these composite types, we develop sample programs, showing how the structure of a problem influences the structure of data associated with that problem and how, in turn, the structure of the data influences the structure of the program. In each case we design sample programs so that by the end of the chapter we will have collections both of specific examples and of general-purpose subprograms, which we can use thereafter to manipulate common and useful data structures.

APPLICATIONS: DISPLAYING INFORMATION

So far our programs have dealt with relatively little information. Most have accepted only a few numbers or characters as input and displayed only a few numbers or characters as output. However, many applications of computing deal with much larger quantities of information. Often they must digest large amounts of raw data as input, produce extensive reports as output, or both.

The following examples illustrate a variety of problems calling for computer programs that manipulate more than a few numbers. Our task in this and later chapters is to learn how best to organize the information required to solve these and related problems.

RECORD KEEPING AND PROCESSING

Many organizations keep extensive records of their activities. Businesses record financial and personnel data, governments record tax and census data, and schools record data for class schedules and grade reports. Nowadays most of these organizations use computers to maintain their records and to display information in useful ways.

In this chapter we consider a particularly simple record-keeping activity. We will use a variety of composite data structures to process moderate quantities of information. Later, in Chapter 9, we will consider information-processing systems in much greater detail and learn how they can rearrange and locate information as well as display it.

For our main example, we suppose that an instructor plans to administer three examinations to a class of six students. The instructor wants to keep grade records for the class and to generate, after each exam, a report such as Table 6.1 to show the individual scores and cumulative average for each student in the class. Using a series of programs *grades1*, *grades2*, and *grades3*, we examine alternative ways of organizing these records and generating the report.

TABLE 6.1 Typical Table of Exam Scores and Averages

Student	Exam 1	Exam 2	Exam 3	Average
Adams	83	87	95	88.33
Brown	90	93	86	89.67
Jones	70	75	83	76.00
Miller	75	76	78	76.33
Smith	99	96	97	97.33
Williams	80	80	80	80.00
Average	82.83	84.50	86.50	84.61

TABLE 6.2   Typical Table Showing Sales of Widgets

Year	Giant	Large	Medium	Small
1980	157	230	581	732
1981	163	185	415	690
1982	175	190	407	638
1983	181	213	398	641
1984	196	247	384	640

For another example, suppose that the widget department in a retail store wants to keep sales records for the four sizes of widgets it stocks. The number of widgets of each type sold during each of the past five years can be displayed as in Table 6.2. Similarly, the cost of manufacturing the widgets and their selling prices can be displayed in a table such as Table 6.3. From Table 6.3, we can easily compute the profit on each widget by subtracting the cost from the selling price. From both tables, we can easily compute the yearly profits of the widget department on the total sales of each type of widget.

GRAPHICS

Tables do not necessarily provide the best way to display information. If "a picture is worth a thousand words," then a graph is worth a thousand numbers. Rather than use a table such as

Year	1972	1974	1976	1978	1980
Cents per bit	0.56	0.28	0.13	0.07	0.03

to display the declining cost of computer memory, we prefer to use a graph such as that in Fig. 6.1, which illustrates just how rapidly that cost is falling. We can also find the equation of a curve that "best fits" those points in order to, for example, predict the future cost of computer memory.

Simple graphic systems allow us to generate graphs such as Figure 6.1. More elaborate graphic systems allow us to produce scale drawings in two and three dimensions. The more elaborate the graphic application, the more elaborate are the ways in which we need to structure the information in that application: simple ap

TABLE 6.3   Typical Table Showing Cost and Price of Widgets

	Giant	Large	Medium	Small
Cost	2.00	1.00	0.75	0.50
Price	3.00	1.50	1.25	1.00

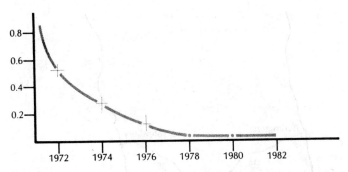

FIGURE 6.1 ■ Cost per bit (in cents) of computer memory

plications require us to keep track of points and lines; more ambitious applications require us to keep track of curves, shapes, surfaces, and solid objects. To generate pictures that are "worth a thousand words," we need data structures that help us describe those pictures and manipulate their components.

TEXT PROCESSING

As we learned in Chapter 5, computers process symbols in addition to numbers. Most record-keeping activities involve symbolic information (such as names and addresses) as well as numbers. And many applications of computing (such as word processing) deal with symbolic information alone. Hence we need ways to deal with sequences of characters rather than just single characters, and we need ways to decompose large amounts of textual information into recognizable units (words, sentences, and paragraphs in English text and identifiers, statements, and subprograms in program text).

OPTIMIZATION

Some applications of computing seek the best or *optimal* way to accomplish a given task, often by systematically examining all the ways to perform that task. Consider, for example, the problem of producing the table of driving distances that typically accompanies a highway map in a road atlas. Using a map of Vermont, such as that in Fig. 6.2, we can construct a list of distances between neighboring cities. With this list, we can explore all the routes between cities and generate a table such as Table 6.4 for inclusion in a road atlas. In this table, the shortest distance from one city to another can be obtained by reading across to the diagonal in the row containing the first city (alphabetically) and then down that column to the row containing the second city. For optimization problems like this, we need to keep track not only of raw information (such as driving distances), but also of our progress toward finding an optimal solution.

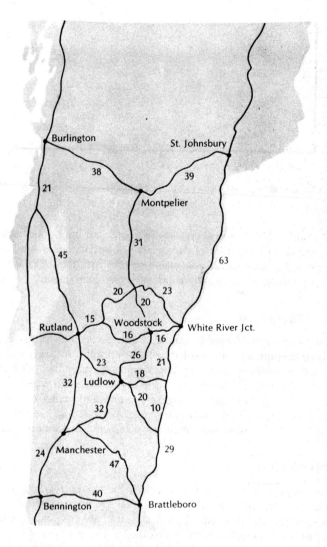

FIGURE 6.2 ■ Map showing distances (in miles) between cities in Vermont

TABLE 6.4 Distances between Cities in Vermont

Bennington	0								
Brattleboro	40	0							
Burlington	122	138	0						
Ludlow	56	49	89	0					
Manchester	24	47	98	32	0				
Montpelier	122	114	38	77	98	0			
Rutland	56	72	66	23	32	66	0		
St. Johnsbury	158	123	77	102	134	39	105	0	
White River Jct.	95	60	92	39	71	54	47	63	0
Woodstock	82	75	89	26	58	51	31	79	16	0

EXERCISES

1. Investigate various means for projecting three-dimensional figures onto a two-dimensional screen. How can we represent those figures? What geometric transformations are required to project them?

2. Verify by hand that Table 6.4 shows the minimum number of miles that a person must drive between cities in Vermont when using the roads on the map in Fig. 6.2.

6.2 DATA STRUCTURES: COMPOSITE TYPES

Implicit in the applications described in Section 6.1 are a variety of composite data structures. For example, a class consists of a number of students, each of whom has a name, grades on several exams, and a cumulative average; a graph or picture consists of a number of lines or curves, each of which is determined by a number of points, each of which in turn has two or three coordinates; and an English text or a program consists of a number of lines, each of which is divided into a number of words, each of which in turn consists of a number of characters. Such hierarchical organizations of data are typical of the structures we need to create when recording and processing information.

We can make two independent choices when assembling individual items of information into a composite data structure. First, we can choose whether to attach a label or index to each item (as we do for books in a library) or not (as we decline to do for anonymous questionnaires). Labels or indices enable us to retrieve specific items directly rather than by searching through the collection of all items. Second, we can choose whether to arrange the items in a particular order (as we do for an alphabetical list of names) or not (as we need not for a list of household furniture).

With two independent choices, there are four possible outcomes. Corresponding to each outcome is a composite data type: arrays, in which items are both indexed and ordered; records, in which items are labeled but not ordered; files, in which items are ordered, but not labeled; and sets, in which items are neither ordered nor labeled. We discuss the first three of these data types in this chapter and the last (sets) in Chapter 12.

In this section we concentrate on describing the objects in each composite data type. Later we will examine operations that enable us to manipulate these objects and their components.

ARRAYS

An *array* is an ordered and indexed collection of objects. Most programming languages require that all objects in an array belong to the same data type (for example, all must be integers or all must be characters).

A one-dimensional array, or *vector*, such as

$$(2, 3, 5, 7, 11, 13, 17, 19)$$

represents a list of objects (in this case, the first eight prime numbers). In ordinary mathematical usage, we denote an element in a vector by attaching a single *index* or *subscript* to a variable that denotes the vector. Thus, for example, if p is the vector just displayed, then

$$p_1 = 2, \quad p_2 = 3, \quad p_3 = 5, \quad p_4 = 7, \quad \ldots, \quad p_8 = 19.$$

A two-dimensional array, or *matrix*, such as

$$\begin{bmatrix} 8 & 1 & 6 \\ 3 & 5 & 7 \\ 4 & 9 & 2 \end{bmatrix}$$

represents a table of objects (in this case a "magic square" in which the sum of the numbers in each row, column, and diagonal is the same). In ordinary mathematical usage, we denote an element in a matrix by attaching two indices or subscripts to a variable that denotes the matrix. The first index indicates the row and the second the column of the matrix in which an element occurs. Thus, for example, if s is the magic square displayed above, then

$$s_{1,1} = 8 \quad s_{1,2} = 1 \quad s_{1,3} = 6$$
$$s_{2,1} = 3 \quad s_{2,2} = 5 \quad s_{2,3} = 7$$
$$s_{3,1} = 4 \quad s_{3,2} = 9 \quad s_{3,3} = 2$$

Higher-dimensional arrays represent more highly structured arrangements of objects. We usually denote elements in such arrays by attaching multiple indices or subscripts to variables that denote the arrays.

Of all composite data structures, arrays are the most frequently used. Following are some ways of using arrays to structure the information associated with the applications of computing discussed in Section 6.1

Student grade records Consider the exam results in Table 6.1 for a class of six students that took three exams. The scores for all students on a single exam constitute a vector with six numeric components, and the scores for all students on all exams constitute a matrix with three columns (one for each examination) and six rows (one for each student).

Each student's name is a vector of characters. For example, `'Smith'` is the vector

$$('S', 'm', 'i', 't', 'h')$$

which contains five characters. Since we frequently use vectors of characters to represent textual information, we distinguish them from other vectors by calling them *strings*. (See Section 6.4.) The list of names of all students in the class is a vector with six string components:

$$(\text{'Adams', 'Brown', 'Jones', 'Miller', 'Smith', 'Williams'})$$

Retail sales   Designations for the widgets in Table 6.2 constitute a vector with four components:

$$(\text{Giant, Large, Medium, Small})$$

The costs of manufacturing the widgets also constitute a vector with four numeric components that indicate, respectively, the costs of giant, large, medium, and small widgets:

$$(2.00, 1.00, 0.75, 0.50)$$

Similarly, the selling prices of the widgets constitute a vector with four numeric components:

$$(3.00, 1.50, 1.25, 1.00)$$

The number of widgets of each type sold during each of the past five years can be represented by a matrix with five rows and four columns, as in Table 6.2. The number of widgets of each type sold during each month of the past five years can be represented by a matrix with 60 rows and four columns or, alternatively, as a three-dimensional array indexed by year, month, and size of widget.

Graphics   The coordinates of a point in a plane can be represented as a vector $<x, y>$ with two components. A list of points in a plane, such as those used in Fig. 6.1 to plot the declining cost of computer memory, may be represented variously as the matrix with two rows and six columns displayed earlier, as a matrix with six rows and two columns,

$$\begin{bmatrix} 1972 & 0.56 \\ 1974 & 0.28 \\ 1976 & 0.13 \\ 1978 & 0.07 \\ 1980 & 0.03 \end{bmatrix}$$

as six two-element vectors, or as two six-element vectors.

RECORDS

Not surprisingly, records as a data type occur most naturally in record-keeping applications of computing. The information concerning each student in a class—a name, a list of grades, and a cumulative average—constitutes a single record:

Name: Adams
Grades: 83 87 95
Average: 88.33

Whereas the components in an array all belong to the same data type, those in a record may come from several different types. The first component in our example is a string, the second a vector of numbers, and the third a single number. And, whereas the subscripts attached to the components of an array impose an order on those components, the labels attached to the components of a record do not. Since we refer to the components of a record by name and not by number, the order in which we list those components matters little. We are not likely to confuse the components of a student's grade record if we list them in a different order:

Name: Adams
Average: 88.33
Grades: 83 87 95

This example shows that a vector may occur as a component of a record. A record may also occur as a component of a vector. For example, we can structure the grade records for an entire class as a vector of records.

Often we have a choice of whether to use arrays or records when structuring information. For example, we can structure the grade records for a class as a collection of related arrays, one containing the students' names, one their grades, and one their averages. Or, as just noted, we can structure them as a single vector of records. Similarly, we can represent a point p in a plane as a coordinate vector with two components p_1 and p_2, or we can represent it as a record with two components p_x and p_y. Which representation we choose is influenced by the way we find it most natural to view the information and the way we want to process that information.

FILES

We can access a component of an array directly by using a subscript and a component of a record directly by using a name. However, direct access can be costly when the number of components in a composite structure is very large. Hence it is appropriate to consider another data structure—the file—which is more suitable for large amounts of data.

In simplest terms, a file is a sequence of items of data. Different programming languages impose different restrictions on the methods we may use to access or change data in a file or on the types of data allowed in a file. But they all involve the same underlying conception of a file as an ordered sequence of items.

Many programming languages, including Pascal, restrict us to accessing data in a file in order, from the first piece of data to the last. To emphasize this restriction, we say that these languages support *sequential files*. We can access data in the middle of a sequential file only after accessing the preceding data. We can append data to the end of a sequential file, but we cannot change data in the middle of such a file without changing the entire file. Thus data in a sequential file are ordered by their appearance in that file, but they are not indexed for direct access.

Some languages, and some dialects of Pascal, support *random* or *direct-access* files in addition to sequential files. We can manipulate such files more like arrays, accessing or changing data in any order. Because direct-access files are so similar to arrays, and because Pascal does not support them, we will not dwell on them. However, from time to time we will mention uses for direct-access files, particularly when we consider strategies for coping with large amounts of data. At those times, we will find that the techniques required to manipulate direct-access files are familiar enough, despite their absence in Pascal, because of our experience with arrays.

From a practical point of view, the most important aspect of files has less to do with how to structure information than with how to preserve it. Files enable us to store information elsewhere than within the body of a program. Such information may consist of data, text, subprograms, or other programs. By placing information in an external file, rather than directly in a program, we achieve several important benefits.

First, by placing information in an external file, we make it accessible to many programs without having to duplicate it within each of those programs. As a result, programs become shorter and more independent of the data they manipulate. This greater degree of independence provides a greater degree of security: routine modifications to a program or to data are less likely to result in accidental modifications to data or programs stored in separate files than to data or programs stored in the same file.

Second, most computer systems place rather more severe limits on the amount of data that we can incorporate into the text of a program, or store in data structures such as arrays, than on the amount of data that we can store in a file. Programs generally reside entirely in primary memory when they are executed, whereas files reside in secondary storage and are brought into primary memory a piece at a time. Since the capacity of secondary storage is far greater than that of primary memory, files can be much larger than arrays.

Third, files are dynamic data structures. Unlike arrays and records, they may grow or shrink in size. Hence we do not need to determine exactly the amount of data that a file will contain when we write programs to manipulate that file; instead, we can determine or change the amount of data that a file contains when we use those programs.

And fourth, programs can modify information that is stored in external files and make the results available for further processing by other programs. In this manner, collections of programs can manipulate and maintain a common base of information.

In fact, we have already been using files without explicitly mentioning it. The identifiers *input* and *output* in Pascal designate files, the first of which supplies input to a program and the second of which receives its output. On a batch system, these files reside in secondary storage like other files. On an interactive system, they are simply pipelines connecting a program to the terminal. On a typical computer system, each of our sample programs would be stored in a separate file. These·files would possess names (most likely the same as those of the programs they contain), enabling us to specify to the computer system which program we wish to examine or execute. Subprogram libraries such as *maxmin* also constitute files, which we can reference in programs such as *minOf4*.

EXERCISES

1. Suppose that an instructor wants to record the performance of 100 students on 10 homework assignments. For what purposes is it most natural to structure the data using 11 arrays or files with 100 entries each, one containing the students' names and the others containing the grades on individual exams? For what purposes is it most natural to structure the data as a single array or file containing 100 records, one for each student?

2. Suppose that we want to rename certain variables in a Pascal program. How should we view that text as a composite data structure in order to expedite our task?

3. Suppose that we need to draw alternative floor plans for a new office building. What data structures might we employ to describe the size, shape, and arrangement of the offices?

6.3 PROGRAMMING: ARRAYS

Most programming languages allow us to manipulate individual objects in an array. Many languages also allow us to manipulate an entire array as a single entity. Some languages, such as APL, provide a large set of operations (such as addition, multiplication, and other arithmetic operations) that we can perform on arrays; others, such as Pascal, provide a much more limited set (such as assignment alone).

Arrays in Pascal are particularly flexible in at least two respects. First, the objects in an array may belong to any data type. Thus we can manipulate not only arrays of integers and arrays of real numbers, but also arrays of characters, arrays of records (Section 6.5), or even arrays of arrays. Second, we can index the objects in an array by elements of any ordinal type. Thus we can index objects in an array not only by integers, but also by characters, days of the week, colors of the rainbow, and the like.

ARRAY VARIABLES

Array variables enable us to manipulate objects in an array without having to assign a separate variable to each object. Instead, we assign a single variable, called an *array variable*, to the array itself and use *subscripts* following the array variable to indicate which objects in the array we wish to manipulate. The typographical limitations of most computer systems do not permit us to display subscripts half a line below an array variable; instead, we must resort to some other notational device.

In Pascal, we enclose subscripts within brackets following an array variable. A singly subscripted array variable, such as *cost*[*i*], refers to an object in a vector. A doubly subscripted variable, such as *sales*[*i, j*], refers to an object in a matrix (in particular, to the object in the row indexed by *i* and the column indexed by *j* of the matrix *sales*). Variables with more subscripts refer to objects in higher-dimensional arrays.

ARRAY DECLARATIONS

The declaration for an array variable in Pascal specifies not only the type of the objects in that array, but also the type and allowable range for the subscripts of that array. For example,

> **var** *profits* : **array** [1980..1984] **of** *real*;

declares *profits* to be a vector with five real components—*profits*[1980], *profits*[1981], *profits*[1982], *profits*[1983], *profits*[1984]—that are indexed by integer subscripts ranging from 1980 to 1984.

The syntax diagram in Fig. 6.3 shows how to construct a type specification for an array variable. As can be seen from the diagram, the types of the subscripts for an array may be arbitrary ordinal types. In most common applications, these ordinal types will be subranges of the integers (for example, 1980..1984, 1..1000, or 0..10). However, in certain applications we may find it handy to use other ordinal types as subscripts. For example, we could use the declaration

> **var** *freq* : **array** [*char*] **of** *integer*;

in a program that counts the frequency of characters that occur in a text: *freq*['d'] would indicate the number of occurrences of a lowercase d in the text. In this example, subscripts belong to the ordinal type *char*.

We could also use the declarations

> **type** *size* = (*Giant, Large, Medium, Small*);
> **var** *sales* : **array** [1980..1984, *size*] **of** *real*;

to create a matrix *sales* with five rows, indexed from 1980 to 1984, and four columns, indexed by the sizes *Giant*, *Large*, *Medium*, and *Small*. In this example, subscripts belong to the enumerated type *size*.

array type

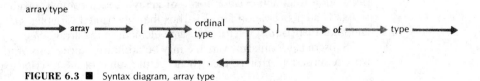

FIGURE 6.3 ■ Syntax diagram, array type

Figure 6.3 also makes it clear that the objects in an array may be of any type. In many applications these objects will be integers, reals, or characters. However, in certain applications we may find it handy to create arrays of other types as well. For example, we could use an array *sizes* declared by

   var *sizes* : **array** [1..100] **of** (*Giant, Large, Medium, Small*);

if we wanted to record the sizes of 100 objects. In this example, the objects of the array come from an enumerated type.

Pascal gives us some flexibility in the construction of array declarations. For example, the preceding declaration is equivalent to the declarations

   type *size* = (*Giant, Large, Medium, Small*);
   var *sizes* : **array** [1..100] **of** *size*;

which assign a name to the enumerated type. Furthermore, the declaration

   var *sales* : **array** [1980..1984, *size*] **of** *real*;

cited earlier is equivalent to the declaration

   var *sales* : **array** [1980..1984] **of array** [*size*] **of** *real*;

or to the declarations

   type *salesBySize* = **array** [*size*] **of** *real*;
   var *sales* : **array** [1980..1984] **of** *salesBySize*;

Thus a comma in an array declaration is really an abbreviation for "] **of array** [", and a matrix is really a vector of vectors, that is, a vector consisting of the rows in that matrix.

USING ARRAY VARIABLES

We can manipulate subscripted array variables and give them values, as we do with ordinary variables. Thus the statement

   profits[*i*] := 2**profits*[*i*]

doubles the *i*th element of the vector *profits* and the statement

   writeln(*profits*[*j* + 1])

displays the value of the ($j + 1$)-st element of *profits*. The syntax diagram in Fig. 6.4 governs the formation of a (possibly) subscripted variable. As a comma in an array declaration is an abbreviation for "] **of array** [", so a comma separating array subscripts is an abbreviation for "][". Thus the subscripted variables *sales*[1980, *Giant*] and *sales*[1980][*Giant*] refer to the same element in the array *sales*.

Subscripts for an array variable may be arbitrary expressions of the appropriate type. A subscript error results whenever the value of a subscript expression falls

variable

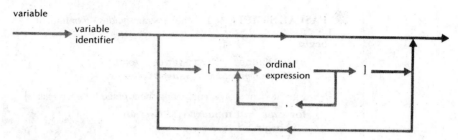

FIGURE 6.4 ■ Syntax diagram, variable (second version)

outside the subrange of permissible values declared for that subscript. On most systems, execution of a Pascal program terminates with an error message whenever a subscript error is detected.

Pascal Sample 6.1, *grades1*, illustrates the use of arrays to produce a table of grade-point averages similar to Table 6.1. (We will write a program that produces this table exactly in Section 6.4 to illustrate the use of strings.) The program expects grades to be entered exam by exam rather than student by student, and it stores these grades in an array until it can display them in the appropriate format.

The declarations in *grades1* specify arrays that are larger than necessary for the purposes of Table 6.1. Such declarations simplify the modifications that we must make to use *grades1* with a different number of students or a different number of examinations. Because it is awkward (and undesirable) to change a program every time the data for the program change, we write *grades1* so that we may change the

PASCAL SAMPLE 6.1   The program *grades1*

{ computes student grade-point averages (simple version) }

program *grades1*(*input, output*);

const *maxStudents* = 50;   { limit on size of class   }
       maxExams   = 9;   { limit on number of exams }
       columnWidth = 12;   { spacing for output   }

var *score* : **array** [1..*maxStudents*, 1..*maxExams*] **of** *integer*;
     ave   : **array** [1..*maxExams*] **of** *real*;

     numberOfStudents : 0..*maxStudents*;
     numberOfExams   : 0..*maxExams*;
     student   : 1..*maxStudents*;
     exam   : 1..*maxExams*;
     grade   : *integer*;
     total   : *real*;

PASCAL SAMPLE 6.1 The program *grades1* (continued)

begin

　　write('Number of students, exams? ');
　　read(*numberOfStudents*, *numberOfExams*);

　　{ get student scores, computing the average for each exam }

　　for *exam* := 1 **to** *numberOfExams* **do**
　　　　begin
　　　　　　total := 0;
　　　　　　writeln;
　　　　　　writeln('Enter scores for exam ', *exam*:1, ':');
　　　　　　for *student* := 1 **to** *numberOfStudents* **do**
　　　　　　　　begin
　　　　　　　　　　read(*grade*);
　　　　　　　　　　score[*student*, *exam*] := *grade*;
　　　　　　　　　　total := *total* + *grade*
　　　　　　　　end;
　　　　　　ave[*exam*] := *total*/*numberOfStudents*

　　　　end;

　　{ display column headings for grade report }

　　writeln;
　　writeln;
　　write('Student', ' ' : *columnWidth* − 7);
　　for *exam* := 1 **to** *numberOfExams* **do**
　　　　write('Exam ', *exam* : 1, ' ' : *columnWidth* − 6);
　　writeln('Average');

　　{ display student scores and cumulative averages }

　　writeln;
　　for *student* := 1 **to** *numberOfStudents* **do**
　　　　begin
　　　　　　write(*student* : 3, ' ' : *columnWidth* − 3);
　　　　　　total := 0;
　　　　　　for *exam* := 1 **to** *numberOfExams* **do**
　　　　　　　　begin
　　　　　　　　　　grade := *score*[*student*, *exam*];
　　　　　　　　　　total := *total* + *grade*;
　　　　　　　　　　write(' ', *grade* : 3, ' ' : *columnWidth* − 4)
　　　　　　　　end;
　　　　　　writeln(' ', *total*/*numberOfExams* : 6:2)
　　　　end;

　　{ display exam averages }

　　writeln;
　　write('Average', ' ' : *columnWidth* − 7);
　　total := 0;

```
for exam := 1 to numberOfExams do
    begin
        write(' ', ave[exam] : 6:2, ' ' : columnWidth − 7);
        total := total + ave[exam]
    end;
    writeln(' ', total/numberOfExams : 6:2)
end.
```

data without having to change the program. In general, good programs require that users be concerned only with data; they do not force users to be programmers.

When supplied with the grades from Table 6.1, *grades1* produces the results shown in Pascal Sample 6.2.

We carefully chose the format controls in the output statements in *grades1* to achieve the output format for Table 6.1. Each line in that table is generated by three output statements: the first displays identification for a student; the second occurs in a **for** loop and displays the student's scores on individual exams; and the third displays the student's cumulative average. The first two output statements fill each column of the table to its proper width, and the last output statement (which invokes *writeln*) terminates the display of that line.

PASCAL SAMPLE 6.2   The program *grades1* (sample use)

```
Number of students, exams? 6 3

Enter scores for exam 1:
83 90 70 75 99 80

Enter scores for exam 2:
87 93 75 76 96 80

Enter scores for exam 3:
95 86 83 78 97 80
```

Student	Exam 1	Exam 2	Exam 3	Average
1	83	87	95	88.33
2	90	93	86	89.67
3	70	75	83	76.00
4	75	76	78	76.33
5	99	96	97	97.33
6	80	80	80	80.00
Average	82.83	84.50	86.50	84.61

ARRAY ASSIGNMENTS

Suppose that we declare a and b to be arrays of the same type, for example,

    var a, b : **array** [1..*maxRows*, 1..*maxCols*] **of** *real*;

Then we can use these variables in an assignment statement such as

    $a := b$

to assign the elements of array b as values to the elements of array a. This single assignment statement is equivalent to a nested loop

```
for i := 1 to maxRows do
    for j := 1 to maxCols do
        a[i, j] := b[i, j]
```

which assigns the elements of array b as values to the elements of array a one at a time.

The two arrays in an array assignment must have the exactly the same type. Even though integer expressions are assignment compatible with real variables in Pascal, integer arrays may not be assigned to real arrays. Thus, for the declarations

    var i : *integer*;
         r : *real*;
         a : **array** [1..10] **of** *integer*;
         x : **array** [1..10] **of** *real*;

the assignment $r := i$ is permissible in Pascal, but the assignment $x := a$ is not.

ARRAY PARAMETERS

We can supply subscripted and unsubscripted array variables as actual parameters to procedures and functions. When we supply a subscripted variable as a parameter for a subprogram, the subscripts for that variable are evaluated just once upon invocation of the subprogram, regardless of whether the parameter is passed by reference or by value. Thus, if we declare a procedure *increment* by

```
procedure increment( var i, j : integer );
    begin
        i := i + 1;
        j := i
    end; { of increment }
```

and invoke *increment* by *increment*(n, $a[n]$) when $n = 2$, then n gets the value 3 as does $a[2]$, the subscript in $a[n]$ having been evaluated upon invocation of *increment* and not upon execution of the statement $j := i$.

When we supply an unsubscripted array variable as a parameter, we must declare the corresponding formal parameter to be an array of the same type. For example, in a program that manipulates vectors of the type declared by

type *vector* = **array** [1..*maxN*] **of** *real*;

we can define a function to return the average of the elements $a[1], \ldots, a[n]$ in one of these vectors as follows:

function *average*(v : *vector*; n : *integer*) : *real*;
   { returns $(v[1] + \cdots + v[n])/n$ assuming $n > 0$ }
  var *sum* : *real*;
     i : *integer*;
  begin
    sum := 0;
    for i := 1 **to** n **do** *sum* := *sum* + $v[i]$;
    average := *sum*/n
  end; { of *average* }

Later in the program we can invoke this function by a statement such as

writeln('Average = ', *average*(*a*,10))

provided we declare *a* to be of type *vector*.

Pascal does not provide a way to define functions having arrays as values. The only way to construct a subprogram in Pascal that returns an array as a value is to construct a procedure with an array as a variable parameter. For example, we could use the following procedure to give the elements in an array an initial value of zero:

procedure *zero*(**var** *a* : *vector*; n : *integer*);
   { sets $a[1], \ldots, a[n]$ to zero }
  var i : *integer*;
  begin
    for i := 1 **to** n **do** $a[i]$:= 0
  end; { of *zero* }

Arrays, like other parameters, are passed in Pascal by value unless the keyword **var** in a subprogram header indicates that a parameter should be passed by reference instead. Passing an array by value to a subprogram is a good way to prevent that subprogram from inadvertently changing the value of elements in the array. However, passing an array by value to a subprogram may be overly expensive in terms of time or space: most implementations of Pascal make a copy of an array passed by value upon invocation of a subprogram. Therefore, in applications where time or space are valuable, we may choose to pass an array by reference to a subprogram and thereby avoid making a copy of the array, even though the subprogram does not modify the array; in such cases, it is good programming practice to document the fact that the array is not changed in a comment at the beginning of the subprogram.

EXERCISES

1. Assume that the type *matrix* has been declared to be **array** [1..*maxRows*, 1..*maxCols*] **of** *real*.

   (a)   Define a function beginning with the header

          function *columnAve*(*a* : *matrix*; *col, n* : *integer*) : *real*;

          having a value that is the average of $a[1, col]$, ..., $a[n, col]$.

   (b)   Define a function beginning with the header

          function *rowAve*(*a* : *matrix*; *row, n* : *integer*) : *real*;

          having a value that is the average of $a[row, 1]$, ..., $a[row, n]$.

2. The instructor in a course has decided to compute final grade-point averages by ignoring each student's lowest examination score and averaging the remaining scores. Modify the program *grades1* so that it computes final averages in this manner.

3. Write a program to compute and print the yearly profits of the widget department from the data in Tables 6.2 and 6.3.

4. Consider the problem of finding elements common to two lists.

   (a)   Write a program to input an integer, n, followed by two lists of n numbers each and then print all the numbers that occur in both lists.

   (b)   Express the number of comparisons your program makes as a function of n.

   (c)   What difference would it make in your answers to parts (a) and (b) if you knew that the numbers in each list were arranged in increasing order?

5. Use arrays to solve the following problems concerning the calendar.

   (a)   Write a program to input three integers representing a month, day, and year (say, to input 5 14 1982, representing May 14, 1982) and then print the day of the week on which that date falls (say, to print Friday). (*Hint:* Create a vector listing the number of days in each month of the year. Recall that every fourth year is a leap year, except that years divisible by 100 and not by 400 are not leap years.)

   (b)   Modify the program you wrote for (a) to input a three-character abbreviation for the month (Jan, Feb, Mar, . . .)

   *(c)   Write a program to determine on which day of the week the thirteenth of the month falls most often. (*Hint:* Show that the calendar cycles every 400 years; then count the number of times the thirteenth falls on each day of the week in a 400-year period.)

6. The following program counts the frequency of positive integers supplied as input and then prints a histogram of the frequency count such as

```
        1 **
        2 ****
        3 ********
        4 ******
        5 ****
   >= 6 *
```

(The first five lines of this histogram indicate that there were 2, 4, 8, 6, and 4 occurrences of the integers 1, 2, 3, 4, and 5, respectively; the last line indicates that there was one occurrence of an integer greater than 5.)

```
program frequency(input, output);
const maxValue = 100;
var i, j, m : integer;
      freq    : array [1..maxValue] of integer;
begin
      write('Enter maximum value for histogram: ');
      read(m);
      for i := 1 to m+1 do freq[i] := 0;
      write('Enter data. Follow last datum immediately ');
      writeln('by a carriage return.');
      while not eoln do
            begin
                  read(i);
                  if i > m then i := m + 1;      { offscale value }
                  freq[i] := freq[i] + 1
            end;
            { display histogram }
            writeln;
            for i := 1 to m+1 do
                  begin
                        if i <= m then write('    ') else write('>=');
                        write(i : 3, '  ');
                        for j := 1 to freq[i] do write('*' : 1);
                        writeln
                  end
end.
```

(a) Modify this program so that it prints the histogram vertically instead of horizontally, for example, as

```
        *
        *
    *   *
    *   *
*   *   *   *
*   *   *   *
*   *   *   *   *
*   *   *   *   *   *
1   2   3   4   5   6 or more
```

(b) If the data for the frequency count consisted of integers between 1 and 1,000,000, it would not be practical to preassign a counter for every possible integer as in this sample program. Design an algorithm that compiles a frequency count for arbitrary integers as data. The algorithm should store only the integers that appear in the data and the frequency count of each such integer.

7. In parts (a)–(c), concerning two-dimensional geometry, we represent a point by a vector with two components; for example, we represent the point <5, 10> by a vector p such that $p[1] = 5$ and $p[2] = 10$. Furthermore, we represent a line segment by specifying its two endpoints.

   (a) Define a function *between* with parameters a, b, and c that has the value 1 if the point c lies on the line segment between the points a and b, the value 0 if it lies on the same line as a and b, but is not between them, and the value -1 if it does not lie on this line. (*Hint:* Any point on the line connecting <$a1$, $a2$> and <$b1$, $b2$> has coordinates of the form <$a1 + t(b1 - a1)$, $a2 + t(b2 - a2)$>, where t is an arbitrary real number; such a point is between <$a1$, $a2$> and <$b1$, $b2$> if t is between 0 and 1.)

   (b) Define a procedure *meet* with two lines, a point, and a variable *status* as parameters that sets *status* to 1 if the two lines intersect, to 0 if they coincide, and to -1 if they are parallel; furthermore, if the lines intersect, *meet* should set the point to the coordinates of their intersection.

   (c) Define a function *inside* with parameters a, b, c, and d that has the value 1 if the point d is inside the triangle determined by the points a, b, and c, and has the value 0 otherwise. (*Hint:* A point is inside a triangle if it is between a vertex and a point on the side opposite that vertex.)

*8. Solve the following problems.

   (a) Write a program to input the coordinates of points in a plane and then determine whether those points are the vertices of a convex polygon, that is, of a polygon that contains entirely any line segment with endpoints lying inside the polygon. (*Hint:* The points are the vertices of a convex polygon if none of them lies inside a triangle determined by three of the other points.)

   (b) Show that the time required by the algorithm suggested in part (a) grows proportionally to n^4, where n is the number of points.

   (c) Can you devise an algorithm that requires less time (for example, time that grows proportionally to n^2)?

9. In parts (a)–(c), concerning three-dimensional geometry, we represent a point by a vector with three components, a line by two points, and a plane by three points not lying on the same line.

   (a) Define a function *between*, as in Exercise 7(a), that determines whether one point lies between, or on the same line as, two other points.

   (b) Define a procedure *meet*, as in Exercise 7(b), that determines whether two lines intersect and, if so, determines their point of intersection.

   (c) Define a procedure *pierce* that determines whether a line intersects a plane and, if so, determines the point of intersection.

*10. Use the geometric functions and procedures developed so far to compute two-dimensional projections of three-dimensional objects, as follows.

   (a) Write a program to compute the projections of the vertices <0, 0, 1>, <0, 1, 1>, <1, 1, 1>, <1, 0, 1>, <0, 0, 2>, <0, 1, 2>, <1, 1, 2>, and <1, 0, 2> of a cube on the *xy*-plane (on the plane where $z = 0$) when viewed from a point in space chosen by the user. If your system has graphic capabilities, have your program draw the edges of the cube.

(b)   Modify the program for part (a) so that it determines which of the vertices of the cube are visible. [*Hint:* Use Exercises 9 and 7(c).] If your system has graphic capabilities, have your program draw the visible edges of the cube.

11.   Write a program to generate a mileage table similar to that in Table 6.4 from the data

```
10
A   40    0    0   24    0    0    0    0    0
B    0   49   47    0    0    0   60    0
C    0    0   38   66    0    0    0
D   32    0   23    0   39   26
E    0   32    0    0    0
F   66   39   54   51
G    0    0   31
H   63    0
I   16
J
```

which gives the direct distance from each of ten cities (identified by letters) to each successive city, where a distance of zero indicates that there is no direct route from one city to another. (*Hint:* Construct a series of tables that show the shortest distances between cities via routes with at most *n* intermediate cities. For $n = 0$ the table is given by the data; the table for $n = m + 1$ can be computed from that for $n = m$.)

12.   One side of a cube is maintained at a temperature of 100°, while the other five sides are maintained at 0°. Find the temperature at the center of the cube. (*Hint:* Divide the cube into a number of smaller cubes and repeatedly compute the temperature at the vertices of these smaller cubes by averaging the temperatures of neighboring vertices. Stop when the temperatures stabilize.)

13.   Write a procedure *permute* with parameters *a* and *n* to generate all permutations of $a[1], ..., a[n]$. Use this procedure to generate all permutations of the integers $1, ..., n$. (*Hint:* Have *permute* call a recursive procedure *perm* with parameters *a*, *m*, and *n* that generates all permutations of $a[1], ..., a[m]$ and, each time a permutation is generated, prints $a[1], ..., a[n]$. To generate all permutations of $a[1], ..., a[m]$ when $m > 1$, *perm* should interchange $a[m]$ with each of $a[i], ..., a[m]$ and then generate all permutations of $a[1], ..., a[m-1]$.)

14.   Write a procedure *subsets* with parameters *a*, *m*, and *n* to generate all *m*-element subsets of $a[1], ..., a[n]$. (*Hint:* Proceed recursively, noting that the *m*-element subsets of $a[1], ..., a[n]$ consist of the *m*-element subsets of $a[1], ..., a[n-1]$ together with the *m*-element sets formed by adding $a[n]$ to an $(m-1)$-element subset of $a[1], ..., a[n-1]$.

15.   Write a variant of the program *sums1* presented in Section 4.6 that does not use recursion, but instead uses an array *sums* such that $sums[n, m]$ is the number of ways to represent *n* as the sum of a nonincreasing sequence of positive integers ranging from 1 to *m*.

So far, we have used strings of characters solely to label output from Pascal programs. In this section we explore further the ways to represent, manipulate, and process strings using computer programs.

Unfortunately it is more difficult to manipulate strings in Pascal than in many other programming languages. In this section we examine the limited set of string-processing tools Pascal does provide. In Section 7.2, we will develop a more powerful and convenient set of tools by designing both our own representation for strings and our own procedures for manipulating these representations. Although this expanded set of tools still does not make string processing as convenient in Pascal as in other languages, it represents a considerable improvement over the tools provided directly by Pascal.

A *string* is simply a sequence of characters. Pascal has no built-in type identifier for strings, as it does for integers, reals, characters, or booleans. However, it does recognize certain arrays of characters as strings, and it does accord special privileges to these arrays. Specifically, a *string* in Pascal is an array of characters such that

- the array is indexed by a subrange of the integers with a lower bound of 1 (characters in a string are numbered from left to right starting with 1);
- the upper bound of the index subrange for the array is at least 2 (strings of length 0 and 1 are not permitted); and
- the array is designated as **packed** (to enable processors to economize on the space required to store strings).

Thus, if we include declarations such as

const *stringLength* = 15;
type *string* = **packed array** [1..*stringLength*] **of** *char*;
var *a*, *b* : *string*;

in a program, we can manipulate the variables *a* and *b* as strings. (Some dialects of Pascal permit omission of the keyword **packed**, but it is generally safest to include it.)

Pascal extends privileges to strings above and beyond those it extends to structured types in general. In particular, it provides constants to denote strings, it allows us to use relational operators to compare strings, and it allows strings as arguments to the *write* and *writeln* procedures. Yet Pascal stops short of allowing strings as arguments to the *read* and *readln* procedures, and it stops short of allowing strings as values of functions.

STRING CONSTANTS

Constants that denote strings consist of sequences of two or more characters bounded by apostrophes (for example, `'Jones'` or `'123.4'`). The presence of apostrophes distinguishes '123.4', which is a string constant, from 123.4, which is a numeric constant.

As noted in Section 2.5, two adjacent apostrophes in a string constant denote a single apostrophe. Thus 'a''b' denotes a string of length 3 consisting of a single apostrophe between the letters a and b.

Constants such as 'a' that contain a single character denote characters and not strings in Pascal. It is precisely to avoid ambiguity over whether 'a' is a constant that denotes a single character (which it is) or a constant that denotes a string of length 1 (which it cannot be) that Pascal requires all strings to contain at least two characters. Furthermore, Pascal does not recognize the constant '' as denoting a string of length 0 because it allows neither the empty subrange [1..0] nor strings of length 0.

STRING ASSIGNMENT

As for arrays in general, we can assign the value of one string variable to another by a simple assignment statement such as $a := b$. The variables a and b do not need to have exactly the same type, as defined in Section 5.6; they need only to be strings of the same length. We can also assign a constant as a value by an assignment such as $a := $ 'dog' provided that the length of the constant matches the declared length for the string variable. (For example, the assignment $a := $ 'dog' is legal only if a is declared to have length 3.)

If we wish to manipulate strings of different lengths in the same program, we must either declare string variables with different (and appropriate) lengths, or extend each string to a common (and appropriate) length (say, by adding trailing spaces). For example, in programs dealing with the calendar, we might use declarations such as

> **const** *stringLength* = 9;
>
> **type** *string* = **packed array** [1..*stringLength*] **of** *char*;
>
> **var** *weekday* : **array** [1..7] **of** *string*;

and assignments such as

> *weekday*[1] := 'Sunday   ';
> *weekday*[2] := 'Monday   ';
> *weekday*[3] := 'Tuesday   ';
> *weekday*[4] := 'Wednesday ';
> *weekday*[5] := 'Thursday   ';
> *weekday*[6] := 'Friday   ';
> *weekday*[7] := 'Saturday   ';

in which we extend the constants that name the days of the week by enough spaces to increase their length to nine. (Some dialects of Pascal automatically extend string constants in assignment statements by spaces to reach the required length, but it is safest not to depend on this being done.)

STRING INPUT AND OUTPUT

We can display the value of a string by using a single output statement in Pascal. Thus, even though *write(a)* ordinarily is not legal when *a* is an array, it is legal when *a* is a string, that is, when *a* is a packed array of characters with a first index of 1. Execution of this statement displays all the characters in the string *a*.

We can display an entire string by using the *write* procedure in Pascal, but we cannot read one by using a single input statement. The statement *read(a)* is no more legal in Pascal when *a* is a string than when *a* is an arbitrary array. Instead, we must read strings a character at a time.

To help us manipulate strings in Pascal, we build a library *stringSubs1* of procedures that perform tasks not handled by the language. One useful procedure in *stringSubs1* is *readString*, which reads a sequence of nonblank characters from the input and assigns this string as the value of its parameter *s*. It skips any initial blanks in the input and stops when a subsequent blank is detected. If necessary, *readString* extends the string being read by blanks to fill up *s*; it also discards extra characters at the end of the string if they won't fit into *s*. Pascal Sample 6.3 shows one way to construct such a procedure; an improved version appears in Section 6.6.

PASCAL SAMPLE 6.3   The library *stringSubs1* (*readString* procedure)

```
procedure readString( var s : string );
    { skips initial blanks in the input and assigns next string of nonblank    }
    { characters as the value of s, truncating strings that are too long for    }
    { s and extending strings that are too short by blanks                      }
    { assumes: not eof                                                          }
    var ch : char;
        i   : 1..stringLength;
    begin
        repeat                                              { skip blanks }
            read(ch)
        until eof or (ch <> ' ');
        for i := 1 to stringLength do { put characters in string }
            begin
                s[i] := ch;
                if ch <> ' ' then read(ch)
            end;
        if ch <> ' ' then
            begin
                writeln;
                writeln('String too long -- excess ignored');
                repeat read(ch) until ch = ' '
            end
    end; { of readString }
```

To illustrate the use of *readString*, we improve the program *grades1* discussed in Section 6.3 so that it displays the names of students along with their grades to reproduce Table 6.1 exactly. Lines in the improved program *grades2* that differ from corresponding lines in *grades1* are marked by asterisks in trailing comments. (See Pascal Sample 6.4.) Pascal Sample 6.5 shows that *grades2* does indeed produce Table 6.1 when supplied with the appropriate data. Thus the conversion of *grades1* to *grades2* is relatively straightforward. The only subtlety occurs in redefining the width of the left-hand column to accommodate the longest possible name, followed by three spaces to separate this column from the next.

STRING EQUALITY AND ORDER

Two strings are equal if they have the same length and contain identical sequences of characters. The order assigned to characters by the collating sequence of a partic-

---

PASCAL SAMPLE 6.4   The program *grades2*

```
{ computes student grade-point averages (improved version) }          {*}
{ changes from grades1 are noted by asterisks in comments  }          {*}

program grades2(input, output);                                       {*}

const  maxStudents = 50;      { limit on size of class       }
       maxExams    =  9;      { limit on number of exams }
       columnWidth = 12;      { spacing for output           }
       stringLength = 15;     { limit on name length         }        {*}

type string = packed array [1..stringLength] of char;                 {*}

var  name : array [ 1..maxStudents ] of string;                       {*}
     score  : array [ 1..maxStudents, 1..maxExams ] of integer;
     ave    : array [ 1..maxExams ] of real;

     numberOfStudents : 0..maxStudents;
     numberOfExams    : 0..maxExams;
     student          : 1..maxStudents;
     exam             : 1..maxExams;
     grade            : integer;
     total            : real;

#include 'stringSubs1';                                               {*}

begin
     write('Number of students, exams? ');
     read (numberOfStudents, numberOfExams);

     { get names of students }                                        {*}

     writeln;                                                         {*}
     writeln('Enter student names.');                                {*}
     for student := 1 to numberOfStudents do                          {*}
          readString(name[student]);                                 {*}
```

■ **PASCAL SAMPLE 6.4** The program *grades2* (continued)

{ get student scores, computing the average for each exam }

```
for exam := 1 to numberOfExams do
    begin
        total := 0;
        writeln;
        writeln('Enter scores for exam ', exam:1, ':');
        for student := 1 to numberOfStudents do
            begin
                read(grade);
                score[student, exam] := grade;
                total := total + grade
            end;
        ave[exam] := total/numberOfStudents
    end;
```

{ display column headings for grade report }

```
writeln;
writeln;
write('Student', ' ' : stringLength − 4);                          {*}
for exam := 1 to numberOfExams do
    write('Exam ', exam : 1, ' ' : columnWidth − 6);
writeln('Average');
```

{ display student scores and cumulative averages }

```
writeln;
for student := 1 to numberOfStudents do
    begin
        write(name[student], ' ' : 3);                             {*}
        total := 0;
        for exam := 1 to numberOfExams do
            begin
                grade := score[student, exam];
                total := total + grade;
                write(' ', grade : 3, ' ' : columnWidth − 4)
            end;
        writeln(' ', total/numberOfExams : 6:2)
    end;
```

{ display exam averages }

```
writeln;
write('Average', ' ' : stringLength − 4);                          {*}
total := 0;
```

```
        for exam := 1 to numberOfExams do
            begin
                write(' ', ave[exam] : 6:2, ' ' : columnWidth − 7);
                total := total + ave[exam]
            end;
        writeln(' ', total/numberOfExams : 6:2)
    end.
```

ular computer system (Section 5.3) extends to an order of all strings. Which of two strings precedes the other in this order is determined by the first character in which those strings differ. Thus

$$\text{'cat'} < \text{'dog'} < \text{'dot'}$$

since, as characters, $\text{'c'} < \text{'d'}$ and $\text{'g'} < \text{'t'}$.

String order bears a strong resemblance to the usual dictionary order. However, important differences stem from the nature of collating sequences for characters.

PASCAL SAMPLE 6.5   The program *grades2* (sample use)

```
Number of students, exams? 6 3

Enter student names.
Adams Brown Jones Miller Smith Williams

Enter scores for exam 1:
83 90 70 75 99 80

Enter scores for exam 2:
87 93 75 76 96 80

Enter scores for exam 3:
95 86 83 78 97 80
```

Student	Exam 1	Exam 2	Exam 3	Average
Adams	83	87	95	88.33
Brown	90	93	86	89.67
Jones	70	75	83	76.00
Miller	75	76	78	76.33
Smith	99	96	97	97.33
Williams	80	80	80	80.00
Average	82.83	84.50	86.50	84.61

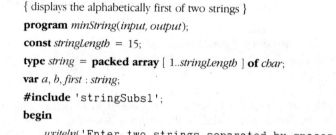

PASCAL SAMPLE 6.6   The program *minString*

{ displays the alphabetically first of two strings }

program *minString(input, output)*;

const *stringLength* = 15;

type *string* = **packed array** [1..*stringLength*] **of** *char*;

var *a*, *b*, *first* : *string*;

#include 'stringSubs1';

begin

> *writeln*('Enter two strings separated by spaces.');
> *readString(a)*;
> *readString(b)*;
> **if** *a* <= *b* **then** *first* := *a* **else** *first* := *b*;
> *writeln*;
> *writeln*('The string "', *first*, '" comes first.')

end.

SAMPLE USE OF *minString*:

```
Enter two strings separated by spaces.
watch this

The string "this           " comes first.
```

First, since either 'A' < 'a' or 'a' < 'A' in a particular collating sequence, either 'Ax' < 'an' or 'ax' < 'An' in the string order induced by that collating sequence. Hence intermixed uppercase and lowercase letters may cause the order of strings to deviate from dictionary order. Second, the order of strings that contain spaces, hyphens, or other punctuation marks may be different from the dictionary order.

We can compare strings of the same length for equality and order in Pascal by using the usual relational operators =, <>, <, <=, >, and >= to form relational expressions. To illustrate the use of strings in relational expressions, we modify the program *minChar* (Section 5.3) to produce a program *minString* that displays the first (alphabetically) of two strings (Pascal Sample 6.6). The comparison performed in this short example forms the basis for algorithms (discussed in Chapter 8) that arrange a list of words in alphabetical order.

FURTHER STRING MANIPULATION PROCEDURES

The extra blanks in the output from *minString* occur because we declared the variable *first* to be a string containing 15 characters. Writing the value of *first* generates 15 characters of output, even if we supplied fewer characters in response to the request for input. (Recall that *readString* pads strings with trailing blanks to bring their length up to that required by the declaration.)

In order to eliminate these extra blanks, we can define two further procedures for inclusion in *stringSubs1*. The first, *length*, is a function that returns the length of its string argument; that is, it returns the index of the last nonblank character in the string. The second, *writeString*, displays a string with the trailing blanks omitted. Pascal Sample 6.7 displays these two procedures.

In order to use these procedures in *minString*, we simply replace the statement

```
writeln('The string "', first, '" comes first.')
```

by the sequence

```
write('The string "');
writeString(first);
writeln('" comes first.')
```

of three statements. This replacement changes the output from *minString* to

```
The string "this" comes first.
```

PASCAL SAMPLE 6.7   The library *stringSubs1* (*length, writeString* procedures)

function *length*(*s* : *string*) : *integer*;
  { returns the length of the string *s* }
  var *i*   : 0..*stringLength*;
    found : *boolean*;
  begin
    i := *stringLength*;
    found := *false*;
    repeat
      if *s*[*i*] = ' ' **then** *i* := *i* − 1 **else** *found* := *true*
    until (*i* = 0) **or** *found*;
    length := *i*
  end;   { of *length* }

procedure *writeString*(*s* : *string*);
  { outputs the string *s*, suppressing trailing blanks }
  var *i* : 1..*stringLength*;
  begin
    for *i* := 1 **to** *length*(*s*) **do** *write*(*s*[*i*])
  end;   { of *writeString* }

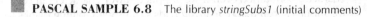

PASCAL SAMPLE 6.8   The library *stringSubs1* (initial comments)

```
{ stringSubs1: procedures for manipulating strings }
{ length(s)          returns index of last nonblank character in s    }
{ readString(s)      reads a sequence of nonblank characters into s   }
{ writeString(s)     writes s without any trailing blanks             }
{     Any program that uses stringSubs1 must contain the following    }
{ declarations:                                                       }
{                                                                     }
{     const stringLength = ...;                                       }
{                                                                     }
{     type string = packed array [1..stringLength] of char;           }
```

We complete our construction of *stringSubs1* by writing comments to go at the beginning of that library. These comments describe the procedures in *stringSubs1* and state the conventions for their use. (See Pascal Sample 6.8.)

EXERCISES

1. Supplement the procedures in *stringSubs1* by defining
   (a) a procedure *writelnString* that displays the characters in a string, as does *writeString*, but with a trailing newline;
   (b) a procedure *readLine* that reads an entire line of input (blanks included); and
   (c) procedures *ucase* and *lcase* that convert all characters in a string to uppercase and lowercase.
2. Write a program that inputs a line of characters and determines whether it is a *palindrome*, that is, whether its characters read the same from left to right as they do from right to left. For example, `level` and `top a pot` are palindromes. (Be careful about trailing blanks.)
3. Extend your solution to Exercise 2 to recognize as palindromes strings that differ only in punctuation, the spacing between words, or capitalization. For example, `Able was I ere I saw Elba` and `A man, a plan, a canal: Panama!` should be recognized as palindromes.

6.5   PROGRAMMING: RECORDS

The use of arrays in Pascal is limited by the requirement that all the components in an array belong to the same data type. In applications concerning inventories, personnel records, and the like, we need to assemble components that belong to several different data types. Since we cannot mix string and numeric components in a single array, we choose to assemble them by using the *record data type*.

Records, like arrays, enable us to assemble several items of data in a single structure. However, arrays and records differ in two important ways: (1) the items in a record may have different types; and (2) the order of items in a record is not as critical as the order of items in an array. Hence we usually identify the components of a record by symbolic names rather than by subscripts.

We can illustrate the way to declare and use records by considering two examples combined into one. Suppose that we want to keep certain information about each employee in a business firm: name, address, date of birth, and salary. The first two items are alphabetic, the last numeric. How can we assemble them into a single structure? And what about the date of birth? How should we represent it?

We know that a date has three components: the day (an integer between 1 and 31), the month (January, February, ...), and the year (also an integer). It is tempting to define a date as a structure with three components named *day*, *month*, and *year*. In Pascal, we can do this by using the record data type, as follows:

```
type months = (Jan, Feb, Mar, Apr, May, Jun, Jul, Aug, Sep, Oct, Nov, Dec);
     date   = record
                 day   : 1..31;
                 month : months;
                 year  : 0..3000
              end;
var birthdate, today : date;
```

With these declarations, we can manipulate the variables *birthdate* and *today* in the same way that we manipulate variables of other types in Pascal. We can assign them to each other with assignments such as

```
birthdate := today;    { Happy Birth Day! }
```

and we can pass them as parameters to functions in statements such as

```
writeln('You are ', howOld(birthday, today) : 1, ' years old.');
```

We can also access the components of a record by adding a period and the name of a component to the name of the record. Thus *today.day*, *today.month*, and *today.year* are the three components of the record *today*. These components are variables in their own right, and we can use them like other variables in statements such as

```
if (today.month = Jan) and (today.day = 1) then
   begin
      writeln('Happy New Year!');
      today.year := today.year + 1
   end
```

Beyond this, we cannot do much syntactically with records in Pascal: there are no constants for denoting records, no operators for forming expressions that involve records, and no functions for returning records as values. (Records are like arrays in these respects.) In particular, since the record data type is not a simple type, we cannot compare two records by using any of the operators $=$, $<>$, $<$, $<=$, $>$, or $>=$. If we need to know whether two records are identical, we must compare them component by component.

Returning to our example, we can create structures to hold information concerning employees in a business firm by using the following declarations.

```
type employee = record
                    name     : string;
                    address  : string;
                    birthdate : date;
                    salary   : real
                end;
var manager : employee;
    clerk    : array [1..10] of employee;
```

Note that a record can have other records as components (*date* is a component of *employee*) and can itself be an element of an array (*clerk* is an array of records). We identify the components of such multilevel structures systematically, using subscripts and component names. Thus, *clerk*[5] is the record containing information about the fifth clerk, *clerk*[5].*birthdate* is that clerk's date of birth, and *clerk*[5].*birthdate.year* is the year in which that clerk was born.

THE SYNTAX OF RECORD DECLARATIONS AND VARIABLES

The syntax diagram in Fig. 6.5 specifies the precise syntax for declaring records. That diagram allows us to compress a declaration such as

```
var time : record
              hour    : 0..24;
              minute : 0..60;
              second : 0..60
          end;
```

record type

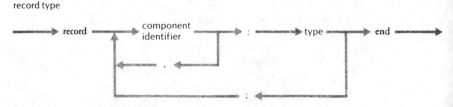

FIGURE 6.5 ■　Syntax diagram, record type (preliminary version)

variable

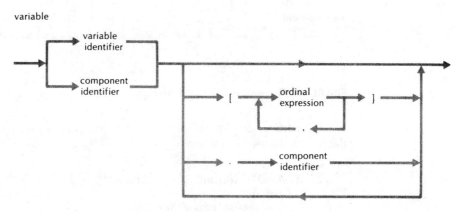

FIGURE 6.6 ■ Syntax diagram, variable (third version)

in which several components have the same type, into a declaration such as

> **var** *time* : **record**
> > *hour*   : 0..24
> > *minute, second* : 0..60
>
> > **end**;

in which both components are declared together. Component identifiers need only to be distinct from the other component identifiers in the same record declaration. They do not need to be distinct from other identifiers declared in the same declaration section. Thus we can declare the data type *date* and variables *today, birthday,* and *day* in the same declaration section. The meaning of the identifier *day* is clear from the context: *day* by itself is a variable, and *today.day* is a component of the record *today*.

The syntax diagram for a variable, as shown in Fig. 6.6, extends that presented in Section 6.3, specifying how to construct variables to range over records, arrays, and their components.

THE WITH STATEMENT

Figure 6.6 allows us to abbreviate references to the components of a record in conjunction with a special statement called the **with** statement. As shown by the syntax diagram in Fig. 6.7, a **with** statement consists of the keyword **with** followed by a list of record variables, the keyword **do**, and a statement that forms the body of the **with** statement. Within the body of a **with** statement we no longer need to mention the listed record variables; we merely name components of those records directly.

with statement

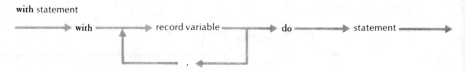

FIGURE 6.7 ■ Syntax diagram, **with** statement

The **with** statement enables us to rewrite the previous statement that advances the year on January 1 as follows:

with *today* **do**
    if (*month* = *Jan*) **and** (*day* = 1) **then**
        begin
            writeln('Happy New Year!');
            year := *year* + 1
        end

If several of the records listed in a **with** statement or in nested **with** statements have components with the same name, abbreviations of components always apply to the record mentioned last; like-named components of other records must be specified in full. Thus

    with *today*, *birthday* **do** *write*(*year*)

is equivalent to *write*(*birthday.year*).

USING RECORD VARIABLES

To illustrate in detail how records provide an alternative to arrays, we modify the program *grades2* (Section 6.4) so that it keeps all the information concerning a single student in a single record. The new program *grades3* produces exactly the same results as *grades2*. But, instead of finding the name of the *n*th student in *name*[*n*], we find it in *students*[*n*].*name*. Instead of finding the score of the *n*th student on the *e*th exam in *score*[*n*, *e*], we find it in *students*[*n*].*score*[*e*]. Lines in *grades3* that differ from the corresponding lines in *grades2* are marked by asterisks in trailing comments. (See Pascal Sample 6.9.)

VARIANT RECORDS (OPTIONAL)

So far, we have considered records with a fixed list of components. However, some applications involve records with varying numbers and types of components. Suppose, for example, that we need to keep information on the students and faculty at a small college. Some items (such as name, address, and date of birth) are common to both students and faculty. Others pertain to one group or the other, but not to both (such as grades for students and salaries, ranks, and departments for faculty).

■ **PASCAL SAMPLE 6.9** The program *grades3* (declarations and input)

```
{ computes student grade-point averages (illustrates records) }        {*}
{ changes from grades2 are noted by asterisks in comments  }            {*}
program grades3(input, output);                                         {*}
const  maxStudents  = 50;      { limit on size of class       }
       maxExams     =  9;      { limit on number of exams }
       columnWidth  = 12;      { spacing for output           }
       stringLength = 15;      { limit on name length         }
type string  = packed array [1..stringLength] of char;
     student = record                                                   {*}
                     name : string;                                     {*}
                     score : array [1..maxExams] of integer             {*}
               end;                                                     {*}

var students                   : array [1..maxStudents] of student;     {*}
    ave                        : array [1..maxExams] of real;           {*}
    numberOfStudents, s        : 0..maxStudents;                        {*}
    numberOfExams, exam : 0..maxExams;                                  {*}
    grade                      : integer;
    total                      : real;
#include 'stringSubs1';
begin
     write('Number of students, exams? ' );
     read(numberOfStudents, numberOfExams);

     { get names of students }

     writeln;
     writeln('Enter student names.');
     for s := 1 to numberOfStudents do readString(students[s].name);    {*}

     { get student scores, computing the average for each exam }

     for exam := 1 to numberOfExams do
        begin
             total := 0;
             writeln;
             writeln('Enter scores for exam ', exam:1, ':' );
             for s := 1 to numberOfStudents do                          {*}
                begin
                     read(grade);
                     students[s].score[exam] := grade;                  {*}
                     total := total + grade
                end;
             ave[exam] := total/numberOfStudents
        end;
```

PASCAL SAMPLE 6.9   The program *grades3* (remainder of program)

```
{ display column headings for grade report }
writeln;
writeln;
write('Student', ' ' : stringLength − 4);
for exam := 1 to numberOfExams do
    write('Exam ', exam : 1, ' ' : columnWidth − 6);
writeln('Average');

{ display student scores and cumulative averages }
writeln;
for s := 1 to numberOfStudents do with students[s] do          {*}
    begin                                                       {*}
        write(name, ' ' : 3);
        total := 0;
        for exam := 1 to numberOfExams do
            begin
                grade := score[exam];                           {*}
                total := total + grade;
                write(' ', grade : 3, ' ' : columnWidth − 4)
            end;
        writeln(' ', total/numberOfExams : 6:2)
    end;

{ display exam averages }
writeln;
write('Average', ' ' : stringLength − 4);
total := 0;
for exam := 1 to numberOfExams do
    begin
        write(' ', ave[exam] : 6:2, ' ' : columnWidth − 7);
        total := total + ave[exam]
    end;
writeln(' ', total/numberOfExams : 6:2)
end.
```

One way to handle such situations is to define records with enough components to handle all cases, but to use only those components that are appropriate to a specific case. Thus we can declare a record to contain an array of grades together with a salary, rank, and department. However, at any given time not all of these components will have meaningful values, and reserving space for more components than we really need is somewhat wasteful of space.

Pascal provides a better way for us to handle such situations, with a device known as a *variant record*. The declaration of a variant record begins with a fixed list of components, as for an ordinary record. But it ends with a construct, called the *variant part* of the record, that resembles a **case** statement and enables us to specify alternative choices for additional components.

We might use a variant record to hold information concerning either students or faculty in the following manner.

```
type categories  = (student, faculty);
     ranks       = (instructor, asstProf, assocProf, professor);
     departments = (english, history, math, physics, ...);
     scores      = array [1..nCourses] of integer;
     person      = record
                      name    : string;
                      address : string;
                      birthday : date;
                      case status   : categories of
                          student : ( score : scores );
                          faculty : ( salary : real;
                                      rank   : ranks;
                                      dept   : departments)
                   end.

var teacher, enrollee : person;
```

The first four components of a record of type *person* are fixed: each person, whether a student or faculty member, has a name, address, date of birth, and status. The number of components that remain in a record of type *person*, and what they are, depends on the value of the component *status*. Suppose that *enrollee.status = student* and *teacher.status = faculty*. Then *enrollee* has one further component, namely, *enrollee.score*, and *teacher* has three further components, namely, *teacher.salary*, *teacher.rank*, and *teacher.dept*.

Figures 6.8 and 6.9 specify the precise syntax for record declarations with variant parts. Note that a component list can have a fixed part, a variant part, neither, or both. Empty component lists make sense when one of the variants of a variant record has no components beyond those in the fixed part. For example,

```
type person = record
                 name : string;
                 case married : boolean of
                     true : ( spouse : string );
                     false : ( )
              end;
```

record type

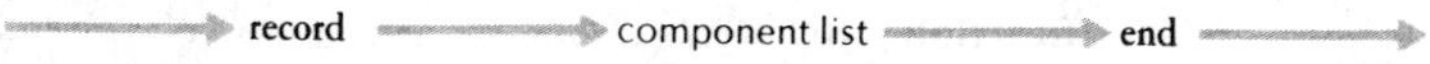

FIGURE 6.8 ■ Syntax diagram, record type (final version)

component list

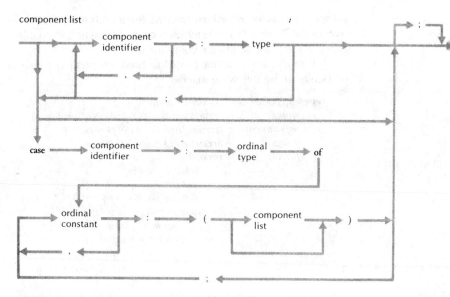

FIGURE 6.9 ■ Syntax diagram, component list

declares a record that has either two or three components, depending on whether the value of the component *married* is *true* or *false*.

The syntax for variant records is somewhat complex. Therefore we will not use variant records in our sample programs lest they obscure more important points. Nonetheless, variant records would make more economical use of space in programs such as those in Section 7.4. We leave their use in those programs to the exercises.

EXERCISES

1. Suppose that *date* is a record data type with components *day, month*, and *year*.

   (a) Define a procedure beginning with the header

   procedure *nextDay*(**var** *d* : *date*);

   that advances the date *d* by one day. Make sure your procedure works properly when *d* is the last day in a month.

   (b) Suppose that *weekday* is the enumerated type (*Su, Mo, Tu, We, Th, Fr, Sa*). Define a function beginning with the header

   function *dayOfWeek*(*d* : *date*) : *weekday*;

   that returns the weekday on which a given date falls. (*Hint:* If the current calendar had been in use then, January 1 in the year 1 would have been a Saturday. Is it a good idea for *dayOfWeek* to invoke *nextDay* repeatedly, or is there a faster way for *dayOfWeek* to compute its result?)

(c) Write a program to test your solutions to parts (a) and (b) by reading a six-digit integer *yymmdd* representing a date and then printing the day of the week on which the next day falls.

2. Suppose that we represent complex numbers using a record type *complex* with two real components, *re* and *im*.

(a) Define a procedure to assign specified values to the real and imaginary components of a complex number.

(b) Define a procedure to print the value of a complex number in the format $x + iy$. Have your procedure omit either the real or imaginary part (but not both!) if it is zero.

(c) Define procedures to add, subtract, multiply, and divide two complex numbers.

(d) Write a program that uses these procedures to find the two roots of the quadratic equation $ax^2 + bx + c = 0$. (*Hint:* See Exercise 11, Section 3.3.)

(e) Design and code an enhancement to *calc2* that performs its operations using complex arithmetic.

3. Suppose that we represent rational numbers using a record type *rational* with two integer components *num* and *den* for the numerator and denominator of a fraction.

(a) Define a procedure to assign specified values to the numerator and denominator of a fraction.

(b) Define a procedure to reduce a fraction to "lowest terms," that is, to remove common factors from the numerator and denominator, and to ensure that the denominator is positive. (*Hint:* Use the *gcd* function written for Exercise 3, Section 4.6.)

(c) Define procedures to print the value of a rational number in either fractional or decimal notation. Have your procedures print integers as integers.

(d) Define procedures that add, subtract, multiply, and divide two rational numbers.

(e) Define boolean-valued functions that test whether two rational numbers are equal or whether one is less than the other.

(f) Modify *calc2* to use rational arithmetic for carrying out its computations.

4. Redo Exercises 7–10, Section 6.3, on coordinate geometry using records, the components of which are the coordinates of a point.

5. One way to represent a hand in a card game such as bridge or poker uses the following declarations.

```
const sizeOfHand = 5;      { 5 for poker, 13 for bridge }
type suit  = (clubs, diamonds, hearts, spades);
     rank  = (ace, two, three, four, five, six, seven, eight,
              nine, ten, jack, queen, king);
     card  = record
                s : suit;
                r : rank
             end;
     hand  = array [1..sizeOfHand] of card;
```

(a) The point count for a bridge hand is defined as follows: each ace is worth four points, each king three points, each queen two points, and each jack one point; in addition, a suit containing two or six cards is worth an extra point, a suit containing one or seven cards is worth two points, and a suit containing no cards or more than seven is worth three points. Define a function that computes the point count of a bridge hand.

(b) We can use an enumerated type to represent the possible values of a poker hand:

type *values* = (*bust, pair, twoPair, threeOfaKind, straight, flush,*
                  fullHouse, fourOfaKind, straightFlush, royalFlush);

A pair consists of two cards with the same rank; three or four of a kind consists of three or four cards with the same rank; a straight is a sequence of five cards with consecutive ranks, the ace counting either low or high; a flush consists of five cards of the same suit; a full house is a pair and three of a kind; a straight flush is a straight that is also a flush; a royal flush is a straight flush that begins with a ten and ends with an ace; and any other hand is a bust. Define a function that computes the value of a poker hand.

6.6   PROGRAMMING: FILES

Pascal is very permissive regarding the types of data we can store in a file. Most languages support *text files*, which are simply sequences of characters. These files are particularly convenient since we can create, inspect, and modify them using an editor. Furthermore, we can transport text files from one computer system to another. In Pascal, the standard files *input* and *output* are examples of text files.

Pascal also recognizes files that are sequences of data from an arbitrary type. Thus Pascal recognizes files of integers, files of arrays of reals, files of records, and the like. Such files do not need to represent all data as strings of characters, so they offer several advantages over text files. Numeric data, for example, can be kept in the format used by a program during its execution (Section 2.9). Programs do not need to convert numbers in such files to and from their decimal representations, and they can write information into, or read it from, these files quickly and with no loss of accuracy. On the other hand, these files are sometimes more difficult to handle than text files. On most computer systems, we must use a Pascal program to create, inspect, or modify them. And since the format of their data is determined by a particular computer system, they are harder to transport from one system to another.

FILE DECLARATIONS

Files, like other types of data, must be declared in a Pascal program. The declarations

```
var myData : file of real;
    f      : file of integer;
    source : file of char;
```

file type

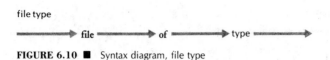

FIGURE 6.10 ■ Syntax diagram, file type

declare the variables *myData*, *f*, and *source* to range, respectively, over files of reals, integers, and characters. Since files of characters are among the most frequently used, Pascal predefines the identifier *text* as **file of** *char*.

Figure 6.10 specifies the precise syntax for describing a file type in Pascal. The type of the data in a file is known as the *base type* of that file. The only restriction on it is that it not be a file type itself or a composite type with file components.

Files used by a Pascal program may be *external* or *internal*. External files have a life of their own, independent of any Pascal program. They must exist before we execute a program that manipulates them, and they continue to exist after the program terminates. Internal files, by contrast, are created by a program and cease to exist when that program terminates.

All external files used by a Pascal program must be listed in the header for that program. The identifiers *input* and *output* appear there to indicate that a Pascal program takes its input from a standard external source and directs its output to a standard external destination. If a Pascal program is to use some other external file *myfile*, the name of that file must also appear in the header:

program *myprogram*(*input, output, myfile*);

All external files other than *input* and *output* used by a Pascal program must be declared at the start of that program (they cannot be declared within procedure or function definitions). The identifiers *input* and *output* are predefined to be of type *text* and should not be declared again in a program.

FILE OPERATIONS

Operations that manipulate files fall into two categories: those associated with reading data in files; and those associated with writing data into files. (See Table 6.5.) In

TABLE 6.5 File Operations in Pascal	
eof(*f*)	*true* if no data remain in file *f*
eoln(*f*)	*true* if no characters remain on line in text file *f*
read(*f, a, b, ...*)	read *a, b, ...* from file *f*
readln(*f, a, b, ...*)	read *a, b, ...* from text file *f*; advance to next line in file
reset(*f*)	prepare file *f* for reading
rewrite(*f*)	prepare file *f* for writing
write(*f, a, b, ...*)	write *a, b, ...* into file *f*
writeln(*f, a, b, ...*)	write *a, b, ..* followed by end-of-line into text file *f*

input statement

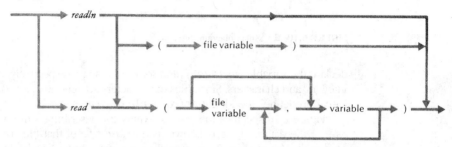

FIGURE 6.11 ■   Syntax diagram, input statement (final version)

Pascal, we cannot assign the value of one file variable to another (Section 5.6); instead, we must read the data in the first file an item at a time and write it into the second file. Likewise, we cannot pass a file by value to a procedure; all file parameters must be passed by reference.

The syntax diagrams in Fig. 6.11 and 6.12 amend those in Section 2.6 to allow the optional first parameter designating a file shown in Table 6.5.

Before manipulating a file in Pascal, we must indicate whether we want to read or write that file. Invoking the procedure *reset(f)* indicates that we want to read the file *f*, and invoking the procedure *rewrite(f)* indicates that we want to write it. After we invoke one of these procedures, we can read or write our way sequentially through the file. We need to invoke *reset* or *rewrite* a second time only if we want to start reading or writing at the beginning of the file once again.

When we execute a program, Pascal automatically prepares the file *input* for reading and the file *output* for writing. The effect of invoking *reset* or *rewrite* for these files is undefined.

output statement

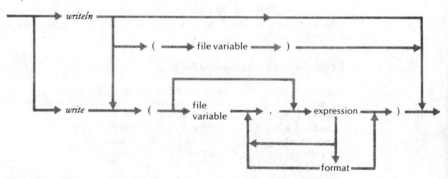

FIGURE 6.12 ■   Syntax diagram, output statement (final version)

Associated with each file is a *file pointer*, which indicates the datum to be affected by the next operation to be performed on that file. The *reset* procedure resets this pointer to the first datum in the file, causing that datum to be the next one read. The *rewrite* procedure erases the previous contents of the file and sets the file pointer to the end of the newly emptied file, causing the next datum written to be appended to the file.

Some dialects of Pascal (such as UCSD Pascal) enhance the *reset* and *rewrite* procedures so that they can select any external file for manipulation, whether or not that file has been named in the program header. Such enhancements enable us to write general-purpose programs, such as editors or interpreters, that can process arbitrary files of text. In these dialects the *reset* and *rewrite* procedures have an optional second argument, which is a string constant or variable that names an external file. The statements

> *reset*(f, 'realdata');
> *rewrite*(*source, newfile*)

associate the named files with the identifiers f and *source* and prepare these files for reading and writing.

File input   The variant *read*(f, ...) of the familiar *read* procedure enables us to read data in a file. The first parameter in an invocation of this variant identifies the file containing the data. Unless this file is a text file, the type of the remaining parameters must be the base type of the file. (Text files, as described farther on, are less restrictive in this respect.) The *read* procedure assigns successive items of data from the file to these parameters, starting with the datum indicated by the pointer for the file and advancing that pointer beyond the last datum assigned.

Pascal Sample 6.10, *fileAve*, illustrates how we read data from a file by computing the average of the list

> 1.2   −3.4   15.002   0.1111   78.9   100.0

of numbers stored in a file *realdata*. The program names that file in its header, declares its type to be **file of** *real*, and prepares it for reading by the statement *reset*(*realdata*). Then the main loop in the program reads the data in *realdata* a datum at a time. When the file pointer reaches the end of the file, the function *eof*(*realdata*) returns the value *true*, terminating this loop. Thus *fileAve* can count the numbers in the file—we do not need to tell it in advance how many there will be. Also, since *fileAve* uses a **while** loop instead of a **repeat** loop to read data from the file, it works properly even if the file *realdata* is empty.

File output   Similarly, the variant *write*(f, ...) of the familiar *write* procedure enables us to write data into a file. The first parameter in an invocation of this variant identifies the file being written. Unless this file is a text file, the type of the remaining parameters must be the base type of the file (again, text files are less restrictive in this respect).

PASCAL SAMPLE 6.10   The program *fileAve*

{ averages a list of numbers in a file }

program *fileAve*(*input, output, realdata*);

var *realdata* : **file of** *real*;   { file containing list }
    count   : *integer*;   { length of list   }
    number : *real*;   { number from list }
    sum   : *real*;   { sum of numbers }

begin
    sum := 0;
    count := 0;   { no numbers yet }
    reset(*realdata*);
    while not *eof*(*realdata*) **do**
        begin
            read(*realdata, number*);
            sum := *sum* + *number*;
            count := *count* + 1
        end;
    if *count* = 0 **then**
        writeln('Empty file.')
    else
        writeln('Average = ', *sum*/*count*:7:5)
end.

SAMPLE USE OF *fileAve*:

```
Average = 31.96885
```

The *write* procedure appends the values of these parameters to the file, advancing the file pointer to the end of the file.

    Pascal Sample 6.11, *makeFile*, illustrates how we can create the file *realdata* used by *fileAve*. Like *fileAve*, it names *realdata* in its header and declares it to be of type **file of** *real*. But it prepares the file for writing using *rewrite*(*realdata*), and then it writes one datum at a time into the file.

    When we create a file of real numbers or a file of integers, we must use a program such as *makeFile*. Since the numbers in these files are not represented as strings of characters, we cannot create them simply by typing characters into a text file.

TEXT FILES

Text files—that is, files of characters—receive special treatment in Pascal. For such files, the *read* and *write* procedures behave as they do for the files *input* and *output*. Indeed, *read*(*a, b, . . .*) is equivalent to *read*(*input, a, b, . . .*), and *write*(*a, b, . . .*) is equivalent to *write*(*output, a, b, . . .*). This means that we are not restricted to reading

---

 PASCAL SAMPLE 6.11   The program *makeFile*

{ creates a file of real numbers }

program *makeFile(input, output, realdata)*;

var *realdata* : **file of** *real*;
 item   : *real*;

begin
    writeln('Enter numbers, one per line, followed by eof.');
    rewrite(realdata);
    while not *eof* **do**
        begin
            readln(item);
            write(realdata, item)
        end

end.

SAMPLE USE OF *makeFile*:

```
Enter numbers, one per line, followed by eof.
1.2
-3.4
15.002
0.1111
78.9
100.0
```
■

and writing characters when we manipulate text files; we can also read or write integer and real values, with Pascal converting these values to and from their character representations.

Text files, like the files *input* and *output*, are composed of lines of characters, each of which ends with an end-of-line marker. The function *eoln(source)* has the value *true* if the pointer for the text file *source* is at the end of a line, that is, if the next character to be read is the end-of-line marker. Furthermore, the *readln* and *writeln* procedures read and write lines in a text file as they do for lines in the files *input* and *output*.

In order to illustrate the use of these built-in procedures, we define a procedure *appendToFile* that appends the contents of one text file to another. We can use this procedure to display a text file on our terminal (by appending the contents of that file to the file *output*) or to insert some lines at the beginning of a text file (by appending the contents of the file to another file containing those lines). In Chapter 7, we will use this procedure several times as we construct a program to edit a file of text.

When writing the procedure *appendToFile* (Pascal Sample 6.12), we must take care to preserve the division of a file into lines. Hence the procedure follows the general pattern for processing text line by line, and character by character within a line (Section 5.3). Both parameters to *appendToFile* are passed by reference and not by value, even though the contents of one of these files remains the same. This is because passing a parameter by value involves an implicit assignment of the value of an actual parameter to a formal parameter, and Pascal permits neither assignment of file values nor file parameters to be passed by value.

We can create further aids for manipulating files of text by modifying the library *stringSubs1* of procedures that manipulate fixed-length strings to handle input from, and output to, arbitrary text files. One revision is straightforward: we simply add a file parameter to the procedure *writeString*. A procedure to enhance the *readString* procedure in *stringSubs1*, so that it can read strings containing spaces, requires more extensive work.

Pascal Sample 6.13 describes the new capabilities of the procedures in the library *stringSubs1*, which we rename as *stringSubs2*. It also shows the routine modifications that we make in the *writeString* procedure.

The new version of *skipBlanks*, displayed as Pascal Sample 6.14, is an enhanced version of the procedure that we wrote in Section 5.4. The earlier version skipped blanks in the text file *input*; the new version skips blanks in an arbitrary text file.

PASCAL SAMPLE 6.12   The procedure *appendToFile*

{ *appendToFile*: appends contents of one text file to another }

procedure *appendToFile*(**var** *destination*, *source* : *text*);

    { appends contents of *source* to *destination* }
    { assumes *destination* prepared for writing }

    var *c* : *char*;

    begin

        reset(*source*);
        while not *eof*(*source*) **do**   { copy next line }
            begin
                while not *eoln*(*source*) **do**
                    begin
                        read(*source*, *c*);
                        write(*destination*, *c*)
                    end;
                readln(*source*);
                writeln(*destination*)
            end

    end;   { of *appendToFile* }

PASCAL SAMPLE 6.13   The library *stringSubs2* (header, *writeString* procedure)

```
{ stringSubs2: procedures for manipulating strings and text files      }
{ length(s)              returns index of last nonblank character in s }
{ readString(f, s)       reads a string s from a text file f           }
{ skipBlanks(f)          skips over blanks in a text file f            }
{ writeString(f, s)      writes s into f without any trailing blanks   }
{     Any program that uses stringSubs2 must contain the following     }
{ declarations:                                                        }
{                                                                      }
{     const stringLength = ...;                                        }
{                                                                      }
{     type string = packed array [1..stringLength] of char;           }
```

```
procedure writeString( var f : text; s : string );
    { writes s to f, suppressing trailing blanks }
    var i : 1..stringLength;
    begin
        for i := 1 to length(s) do write( f, s[i])
    end;   { of writeString }
```

PASCAL SAMPLE 6.14   The library *stringSubs2* (*skipBlanks* procedure)

```
{ skipBlanks: skips over blanks in a text file }
procedure skipBlanks( var f : text );
    { advances the pointer for f to the next nonblank character }
    { or to the end of the file if only blanks remain           }
    var done  : boolean;
        space : char;
    begin
        done := false;
        repeat
            if eof(f) then
                done := true
            else if f↑ = ' ' then
                read( f, space)
            else
                done := true
        until done
    end;   { of skipBlanks }
```

We will examine the buffer variable $f\uparrow$, which the new version of *skipBlanks* uses to look one character ahead in f, just as the old version used *input* $\uparrow$ to look one character ahead in *input*. But first we use this variable to construct a new version of *readString*, thereby completing the development of *stringSubs2*. The earlier version of *readString* did not enable us to read strings that contained blanks—a serious shortcoming if we are to supply strings such as New York as input to a program. We enhance *readString* both to take a file parameter and also to recognize two kinds of strings: sequences of nonblank characters, as before, and arbitrary sequences of characters surrounded by apostrophes, as for string constants in Pascal.

Pascal Sample 6.15 contains the new *readString* procedure for *stringSubs2*. To streamline the logic for that procedure, we have defined a function *inString* (Pascal Sample 6.16) that recognizes the various ways a string might end: at the end of the file; at the end of a line; at a space; or at an apostrophe followed by some character other than an apostrophe. With *inString* handling the laborious work, the rest of *readString* can place characters from f in the string s, truncating the string or filling it with blanks as necessary.

FILE BUFFER VARIABLES

By inspecting the buffer variable $f\uparrow$ for the file f in *inString*, we were able to detect the end of a string without reading one character beyond the end of that string. And by inspecting the buffer variable *input* $\uparrow$ in Section 5.3, we were able to avoid problems that arise when we attempt to detect the end of the input.

To recall the nature of these problems, consider what happens if we try to modify *fileAve* so that it averages a list of numbers in a text file rather than a list of numbers in a file of reals or integers. If we simply change the declaration for the file *realdata* from **file of** *real* to *text*, the program will not work: *eof(realdata)* will not be true after we read the last number in the file because at least one character—the end-of-line marker—remains in the file. If we also read numbers using *readln* instead of *read*, the end-of-line marker will not get in the way. But then our program, like *average4* in Section 2.5, will work only if *realdata* contains a single number on each line and does not end with a blank line. In order to detect the end of a text file reliably, we must use *skipBlanks* to advance the file pointer to the next nonblank character in that file or to the end of the file if only blanks remain; then we can test *eof* to determine whether any numbers remain in the file. (See Exercise 6, Section 5.3.)

When constructing procedures like *skipBlanks* and *readString*, we need to inspect the next character in a text file. In some cases we need to read it and get to the next character; in other cases we can leave it alone. Fortunately, Pascal enables us to do this. In fact, Pascal enables us to inspect the item that will be read next from an arbitrary file without actually reading that item.

Suppose that f is a file with base type *fType*. Associated with f is a variable $f\uparrow$ of type *fType*, called the *buffer variable* for f. When f is reset to prepare it for reading, the value of $f\uparrow$ is the first item in the file; thereafter, the value of $f\uparrow$ is

PASCAL SAMPLE 6.15   The library *stringSubs2* (*readString* procedure)

procedure *readString*(**var** *f* : *text*; **var** *s* : *string*);

{ skips initial blanks in *f* and assigns the next "string" as the value of *s*,   }
{ truncating strings that are too long for *s* and extending strings that are   }
{ too short by blanks   }

{ If the next nonblank character in *f* is an apostrophe, then the "string"   }
{ contains all characters up to, but not including, the next single   }
{ apostrophe or end-of-line; doubled-up apostrophes in such a string are   }
{ reduced to a single apostrophe. If the next nonblank character in *f* is   }
{ not an apostrophe, then the "string" contains all characters up to, but   }
{ not including, the next blank or end-of-line. The file pointer is left in   }
{ position on the character following the string.   }

const *apostrophe* = ' ' ' ';

var *quoted* : *boolean*;   { *true* if string begins with apostrophe }
   i, n   : *integer*;   { character positions in string   }
   junk   : *char*;   { discarded character   }

{ declaration for *inString* goes here; returns *true* if *f*↑ is in the string }

begin
   skipBlanks(*f*);
   if not *eof*(*f*) **then**   { determine type of string }
      begin
         quoted := (*f*↑ = *apostrophe*);
         if *quoted* **then** *read*(*f*, *junk*)
      end;
   n := 0;
   while *inString* **do**   { add next character to string if it fits }
      begin
         n := *n* + 1;
         if *n* <= *stringLength* **then** *read*(*f*, *s*[*n*]) **else** *read*(*f*, *junk*)
      end;
   for *i* := *n* + 1 **to** *stringLength* **do** *s*[*i*] := ' ';   { fill string }
   if *n* > *stringLength* **then**
      begin
         writeln;
         writeln('String too long -- excess ignored');
      end
end;   { of *readString* }

always the item that will be read next from the file. In particular, if *f* is a text file, then *f*↑ is the next character in the file. When *eof*(*f*) is *true*, *f*↑ is undefined.

We can manipulate the buffer variable for a file in the same way that we manipulate other variables in Pascal. If the base type of the file is a composite type, we can

PASCAL SAMPLE 6.16   The library *stringSubs2* (local *inString* function)

function *inString* : *boolean*;
    { returns *true* if $f\uparrow$ is in the string }
   begin
       if *eof*(*f*) **then**
          inString := *false*
       else if *eoln*(*f*) **then**
          inString := *false*
       else if *quoted* **then**
         if $f\uparrow$ = *apostrophe* **then**
           begin
             read(*f*, *junk*);
             inString := ($f\uparrow$ = *apostrophe*)
           end
         else
           inString := *true*
       else
         inString := ($f\uparrow$ <> ' ')
   end;   { of *inString* }

subscript its buffer variable (as in $f\uparrow[3]$ if f is a file of arrays) or extract a component (as in $f\uparrow.name$ if f is a record). Figure 6.13 incorporates this use of a buffer variable into the specifications for the syntax of a variable in Pascal.

It is impossible to change the contents of a file simply by assigning values to its buffer variable. Changes to the buffer variable are made in the file only if we invoke

variable

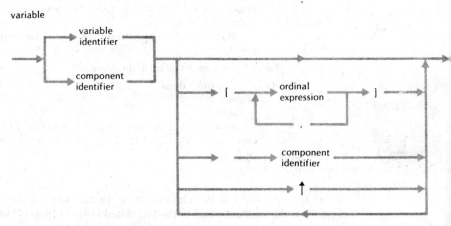

FIGURE 6.13 ■ Syntax diagram, variable (final version)

a special primitive procedure supplied by Pascal. This explains why buffer variables are named as they are; they act as a "buffer" between us and the file. In order to transfer values between a file and its buffer variable, we can invoke the following primitive procedures in Pascal:

$get(f)$ assigns the next value in the file f to $f\uparrow$
            assumes: f prepared for reading and not $eof(f)$

$put(f)$ appends $f\uparrow$ to the end of f, making $f\uparrow$ undefined
            assumes: f prepared for writing

Pascal, in fact, defines the *read* and *write* procedures in terms of the buffer variable and these primitive procedures. Invoking $get(f)$ assigns the next value in the file f to the buffer variable $f\uparrow$. Hence the statement $read(f, x)$ is equivalent to the sequence

$x := f\uparrow;$ { assign the next value in the file f to x }
$get(f)$ { advance file pointer, assigning new value to $f\uparrow$ }

of more primitive statements. Invoking $put(f)$ appends the value of the buffer variable to the end of the file. (This is the only way in which a change in the value of the buffer variable results in a change to the file.) Hence the statement $write(f, x)$ is equivalent to the sequence

$f\uparrow := x;$ { assign value to be written to buffer variable }
$put(f)$ { append this value to the file f }

of more primitive statements.

We will use *put* and *get* procedures sparingly, preferring to use the more natural procedures *read* and *write*. But, on several occasions, we will find that the ability to look ahead in a file, using its buffer variable, is an indispensable feature of Pascal.

EXERCISES

1. Write a program to display the contents of a file of integers.

2. Write a program to input the name of a text file and print the number of lines, words, and characters in that file.

3. Write a program to input the names of two files and determine whether the files have identical contents.

4. Modify the program *grades2* to obtain its data from a text file rather than from the terminal. What are the advantages of supplying data to *grades2* in this manner rather than interactively?

5. Use files to create a more flexible set of grading programs, as follows:

   (a) Define a file type that is suitable for holding the grade records for the students in a course. (*Hint:* Use a file of records.)

   (b) Write a program to create a file of grade records from a text file that contains the names of the students in the course and their grades on the first exam.

(c) Write a program to add the results of a new exam to this file.

(d) Write a program to produce a grade report from the exam scores currently on file.

(e) Write a program that enables the instructor to correct the file of grade records by changing a grade, adding the name of a new student, or deleting the name of a student who has dropped the course.

(f) What alternatives did you have for recording the number of students and exams in the file of grade records? Why did you choose the alternative you did?

6. Write a program to read a text file that contains a Pascal program with **#include** statements and to produce a file in which each **#include** statement has been replaced by the contents of the file named in that statement.

7. Extend your solution to Exercise 6 by having your program process **#include** statements found in included files. What is the best strategy for dealing with nested **#include** files? What happens if someone inadvertently includes a file in itself?

*8. Write a program that prints a copy of itself. Can you do this without using files?

6.7 SYSTEMS: HOW COMPUTERS REPRESENT COMPOSITE DATA

Composite data types enable us to tailor data structures to the problem at hand. Even though different programs use different data structures to solve different problems, we expect one computer system to execute any of those programs. Therefore computer systems need a uniform way of representing the structures that we create and accessing the components of those structures. We consider in turn how they do this for arrays, records, and files.

ARRAYS

To consider a simple case first, suppose that we have declared a to be an array that contains five integers, using the following declaration.

> **var** a : **array** [1..5] **of** *integer*;

A computer with single-precision integers will devote five consecutive words of memory to the array a. Figure 6.14 depicts such a representation when $a[n]$ has the value n^2 for $n = 1, 2, \ldots, 5$.

Suppose now that we wish to change one of the elements in this array, say, by executing the statement $a[i] := n$. Recall that the simpler assignment $i := n$ can be carried out by a sequence of two machine-language instructions; if the values of i and n are stored in locations 210 and 211, then the instructions

```
LDA 211    { load A with n }
STA 210    { store A in i  }
```

load the value of n into the A register and store this value in the location assigned to i. To assign the value of n to $a[i]$ instead of to i, the STA instruction requires a

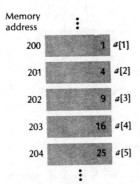

FIGURE 6.14 ■ Storing a five-element array in memory

different address. In fact, since the value of i can vary, we must compute this address just before executing the STA instruction. One way to do this is to use indirect addressing (Section 4.8) and two additional words of memory: one (say, location 212) to hold the *base address* of the array a, that is, the address (199 in this example) of a fictional element $a[0]$ in the array; and another (say, location 213) to hold the computed address of $a[i]$. With these additional words of memory, the instructions

```
LDA  210    { load A with i        }
ADD  212    { add base address of a }
STA  213    { store address of a[i] }
LDA  211    { load A with n         }
STAI 213    { store A indirectly in a[i] }
```

carry out the assignment by computing the address of $a[i]$, loading the value of n into the A register as before, and storing this value indirectly into the location with the address just computed.

In general, arrays are represented and manipulated in much the same way as in this simple case, the principal difference being that the individual elements in an array may occupy more or less than a single word of memory. However, the feature that distinguishes arrays from other data structures is that each element in an array occupies exactly the same amount of memory. Hence we can compute the address of any element in an array if we know its subscript. This computation is particularly easy if each element in the array occupies entirely a number of consecutive words. Then, in order to find the address of the ith element in an array, we simply multiply i by the number of words needed for a single element and add the base address of the array.

In certain cases, elements in an array do not need to occupy a full word. For example, an element in a boolean array needs to occupy only a single bit, and an element in a string (a character) needs to occupy only a single byte. In such cases we can choose to conserve storage by packing as many elements into a word as will

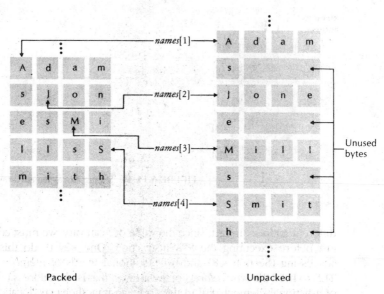

FIGURE 6.15 ■ Alternate representations in memory for an array of strings

fit, or we can choose to access the elements in the array more readily by storing them one per word. Pascal provides this option by the keyword **packed**: if we want to conserve space, we declare an array to be packed; otherwise, we let Pascal put each element in the array at the beginning of a new word, thereby making it easier to find and manipulate those elements.

In still other cases, elements in an array may occupy a fractional number of words. In such cases, packed arrays again conserve space, whereas unpacked arrays devote an extra fraction of a word to each element to simplify accessing those elements. Suppose, for example, that we want to create an array *names* containing the four 5-character strings Adams, Jones, Mills, and Smith. Strings in Pascal are packed arrays of characters, and a 5-character string will occupy 1.25 words on a computer with four bytes per words. As shown by Fig. 6.15, *names* will occupy five words if it is packed and eight words if it is not.

RECORDS

The components of a record, unlike those of an array, do not need to occupy the same amount of space. Nevertheless, a record is stored in memory just like an array, with its components occupying consecutive locations. Since we know how much space is required for each component, it is easy to compute where they begin.

For purposes of illustration, suppose that we are given the following declaration for a record.

var *person* : **record**
　　　　　　name　　: **packed array** [1..16] **of** *char*;
　　　　　　address　: **packed array** [1..34] **of** *char*;
　　　　　　age　　　: 0..100;
　　　　　　married : *boolean*
　　　end;

Then Fig. 6.16 shows an unpacked representation for this record on a computer with four bytes per word.

The *base address* of a record is the address of the first word in the record. We find the address of any component in an unpacked record by computing the number

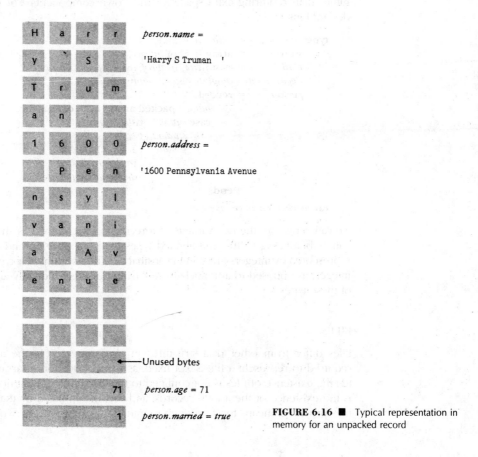

person.name =

'Harry S Truman　　'

person.address =

'1600 Pennsylvania Avenue

──Unused bytes

person.age = 71

person.married = true

FIGURE 6.16 ■ Typical representation in memory for an unpacked record

of words of storage occupied by the preceding components in the record and adding that number to the base address.

As for arrays, declaring a record to be packed conserves space by making its components fit together as tightly as possible. For example, in Fig. 6.16, we could pack the last two components of the record into the two unused bytes in the last word devoted to *person.address*, thereby saving two words of storage. However, this increases the amount of time required to access the components of a record: on most computer systems it is easier to access an entire word than part of a word.

In some situations we can conserve space with no loss in efficiency. When the number and types of the components in a record vary, depending on the contents of that record, we do not need to reserve space for all possible components. Instead, we can conserve space by using variant records, which require only as much storage for the variant part as is required by the longest variant. The other variants use as much of this space as necessary, *overlapping* each other in their use of this space rather than requiring extra space for their own components. For example, for the declarations

```
type categories  = (student, faculty);
     scores       = array [1..5] of integer;
     ranks        = (instructor, asstProf, assocProf, professor);
     department = (english, history, math, physics, ...);
     person       = record
                        name : packed array [1..20] of char;
                        case status  : categories of
                           student : ( score : scores );
                           faculty  : ( born : 1800..2000;
                                        rank  : ranks;
                                        dept  : departments )
                     end;
     var teacher, enrollee : person;
```

we can represent the two variants of a record of type *person* as shown in Fig. 6.17. Values belonging to the enumerated types *categories, ranks*, and *departments* are represented by integers giving their ordinal positions within their types. Thus a single integer, as opposed to a multicharacter string, suffices to identify an element of any of these types.

FILES

Files differ from other data structures in two respects: (1) the amount of space required to represent a file is not fixed, as is the space for an array or record; and (2) the existence of files is not confined to the execution of a particular program, as is the existence of the arrays, records, and sets manipulated by that program. Thus files provide a means for a program to interact with the outside world.

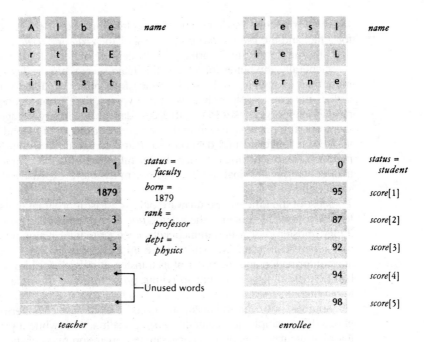

FIGURE 6.17 ■ Representations of variant records

Because of these characteristics, files are kept on secondary storage devices, such as disks, rather than in primary memory. And, as noted previously, secondary storage has a far greater capacity than primary memory. Thus files can grow in size, and many files can remain in existence for long periods of time. The operating system for a computer keeps track of which files are stored and where they are stored in secondary storage, allocating more space as needed for new files or for files that need to grow, and reclaiming space from files that disappear or wish to shrink.

Programs that manipulate files need some way to bridge the gap between primary memory, where programs reside during execution, and secondary storage, where files reside. If a file were sufficiently small, a program could make a copy of that file in primary memory, modify it as necessary, and then replace the external file with the modified copy. But one of the primary attractions of files is that they can hold more data than can primary memory, and this simple strategy will not work for every file.

To handle files of any size, programs manipulate all files a piece at a time. Rather than copy an entire file into memory, they copy a small piece at a time into a region of memory known as a *buffer*. They can then inspect the contents of the buffer, change these contents, and copy the new contents back into the file. The buffer variable for a file in Pascal permits a program to inspect or change data in the buffer for a file, and the *get* and *put* procedures, or the *read* and *write* procedures, enable that program to transfer information between the buffer and the file.

Generally, the buffer for a file will contain several hundred words of storage, or more than enough to hold a single value of the buffer variable for that file, because it does not pay to read only a word or two at a time from secondary storage into primary memory. It takes longer to access data on secondary storage than in primary memory—the price we pay to utilize the greater capacity of secondary storage—and it takes far longer to find data on secondary storage than to transfer that data into memory. Hence copying one large buffer full of information is much less expensive than copying many small buffers and not much more expensive than copying one small buffer.

Most of the time we are unaware of how a Pascal program transfers information to and from its file buffers. The *get* and *put* or *read* and *write* procedures behave as if they transfer information immediately: if we write information into a file, reset that file, and read it again, we will find the information we just wrote. Buffers do not affect information and the order of its transfer; at most they cause some slight delays between the time we execute an output procedure and the time data actually gets into a file.

At times, however, the delays associated with the use of buffers cause noticeable effects. For example, if a computer system malfunctions while a program is writing information into a file, or if that program terminates prematurely because of an error, we cannot be sure exactly of what information reached the file and what remains in the buffer. Good computer systems try to ensure the timeliness of information in a file, but no computer system is immune from the effects of a breakdown.

If we write information slowly into a file, the rate at which that information actually appears in the file will vary according to the size of buffer. An experiment such as that suggested by Exercise 5 at the end of this section shows that, when writing characters into the text file *output*, we can depend on the order in which those characters appear, but not on the speed with which they do so. Some systems will print each character immediately, making the characters appear at evenly spaced intervals of time. Others will print the characters a buffer at a time, making the characters appear in spurts. And still others will print the characters that are in the buffer each time we invoke the *writeln* procedure. Hence programs that drive a video display at a fixed rate are difficult to write in standard Pascal.

EXERCISES

1. Suppose that *a* is a two-dimensional array declared as follows:

   var *a* : **array** [*low1..high1, low2..high2*] **of** *integer*;

   (a) How many elements are there in the array *a*?

(b) Let n be the number of elements in the array a. Then we can view the memory needed to represent a as a one-dimensional array b with n elements. Define a function *subscript* beginning with the header

> **function** *subscript*(i, j : *integer*) : *integer*;

which maps the array a onto the array b so that

- $a[i, j]$ corresponds to $b[subscript(i, j)]$,
- $subscript(low1, low2) = 1$, and
- $subscript(high1, high2) = n$.

2. Suppose that a is an M-dimensional array declared as follows:

> **var** a : **array** [$low1..high1, ..., lowM..highM$] **of** *integer*;

(a) How many elements are there in the array a?

(b) Let n be the number of elements in the array a. Then we can view the memory needed to represent a as a one-dimensional array b with n elements. Define a function *subscript* beginning with the header

> **function** *subscript*($i1, ..., iM$: *integer*) : *integer*;

which maps the array a onto the array b so that

- $a[i1, ..., iM]$ corresponds to $b[subscript(i1, ..., iM)]$,
- $subscript(low1, ..., lowM) = 1$, and
- $subscript(high1, ..., highM) = n$.

3. Investigate the amount of space your system uses, and makes available, for different data types.

(a) How many bits are there in a word on your system? (*Hint:* Examine the value of *maxint*.)

(b) Will your system execute the following program?

```
program test(input, output);
var a : array [1..16000] of integer;
begin
end.
```

What is the maximum size it will accept for the array a? What does this say about the number of words available for storing data on your system?

(c) How is your answer to part (b) affected if a is an array of boolean values? Characters? Reals?

(d) How are your answers to parts (b) and (c) affected if you declare a to be packed?

4. Among the alternatives for representing a structure that contains three positive integers, one with a single digit, one with at most two digits, and one with at most four digits, are

(a) as an array with three components;

(b) as a record with three components;

(c) as a string containing seven characters; and

(d) as a single integer with up to seven digits.

For each of these possibilities, determine the number of words of memory that are required to store the structure. Furthermore, define a procedure *create(a, b, c, s)* that creates a structure *s* containing the integers *a*, *b*, and *c*, and define a function *extract(s, i)* that extracts the value of the *i*th integer in the structure.

5. Investigate how your system buffers output to the terminal by executing the following program.

```
program timer(input, output);
const n = 1000;
var i, j : integer;
    x   : real;
begin
    x := 1;
    for i := 1 to 2000 do
        begin
            write( chr( ord('0') + i mod 10 ) );
            for j := 1 to n do x := sin(x)
        end
end.
```

(a) Do the characters appear at evenly spaced intervals of time?

(b) Does the value of the constant *n* affect the amount of time it takes for characters to appear?

(c) Do characters appear more or less evenly in time if the *write* procedure is changed to *writeln*?

(d) Do characters appear more or less evenly in time if a statement

     if *i* mod 50 = 0 then *writeln*

is added at the end of the loop?

SUMMARY

Just as primitive actions can be assembled into larger composite actions, so can primitive data types be combined into larger composite data types. As with the primitive data types, each composite type is characterized by a collection of similar objects together with a collection of operations for manipulating those objects. The mechanisms for forming composite types in Pascal include

▪ arrays, which have

1. objects that are indexed collections of objects from a common data type and

2. operations of := and subscripting (to yield an element in an array);

■ strings, which have

   1. objects that are fixed-length arrays of characters and

   2. operations of *write*, := , subscripting, and order relations;

■ records, which have

   1. objects that are named collections of objects from possibly different data types and

   2. operations of := and component extraction (to yield an element in a record); and

■ files, which have

   1. objects that are unindexed sequences of objects from a common data type and

   2. operations of preparing a file for reading (*reset*) or writing (*rewrite*), reading an object from a file; writing an object to a file, and testing for the end of a file.

Some dialects of Pascal provide additional composite data types such as variable-length strings or direct-access files.

Composite data types can themselves be combined into still larger data types. Objects in a composite data type can be supplied as parameters to functions and procedures. However, in Pascal, they cannot be returned as values of functions.

ON ABSTRACT DATA ABSTRACT ACT
BSTRACT DATA ABSTRACT ACTION
ATA ABSTRACT ACTIONS ON ABST
ONS ON ABSTRACT DATA ABSTRAC
ON ABSTRACT DATA ABSTRACT AC
BSTRACT DATA ABSTRACT ACTIO
ATA **ABSTRACT ACTIONS ON** ABS
ONS ON **ABSTRACT DATA** ABSTRA

C   H   A   P   T   E   R

7

*S*o far our use of data structures has not been as imaginative as our use of procedures. We have learned how to define procedures and functions so that we may deal with problems in our own terms rather than in the terms imposed by a particular programming language. But we have not yet done the same with data structures. Instead, we have learned solely how to deal with particular data structures using the facilities provided by a particular programming language.

In this chapter we turn our attention to dealing with data as well as actions in our own terms. Before, we concentrated on how to represent data; now, we concentrate on what we intend to do with that data. Our objective is to create *abstract data types*, defining both representations for abstract objects and operations that manipulate those objects.

In terms of programming, an abstract data type is a library of procedures that perform abstract operations on abstract data. The procedures in that library share information about the representation of that data but, insofar as possible, they hide this information from programs that invoke them. Such programs are concerned only with what the procedures in the library can do, not with how they do it.

In this chapter we examine several ways to treat sequences of symbols as an abstract data type: as representations for multiple-precision integers; as variable-length strings of characters; as lines in a file of text; and as sequences of operations and operands in an arithmetic expression. Later, in Part II, we will represent several important data structures as abstract data types. Although the underlying representations in many of these applications bear a superficial resemblance to each other, the ways in which we manipulate those representations differ considerably. Hence by focussing our attention on operations and not on representations, we will see more clearly the distinctive features of data structures.

Most computer systems provide only seven or eight decimal digits of precision when performing arithmetic operations. If we desire greater precision, we cannot rely on ordinary numeric variables and the ordinary operations of addition, subtraction, multiplication, and division. Instead we must devise a way to represent numbers more precisely, and we must write procedures to perform arithmetic operations with as much precision as we desire.

In this section we develop a representation for multiple-precision positive integers, that is, for positive integers having a precision beyond that of the *integer* data type. Furthermore, we develop a library of procedures to manipulate these integers. Our objective is to illustrate how several procedures can share a concrete representation for abstract data and how, by hiding the details of that representation, they can help us raise the level of abstraction in our programs.

For a first approach to multiple-precision integer arithmetic, we choose a particularly simple representation for our data, namely, we choose to represent integers with up to 20 digits as vectors with subscripts ranging from 0 to 19. For any such vector x, $x[0]$ will contain the unit's digit in decimal representation of an integer, $x[1]$ the ten's digit, and so on; thus x will represent

$$\sum_{n=0}^{19} 10^n x[n].$$

For example, to represent 100,718, we will set

$$x[0] = 8$$
$$x[1] = 1$$
$$x[2] = 7$$
$$x[3] = 0$$
$$x[4] = 0$$
$$x[5] = 1$$
$$x[6] = x[7] = \cdots = x[19] = 0$$

Our procedures for multiple-precision integer arithmetic will manipulate these vectors using algorithms for addition and multiplication based on those we learned in elementary school.

Before writing these procedures, we examine a sample program that calls them. Pascal Sample 7.1, *power1*, computes powers of integers by repeated multiplication and is based on the simplified program fragment

```
y := 1;                    { y = x**0 }
for i := 1 to n do y := y*x   { y = x**i }
```

from *intPower* in Section 3.4 that sets y equal to x^n. To create *power1*, we transform the variables x and y into vectors of type *longInt* that hold the digits in the decimal representations of positive integers; the constant and type declarations in *power1*

■ **PASCAL SAMPLE 7.1**   The program *power1*

```
{ finds powers of integers using multiple-precision arithmetic }
program power1(input, output);
const base     = 10;                    { base for arithmetic    }
      lastDigit = 19;                    { number of digits − 1 }
type posInt  = 0..maxint;
     longInt = array [0..lastDigit] of posInt;
var number, n, i : posInt;              { single precision    }
    x, y          : longInt;            { multiple precision }
#include 'arith1';                      { arithmetic procedures }
begin
    write('Enter base, exponent: ');
    read(number, n);
    convert(number, x);
    convert(1, y);                                  { y = x**0 }
    for i := 1 to n do multiply(y, x, y);           { y = x**i }
    writeln;
    write(number:1, ' ** ', n:1, ' = ');
    print(y);
    writeln
end.
```

SAMPLE USE OF *power1*:

```
Enter base, exponent:  2 60

2 ** 60 = 1152921504606846976
```

supply the details of this representation. We also transform the assignment statements involving the variables *x* and *y* into calls of procedures that perform the desired tasks.

We may want many programs in addition to *power1* to use multiple-precision integer arithmetic, so we store our procedures to perform arithmetic operations in a separate library called *arith1*. The **#include** statement in *power1* tells where to find these procedures. From the standpoint of *power1*, the precise representation of multiple-precision integers used by these procedures matters very little. True, we must start *power1* with two constant declarations and two type declarations, as required by these procedures, and we must declare the variables *x* and *y* to be of type *longInt*. But only the procedures in *arith1* are affected by how *longInt* is declared.

The program *power1* manipulates multiple-precision integers using the procedures in *arith1* without regard to the details of their declaration. Hence we can grasp what *power1* does in terms of which operations it performs without getting bogged down in the details of how those operations are carried out. Furthermore, by separating the procedures in *arith1* from the program *power1*, we make it easier to replace them with improved or slightly different versions. More importantly, by treating multiple-precision integers as an abstract data type—that is, as a data type defined in terms of operations that manipulate data rather than in terms of representations for that data—we make it easy to change or improve the way we handle these integers. If we were to develop a better representation for multiple-precision integers, or better procedures to handle them, we could store these procedures in a library *arith2* and convert *power1* to use them simply by changing a few declarations and including *arith2* rather than *arith1*. In fact, we will do just this in the exercises at the end of this section and in Section 13.1.

Let us turn our attention now to the operation of *power1*. The calls of the *convert* procedure in *power1* convert the single-precision integers *number* and 1 into vectors of digits, which we can manipulate as multiple-precision integers. The *multiply* procedure multiplies the integers represented by the first two parameters and assigns a representation for the result to the third parameter (which is passed by reference). The *print* procedure prints the integer represented by its parameter. In a sense, these procedures expand the Pascal language: invoking one of them takes the place of executing a statement that might have been, but unfortunately is not, part of Pascal.

Details of how these procedures carry out the required operations are found in the library *arith1*, which is a collection of procedure definitions. Comments at the beginning of *arith1* describe its purpose and its contents (Pascal Sample 7.2), concentrating first on how to use multiple-precision integers as an abstract data type and only later providing details about how multiple-precision integers are represented.

■ **PASCAL SAMPLE 7.2**   The library *arith1* (initial comments)

```
{ arith1: procedures for multiple-precision positive integer arithmetic   }

{      The following procedures manipulate multiple-precision positive   }
{ integers x, y, z whose type longInt is described below. The variable   }
{ n represents a single-precision positive integer.                       }

{      Procedure              Action or value                            }
{      add(y,z,x)             x := y + z                                 }
{      convert(n,x)           x := n                                    }
{      multiply(y,z,x)        x := y*z                                  }
{      print(x)               display x                                 }

{      Any program using these procedures must contain the following    }
{ declarations:                                                          }
{                                                                        }
{      const base    = 10;     (base for arithmetic)                    }
{            lastDigit = 19;    (number of digits − 1)                  }
{                                                                        }
{      type posInt = 0..maxint;                                         }
{           longInt = array [0..lastDigit] of posInt;                   }
```

PASCAL SAMPLE 7.2   The library *arith1* (initial comments, continued)

```
{     These declarations represent integers with up to 20 digits as    }
{ vectors with subscripts ranging from 0 to 19. Each element of such   }
{ a vector x contains a single decimal digit, with x[0] containing the }
{ least significant digit (the unit's digit) and x[19] the most significant }
{ digit. Thus the integer represented by the vector x is the sum of    }
{ x[i]*10**i for i ranging from 0 to 19.                               }

{     The two constant declarations make it easy to change both the    }
{ number of digits allowed in the representations (say, to 100) and    }
{ the base of the number system (say, to 2 for binary arithmetic or    }
{ to 1000 to store three decimal digits per element in a vector).      }
```

The procedure definitions follow these comments. The *convert* procedure (Pascal Sample 7.3) unpacks the digits in the decimal representation of an integer n and stores these digits in the vector x, the unit's digit going in $x[0]$, the ten's digit in $x[1]$, and so on. Leading zeroes are added to decimal representations so that all numbers are stored using exactly 20 digits. This simplifies the coding, but makes execution of some procedures very inefficient. We will address this inefficiency in Exercise 14 at the end of this section and in Section 13.1.

The definition of *convert* uses the **mod** and **div** operations to compute the digits in the decimal representation of a number: n **mod** 10 gives the unit's digit in the decimal representation of n and n **div** 10 gives the preceding digits. (See Section 2.7.) By utilizing these operations repeatedly, *convert* peels off the digits in the decimal representation of n from right to left.

We take care in *convert* to ensure that the value of n can be represented by no more digits than the vector x will hold. If this is not the case, we report an error. It is good programming practice to detect and report errors as soon as they are found and not let their effects propagate in mysterious ways throughout a program.

PASCAL SAMPLE 7.3   The library *arith1* (*convert* procedure)

```
procedure convert( n : posInt; var x : longInt );
      { converts an integer n to its vector representation x }
      var digit : 0..lastDigit;
   begin
      for digit := 0 to lastDigit do
            begin
                  x[digit] := n mod base;
                  n        := n div base
            end;
      if n > 0 then writeln('Overflow in conversion')
   end;   { of convert }
```

PASCAL SAMPLE 7.4   The library *arith1* (*add* procedure)

```
procedure add( y, z : longInt; var x : longInt );
    { sets x to the representation of the sum of }
    { the integers represented by y and z       }
    var sum, carry : posInt;
        digit        : 0..lastDigit;
    begin
        carry := 0;
        for digit := 0 to lastDigit do
            begin
                sum    := y[digit] + z[digit] + carry;
                x[digit] := sum mod base;
                carry  := sum div base
            end;
        if carry > 0 then writeln('Overflow in addition')
    end;   { of add }
```

The *add* procedure (Pascal Sample 7.4) adds two representations for integers, a digit at a time, starting with the least significant digit and propagating a carry as necessary. Again we take care to ensure that no more digits are needed to represent the result than can be stored in the vector *x*.

The *print* procedure (Pascal Sample 7.5) prints a multiple-precision integer by finding its first nonzero digit and printing it together with all following digits. The variable *printed* becomes true when a digit has been printed, enabling *print* to sup-

---

PASCAL SAMPLE 7.5   The library *arith1* (*print* procedure)

```
procedure print( x : longInt );
    { prints the integer represented by x }
    { assumes base <= 10                  }
    var digit    : 0..lastDigit;
        printed : boolean;
    begin
        printed := false;
        for digit := lastDigit downto 1 do
            if printed or (x[digit] > 0) then
                begin
                    write(x[digit]:1);
                    printed := true
                end;
        write(x[0]:1)
    end;   { of print }
```

press zeroes until it prints a nonzero digit. It always prints the unit's digit in case the integer represented is 0.

If we want the *print* procedure to work for arithmetic to some base larger than 10, we must invent notations for digits beyond 9 and modify the invocations of *write* in *print* to generate these notations. (See Exercise 4 at the end of this section.)

Finally, the *multiply* procedure (Pascal Sample 7.6) is the most complicated procedure in *arith1*. Of the many ways that we can code this procedure, we choose the following. We multiply each digit of one factor in a product by each digit of the other factor and add the result to the appropriate digit in the product, propagating a carry to the left when necessary. Since the product of two n-digit integers can contain $2n$ digits, we must avoid exceeding the length of the vector that represents the result.

■ **PASCAL SAMPLE 7.6**   The library *arith1* (*multiply* procedure)

procedure *multiply*(*y, z* : *longInt*; **var** *x* : *longInt*);

{ sets *x* to the representation of the product of }
{ the integers represented by *y* and *z* }

var *xDigit*   : *posInt*;
    yDigit, zDigit : 0..*lastDigit*;
    overflow   : *boolean*;

procedure *incrementDigit*(*xDigit, increment* : *posInt*);

{ adds *increment* to *x*[*xDigit*], propagating a carry if }
{ necessary; makes *overflow* true if carry goes too far }

begin

    while (*increment* > 0) **and** (*xDigit* <= *lastDigit*) **do**
      begin
        increment := *increment* + *x*[*xDigit*];
        x[*xDigit*] := *increment* **mod** *base*;
        increment := *increment* **div** *base*;
        xDigit   := *xDigit* + 1
      end;
    if *increment* > 0 **then** *overflow* := *true*

end;   { of *incrementDigit* }

begin

    for *xDigit* := 0 **to** *lastDigit* **do** *x*[*xDigit*] := 0;
    overflow := *false*;

    for *yDigit* := 0 **to** *lastDigit* **do**
      for *zDigit* := 0 **to** *lastDigit* **do**
        incrementDigit(*yDigit* + *zDigit*, *y*[*yDigit*]*z[*zDigit*]);

    if *overflow* **then** *writeln*('Overflow in multiplication')

end;   { of *multiply* }

The procedures in *arith1* are far from the most efficient we can provide. For example, they must add 20 digits to add two integers and perform 20 × 20 multiplications to multiply two integers. This is clearly inefficient if the integers involved have only a few significant digits. More efficient procedures would keep track of how many significant digits there were in a vector representing an integer and use this information to cut down on the work needed to perform arithmetic operations. (See Exercise 14 at the end of this section.) More efficient procedures yet, such as we will develop in Section 13.1, would use only as much space as was required to hold the digits in the decimal representation for an integer.

The procedures in *arith1* are further limited by the fact that they perform only a few of the standard arithmetic operations—and these only on positive integers. Some of the following exercises call for constructing procedures to perform further operations, both on multiple-precision integers and on other types of numbers.

EXERCISES

1. Write a program that uses the procedures in *arith1* to compute multiple-precision factorials of integers supplied as input to the program. (*Hint:* Modify *fact1* or *fact2*.)

2. Modify the procedures in *arith1* to make more economical use of storage by performing arithmetic to the base 100 or 1000, thereby packing several digits of the representation for an integer into a single element of a vector. What changes must be made in the *print* procedure for it to produce the correct results?

3. Modify the procedures in *arith1* to perform arithmetic in the binary number system. Write a program that uses these procedures to convert a decimal number into binary.

4. Modify the *print* procedure in *arith1* to print representations for integers when the base of the representation is greater than 10. Use the lowercase letters a, ..., z to represent digits with values from 10 to 35.

5. Why does the definition of *multiply* declare *xDigit* to have the type *posInt* rather than 0..*lastDigit*?

6. Modify the *multiply* procedure in *arith1* to employ the following algorithm. For each digit in the product of two integers, find the pairs of digits in the integers that themselves contribute to that digit in the product, multiply these digits together, and add the results to produce the desired digit in the product together with a carry. Be careful to check for overflows. Try to perform as few multiplications as possible.

7. The *multiply* procedure in *arith1* performs n^2 multiplications of digits to multiply two *n*-digit integers. This is clearly wasteful if we want to compute, say, 10*x*.

   (a) Devise a way to compute 10*x*, where *x* is a multiple-precision integer, without using multiplications.

   (b) How can *multiply* be modified to be more efficient when *x* represents a number that contains a lot of zero digits?

8. Recode the multiplication procedure in *arith1* to multiply the integer represented by *y* by one digit of *z* at a time, summing the results using *add*. [*Hint:* Use a procedure

beginning with the header

> **procedure** *mult1*(*y* : *longInt*; *n* : *posInt*; **var** *x* : *longInt*);

that multiplies the integer represented by *y* by the single-precision integer *n* and places the result in *x*. Also use the result of Exercise 7(a).]

9. Write a more efficient version of *power1* based on the recursive method for computing integral powers described in Exercise 6, Section 4.6. Create a procedure beginning with the header

> **procedure** *power*(*y* : *longInt*; *n* : *posInt*; **var** *x* : *longInt*);

suitable for inclusion in *arith1* that raises the integer represented by *y* to the *n*th power and places the result in *x*.

10. Write a procedure *halve* beginning with the header

> **procedure** *halve*(*y* : *longInt*; **var** *x* : *longInt*);

that divides the multiple-precision integer represented by *y* by 2, discards the fractional part, if any, and places the result in *x*.

11. Write a function *compare* beginning with the header

> **function** *compare*(*x*, *y* : *longInt*) : *integer*;

with a value of 1 if the integer coded by *x* is greater than that coded by *y*, 0 if the integers are equal, and -1 if the integer coded by *x* is less than that coded by *y*. (*Hint:* How would you go about subtracting *y* from *x*, and what would happen if you did?)

12. Write a program that inputs an integer *n* and then uses the procedures in *arith1* together with *halve* and *compare* to compute the square root of 10^n to the nearest integer. (*Hint:* Use the method of bisection.)

13. Devise a procedure for inclusion in *arith1* that divides one multiple-precision integer by another, returning both the greatest integer in the quotient and a remainder.

14. The representations chosen for multiple-precision integers in this section lead to somewhat inefficient algorithms. Since we add leading zeroes to bring all representations up to the same length, we wind up performing many superfluous arithmetic operations involving those leading zeroes. Suppose, instead, that we represent a multiple-precision integer using the following declarations.

```
const base    = 10;        { base for arithmetic  }
      maxDigit = 19;        { max no. of digits − 1 }

type posInt = 0..maxint;
     longInt = record
                    digit     : array [0..maxDigit] of posInt;
                    lastDigit : 0..maxDigit
               end;
```

(a) Rewrite the procedures in *arith1* using this representation, performing as few arithmetic operations on digits as possible when adding or multiplying two multiple-precision integers.

(b) Convert the program *power1* to use the procedures you wrote for (a).

(c) What aspects of the design of *power1* made it easy to convert the program as required in (b)?

(d) What difference do your procedures make in the execution time of *power1*?

(e) What difference do your procedures make in the execution time of *power1* if *maxDigit* is 99 instead of 19?

15. Design representations and procedures for performing multiple-precision arithmetic on the following numeric data types:

(a) signed integers

(b) fixed-point real numbers (specify a maximum number of digits for the decimal part; do not keep trailing zeroes)

(c) floating-point real numbers (use multiple-precision for the significand and single-precision for the exponent)

16. Modify the program *calc2* to use multiple-precision arithmetic in carrying out its computations.

7.2 VARIABLE-LENGTH STRINGS

Many applications that involve strings require us to manipulate strings of different lengths. For example, we form the past tense of many verbs by adding the letters 'ed' to the end of a string. Some languages—Pascal among them—make it difficult to manipulate strings of different lengths by requiring that all strings assigned as values to a particular variable have the same length. Even though strings assigned as values to different variables may have different lengths, those assigned to a particular variable must have the same length. Such languages are said to support *fixed-length* strings.

The term "fixed-length string" is something of a misnomer. By definition, the length of every string is fixed to be the number of characters in that string. When we say that a language supports fixed-length strings, we really mean that it supports variables with values that are strings, but the strings associated with each such variable have a common fixed length.

When using fixed-length strings, we must know the length of each string in advance, and we must take care to assign only strings of the appropriate lengths to string variables. This is often a cumbersome task. But since Pascal supports fixed-length strings directly, it is tempting to get by with the tools described in Section 6.4 whenever we can.

Other languages allow us to assign strings of arbitrary lengths as values to a single string variable. Such languages are said to support *variable-length* strings. It is much more convenient to employ such strings in many applications; hence we provide a representation for variable-length strings using type definitions in Pascal and develop a set of procedures to manipulate these representations. In the course of developing this set of tools, we will learn a lot that is applicable to string processing in any language.

However, before getting involved with the details of processing variable-length strings in Pascal, we need to take a general look at strings as a data type and at several fundamental operations associated with strings. For the remainder of this section, when we talk about strings, we mean variable-length strings rather than the more restricted fixed-length strings supported by Pascal.

CHARACTERS AND STRINGS

Recall that a *string* is simply a sequence of characters. The *length* of a string is the number of characters in that string. We denote the length of a string s by $len(s)$.

A string that contains no characters (that is, the string ' ') is called a *null* or *zero-length* string. Just as the number zero plays an important role in numeric operations, so the null string plays an important role in string operations.

STRING EQUALITY AND ORDER

We have already defined two strings to be equal if they have the same length and contain identical sequences of characters. And we have defined one string to be "less than" another of the same length if, for some n, the first n characters in the two strings agree and the nth character in the first string collates before the nth character in the second. Now we extend this definition by removing the restriction that the two strings have the same length, and we define one string to precede another if the second string extends the first. Thus

'box' < 'boxes' < 'boy'

and the null string precedes any other string.

Although the order of the digits as single-character strings coincides with their order as numbers, we should note that the same is not true for numbers in general. For example, '10' < '2', since their first characters differ and 1 collates before 2.

SUBSTRINGS

Sometimes we want to take a string apart by extracting some of its characters. For example, to check for spelling mistakes in a sentence, we might extract individual words from that sentence and look them up in a dictionary. We say that one string is a *substring* or *segment* of another if it consists of a contiguous subsequence of characters from that other string. Thus 'abra', 'c', and 'dab' are substrings of 'abracadabra', but 'abcd' is not: its characters occur in order in the longer string but not contiguously.

We will use the notation $seg(s, i, j)$ to denote the segment of the string s that consists of those characters in s from character position i to character position j, inclusive. (We number character positions in a string from left to right, starting with 1.) For example, if s = 'income ', then $seg(s, 1, 2)$ = 'in' and $seg(s, 5, 7)$ = 'me '.

It is convenient for $seg(s, i, j)$ to make sense regardless of the values that i and j may have. Hence we employ special conventions when either i or j refers to a nonexistent character position. In such cases, $seg(s, i, j)$ contains the characters that exist in the string s, starting at character position i and continuing through character position j; if s has no characters in positions i through j, or if $j < i$, then $seg(s, i, j)$ is the null string. Thus, for example, if s = 'abcde', then $seg(s, 5, 10)$ = 'e' and $seg(s, 6, 10)$ = $seg(s, 2, 1)$ = ' '.

A common application illustrates the utility of these conventions. Whatever the value of i may be, $seg(s, 1, i - 1)$ contains those characters that occur before the ith character in s, and $seg(s, i + 1, len(s))$ contains those characters that occur after it. One or the other of these substrings may be null if i equals 1 or $len(s)$, but in neither case will the value of seg be undefined.

CONCATENATION

In addition to taking strings apart, we may want to put them back together. For example, we may want to reconstruct a sentence after correcting the spelling of individual words. The result of joining two strings is termed the *concatenation* of those strings. To *concatenate* two strings s and t is to join them or, equivalently, to append the characters in t to those in s. We use the notation $s \& t$ to denote the concatenation of s and t. For example, if s is 'in' and t is 'come ', then $s \& t$ is 'income ', while $t \& s$ is 'come in'.

STRINGS AS AN ABSTRACT DATA TYPE

The preceding terminology concerning strings is surprisingly powerful. Whether a programming language allows us to perform the fundamental operations of concatenation, substring extraction, and string comparison directly, or whether we must construct procedures that perform these operations, they form the basis for all string processing. In addition to these operations, we need facilities only for supplying strings as input to a program, for displaying them as output, for assigning them as values to variables, and for passing them to and from procedures and functions.

Since Pascal does not permit us to manipulate variable-length strings directly, we must provide our own tools for manipulating such strings in applications for which fixed-length strings will not work. Therefore we use type definitions in Pascal to define a representation for variable-length strings, and we develop a library *string-Subs3* of functions and procedures to manipulate these representations.

As we construct this library, we will be guided primarily by what we want to do rather than by how we might do it. For this reason the set of functions and procedures we choose is more important than the representation we choose for the strings themselves. Our library should enable us to deal with strings as an abstract data type, that is, in terms of the operations we can perform rather than in terms of the particular way we choose to represent strings.

The primary benefits of abstraction are clarity of purpose and clarity of programs. Our programs will be much clearer, and our efforts much simpler, if we separate the task of building good tools from the task of using them well. If we ever decide to change our representation for strings (say, for reasons of efficiency), successful use of abstraction would ensure that we need to change only the definitions of the procedures and functions in our library; we would not need to change the many programs that use these subprograms because those programs will continue to work as long as they make no direct reference to the underlying representation.

SPECIFYING OPERATIONS TO MANIPULATE STRINGS

To guide us in specifying the contents of our library, it is helpful to consider how we might solve a simple problem in string manipulation. Suppose we want to form the past tense of a verb by adding the letters 'ed' to the end of that verb. The solution would be as simple as the problem if we could write a statement such as

pastTense := *verb* & 'ed'

that concatenates the verb with the string 'ed'. Unfortunately, Pascal does not allow so simple a solution. Yet this "solution" does suggest tools for our library and typical uses for those tools.

Since Pascal does not provide a built-in function that concatenates strings, it is natural to attempt to define such a function ourselves and to recast our "solution" as a statement

pastTense := *concatenation*(*verb*, 'ed')

using that function. However, we cannot do this without knowing more than we presently know. Functions in Pascal cannot return composite data structures as values, and until we study pointers in Chapter 11 we have no way of returning a string as the value of a function. Hence we are forced at present to code concatenation as a procedure rather than as a function.

In order to code concatenation as a procedure, we must choose how to return a value from that procedure. One alternative is to define a procedure *concatenate* with three parameters that concatenates the values of the first two and assigns the result to the third, enabling us to write

concatenate(*verb*, 'ed', *pastTense*)

as our "solution." Another is to define a procedure *append* with two parameters that appends the value of the second to the first, enabling us to write

> *pastTense* := *verb*;
> *append*(*verb*, 'ed')

as our "solution." Which of these two alternatives we choose is largely a matter of convenience. We will use the second because it is easier to remember the roles of parameters when there are fewer of them.

Our "solution" is still not complete: the constant 'ed' in Pascal denotes a fixed-length string of length two, and we want the arguments of the procedure *append* to be variable-length strings. Since Pascal does not give us a way to construct constants for user-defined types, we must use constants for characters and define a procedure *appendChar* that tacks characters onto the end of a string one at a time. Then we can write

> *pastTense* := *verb*;
> *appendChar*(*verb*, 'e');
> *appendChar*(*verb*, 'd')

as the final solution to our problem.

It is worth emphasizing that this particular solution and the choice of this particular tool are less important than our approach to finding them. We started with a clear understanding of what we wanted to do; only then did we try to find a way to do it in Pascal. Such an approach is far better than fumbling around with the features of Pascal (or any other language) until we stumble across a combination that seems to do what we want. In short, we should shape the language to fit the task, not the task to fit the language.

PRIMITIVE TOOLS

The preceding problem, together with others like it, demonstrates that our library must contain tools that enable us to put characters into, and to take characters out of, strings. Four such primitive tools form a basis from which all other tools can be constructed:

appendChar(*a*, *c*)	appends the character *c* to the end of the string *a*
getChar(*a*, *n*)	returns the *n*th character in the string *a*
len(*a*)	returns the length of the string *a*, that is, the number of characters in *a*
nullify(*a*)	sets *a* to the null string

The operations *appendChar* and *getChar* enable us to put characters into a string and to take them out again. The operation *nullify* lets us construct a null string, to which we can append characters and thereby form other strings. The *len* function enables us to determine how many characters we may extract from a string.

FURTHER TOOLS

Any string operation can be constructed from these four primitive tools. Because strings are nothing more than sequences of characters these four tools, together with those tools that Pascal provides for manipulating characters, are sufficient to construct all others. For example, we can define a procedure *append* that appends one variable-length string, *t*, to another, *s*, in terms of these primitives. With the primitive tools *len*, *appendChar*, and *getChar*, we do not need to know anything about the representation of the data type *varyingString*.

```
procedure append( var s : varyingString;  t : varyingString );
    { appends the string t to the end of s }
    var i : integer;
    begin
        for i := 1 to len(t) do appendChar(s, getChar(t, i))
    end;
```

Even though these four primitive tools are enough, it is still worthwhile to include other tools, such as *append*, in our library. Some tasks simply require tools that are more powerful than a saw, a hammer, and some nails. We can define these more powerful tools in terms of the primitive four, but it is still worthwhile to define some of them directly in terms of the (still to be chosen) representation for strings. Some tools are used so often that it pays to define them in the most efficient manner possible.

Comments at the beginning of the library *stringSubs3* describe the tools we will provide to manipulate variable-length strings. (See Pascal Sample 7.7.)

REPRESENTATIONS FOR VARIABLE-LENGTH STRINGS

The descriptions of the tools in *stringSubs3* mention what these tools do, not how they are constructed. In particular, there is no mention of the underlying representation for strings. The definitions of the functions and procedures in *stringSubs3* will refer to this representation, and programs calling these procedures and functions must contain appropriate type declarations. But the choice of a representation is secondary to the choice of the tools and is of correspondingly less concern to someone who wants to use these tools.

When representing variable-length strings, we have several alternatives. One simple alternative is to represent variable-length strings as packed arrays of characters, as for fixed-length strings, but to mark the end of a string by a special character such as #. (See Exercise 15 at the end of this section.)

One advantage of this alternative is that we may compare string representations directly by using the relational operators provided by Pascal instead of having to define a special function *lessThan*. If the special character that marks the end of a string collates before all other characters, such comparisons even lead to correct conclusions in comparisons such as `'box'` < `'boxes'`, since this character would collate before the letter e. But, it is hard enough to find a special character that will

PASCAL SAMPLE 7.7   The library *stringSubs3* (header)

{ *stringSubs3*: subprograms to manipulate variable-length strings }

{ Procedures:		}
{		}
{	*append*(*a*, *b*)	appends the string *b* to the string *a* }
{	*appendChar*(*a*, *c*)	appends the character *c* to the string *a* }
{	*intRep*(*a*, *n*)	sets *a* to the decimal representation of the integer *n* }
{	*nullify*(*a*)	sets *a* to the null string }
{	*readLine*(*f*, *a*)	assigns the next line from the text file *f* to *a* }
{	*readString*(*f*, *a*)	assigns the next string from the text file *f* to *a* }
{	*replace*(*a*, *b*, *c*)	replaces all occurrences in *a* of the string *b* by the }
{		string *c* }
{	*skipBlanks*(*f*)	skips over blanks in text file *f* }
{	*substr*(*a*, *m*, *n*)	sets *a* to the substring of itself consisting of }
{		characters *m* through *n* }
{	*writeString*(*f*, *a*)	writes the string *a* to the text file *f* }
{	*writelnString*(*f*, *a*)	writes *a* followed by an end-of-line to *f* }

{ Functions:		}
{		}
{	*equal*(*a*, *b*)	*true* if *a* = *b*; *false* otherwise }
{	*getChar*(*a*, *n*)	the *n*th character in the string *a* }
{	*len*(*a*)	the length of the string *a* }
{	*lessThan*(*a*, *b*)	*true* if *a* < *b*; *false* otherwise }
{	*pos*(*a*, *b*)	the position of the first character of the first }
{		occurrence of the string *b* in the string *a* }
{		(0 if *b* does not occur in *a*) }

never appear in the strings we want to manipulate, let alone to find one that occurs first in all collating sequences. Hence, for generality, it is still desirable to define our own procedure *lessThan*.

A disadvantage of this first alternative is the expense of certain simple operations: in order to compute the length of a string we have to examine each character in that string. A second alternative allows us to construct more efficient tools. We choose to represent variable-length strings in Pascal by using records, keeping two quantities in each record: the length of the string and a packed array containing the characters in the string. These packed arrays all have the same length, and each reserves enough space to accommodate the longest string that will be manipulated by a program. As such, the representation is somewhat wasteful of storage. In Chapter 11, we will learn how to define another representation that makes more economical use of storage and does not impose any predetermined limit on the length of a string. The next few lines of *stringSubs3* describe our representation for variable-length strings. (See Pascal Sample 7.8.)

■ **PASCAL SAMPLE 7.8**   The library *stringSubs3* (conventions for use)

```
{      Any program calling one of the above procedures or functions must    }
{ contain the declarations                                                  }
{                                                                           }
{      const maxChars = . . . ;                                            }
{                                                                           }
{      type varyingString = record                                         }
{                                    length : integer;                     }
{                                    chars  : packed array [1..maxChars] of char }
{                           end;                                           }
{                                                                           }
{                                                                           }
{ Here maxChars is the maximum number of characters in a string.           }

{      The packed array is blank-filled even though the length of a string is }
{ recorded in its representation. Internally, this ensures that string equality }
{ can be detected by a comparison such as a = b.                           }
```

The remainder of *stringSubs3* is devoted to the definitions of the procedures and functions in that library. Within *stringSubs3* these definitions occur in alphabetical order within two groups: the definitions that refer directly to the representation appear first (*append, appendChar, equal, getChar, len, lessThan, nullify, pos,* and *substr*), and those that are independent of the representation appear last (*intRep, readLine, readString, replace, writeString,* and *writelnString*). This organization makes it easy to locate subprograms within *stringSubs3* and to maintain those subprograms. Let us now examine the definitions in *stringSubs3*, grouped according to their use.

DEFINITIONS OF PRIMITIVE OPERATIONS

The definition of the *len* function is the simplest in *stringSubs3*. (See Pascal Sample 7.9.) Since this definition is so short, why do we bother defining a function *len* at all? Why not just refer to *a.length* directly instead of computing *len(a)*? We define *len* to achieve our desired level of abstraction in dealing with strings. With this level

---

■ **PASCAL SAMPLE 7.9**   The library *stringSubs3* (*len* function)

```
function len( a : varyingString ) : integer;
    { returns the length of the string a }
begin
    len := a.length
end;   { of len }
```

PASCAL SAMPLE 7.10   The library *stringSubs3* (*nullify* procedure)

procedure *nullify*(**var** *a* : *varyingString*);

   { assigns the null string to *a* }

   var *i* : 1..*maxChars*;

   begin
      a.length := 0;
      { the next statement ensures that *a* = *b* will be *true* }
      { if *a* and *b* are both null strings   }
      for *i* := 1 **to** *maxChars* **do** *a.chars*[*i*] := ' '
   end;   { of *nullify* }

of abstraction, we do not need to know which functions are easy to compute and which are not. And with this level of abstraction we have the freedom to change the underlying representation for strings (for example, to one that does not use a record structure) without invalidating, or having to change, programs that require the length of a string.

The definition of the *nullify* procedure is almost as short. (See Pascal Sample 7.10.) In it we call attention to the purpose of a seemingly superfluous statement lest an overzealous programmer remove that statement in the interest of efficiency. Though comments at the beginning of *stringSubs3* have already alluded to this purpose, the comment in the definition of *nullify* pinpoints one statement that serves this purpose and, in so doing, provides valuable documentation for programmers who wish to modify *stringSubs3*. A similar comment in the definition of *substr* calls attention to another statement serving the same purpose.

The *appendChar* procedure and *getChar* function are also easy to define. (See Pascal Samples 7.11–7.13.) We have each definition report anomalous situations as errors: when necessary, *appendChar* invokes the procedure *overflow* to report that the length of the string is exceeded, and *getChar* reports that a nonexistent character

PASCAL SAMPLE 7.11   The library *stringSubs3* (*overflow* procedure)

procedure *overflow*;
   { procedure used locally to report overlength strings }
   begin
      writeln;
      writeln('String overflow -- excess ignored')
   end;   { of *overflow* }

PASCAL SAMPLE 7.12   The library *stringSubs3* (appendChar procedure)

procedure *appendChar*(**var** *a* : *varyingString*; *c* : *char*);
  { appends the single character *c* to the string *a* }
  begin
    if *a.length* = *maxChars* **then**
      overflow
    else
      begin
        a.length := *a.length* + 1;
        a.chars[*a.length*] := *c*
      end
  end;   { of *appendChar* }

is requested. Without these responses, programmers would have much greater difficulty in discovering and locating what are almost surely mistakes in their programs.

DEFINITIONS OF INPUT AND OUTPUT PROCEDURES

We define the input and output procedures *readLine*, *readString*, *writeString*, and *writelnString* in terms of the four primitive procedures *len*, *appendChar*, *getChar*, and *nullify* rather than directly in terms of the representation for strings. These input and output procedures are not invoked frequently enough for us to be concerned about efficiency. By referring to lower-level primitives rather than to the representation of variable-length strings, we reduce the number of definitions in *stringSubs3* that we must modify if we change the representation for strings.

PASCAL SAMPLE 7.13   The library *stringSubs3* (getChar procedure)

function *getChar*(*a* : *varyingString*; *n* : *integer*) : *char*;
  { returns the *n*th character in the string *a* }
  begin
    if (1 <= *n*) **and** (*n* <= *a.length*) **then**
      getChar := *a.chars*[*n*]
    else
      begin
        writeln;
        writeln('String index out of range');
        getChar := ' '
      end
  end;   { of *getChar* }

PASCAL SAMPLE 7.14 The library *stringSubs3* (input and output procedures)

procedure *readLine*(**var** *f* : *text*; **var** *a* : *varyingString*);
  { reads a line from a text file *f* and assigns it to *a* }
  var *c* : *char*;
  begin
      nullify(*a*);
      while not *eoln*(*f*) **and** (*len*(*a*) < *maxChars*) **do**
          begin
              read(*f,c*);
              appendChar(*a,c*)
          end;
      if not *eoln*(*f*) **then** *overflow*;
      readln(*f*)
  end; { of *readLine* }

procedure *writeString*(**var** *f* : *text*; *a* : *varyingString*);
  { writes *a* to *f* }
  var *i* : 1..*maxChars*;
  begin
      for *i* := 1 **to** *len*(*a*) **do** *write*(*f, getChar*(*a, i*))
  end; { of *writeString* }

procedure *writelnString*(**var** *f* : *text*; *a* : *varyingString*);
  { writes *a* followed by an end-of-line to *f* }
  begin
      writeString(*f, a*);
      writeln(*f*)
  end; { of *writelnString* }

The definitions of *writeString* and *writelnString* are straightforward. That of *readLine* generates a single overflow message when a line of input is too long for a string. (See Pascal Sample 7.14.)

The definition of *readString* in *stringSubs3* is similar to that for fixed-length strings in *stringSubs2*. We leave it to the exercises at the end of this section. (See Exercise 2 at the end of this section.)

DEFINITIONS OF STRING EQUALITY AND ORDER

Since we take care to blank fill the packed array in the representation of a string, we can determine whether two strings *a* and *b* with the same length are equal simply by evaluating the expression *a.chars* = *b.chars*. Without blank filling, a sequence of

---

PASCAL SAMPLE 7.15　The library *stringSubs3* (*equal* function)

function *equal*(*a*, *b* : *varyingString*) : *boolean*;
　{ returns *true* if *a* and *b* represent the same string }
　begin
　　equal := (*a.length* = *b.length*) **and** (*a.chars* = *b.chars*)
　end;　{ of *equal* }

---

statements such as

　nullify(*a*);
　nullify(*b*)

would produce strings that should be equal, but for which representations might differ if the former values of *a* and *b* differed. However, such details are best hidden within *stringSubs3*. Hence we include a function *equal* (Pascal Sample 7.15) in *stringSubs3* that we can invoke in order to determine whether two strings are in fact equal (and that enables us to represent strings differently, if we choose to do so).

The function *lessThan* determines which of two strings comes earlier in the order of all strings induced by the collating sequence for characters. It does this by finding the left-most point of difference between two strings and analyzing the cause of the difference. (See Pascal Sample 7.16.)

PASCAL SAMPLE 7.16　The library *stringSubs3* (*lessThan* function)

function *lessThan*(*a*, *b* : *varyingString*) : *boolean*;
　{ returns *true* if $a < b$ }
　var *same* : *boolean*;
　　i　　: *integer*;
　begin
　　same := *true*;
　　i := 1;
　　while (i <= *a.length*) **and** (i <= *b.length*) **and** *same* **do**
　　　if *a.chars*[*i*] = *b.chars*[*i*] **then**
　　　　i := *i* + 1
　　　else
　　　　same := *false*;
　　if *same* **then**　　{ one string is a substring of the other }
　　　lessThan := (*a.length* < *b.length*)
　　else　　　　　　{ strings differ first in *i*th character　　}
　　　lessThan := (*a.chars*[*i*] < *b.chars*[*i*])
　end;　{ of *lessThan* }

Although these definitions could rely on the *getChar* and *len* functions, they refer directly to the representation of strings, thereby avoiding expensive multiple invocations of these primitives. Such steps to improve efficiency are often warranted when we define procedures that will be invoked frequently.

DEFINITION OF CONCATENATION

Concatenation is another operation used frequently enough to warrant an efficient definition. The definition of *append* avoids the multiple invocations of *getChar* and *appendChar* that would result from our earlier definition of *append* in terms of these primitives. (See Pascal Sample 7.17.)

DEFINITIONS RELATED TO SUBSTRINGS

The *substr* procedure allows us to compute values of the *seg* function defined at the beginning of this section. In particular, the statements

$t := s$;
$substr(t, m, n)$

are equivalent to the pseudo-statement

$t := seg(s, m, n)$

that Pascal prevents us from writing because a string cannot be returned as the value of a function.

PASCAL SAMPLE 7.17 The library *stringSubs3* (*append* procedure)

procedure *append*(**var** a : *varyingString*; b : *varyingString*);
  { appends the string b to the string a }
  var *copyLen* : 0..*maxChars*;
    i : 1..*maxChars*;
  begin
      copyLen := *b.length*;
      if *a.length* + *copyLen* > *maxChars* **then**
        begin
            copyLen := *maxChars* − *a.length*;
            overflow
        end;
      for i := 1 **to** *copyLen* **do** *a.chars*[*a.length* + i] := *b.chars*[i];
      a.length := *a.length* + *copyLen*
  end; { of *append* }

Substring extraction, like concatenation, is performed frequently enough to warrant a direct definition in terms of the representation for strings. The definition of *substr* observes the conventions for treating out-of-range values for *m* and *n*, and it avoids extraneous copying when *m* = 1. (See Pascal Sample 7.18.)

The procedure *substr* enables us to extract a specified substring from a string *s*. But how can we find the substrings that we want to extract? For example, suppose that we want to extract the first word from the string *s*, that is, to extract all characters up to, but not including, the first space in *s*. How would we find that first space? Alternatively, suppose that we want to extract the first sentence from the string *s*, that is, to extract all characters up to the first period in *s* that is followed by two spaces. How would we find the end of that first sentence?

To find a specific sequence of characters in a string, we could employ a loop that checked, in turn, each character in the string until it found the specified sequence. Alternatively, we could employ a loop that extracted successive substrings of the string until the substring matched the specified sequence of characters. (See Exercise 4 at the end of this section.)

Locating substrings is such a common task that it pays to provide a function *pos* (Pascal Sample 7.19) tailor-made for this task: *pos(a, b)* is the position of the first character of the first occurrence of the string *b* in the string *a*, provided that *b* is a substring of *a*; if *b* is not a substring of *a*, then *pos(a, b)* is zero. For example, if *a* is

---

PASCAL SAMPLE 7.18   The library *stringSubs3* (*substr* procedure)

procedure *substr*(**var** *a* : *varyingString*; *m, n* : *integer*);

    { extracts the substring of *a* consisting of whatever }
    { characters occupy positions *m* through *n* in *a*   }

    var *oldLength* : 0..*maxChars*;
         i   : 1..*maxChars*;

   begin

      oldLength := *a.length*;
      if *m* < 1 **then** *m* := 1;
      if *n* > *a.length* **then** *n* := *a.length*;
      a.length := *n* − *m* + 1;
      if *a.length* < 0 **then** *a.length* := 0;

      if *m* > 1 **then** { move substring down }
         for *i* := 1 **to** *a.length* **do**
            a.chars[*i*] := *a.chars*[*i* + *m* − 1];

      { ensure that tests for equality work }

      for *i* := *a.length* + 1 **to** *oldLength* **do** *a.chars*[*i*] := ' '

   end; { of *substr* }

PASCAL SAMPLE 7.19   The library *stringSubs3* (*pos* function)

function *pos*(*a, b* : *varyingString*) : *integer*;
    { finds the first character of the first occurrence of *b* }
    { as a substring of *a*, returning its index if found and }
    { returning 0 if not   }
  var *match* : *boolean*;
        start   : 0..*maxChars*;

  procedure *compare*;
        { sets *match* true if *b* matches the substring of *a* }
        { that begins at character position *start*   }
    var *i* : *integer*;
    begin
        match := *true*;
        i := 1;
        while ($i <=$ *b.length*) **and** *match* **do**
            if *a.chars*[*start* + *i* − 1] = *b.chars*[*i*] **then**
                i := *i* + 1
            else
                match := *false*
    end; { of *compare* }

  begin
        match := *false*;
        start := 0;
        while (*start* + *b.length* $<=$ *a.length*) **and not** *match* **do**
            begin
                start := *start* + 1;
                compare
            end;
        if *match* **then** *pos* := *start* **else** *pos* := 0
  end; { of *pos* }

'abracadabra', then *pos*(*a*, 'ra') = 3 and *pos*(*a*, 'x') = 0. (Here we use notations—string constants of varying lengths as arguments to a function—that are not legal in standard Pascal but are legal in many dialects and the meaning of which is clear.)

    The *pos* function makes it easy to determine whether one string occurs as a substring of another. For example, if we want to know whether *s* contains the substring the, we could evaluate *pos*(*s*, 'the') and see whether it is nonzero. If we need more information—for example, whether the string *s* begins with the characters the—we could examine the value of *pos(s*, 'the') more closely. Note, however, that *pos*('whether', 'the') = 4, so that from *pos(s*, 'the') ≠ 0 we can conclude only that the is a substring of *s*, not that the word the occurs in the string *s*.

Using the *pos* function, we can easily extract those characters preceding the first space in a string *s*: if *space* = ' ', then the first space in *s* occurs in the position *pos(s, space)* and the statement *substr(s*, 1, *pos(s, space)*) − 1) extracts those characters that precede this space. However, we must be careful in identifying the substring extracted as the first word in *s*. If *s* begins with a space, this substring is the null string (no characters precede the first character in a string). Furthermore, if *s* does not contain a space, then *pos(s, space)* = 0, and this substring is also the null string. Exercise 8(d) at the end of this section asks for the construction of a procedure that correctly identifies and extracts the first word in a string.

Let us examine further the combined use of the *pos* function and *substr* procedure by looking at the definition of the procedure *replace* in *stringSubs3*. (See Pascal Sample 7.20.) This procedure finds all occurrences of the string *old* in the string *a*, replacing each occurrence of *old* by another string *new*. Such a procedure is useful if we want to correct spelling mistakes in a text: we could simply replace all occurrences of a misspelling such as misteak by the correct spelling mistake.

This definition uses the *pos* function to search the string *a* for all occurrences of the string *old*. Each time it finds an occurrence of *old*, it appends part of *a*—either

---

PASCAL SAMPLE 7.20   The library *stringSubs3* (replace function)

procedure *replace*(**var** *a* : *varyingString*; *old*, *new* : *varyingString*);
    { replaces all occurrences in *a* of the string *old* by the string *new* }
        var *p*   : *integer*;
            head : *varyingString*;
            result : *varyingString*;
    begin
        nullify(result);
        p := *pos(a, old)*;
        while *p* > 0 **do**
            begin
                head := *a*;
                substr(head, 1, *p* − 1);   { *head* = *seg(a*, 1, *p* − 1) }
                append(result, head);
                append(result, new);   { new *result* = *result* & *head* & *new* }
                substr(a, p + *len(old), len(a))*;   { new *a* = *seg(a, p* + *len(old), len(a))* }
                p := *pos(a, old)*
            end;
        append(result, a);
        a := *result*
    end;   { of *replace* }

from the first character of *a*, or from the first character after the last occurrence of *old*, and continuing up to the character before the occurrence of *old* just found—to the result being accumulated in *result*. Then it appends *new* to *result* in place of *old* and shortens *a* prior to searching the remainder for another occurrence of *old*. After the last occurrence of *old* has been found, the desired new value for *a* is the result that has been accumulated so far, extended by the characters that remain in *a*.

STRINGS AND NUMBERS

At times it is necessary to pass back and forth between numbers and their decimal representations. For this purpose we provide a procedure *intRep* in *stringSubs3* to generate a string that contains the decimal representation of an integer. Further such procedures are left to the exercises at the end of this section. [See Exercises 8(d), 8(e), 9(e), and 9(f) at the end of this section.]

The action performed by *intRep* is similar to that performed by the procedure *convert* encountered in our discussion of multiple-precision arithmetic in Section 7.1. That procedure generated the digits in the decimal representation for an integer, starting with the least significant digit, and placed these digits into an array representing a multiple-precision integer. The task of *intRep* is somewhat more complicated because we need to produce a string that starts with the most significant digit, not the least significant.

We could define *intRep* by generating the digits in a decimal representation from least significant to most significant, as in *convert*, and then reversing the order of these digits. (See Exercise 10 at the end of this section.) We choose instead to proceed more directly by employing recursion. (See Pascal Sample 7.21.) The definition of

---

■ **PASCAL SAMPLE 7.21**   The library *stringSubs3* (*intRep* procedure)

procedure *intRep*(**var** *a* : *varyingString*; *n* : *integer*);

    { sets *a* to the decimal representation of the integer *n* }

    begin

        { set leading digits and sign of integer }

        if *abs*(*n*) < 10 **then**   { no leading digit }

            begin

                nullify(*a*);

                if *n* < 0 **then** *appendChar*(*a*,'−');

            end

        else   { set leading digits }

            intRep(*a*, *n* **div** 10);

        { append final digit }

        appendChar(*a*, *chr*(*ord*('0')+*abs*(*n* **mod** 10)));

    end;   { of *intRep* }

intRep depends on the fact that the digits occupy consecutive positions, starting with *ord*('0'), in all collating sequences. This allows us to use the *chr* function to generate character representations for individual digits.

STRINGS AND RECURSION

Recursion and iteration provide complementary means for processing strings. Using iteration, we can proceed through a string, a character, or a substring at a time, processing those characters and substrings as we go. Using recursion, we can split a string into smaller pieces and process those pieces recursively.

For most of the definitions in *stringSubs3* we utilize iteration to process strings. For example, the definition of *replace* iteratively appends successive substrings of *a* to an initially empty string *result*, replacing each substring equal to *old* by one equal to *new*. If we had chosen to define this function recursively instead of iteratively, we could have reduced the task of replacing all occurrences of *old* in *a* by *new* (say, *n* occurrences) to the tasks of replacing the first occurrence directly and then replacing the remaining *n* − 1 by recursion. This approach leads to the following alternative definition of the function *replace*.

```
procedure replace( var a : varyingString; old, new : varyingString );
    { replaces all occurrences in a of the string old by the string new }
    var p    : integer;
        tail : varyingString;
    begin
        p := pos(a, old);
        if p > 0 then
            begin
                tail := a;
                substr(a, 1, p − 1);
                append(a, new);
                substr(tail, p + len(old), len(tail));
                replace(tail, old, new);
                append(a, tail)
            end
    end;   { of replace }
```

Here, as is typical in definitions by recursion, we perform a task directly in the simplest case and reduce the task to simpler instances of the same task in more complicated cases. We present this recursive definition of *replace* not because it represents any real improvement over the iterative version (it is somewhat shorter), but because it illustrates a different approach to the solution of a problem. This different approach helps considerably in situations such as the definition of *intRep*, where iterative approaches are not nearly as straightforward. (See Exercise 10 at the end of this section.)

Recursion also helps considerably in applications such as the following. In Section 4.6 we developed a program *sums1* that used recursion to compute the number of different ways to represent an integer n as the sum of a nonincreasing sequence of positive integers. We now modify that program to produce a program *sums2* (Pascal Sample 7.22) that displays the representations for n instead of counting them. The key to the modification is to pass an additional string parameter to the defined function *sums*. That parameter records an initial part of a representation for n, and the revised procedure *sums* completes that representation in all possible ways.

Exercise 19 at the end of this section asks you to produce the same results using iteration instead of recursion. The difficulty of that exercise provides a clear illustration of the power of recursion.

PASCAL SAMPLE 7.22   The program *sums2*

```
{ displays the different ways to represent an integer n as the }
{ sum of a nonincreasing sequence of positive integers       }
program sums2(input, output);

const maxChars = 100;

type varyingString = record
                        length : integer;
                        chars  : packed array [1..maxChars] of char
                     end;

var n : integer;
    s : varyingString;

#include 'stringSubs3';

procedure sums( partialSum : varyingString; n, m : integer );

   { displays partialSum extended by all ways to represent n as  }
   { a sum of a nonincreasing sequence of integers from 1 to m }

   var mRep : varyingString;

   begin
       if n = 0 then                               { display sum }
           writelnString(output, partialSum)
       else if (n > 0) and (m > 0) then            { extend sum }
           begin
               { generate sums without using m }
               sums( partialSum, n, m - 1 );
               { generate sums using m }
               if len( partialSum ) > 0 then appendChar( partialSum, '+' );
               intRep( mRep, m );
               append( partialSum, mRep );
               sums( partialSum, n - m, m )
           end
   end;  { of sums }
```

PASCAL SAMPLE 7.22   The program *sums2* (continued)

begin

    write('Enter an integer: ');

    read(n);

    writeln;

    nullify(s);

    sums(s, n, n)

end.

SAMPLE USE OF *sums2*:

```
Enter an integer: 4

1+1+1+1
2+1+1
2+2
3+1
4
```

EXERCISES

1. Define a procedure *deblank* to remove all blanks from a string. For example, if *s* has the value 'Watch this space.   ', then *deblank*(*s*) should change the value of *s* to 'Watchthisspace.'

2. Modify the definition of the procedure *readString* in *stringSubs2* to make it suitable for inclusion in *stringSubs3*.

3. Construct alternative definitions of the *lessThan* function and the *substr* procedure in *stringSubs3* using only the four primitive string operations. Do not refer directly to the representation employed for strings.

4. Construct alternative definitions of the *pos* function in *stringSubs3*

   (*a*) using the *len* and *getChar* functions alone; and

   (*b*) using the *len* function and the *substr* procedure.

5. Why is *i* declared to be of type *integer* rather than 1..*maxChars* in the definitions of *lessThan* and *pos*?

6. Verify the correctness of the definition of *lessThan* by constructing an invariant assertion for the **while** loop in that definition.

7. Analyze the complexity of computing the *pos* function as follows.

   (a) Show that the number of times a character from *a* is compared with a character from *b* in computing the value of *pos*(*a*, *b*) is bounded by *len*(*a*) times *len*(*b*).

   *(b)   Construct another definition for the *pos* function in which the number of comparisons performed is bounded by *len*(*a*) times the number of different characters in *b*.

8. Produce definitions, suitable for inclusion in *stringSubs3*, of the following functions.

(a) *rpos(a, b)*   the position of the first character of the last occurrence of *b* in *a* (0 if *b* is not a substring of *a*); for example, *rpos*('abracadabra', 'ab') is 8

(b) *findchar(a, b)*   the position of the first character in *a* that also occurs in *b* (0 if no character in *a* also occurs in *b*); for example, *findchar*('abracadabra', 'cd') is 5

(c) *misschar(a, b)*   the position of the first character in *a* that does not occur in *b* (0 if all characters in *a* also occur in *b*); for example, *misschar*('abracadabra', 'abc') is 3

(d) *intValue(a)*   the value of the integer represented by the string *a*

(e) *realValue(a)*   the value of the real number represented by the string *a*

(f) *dictLess(a, b)*   *true* if *a* < *b* in dictionary order (case distinctions and all characters other than digits should be ignored when comparing *a* and *b*)

9. Produce definitions, suitable for inclusion in *stringSubs3*, of the following procedures.

(a) *replicate(a, n)*   sets *a* to *n* copies of itself

(b) *reverse(a)*   reverses the order of the characters in *a*; for example, if *a* is 'abcd', then *reverse(a)* should set *a* to 'dcba'

(c) *code(a, b, c)*   replaces in *a* each character that occurs in *b* by the character in the corresponding position in *c*; for example, *code(a*, 'abc', 'ABC') capitalizes all lowercase a's, b's, and c's in *a*

(d) *nextword(a, b)*   finds the first word in the string *b*, assigns this word as the value of *a*, and removes it from the string *b* (define a word to be a string that contains at least one character, contains no spaces, and is separated from adjacent words by one or more spaces)

(e) *realRep(a, x)*   sets *a* to the floating-point representation for the real number *x* [that is, to the representation for *x* generated by the statement *write(x)*]

(f) *decRep(a, x, m, n)*   sets *a* to the decimal representation for the real number *x* generated by the statement *write(x:m:n)*

10. Provide iterative definitions of the procedure *intRep* in *stringSubs3* based upon the following ideas.

(a) Generate a string that contains the digits in the decimal representation of *n* from least significant to most significant, as in *convert* (Section 7.1), and then reverse the order of the digits.

(b) Compute the number of digits in the decimal representation of *n* before generating them.

(c) Define and use a function *prefixChar(a, c)* that inserts the character *c* in the string *a* before the first character of *a*.

11. Define a procedure suitable for inclusion in *arith1* that converts a string representing an integer into the multiple-precision vector representation for that integer.

12. Variable-length strings provide another representation for multiple-precision integers. Recode the subprograms in *arith1* to perform multiple-precision arithmetic on strings that contain decimal representations for integers. How do the recoded subprograms compare with the originals?

13. The *pos* function in *stringSubs3* enables us to locate patterns in a string, but it requires us to specify those patterns exactly. If we are unsure of one or more characters in the string, we need a more sophisticated algorithm for locating patterns.

   (a) Define a procedure *match* such that *match*(*a*, *b*, *c*) sets *c* to the left-most substring of *a* that matches the pattern specified by *b*; *match*(*a*, *b*, *c*) should set *c* to the null string if no substring matches the pattern. Letters, digits, and spaces in a pattern match the corresponding characters in the string. A question mark in a pattern is a "wild card" that matches any character. Thus the pattern a?a? matches the substrings acad and adab of abracadabra, and *match*('abracadabra', 'a?a?', *c*) should set *c* to acad.

   (b) Extend your solution of (a) to handle asterisks in patterns acting as wild cards that match any sequence of zero or more characters. Thus the pattern a∗a matches any string with at least two characters that begins and ends with an a, so that *match*('abracadabra', 'a∗a', *c*) should set *c* to abra, this being the left-most substring of abracadabra that begins and ends with an a.

14. Modify *stringSubs3* so that the representation for strings no longer fills the packed array with blanks. Which subprograms must be changed?

15. Recode the subprograms in *stringSubs3* to employ the alternative representation for variable-length strings mentioned in this section (that is, represent a string by a packed array of characters, as for a fixed-length string, but mark the end of the string by a special character, such as #).

16. Write a program to convert Roman numerals into Arabic numerals.

17. Write a program to convert Arabic numerals into Roman numerals.

18. Write a program to input the number *n* and solve the Tower of Hanoi problem for *n* discs, displaying the contents of the three needles after each move. (See Exercise 8, Section 4.6.)

19. Write a program to produce the same results as *sums2*, but without using recursion. [*Hint:* Modify your solution to Exercise 15, Section 6.3, by creating an array *reps* such that *reps*(*n*, *m*, *i*) is the *i*th representation of *n* as a sum of positive integers from 1 to *m*.]

20. Write a program that inputs a line of a Pascal program and prints a list of all the identifiers that occur in that line.

7.3   **TEXT EDITING**

We illustrate the utility of variable-length strings as an abstract data type by constructing two simple programs, a rudimentary *editor1* and an improved *editor2*, that edit arbitrary files of text. Our discussion will reveal the way that editors work and will

---

■ **PASCAL SAMPLE 7.23**   The program *editor1* (initial comments)

```
{ edits a file of text (preliminary and incomplete version)        }
{ The following commands are available to edit a file of text:     }
{ e                       exit from editor                         }
{ f filename              prepare to edit the named file           }
{ p                       print the contents of the file           }
{ r oldstring newstring   replace all occurrences of oldstring     }
{                         in the file by newstring                 }
{ s string                selectively print those lines in the     }
{                         file containing the string               }

{ Strings for the r and s commands should be enclosed within       }
{ apostrophes if they contain spaces or apostrophes; apostrophes   }
{ in such strings should be doubled. Thus                          }
{     r ab c              replaces every 'ab' by 'c'               }
{     r 'ab c' d          replaces every 'ab c' by 'd'            }
{     r '''' ''           deletes every apostrophe                 }
{ The user will be prompted for any missing information.           }
```

provide another example of the organization and development of large programs in a top-down fashion.

In order to clarify what we eventually want *editor2* to do, we first write comments (Pascal Sample 7.23) to describe its capabilities. By placing these comments at the beginning of *editor1*, we create a handy checklist of work to be done while we are building and improving that program; and after *editor2* has been finished, the comments constitute a handy reminder of what the program does.

As the comments show, we want our editor to be *command driven*, that is, to accept directions from the user. In general, command-driven programs are easier to use than programs that ask a barrage of questions such as

```
What file do you wish to edit?
Do you wish to list the file?
Do you wish to change the file?
```

in some fixed and predetermined order.

We proceed to build our editor in a top-down manner, writing the main program for *editor1* before writing any subsidiary procedures. The main program will convey the general nature of *editor1*—a command-driven program to edit files—and it will identify procedures that carry out the necessary work. But it will do little else. Using a simple main program, we can add the procedures to do the real work one at a time. By testing these additions as we go, we can always be sure of where we stand.

A first try at the main program for an editor is displayed as Pascal Sample 7.24. That program responds to only three of the five commands, largely using tools we have already created to decipher and carry out these commands. The two other commands are named, but the program does not yet respond to those commands.

PASCAL SAMPLE 7.24 The program *editor1* (main program)

```
program editor1(input, output, textfile);
const maxChars = 200;                    { limit on length of a line of text }
type varyingString = record
                        length : integer;
                        chars  : packed array [1..maxChars] of char
                     end;
var textfile  : text;                    { file to edit          }
    command : char;                      { editing command      }
    pattern   : varyingString;           { string to match      }
#include 'stringSubs3';          { string manipulation procedures }
#include 'appendToFile';         { file manipulation procedure    }
{ declaration for selectLines goes here }
begin
    repeat
        writeln;
        write('Command: ');
        read(command);
        case command of
        'e' : writeln('bye');
        'f' : writeln('Not implemented');
        'p' : appendToFile(output, textfile);
        'r' : writeln('Not implemented');
        's' : begin
                  readString(input, pattern);
                  selectLines(textfile, pattern)
              end
        end;
        readln
    until command = 'e'
end.  { of editor1 }
```

We must and will improve upon this main program, enabling it to respond to all five commands and making several other minor improvements. For example, we will have it print an informative error message when a user enters an unrecognizable command. We could make other improvements as well, all of which would make our use of the editor easier. We could recognize an additional command such as '?', responding with a summary of the legal commands. Or we could enable users to supply commands piece by piece, prompting them for each missing piece. Such aids are particularly helpful for new users, who may have trouble remembering the cryptic commands that the editor understands.

Attractive as these improvements may be, we should not get sidetracked into making them now. Our first priority is to get *editor1* to work. Getting it to work better can come later. Writing large programs is easier if we have an early working prototype. Although a main program that accepts a lot of intricate commands could be construed as a working prototype, it wouldn't be a very useful one if it couldn't carry out any of those commands. Hence we will defer working on bells and whistles until we have put more of the basic structure in place.

With the *appendToFile* procedure, *editor1* can easily respond to the p command: it displays the contents of the file *textfile* by appending it to the file *output*. By implementing the p command first, we can determine whether the other commands work when we get to them by noting the effect they have on the file. Again, we resist the temptation to indulge prematurely in refinements such as enhancing the p command so that it can display selected lines in a file (say, the last line alone or the tenth through twentieth lines).

To display only those lines in *textfile* that contain a specified string requires more work. We can use the procedure *readString* in *stringSubs3* (Exercise 2, Section 7.2) to get this string, but the task of finding this string in *textfile* is best farmed out to a subsidiary procedure *selectLines*. Fortunately, the tools in *stringSubs3* make it easy for us to write that procedure: we can retrieve lines from a text file one at a time using the procedure *readLine*, determine which lines contain the specified string using the *pos* function, and display those lines using the procedure *writelnString*. (See Pascal Sample 7.25.) Thus we are amply repaid for the time we invested in developing a good set of tools.

We could enhance the s command in several ways. We could provide an option for finding only the first occurrence of the string, we could search only a specified range of lines in the file for the string, or we could search for strings that match some sort of pattern. But once again, we simply note what we could do and refrain from doing it just yet.

PASCAL SAMPLE 7.25 The program *editor1* (*selectLines* procedure)

```
procedure selectLines( var f : text; s : varyingString );
    { displays all lines in the file f containing the string s }
    var line : varyingString;
    begin
        reset(f);
        while not eof(f) do
            begin
                readLine(f, line);
                if pos(line, s) > 0 then writelnString(output, line)
            end
    end; { of selectLines }
```

■ **PASCAL SAMPLE 7.26**   The program *editor1* (sample use)

```
Command? p
"The time has come," the Walrus said,
    "To talk of many things:
Of shoes -- and ships -- and sealing wax --
    Of cabbages -- and kings --
And why the sea is boiling hot --
    And whether pigs have wings."

Command? s wax
Of shoes -- and ships -- and sealing wax --

Command? s the
"The time has come," the Walrus said,
And why the sea is boiling hot --
    And whether pigs have wings."

Command? s abracadabra

Command? e
bye
```

The first draft of *editor1* is now complete. Much more work must be done to turn *editor1* into a truly useful editor, but we at least have a prototype editor at hand—one that we can test, use to gain experience with editors, and refine a little at a time. Pascal Sample 7.26 illustrates the use of *editor1* to manipulate a short file of text.

This session with *editor1* brings to light two aspects of the *selectLines* procedure. First, the *pos* function, and hence the *selectLines* procedure, searches for strings as opposed to words; as a result, it finds the string the in the middle of the word whether. And second, when the *selectLines* procedure does not find the specified string, it does not print anything. If we are unhappy with this result, we should make a note to modify *selectLines*; otherwise we should leave it alone.

Having produced *editor1* as a prototype editor and having noted where improvements can be made, we are now in a position to refine that prototype. We do so by transforming it piece by piece into a program *editor2*, making improvements as we go. We do not attempt to make all the improvements possible because that would bog us down in too many details at once.

The main program in *editor2*, displayed as Pascal Samples 7.27 and 7.28, differs from that in *editor1* in four respects: (1) it uses a new procedure *getString* instead of *readString* to obtain strings from users, with *getString* reminding the users to supply the required strings if they haven't already; (2) it responds to the f command, allowing users to select the files they want to edit, using the enhanced version of the *reset* procedure described in Section 6.6; (3) it calls a new procedure *changeLines* in response to the r command; and (4) it prints an informative error message in case the user enters an illegal command. By putting off details about how *getString* and *changeLines* will operate to subsidiary procedures, we can concentrate first on the overall structure of the program.

The program *editor2* invokes the same procedures that *editor1* does to display a file or to display selected lines in a file. Since these procedures work reasonably well in *editor1*, we choose not to tamper with them as we attend to other details. Before tackling the new features of *editor2*, we write skeleton declarations for the

---

PASCAL SAMPLE 7.27   The program *editor2* (initial comments and declarations)

```
{ edits a file of text (improved version) }
{ The following commands are available to edit a file of text:    }
{ e                           exit from editor                    }
{ f  filename                 prepare to edit the named file       }
{ p                           print the contents of the file       }
{ r  oldstring newstring      replace all occurrences of oldstring }
{                             in the file by newstring             }
{ s  string                   selectively print those lines in the }
{                             file containing the string           }

{ Strings for the r and s commands should be enclosed within  }
{ apostrophes if they contain spaces or apostrophes; apostrophes }
{ in such strings should be doubled. Thus                      }
{     r  ab c                 replaces every 'ab' by 'c'         }
{     r 'ab c' d              replaces every 'ab c' by 'd'       }
{     r '''' ''               deletes every apostrophe           }
{ The user will be prompted for any missing information.       }

program editor2(input, output, textfile);

const maxChars = 200;                  { limit on length of a line of text }

type varyingString = record
                        length : integer;
                        chars  : packed array [1..maxChars] of char
                     end;
     message      = packed array [1..messageLength] of char

var textfile    : text;             { file to edit           }
    filename    : varyingString;    { its name               }
    command : char;                 { editing command        }
    pattern     : varyingString;    { string to match        }
    newString : varyingString;      { its replacement        }

#include 'stringSubs3';    { string manipulation procedures }
#include 'appendToFile';   { file manipulation procedure    }

{ declarations for changeLines, getString, and selectLines go here }
```

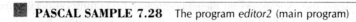

PASCAL SAMPLE 7.28   The program *editor2* (main program)

```
begin
  repeat
    writeln;
    write('Command: ');
    skipBlanks(input);
    read(command);
    if command in ['e', 'f', 'p', 'r', 's'] then
      case command of
        'e' : writeln('bye');
        'f' : begin
                getString('Which file: ', filename);
                reset(textfile, filename.chars)
              end;
        'p' : appendToFile(output, textfile);
        'r' : begin
                getString('Old string: ', pattern);
                getString('New string: ', newString);
                changeLines(textfile, pattern, newString)
              end;
        's' : begin
                getString('Search for: ', pattern);
                selectLines(textfile, pattern)
              end
      end
    else
      begin
        writeln('Unrecognizable command. Legal commands are: ');
        writeln('e(xit), f(ile), p(rint), r(eplace), s(earch)')
      end;
    readln
  until command = 'e'
end.   { of editor2 }
```

two new procedures *getString* and *changeLines*. With these declarations, displayed as Pascal Sample 7.29, *editor2* becomes a working program—one that we can test and refine, a procedure at a time.

Let us tackle the *changeLines* procedure first. This procedure must replace all occurrences of one string in the file *f* by another string. Since files in Pascal are sequential, we must copy the entire file twice to change it: once to make the changes, and a second time to return the changes to the original file. A file variable *temp* local to *changeLines* provides scratch space for making the changes. This file is created upon invocation of *changeLines* and disappears upon exit. In the first half of *changeLines*,

---

PASCAL SAMPLE 7.29   The program *editor2* (skeleton procedure declarations)

procedure *getString*(*m* : *message*; **var** *s* : *varyingString*);
  { gets a string from the user, prompting with the message *m* }
  { when no input remains on the current line of input   }
  begin
      readString(*input*, *s*)   { skip message for now }
  end; { of *getString* }

procedure *changeLines*(**var** *f* : *text*; *old*, *new* : *varyingString*);
  { replaces all occurrences of the string *old* by the string *new* }
  { in the file *f*   }
  begin
      writeln('Not implemented yet')
  end; { of *changeLines* }

we retrieve lines from *f* one at a time using *readLine*, make the necessary replacements of one string by another string using the procedure *replace* in *stringSubs3*, and write the modified line into *temp*. Then we copy the modifications stored in *temp* back into *f* using *appendToFile*. (See Pascal Sample 7.30.)

PASCAL SAMPLE 7.30   The program *editor2* (*changeLines* procedure)

procedure *changeLines*(**var** *f* : *text*; *old*, *new* : *varyingString*);
  { replaces all occurrences of the string *old* by the string *new* }
  { in the file *f*   }

  var *line* : *varyingString*;
       temp : *text*;

  begin
      reset(*f*);
      rewrite(*temp*);
      while not *eof*(*f*) **do**
          begin
              readLine(*f*, *line*);
              replace(*line*, *old*, *new*);
              writelnString(*temp*, *line*)
          end;
      rewrite(*f*);
      appendToFile(*f*, *temp*)
  end; { of *changeLines* }

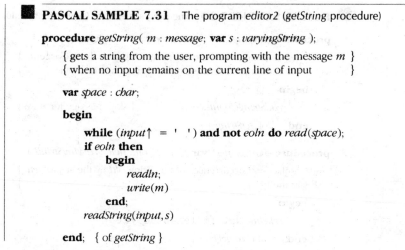

PASCAL SAMPLE 7.31   The program *editor2* (*getString* procedure)

procedure *getString*(*m* : *message*; **var** *s* : *varyingString*);
    { gets a string from the user, prompting with the message *m* }
    { when no input remains on the current line of input   }

    var *space* : *char*;

    begin
        while (*input*↑ = ' ') **and not** *eoln* **do** *read*(*space*);
        if *eoln* **then**
            begin
                readln;
                write(*m*)
            end;
        readString(*input*, *s*)
    end;   { of *getString* }

Finally we tackle the *getString* procedure. (See Pascal Sample 7.31.) If anything other than blanks remains on the line of input containing the command, then *getString* simply returns the next string on that line. Otherwise, it reminds the user of the additional input that is required before attempting to read a string. This simple strategy enables a single program to meet the needs of both novices and experts. Frequent users can circumvent a lot of questions by supplying all the necessary information with a command, whereas inexperienced users receive automatic guidance about what to do next.

EXERCISES

1. Make the following improvements in *editor2*.

  (a) Have *editor2* recognize commands in either lowercase or uppercase.

  (b) Have *editor2* recognize any abbreviation to one or more letters for the words `exit`, `file`, `print`, `replace`, and `select` as commands.

  (c) Add a `help` command to print the contents of a separate file of information describing how to use *editor2*.

  (d) Add a `delete` command that enables the user to delete specified lines from the file. For example, the command `delete 3` should delete the third line from the file, and the command `delete 10-20` should delete the tenth through twentieth lines.

  (e) Enhance the `print` command to enable the user to print specified lines in the file using the conventions just described for the `delete` command.

  (f) Enhance the `select` command to enable the user to locate strings that match specified patterns. (See Exercise 13, Section 7.2.)

(g) Add an `append` command that enables the user to append lines to the end of the file.

(h) Add an `insert` command that enables the user to insert additional lines before a specified line in the file.

(i) Design and implement additional enhancements to *editor2*.

2. Write a program to reformat and print lines of English text stored in a file. Each printed line should contain as many words as will fit within a 65-character limit. (A standard page is 8.5 inches wide and a standard terminal prints ten characters per horizontal inch; thus 65 characters can be printed on a page and still leave one-inch margins.) Words from the source text that will not fit on the current line of output should be printed on the next line. Lines of output that can accommodate more words should be filled with words from successive lines in the source text. Adjacent words in the output should be separated by a single space.

3. Enhance the program you wrote for Exercise 2 as follows.

   (a) Two spaces, rather than a single space, should separate the last word in a sentence from the first word in the next sentence. Assume that sentences in the source text always end with a period, question mark, or exclamation point and are followed by two spaces or the end of a line.

   (b) Stop filling lines of output with words from successive lines of the source text when you reach a blank line or a line beginning with a space. Treat a line beginning with a space as the first line in a new paragraph; preserve any spaces at the beginning of that line to indent the paragraph and begin filling once again. Preserve blank lines in the source text to separate paragraphs in the output.

   (c) Justify both the left and right margins of all lines of text except those that end paragraphs. Do this by inserting extra spaces as evenly as possible between words on each line except the last in a paragraph to align the last character of the line in the 65th character position.

4. Write a program to paginate a file of text as follows. The text should be typed on standard 8½ × 11-inch paper, with one-inch margins at the top and bottom. Since terminals print 6 lines per vertical inch, this means that a page can accommodate 54 lines. All pages except the first should have a page number centered in the second line of the bottom margin, that is, four lines above the bottom of the page. Your program should provide an option whereby it will either print a line of hyphens every 11 inches to indicate where a continuous role of paper should be cut into pages or merely space over perforations that occur every 11 inches in the paper.

5. Combine the programs you wrote for Exercises 3 and 4 into a single program that both paginates and formats a file of text. Do not print blank lines when they occur at the top of a page of output.

6. Enhance the program you wrote for Exercise 5 to recognize and process commands embedded in the input file. Any line of that file beginning with a period should be interpreted as containing a command. You should recognize the following commands.

   (a) `.page`
   The next line of output should occur at the top of a page. If the next line would already be at the top of a page, this command does nothing. (Note that two `.page` commands in a row will not leave a blank page.)

(b) `.center`
Center the next line of text.

(c) `.nofill`
Start copying input lines to the output, without changing their spacing or filling them (This command allows us to include such things as tables where spacing matters.)

(d) `.fill`
Undo a `.nofill` command and go back to filling lines normally.

7. Enhance the program you wrote for Exercise 5 or Exercise 6 to allow the user to specify the number of characters printed per line, the number of lines printed per page, and the size of the top and bottom margins.

8. Enhance the program you wrote for Exercise 7 to allow the user to specify that output is to occur in either one or two columns per page.

7.4   TOKENS AND SCANNERS

The program *calc2* in Chapter 5 simulated a pocket calculator with limited, but instructive, capabilities. It could evaluate a sequence of arithmetic operations. But it could evaluate only one such sequence, it was extremely sensitive to typing mistakes, it lacked a memory in which to store the results of intermediate computations, and it recognized neither parentheses nor the usual precedence of arithmetic operators.

In this section we will construct an improved version *calc3* of *calc2* that overcomes most of these limitations. In particular, *calc3* can evaluate several sequences of operations in a row, it can store the results of intermediate computations in a memory consisting of 26 single-character variables, and it can recall the values of these variables in later computations. Furthermore, it can recover from typing mistakes. Pascal Sample 7.32 shows an interaction with *calc3*, which prints the symbol > to prompt the user for a line of input and then evaluates the operations on that

---

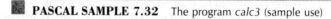

PASCAL SAMPLE 7.32   The program *calc3* (sample use)

```
> 1+2+3 @ a

> a*a + 1
37.00000

> 3a/2 - 4
    ↑
Need an operator here

> 3*a/2 - 4
5.00000

> ■
Done.
```

line from left to right. If a line of input ends with the symbol @ followed by a single-character variable, then *calc3* assigns the result of its calculation to that variable as its value; otherwise it prints the result.

Whenever *calc3* detects an error in the input, it prints an error message together with an indication of where the error occurred. In Chapter 13 we will enhance *calc3* a final time to recognize parentheses and the usual precedence of arithmetic operators.

The principal problems that we must solve in writing *calc3* involve the operands in input such as $x/2 + y - 1.5$, which can be either numbers or variables. Therefore we cannot use a single statement *read(operator, operand)* as we did in *calc2* to read a symbol that denotes an operator and a numeric value for the next operand. Before we can extract an operand from the input and get its value, we must determine whether it is a number or a variable. Furthermore, in order to issue our desired error messages, we must keep track of where symbols occur in a line of input. Hence we cannot use the *read* procedure to read numbers because it might consume unknown quantities of input; instead we must read everything a character at a time.

In order to solve these problems we design a procedure, known as a *scanner*, that extracts successive operators and operands from the input. Whereas *calc2* viewed its input as a sequence of numbers separated by operators, *calc3* views its input more generally as a sequence of abstract symbols, known as *tokens*, each of which is a sequence of characters. For our present application, a token can be a number, a variable, a symbol denoting an operation, or a mark such as end-of-line or end-of-file. For other applications, we might choose to define tokens differently; for example, a program that processed English text might recognize words, spaces, and punctuation marks as tokens. The job of a scanner is to deliver successive tokens from the input to a program without involving that program in processing individual characters.

In Pascal, it is natural to represent a token as a record. One component of the record identifies the kind of token it represents. Other components in the record identify the value of a numeric token or the name of a variable. The precise definition of a token for *calc3*, and how we choose to represent it, appears in Pascal Sample 7.33, which contains comments describing a library *scanner* that delivers tokens to *calc3*. This library, like those for multiple-precision integers or variable-length strings, requires certain type declarations that describe the objects it will manipulate. Unlike those earlier libraries, it also requires declarations for certain global variables. The procedures in this library must retain a small amount of information from one invocation to the next. In Pascal, global variables provide the least obtrusive place to store this information.

The library *scanner* is more general than we need right now because it also recognizes parentheses as tokens. But this generality will serve us well in Chapter 13 when we will use the same library to construct a more sophisticated calculator. We could, in fact, construct an even more general scanner: one that recognizes every kind of token that appears in a Pascal program (such as string constants and multi-

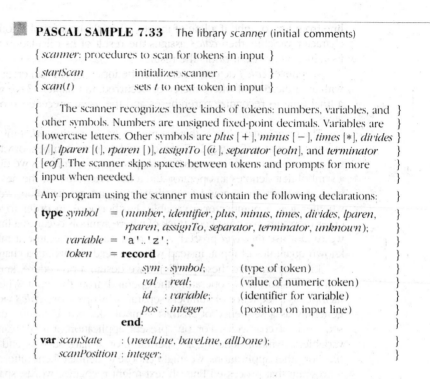

PASCAL SAMPLE 7.33   The library *scanner* (initial comments)

```
{ scanner: procedures to scan for tokens in input }
{ startScan            initializes scanner              }
{ scan(t)              sets t to next token in input }

{     The scanner recognizes three kinds of tokens: numbers, variables, and  }
{ other symbols. Numbers are unsigned fixed-point decimals. Variables are    }
{ lowercase letters. Other symbols are plus [ + ], minus [ − ], times [*], divides }
{ [/], lparen [(], rparen [)], assignTo [@], separator [eoln], and terminator }
{ [eof]. The scanner skips spaces between tokens and prompts for more         }
{ input when needed.                                                          }

{ Any program using the scanner must contain the following declarations:     }

{ type symbol   = (number, identifier, plus, minus, times, divides, lparen,   }
{                     rparen, assignTo, separator, terminator, unknown);       }
{      variable = 'a'..'z';                                                    }
{      token    = record                                                       }
{                    sym : symbol;        (type of token)                      }
{                    val : real;          (value of numeric token)             }
{                    id  : variable;      (identifier for variable)            }
{                    pos : integer        (position on input line)             }
{                 end;                                                         }
{ var scanState    : (needLine, haveLine, allDone);                           }
{     scanPosition : integer;                                                 }
```

character identifiers) and that can skip over comments as well as spaces. we have
allowed ourselves some leeway for such generality in the design of our scanner: by
using an enumerated type rather than a set of characters to represent the symbols
known to the scanner, we can treat keywords such as **not** and **mod**, or multicharacter
operators such as := and <>, as single symbols. We will leave the details of constructing more general scanners to the exercises at the end of this section.

AN IMPROVED POCKET CALCULATOR

Before discussing the details of our scanner, we will use it to construct the promised
enhancement *calc3* of *calc2*. Comments at the beginning of *calc3* describe the capabilities of that more sophisticated calculator. (See Pascal Sample 7.34.) Declarations
that follow these comments conform to the requirements of the library *scanner*. The
body of *calc3* is very short, delegating all its work to a subsidiary procedure, *calculate.*
Since *scanner* uses several global variables (which do not concern the rest of *calc3*),
we prefer to separate them from the variables required by *calc3* (which do not
concern the procedures in *scanner*). By hiding the latter variables in the procedure

PASCAL SAMPLE 7.34   The program *calc3* (main program)

{ simulates a pocket calculator with memory }

{   Calculations are specified on separate lines as sequences of decimal }
{ numbers, variables, and operators. Variables are lowercase letters. The }
{ operators on a line are evaluated from left to right, with each operator }
{ + − * / @ affecting the result *r* of the calculation as follows (here *x* is}
{ the number or variable that follows the operator):   }
{   + $r := r + x$ * $r := r * x$ }
{   − $r := r - x$ / $r := r / x$ }
{   @ $x := r$ (*x* must be a variable)   }
{ Spaces can occur anywhere other than within numbers. The value of   }
{ each calculation is printed unless the last operator on the line was @   }
{ The program recovers automatically from typing mistakes.   }

program *calc3*(*input*, *output*);

{ The following declarations are required by *scanner*. }

type *symbol*   = (*number*, *identifier*, *plus*, *minus*, *times*, *divides*, *lparen*,
                       rparen, *assignTo*, *separator*, *terminator*, *unknown*);
     variable = 'a'..'z';
     token   = **record**
                       sym : *symbol*;   { type of token   }
                       val : *real*;   { value of numeric token }
                       id   : *variable*;   { identifier for variable }
                       pos : *integer*   { position on input line }
                   end;

var *scanState*   : (*needLine*, *haveLine*, *allDone*);
     scanPosition : *integer*;

#include 'scanner';   { *startScan* and *scan* procedures }

{ The declaration for *calculate* goes here. }

begin
     startScan;
     calculate
end.

calculate, we avoid accidents or lapses of memory that sometimes occur when we have too many global variables.

As a guide to writing the *calculate* procedure, we redisplay *calc2* as Pascal Sample 7.35. The key statements that we must modify are identified by numbers in comments.

PASCAL SAMPLE 7.35   The program *calc2*

{ simulates a pocket calculator that evaluates, from left to right, an   }
{ expression on a single line consisting of numbers separated by   }
{ the operators +, −, *, /   }

program *calc2*(*input, output*);

var *result* : *real*;	{ result so far }	
operator : *char*;	{ next operation to perform }	{1}
operand : *real*;	{ operand for that operation }	{1}

#include `'skipSpaces'`;   {2}

begin

   write(`'Expression: '`);   {2}
   read(*result*);   {3}
   skipSpaces;   {2}
   while not *eoln* **do**   {3}
     begin
      read(*operator, operand*);   {4}
      case *operator* **of**   {5}
        `'+'` : *result* := *result* + *operand*;   {6}
        `'−'` : *result* := *result* − *operand*;
        `'*'` : *result* := *result* * *operand*;
        `'/'` : *result* := *result* / *operand*
     end;
     skipSpaces   {2}
   end;
   writeln;
   writeln(`'Result = '`, *result*:7:5)   {3}

end.

Now, to turn *calc2* into a definition of the *calculate* procedure in *calc3*, we make the following modifications.

1. We want to view the input to *calc3* more abstractly as a sequence of tokens, thereby allowing an operand to be either a number or a variable. Hence we declare *operator* and *operand* to be tokens rather than characters and real numbers.

2. The procedure *scan* will take care of prompting the user for input and of skipping spaces in the input. Hence we delete the invocations of *skipSpaces* and the statement *write*(`'Expression: '`).

3. So that we may perform several calculations in a row, we treat the end-of-line as an operator (called a *separator* by *scanner*) signalling the beginning of a new

calculation. We use the operand that follows this operator to initialize the variable *result*. Hence the statements that initialize and display *result* both move inside the loop. Furthermore, the loop is terminated by an appearance of an end-of-file (called a *terminator* by *scanner*) where we would ordinarily expect an operand, rather than an end-of-line where we would ordinarily expect an operator.

4. Since *operator* and *operand* are now tokens, we replace the invocation of *read* by invocations of *scan* to extract them from the input.

5. Since *operator* is now a token rather than a character, we change the labels in the **case** statement to the elements of the enumerated type *symbol*. Also, we add two new cases to correspond to the new operators *assignTo* (the symbol @ for assigning a value to a variable) and *separator* (an *eoln* for terminating one calculation and beginning another).

6. Finally, since *operand* is now a token, we define a function *value* to return the value of that token and use *value*(*operand*) instead of *operand* itself in carrying out a computation. We can easily find the value of a numeric token. In order to find the value of a variable, we maintain an array *memory* indexed by the variables a, ..., z themselves; thus *memory*['x'] contains the value of the variable x.

Pascal Sample 7.36 displays the results of these modifications in *calc2*.

This completes our initial development of *calc3*. Although *calc3* does much more than *calc2*, it is not that much more complicated a program. Its simplicity results from the fact that it does not get bogged down in reading its input character by character; instead, it utilizes the services of *scan* to read its input token by token.

PASCAL SAMPLE 7.36   The program *calc3* (*calculate* procedure)

procedure *calculate*;
    { performs calculations specified by the user }
        var *memory* : **array** [*variable*] **of** *real*;   { values of variables   }
            result   : *real*;   { result of computation   }
            lastOp   : *symbol*;   { pending operation   }
            operand : *token*;   { operand for the operation }
            operator : *token*;   { next operation   }

        function *value*(*t* : *token*) : *real*;
            { assumes: *t.sym* **in** [*number*, *identifier*] }
            { returns: numeric value of token *t*   }
        begin
            if *t.sym* = *number* **then**
                value := *t.val*
            else
                value := *memory*[*t.id*]
        end; { of *value* }

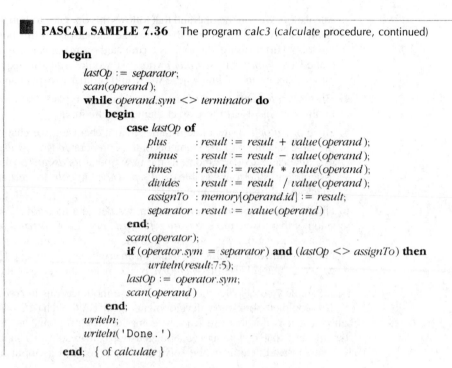

PASCAL SAMPLE 7.36 The program *calc3* (*calculate* procedure, continued)

```
begin
    lastOp := separator;
    scan(operand);
    while operand.sym <> terminator do
        begin
            case lastOp of
                plus      : result := result + value(operand);
                minus     : result := result − value(operand);
                times     : result := result * value(operand);
                divides   : result := result  / value(operand);
                assignTo  : memory[operand.id] := result;
                separator : result := value(operand)
            end;
            scan(operator);
            if (operator.sym = separator) and (lastOp <> assignTo) then
                writeln(result:7:5);
            lastOp := operator.sym;
            scan(operand)
        end;
    writeln;
    writeln('Done.')
end;   { of calculate }
```

Before we finish *calc3*, enabling it to recover from typing mistakes, we will write the procedure *scan* to extract these tokens from the input.

SCANNING FOR TOKENS

For guidance in constructing a token scanner, we consider methods for recognizing when an integer occurs next in the input and for reading that integer a character at a time. An integer occurs next if the next nonblank character in the input is a digit. Thus one way to proceed is to skip over blanks using a statement such as

```
repeat read(ch) until ch <> ' '
```

and then to examine the character *ch* to see whether it is a digit. If it is a digit, that is, if *ch* **in** ['0'..'9'], then the following loop finds the value of the integer beginning with that digit.

```
value := 0;
while ch in ['0'..'9'] do
    begin
        value := 10*value + ord(ch) − ord('0');
        read(ch)
    end
```

Significantly, we can detect the end of the integer only by reading one character too many. Furthermore, unless this character is a space, it will be the first character in the next token, and we will have to remember this character until we are ready to read that token. We could proceed along these lines and build a successful scanner by always reading one character ahead, retaining this extra character from one invocation of *scan* to the next. To do so would require us to declare *ch* as a global variable and to have the procedure *startScan* initialize *ch*.

In general, we use global variables reluctantly and sparingly. Poorly or overly used, they make a program unreliable and hard to understand: any subprogram can read or change their values, accidentally or intentionally, with or without a need or a right to do so. Parameters provide much more secure communication between one subprogram and another. But sometimes a subprogram, or a library of subprograms, needs to communicate some information to a later invocation of itself. Some languages provide a mechanism for doing this in a way that keeps this information hidden from all other subprograms. Unfortunately, Pascal does not. Therefore we resort to global variables to overcome this limitation in Pascal, preferring not to clutter up the parameter lists for our subprograms with information that no other subprogram needs to know.

In *scanner* we can avoid making *ch* a global variable by using the buffer variable *input*↑ to look ahead in the input. But we cannot avoid using global variables altogether. To keep track of where we are on a line of input, we must use a global variable *scanPosition* that retains its value from one invocation of *scan* to the next. Because of the peculiarities of reading input in Pascal, we must also use another global variable *scanState* to remember whether *scan* must prompt the user for a new line of input upon its next invocation.

When we have to use global variables, we should limit severely the number of subprograms that inspect those variables. We should limit even more severely the number of subprograms that can change their values. Things are less likely to go wrong, and are easier to fix if they do, if we assign responsibilities clearly and to as few subprograms as possible. In the case of *scanner*, we assign responsibility for maintaining *scanPosition* and *scanState* to a single subprogram *nextChar*, exhibited as Pascal Sample 7.37, which extracts the next character from the input and returns this character as its value.

The comments at the beginning of *scanner* do not advertise the existence of the *nextChar* function. This is appropriate because that function exists only to help *scan* do its job. In programs using *scanner* we should care about tokens and not about characters; any temptation to look at characters should lead us to redefine *token,* not to invoke *nextChar*.

The function *nextChar* helps us to construct *scan*. The design of that procedure is guided by a syntax diagram (Fig. 7.1), which specifies the syntax for the tokens recognized by *scan*. So far, we have used syntax diagrams to describe the construction of parts of a Pascal program. We now use them to design procedures that recognize those parts. Such a design is straightforward if, wherever we have a choice of arrows to follow in a syntax diagram, the next character in the input determines which route

---

■ **PASCAL SAMPLE 7.37**   The library *scanner* (*nextChar* procedure)

function *nextchar* : *char*;
    { returns: next character in line of input, space at end of line   }
    { affects: *scanPosition* = position of returned character   }
    {   *scanState* = *needLine* when new input line is needed   }
    {   = *haveLine* when more remains on current line }
    {   = *allDone* when *eof* has been detected   }
    var *ch* : *char*;
    begin
        if *scanState* = *needLine* **then** { prompt user for input }
            begin
                writeln;
                write(' > ');
                scanState := *haveLine*;
                scanPosition := 0
            end;
        if *eof* **then**
            scanState := *allDone*
        else
            begin
                if *eoln* **then** *scanState* := *needLine*;
                scanPosition := *scanPosition* + 1;
                read(*ch*);
                nextChar := *ch*
            end
    end;   { of *nextChar* }

we must take. In the procedure *scan* (Pascal Sample 7.38) we list the possible values for this character by using the notation that Pascal provides for sets of characters.

The procedure *scan* delegates the task of extracting the value of a number from the input to a function *nextNumber*. Another syntax diagram (Fig. 7.2), which de-

token

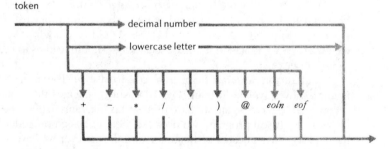

FIGURE 7.1 ■ Syntax diagram for tokens recognized by *scan*

PASCAL SAMPLE 7.38   The library *scanner* (*scan* procedure)

procedure *scan*(**var** *t* : *token*);
   { returns: *t* = next token in input }
  var *ch* : *char*;
  { declaration for *nextNumber* goes here }

begin
    repeat { skip spaces in line }
      ch := *nextChar*
    until (*ch* <> ' ') **or** (*scanState* <> *haveLine*);

    t.pos := *scanPosition*;
    if *scanState* = *allDone* **then**
      t.sym := *terminator*
    else if *ch* **in** ['0'..'9'] **then**
      begin
        t.sym := *number*;
        t.val := *nextNumber*(*ch*)
      end
    else if *ch* **in** ['a'..'z'] **then**
      begin
        t.sym := *identifier*;
        t.id := *ch*
      end
    else if *ch* **in** ['+', '−', '*', '/', '(', ')', '@', ' '] **then**
      case *ch* **of**
        '+' : *t.sym* := *plus*;   '(' : *t.sym* := *lparen*;
        '−' : *t.sym* := *minus*;   ')' : *t.sym* := *rparen*;
        '*' : *t.sym* := *times*;   '@' : *t.sym* := *assignTo*;
        '/' : *t.sym* := *divides*;   ' ' : *t.sym* := *separator*
      end
    else
      t.sym := *unknown*
  end; { of *scan* }

decimal number

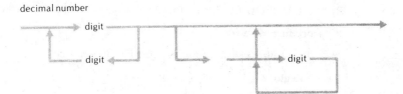

FIGURE 7.2 ■ Syntax diagram for decimal numbers recognized by *scan*

PASCAL SAMPLE 7.39   The library *scanner* (*nextNumber* function)

function *nextNumber*(*firstDigit* : *char*) : *real*;

    { returns the value of the number in the input beginning with *firstDigit* }

    var *value* : *real*;
        scale, i : *integer*;
        period : *char*;

    begin
        value := *ord*(*firstDigit*) − *ord*('0');
        while *input*↑ **in** ['0'..'9'] **do** { read integer part }
            value := 10*value* + *ord*(*nextChar*) − *ord*('0');
        if *input*↑ = '.' **then**
            begin
                read(*period*);
                scale := 0;
                while *input*↑ **in** ['0' '9'] **do** { read decimal part }
                    begin
                        value := 10*value* + *ord*(*nextChar*) − *ord*('0');
                        scale := *scale* + 1
                    end;
                for *i* := 1 **to** *scale* **do** *value* := *value*/10
            end;
        nextNumber := *value*
    end;   { of *nextNumber* }

scribes the decimal numbers recognized by *calc3*, underlies the definition of this function. Note that these numbers, unlike decimal constants in Pascal, do not need to have a digit after the decimal point. Thus, in *nextNumber*, a **while** loop picks off digits in the integer part of a number until none remains, and then an **if** statement picks off the decimal part if the next character is a period. (See Pascal Sample 7.39.)

    Finally, to round out the construction of *scanner*, we define a procedure, *startScan*, that initializes the global variable *scanState* used by *scan*. (See Pascal Sample 7.40.) With this procedure, programs such as *calc3* are not involved in the inner workings

---

PASCAL SAMPLE 7.40   The library *scanner* (*startScan* procedure)

procedure *startScan*;

    { initializes global variable associated with token scan }

    begin
        scanState := *needLine*
    end;   { of *startScan* }

of *scan*; by invoking *startScan*, however short it may be, they can take care of whatever initialization *scan* requires.

From a programmer's point of view, the most interesting thing about our scanner is how it transforms the input to a program into an abstract data type. By enabling us to pick off the successive components of an arithmetic expression one at a time, it helps us deal with that expression at a high level of abstraction.

HANDLING ERRORS

We conclude our development of *calc3* by providing a mechanism that handles typing mistakes. Since *calc3* expects a line of input to consist of a sequence of numbers and variables separated by operators, three types of errors can arise: (1) an operator may be missing, as in **3x** + **7** (*calc3* requires an explicit operator for multiplication); (2) an operand may be missing, as in **4** * **−3** (*calc3* does not recognize unary plus and minus signs); or (3) a variable may be missing, as in **1@2** (*calc3* requires that a variable follow the assignment operator **@**). In fact, if we choose to diagnose errors in terms of what *calc3* expects, rather than in terms of what the user intends (which may be hard to determine), these three types of errors cover all possibilities.

In order to avoid obscuring the design of *calc3* by the details of error recovery, we assign to a procedure, *error,* the tasks of printing an error message and deciding what to do next. We pass two parameters to *error*: (1) a member of an enumerated type, *errors* = (*needOperator, needValue, needVariable*), which describes the nature of the error; and (2) the token the evaluation of which produced the error. By passing this token to *error*, we enable it to report where the error occurred.

Pascal Sample 7.41 shows the final version of the *value* function from *calc3*. In this version we are more careful than in the last, making sure that the token *t* is a number or a variable before attempting to find its value. If *t* is some other token, *value* invokes *error* to report the problem.

Except for one detail, the *error* procedure and the rest of *calculate* would be easy to write. We can easily have *error* report the nature of an error. However, we

---

 PASCAL SAMPLE 7.41   The program *calc3* (*value* function, final version)

function *value*(*t* : *token*) : *real*;

   { returns numeric value of token *t* }

   begin
      if *t.sym* = *number* **then**
         value := *t.val*
      else if *t.sym* = *identifier* **then**
         value := *memory*[*t.id*]
      else
         error(*needValue, t*)
   end;   { of *value* }

must also have *error* take corrective action so that *calculate* can resume useful work. The difficulty lies not so much in·deciding what corrective action to take (such as discarding the rest of the line that contains the error), but in returning control properly from *error* to *calculate*. We cannot have *error* return control to *value* as if there had been no error. It should return control to the beginning of *calculate* so that we can start all over again with a new line of input.

But how do we get back to the beginning of the *calculate* procedure from within *error*? We could invoke *calculate* recursively, but that hardly seems appropriate since we do not wish to return to *error* when *calculate* terminates. We just want to go back and start over again.

For exceptional situations such as this, Pascal and other languages provide a statement known as the **goto** statement. Earlier programming languages, such as Fortran and Basic, had initial dialects that lacked adequate control structures for constructing conditionals and loops; they relied heavily on the **goto** statement to alter the usual sequential order of executing statements. However, programs in those languages were hard to read because there was no way to know where a **goto** statement might go. Now, good programmers reserve the use of the **goto** statement for those few exceptional situations in which it is nearly impossible to get cleanly to where they need to be. In this book, we use the **goto** statement only to recover from errors.

The definition of the *error* procedure displayed as Pascal Sample 7.42 illustrates how we use the **goto** statement. The statement **goto** 9999 at the end of the procedure overrides the normal execution of *calc3* by specifying that execution continue with the statement that bears the label 9999.

Now we can finish writing the final version of the *calculate* procedure. We declare 9999 as a label at the beginning of the procedure and attach it to the first

---

■ **PASCAL SAMPLE 7.42**   The program *calc3* (error procedure)

procedure *error*(*trouble* : *errors*; *t* : *token*);

    { prints a message indicating the location and nature of trouble }
    { detected upon processing the token *t*; then skips to the end   }
    { of the current line and resumes processing   }

    const *promptLength* = 2;   { length of '> ' }

    begin
        writeln(' ↑ ' : *promptLength* + *t.pos*);
        case *trouble* **of**
            needValue   : *writeln*('Need a value here');
            needOperator : *writeln*('Need an operator here');
            needVariable : *writeln*('Need a variable here')
        end;
        while not (*t.sym* **in** [*separator*, *terminator*]) **do** *scan*(*t*);
        goto 9999

    end; { of *error* }

statement in the procedure. We also insert two new conditional statements to detect missing operators and variables; in case of trouble, these statements simply invoke *error*, as in Pascal Sample 7.43. By holding such new statements to a minimum, and

---

PASCAL SAMPLE 7.43   The program *calc3* (*calculate* procedure, final version)

procedure *calculate*;

    { performs calculations specified by the user }

    label 9999;   { where to resume following an error }

    type *errors* = (*needOperator*, *needValue*, *needVariable*);

    var *memory* : **array** [*variable*] **of** *real*;   { values of variables   }
          result   : *real*;   { result of computation   }
          lastOp   : *symbol*;   { pending operation   }
          operand : *token*;   { operand for the operation }
          operator : *token*;   { next operation   }

    { The declarations for *error* and *value* go here. }

  begin

      9999: { resume processing here following an error }
      lastOp := *separator*;
      scan(*operand*);
      while *operand.sym* <> *terminator* **do**
        begin
          case *lastOp* **of**
            plus   : *result* := *result* + *value*(*operand*);
            minus   : *result* := *result* − *value*(*operand*);
            times   : *result* := *result* * *value*(*operand*);
            divides : *result* := *result* / *value*(*operand*);
            assignTo : **if** *operand.sym* = *identifier* **then**
                          memory[*operand.id*] := *result*
                else
                      error(*needVariable*, *operand*);
            separator : *result* := *value*(*operand*)
          end;
          scan(*operator*);
          if (*operator.sym* = *separator*) **and** (*lastOp* <> *assignTo*) **then**
            writeln(*result*:7:5);
          lastOp := *operator.sym*;
          if not (*lastOp* **in** [*plus*, *minus*, *times*, *divides*, *assignTo*, *separator*])
          then
            error(*needOperator*, *operator*);
          scan(*operand*)
        end;
      writeln;
      writeln('Done.')
  end; { of *calculate* }

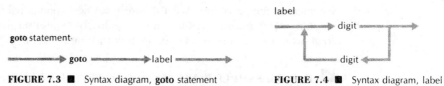

goto statement

FIGURE 7.3 ■ Syntax diagram, **goto** statement

FIGURE 7.4 ■ Syntax diagram, label

by refusing to distort the rest of *calculate*, we avoid obscuring the normal cases with the abnormal. Thus, by using the **goto** statement, we enable *calc3* to recover from errors without having to change the structure of that program dramatically.

THE GOTO STATEMENT

The rules for using **goto** statements in Pascal are fairly straightforward. The syntax diagrams in Figs. 7.3 and 7.4 show that a **goto** statement consists of the keyword **goto** followed by a label, which is a sequence of digits.

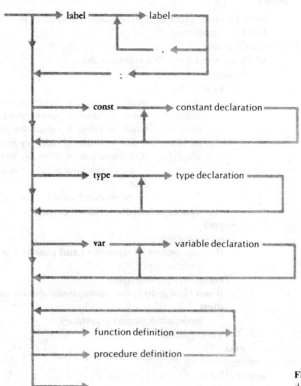

declaration section

FIGURE 7.5 ■ Syntax diagram, declaration section (final version)

compound statement

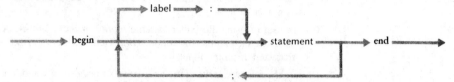

FIGURE 7.6 ■ Syntax diagram, compound statement (final version)

We must declare all labels used within a program or a subprogram at the beginning of the declaration section for that program or subprogram, as shown by Fig. 7.5.
Once we have declared a label, we can attach it to any statement in the body of a
compound statement. And we can go to that label from anywhere else within that
compound statement. (See Figure 7.6.) However, we cannot go to a label from outside
the compound statement in which it appears. (Pascal actually allows us to attach labels
to other statements, but doing so complicates the rules for using the **goto** statement
beyond all reason.)

EXERCISES

1. Modify *scan* so that it recognizes =: rather than @ as the assignment operator. In what
   ways does declaring the enumerated type *symbol* make this change easy? How could we
   make the change if we do not use an enumerated type?

2. Enhance *scan* so that it returns successive tokens occurring in a Pascal program, as follows.

   (a) Have *scan* recognize multicharacter identifiers rather than single character variables,
       returning the name of an identifier as a string of characters.

   (b) Have *scan* recognize string constants, returning the string denoted by a constant as
       a string of characters. (Be careful of double apostrophes in string constants.)

   (c) Have *scan* skip over comments just as it skips over spaces.

3. Enhance *calc3* to report the errors

   (a) division by zero; and

   (b) use of a variable in a calculation before the variable has a value.

4. Enhance *calc3* and *scanner* to recognize ** as the exponentiation operator.

5. Modify *calc3* and *scanner* to terminate a calculation with a semicolon rather than an end-
   of-line, thereby allowing several calculations per line or one calculation to extend over
   several lines. Discuss how the design of *calc3* and *scanner* help and/or hinder this modification.

6. Rewrite *scanner* using the following alternative strategies.

   (a) Instead of using the buffer variable *input↑* in *nextNumber*, use a global variable *ch*
       as suggested in this section to hold the next character in the input. Be careful at the
       end of a line, so that *calc3* still prints the result of a calculation before requesting a
       new line of input.

(b) Instead of reading input a character at a time, read it a line at a time. Use a string variable to remember the current line of input, and have *nextChar* extract characters from that string.

(c) Instead of using the buffer variable *input*↑ in *nextNumber*, devise a way to "push back" characters into the input. (*Hint:* Define a new abstract data type for reading characters from the input.)

7. Discuss the relative merits of the alternative strategies suggested in Exercise 6 for writing *scanner*. Discuss also the effect of these strategies on the design of *calc3*.

8. Rewrite *scanner* and *calc3* to represent a token by a record with a variant part.

9. Discuss the problems we encountered in modifying *calc3* to recover from errors. How difficult is it to make a program "idiot proof"? How much of *calc3* is devoted to handling the unexpected as opposed to the expected? How can we handle errors other than by resorting to the **goto** statement?

10. Design and write a scanner that returns successive words and punctuation marks occurring in English text supplied as input. Think carefully about what constitutes a word. Are short-lived and I've each one word or two?

11. Design and write a program that uses the scanner you constructed for Exercise 10 to count the number of words and sentences that occur in the input. Think carefully about how to detect the end of a sentence. Are the problems you encounter in doing this correctly handled better in the main program or in the definition of a token?

SUMMARY

The data types introduced in Chapter 5 and 6 are concrete data types with specific representations for objects and specific operations provided by a programming language. An abstract data type, by contrast, consists of object and operations specified by a programmer. Its operations are performed by functions and procedures that hide the details of the data type from the rest of a program. In particular, an abstract data type hides

▪ the specific representation of its objects,

▪ the details of how it performs its operations, and

▪ any data its procedures share and preserve from one invocation to another.

Examples of abstract data types and their applications include

▪ multiple-precision integers, which have

    1. objects that are integers with decimal representations containing at most some fixed number of digits,

    2. operations of :=, input, output, addition, and multiplication, and

    3. applications such as raising the integer 2 to a large power;

▪ variable-length strings, which have

    1. objects that are sequences of characters with varying lengths,

    2. operations of :=, input, output, concatenation, substring extraction, substring search, order relations, and length, and

      3. applications such as text editing; and

■ syntactic tokens, which have

      1. objects that are sequences of characters specified by certain simple syntax diagrams (for example, variables, constants, and operators),

      2. operations of := and reading and identifying a token, and

      3. applications such as simulating a multiple-function calculator with a memory.

In Pascal, abstract data types are best implemented as libraries of procedures and functions. A program that uses an abstract data type

■ supplies the constant, type, and shared variable declarations that the library requires;

■ declares variables ranging over objects in the data type to have the appropriate types; and

■ manipulates these variables only by invoking procedures and functions in the library.

With these conventions, programs achieve

■ clarity, by dealing with objects and operations on a conceptual level;

■ flexibility, by making it easy to provide more efficient implementations for data types;

■ uniformity, by using the same data types as other programs; and

■ reliability, by using thoroughly tested procedures to manipulate data.

GORITHMS AND DATA STRUCTURE

MS AND DATA STRUCTURES ALGO

RES ALGORITHMS AND DATA STR

ND DATA STRUCTURES ALGORITH

GORITHMS AND DATA STRUCTURE

MS AND DATA STRUCTURES ALGO

RES **ALGORITHMS AND DATA** STRU

ND DATA **STRUCTURES** ALGORITH

P   A   R   T

II

RCHING AND SORTING SEARCHIN
SORTING SEARCHING AND SORTIN
HING AND SORTING SEARCHING A
G SEARCHING AND SORTING SEA
ARCHING AND SORTING SEARCHIN
SORTING SEARCHING AND SORTI
HING AND SORTING SEARCHING A

G SEARCHING AND SORTING SEA

C H A P T E R

8

Computer programs cannot create information, but they can manipulate, transform, or rearrange information. They can even surprise us by presenting information in a new light or by extracting useful information from data we supply. Much of this book, in fact, concerns itself with algorithms that seem to produce new information, but which only help us to extract information from what we already know.

In the next chapter we will examine the connection between programs and information, and we will build a prototype information retrieval system. Such systems are important commercial applications of computing, and for that reason alone they merit examination. As important to us is the fact that the algorithms required for these systems are among the most useful and widely studied in computer science. By developing these algorithms and embedding them in a prototype system, we engage in a process that is itself a prototype of the general activity of algorithm development, analysis, and utilization.

In this chapter, we develop the algorithms needed for our study of information retrieval. First, we consider how we can organize information and how this affects our ability to retrieve specific items of information from a large collection. Then we learn how we can reorganize information in the light of what we've learned to present it in a different, more useful, or more logical order. As we will see, retrieving and reorganizing information can be a challenge when large quantities of it are involved, particularly if we are concerned with the efficiency of our algorithms. What at first appear to be routine problems lead to many interesting questions that will motivate much of our subsequent study.

Long before the advent of computers, human beings collected information. The U.S. census, the Library of Congress card catalog, the price and inventory list in a local supermarket, or this year's grade reports for students in a college are but a few examples of information that is collected for some specific purpose. We can extract two fundamentally different types of information from a collection of individual items of data. One type provides an aggregate or summary view of all the items in the collection; the other type, a detailed view of one particular item. For example, from the collections of data mentioned, we could extract the age distribution of the population of the United States or the ages of the members of your family, the total number of books in the Library of Congress or the call number of a particular book, the value of the current inventory of a supermarket or the cost of the items in your shopping cart, and the average grades given in all courses at your school or the grades you received in your courses.

The type of information that can be extracted from a collection of data, and to whom it can be provided, are decisions that must be made by those ultimately responsible for the data and its use. How that information can be extracted and provided are questions that involve algorithms.

When aggregate information is required, an entire collection of data must be processed. On the other hand, when individual information is required, it is not necessary to process the entire collection; instead we need to locate the desired information in, and extract it from, the collection. The process of locating particular information in a collection of data is known as *searching*.

Whether you have thought about it in these terms or not, you are already familiar with several different approaches to searching for information. The way you locate a telephone number in a telephone directory differs from the way you find the ace of spades in a newly shuffled deck of cards, and both differ from the way you look for the solution to a puzzle. As these examples show, the way we search for information depends on how that information is organized. Furthermore, by organizing information properly we can enhance greatly our ability to find what we seek. Just consider what it would be like to use a telephone directory that listed telephone numbers in the order in which they were assigned.

In a typical setting for conducting a search, we are presented with a list $a[1], \ldots,$ $a[n]$ of items of data and seek to determine whether a given item x occurs in this list. If x does occur in the list, then we may also want to identify where it occurs by producing an index i such that $x = a[i]$; such an index is useful if we want to modify the entry containing x in the list (say, to correct a misspelled name) or to access information (such as a telephone number) concerning x in a separate list $b[1], \ldots,$ $b[n]$ associated with the list $a[1], \ldots, a[n]$. In more elaborate settings, searches have the same characteristics as in this simple setting: they seek an item of data that has a particular property (say, a structure with a component equal to x) and, if successful, they return some information about that item (such as where it was found).

In this section we will concentrate on searching for items of data in collections organized as simple lists. We will see that different methods can be used, depending on whether the items in the lists occur in any particular order, as they do in a telephone directory, or whether they occur in no particular order, as they do in a shuffled deck of cards. In later chapters we will generalize these techniques to ones appropriate for more elaborate organizations of data and learn how these more elaborate organizations can be used to expedite certain searches.

THE LINEAR SEARCH

When we have to search a list in the absence of any information about the order of the items in that list, we have little recourse but to start at the beginning of the list and examine its entries one by one. A search conducted in this fashion is known as a *linear search* since it proceeds in a linear, or straight-line, manner through a list.

The exact details of a search procedure are of interest to us now as we implement and analyze various searching algorithms. However, they will be of considerably less interest to us when we use searching algorithms in larger programs; then we will be interested more in what a search does than in how it does it. Hence we will place searching algorithms in interchangeable libraries, *search0*, *search1*, . . . , coding them as procedures that we can invoke in a uniform manner by the statement $search(a, n, x, i)$ where

- a is a list containing n items of data;
- x is the item being sought; and
- i is an index to be set by the search procedure so that $x = a[i]$ if x is among $a[1], \ldots, a[n]$ and $i = 0$ otherwise.

Rather than to decide in advance whether we will use these procedures to search for integers, strings, or some other type of items, we will use type declarations in Pascal to defer this decision until we embed a search procedure in a program; that program must contain the declarations

```
const maxlen  = ... ;            { maximum length of list }
type  itemType = ... ;           { type of data in list        }
      index    = 0..maxlen;
      itemList = array [1..maxlen] of itemType;
```

to pin down the details.

A naive attempt to code a linear search in this manner results in a procedure that examines each item in the list a in succession, setting the value of i to an index for the item x if it finds x in a and setting the value of i to 0 if it never finds x. This version of the linear search is contained in the library *search0*, displayed as Pascal Sample 8.1.

The linear search performed by *search0* is clearly inefficient: it searches the entire list a, even if it finds the desired item x early in the list. Furthermore, since the parameter a is passed by value, an entire vector is copied each time we invoke *search*.

■ **PASCAL SAMPLE 8.1**   The library *search0* (inefficient linear search)

{ *search0*: linear search for x among $a[1], ..., a[n]$ }

{ assumes: $n <= maxlen$ }
{ returns: i such that $x = a[i]$ if x is among $a[1], ..., a[n]$ }
{ $i = 0$ otherwise   }

{ (inefficient version)   }

procedure *search*(a : *itemList*;   { list of items }
                                  n : *index*;   { length of list }
                                  x : *itemType*;   { item to find   }
                          var i : *index*);   { index of x }

       var j : *index*;   { auxiliary index }

       begin

              $i := 0$;
              for $j := 1$ **to** n **do if** $x = a[j]$ **then** $i := j$

       end;   { of *search* }

even though that vector is not changed by *search*. A more efficient version of the linear search passes the parameter a by reference and quits as soon as it finds the desired item. This version is contained in the library *search1*, displayed as Pascal Sample 8.2. A comment accompanying the declaration of a as a **var** parameter notes that we do not change its value.

■ **PASCAL SAMPLE 8.2**   The library *search1* (linear search)

{ *search1*: linear search for x among $a[1], ..., a[n]$ }

{ assumes: $n <= maxlen$ }
{ returns: i such that $x = a[i]$ if x is among $a[1], ..., a[n]$ }
{ $i = 0$ otherwise   }

procedure *search*(**var** a : *itemList*;   { list (unchanged) }
                                   n : *index*;   { length of list   }
                                   x : *itemType*;   { item to find   }
                          var i : *index*);   { index of x }

       var j : *index*;   { auxiliary index }

       begin

              $i := 0$;
              $j := 1$;
              while ($j <= n$) **and** ($i = 0$) **do**
                     if $x = a[j]$ **then**
                            $i := j$ { $x = a[i]$ }
                     else
                            $j := j + 1$ { $x <> a[1], ..., a[j-1]$ }

       end;   { of *search* }

When used repeatedly to find a large number of items distributed uniformly throughout a list, the *search* procedure in *search1* expends only half the effort as does the procedure in *search0*: on the average it will find an item roughly halfway through the list, enabling it to ignore the rest of the list.

A concern for efficiency can lead to many variations in the way we code a linear search. For example, we might be tempted to recode the body of the search as

```
i := 1;
while (i <= n) and (x <> a[i]) do i := i + 1;
if i > n then i := 0
```

In this variation we do away with the auxiliary variable *j*, thereby shortening the code, and we reduce from three to two the number of relations evaluated on each pass through the loop, thereby shortening the execution time of the procedure. Unfortunately this revision, while successful in some programming languages, leads to a subtle error in Pascal. If $n = maxlen$ and x is not in the list, then the final pass through the loop with $i = n$ will assign the value $maxlen + 1$ to i, violating the subrange type $0..maxlen$ of i. Amending the type of i to $0..maxlen + 1$ does not solve the problem, since the condition governing the loop will then be evaluated once more for $i = maxlen + 1$, violating the range $1..maxlen$ of subscripts for the list a. We could patch the variation still further, but further patches would sufficiently violate the specification for the linear search so as to raise doubts about the merits of the "improvement."

In languages where this revision works, subscript indices are simply integers and are not restricted to a subrange. Furthermore, the evaluation of logical expressions proceeds from left to right, stopping as soon as the truth or falsity of the expression can be determined. Thus, when $i = n + 1$, evaluation of the term $i <= n$ is sufficient to determine that the entire logical expression $(i <= n)$ and $(x <> a[i])$ is false, so that $x <> a[i]$ does not need to be evaluated and thereby cause a subscript error.

Given the problems with this particular variation of the linear search, it is wise to avoid it and use a safer version, such as that in *search1*. Another such variation, which is both safe and efficient, is motivated by a common application. Often when searching for an item in a list we want to add that item to the list if it is not already there; for instance, we could be compiling an index for a book and need to make new entries in the index, as well as to add new citations for old entries. It is for this reason that our search procedures seek x only among $a[1], \ldots, a[n]$ rather than among $a[1], \ldots, a[maxlen]$; the remaining items $a[n + 1], \ldots, a[maxlen]$ are reserved for future additions to the list. It is also for this reason that we are careful to have our search procedures work even if $n = 0$, so that adding the first item to a list does not have to be treated as a special case.

If we wish to add an item to a list when it is not already there, it helps to place a copy of that item at the end of the list before beginning the search. If we find the item where we placed it and not before, then we know that it was not already in the list, and we can make its addition permanent simply by increasing the length of the

---

PASCAL SAMPLE 8.3   The library *search2* (linear search with sentinel)

```
{ search2: linear search for x among a[1], ..., a[n] }
{          adds x to list if not there already      }

{ assumes:  n < maxlen                                       }
{ returns:  i such that x = a[i]                             }
{           n = old n + 1 if x not among a[1], ..., a[old n] }
{           a[old n + 1] = x                                 }
procedure search( var a : itemList;        { list of items  }
                  var n : index;           { length of list }
                      x : itemType;        { item to find   }
                  var i : index );         { index of x     }
   begin
       a[n + 1] := x;                      { place x at end }
       i := 1;                             { find first x   }
       while x <> a[i] do i := i + 1;
       if i > n then                       { keep x if new }
           if n + 1 < maxlen then
               n := n + 1
           else
               writeln('List full')
   end;   { of search }
```

list by one. On the other hand, if we find it earlier in the list, we do not need to retain the copy. This strategy has an additional benefit. Having placed the item at the end of the list, even if temporarily, we are sure to find it. Hence we can reduce to one the number of relations evaluated on each pass through the loop. The precondition for the procedure *search* in the library *search2* notes the price we pay for this gain in efficiency: we require $n < maxlen$ to ensure that there is room for the item being sought at the end of the list. (See Pascal Sample 8.3.)

The item placed at the end of the list in this version of the linear search is known as a *sentinel* because it guards against the loop being executed too many times. When they can be used, sentinels often provide a means to increase the efficiency of loops.

THE BINARY SEARCH

If the items in a list occur in ascending numeric or alphabetic order, a linear search of that list can stop as soon as it finds the desired item or as soon as it passes the last place the item could occur. This strategy results in a savings when the desired item is not in the list, as the search needs to examine only those items that would precede the item and not those that would follow it. However, another strategy leads to greater savings.

The *binary search* of an ordered list is based on a divide-and-conquer strategy and resembles the bisection method for finding a zero of a continuous function. In a binary search we compare the item being sought with the item midway through the list. If the two items are identical, then the search ends successfully. If the item being sought is less than the one in the middle, then we look further in the first half of the list; if it is greater, then we look further in the second half. The fact that the list is in ascending order guarantees that we can ignore the other half of the list. We continue in this manner, continually restricting our attention to smaller and smaller portions of the list, knowing that the item being sought cannot occur outside these portions. Eventually we will either find the item (for example, midway through a portion of the list that contains a single element) or reduce the size of the portion

---

PASCAL SAMPLE 8.4   The library *search3* (binary search)

```
{ search3: binary search for x among a[1], ..., a[n] }
{ assumes:  n <= maxlen                                      }
{           a[1] <= a[2] <= ... <= a[n]                       }
{ returns:  i such that x = a[i] if x is among a[1], ..., a[n] }
{           i = 0 otherwise                                    }

procedure search(var a : itemList;      { list (unchanged) }
                     n : index;·         { length of list   }
                     x : itemType;       { item to find     }
                 var i : index );        { index of x       }

    var first, last : index;            { bounds for search }
        middle  : index;                { halfway point     }

    begin
        i := 0;                          { x not found yet   }
        first := 1;                      { search whole list }
        last := n;

        while ( first <= last) and (i = 0) do
            begin
                { Now x <> a[j] if j < first or last < j.        }
                { Hence we seek x among a[first], . . ., a[last]. }

                middle := ( first + last) div 2;
                if x = a[middle] then
                    i := middle                      { x = a[i] }
                else if x < a[middle] then
                    last := middle - 1
                else
                    first := middle + 1
            end
    end;   { of search }
```

in which it can occur to zero, in which case we can conclude that the item was not in the list.

This description of the binary search appears to call for recursion, but we can define it easily using iteration. The library *search3*, displayed as Pascal Sample 8.4, contains such a definition. The assertion in the comment at the beginning of the loop in that definition clarifies the progress that the binary search has made toward finding the desired item *x*.

EXERCISES

1. Describe in detail how you would search for
    (a) someone's telephone number;
    (b) the name of the person with a given telephone number;
    (c) a book in the library, by title;
    (d) a book you once came across in the library having something to do with algorithms and written by someone whose last name begins with the letter K;
    (e) a book you once came across in the library having something to do with numerical computations and bound in a red cover;
    (f) the longest book in the library;
    (g) the most recent book on data structures in the library;
    (h) the telephone number of the author of that book;
    (i) the annual income of the author of that book;
    (j) the religion of the author of that book; and
    (k) a two bedroom apartment in a convenient location, at a price you can afford.

2. Which of the above searches are easy to perform and which are difficult? Why?

3. How could information be organized to simplify the more difficult of these searches? What factors govern whether information should be organized in that fashion?

4. Modify the linear search so that it searches backward rather than forward through the list. How does this modification shorten the code?

5. Show that the linear search procedures presented in this section work even when $n = 0$.

6. Under what conditions does the following version of the linear search perform correctly?

    ```
    i := 1;
    while (i < n) and (x <> a[i]) do i := i + 1;
    if x <> a[i] then i := 0
    ```

7. Modify the linear search so that it places a sentinel in $a[0]$ and searches backward through the list. What are the advantages and disadvantages of this modification?

8. In a *self-organizing* search, items that are accessed frequently migrate to locations where they can be found quickly. Construct a self-organizing linear search in which items are moved forward one position in the list each time they are found.

9. Recode the binary search using a recursive subprocedure *bsearch* such that *bsearch*(*a, first, last, x, i*) searches for *x* in the ordered list *a*[*first*], ..., *a*[*last*], returning an index *i* such that *x* = *a*[*i*] if it finds *x* and *i* = 0 otherwise.

10. How does the binary search behave when given

    (a) an empty list?

    (b) an unordered list?

    (c) a list containing duplicate items?

11. Recode the binary search to return an index *i* such that *x* = *a*[*i*] if *x* is in the list and such that *a*[*i*] is the largest item less than *x* in the list otherwise.

12. Which of the following variants of the binary search behave correctly when *n* > 0? When *n* = 0? For those that are incorrect, describe conditions under which they fail. For those that are correct, construct an assertion that is true at the end of each pass through the loop.

    (a) *first* := 1; *last* := *n*;
        middle := (*first* + *last*) **div** 2;
        while (*first* <= *last*) **and** (*x* <> *a*[*middle*]) **do**
            begin
                if *x* < *a*[*middle*] **then**
                    last := *middle* − 1
                else
                    first := *middle* + 1;
                middle := (*first* + *last*) **div** 2
            end;
        if *last* < *first* **then** *i* := 0 **else** *i* := *middle*

    (b) *first* := 1; *last* := *n*;
        repeat
            middle := (*first* + *last*) **div** 2;
            if *x* < *a*[*middle*] **then**
                last := *middle* − 1
            else
                first := *middle* + 1
        until (*x* = *a*[*middle*]) **or** (*last* < *first*);
        if *x* = *a*[*middle*] **then** *i* := *middle* **else** *i* := 0

    (c) *first* := 1; *last* := *n*;
        repeat
            middle := (*first* + *last*) **div** 2;
            if *x* < *a*[*middle*] **then**
                last := *middle* − 1
            else
                first := *middle* + 1
        until (*x* = *a*[*middle*]) **or** (*last* < *first*);
        if *last* < *first* **then** *i* := 0 **else** *i* := *middle*

(d) *first* := 1; *last* := *n*;
    while *first* <= *last* **do**
        begin
            middle := (*first* + *last*) **div** 2;
            if *x* <= *a*[*middle*] **then** *last* := *middle* − 1;
            if *x* >= *a*[*middle*] **then** *first* := *middle* + 1
        end;
    if *x* = *a*[*middle*] **then** *i* := *middle* **else** *i* := 0

(e) *first* := 0; *last* := *n* + 1;
    while *first* < *last* **do**
        begin
            middle := (*first* + *last*) **div** 2;
            if *x* < *a*[*middle*] **then**
                first := *middle*
            else
                last := *middle* − 1
        end;
    if *x* = *a*[*middle*] **then** *i* := *middle* **else** *i* := 0

13. How does the efficiency of each of the correct variants of the binary search in Exercise 12 compare with the efficiency of the variant described in the text? (*Hint:* How many comparisons are needed to find each of the items in the list <1, 2, 3, 4, 5>?)

14. In some situations the beginning of a list might not be the best place to begin a search. For example, when seeking someone's telephone number, we generally guess where to begin looking in a directory based on the first letter of the person's last name.

    (a) Write a function *startingplace*(*word*, *n*) that computes a good place to begin looking for the string *word* in an ordered list with *n* entries. (*Hint:* Make the simplifying assumption that each letter of the alphabet occurs with equal frequency as the first letter of a word in the list.)

    (b) Construct a procedure to conduct a linear search for a word in an ordered list of length *n*, beginning at *startingplace*(*word*, *n*) and searching forward or backward in the list either until the word is found or until it is determined that it cannot be in the list.

15. Enhance the *scan* procedure written in Section 7.4 to recognize keywords in Pascal. (*Hint:* Use a binary search of a list of keywords.)

8.2   **ANALYSIS OF SEARCHING ALGORITHMS**

Intuitively, a binary search of an ordered list is more efficient than a linear search since it examines fewer items in the list. But how much more efficient is it? To find out, we proceed to analyze searching algorithms using the two methods discussed in Section 3.8: empirically, by observing the algorithms in actual use; theoretically, by reasoning about the amount of work they must do.

EMPIRICAL ANALYSIS

We conduct an empirical analysis first by writing a program *search* to determine the average time required by the searching algorithms in the libraries *search0* through *search3*. (See Pascal Sample 8.5.) This program measures the time it takes an algorithm to find all items in a list and then divides this time by the number of items in

PASCAL SAMPLE 8.5   The program *search*

```
{ program to test and time search subroutines }
program search(input, output);
const maxlen = 1001;              { max length of list }
type itemType = 1..maxlen;        { type of data in list }
     index    = 0..maxlen;
     itemList = array [1..maxlen] of itemType;
var list     : itemList;          { list to search      }
    length   : index;             { length of list      }
    item     : itemType;          { item to find        }
    position : index;             { where found         }
    start    : integer;           { time search starts  }
    done     : integer;           { time search stops   }
#include 'searchl';               { search procedure    }
begin
    write('Length of list: ');
    read(length);
    { set up list containing integers 1..length in order }
    for item := 1 to length do list[item] := item;
    { try to find each item in list }
    start := clock;
    for item := 1 to length do
        begin
            search(list, length, item, position);
            if item <> position then
                if position = 0 then
                    writeln(item, ' not found')
                else
                    writeln(item, ' found erroneously at ', position)
        end;
    done := clock;
    writeln;
    writeln('Average search time = ', (done - start)/length:4:2)
end.
```

PASCAL SAMPLE 8.6   The program *search* (sample use)

```
Length of list: 100

Average search time = 1.33
```

---

the list to obtain the average searching time. To do this, we use the function *clock* provided by Berkeley Pascal to measure the amount of computing time (in milliseconds) consumed since the program began; this function is not standard from system to system, so you may have to adapt the statements in *search* that involve this function to the conventions of the system you have available.

We can use the program *search* to test a particular search procedure simply by changing the name of the library in the **#include** statement, or by replacing this statement by the contents of the library if our version of Pascal does not support this feature of Berkeley Pascal. Pascal Sample 8.6 shows the results of using *search* to test the linear search in *search1*.

Using *search*, we can measure the average searching time required by the search algorithms we have developed. Table 8.1 shows the average times required by these algorithms to find an item in a list with 100, 500, and 1000 entries, using a VAX 11/780 and running Berkeley Pascal.

As expected, the average searching time for each version of the linear search grows roughly linearly with the length of the list: the time needed to find an item in a list of length 1000 is roughly twice that needed to find an item in a list of length 500. The growth is not exactly linear because there is a certain amount of overhead associated with the measurement process (the overhead required to evaluate the *clock* function). This overhead becomes less significant as the list becomes longer, since it is spread out over more items, but for short lists makes it appear that searches take longer than they actually do; hence the times listed for $n = 100$ are slightly on the high side.

Contrary to what we might have expected, the average searching time for the "more efficient" linear search *search1* is more than half that of the "less efficient"

TABLE 8.1.   Average Time (in Milliseconds) Required to Search *n*-Item List

Algorithm	$n = 100$	$n = 500$	$n = 1000$
Inefficient linear search (*search0*)	2.83	10.53	20.72
Linear search (*search1*)	1.33	6.50	12.27
Linear search with sentinel (*search2*)	1.00	4.57	9.15
Binary search (*search3*)	0.33	0.43	0.53

version *search0*. Examination of 50 percent fewer items in the list on the average should lead to a 50 percent improvement in the efficiency of the algorithm, but experimentation shows an improvement of only about 40 percent. What happened? A close examination of the Pascal system used to conduct the experiment reveals that this system handles the **for** loop in *search0* more efficiently than it handles the **while** loop in *search1*. As a result, the advantage we had hoped to gain by reducing the number of passes through the loop is partially offset by the increased amount of work performed on each pass. In fact, some systems handle the **for** loop in *search0* so much more efficiently that this "inefficient" linear search actually requires less time than *search1*.

This experiment shows that, even though we can improve the efficiency of an algorithm in the abstract (say, by using a sentinel or by having it examine 50 percent fewer items), it is difficult to predict exactly the effect of such an "improvement" on the execution time of the algorithm. The most we can conclude in the abstract about an algorithm with a linear time requirement is that its execution time will grow linearly. In order determine the actual rate of growth for its execution time, we have to measure the performance of the algorithm in actual use.

By contrast, the experiment suggests that we can obtain dramatic increases in efficiency by using a different algorithm. The average searching time of the binary search grows much less rapidly than that of the linear search. We can determine the reason for this and the actual rate of growth by examining the algorithm theoretically rather than empirically.

THEORETICAL ANALYSIS

To analyze an algorithm theoretically, we count the number of times it must perform some essential step. Since search algorithms must compare items of data, we count the number of such comparisons and express this number as a function of the length of the list being searched. We do this first for the worst case of the binary search and then for its average case.

Worst-case analysis of the binary search   To determine the worst case of the binary search we count the number of items in a list that can be found with at most *m probes* into the list, that is, by examining at most *m* items in the list. If we are allowed only one probe into the list, we can find at most one item, namely, that midway through the list. If we are allowed two probes into the list, we can find two more items, namely, those one-fourth and three-fourths of the way through the list. Each additional probe enables us to find twice as many items as the previous probe. In summary,

$$
\begin{array}{llll}
1 \text{ probe finds} & 1 & \text{item;} & \\
2 \text{ probes find} & 2 & \text{more, for a total of} & 3 & \text{items;} \\
3 \text{ probes find} & 4 & \text{more, for a total of} & 7 & \text{items;} \\
\vdots & \vdots & & \vdots & \\
m \text{ probes find} & 2^{m-1} & \text{more, for a total of} & 2^m - 1 & \text{items.}
\end{array}
$$

Thus the binary search can find an arbitrary item in a list containing $2^m - 1$ items using no more than m probes. Put another way, if a list contains n items, the binary search in its worst case will use m probes, where m is the smallest integer such that

$$2^m - 1 \geq n.$$

Solving this inequality for m, we find that

$$2^m \geq n + 1 \quad \text{or} \quad m \geq \log_2(n+1),$$

where $\log_2(x)$ is the logarithm to the base 2 of x. Finally,

$$m = \lceil \log_2(n+1) \rceil,$$

where $\lceil x \rceil$ is the *ceiling* of x, that is, the smallest integer greater than or equal to x. The $\log_2$ and ceiling functions occur frequently in the analysis of algorithms, but they are not provided as standard functions in many programming languages. However, it is an easy matter to define them in terms of functions that are provided. (See Exercises 1 and 2 at the end of this section.)

From this analysis we can see that the binary search requires *logarithmic* time in its worst case as opposed to the *linear* time required by the linear search; that is, the binary search uses time that grows proportionally to $\log_2(n+1)$, where n is the number of items in the list, whereas the linear search requires time that grows proportionally to n.

Measuring the time requirements of algorithms Table 8.2 shows that there are striking differences in the resources required by algorithms with execution times that grow proportionally to various functions of n. Algorithms with logarithmic time requirements clearly are much more efficient than algorithms with linear time requirements. Even if an algorithm with a logarithmic time requirement must work much harder on each pass through a loop than an algorithm with a linear time requirement (as the binary search works harder than the linear search on each pass through its loop), that algorithm is still faster for large values of n. A linear-time algorithm must be 15 times faster on each pass through a loop to keep pace with a logarithmic-time algorithm when $n = 100$; when $n = 1000$, it must be 100 times faster on each pass through a loop.

TABLE 8.2 Comparison of Growth Rates

Growth rate	$n = 10$	$n = 100$	$n = 1000$
Logarithmic: $\log_2(n)$	3.3	6.6	10
Linear: n	10	100	1,000
Quadratic: n^2	100	10,000	1,000,000
Exponential: 2^n	1,024	2^{100}	2^{1000}

Logarithmic functions simply have a much slower growth rate than linear functions. Whether we cut the work performed by a linear-time algorithm by a factor of 2, 10, or 1000, it will still be less efficient than a logarithmic-time algorithm when n is large. Similarly, linear functions have a slower growth rate than quadratic functions, and quadratic functions have a slower growth rate than exponential functions. There is no point in optimizing an algorithm with a fast-growing time requirement if we can find another algorithm for the same task with a slower-growing time requirement.

Finally, exponential-time algorithms are clearly impractical for all but very small values of n; for example, 2^{100} equals $(2^{10})^{10}$, or 1024^{10}, which is approximately 10^{30}. Even if we could perform each step in an exponential-time algorithm exceedingly quickly, there simply is not enough time to perform such a huge number of steps. There are only 3×10^7 seconds in a year and 3×10^{15} microseconds in a century.

Average-case analysis of the binary search   We turn our attention now to determining the average case for the binary search. To do this, we count the number of probes required to find each of the items in a list with n items and average the results. For simplicity, let us assume that $n = 2^m - 1$. Then an extension of our worst-case analysis behavior of the binary search produces the results in Table 8.3. The total number of probes required to find all the items in the list is

$$s = (1 \times 1) + (2 \times 2) + (3 \times 4) + \cdots + m\,2^{m-1}.$$

To express this sum s as a function of n, we note that

$$2s = (1 \times 2) + (2 \times 4) + \cdots + (m - 1)2^{m-1} + m2^m.$$

Subtracting s from $2s$, we find that

$$s = -1 - 2 - 4 - \cdots - 2^{m-1} + m2^m.$$

Recalling that

$$n = 2^m - 1 = 1 + 2 + 4 + \cdots + 2^{m-1},$$

we see that

$$s = m2^m - n \quad \text{or} \quad (n + 1)\log_2(n + 1) - n.$$

TABLE 8.3   Analysis of Binary Search

Exact number of probes	Number of items that can be found	Total number of probes to find all items
1	1	$1 \times 1 = 4$
2	2	$2 \times 2 = 4$
3	4	$3 \times 4 = 12$
$\vdots$	$\vdots$	$\vdots$
m	2^{m-1}	$m \times 2^{m-1}$

Thus the average number of probes required to find an item in a list of length $n = 2^m - 1$ is s/n or

$$\log_2(n+1) - 1 + \frac{\log_2(n+1)}{n},$$

which is only a fraction of a probe less than the number of probes required in the worst case. This result should not be surprising since the binary search uses the maximum number of probes to find half the items in a list of length $2^m - 1$.

An analysis of the general case, in which $n = 2^m + k$ for $k < 2^m$, shows the same to be true, namely, that the number of probes made by the binary search in the average case is at most one fewer than the number made in the worst case. (See Exercise 3 at the end of this section.) Hence the binary search requires logarithmic time in its average case as well as in its worst case. This analysis explains the results of our empirical analysis of the binary search: $\lceil \log_2(500) \rceil - 1$ is only 33 percent greater than $\lceil \log_2(100) \rceil - 1$, and the binary search requires 33 percent more time on the average to find an item in a list of 500 items than in a list of 100 items.

Reflecting on this analysis, we see that we can explain the observed action of an algorithm by theoretical analysis. Furthermore, we can use theoretical analysis to extrapolate estimates of an algorithm's action to untested cases. For example, to search a list with 10,000 items using a binary search should take 44 percent more time on the average than to search a list with 1000 items since $\lceil \log_2(10000) \rceil - 1$ is 44 percent greater than $\lceil \log_2(1000) \rceil - 1$. Experimentation confirms this prediction: it takes 0.69 milliseconds on the average to find an item in a list of 10,000 items using the binary search.

Finally, we learned that worst-case analysis of an algorithm is somewhat easier than average-case analysis. Average-case analyses involve very careful counting, and they may involve sophisticated summation techniques. For this reason, we will generally content ourselves with performing worst-case analyses.

EXERCISES

1. Write a definition for the function *log2* such that $log2(x) = \log_2(x)$. [*Hint:* Find a constant, c, such that $\log_2(x) = c \log(x)$.]

2. Write a definition for the function *ceil* such that $ceil(x) = \lceil x \rceil$. (*Hint:* Use the *trunc* function.)

3. Show that, regardless of the length of a list, the binary search requires at best one less probe in its average case than in its worst case.

4. We say that an algorithm is $O(f(n))$ [pronounced "Oh of $f(n)$)"] if there is a constant, c, such that, except for finitely many values of n, the algorithm always solves a problem of size n in at most $cf(n)$ steps. For searching algorithms, we determine the size of the problem by the length of the list we want to search. Thus an algorithm has a linear time requirement if it is $O(n)$, a logarithmic time requirement if it is $O(\log(n))$, a quadratic time requirement if it is $O(n^2)$, and an exponential time requirement if it is $O(2^{kn})$ for some constant k.

(a) Show that an $O(n)$ algorithm is faster than an $O(n^2)$ algorithm when n is large.

(b) Must an $O(n)$ algorithm be faster than an $O(n^2)$ algorithm when n is small?

(c) Suppose that $f(n) = an^2 + bn + c$. Show that any $O(f(n))$ algorithm is also $O(n^2$

(d) Show that for any $a, b > 1$, an algorithm is $O(\log_a(n))$ if it is $O(\log_b(n))$.

(e) Suppose that $f(n) = m^n$ for some positive integer m. Show that any $O(f(n))$ alg rithm has an exponential time requirement.

8.3   ELEMENTARY SORTING ALGORITHMS

As we learned in Section 8.1, the way in which information is arranged affects th ways in which we can access that information. A telephone directory that lists name in alphabetic order makes it easy for us to determine a person's telephone numbe a directory that lists phone numbers in increasing number order makes it easy fo us to determine who has a given phone number. Either directory can be used fo either task, but it can be used much more conveniently and efficiently for its intende task.

The process by which a list is arranged in a particular order is known as *sorting* When a list contains alphabetic information, sorting that list amounts to alphabetizing it. When a list contains numeric information, sorting that list amounts to arranging in increasing order.

Sorting algorithms have been studied widely, partly because they have such im portant applications and partly because there are a great many ways in which they can be constructed. In this section we will examine a number of sorting algorithms all of which are simple and easy to understand, but relatively inefficient. In late sections we will consider sorting algorithms that are much more sophisticated and efficient.

Most simple sorting algorithms proceed by interchanging entries in the list to be sorted, either to put one of these entries in its proper place or to move it closer to that place. Three of these algorithms—the selection sort, the exchange (or bubble sort, and the insertion sort—are based on intuitive procedures that we could carry out by hand.

As in our treatment of searching, we will code sorting algorithms as procedures that can be invoked in a uniform manner by the statement $sort(a, n)$, where a is a list containing n items of data; we will package sorting algorithms in separate libraries $sort1, sort2, \ldots$ Again, we presume that a program using one of these libraries contains the declarations

```
const maxlen  = ...;        { maximum length of list }
type   itemType = ...;        { type of data in list     }
       index    = 0..maxlen;
       itemList = array [1..maxlen] of itemType;
```

which are needed to construct the header for that procedure. We also presume that items of type *itemType* can be compared using the relational operators < and > (that *itemType* is the type *real*, an ordinal type, or a string type).

THE SELECTION SORT

Perhaps the easiest of all sorting algorithms to understand is the selection sort. To put a list $a[1], \ldots, a[n]$ in order, we first find the smallest item in the list and put it at the beginning; in order to make room for it there, without losing the value of $a[1]$ and without creating a hole in the list where the smallest item used to be, we simply interchange that item with $a[1]$. Next we find the second smallest item and make it the second item in the list by interchanging it with $a[2]$. We continue in this manner, finding the smallest item in the remainder of the list and putting it in its proper position, until all the items in the list are in order.

To arrange a list completely in order by a selection sort, we must make $n - 1$ passes through a list $a[1], \ldots, a[n]$. On the ith pass, we find the ith smallest item in the list and interchange it with $a[i]$. At the end of $n - 1$ passes, the smallest $n - 1$ items in the list have been moved into place; the largest item in the list is automatically in its proper place, so no further work needs to be done.

Figure 8.1 illustrates the action of the selection sort by displaying the state of a 5-item list before and after each pass through that list. It also shows which items in the list are interchanged on each pass. When coded as a procedure to place $a[1], \ldots, a[n]$ in order, the selection sort takes the form of the procedure *sort* in the library *sort1* displayed as Pascal Sample 8.7.

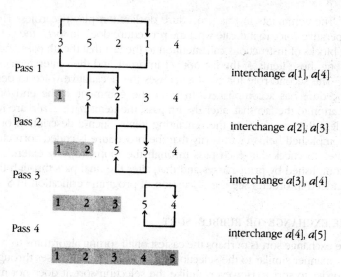

FIGURE 8.1 ■ Interchanges performed by a selection sort on a 5-item list

---

■ **PASCAL SAMPLE 8.7**   The library *sort1* (selection sort)

{ *sort1*: selection sort of $a[1], ..., a[n]$ }

```
procedure sort(var a : itemList;        { list to sort       }
                    n : index );        { length of list     }

        var i, j, p : index;            { auxiliary indices }
            item   : itemType;          { item from list    }

    begin
        for i := 1 to n - 1 do
            begin
                { find minimum a[p] of a[i], ..., a[n] }
                p := i;
                for j := i + 1 to n do if a[j] < a[p] then p := j;
                { interchange a[i] and a[p] }
                item := a[p];
                a[p] := a[i];
                a[i]  := item
                { now a[1] <= ... <= a[i] and   }
                { a[i] <= a[j] when i < j <= n }
            end
    end;    { of sort }
```

The comments in this procedure declaration play two roles. The first uses the imperative voice to indicate what the procedure does. In *sort1*, the comments preceding blocks of instructions call attention to the fact that the *i*th pass finds the least item among those items of the list not yet in order and then interchanges this item with $a[i]$. The second role for comments uses the declarative voice to describe what the procedure has accomplished. In *sort1* the comment at the end of the loop calls attention to the fact that, after the *i*th pass, the items $a[1], ..., a[i]$ are in order and are all less than or equal to the remaining items. Such a description of what has been accomplished helps us to verify that the procedure is coded correctly: it is a simple matter to check that each pass through the loop properly extends what has been accomplished by prior passes and that, after the final pass through the loop, the list is indeed in order. (See the discussion of program verification in Section 3.7.)

THE EXCHANGE (OR BUBBLE) SORT

The exchange sort is perhaps the easiest of all sorting algorithms to code. It proceeds in a manner similar to the selection sort, making $n - 1$ passes through an n-item list in order to sort it. However, unlike the selection sort, it does not move items over long distances to place them in the proper position; rather, it moves items at most

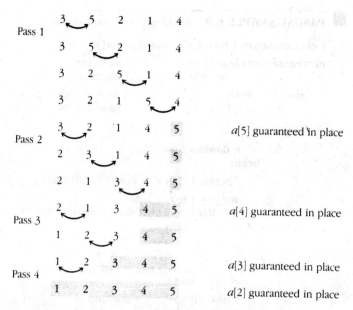

FIGURE 8.2 ■ Comparisons performed by an exchange sort for a 5-item list

one position at a time in order to correct local discrepancies in the sequence and to move items closer to their proper position. On each pass the exchange sort moves through the list, comparing adjacent items and interchanging them if they are out of order. At the end of the first pass, the largest item has risen like a "bubble" to the end of the list; at the end of the second pass, the second largest item has risen to the next-to-last position; and so on, until at the end of the $(n-1)$st pass the second smallest item has risen to the second position in the list and the smallest item occupies the one remaining position at the beginning of the list. Figure 8.2 illustrates the action of the exchange sort. The items being compared in each step of the algorithm are indicated by the double-headed arrows.

Note that on each successive pass through the list we can stop the bubbling process one item before we stopped on the last pass. At the time of the ith pass, the largest $i-1$ items in the list have already bubbled to their proper place; hence only the first $n-i+1$ items need to be compared to see whether any further exchanges are required. Note also that passes continue to compare items even when no further exchanges are necessary since continued comparisons are needed to ensure that this is indeed the case.

Pascal Sample 8.8 displays the library *sort2*, which contains the exchange sort coded as a procedure in Pascal. Here again comments describe not only what each pass through the list is going to do, but also what has been accomplished by the end of each pass.

PASCAL SAMPLE 8.8   The library *sort2* (exchange sort)

{ *sort2*: exchange or bubble sort of $a[1], ..., a[n]$ }

```
procedure sort(var  a : itemList;          { list to sort       }
                    n : index );           { length of list     }

        var i, j  : index;                 { auxiliary indices }
            item  : itemType;              { item from list    }

    begin
        for i := n downto 2 do
            begin
                { bubble largest item in a[1], ..., a[i] to a[i] }
                for j := 1 to i − 1 do
                    if a[j] > a[j + 1] then { exchange items }
                        begin
                            item     := a[j];
                            a[j]     := a[j + 1];
                            a[j + 1] := item
                        end
                { now a[i] <= ... <= a[n] and   }
                { a[j] <= a[i] when 1 <= j < i }
            end

    end;   { of sort }
```

Examination of the exchange sort suggests ways for improving the algorithm. For example, if the bubbling process were to arrange all items in the proper order in fewer than $n − 1$ passes, we can detect this by determining whether any bubbles move during a pass through the list; if no bubbles move, then no more passes are needed. This suggestion results in the modification to the exchange sort contained in the library *sort3*. (See Pascal Sample 8.9.)

As it turns out, the savings achieved by this modification to the exchange sort are more apparent than real. The only attractions of the exchange sort are that it is easy to code and that it has the catchy nickname "bubble sort." As we will see, there are far more efficient ways to sort large lists, and even the selection sort is better for sorting short lists.

THE INSERTION SORT

The insertion sort is based on the way a card player arranges a hand of cards. It creates successively longer sorted initial segments $a[1], ..., a[i]$ of a list $a[1], ..., a[n]$ by taking each item $a[i]$ in turn and inserting it in the appropriate position in the

PASCAL SAMPLE 8.9 The library *sort3* (improved exchange sort)

{ *sort3*: improved exchange or bubble sort of $a[1], ..., a[n]$ }

```
procedure sort(var a : itemList;        { list to sort         }
                    n : index );        { length of list        }
          var i, j    : index;          { auxiliary indices     }
              item    : itemType;       { item from list        }
              bubble  : boolean;        { indicates movement    }

          begin
              i := n;
              repeat
                  { bubble largest item in a[1], ..., a[i] to a[i], }
                  { setting bubble = true if anything moves  }
                  bubble := false;                  { no movement yet }
                  for j := 1 to i - 1 do
                      if a[j] > a[j + 1] then        { exchange items  }
                          begin
                              item     := a[j];
                              a[j]     := a[j + 1];
                              a[j + 1] := item;
                              bubble   := true
                          end;
                  { now a[i] <= ... <= a[n] and a[j] <= a[i] }
                  { when 1 <= j < i; also, if bubble = false,  }
                  { then a[1] <= ... <= a[n]                 }
                  if i > 1 then i := i - 1
              until (i <= 1) or not bubble
          end;   { of sort }
```

sorted segment $a[1], ..., a[i - 1]$ that precedes it. It finds this position by searching the list $a[1], ..., a[i - 1]$; if this search determines that $a[i]$ belongs in position j, then it makes room for $a[i]$ there by shifting the items $a[j], ..., a[i - 1]$ to occupy positions $j + 1, ..., i$.

Figure 8.3 illustrates the action of the insertion sort. On each pass through the list, the item at the tail of the leftward pointing arrow is moved to the position at the head of the arrow, with the items in between being shifted right one position to make room for it. When implemented as a procedure in Pascal, the insertion sort takes the form of the procedure *sort* in the library *sort4*. (See Pascal Sample 8.10.) Note that by searching backward through $a[1], ..., a[i - 1]$ in order to find the position j at which $a[i]$ belongs, we can shift the items $a[i - 1], ..., a[j]$ out of the way as we search.

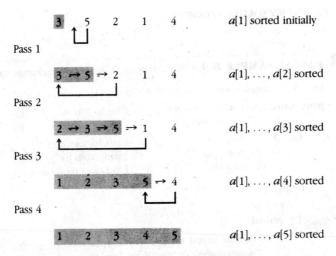

Pass 1 — 3 5 2 1 4 — a[1] sorted initially

Pass 2 — 3 → 5 ⇒ 2 1 4 — a[1], ..., a[2] sorted

Pass 3 — 2 → 3 → 5 → 1 4 — a[1], ..., a[3] sorted

Pass 4 — 1 2 3 5 → 4 — a[1], ..., a[4] sorted

1 2 3 4 5 — a[1], ..., a[5] sorted

FIGURE 8.3 ■ Insertions performed by the insertion sort for a 5-item list

---

■ **PASCAL SAMPLE 8.10** The library *sort4* (insertion sort)

```
{ sort4: insertion sort of a[1], ..., a[n] }
procedure sort( var a : itemList;              { list to sort        }
                     n : index );              { length of list      }

    var i, j  : index;                         { auxiliary indices }
        item  : itemType;                      { item from list    }
        found : boolean;

    begin
        for i := 2 to n do
            begin
                { insert a[i] in the sorted subsequence a[1], ..., a[i−1] }
                item := a[i];                  { item to insert     }
                j := i;                        { insertion pointer  }
                found := false;
                while ( j > 1 ) and not found do
                    if a[j−1] <= item then      { item should be a[ j]}
                        found := true
                    else
                        begin
                            a[j] := a[j−1];      { move a[j−1] up    }
                            j := j−1
                        end;
                a[j] := item                    { insert item       }
                { now a[1] <= ... <= a[i] }

            end

    end;  { of sort }
```

1. Modify the selection sort so that it arranges the list in decreasing order instead of in increasing order.

2. Modify the way the selection sort is coded so that it
   (a) finds the *i*th largest item on the *i*th pass, and
   (b) interchanges $a[p]$ and $a[i]$ only if $i \neq p$.

3. A sorting algorithm is *stable* if two items in a list that are equal in value retain their original order as the list is sorted. Which of the sorting algorithms in this section are stable?

4. Improve the exchange sort further by making the following modifications.
   (a) On each pass keep track of where the first and last bubbles moved. The next pass needs to bubble only the items between those positions. (Why?)
   (b) Reverse the direction of the bubbling process on each pass through the list. In this way small items will move toward the beginning of the list as rapidly as large items move toward the end. (This version of the exchange sort is sometimes known as the *cocktail shaker* sort.)

5. Would the improved exchange sort still be correct if the last statement inside the loop were simply $i := i - 1$? (*Hint:* What happens if $n = 0$?)

6. Modify the insertion sort to use a binary search rather than a linear search to find the point of insertion for each item in the subsequence that precedes it.

7. What goes wrong if we code the loop in the insertion sort more simply as follows?

   ```
   while ( j > 1) and (a[ j − 1] > item) do
       begin
           a[ j] := a[ j − 1];
           j := j − 1
       end
   ```

   (*Hint:* What happens if *item* belongs first in the list?)

8. What gains can be made in the efficiency of the insertion sort by declaring *itemList* so that the subscripts for *a* range from 0 to *maxlen* and then posting each item to insert as a sentinel in $a[0]$?

ANALYSIS OF ELEMENTARY SORTING ALGORITHMS

The sorting algorithms that we have examined so far work best when sorting a list that is already in order and worst when sorting a list that is arranged in decreasing, rather than increasing, order. Hence, we can analyze the best and worst cases of these sorting algorithms empirically by simply measuring the time it takes them to sort ordered and inversely ordered lists.

However, in order to analyze the average case for a sorting algorithm, we cannot measure and average the time it takes to sort lists in all possible orders: there are too many possible orders even for lists of moderate length, and to sort them all would be prohibitively expensive. Instead, we measure the time it takes to sort a list arranged in a random order.

■ **PASCAL SAMPLE 8.11**   The procedure *shuffle*

procedure *shuffle*(**var** *a* : *itemList*; *n* : *index*);
  { rearranges *a*[1], ..., *a*[*n*] randomly }
  var *i, j* : *index*;
    item : *itemType*;
  begin
    for *i* := *n* **downto** 2 **do**   { move random item to *a*[*i*] }
      begin
        j   := *randomInt*(1, *i*);
        item := *a*[*j*];
        a[*j*] := *a*[*i*];
        a[*i*] := *item*
      end
  end;   { of *shuffle* }

How do we arrange a list in a random order? We appeal to a function, *randomInt*, which we will define in Chapter 10. Successive evaluations of *randomInt*(*m*, *n*) produce integers *i* such that $m \leq i \leq n$, with any such integer as likely to be produced by each evaluation as any other. In a sense, evaluating *randomInt* is like picking a card at random from a deck that contains cards labeled with the integers from *m* to *n*.

Now, to arrange a list in random order, we employ a "shuffle" or "unsorting algorithm" based on the selection sort. The procedure *shuffle* (Pascal Sample 8.11) successively selects values for *a*[*n*], . . . , *a*[2] by selecting, for *i* ranging from *n* down to 2, a random item from among the first *i* items in the list and interchanging this item with *a*[*i*]. This procedure shuffles the items in a list, not quite in the same way a card player would shuffle them, but equally randomly. It is a much more efficient method for shuffling a list than one that removes random items from a list until that list is exhausted; unless the list is collapsed each time an item is removed, it may take a very long time to locate and remove the last few items.

With this means of constructing a list in random order, we are able to write a program, *sort*, that checks sorting algorithms for accuracy and measures the time required by these algorithms to sort ordered, inversely ordered, and randomly ordered lists. (See Pascal Sample 8.12.) The heart of the program *sort* is the *check* procedure, which sorts and checks lists that are set up by the main program.

When *sort* is used to measure the time required to sort lists of length 100 and 200 on a VAX 11/750, running Berkeley Pascal, it produces the results shown in Table 8.4.

From these results we see that the selection and insertion sorts compete for the best overall performance. Although the improved exchange sort requires less time to sort an already sorted list, the others are quicker in the more common cases where

---

PASCAL SAMPLE 8.12 The program *sort*

{ program to test and time sort subroutines }

program *sort*(*input*, *output*);

const *maxlen* = 1001;   { max length of list }
type *itemType* = 1..*maxlen*;   { type of data in list }
    index   = 0..*maxlen*;
    itemList = **array** [1..*maxlen*] **of** *itemType*;

var *list*   : *itemList*;   { list to sort   }
    length   : *index*;   { length of list }
    i   : *index*;
    randomSeed : *integer*;   { for *random* }

#include 'sort1';   { *sort* procedure }
#include 'random';   { *randomInt* }

{ declaration for *shuffle* goes here }

procedure *check*(**var** *a* : *itemList*; *n* : *index*);
    { procedure to sort a list containing the integers }
    { from 1 to *n*, time the sort, and check the result }
    { assumes *n* < *maxlen*   }

    var *i*   : *index*;
        start : *integer*;   { time sort starts }
        done : *integer*;   { time sort stops }

    begin
        start := *clock*;
        sort(*a*, *n*);
        done := *clock*;
        writeln;
        writeln('Time = ', *done* − *start*:1);

        i := 1;
        while (*i* <= *n*) **and** (*a*[*i*] = *i*) **do** *i* := *i* + 1;

        if *i* > *n* **then**
            writeln('Sort successful')
        else
            begin
                writeln('Sort fails');
                for *i* := 1 **to** *n* **do** *writeln*(*a*[*i*])
            end;
        writeln
    end;   { of *check* }

■ **PASCAL SAMPLE 8.12**   The program *sort* (continued)

begin

    write('Length of list: ');
    read(*length*);

    { Test 1: presorted list }

    for *i* := 1 **to** *length* **do** *list*[*i*] := *i*;
    writeln;
    writeln('Sorting presorted list');
    check(*list*, *length*);

    { Test 2: reverse sorted list }

    for *i* := 1 **to** *length* **do** *list*[*i*] := *length* − *i* + 1;
    writeln;
    writeln('Sorting reverse sorted list');
    check(*list*, *length*);

    { Test 3: random list }

    for *i* := 1 **to** *length* **do** *list*[*i*] := *i*;
    randomize(*true*);
    shuffle(*list*, *length*);
    writeln;
    writeln('Sorting shuffled list');
    check(*list*, *length*)

end.

TABLE 8.4   Time Required (in Milliseconds) by Various Sorting Algorithms

Length of list = 100

Method	In order	Reverse order	Random order
Selection sort	217	217	217
Exchange sort	216	500	384
Improved exchange	16	517	350
Insertion sort	16	317	167

Length of list = 200

Method	In order	Reverse order	Random order
Selection sort	833	884	850
Exchange sort	900	2000	1433
Improved exchange	16	2017	1450
Insertion sort	17	1384	666

the list is in reverse or random order. The results also show that the "improved" exchange sort does not live up to its name: it requires roughly the same amount of time as the unimproved exchange sort except when the list is already in order.

WORST-CASE ANALYSIS OF SORTING ALGORITHMS

A closer examination of the results in Table 8.4 shows that the time required to sort a list quadruples when the length of the list is doubled. This suggests that the time required to sort, as opposed to search, a list with n items is proportional to n^2 rather than to n or to $\log_2(n)$. To explain and justify this observation, we must examine the workings of the sorting algorithms and measure the amount of work actually performed in sorting a list of length n.

There are two measures of the work performed by a sorting algorithm. The first counts the number of comparisons (C) made between items in the list. The second counts the number of times (M) an item in the list is moved from one position to another. Obviously, the more comparisons that are made and the more times an item in the list is moved, the longer a sorting algorithm will take.

Let us first consider the selection sort. On its first pass through a list, when it selects the minimum item in that list, it must perform $n - 1$ comparisons. On its second pass, it performs only $n - 2$ comparisons to find the second least item in the list. In general, on the ith pass through the list, $n - i$ comparisons are required to find the ith least item. Hence the total number of comparisons made in all $n - 1$ passes is

$$C_{\text{selection}} = (n - 1) + (n - 2) + \cdots + 2 + 1.$$

We can find a better expression for $C_{\text{selection}}$, in terms of n, by doubling it.

$$
\begin{array}{rcccccccc}
C_{\text{selection}} = & (n-1) & + & (n-2) & + \cdots + & 2 & + & 1 \\
+ C_{\text{selection}} = & 1 & + & 2 & + \cdots + & (n-2) & + & (n-1) \\
\hline
2C_{\text{selection}} = & n & + & n & + \cdots + & n & + & n
\end{array}
$$

or

$$C_{\text{selection}} = \frac{n(n-1)}{2}.$$

Thus the number of comparisons performed by the selection sort does indeed grow as n^2 rather than n. The number of times an item in the list is moved by the selection sort is

$$M_{\text{selection}} = 3(n - 1)$$

because each of the $n - 1$ passes performed by the selection sort interchanges two items in the list, and each interchange requires three movements.

The number of comparisons and movements made by the selection sort is unaffected by the order of the items in the list being sorted, so that the best, worst, and average cases require essentially the same amount of time. The slight differences in the times observed for these cases in our empirical analysis can be traced to the number of times the selection sort is forced to revise its guess as to which of the remaining items in the list is the least; this occurs much more frequently when the list is in reverse order, earning it the distinction of being the worst case.

In the exchange sort, and more so in the improved exchange sort, the number of comparisons and movements made is affected by the order of the items in the list. To understand the worst case for this algorithm, we observe that it makes as many comparisons as does the selection sort: on the ith of $n - 1$ passes, $n - i$ comparisons are made while bubbling the ith largest item into position. Hence

$$C_{\text{exchange}} = \frac{n(n - 1)}{2}$$

as for the selection sort. Moreover, in the worst case, two items are interchanged each time a comparison is made. Hence

$$M_{\text{exchange}} = \frac{3n(n - 1)}{2}$$

since three movements are required for each interchange. The large number of movements made by the exchange sort explain why it performs so much more poorly than the selection sort. What is somewhat surprising is that the exchange sort in the average case is not much better than it is in the worst case. The mathematical analysis that establishes this fact is beyond the scope of this book, but our empirical analysis provides strong evidence that this is indeed the case.

The insertion sort performs between 1 and i comparisons on its ith pass. Hence

$$n - 1 \leq C_{\text{insertion}} \leq \frac{n(n - 1)}{2}$$

for the insertion sort. On each pass, the insertion sort moves the item to be inserted twice. In the best case, the insertion sort involves no further movements of data; in the worst case, it moves one additional item with each comparison it performs. Hence

$$2(n - 1) \leq M_{\text{insertion}} \leq 2(n - 1) + \frac{n(n - 1)}{2}$$

$$= \frac{(n + 4)(n - 1)}{2}.$$

In its average case the insertion sort performs approximately one-half the work it performs in its worst case: when inserting an item in a sorted initial sequence, it needs to look only halfway through that sequence. This explains why, when comparisons and movements are equally costly, the selection and insertion sorts give roughly the same average-case results.

The larger number of movements made by the insertion sort explains why it performs less well than does the selection sort in the worst case or when movements cost more than comparisons. The insertion sort performs better than the exchange sort because it moves items about a third as often.

Thus our theoretical analyses of the sorting algorithms studied so far bear out our empirical observations. In each case the variations in execution times for the algorithms are traceable directly to the amount of work being done by the algorithms. This correlation between empirical and theoretical analyses gives us the confidence to predict the time required by various algorithms when they are used to sort lists containing 1000, 10,000, or even more items.

For example, in the case of the selection sort, the amount of work required to sort a list with n items is proportional to $n(n - 1)/2$. From our empirical observations, we see that the constant of proportionality is approximately 0.043 seconds. Hence we would expect the selection sort to take about 21 seconds to sort a list with 1000 items. Experimentation with the program *sort* bears out this expectation.

EXERCISES

1. How many comparisons does the improved exchange sort make when sorting a list that is already in order?

2. Improve the efficiency of the selection and insertion sorts by having them move an item $a[i]$ only if that item is not already in place. How do these improvements affect the empirical and analytical measures of the efficiency of these algorithms?

3. Analyze empirically the behavior of the sorting algorithms developed for Exercises 4 and 6, Section 8.3.

4. Determine the worst case, in terms of the length n of the list being sorted, for the algorithms analyzed in Exercise 3.

5. Determine analytically the numbers C of comparisons and M of movements made by the insertion sort in the average case.

8.5 SORTING WITH AN INDEX

Often we would like to sort lists of items that are composed of many separate pieces of information, some of which we use to determine the order of the items in the list and some of which we merely carry along as auxiliary information. For example, we may want to arrange student records in alphabetic order, either according to their surnames or according to their home states. The piece of information used to determine the desired order is known as the *key* or basis of comparison for the sort.

If such composite items of data contain a single key, we may structure them as records in Pascal using a declaration such as

```
type itemType = record
                  key : keyType;
                  ⋮
              end;
```

We can then easily modify our sorting algorithms to order such items according to their keys. We simply change comparisons such as

if $a[j] < a[p]$ **then** . . .

to

if $a[j].key < a[p].key$ **then** . . .

and leave the rest of the algorithm unchanged.

If such composite items of data contain multiple keys, use of the record structure in Pascal poses certain problems. For example, if we structure the items to be sorted using a declaration such as

type *itemType* = **record**
    key1 : *keyType*;
    key2 : *keyType*;
        ⋮
    end;

there is no convenient way in Pascal for us to designate to a sorting procedure which key we want to use for a sort. In such cases it may be more convenient to structure the items as vectors than as records; we can then pass to a subroutine an index of the component of the vector we want to use as the key.

If an item is a vector, then a list of items is a matrix, with the rows in that matrix containing the items and the columns containing particular pieces of information (such as names, ages, and addresses of students) about the items. To sort such a matrix of information so that the entries in a particular column (say, that containing the names of the students) are in order, we may have to move substantial amounts of data during the sort. In the selection or exchange sorts we must interchange entire rows in the matrix, not just the entries in the column being used as a key. Otherwise, we would lose track of which information pertains to which key.

For example, let us begin with the matrix in Table 8.5, which contains four rows of student records. After we sort these rows using the first column as a key, we should

TABLE 8.5   Unsorted Matrix of Data

		Column 1	Column 2	Column 3
Row	1	Jones	John	New York
	2	Adams	Ann	Vermont
	3	Smith	Susan	New York
	4	Baker	Barry	Texas

TABLE 8.6   Matrix Sorted Using Column 1 as a Key

		Column		
		1	2	3
	1	Adams	Ann	Vermont
	2	Baker	Barry	Texas
Row	3	Jones	John	New York
	4	Smith	Susan	New York

arrive at the matrix in Table 8.6, which contains the same four rows but in a different order.

The procedure *sortRows* in the library *xsort0* (Pascal Sample 8.13) is a modification of the selection sort in *sort1*. It arranges the rows of a matrix so as to place the entries in a specified column in order, presuming the existence of the declarations

```
const maxRows = ...;      { maximum number of rows    }
      maxCols = ...;      { maximum number of columns  }
type  itemType = ...;
      rowIndex = 0..maxRows;
      colIndex = 0..maxCols;
      table    = array [1..maxRows, 1..maxCols] of itemType;
```

in the main program that specify the types of its parameters. As can be seen, the interchanges performed by this sorting algorithm become progressively more expensive as the number of columns in the matrix increases.

In order to avoid the multiple interchanges of data required by *xsort0*, we employ an *index* to the data being sorted. An index is a list $x[1], \ldots, x[n]$ of pointers to data (for example, to rows in a matrix). In order to sort data using a particular component as a key, we interchange indices in the index rather than interchange items of data. It costs more to refer to data through an index, but it costs less to interchange indices than to interchange large amounts of data. Thus the use of an index reduces the overall time required to sort a collection of data comprising many components.

The index sort *xsort* in the library *xsort1* is based on the selection sort. (See Pascal Sample 8.14.) In it, data in the array are always accessed through the index x, never directly. It presumes the existence of the type declaration

```
type indexType = array [1..maxRows] of 1..maxRows;
```

in the main program to specify the type of the index x.

Although the array a is not changed during the index sort, it is passed by reference (rather than by value) to the sorting procedure in order to avoid the expense

---

PASCAL SAMPLE 8.13   The library *xsort0* (sorts rows in an array)

```
{ xsort0: sorts rows in an n by m array a using keys in column k }
{ assumes: 1 <= k <= m                      }
{ returns:  a with rows rearranged so that  }
{          a[1, k] <= a[2, k] <= ... <= a[n, k] }
procedure sortRows( var a : table;          { array of items   }
                 n : rowIndex;              { no. of rows      }
                 m : colIndex;              { no. of columns   }
                 k : colIndex );            { column for key   }
       var i, j, p : rowIndex;
           c       : colIndex;
           item    : itemType;
       begin
           for i := 1 to n−1 do
              begin
                 { find row p containing minimum of a[i, k], ..., a[n, k] }
                 p := i;
                 for j := i+1 to n do if a[j, k] < a[p, k] then p := j;
                 { interchange row i with row p }
                 for c := 1 to m do
                    begin
                       item    := a[i, c];
                       a[i, c] := a[p, c];
                       a[p, c] := item
                    end
                 { now a[1, k] <= ... <= a[i, k] and  }
                 { a[i, k] <= a[j, k] when i < j <= n }
              end
       end;   { of sortRows }
```

of copying it over each time the procedure is called. Tables 8.7–8.10 illustrate the action of *xsort1* by displaying the states of the index and the array after each pass of the selection sort when column 1 is used as the key.

Thus, at the end of the sorting process, the index contains pointers to the rows in the matrix, with the first pointer pointing to the row that comes first in the desired order, the second pointer pointing to the row that comes second, and so on. The rows in the matrix remain unchanged.

In an actual experiment, both *xsort0* and *xsort1* were applied to matrices with 80 columns. The index sort *xsort1* required less than one-fifth the time used by *xsort0* to sort a matrix with 50 rows and less than one-third the time to sort a matrix with 100 rows.

PASCAL SAMPLE 8.14   The library *xsort1* (index sort)

```
{ xsort1: sorts index x to rows in array a using keys in column k }
{ returns: x rearranged so that                              }
{          a[x[1], k] <= a[x[2], k] <= ... <= a[x[n], k] }
procedure xsort( var a : table;              { table of items   }
                                             { (not changed)    }
                 var x : indexType;          { index to table   }
                     n : rowIndex;           { length of table  }
                     k : colIndex );         { column for key   }
    var i, j, p : rowIndex;
        item  : itemType;
    begin
        for i := 1 to n − 1 do
            begin
                { find minimum a[x[p], k] of a[x[i], k], ..., a[x[n], k] }
                p := i;
                for j := i + 1 to n do if a[x[j], k] < a[x[p], k] then p := j;
                { interchange x[i] and x[p] }
                j    := x[i];
                x[i] := x[p];
                x[p] := j;
                { now a[x[1], k] <= ... <= a[x[i], k] and   }
                { a[x[i], k] <= a[x[j], k] when i < j <= n }
            end
    end;   { of xsort }
```

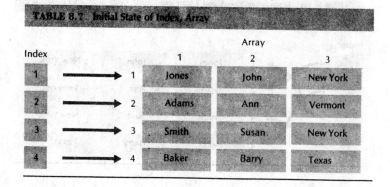

TABLE 8.7 Initial State of Index, Array

Index		Array 1	2	3
1	→ 1	Jones	John	New York
2	→ 2	Adams	Ann	Vermont
3	→ 3	Smith	Susan	New York
4	→ 4	Baker	Barry	Texas

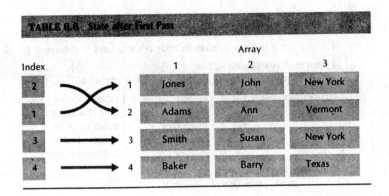

TABLE 8.8   State after First Pass

Index			Array 1	Array 2	Array 3
2	→	1	Jones	John	New York
1	→	2	Adams	Ann	Vermont
3	→	3	Smith	Susan	New York
4	→	4	Baker	Barry	Texas

TABLE 8.9   State after Second Pass

Index			Array 1	Array 2	Array 3
2	→	1	Jones	John	New York
4	→	2	Adams	Ann	Vermont
3	→	3	Smith	Susan	New York
1	→	4	Baker	Barry	Texas

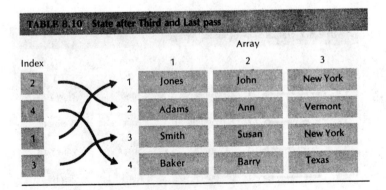

TABLE 8.10   State after Third and Last pass

Index			Array 1	Array 2	Array 3
2	→	1	Jones	John	New York
4	→	2	Adams	Ann	Vermont
1	→	3	Smith	Susan	New York
3	→	4	Baker	Barry	Texas

As we will see later, indices have many uses. When we need to manipulate long lists of information, we can use indices to restrict attention to sublists of interest, which we can search or sort more rapidly than the entire list.

1. Write programs to time the procedures in *xsort0* and *xsort1* for matrices of varying sizes. How many columns must a matrix contain for an index sort to be more efficient than an ordinary sort of the rows in the matrix?

2. Modify the exchange and insertion sort so that they, too, sort rows in an array both with and without an index. Since these algorithms perform more data movements than does the selection sort, use of an index should result in a greater improvement in efficiency.

3. Often a list to be sorted contains items with identical keys. For example, the surname Smith may occur several times in a list. In such cases we may chose to resolve the "tie" resulting from a comparison of keys by referring to some other piece of information, known as a *secondary key*, associated with the items (say, to a first name). Rewrite either *xsort0* or *xsort1* to accept an additional parameter specifying a secondary key and use that key within the sort to determine the order of two items with identical primary keys.

4. Another method for resolving ties among primary keys does not require any modifications to a sorting algorithm. Show how a stable sorting algorithm can be used to resolve ties. (*Hint:* Try invoking a stable sort more than once.)

8.6 EFFICIENT SORTING ALGORITHMS

The sorting algorithms considered so far all require time proportional to n^2 to sort a list with n entries. Two algorithms, which employ a "divide and conquer" strategy, are much more efficient, requiring on the average time proportional to $n \log_2(n)$.

SORTING BY REPEATED MERGING

To a limited extent the selection sort employs a "divide and conquer" approach to sorting. It divides the problem of sorting a list with n items into two subproblems: (1) placing the least item in the list in the first position; and (2) sorting the remaining list of $n - 1$ items. The reason that the selection sort is not particularly efficient is that these two subproblems are not of equal difficulty, the first being much easier than the second. Intuition suggests that if we can divide a problem into two more or less equal subproblems, then we can solve that problem (for example, by two people working independently) more quickly than we can solve it if one of the subproblems is almost as complicated as the original problem.

How, then, can we divide the problem of sorting a list with n items into two subproblems of equal size? One approach is to divide that list into two sublists, each with $n/2$ items. We can then sort those sublists separately and merge the results to produce a single sorted list containing all n items. As long as the merging process is not too expensive, we might expect a reduction in the total time required to sort the list.

To implement such an approach, we need to revise the parameter lists for our sorting procedures. Since these procedures must now be able to sort a sublist of the entire list, they need to be given the indices of the first and last items in the sublist to be sorted rather than those of the entire list. Exercise 1 at the end of this section asks for a revision of the selection sort that begins with the procedure header

> **procedure** *ssort*(**var** *a* : *itemList*; *first*, *last* : *index*);

and sorts the items *a*[*first*], ..., *a*[*last*] into the proper order. We can invoke *ssort* with a statement *ssort*(*list*, 1, *n*) to sort an entire list using $n(n - 1)/2$ comparisons. But, in an effort to find a more efficient sorting algorithm, we choose instead to use *ssort* to sort the first and second halves of the list and then to use a separate procedure *merge* to merge the results.

> **procedure** *msort1*(**var** *a* : *itemList*; *first*, *last* : *index*);
>   **var** *middle* : *index*;
>   **begin**
>   *middle* := (*first* + *last*) **div** 2;
>   *ssort*(*a*, *first*, *middle*);
>   *ssort*(*a*, *middle* + 1, *last*);
>   *merge*(*a*, *first*, *middle*, *last*)
>   **end**;

Exercise 3 at the end of this section calls for the construction of a procedure *merge*, that performs at most *n* comparisons when merging two sorted sublists to produce a single sorted list with *n* items. With such a procedure, the total number of comparisons required by *msort1* to sort a list with *n* items (Fig. 8.4) includes $n(n - 2)/4$ comparisons to sort the two halves of the list and at most *n* comparisons to merge them, for a total of at most $n(n + 2)/4$ comparisons. Hence *msort1* requires approximately half the number of comparisons as does *ssort*.

Since we were able to reduce the time required to sort the entire list by dividing it into two sublists, sorting and merging them, it is tempting to sort the sublists in the same way. To do this, we construct the procedure *msort2*

> **procedure** *msort2*(**var** *a* : *itemList*; *first*, *last* : *index*);
>   **var** *middle* : *index*;
>   **begin**
>   *middle* := (*first* + *last*) **div** 2;
>   *msort1*(*a*, *first*, *middle*);
>   *msort1*(*a*, *middle* + 1, *last*);
>   *merge*(*a*, *first*, *middle*, *last*)
>   **end**;

which invokes *msort1* to sort each of the two halves of the list. The effect in *msort2* (Fig. 8.5) is to sort the entire list by sorting four sublists, each with *n*/4 items, merging

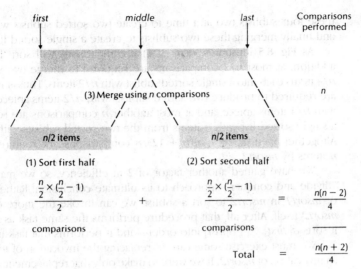

$$\frac{\frac{n}{2} \times (\frac{n}{2} - 1)}{2} + \frac{\frac{n}{2} \times (\frac{n}{2} - 1)}{2} = \frac{n(n-2)}{4}$$

comparisons   comparisons

$$\text{Total} = \frac{n(n+2)}{4}$$

FIGURE 8.4 ■ Stages in sorting an *n*-item list using *msort1*: (1) sort first half using *ssort*; (2) sort second half using *ssort*; and (3) merge sorted sublists using *merge*

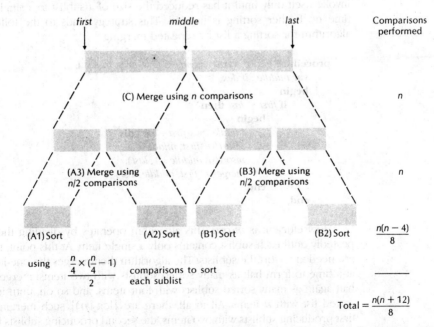

$$\frac{n(n-4)}{8}$$

using $\frac{\frac{n}{4} \times (\frac{n}{4} - 1)}{2}$ comparisons to sort each sublist

$$\text{Total} = \frac{n(n+12)}{8}$$

FIGURE 8.5 ■ Stages in sorting an *n*-item list using *msort2*: (A) sort first half using *msort1*; (B) sort second half using *msort1*; and (C) merge sorted sublists using *merge*

these four sublists two at a time to create two sorted sublists with $n/2$ items ea
and finally merging these two sublists to create a single sorted list.

As Fig. 8.5 illustrates, $n(n - 4)/8$ comparisons will sort the four sublists.
addition, at most $n/2$ comparisons are required to merge two sorted sublists w
$n/4$ items each into a single sorted sublist with $n/2$ items. Thus at most n compariso
are required to produce two sorted sublists with $n/2$ items apiece from four subli
with $n/4$ items apiece, and at most another n comparisons are required to produ
a single sorted list with n items from the two sorted sublists with $n/2$ items apie
Altogether then, at most $n(n + 12)/8$ comparisons are required to sort a list
n items by *msort2*.

We have gained another factor of 2 in efficiency, so we may as well carry t
"divide and conquer" approach to its ultimate conclusion. Rather than invoke *ss*
or *msort1* in *msort2* to sort a sublist, we can invoke the more efficient procedu
msort2 itself. After all, that procedure performs the same task as *ssort* and *msort1-*
it sorts $a[first], \ldots, a[last]$ into order—and it performs that task more efficiently.

We must exercise some care in replacing the invocation of *msort1* in *msort2* b
an invocation of *msort2*. If we were to make only that replacement, the sorting proce
would never stop, as *msort2* would invoke itself endlessly. But, if we invoke *msor*
only when the sublist to be sorted contains more than a single item, then *msort2* w
invoke itself only until it has reduced the size of a sublist to a single item, at whic
time no further sorting is needed. This strategy leads to the following recursiv
algorithm for sorting a list by repeated merging.

```
procedure msort( var a : itemList; first, last : index );
    var middle : index;
    begin
        if first < last then
            begin
                middle := ( first + last) div 2;
                msort(a, first, middle);
                msort(a, middle + 1, last);
                merge(a, first, middle, last)
            end
    end;
```

How efficient is *msort*? This algorithm operates by dividing the list in half re
peatedly until each sublist contains only a single item. At this point, no comparison
are needed to sort the sublists. The algorithm then merges the one-item sublists tw
at a time to form half as many sorted sublists with two items, merges these to forr
half again as many sorted sublists with four items, and so on, until it forms a singl
sorted list with n items. All in all, there are $\lceil \log_2(n) \rceil$ such merging activities, th
first producing sublists with two items, the second producing sublists with four item:
and so on. Each of these merging activities, as in *msort2* above, requires at most *n*
comparisons. Hence *msort* requires a total of at most $n \lceil \log_2(n) \rceil$ comparisons.

TABLE 8.11	Growth Rate of Sorting Times	
Length of list n	**Slow sorting** n^2	**Fast sorting** $n \lceil \log_2(n) \rceil$
10	100	14
100	10,000	700
1,000	1,000,000	10,000
10,000	100,000,000	140,000
100,000	10,000,000,000	1,700,000

The advantage of *msort* over *ssort* is striking if we compute the values of n^2 and $n \lceil \log_2(n) \rceil$ for various values of n. (See Table 8.11.) We see that the selection sort requires on the order of 10 billion comparisons to sort a list with 100,000 entries, whereas the recursive merge sort requires fewer than 2 million comparisons. Thus the "divide and conquer" approach to sorting does indeed provide a tremendous increase in efficiency.

However, this increase does have a cost: the procedure *merge* invoked by *msort* requires a sizable amount of auxiliary storage in order to merge two sublists in linear time. (See Exercise 3 at the end of this section.) This trade-off is typical in computing, when we often are able to reduce the execution time required to perform a certain task if we use additional storage to keep track of the information needed by a more efficient algorithm. However, if *msort* were to be used to sort a list with 100,000 items, the cost of providing an additional 100,000 items of storage might be prohibitive. Fortunately, there is a way (*quicksort*) to sort, with an average time proportional to $n \log_2(n)$, that does not require any additional storage.

The construction of *msort* demonstrates that a list may be sorted quite efficiently by repeated merging. Despite the efficiency of *msort* for long lists, the selection sort is still faster for short lists. Hence we can improve *msort* slightly if we stop the recursion when the sublists to be sorted get "small enough" and use a selection sort for these sublists. How small is "small enough" can be determined by experimentation. (See Exercise 8 at the end of this section.)

Although the recursive merge sort is primarily of educational interest, sorting by repeated merging is used extensively to sort long files that are kept in secondary storage. We will examine how this is done in Section 8.7.

QUICKSORT

The *quicksort* algorithm, like the recursive merge sort, requires a number of comparisons proportional to $n \log_2(n)$ on the average to sort a list with n items. In one sense it is better than the recursive merge sort because it requires no auxiliary storage; furthermore, experiments have shown it to be the sorting algorithm with the best average-case results. However, in its worst case, it is worse than the recursive merge sort because it requires n^2 comparisons to sort a list with n items.

The *quicksort* algorithm operates by recursion as in sorting by repeated merging, but it avoids the need for merging: it divides the list to be sorted into two sublists so that all items in the first sublist precede all items in the second. In pseudocode, the quicksort algorithm proceeds as follows.

```
{ quicksort algorithm }
if list is nonempty then
    begin
            divide list in two so that items in first half come before items in second half;
            sort first half of list;
            sort second half of list
    end
```

For example, in the list

$$25 \quad 36 \quad 22 \quad 41 \quad 57 \quad 48 \quad 52$$

the first three items are less than 41, which is less than the last three items. Therefore it is sufficient to sort the items to the left of 41 and then to sort the items to its right. The list is then in order, and subsequent merging is not needed.

In general, we will not be presented with lists that divide so nicely. Instead, we must rearrange lists so that their smallest items occur in the first half and their largest items occur in the second. We can perform such a rearrangement fairly efficiently by the following procedure.

Suppose that we are given a list of six numbers.

$$17 \quad 36 \quad 22 \quad 41 \quad 12 \quad 24$$

Let us try to put 24 in its proper place by rearranging the list so that its first items are all smaller than 24 and the remaining items are all larger. We first move 24 to a temporary location and set two markers, *left* and *right*, at the ends of the list to keep track of where we are.

$$17 \quad 36 \quad 22 \quad 41 \quad 12 \quad ** \quad \quad 24$$
left   *right*

Now we move the marker *left* to the right until we discover an item larger than 24.

$$17 \quad 36 \quad 22 \quad 41 \quad 12 \quad ** \quad \quad 24$$
      left   *right*

We move this large item to the "hole" where 24 was originally.

$$17 \quad ** \quad 22 \quad 41 \quad 12 \quad 36 \quad \quad 24$$
      left   *right*

Next we move the marker *right* to the left until we discover an item smaller than 24.

$$17 \quad ** \quad 22 \quad 41 \quad 12 \quad 36 \quad \quad 24$$
      left   *right*

We move this small item to the hole now above the marker *left*.

17	12	22	41	**	36	24
	left			*right*		

At this point we have made some progress: the markers *left* and *right* are closer together, the items to the left of *left* are less than 24, the items to the right of *right* are greater, and there is a place for 24 above the marker *right*. We repeat these steps, moving *left* to the right until we find an item larger than 24.

17	12	22	41	**	36	24
			left	*right*		

We put this large item in the hole above the marker *right*.

17	12	22	**	41	36	24
			left	*right*		

We then move *right* to the left. When the markers meet at the hole, we put 24 there and note that all items to the left of 24 are less than or equal to it, while all items to the right are greater than or equal to it.

17	12	22	24	41	36	**
			left			
			right			

Hence, to sort the entire list, we can now sort the items to the left of 24 and the items to the right of 24. Indeed, we can do this recursively, utilizing the process we have just described. The procedure *split* (Pascal Sample 8.15) rearranges a list as required by this process.

Using *split*, we can construct a recursive procedure *quicksort* that sorts an n-item list recursively. This procedure is contained in the library *sort5*. (See Pascal Sample 8.16.)

The procedure *split* requires $n - 1$ comparisons and at most $n + 1$ data movements to split an n-item list in two. On the average this algorithm splits the list into two sublists of nearly equal size; thus *quicksort* requires an average number of comparisons and data movements proportional to $n \log_2(n)$, as does the recursive merge sort. However, since the algorithm that splits the list requires fewer data movements than does the merge algorithm, *quicksort* is faster, on the average, than the recursive merge sort.

Unfortunately, in its worst case *quicksort* can be very slow. This worst case occurs when the list to be sorted is already in order: the right-most item in the list is already in its proper place and the recursion, instead of sorting two half-size sublists, must sort a sublist with only one less item. The worst case can be hidden somewhat by having *split* place a random item from the list in its final resting place, but even then there are still cases where sorting takes on the order of n^2 comparisons.

■ **PASCAL SAMPLE 8.15** The procedure *split*

```
procedure split( var a          : itemList;         { list to split    }
                     first, last : index;           { bounds for list }
                     var middle  : index );         { dividing point  }
{ rearranges a[first], ..., a[last] in linear time and sets middle so that }
{ a[first], ..., a[middle − 1] <= a[middle] <= a[middle + 1], ..., a[last] }
var left, right : index;
    x           : itemType;                         { choice for a[middle] }
begin
    { First choose an x in the list and markers left, right so that }
    { (1) a[i] <= x if first <= i < left                            }
    { (2) x <= a[j] if right < j <= last                            }
    { (3) a place exists for x at a[right]                          }

    x     := a[last];
    left  := first;
    right := last;
    { now squeeze left and right together, preserving (1) through (3) }

    while left < right do
        begin
            { move left marker to the right }

            while (left < right) and (a[left] <= x) do
                left := left + 1;
            if left < right then
                begin
                    a[right] := a[left];            { move big item   }
                    right    := right − 1
                end;
            { move right marker to the left }

            while (left < right) and (x <= a[right]) do
                right := right − 1;
            if left < right then
                begin
                    a[left] := a[right];            { move small item }
                    left    := left + 1
                end
        end;
    middle      := right;                           { place for x     }
    a[middle] := x

end;  { of split }
```

PASCAL SAMPLE 8.16   The library *sort5* (quicksort)

{ *sort5*: quicksort of *a*[1], ..., *a*[*n*] }

```
procedure sort( var a : itemList;                 { list to sort   }
                   n : index );                    { length of list }
    { declaration of split goes here }
    procedure quicksort( var a : itemList; first, last : index );
        { sorts a[first], ..., a[last] recursively }
        var middle : index;                        { set by split   }
        begin
            if first < last then
                begin
                    split(a, first, last, middle);
                    quicksort(a, first, middle − 1);
                    quicksort(a, middle + 1, last)
                end
        end;   { of quicksort }
    begin
        quicksort(a, 1, n)
    end;   { of sort }
```

ANALYSIS OF TIME NEEDED TO SORT

By analyzing a specific algorithm we can establish an upper limit on the length of time required to sort a list; we know that we can do at least as well as that algorithm does. But, if we analyze the problem, we can show that all algorithms require at least a certain amount of time; that is, we can do no better.

To sort a list, an algorithm must ask questions about entries in the list. We have been considering algorithms that ask questions only of the form "Is $a[i]$ less than $a[j]$?" Such algorithms are said to sort *by comparison*.

Some of these algorithms perform on the order of $n(n - 1)/2$ comparisons in their worst case and others perform on the order of $n \log_2(n)$ comparisons. Can we do any better? If we are clever enough, can we devise a method for sorting by comparison that, in its worst case, performs a number of comparisons that grows less rapidly than $n \log_2(n)$? As it turns out, the answer is no.

There are $n! = n(n - 1)(n - 2) \times \cdots \times 2 \times 1$ ways to order n objects. Sorting n objects amounts to determining which of these $n!$ orderings puts the objects in the proper sequence. Hence we must perform enough comparisons to distinguish $n!$

different cases. For example, if we are to sort three objects, we must perform enough comparisons to distinguish six cases.

How many comparisons are required to distinguish six cases? With one comparison we can distinguish two cases. With two comparisons we can distinguish four cases: two possibilities for the outcome of the first comparison and two for the outcome of the second. Even if we choose the objects to compare second after we know the results of the first comparison, there are still only four possible outcomes from two comparisons. Therefore any algorithm that is limited to performing two comparisons cannot distinguish six cases, and an algorithm for sorting three objects must, at least in some cases, perform three comparisons.

In general we can distinguish 2^c cases by performing c comparisons. If we are to sort n objects using no more than c comparisons in the worst case, then we must have

$$2^c \geq n!$$

since there are $n!$ ways to arrange n objects. Equivalently, we must have

$$c \geq \log_2(n!).$$

Since the logarithm of a product is the sum of the logarithms of the factors in that product, we must have

$$c \geq \log_2(n) + \log_2(n - 1) + \cdots + \log_2(2) + \log_2(1).$$

To estimate the size of this sum, we note that its first $n/2$ terms

$$\log_2(n), \ldots, \log_2\left(\frac{n}{2} + 1\right)$$

are all greater than $\log_2(n/2)$, that $\log_2(1) = 0$, and that the remaining $(n/2) - 1$ terms

$$\log_2\left(\frac{n}{2}\right), \ldots, \log_2(2)$$

are all greater than or equal to $\log_2(2)$, which equals 1. Hence

$$c \geq \frac{n}{2} \log_2\left(\frac{n}{2}\right) + \frac{n}{2} - 1 \quad \text{or} \quad c \geq \frac{n}{2} \log_2(n) - 1$$

since $\log_2(n/2) = \log_2(n) - 1$. Thus we have succeeded in showing that, in the worst case, the number of comparisons required to sort a list containing n objects must grow proportionally to $n \log_2(n)$.

The result of this analysis (and a similar, but more difficult analysis of the average time requirements for sorting by comparison) is that we cannot expect to find algorithms that are as much more efficient than *quicksort* or the recursive merge sort as these algorithms are more efficient than the selection, exchange, or insertion sort. All algorithms that sort by comparison require time proportional to $n \log_2(n)$, and these two algorithms require no more time than that.

This does not mean that these two algorithms are the ultimate sorting methods. Each has its limitations: *quicksort* performs poorly in its worst case, and the recursive merge sort requires a large amount of additional storage. Thus we may still need algorithms that are better suited to certain situations than either *quicksort* or the recursive merge sort. We will develop such algorithms later in this book: the merge sort for sequential files will be considered later in this chapter and the heapsort will be considered in Chapter 12.

EXERCISES

1. Analyze the behavior of the selection sort procedure required by *msort* as follows.

   (a) Write a procedure *ssort* that arranges $a[first]$, ..., $a[last]$ in order using a selection sort.

   (b) Measure the execution time required by *ssort* using a variant of the program *sort*, which was developed in Section 8.4.

   (c) Use the results of (b) to determine a constant A such that *ssort* requires approximately An^2 seconds to sort a list of length n.

2. Write a procedure *merge* beginning with the header

   procedure *merge*(**var** a, b, c : *itemList*; n, m: *index*);

   such that, whenever

   $$a[1] \leq a[2] \leq \cdots \leq a[n] \quad \text{and} \quad b[1] \leq b[2] \leq \cdots \leq b[m],$$

   merge will merge $a[1]$, ..., $a[n]$ and $b[1]$, ..., $b[m]$ into a single sorted list occupying $c[1]$, ..., $c[n + m]$ and use at most $n + m$ comparisons.

3. Write a procedure *merge* beginning with the header

   procedure *merge*(**var** a : *itemList*;
                          $first$, $middle$, $last$: *index*   );

   such that, whenever

   $first \leq middle \leq last$,
   $a[first] \leq \cdots \leq a[middle]$, and
   $a[middle + 1] \leq \cdots \leq a[last]$,

   merge will merge the two sorted sublists into a single sorted list occupying $a[first]$, ..., $a[last]$ and use at most $last - first + 1$ comparisons. (*Hint:* You will need to use an auxiliary list to hold items from a during the merging process.)

4. Compute the minimum and maximum number of comparisons and movements made by your solution to Exercise 3 when merging the two halves of an n-item list. (*Hint:* These should be linear functions of n.)

5. Write a program to compute the execution time required by *merge* when creating lists with 10, 100, and 1000 items. Use your results to determine a constant B such that *merge* requires approximately Bn seconds to merge n items into a single list.

6. Use the program *sort*, which was developed in Section 8.4, to measure the time required by *msort1*, *msort2*, and *msort* when sorting lists of various lengths. Verify that *msort1* and *msort2* require time proportional to n^2 to sort an n-item list, but that *msort* only requires time proportional to $n \log_2(n)$.

7. If A and B are the constants determined in Exercises 1 and 5, then *msort1* should be faster than *ssort* when

$$2A\left(\frac{n}{2}\right)^2 + Bn < An^2,$$

that is, when the time to sort and merge two half lists is less than the time to sort the entire list using *ssort*.

   (a) Simplify the expression and use it to predict when *msort1* is faster than *ssort* on your system.

   (b) Compare the times required by *ssort* and *msort1* to determine the accuracy of your prediction.

8. Experiment with making *msort* faster as follows.

   (a) Estimate how long a list must be before *msort* is faster than *ssort*.

   (b) Modify *msort* to sort short lists using *ssort* when it is faster to do that than to divide the lists further. By how much does this improve the execution time of *msort*?

9. The action of the recursive merge sort is easiest to visualize when the length n of the list being sorted is a power of 2. Describe what happens when n is not a power of 2.

10. Is the recursive merge sort a stable sorting method?

11. Modify the procedure *split* in *quicksort* to pick an item at random from a list for use as the "median."

12. Modify the procedure *split* in *quicksort* to use the median of the first, last, and middle items in the list as the "median."

13. Measure the time required by *quicksort*, using the original and modified versions of the *split* procedure. Which version is fastest?

14. Is *quicksort* a stable sorting algorithm?

15. We have learned that three comparisons are required in the worst case to sort a list with three items. How many comparisons are required in the worst case to sort lists with 4, 5, 6, and 7 items?

16. How do your answers to Exercise 15 compare with the lower bound of $(n/2)\log_2(n) - 1$ established in this section for the number of comparisons?

8.7 SORTING LARGE AMOUNTS OF DATA

The algorithms we have studied so far enable us to sort moderate amounts of data. Since they require us to store the items being sorted in an array, they cannot cope with large amounts of data. The space available in primary memory for a program and its data generally prevents us from storing more than several thousand items in an array. To store and sort more information—say 10,000 or 100,000 items—we must find a way to use files residing in secondary storage rather than arrays residing in primary memory.

Of the algorithms we have studied so far, the exchange (or bubble sort) algorithm can be most readily adapted to work with files. For a file with n items of data we can copy that file $n - 1$ times, bubbling large items toward the end of the file each time we copy it. But the bubble sort is the least efficient of the algorithms we know, and copying a file several thousand times would be prohibitively expensive. Hence we seek to adapt a more efficient algorithm to work with files.

Of the two efficient algorithms we know, *quicksort* is not a likely candidate for use with files. Its rearrangement procedure can force us to move items from one end of a list to the other—a difficult maneuver in a sequential file and a costly maneuver in a direct-access file. Thus we elect to adapt the recursive merge sort to work with files. Figure 8.6 shows how that algorithm arranges in order an 8-element list by dividing the list in half, sorting each half, and then merging the results.

In order to sort an n-element list, the recursive merge sort requires $\lceil \log_2(n) \rceil$ levels of recursion to divide the list into sorted pieces containing one item each. Since n comparisons at each level can merge these sorted pieces two by two into sorted pieces that are twice as large, the recursive merge sort requires at most $n \lceil \log_2(n) \rceil$ comparisons to sort a list of length n.

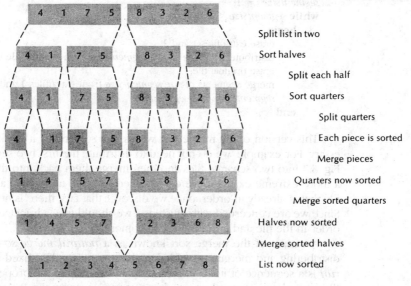

FIGURE 8.6 ■ Recursive merge sort of 8-element list

If we organize the work of the merge sort somewhat differently, we can dispense with both recursion and arrays, using iteration and files instead. To illustrate how this might work, suppose we are given a file containing the unsorted list depicted in Fig. 8.6. Initially we regard the file as a sequence of eight sorted segments containing one item each, as shown in the middle of Fig. 8.6. On successive passes over that file, we arrange to merge these segments two by two, first into four sorted segments with two items each, then into two sorted segments with four items each, and finally into a single sorted segment with all eight items, as shown at the bottom of Fig. 8.6.

We need a strategy for keeping track of the segments in the file as we merge them. One such strategy uses two extra files and divides each pass over the file into two phases: a distribution phase, in which we distribute sorted segments from the file between these two extra files, and a merge phase, in which we merge successive segments from one extra file with successive segments from the other to create sorted segments of twice the length in the original file. By placing the segments in files rather than in arrays, we do not have to limit their lengths. Figure 8.7 illustrates how this strategy arranges the 8-element list in order in three passes, distributing and merging segments of size 1, 2, and 4 on the first, second, and third pass, respectively. What makes this strategy particularly suited to working with files is that, during each phase, we read and write segments in the files sequentially. Hence we do not require the direct-access capability of an array.

In general, to sort a file containing n items using this iterative version of the merge sort, we proceed as follows.

```
segmentSize := 1;
while segmentSize < n do
    begin
        erase extra files 1 and 2;
        distribute segments of size segmentSize from original file to extra files 1 and 2;
        erase original file;
        merge segments of size segmentSize from extra files 1 and 2 into original file;
        segmentSize := 2*segmentSize
    end
```

This version of the merge sort works, but sometimes it works harder than necessary. For example, we do not need to distribute the first two segments in Pass 2 in Fig. 8.7 into two separate files and then merge them back into the original file. For a more extreme example, we do not need to make more than a single pass over a file that is already in order: once we discover that fact, there is no more work to do. Since we are concerned with efficiency, we should take advantage of any preexisting order in the file and avoid unnecessary merging.

A variant of the merge sort known as a *natural merge sort* does just this by distributing and merging variable-length *runs* rather than fixed-length segments. A *run* is a sequence of items in the file that is already in the proper order. Figure 8.8 illustrates how a natural merge sort arranges in order the 8-element list with two,

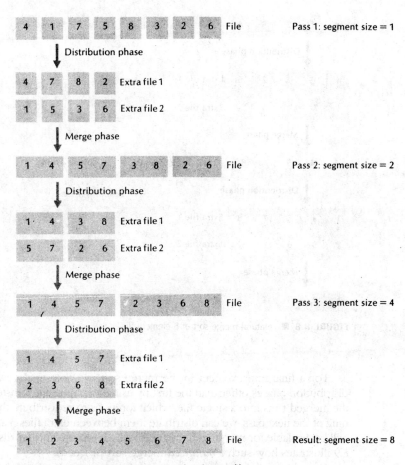

FIGURE 8.7 ■ Iterative merge sort of 8-element file

rather than three, passes. Pass 1 distributes five runs, not eight segments, to the two extra files; furthermore, the first and third runs coalesce, leaving us with only four runs to merge. In general, a natural merge sort employs the following strategy:

repeat
    erase extra files 1 and 2;
    distribute runs from original file to extra files 1 and 2;
    erase original file;
    merge runs from extra files 1 and 2 into original file;
    runCount := number of resulting runs
until *runCount* = 1

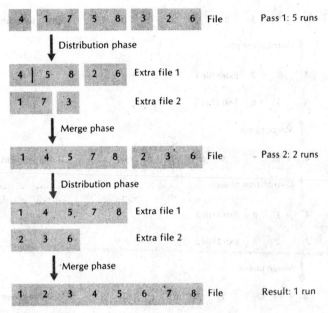

FIGURE 8.8 ■ Natural merge sort of 8-element file

For a final improvement in the merge sort, we note that we can eliminate all distribution phases other than the first by using two more files. Instead of placing all the merged runs into a single file, which forces us to redistribute them at the beginning of the next pass, we can distribute them between extra files 3 and 4, where they will be available for merging in the next pass without any further distribution. Figure 8.9 illustrates how such a *balanced* merge sort proceeds.

Now that we have developed a sorting strategy appropriate for large amounts of data, we convert that strategy into a Pascal program *sortMerge* that performs a balanced natural merge sort on an external file. Our program will employ four subsidiary procedures: *copyItem* to copy an item from one file to another, noting whether or not that item is the last in a run; *distribute* to perform the initial distribution of runs to two auxiliary files; *createRun* to merge two runs from a pair of auxiliary files and put the result in a specified file; and *mergePass* to perform one pass over a pair of auxiliary files, merging pairs of runs and distributing them between two more auxiliary files. Pascal Sample 8.17 displays the main program in *sortMerge*. Liberal comments in that program remind us of the general strategy for a balanced natural merge sort.

The *distribute* procedure, displayed as Pascal Sample 8.18, uses the *copyItem* procedure to copy an item from the source file to one of two output files. That

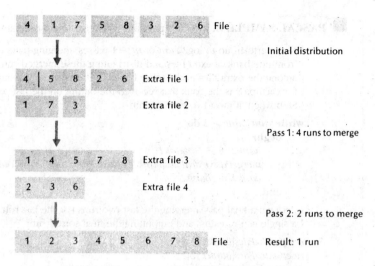

FIGURE 8.9 ■ Balanced natural merge sort of 8-element file

PASCAL SAMPLE 8.17   The program *sortMerge* (main program)

{ balanced natural merge sort of data in an external file }

{ sorts data in *source*, putting results in *destination* }
{ uses four extra files arranged in two banks of two files each }

program *sortMerge*(*input, output, source, destination*);

type *dataType* = *integer*;
    fileType = **file of** *dataType*;
    fileBank = **array** [1..2] **of** *fileType*;

var *source, destination* : *fileType*;
    extraFiles   : **array** [1..2] **of** *fileBank*;
    bank1, bank2   : 1..2;
    runCount   : *integer*;

{ declarations of *distribute, mergePass, copyItem*, and *createRun* procedures go here }

begin

    { Distribute runs (i.e., ordered sequences of data) from the source file }
    { alternately to the files in the first bank of extra files, counting how   }
    { many runs there are.   }

    bank1 := 1;
    distribute(*source, extraFiles*[*bank1*], *runCount*);

PASCAL SAMPLE 8.17   The program *sortMerge* (main program, continued)

{ Now perform up to log2(*runCount*) − 1 passes, merging pairs of runs }
{ from one bank of extra files and distributing these merged runs   }
{ among the extra files in the other bank. The bank serving as input   }
{ for each pass is the bank that received the output on the last pass.   }
{ Stop when at most two runs remain.   }

while *runCount* > 2 **do**
    begin
        bank2 := 3 − *bank1*;
        mergePass(*extraFiles*[*bank1*], *extraFiles*[*bank2*], *runCount*);
        bank1 := *bank2*
    end;

{ Perform a final pass, merging the last two runs (or the last run if }
{ a single run remains) and outputting the final sorted run.   }

reset(*extraFiles*[*bank1*][1]);
reset(*extraFiles*[*bank1*][2]);
rewrite(*destination*);
createRun(*extraFiles*[*bank1*], *destination*)

end.   { of *sortMerge* }

PASCAL SAMPLE 8.18   The program *sortMerge* (*distribute* procedure)

procedure *distribute*(**var** *infile*   : *fileType*;
                      var *outfiles* : *fileBank*;
                      var *runs*   : *integer*);

{ distributes runs from *infile* to *outfiles*[1] and *outfiles*[2]   }
{ returns: *runs* = number of resulting runs   }
{ (could be improved by using an internal sort to lengthen the runs) }

var *newRun* : *boolean*;

begin
    runs := 0;
    newRun := *true*;
    reset(*infile*);
    rewrite(*outfiles*[1]);
    rewrite(*outfiles*[2]);

    { copy items to the output files until none remain, }
    { counting the number of runs   }

    while not *eof*(*infile*) **do**
        begin
            if *newRun* **then** *runs* := *runs* + 1;
            copyItem(*infile*, *outfiles*[2 − *runs* **mod** 2], *newRun*)
        end
end;   { of *distribute* }

PASCAL SAMPLE 8.19 The program *sortMerge* (*copyItem* procedure)

```
procedure copyItem( var infile, outfile : fileType;
                    var endOfRun    : boolean );
    { copies item of data from infile to outfile, setting endOfRun true }
    { if the next item from infile does not belong to the current run  }
    var item : dataType;
    begin
        read(infile, item);
        write(outfile, item);
        if eof(infile) then
            endOfRun := true
        else
            endOfRun := (infile↑ < item)
    end;   { of copyItem }
```

procedure sets *newRun* true if the next item in the source file begins a new run so that *distribute* can alternate writing successive runs to the two output files: the expression 2–*runs* **mod** 2 alternates in value between 1 and 2. We can modify *distribute* to read batches of items into an array, sort the array using *quicksort*, and distribute the manufactured runs instead of the shorter ones that occur accidentally in the source. By generating longer runs prior to the first merging pass, we can reduce the total number of passes required to sort the files. (See Exercise 4 at the end of this section.)

The *copyItem* procedure, displayed as Pascal Sample 8.19, is fairly straightforward. Since both *distribute* and *createRun* must copy items and detect ends of runs, it pays to isolate these details in a single procedure.

The *mergePass* procedure is similar to the *distribute* procedure. It relies on *createRun* to handle the actual merging of runs, and it does not stop before it has exhausted the runs in both input files. (See Pascal Sample 8.20.)

Finally, the *createRun* procedure is the most delicate in *sortMerge*. It must merge two runs, keeping track of the various ways in which they can end, and consuming

---

PASCAL SAMPLE 8.20 The program *sortMerge* (*mergePass* procedure)

```
procedure mergePass( var infiles, outfiles : fileBank;
                     var runs              : integer );
    { merges pairs of runs from infiles[1] and infiles[2], putting the  }
    { resulting merged runs alternately into outfiles[1] and outfiles[2] }
    { returns: runs = number of runs produced                            }
    { (It is not necessary that infiles[1] and infiles[2] contain equal  }
    { numbers of runs.)                                                   }
```

PASCAL SAMPLE 8.20 The program *sortMerge* (*mergePass* procedure, cont.)

```
begin
    runs := 0;
    rewrite(outfiles[1]);
    rewrite(outfiles[2]);
    reset(infiles[1]);
    reset(infiles[2]);

    while not (eof(infiles[1]) and eof(infiles[2])) do
        begin
            runs := runs + 1;
            createRun(infiles, outfiles[2 - runs mod 2])
        end
end;  { of mergePass }
```

those runs completely, even if one runs out before the other. Like *copyItem*, *createRun* looks ahead in a file using a buffer variable to detect the end of a run. (See Pascal Sample 8.21.)

To sort a file containing n items of data, *sortMerge* requires at most $\lceil \log_2(n) \rceil$ merging passes. Since $2^{17} > 2^7 \times 1000 > 100{,}000$, *sortMerge* can sort a file containing

---

PASCAL SAMPLE 8.21 The program *sortMerge* (*createRun* procedure)

```
procedure createRun( var infiles : fileBank;
                     var outfile : fileType );

{ merges the next runs from infiles[1] and infiles[2], }
{ putting the result in outfile                        }
{ assumes: not (eof(infiles[1]) and eof(infiles[2]))   }

var endOfRun1, endOfRun2 : boolean;

begin
    endOfRun1 := eof(infiles[1]);
    endOfRun2 := eof(infiles[2]);
    repeat
        if endOfRun1 then
            copyItem(infiles[2], outfile, endOfRun2)
        else if endOfRun2 then
            copyItem(infiles[1], outfile, endOfRun1)
        else if infiles[1]↑ <= infiles[2]↑ then
            copyItem(infiles[1], outfile, endOfRun1)
        else
            copyItem(infiles[2], outfile, endOfRun2)
    until endOfRun1 and endOfRun2
end;  { of createRun }
```

100,000 entries with at most 17 merging passes. Thus this algorithm represents a considerable improvement over the bubble sort, which would require 100,000 passes.

Many commercial sorting packages rely on the merge sort to sort large amounts of data and *quicksort* to sort smaller amounts. Efficient algorithms such as these make otherwise formidable tasks a matter of routine.

EXERCISES

1. Write a program to sort a file using a modified version of the bubble sort.

2. Compare the time required to sort a list of 1000 integers using the recursive sort merge, *quicksort, sortMerge,* and your solution to Exercise 1.

3. Rewrite *sortMerge* so that it alphabetizes a list of words stored one per line in a text file.

4. Rewrite the *distribute* procedure, as suggested in this section, to generate longer runs using *quicksort.* How does this strategy affect the execution time of *sortMerge?*

5. Is *sortMerge* a stable sorting algorithm?

6. Investigate the effect of using additional auxiliary files in the merge sort algorithm.

   (a) Devise a procedure that merges m runs stored in m separate files into a single run in another file.

   (b) Rewrite *sortMerge* to use $2m$ extra files, performing an m-way merge on each pass and distributing the resulting runs among m of the extra files. Declare m as a symbolic constant in your program.

   (c) How many passes does the revised *sortMerge* make when sorting a file with n items?

   (d) How does using more files affect the execution time of *sortMerge?* What is an optimum value for m?

7. Suppose that you are given a dictionary file containing an alphabetical list of the 40,000 most common words in the English language.

   (a) Design a program to check the spelling of words in an arbitrary file of text. Consider a word to be spelled correctly if it is in the dictionary and to be spelled incorrectly otherwise.

   (b) Estimate how long it would take your program to check the spelling of the words in a text file containing 2000 words, 600 of which are distinct. To help in making your estimates, you may want to time how long it takes to read a file containing 40,000 words and how long it takes to sort a list of 600 or 2000 words. Do not implement your design before making such an estimate. Estimation may show that your algorithm is impossibly slow and that you had better design a more efficient one.

SUMMARY

Searching algorithms locate items in lists. Sorting algorithms arrange lists in alphabetic or numeric order. A study of searching and sorting produces

▨   useful algorithms for a variety of applications; and

■ guidance for developing algorithms to solve other problems, particularly when

  1. several approaches exist to a problem, and

  2. analysis is required to select the best approach

Different algorithms require different amounts of time and space. The resources required to solve a problem usually increase with the size of the problem. For example, it takes longer to search or sort a list of 1000 items than it does a list of 100 items. How much longer depends on the algorithm.

■ Linear-time algorithms take time proportional to n to process a list of length n.

■ Quadratic-time algorithms are slower and take time proportional to n^2.

■ Logarithmic-time algorithms are faster and take time proportional to $\log n$.

■ Constant-time algorithms are fastest and take time independent of n.

An empirical or theoretical analysis of the time required to process a list in the

■ worst case bounds the time required to process any list of length n, and in the

■ average case estimates the time required to process a typical list of length n.

The applicability and efficiency of search algorithms depend on the nature of the list being searched.

■ Linear search

  1. is appropriate for lists of any length stored in arrays or files, and

  2. requires linear time in its worst and average cases.

■ Binary search

  1. is appropriate for ordered lists stored in arrays, and

  2. requires logarithmic time in its worst and average cases.

The applicability and efficiency of sorting algorithms depend on the method used.

■ Selection, exchange, and insertion sort

  1. are appropriate for short lists,

  2. are easy to code, but inefficient for longer lists, and

  3. require quadratic time in their worst and average cases.

■ Merge sort

  1. is appropriate for lists of any length, with the

  (a) recursive variant appropriate for sorting arrays and the

  (b) external variant appropriate for sorting files;

  2. requires time proportional to $n \log n$ in all cases; and

  3. requires linear amount of additional storage for items in list.

■ Quicksort

  1. is appropriate for lists stored as arrays;

    2. is generally faster than merge sort, requiring

       (a) time proportional to $n \log n$ on the average and

       (b) quadratic time in the worst case; and

    3. requires no additional storage for items in list.

Any algorithm that sorts a list by comparing items in that list requires time proportional at least to $n \log n$ in its worst case.

DY: A PROTOTYPE DATABASE MAN
ASE MANAGEMENT SYSTEM CASE
T SYSTEM CASE STUDY: A PROTO
DY: A PROTOTYPE DATABASE MAN
ASE MANAGEMENT SYSTEM CASE
T SYSTEM CASE STUDY: A PROTO
DY: A PROTOTYPE DATABASE MAN
ASE MANAGEMENT SYSTEM CASE

C   H   A   P   T   E   R

*I*n this chapter we will develop a sizable program, using data structures and algorithms introduced in earlier chapters. Our aim is to illustrate the general applicability of the tools developed so far; to motivate the use of further, more sophisticated tools; and to come to grips with the problems of developing large programs.

The third of these aims will occupy most of our attention. When writing short programs, we may be able to proceed with a minimum of prior thought and organization. Viewed optimistically, the time we waste in occasional disorganized attacks on problems that are more difficult than anticipated is offset by the time we save by writing many short programs quickly. Even with short programs, this view may be overly optimistic and lead to inferior programs. In the case of long programs the dangers of getting lost, wasting considerable amounts of time, and producing decidedly inferior programs are simply too great and require that we proceed in an organized manner.

Hence, in this chapter, we develop guidelines for structuring a large program as an integrated collection of well-designed subprograms. These subprograms must fit together well to accomplish their intended task, and we should be able to construct, test, and modify them in an orderly fashion. Ideally we should be able to tackle a large problem a piece at a time with some assurance that, when we are done, the pieces will fit together properly.

We illustrate the process of program construction by writing a prototype database management system. Some other applications that would serve equally as well are suggested in the exercises at the end of Section 9.4.

Databases contain information such as personnel records, student grade transcripts, inventories, and financial records. A *database management system* (DBMS) provides a means for organizing databases, for permitting convenient access to information in databases, and for maintaining databases. A single general-purpose DBMS can provide a common interface to a large number of databases. Developing such a DBMS generally involves writing many interrelated programs, some of which may be quite large.

Database management systems provide a variety of services. They enable users to retrieve selected information from a database, to generate reports, and to update a database by adding, deleting, or changing data. They should also present users with a coherent view of databases, while at the same time allowing databases to be organized efficiently. Users of a DBMS need to know only the logical organization of a database, not its physical representation in terms of specific and file structures.

In general terms, a database contains information about a collection of *entities* such as employees, students, stock items, or financial accounts. This information supplies the values of various *attributes* of the entities. For example, a personnel database may contain the name, address, job title, and salary of each employee; a student database may contain the name, courses taken, and grades of each student; an inventory database may contain the stock number, wholesale and retail prices, source of supply, and quantity in stock of each item in the inventory; and a financial database may contain the account code, the amount budgeted for the year, and the amount spent to date for each account in the budget.

Logically, a database is a matrix. The rows in the matrix correspond to the entities in the database, and the columns correspond to the attributes. Table 9.1 illustrates the logical organization of a simple database of information about classrooms at a small college.

TABLE 9.1   Sample Database: Classrooms at Small College

Building	Room	Seats	TV	Microphone
Humanities	100	75	yes	yes
Humanities	101	20	no	no
Humanities	105	15	no	no
Humanities	201	30	yes	no
Humanities	205	15	no	no
Sciences	120	75	yes	yes
Sciences	130	75	yes	no
Sciences	140	40	yes	no
Campus Center	10	1000	yes	yes
Campus Center	15	100	yes	yes
Campus Center	101	50	no	yes
Campus Center	102	25	no	no

TABLE 9.2   Sample Physical Representation of *classrooms* Database

```
Humanities    100   75yesyes
Humanities    101   20no no
Humanities    105   15no no
Humanities    201   30yesno
Humanities    205   15no no
Sciences      120   75yesyes
Sciences      130   75yesno
Sciences      140   40yesno
Campus Center 101000yesyes
Campus Center 15 100yesyes
Campus Center101   50no yes
Campus Center102   25no no
```

Physically, a database may be stored in a variety of ways. It may be stored row by row in a sequential or direct-access file. In such an organization, the information concerning each entity in the database constitutes a *physical record* that is broken into a number of *fields,* each field containing the value of a particular attribute for that entity. For example, the *classrooms* database may be stored in a text file such as that displayed in Table 9.2. Each physical record in that file contains 27 characters and is divided into five fields with 14, 3, 4, 3, and 3 characters. Since these fields are just wide enough to hold the values of the attributes, it is somewhat tedious to read the file directly. But producing a readable version of a database is the job of a DBMS, not of the physical representation of the database.

Alternatively, a database may be stored column by column in a *transposed* file, with the values of one attribute for all entities in the database occurring contiguously. Table 9.3 contains a transposed representation of the *classrooms* database in which the values of certain attributes have been abbreviated to conserve space. More complex databases may be organized using other representations, more than one file, or a hierarchical arrangement.

The choice of a particular physical representation for a database is influenced by the ways in which that database will be used. If the most common operation involves finding the values of all attributes for a single entity, then a row by row organization, which stores all those values together, makes the most sense. If the most common operation involves locating all records that have specified values for some particular attributes, then a transposed column by column organization, which stores all the

TABLE 9.3   Sample Transposed Representation of *classrooms* Database

```
HHHHHSSSCCCC
100 101 105 201 205 120 130 140 10 15 101 102
75 20 15 30 15 75 75 40 1000 100 50 25
ynnynyyyynn
ynnnnynnyyyn
```

values of the attributes of interest together, may make the most sense. For large databases, more sophisticated physical representations may be necessary to allow easy access to the data. The designer of a database application must therefore know something about the expected use of a database in order to choose the most efficient physical representation. And the designer of a database management system—who is distinct from the more numerous designers of applications of that system or from the even more numerous users of those applications—must build enough flexibility into the DBMS to meet the needs of those who will rely on that system.

The designer of a database management system must, in fact, address many issues. Some of these issues are purely technical in nature. For example, construction of a DBMS that handles very large databases requires a strategy for determining which records from the database belong in primary memory, when, and for how long. Normally, users of a DBMS are aware of the resolution of such technical issues only through the performance characteristics (such as responsiveness and cost of use) of the DBMS.

Most design issues have managerial as well as technical implications. For example, a typical DBMS should include features that enhance the accuracy and integrity of the data it handles. The way in which such features can be provided is a technical issue. Whether the features are cost effective, or whether they are compatible with an organization's means of doing business, is a managerial issue. Technically, *back-up* copies of a database can be retained to help recreate a database that has been destroyed. And *audit trails* of changes made to the database aid in determining the cause of inaccuracies in it or in bringing a back-up copy up to date. Managerially, procedures for updating and restoring a database must be formalized and enforced in order to prevent inaccurate data from entering a database and to ensure that a recreated database contains accurate and up-to-date information.

The *security* of data in a database presents another problem. Owners of a database may have the right or obligation to restrict access to the data to those with a legitimate need to know. People about whom information is kept may have a legitimate right regarding the *privacy* of that information. A database management system must provide mechanisms for ensuring these rights. Often the simplest solution is to restrict physical access to the database to a small group of people. If a larger group must have access, individual users may be required to supply a *password* before being allowed access to sensitive data. Or the data in a database may be encrypted so as to be unreadable by anyone not having access to a decryption mechanism.

Finally, for a database management system to be usable, there must be some way for a user to interact with that system. Database management systems are typically command-driven systems, but the flexibility and convenience of command protocols vary widely from one DBMS to another. Pascal Sample 9.1 shows a sample interaction with a command-driven DBMS *info,* which we will write in this chapter, to interrogate the *classrooms* database.

Computer scientists are currently developing natural language interfaces to database management systems. These interfaces allow users to phrase their questions in or-

PASCAL SAMPLE 9.1   The program *info* (use of command-driven DBMS)

```
Database: classrooms

Command: select TV yes
7 entities selected

Command: print building room

building          room
--------------    ----
Humanities        100
Humanities        201
Sciences          120
Sciences          130
Sciences          140
Campus Center     10
Campus Center     15

Command: stop

bye
```

dinary English instead of as a sequence of commands. For example, a user might type

```
What classrooms are equipped with television?
```

instead of the sequence of commands

```
base classrooms
select TV yes
print building room
```

to obtain the information in Pascal Sample 9.1. The job of a natural language interface is to translate questions that users want to ask into commands that can be understood by a DBMS. Given the complexity and ambiguity of the English language, the design of a natural language interface poses many challenging problems.

The remainder of this chapter is devoted to construction of a prototype database management system. This prototype will provide only a few of the services of a DBMS, namely, the ability to select, sort, and print information from databases similar to the *classrooms* database. Enhancements that enable the prototype to compute useful statistics, to update information in a database, or to handle other physical organizations for a database, are left to the exercises. Nonetheless, constructing even this rudimentary prototype will require us to write a substantial Pascal program. In the course of writing this program, we will gain an understanding of how the services of a DBMS can be provided and, more importantly, of how to go about designing and constructing large programs.

EXERCISES

1. Describe the roles that back-up copies and audit trails might play in maintaining databases for
   (a) bank checking accounts,
   (b) student grade records,
   (c) inventories, and
   (d) census data.

   In each case discuss whether back-up copies and audit trails are needed and why. Pay particular attention to the importance and difficulty of recreating a database that has been accidentally destroyed.

2. An audit trail for a database can be maintained as a separate file that lists the date, time, and nature of changes made to data in the database. Explain how to recreate a database from a back-up copy of the database and an audit trail of changes made to the database.

3. Different strategies for maintaining audit trails are possible. We may change a database first and then record the change in the audit trail. We may note a required change in the audit trail and then change the database. Or we may do both. Care is required if we are to reconstruct exactly a database when a catastrophe (caused, say, by a power failure) occurs while we are changing the database.
   (a) What problems can arise if we change the database first and then record the change in the audit trail?
   (b) What problems can arise if we perform these actions in the reverse order?
   (c) Can you devise a mixed strategy that is impervious to these problems?

4. Passwords that restrict access to sensitive data are themselves sensitive data.
   (a) In what ways might passwords become known to unauthorized users?
   (b) What are the advantages and disadvantages of changing passwords frequently to reduce unauthorized access to data?

5. A system that uses passwords to restrict access to data must itself have some form of access to the passwords. One strategy is simply to store the passwords themselves in a file. Another is to store versions of the passwords that have been scrambled so as to make them unreadable.
   (a) Describe how a system might use scrambled passwords to restrict access to data.
   (b) What are the relative advantages and disadvantages of storing scrambled passwords as opposed to storing the actual passwords?

9.2 DATA STRUCTURES: PICKING THE APPROPRIATE ONES

In order to construct a database management system, we must define two data structures: one for the permanent storage of information in external files and one for the internal structures manipulated by the DBMS. These two structures may bear a strong resemblance to one another, or they may differ substantially because of differing constraints imposed by primary and secondary memories or to requirements for efficient access to the data.

The most important thing to remember as we begin to design a prototype DBMS is the need to remain flexible. As we proceed we will run into situations that are difficult to predict, and we may need to modify our data structures in order to overcome problems or take advantage of opportunities. But if we lock ourselves into a rigid design too early, or if we build this design too thoroughly into our program, we may find that changing our minds is very difficult. Hence we will try to limit the impact of data-structure design on program design. And we will avoid premature complications by starting with reasonably simple data structures.

Let us design first the format for external files that contain particular databases. To simplify creating such files, which we will need to test our prototype, we choose initially to make them text files. More importantly, we choose to make them *self-identifying;* that is, we build our knowledge about the number and nature of the database's attributes and entities into the database itself and do not put this information in the database management system. By separating the data from the program in this way, we make it possible for a single DBMS to handle more than one database.

In practical terms, to make the *classrooms* database self-identifying, we must add several lines of information to those shown in Table 9.2. Pascal Sample 9.2. displays the contents of the text file *classrooms,* which we use to begin constructing our prototype DBMS. We reserve the right to change the format of that file as the need arises, but for now it helps to have a specific—even though preliminary—format.

The first line in Pascal Sample 9.2 is a descriptive title for the database. The second line gives the number of entities in the database (12) and the number of attributes applying to each entity (5). The third line specifies the maximum number of characters required to hold the names and values of each attribute. This information controls the format of the remaining lines in the file, and it will help our DBMS produce good-looking output. The fourth line specifies the names of the attributes, that is, the code words that users of our DBMS must know to retrieve information. In the *classrooms* database, the value of the attribute building is the name of a building, the value of the attribute room is the number of a room in that building, the value of the attribute seats is the seating capacity of that room, and the values of the attributes TV and microphone indicate whether the room is equipped with television or voice amplification. These names appear on the fourth line, left-aligned within a field of the width specified on the third line. The remaining 12 lines of the file contain the values of the 5 attributes for each of the 12 entities, again left-aligned within their fields.

Another example of a database is the larger file *USAdata* (Pascal Sample 9.3) of information concerning the 50 states in the United States. The format of this file is the same as that of *classrooms,* with the first 4 lines providing descriptive information about the database and the remaining 50 lines providing the values of 4 attributes for each of 50 entities. The value of the attribute area is the area in square miles of the state, and that of date is the year in which the state first joined the Union.

PASCAL SAMPLE 9.2   The file *classrooms* (preliminary version, *classrooms1*)

```
Classrooms database
12 5
13          4   5    3  10
building     roomseatsTV microphone
Humanities   100 75   yesyes
Humanities   101 20   no no
Humanities   105 15   no no
Humanities   201 30   yesno
Humanities   205 15   no no
Sciences     120 75   yesyes
Sciences     130 75   yesno
Sciences     140 40   yesno
Campus Center10  1000 yesyes
Campus Center15  100  yesyes
Campus Center101 50   no yes
Campus Center102 25   no no
```

PASCAL SAMPLE 9.3   The file *USAdata* (preliminary version)

```
States of the USA
50  4
14             14           6      4
state          capital      area  date
alabama        montgomery   51609 1819
alaska         juneau       5864121959
arizona        phoenix      1139091912
arkansas       little rock  53104 1836
california     sacramento   1586931850
colorado       denver       1042471976
connecticut    hartford     5009  1788
delaware       dover        2399  1787
florida        tallahassee  58560 1845
georgia        atlanta      58197 1788
hawaii         honolulu     6450  1959
idaho          boise        83557 1890
illinois       springfield  56400 1818
indiana        indianapolis 36291 1816
iowa           des moines   56290 1846
kansas         topeka       82264 1861
kentucky       frankfort    40395 1792
louisiana      baton rouge  48523 1812
maine          augusta      33215 1820
maryland       annapolis    10577 1788
```

PASCAL SAMPLE 9.3   The file *USAdata* (preliminary version, continued)

```
massachusetts boston         8093  1788
michigan       lansing       58216 1837
minnesota      st. paul      84068 1858
mississippi    jackson       47716 1817
missouri       jefferson city69686 1821
montana        helena        1471381889
nebraska       lincoln       77227 1867
nevada         carson city   1105401864
new hampshire  concord       9304  1788
new jersey     trenton       7836  1787
new mexico     santa fe      1216661912
new york       albany        49576 1788
north carolinaraleigh        52586 1789
north dakota   bismarck      70665 1889
ohio           columbus      41222 1803
oklahoma       oklahoma city 69919 1907
oregon         salem         96981 1859
pennsylvania   harrisburg    45333 1787
rhode island   providence    1214  1790
south carolinacolumbia       31055 1788
south dakota   pierre        77047 1889
tennessee      nashville     42244 1796
texas          austin        2673391845
utah           salt lake city84916 1896
vermont        montpelier    9609  1791
virginia       richmond      40817 1788
washington     olympia       68192 1889
west virginia  charleston    24181 1863
wisconsin      madison       56154 1848
wyoming        cheyenne      97914 1890
```

We now turn our attention to designing the data structures that will be used within our database management system. In the absence of specific requirements for a more elaborate data structure—which might be present if we were building more than a prototype DBMS or if we knew something about its expected use—it is wisest and safest to design simple data structures that reflect the logical organization of databases in general. That way we will not box ourselves into a corner unnecessarily. We choose to represent information from a particular database as a matrix; the rows correspond to the entities in the database and the columns correspond to the attributes. The item in row *e* and column *a* of this matrix will be a string that gives the value of attribute *a* for entity *e*. We call this internal representation the *working database*.

We choose to structure the working database as a matrix of strings—rather than as a vector of records with mixed string, numeric, and boolean components—to maintain the independence of our prototype DBMS from particular databases. Since Pascal requires that we name the components of a record when we write a program (not when we use it), a single program cannot use a vector x of entities that refers to boolean values of the fourth attribute in the *classrooms* database using $x[e].TV$ and also refers to integer values of the fourth attribute in the *USAdata* database using $x[e].date$. But we can have a matrix x of strings that refers to these values using $x[e,4]$. If we need to distinguish among the types of these values later on, we will have to find some way to do so that is independent of the particular database.

We will know the size of a database only when we use our DBMS, and not when we are writing it. Thus we must declare a sufficiently large maximum size for the working database and then determine its actual size for each specific use. For example, when we use our DBMS in conjunction with the *classrooms* database, the working database will contain 12 rows and 5 columns; when we use it with the *USAdata* database, it will contain 50 rows and 4 columns. Strictly speaking, the working database is more than just a table: the size of this table, together with any other information that helps to identify and describe a database, also belongs in the working version of that database.

Pascal Sample 9.4 contains declarations that describe one possible structure for a working database, showing that it contains self-identifying information and a table giving the values of all attributes for each entity. In fact, we will incorporate these specific declarations in the first draft, *info1*, of our prototype DBMS.

PASCAL SAMPLE 9.4   The program *info1* (definition of working database)

```
const maxAttributes = 10;
      maxEntities  = 50;
      stringLength = 20;          { maximum attribute width }

type string    = packed array [1..stringLength] of char;
     itemType  = string;
     table     = array [1..maxEntities, 1..maxAttributes] of itemType;
     rowIndex  = 0..maxEntities;
     colIndex  = 0..maxAttributes;
     baseType  = record
                    title      : string;
                    attributes : colIndex;
                    entities   : rowIndex;
                    names      : array [1..maxAttributes] of string;
                    widths     : array [1..maxAttributes] of 0..stringLength;
                    items      : table
                 end;
```

PASCAL SAMPLE 9.5 The program *info1* (definition of index)

indexType = **record**
    size : *rowIndex*;
    ptrs : **array** [1..*maxEntities*] **of** *rowIndex*
  end;

By packaging the working database—complete with descriptive information—a single structure of type *baseType,* we can pass it to procedures in *info1* as a sing parameter. This will keep our parameter lists short and allow us to change the form of the working database, or the amount of descriptive information it contains, whe necessary, without having to change every parameter list. It also allows us to mak local changes to the declaration of *baseType* and to make local changes to thos procedures, and only those procedures, that are affected by the changes in the de laration.

Finally, in order to keep track of the entities in the working database that ar currently of interest, and the order in which we intend to process these entities, w will maintain an index to these entities in *info1*. By using an index we will be abl to select and sort information in the working database without having to modify c rearrange that information. As in Section 8.5, the index will be a vector with a ma imum length equal to the number of entities in the database. (See Pascal Sampl 9.5.) We do not make the index a part of the working database so that we may, necessary, maintain several indices to a single working database.

These data structures—a text file for the external representation and an arra with an index for the internal representation—are among the simplest that can b chosen to manage a prototype database. They reflect closely the logical organizatio of a database, while at the same time allowing us to manipulate the database efficient using an index.

EXERCISES

1. Write programs to transpose a data file with the format shown in Pascal Sample 9.2, th is, to produce a data file with the same first two lines, but with one line thereafter f each attribute and with all information concerning the attribute on that line.

2. On the basis of your results in Exercise 1, describe how you might coordinate changir the format of external files used by a database management system and changing th database management system itself.

3. Design a way to distinguish numeric data from string data, both in external files and the working database.

4. The declaration of the working database utilizes fixed-length strings for the values of th attributes. What would be the relative advantages and disadvantages of using variabl length strings instead?

ALGORITHMS: MAKING USE OF TOOLS

Our prototype DBMS *info* will make use of the tools that we developed in our study of strings, files, searching, and sorting. By using general purpose tools, rather than by reinventing them or disguising them, we can speed the process of program construction and make the resulting program recognizable to others who are familiar with our tools.

Specifically, we will rely on the subprograms that we developed in Section 6.6 to extract information from files; we will rely on the techniques that we developed in Section 8.5 to sort indices to information in a database. Furthermore, as we construct *info*, we should look for opportunities to construct other general purpose tools. We can obtain two benefits from designing and constructing such tools to solve problems that at first appear specific to *info*: (1) by maintaining a high level of generality we will be led to a logical and flexible design for *info*, one that is easy to understand and likely to lead to a working program; and (2) we will earn a bonus in the form of an enlarged tool kit that we can employ in the construction of future programs.

Even before we begin to construct *info*, we can see the need for a few general tools for manipulating indices in addition to an index sort. We package them, together with a revised version of *xsort*, into a library *indexSubs* where they will be available when we need them. Comments at the beginning of *indexSubs*, shown as Pascal Sample 9.6, describe the procedures in that library and specify the types of their arguments.

■ **PASCAL SAMPLE 9.6**   The library *indexSubs* (initial comments)

```
{ indexSubs: procedures to maintain an index to a table }
{ Procedures:                                                                            }
{    xcreate(x, n)        creates index x with entries 1, ..., n                         }
{    xselect(t, x, k, v)  thins x to those entries pointing to the rows in the           }
{                         table t containing the value v in column k                     }
{    xsort(t, x, k)       sorts the index x using the values in column k of the          }
{                         table t as keys                                                }
{ Any program calling one of these procedures must contain the following type }
{ declarations (maxRows and maxCols specify the maximum size of the table,    }
{ but may be replaced by other identifiers or constants).                     }
{                                                                             }
{ type rowIndex  = 0..maxRows;                                                }
{'     colIndex  = 0..maxCols;                                                }
{      itemType  = ...;                                                       }
{      table     = array [1..maxRows, 1..maxCols] of itemType;                }
{      indexType = record                                                     }
{                      size : rowIndex;                                       }
{                      ptrs : array [1..maxRows] of rowIndex                  }
{                  end;                                                       }
```

■ **PASCAL SAMPLE 9.7**   The library *indexSubs* (*xcreate* procedure)

procedure *xcreate*(**var** *index* : *indexType*; *n* : *rowIndex*);
   { creates an index to rows 1 through *n* }
   var *e* : *rowIndex*;
   begin
      for *e* := 1 **to** *n* **do** *index.ptrs*[*e*] := *e*;
      index.size := *n*
   end;   { of *xcreate* }

The first procedure, *xcreate,* in *indexSubs* creates an index to a table. (See Pascal Sample 9.7.) We will invoke this procedure in *info* whenever we create a working database.

The next procedure, *xselect,* will prove useful whenever we want to focus attention on a subset of a database (for example, when we want to find those rooms in the *classrooms* database that are equipped with television). Since we may want to shift our focus later, we should not eliminate the entities outside this subset from the working database. Instead, we simply eliminate them from the index. Later, if we need them back, we can call the *xcreate* procedure to restore all the entities to the index.

Before coding *xselect,* let us consider how it might operate. Suppose that we start with the indexed table displayed in Section 8.5 (Table 8.7, shown here as Fig. 9.1). Then, to focus our attention on the residents of New York, we can try to transform this indexed table into the one shown as Fig. 9.2.

How can we make such a transformation? We could copy the indices of interest into a new index, but it is more economical simply to "squeeze" the undesired pointers out of the old index. We can use two variables, *nextEntry* and *newSize,* to indicate which entry in the old index we want to examine next and the current size of the new index. Initially, *nextEntry* = 1 and *newSize* = 0. Two actions are possible

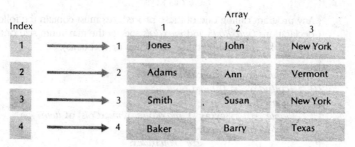

FIGURE 9.1 ■ Sample table with index created by *xcreate*

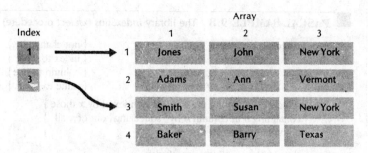

FIGURE 9.2 ■ Sample table with reduced index

when we examine an entry in the old index: (1) we can eliminate it from the new index by passing over it to examine the next entry; or (2) we can retain it by adding one to *newSize* and moving the entry to an earlier position in the index, if necessary, to overwrite an eliminated entry. Figure 9.3 illustrates the successive values of *nextEntry*

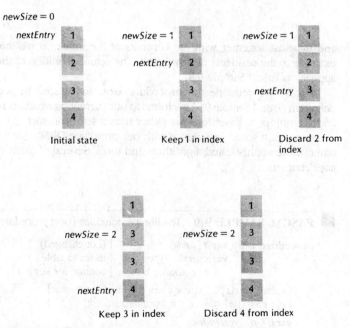

FIGURE 9.3 ■ Steps in squeezing entries out of index

PASCAL SAMPLE 9.8   The library *indexSubs* (*xselect* procedure)

```
procedure xselect( var a : table;                    { not changed   }
                   var x : indexType;                { index to table }
                   k : colIndex;                      { column to use }
                   v : itemType );                    { value to seek }
   { selects from among the rows of a indexed by x those }
   { containing v in column k by "squeezing" out of x all }
   { pointers to undesired rows                           }

   var newSize, nextEntry : rowIndex;
   begin
       newSize := 0;
       for nextEntry := 1 to x.size do
           if v = a[x.ptrs[nextEntry], k] then { keep in index }
              begin
                  newSize := newSize + 1;
                  x.ptrs[newSize] := x.ptrs[nextEntry]
              end;
       x.size := newSize
   end;   { of xselect }
```

and *newSize,* together with the contents of the index, as we thin the index in our example to the residents of **New York**. The actual definition of the procedure *xselect* appears as Pascal Sample 9.8.

Finally, we redefine the procedure *xsort* introduced in Section 8.5. The new definition (Pascal Sample 9.9) conforms to our current conventions regarding *indexType,* and it employs an insertion sort rather than a selection sort.

As we gain some experience with our prototype DBMS, we will see the need for other, more sophisticated algorithms and tools. Several of them will be discussed in later chapters.

PASCAL SAMPLE 9.9   The library *indexSubs* (*xsort* procedure)

```
procedure xsort( var a : table;              { (not changed)  }
                 var x : indexType;          { index to table }
                 k : colIndex );             { column for key }
   { sorts x.ptrs[1], ..., x.ptrs[x.size] by insertion so that}
   { a[x.ptrs[1], k] <= ... <= a[x.ptrs[x.size], k]          }

   var i, j, p : rowIndex;
       key    : itemType;              { key for insertion     }
       found : boolean;                { found location for key }
```

```
begin
    for i := 2 to x.size do
        begin
            p := x.ptrs[i];              { pointer to key   }
            key := a[p, k];
            j := i;                       { insertion pointer }
            found := false;
            while (j > 1) and not found do
                if a[x.ptrs[j−1], k] <= key then
                    found := true
                else
                    begin
                        x.ptrs[j] := x.ptrs[j−1];
                        j := j−1
                    end;
            x.ptrs[j] := p
            { now a[x.ptrs[1], k] <= ... <= a[x.ptrs[i], k] }
        end
    end;  { of xsort }
```

EXERCISES

1. Design and construct procedures that perform the following transformations on indices x and y to a table t.

   (a) Construct an index z to those entries that appear in either x or y.

   (b) Construct an index z to those entries that appear in both x and y.

   (c) Construct an index z to those entries that appear in x but not in y.

   Assume that the entries in x and y appear in increasing order, that is,

   $$x.ptrs[1] \leq x.ptrs[2] \leq \cdots \leq x.ptrs[x.size]$$

   and

   $$y.ptrs[1] \leq y.ptrs[2] \leq \cdots \leq y.ptrs[y.size].$$

   Ensure that the entries in z also appear in increasing order.

2. Redo Exercise 1 without the assumption and requirement that entries in an index occur in increasing order. What effect does this change in specification have on the efficiency and difficulty of coding your procedures?

3. Suppose that we want to create an index to the rows in a table that contain the value $v1$ in column $k1$ and the value $v2$ in column $k2$.

   (a) Describe how we could do this using the procedure constructed in Exercise 1(b).

   (b) Describe how we could do this using $xselect$ alone.

4. Describe how to create an index to the rows in a table that contain either the value $v1$ or the value $v2$ in column k.

5. In a more general setting, we may want to select those entries in an index that satisfy an arbitrary condition. One way to do this is to define a boolean-valued function *retain* such that *retain*(v) is *true* if a pointer to a value of v should be retained.

   (a) Modify *xselect* to treat the function *retain* as a formal parameter and to select those entries pointing to values v for which *retain*(v) is *true*.

   (b) How can this modification of *xselect* be used in solving Exercises 1–4?

   (c) What are the advantages and disadvantages of this approach?

6. What advantage is there in using an insertion sort to sort an index rather than a selection sort? (*Hint:* What happens if *xsort* is invoked twice in succession, first with column 1 containing the key and then with column 2 containing the key?)

9.4   PROGRAMMING: PUTTING IT ALL TOGETHER

We construct *info,* our prototype DBMS, top-down, as described in Section 4.2. There we identified four stages in developing a large program:

1. develop clear specifications for what the program must do;

2. write an outline for the program;

3. write a rough draft of the program; and

4. fill in and refine the details in the rough draft.

The purpose of staged development is to give us, and help us maintain, a clear idea of where we are heading. Without a clear sense of direction we may wind up with a program that does not suit our needs or, worse yet, does not work at all. Furthermore, without a clear sense of direction, we risk wasting time and energy trying to figure out what to do next or, worse yet, redoing work that went off in the wrong direction.

A good strategy for staged development is to get a skeleton program working early and to enhance that skeleton gradually and methodically, testing each enhancement as we go. By maintaining a program that always works (even though it may not do much at the outset), we provide ourselves with a framework within which we can create new subprograms, enhance old subprograms, and test our changes. In the event that some enhancement results in a disaster, we can always undo that enhancement and fall back to solid ground. It is far easier to keep our bearings in such a setting than in one without a fall-back position and without any real feeling for how or whether our subprograms fit together.

A staged development embodies a top-down approach to programming. We start at the highest level of generality with an outline that gives an overview of a program and then refine the outline to produce the program. In a bottom-up approach, by contrast, we start by constructing a collection of specific low-level procedures and then attempt to assemble those procedures into a program. We already have a collection of low-level procedures in our tool kit, but they do not need to influence us toward using a bottom-up approach. We are more likely to build a program that does what we want it to do if we start with a clear idea of our objectives, and then use our tools to reach those objectives, than if we start with our tools and then try to find out what they will let us do. And, with a top-down approach, we will have a clear idea of where we are going rather than a hazy idea of where we have been.

STEP 1: SPECIFICATION

We begin our development of *info* by specifying exactly what it will do. Simply saying that *info* is a prototype DBMS is not enough. Database management systems can have many capabilities, and we need to specify which ones this particular DBMS will have.

For very long programs, it is a good idea to write specifications in the form of a users' manual before beginning to write the program. For a medium-sized program such as *info,* we can save some effort initially by writing specifications in the form of comments to be incorporated as documentation in the program itself. However we write them, our initial specifications should be addressed to potential users of our program. If we cannot explain to them what the program will do, we do not have a clear enough idea ourselves of what we must do to create our program.

Pascal Sample 9.10 contains comments that we will place at the beginning of *info* to give an overview of the entire program. In particular, these comments describe

---

■ **PASCAL SAMPLE 9.10**   The program *info* (initial comments)

```
{ info: a prototype database management system }
{      The program info allows users to retrieve information from specified }
{ files and then select, sort, or print subsets of this information. The     }
{ information itself consists of the values of certain attributes for a      }
{ collection of entities.                                                     }
{ The commands understood by info are as follows:                            }
{      base filename       retrieves data from named file                    }
{      describe            describes data in database                        }
{      help                prints these instructions                         }
{      print all           prints values of all attributes for the selected  }
{                          entities                                          }
{      print att1 att2 ... prints values of the named attributes for the     }
{                          selected entities                                 }
{      restore             selects all entities                              }
{      select att value    selects those entities having the specified       }
{                          value for the named attribute from among the      }
{                          currently selected entities                       }
{      size                prints the number of selected entities            }
{      sort att            sorts the selected entities with the named        }
{                          attribute as key                                  }
{      stop                terminates info                                   }
{ All commands may be abbreviated by their first three letters. Each         }
{ command occupies a single line.                                            }
```

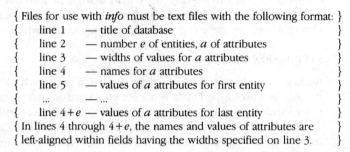

PASCAL SAMPLE 9.11   The program *info* (further comments, initial version)

```
{ Files for use with info must be text files with the following format: }
{     line 1      — title of database                                   }
{     line 2      — number e of entities, a of attributes               }
{     line 3      — widths of values for a attributes                   }
{     line 4      — names for a attributes                              }
{     line 5      — values of a attributes for first entity             }
{     ...         — ...                                                  }
{     line 4+e — values of a attributes for last entity                 }
{ In lines 4 through 4+e, the names and values of attributes are        }
{ left-aligned within fields having the widths specified on line 3.     }
```

the commands that *info* will process. (Pascal Sample 9.1 in Section 9.1 illustrates the use of these commands to retrieve information from the *classrooms* data base.)

Specifications for a program should describe not only how to use the program, but also what must be done to prepare the program for use. In the case of *info,* we need to specify the format of the files containing the databases we intend to access. We have already done this in Section 9.2, and the next set of comments in *info* (Pascal Sample 9.11) records the decisions we made there. By keeping all the specifications for a program in a single place, we can find them when the need arises. For moderate-sized programs there is no better place to keep specifications than as comments in the program itself. Then, if we refine or change our specifications as we construct the program, we can easily find and revise these comments.

STEP 2: OUTLINE

The second step in constructing a large program is to develop an outline for the program. The outline should show how the program will be decomposed into subprograms, what those subprograms will do, and how they will communicate. Details of how the subprograms work, or of how to structure the data they pass back and forth, is unimportant at this stage. In fact, the longer we can defer making decisions about details, the more lasting will be our decisions when we make them.

Pascal Sample 9.12 contains an outline for *info1,* a preliminary version of *info.* The outline shows that this skeleton DBMS will do nothing more than interpret two of the specified commands, namely, those that let us create a working database and display its contents. That may not seem like much for a DBMS, but it will allow us to test other features as we add them. And it is enough (once we get it working) to give us confidence that our goal is in sight. Furthermore, to fill in this outline is, by choice, a small enough task that we can gain this confidence quickly.

Note that the outline for *info1,* in addition to describing how *info1* will be structured, is itself a working program. It may not do anything, and we may have cheated in writing its type declarations, but the outline is all the more believable and informative since we can execute it as well as read it. A working program is more convincing than a recipe for constructing a program, and it is not much more difficult to write. So, just as we wrote the specifications for *info* as comments that form part of the program, we write its outline as part of the program.

The outline conveys information in two ways: through comments and through *procedure stubs,* that is, through mock-up or dummy procedures that reserve a place for the procedures we must write. Accurate comments in the outline serve several useful purposes. First, writing them forces us to think carefully about what we must do, particularly if we phrase our comments (as we should) precisely and concisely.

■ **PASCAL SAMPLE 9.12**   The program *info1* (outline)

```
{ info1: a rough draft of the prototype DBMS info }
{ implements rudimentary base and print commands only }

program info1(input, output, datafile);
type baseType  : real;        { must define this properly }
     indexType : real;        { ditto                     }
var datafile : text;          { permanent database        }

procedure base( var db : baseType;  var x : indexType );
     { creates working database and index for user }
     begin
     end;  { of base }

procedure print( db : baseType;  x : indexType );
     { prints values of attributes for entities indexed in x }
     begin
     end;  { of print }

procedure commandAnalysis;
     { interprets user's commands }
     var wbase : baseType;         { working database   }
         index : indexType;        { of selected entities }
     begin
     end;  { of commandAnalysis }

begin  { main program }
     commandAnalysis
end.  { of info1 }
```

Second, comments serve as natural reminders of work that we still have to do; to fill out the outline, we simply write procedures that do what the comments require. And third, good comments in the outline will serve as good documentation in the final version of the program. It pays to think first, document second, and code last.

Placing procedure stubs in the outline, rather than simply writing comments such as

{ command analysis procedure goes here }

also serves several useful purposes. First, a comment such as

{ interprets user's commands }

in the stub tells us what the procedure will do, and we can retain such a comment in the finished program. Second, procedure stubs contain parameter lists that specify the information that is passed between procedures. And, third, the existence of procedure stubs allows us to write procedures one at a time, insert them in the outline in place of the stubs, and still have a program that we can compile and test. When we write one procedure that must call another, we can have it call the already constructed stub and not have to worry immediately about writing that other procedure.

The procedure stubs in Pascal Sample 9.12 do not do anything when executed. As we fill in the outline for *info*, we may have occasion to construct stubs that do some work. The following are useful types of procedure stubs, all of which are easier to write than a complicated procedure.

■ A procedure stub that prints its name and the values of key parameters helps us to verify that a procedure is called when expected and with the proper values.

■ In an interactive environment, a procedure stub that prints this information and then asks us to supply the values it must generate helps us to test other procedures that depend on this one.

■ Likewise, a procedure stub that computes approximations to the values it must generate, finds those values in a table, or computes them inefficiently helps us to test other procedures that depend on this one.

Stubs such as these are examples of *throw-away* code. The effort that we invest in writing these stubs helps considerably in getting a long program to work, but is small enough that we do not mind throwing the stubs away when we are done with them.

The procedure stubs in the outline for *info1* disclose an interesting aspect of the design for that program, namely, that we have chosen to use as few global variables as possible. Although Pascal forces us to declare the external file *datafile* globally, we are extremely reluctant to utilize other global identifiers for three reasons.

First, global variables are particularly dangerous in a large program. For example, we might be tempted to shorten parameter lists by declaring the frequently used variables *wbase* and *index* globally, rather than within *commandAnalysis*. However, we would run the risk of being baffled by an error caused by an obscure subprogram that used another variable named *index* but forgot to declare that variable. If we were unlucky, the two uses of *index* would have compatible types, and it would take us a long time indeed to discover that the error resulted from a missing declaration. (The author once spent the better part of a day tracking down such an error and now believes in making the body of a long Pascal program as short as possible—say, a single procedure call—just to avoid the need for global variables.)

Second, overuse of global variables destroys generality. If we are too lazy to pass *wbase* and *index* to those procedures that need them, choosing instead to make these variables global, we make it extremely difficult to enhance *info1* so that it can manipulate several indices or working databases at once.

Third, by avoiding global variables and utilizing explicit parameter lists, we document the information used by each of the subprograms in our program. That way we can see at a glance which subprograms need to be changed if we change the declaration for a particular variable. We do not have to search exhaustively through all of the subprograms to uncover hidden references to global variables, but instead can focus our attention on the subprograms in which we changed declarations.

STEP 3: ROUGH DRAFT

To turn the outline for *info1* into a program that will actually accept input and produce output, we must provide accurate declarations for the types *baseType* and *indexType*; we must also provide code for the three procedure stubs *base, print,* and *commandAnalysis.* The declarations of *baseType* and *indexType* in Section 9.2 meet our present needs, so we go directly to coding the procedures.

We turn our attention first to *commandAnalysis.* That procedure is at the heart of our prototype DBMS. It enables users to enter commands, it interprets those commands, and it calls other procedures to process those commands. Hence this procedure gives an overview of the entire DBMS by specifying the commands that it can process and the routines that process them. In the version of *commandAnalysis* displayed as Pascal Sample 9.13, we have chosen to recognize all of the commands that *info* will eventually accept but to print a simple message in response to all commands except `base` and `print`. Such messages are stubs with the same purpose as procedure stubs: they serve as gentle reminders of work that remains to be done.

Note that our first try at *commandAnalysis* is not particularly elegant about how it obtains its commands: everything beyond the first three characters in a command line is thrown away, making it impossible for us to enter a command like `base classrooms` on a single line. Such a design would be intolerable in a finished product, but it enables us to get a prototype working quickly and to use the prototype, though somewhat awkwardly, in debugging code as we write it. Refinements can wait for later versions of *commandAnalysis.*

Next we code the *base* procedure to get the name of a database from the user, extract information from the named permanent database, place it in the working

■ **PASCAL SAMPLE 9.13**   The program *info1* (*commandAnalysis* procedure)

```
procedure commandAnalysis;
    { interprets user's commands }
    var wbase     : baseType;              { working database }
        index     : indexType;             { of selected entities}
        command : array [1..3] of char;
    begin
        repeat
            write('Command: ');
            readln(command[1], command[2], command[3]);
            if command = 'bas'    then base(wbase, index)
            else if command = 'des' then writeln('Can''t do it.')
            else if command = 'hel' then writeln('Can''t do it.')
            else if command = 'pri' then print(wbase, index)
            else if command = 'res' then writeln('Can''t do it.')
            else if command = 'sel' then writeln('Can''t do it.')
            else if command = 'siz' then writeln('Can''t do it.')
            else if command = 'sor' then writeln('Can''t do it.')
            else if command = 'sto' then writeln('bye')
            else writeln('Illegal command')
        until command = 'sto'
    end;    { of commandAnalysis }
```

database, and create an index to the data. (See Pascal Sample 9.14.) Since *base* must accomplish several distinct tasks, it is natural to farm these tasks out to several other procedures: obtaining input from the user is delegated to the procedure *readChars,* which assigns a given number of characters to a string from a line in a file; creating the working database is delegated to the procedure *loadBase;* and creating an index

■ **PASCAL SAMPLE 9.14**   The program *info1* (*base* procedure)

```
procedure base( var db : baseType; var x : indexType );
    { creates working database for user }
    var baseName : string;
    begin
        write('Database: ');
        readChars(input, stringLength, baseName);
        readln;
        loadBase(db, baseName);
        xcreate(x, db.entities)
    end;    { of base }
```

to the database is delegated to the procedure *xcreate,* which we developed in Section 9.3.

The point of coding *loadBase* as a separate procedure, rather than incorporating it into *base,* is to separate the details of interacting with the user from the details of extracting information from a permanent database. By not tying these two operations together in a single procedure, we can modify one independently of the other. Pascal Sample 9.15 contains the *loadBase* procedure, which also invokes the procedure *readChars* to extract the names and values of the attributes from the file. The *readChars* procedure, called by both the *base* and *loadBase* procedures, is straightforward. (See Pascal Sample 9.16.)

For *info1,* we choose to code the *print* procedure as a procedure stub that prints the values of all attributes for the indexed entities. We will want to enhance this procedure soon, but for now we need only a procedure that lets us see what we have. (See Pascal Sample 9.17.)

With these few procedures, we have transformed our outline for *info1* into a skeleton DBMS that will serve as a rough draft in our development of *info.* We have barely begun to code *info,* but already we have a skeleton that does something

---

PASCAL SAMPLE 9.15   The program *info1* (*loadBase* procedure)

```
procedure loadBase( var db        : baseType;
                       filename : string );
   { creates working database from file with given name }
   var a : 0..maxAttributes;
       e : 0..maxEntities;
   begin
       reset(datafile, filename);
       readChars(datafile, stringLength, db.title);                    { line 1 }

       readln(datafile, db.entities, db.attributes);                   { line 2 }

       for a := 1 to db.attributes do
           read(datafile, db.widths[a]);
       readln(datafile);                                               { line 3 }

       for a := 1 to db.attributes do
           readChars(datafile, db.widths[a], db.names[a]);
       readln(datafile);                                               { line 4 }

       for e := 1 to db.entities do
           begin
               for a := 1 to db.attributes do
                   readChars(datafile, db.widths[a], db.items[e, a]);
               readln(datafile)                                        { line 4+e }
           end
   end;   { of loadBase }
```

PASCAL SAMPLE 9.16   The program *info1* (*readChars* procedure)

```
procedure readChars( var f : text;
                          n : integer;
                     var s : string );
  { reads the next n characters on the current line of the text }
  { file f and assigns them to s                               }
  var i : integer;
  begin
    for i := 1 to stringLength do
      if (i <= n) and not eoln(f) then
        read(f, s[i])
      else
        s[i] := ' '
  end;   { of readChars }
```

interesting: it accepts commands and displays the contents of databases. No matter how clumsy it may be, we can use this skeleton to keep track of our progress. Furthermore, others can test the skeleton and give us feedback regarding the specifications for our program. Far from being a source of annoyance, such feedback can lead to desirable changes in the specifications while there is still time to make them and before we have invested a lot of energy (and ego) in writing programs to carry out imperfect specifications. Pascal Sample 9.18 shows the results of executing the skeleton *info1* in an attempt to reproduce the results displayed Pascal Sample 9.1.

It is apparent from Pascal Sample 9.18 that *info1* handles neither input nor output particularly well. It ignores all but the first three characters on a line of input, and

PASCAL SAMPLE 9.17   The program *info1* (*print* procedure)

```
procedure print( db : baseType; x : indexType );
  { prints all attributes for entities indexed by x }
  var e : rowIndex;
      a : colIndex;
  begin
    for e := 1 to x.size do
      begin
        for a := 1 to db.attributes do
          write(db.items[x.ptrs[e], a] : db.widths[a]);
        writeln
      end
  end;   { of print }
```

PASCAL SAMPLE 9.18   The program *info1* (sample use)

```
Command: base classrooms1
Database: classrooms1
Command: select TV yes
Illegal command
Command: print building room
Humanities     100 75    yesyes
Humanities     101 20    no no
Humanities     105 15    no no
Humanities     201 30    yesno
Humanities     205 15    no no
Sciences       120 75    yesyes
Sciences       130 75    yesno
Sciences       140 40    yesno
Campus Center10  1000    yesyes
Campus Center15  100     yesyes
Campus Center101 50      no yes
Campus Center102 25      no no
Command: stop
bye
```

its output is difficult to read. But then we did not expect our first attempts at *commandAnalysis* and *print* to do anything fancy. However, Pascal Sample 9.18 does assure us that *info1* can handle a sequence of commands and that it can extract information reliably from a database. That in itself is enough to give us confidence to proceed.

STEP 4: FILLING IN THE ROUGH DRAFT

So many aspects of *info1* need improvement that it is difficult to know where to begin. Should we make the output easier to read, improve the analysis of commands, add a procedure to process the `select` command, or attack one of the other missing procedures first?

A good rule of thumb is to fill in major portions of a rough draft before beginning to polish any one portion. Thus we should concentrate first on writing procedures that add new functionality to the draft, say, on a procedure to process the `select` command. It would be a mistake to spend time now cleaning up the *print* and *commandAnalysis* procedures. These procedures were not meant to be finished products at this stage, and our ideas for improving them may change as we construct other procedures. Furthermore, no matter how much we improve these procedures before attacking the others, *info1* will not do very much of interest. So, we may as well live with their known inadequacies and concentrate on more important work. If we are afraid that we will forget the improvements that must be made, we can always write comments such as

{ needs to handle multiple-word commands }

in our rough draft to serve as reminders.

For *info* to process the `select` command, we provide an interface to the *xselect* procedure that we developed in Section 9.3. As in the case of the procedures *base* and *loadBase,* we separate the details of determining what the user wants to do from the details of carrying out the request. Hence we have *commandAnalysis* call a procedure *select* that obtains the information necessary for a selection from the user and then calls *xselect* to carry out the selection.

It would be natural to begin *select* in much the same way as *base,* namely, with a sequence of statements

```
write('Attribute: ');
readChars(input, stringLength, attribute);
readln;
write('Value to select: ');
readChars(input, stringLength, value);
readln;
```

that prompt the user for the necessary information. However, our experience with *info1,* which could not handle more than one response per line of input, makes us uneasy with such a rigid approach. Eventually we will need a more general approach, and the only question is whether to develop that approach now or later.

Exercising considerable self-discipline, we decide that the proper answer to this question is "later." After all, we set out to make *info1* handle the `select` command, and we should not get sidetracked from this objective (lest we get sidetracked from the sidetrack and never return). But how do we write *select* without creating additional headaches for ourselves later on? If we build *readChars* solidly into this and further procedures, won't major surgery be required to provide more flexible input?

The top-down philosophy to programming provides a solution to this dilemma. We can have *select* call yet another procedure *getResponse* to obtain each piece of information needed from the user, and we can worry about how to code *getResponse* later. Similarly, when we realize that *select* needs to know the column in the working database that contains a specified attribute (not just the name of that attribute), we can delegate the task of determining the column number to a function, *att,* which we will also write later. In programming, in contrast to other activities, it is often wisest to avoid doing today what can be done tomorrow.

With these acts of creative procrastination, we can finish the job of writing the *select* procedure in short order. The result is displayed as Pascal Sample 9.19. Although the parameter *db* is not modified by *select,* we pass it by reference to avoid the expense of copying a large matrix each time *select* is called. A comment in the procedure header calls attention to what we have done and serves as a reminder that we can make a similar improvement in *print.*

PASCAL SAMPLE 9.19   The program *info1* (*select* procedure)

```
procedure select( var db : baseType;              { not changed }
                  var x  : indexType );
    { enables user to thin out the index x }
    var attribute, value : string;
    begin
        getResponse('Attribute:              ',attribute);
        getResponse('Value to select:        ',value);
        xselect(db.items, x, att(db, attribute), value);
        writeln(x.size:1, ' entities selected')
    end;   { of select }
```

In order to test *select,* we need versions of *getResponse* and *att* because *select* won't work without them. We were reluctant to divert our attention from writing *select* by paying premature attention to these procedures, and we are likewise reluctant to divert our attention from testing *select.* Hence we write short stubs for these procedures.

The stub for *getResponse,* shown as Pascal Sample 9.20, is no more sophisticated than the code it allowed us to eliminate from *select.* But by packaging this clumsy code in a separate procedure, we make it that much easier to replace. The fact that the type of the parameter *message* to *getResponse* is a *string* explains why the string arguments in Pascal Sample 9.19 end with so many spaces: strings in Pascal have fixed lengths, and string constants supplied as parameters must have the appropriate length.

The stub for *att* (Pascal Sample 9.21), when given the name of an attribute, uses a linear search to find that name in the list of all attribute names. For the moment we do not worry about what happens if the value of *attribute* is not a valid attribute name; we can add an error recovery function later.

PASCAL SAMPLE 9.20   The program *info1* (*getResponse* stub)

```
procedure getResponse( message : string; var value : string );
    { gets a string value from the user, prompting with message }
    begin
        write(message);
        readChars(input, stringLength, value);
        readln
    end;   { of getResponse }
```

PASCAL SAMPLE 9.21   The program *info1* (att stub)

```
function att( var db        : baseType;                    { not changed   }
                 attribute : string ) : colIndex;
    { returns the number of the column in db holding the given attribute }
    { (returns 0 if an illegal attribute is given)                       }
    var a, col : colIndex;
    begin
        col := 0;
        a := 1;
        while (a <= db.attributes) and (col = 0) do
            if attribute = db.names[a] then
                col := a
            else
                a := a + 1;
        att := col
    end;   { of att }
```

With these two stubs, we can test our ability to handle the select command properly. We install the *select* procedure in *info1*, changing the line

else if *command* = 'sel' **then** *writeln*('Can''t do it.')

in *commandAnalysis* to

else if *command* = 'sel' **then** *select*(*wbase, index*)

PASCAL SAMPLE 9.22   The program *info1* (testing the select command)

```
Command: base
Database: classrooms1
Command: select
Attribute:          TV
Value to select:    yes
7 entities selected
Command: print
Humanities     100  75    yesyes
Humanities     201  30    yesno
Sciences       120  75    yesyes
Sciences       130  75    yesno
Sciences       140  40    yesno
Campus Center10  1000    yesyes
Campus Center15   100    yesyes
```

PASCAL SAMPLE 9.23   The program *info1* (*sort* procedure)

procedure *sort*(**var** *db* : *baseType*;   { not changed }
                   var *x* : *indexType*);

    { enables user to sort indexed entities }

    var *attribute* : *string*;

    begin

        getResponse('Attribute to sort: ', *attribute*);
        xsort(*db.items*, *x*, *att*(*db*, *attribute*))

    end;   { of *sort* } .

and test the result. Pascal Sample 9.22 presents evidence that we have succeeded in constructing *select,* and more thorough testing convinces us of this fact. Pascal Sample 9.22 also discloses a quirk in the operation of *getResponse,* namely, that it prints extra spaces after the message. This quirk does not have anything to do with *select,* so we feel comfortable making a note of the quirk and moving on.

We next construct an interface *sort* to the *xsort* procedure. This interface is similar to *select,* relying again on the subprograms *getResponse* and *att* for assistance. (See Pascal Sample 9.23.)

When we install *sort* in *info1* and test it, we discover a problem with the way it arranges numeric data. (See Pascal Sample 9.24.) A little thought shows that the problem arises because we treat all items in a database as strings: '1000' precedes '15' in string order, even though 15 < 1000 in numeric order.

PASCAL SAMPLE 9.24   The program *info1* (problem with sort command)

```
Command: base
Database: classrooms1
Command: sort
Attribute to sort:  seats
Command: print
Campus Center15  100  yesyes
Campus Center10  1000 yesyes
Humanities     105 15  no no
Humanities     205 15  no no
Humanities     101 20  no no
Campus Center102 25  no no
Humanities     201 30  yesno
Sciences       140 40  yesno
Campus Center101 50  no yes
Humanities     100 75  yesyes
Sciences       130 75  yesno
Sciences       120 75  yesyes
```

For a "quick fix" to this problem, we could try right-aligning values of numeric attributes in their fields in the external database. Since a space collates before a digit, the string order of right-aligned, fixed-length strings of digits agrees with their numeric order: ' 15' < '1000'. Pascal Sample 9.25 shows how the *classrooms* database would look with this revision.

When we test *sort* with this revised database, our problems seem to have been corrected. (See Pascal Sample 9.26.) But we should not leap to conclusions and believe just yet that all is well. Perhaps, while correcting the problem with *sort,* we introduced a problem somewhere else. When we make a change in a program or its data, we should test *all* aspects of the program, not just those we think might be affected by the change.

More complete testing, as shown in Pascal Sample 9.27, does in fact uncover a problem: the `select` command no longer produces the correct result when looking for particular values of numeric attributes. Since the *select* procedure worked before we changed the format of the *classrooms* database, we have a good idea of where to look for the trouble. (Here we see the value of making a single enhancement at a time and testing that enhancement immediately: when something goes wrong, it's clear what to suspect.) Sure enough, *select* fails because it supplies *xselect* with a left-aligned value '75 ' for an attribute of width four, and *xselect* compares this value with right-aligned strings ' 75' extracted from the revised database.

We could fix *select* by right-aligning the values of all attributes, but then *sort* would fail to work for attributes with alphabetic values. We appear to have no recourse other than to distinguish between string and numeric data, both in external databases and in the working database. Accordingly, we decide to add a fifth line of self-identifying information to each external database and to indicate on that line which attributes are alphabetic (by the letter **A**) and which are integers (by the letter

---

■ **PASCAL SAMPLE 9.25**   The file *classrooms* (possible revision, *classrooms2*)

```
Classrooms database
' 12 5
13           4   5    3   10
building     roomseatsTV microphone
Humanities   100   75yesyes
Humanities   101   20no no
Humanities   105   15no no
Humanities   201   30yesno
Humanities   205   15no no
Sciences     120   75yesyes
Sciences     130   75yesno
Sciences     140   40yesno
Campus Center  10 1000yesyes
Campus Center  15 100yesyes
Campus Center 101   50no yes
Campus Center 102   25no no
```

PASCAL SAMPLE 9.26   The program *info1* (successful sort of *classrooms2*)

```
Command: base
Database: classrooms2
Command: sort
Attribute to sort:   seats
Command: print
Humanities      105    15no no
Humanities      205    15no no
Humanities      101    20no no
Campus Center   102    25no no
Humanities      201    30yesno
Sciences        140    40yesno
Campus Center   101    50no yes
Sciences        120    75yesyes
Sciences        130    75yesno
Humanities      100    75yesyes
Campus Center   15    100yesyes
Campus Center   10   1000yesyes
```

I). We continue to right-align values of numeric attributes and left-align values of alphabetic attributes. Pascal Sample 9.28 shows the effect of this revision on the *classrooms* database.

To cope with, and make use of, this change in the external database, we must make several changes in *info1*. The *loadBase* procedure must do something with the new information, the declaration for the working database must be changed if we are to keep the new information, and the *select* procedure must use the new information to rectify the problem that prompted us to distinguish between numeric and alphabetic attributes. Furthermore, we should revise the comments shown in Section 9.2 to reflect the new format of external data files. This may seem like a lot of work, but it is well-defined work and it is limited to specific parts of *info1*; subprograms such as *sort, print, commandAnalysis,* and *att* are not affected at all. Hence a good modular design for *info1* aids us when we make major as well as minor changes.

Since extensive changes are required in *info1*, perhaps this is a good time to convert *info1*, which was intended to be only a rough draft, into *info*, which will be a more polished prototype DBMS.

PASCAL SAMPLE 9.27   The program *info1* (bug caused by too quick a fix)

```
Command: base
Database: classrooms1
Command: select
Attribute:           seats
Value to select:     75
0 entities selected
```

PASCAL SAMPLE 9.28   The file *classrooms* (final version)

```
Classrooms database
12 5
13              4   5   3 10
building        roomseatsTV microphone
A               I   I   A  A
Humanities     100   75yesyes
Humanities     101   20no no
Humanities     105   15no no
Humanities     201   30yesno
Humanities     205   15no no
Sciences       120   75yesyes
Sciences       130   75yesno
Sciences       140   40yesno
Campus Center   10 1000yesyes
Campus Center   15  100yesyes
Campus Center  101   50no yes
Campus Center  102   25no no
```

STEP 4 (CONTINUED): REFINING THE DRAFT

Before beginning to polish our prototype DBMS, let us list the improvements we want to make. Then we can set about making these improvements one at a time.

1. Distinguish between numeric and alphabetic attributes by changing the declaration of the working database and modifying the procedures *loadBase* and *select*.

2. Handle the `describe`, `help`, and `restore` commands.

3. Permit more flexible command entry by using *getResponse* in *commandAnalysis* and *base*, and by modifying *getResponse* to retain all input supplied by the user.

4. Improve the appearance of output by printing labels and by allowing *print* to display the values of specified attributes.

5. Provide better error recovery in case the user mistypes the name of an attribute.

Rather than examining these changes one at a time, we will simply display the entire text of the resulting program *info*. (See Pascal Sample 9.29.) Careful study of that program will disclose how the improvements were made. However, a few comments about some of these improvements are in order.

1. The *select* procedure now calls a new procedure *rightAlign* to align numeric values before calling *xselect*.

2. The `restore` command is easy to implement, given the existence of the *xcreate* procedure. The *describe* procedure is straightforward, but we have to work at making its output look good. The `help` command is easiest to handle if we place

instructions for the user in a separate text file *helpinfo* and use the *appendToFile* procedure from Section 6.6 to display this file whenever help is requested.

3. To enable *getResponse* to determine whether to issue a message before getting a response, we introduce a boolean variable *needInput*. Whenever *getResponse* finishes supplying a response, it makes *needInput false* if there is more input on the line supplied by the user and *true* otherwise. Since the value of *needInput* must be preserved from one call of *getResponse* to the next, Pascal forces us to make it a global variable and to initialize it to *true* at the beginning of the main program.

4. To produce attractively formatted output, we must pay attention to details in *print*. This procedure calls a subsidiary procedure *getCols* to determine the attributes that the user wants printed.

5. Better error recovery results from having *att* interact with the user in case the name of an attribute was misspelled.

Since *info* is such a long program, we have divided it into levels that contain command handling routines (such as *print* and *sort*), command decoding routines (such as *getResponse* and *att*), command processing routines (such as *loadBase* and *xsort*), and auxiliary routines (such as *rightAlign*). Comments separate each of these levels from the others, making it possible to read *info* one level at a time.

■ **PASCAL SAMPLE 9.29**   The program *info* (final version)

```
{     The program info allows users to retrieve information from specified }
{ files and then select, sort, or print subsets of this information. The   }
{ information itself consists of the values of certain attributes for a     }
{ collection of entities.                                                   }
{                                                                           }
{ The commands understood by info are as follows:                          }
{       base filename          retrieves data from named file              }
{       describe               describes data in database                  }
{       help                   prints these instructions                   }
{       print all              prints values of all attributes for the selected }
{                              entities                                     }
{       print att1 att2 ...    prints values of the named attributes for the    }
{                              selected entities                            }
{       restore                selects all entities                        }
{       select att value       selects those entities having the specified }
{                              value for the named attribute from among the }
{                              currently selected entities                  }
{       size                   prints the number of selected entities      }
{       sort att               sorts the selected entities with the named  }
{                              attribute as key                            }
{       stop                   terminates info                             }
{ All commands may be abbreviated by their first three letters. Each       }
{ command occupies a single line.                                          }
```

■ **PASCAL SAMPLE 9.29**   The program *info* (final version, continued)

```
{ Files for use with info must be text files with the following format:  }
{     line 1          — title of database                                }
{     line 2          — number e of entities, a of attributes            }
{     line 3          — widths of values for a attributes                }
{     line 4          — names for a attributes                           }
{     line 5          — types for a attributes (I for integer, A for alphabetic)}
{     line 6          — values of a attributes for first entity          }
{     ...             — ...                                              }
{     line 5+e        — values of a attributes for last entity           }
{ In lines 4 through 5+e, attribute names and the values of alphabetic   }
{ attributes are left-aligned within fields having the widths specified on }
{ line 3. The values of numeric attributes are right-aligned in these fields. }
```

program *info*(*input*, *output*, *datafile*, *helpinfo*);

const *maxAttributes* = 10;
     maxEntities   = 50;
     stringLength = 20;   { maximum attribute width }

type *string*   = **packed array** [1..*stringLength*] **of** *char*;
    itemType   = *string*;
    table   = **array** [1..*maxEntities*, 1..*maxAttributes*] **of** *itemType*;
    rowIndex   = 0..*maxEntities*;
    colIndex   = 0..*maxAttributes*;
    colList   = **array** [1..*maxAttributes*] **of** *colIndex*;
    attType   = (*intAtt*, *strAtt*);
    baseType   = **record**
            title   : *string*;
            attributes : *colIndex*;
            entities : *rowIndex*;
            names   : **array** [1..*maxAttributes*] **of** *string*;
            widths   : **array** [1..*maxAttributes*] **of** 0..*stringLength*;
            attTypes : **array** [1..*maxAttributes*] **of** *attType*;
            items   : *table*
      end;
    indexType = **record**
            size : *rowIndex*;
            ptrs : **array** [1..*maxEntities*] **of** *rowIndex*
      end;

var *datafile*   : *text*;   { permanent database }
   helpinfo   : *text*;   { help for using *info* }
   needInput : *boolean*;   { used by *getValue* }

{ ***** Auxiliary Routines ***** }

#include 'stringSubs2';   { *length*, *readString*, *writeString* }
#include 'appendToFile';   { *appendToFile* }

```
procedure readChars( var f : text;
                         n : integer;
                     var s : string );
    { reads the next n characters on the current line of the text }
    { file f and assigns them to s                               }
    var i : integer
    begin
        for i := 1 to stringLength do
            if (i <= n) and not eoln(f) then
                read(f,s[i])
            else
                s[i] := ' '
    end;   { of readChars }


{ ***** Command Processing Routines ***** }

procedure loadBase( var db         : baseType;
                        filename : string );
    { creates working database from file with given name }
    var a : 0..maxAttributes;
        e : 0..maxEntities;
        t : string;
    begin
        reset(datafile,filename);
        readChars(datafile,stringLength,db.title);              { line 1 }
        readln(datafile,db.entities,db.attributes);             { line 2 }
        for a := 1 to db.attributes do
            read(datafile,db.widths[a]);
        readln(datafile);                                       { line 3 }
        for a := 1 to db.attributes do
            readChars(datafile,db.widths[a],db.names[a]);
        readln(datafile);                                       { line 4 }
        for a := 1 to db.attributes do
            begin
                readChars(datafile,db.widths[a],t);
                if t[1] = 'A' then
                    db.attTypes[a] := strAtt
                else if t[1] = 'I' then
                    db.attTypes[a] := intAtt
                else
                    writeln('Illegal type in database for ', db.names[a])
            end;
        readln(datafile);                                       { line 5 }
```

▉ **PASCAL SAMPLE 9.29**　The program *info* (final version, continued)

```
            for e := 1 to db.entities do
              begin
                for a := 1 to db.attributes do
                    readChars(datafile, db.widths[a], db.items[e, a]);
                readln(datafile)                                        { line 5+e }
              end
          end;  { of loadBase }

      procedure rightAlign( var s : string;  n : integer );
          { right-aligns the first n characters in the string s }
          var i, j : 0..stringLength;
          begin
              { find rightmost nonblank }
              i := n;
              while (s[i] = ' ') and (i > 1) do i := i − 1;
              if i < n then                                            { shift string }
                  for j := n downto 1 do
                      if i > 0 then
                          begin
                              s[ j] := s[i];
                              i := i − 1
                          end
                      else
                          s[ j] := ' '
          end;  { of rightAlign }

      #include 'indexSubs';                                 { xcreate, xselect, xsort }

      { ***** Command Decoding Routines ***** }

      procedure abbreviate( var s : string );
          { abbreviates s to its first three characters }
          var i : 1..stringLength;
          begin
              for i := 4 to stringLength do s[i] := ' '
          end;  { of abbreviate }
```

```
function att( var db        : baseType;                        { not changed }
              attribute : string ) : colIndex;
    { returns the number of the column in db holding the given attribute }
    { (requests that the attribute be resupplied if it is misspelled)     }
    var a, col : colIndex;
    begin
        repeat
            col := 0;
            a := 1;
            while (a <= db.attributes) and (col = 0) do
                if attribute = db.names[a] then
                    col := a
                else
                    a := a + 1;
            if col = 0 then
                begin
                    write('Don''t recognize ');
                    writeString(output, attribute);
                    write('. Re-enter it: ');
                    readString(input, attribute);
                end
        until col > 0;
        att := col
    end;  { of att }


procedure getResponse( message : string; var value : string );
    { gets a string value from the user, prompting with message if needInput }
    { is true (needInput is global so that its value is retained from one call }
    { of getResponse to the next)                                              }
    begin
        if needInput then
            begin
                writeString(output, message);
                write(' ')
            end;
        readString(input, value);
        needInput := eoln
    end;  { of getResponse }
```

■ **PASCAL SAMPLE 9.29**   The program *info* (final version, continued)

```
procedure getCols( var db  : baseType;                               { not changed }
                   var cols : colList;
                   var n    : colIndex );
    { constructs a list of n column numbers for attributes specified by the user }
    var i       : colIndex;                              { .cols subscript       }
        attName : string;                                { name of attribute     }
        done    : boolean;
    begin
        { find which attributes user wants }
        getResponse('Attributes:          ', attName);
        if attName = 'all' then                          { all of them  }
            begin
                n := db.attributes;
                for i := 1 to db.attributes do cols[i] := i
            end
        else                                             { named ones }
            begin
                n := 0;
                done := false;
                repeat
                    n := n + 1;
                    cols[n] := att(db, attName);
                    if needInput then
                        done := true
                    else
                        getResponse('Attribute:          ', attName);
                until done
            end
    end;   { of getCols }

{ ***** Command Handlers ***** }

procedure base( var db : baseType;
                var x  : indexType );
    { creates working database for user }
    var baseName : string;
    begin
        getResponse('Database:          ', baseName);
        loadBase(db, baseName);
        xcreate(x, db.entities)
    end;   { of base }
```

```
procedure describe( var db : baseType );
    { describes contents of database }
    const pageWidth = 75;
    var a        : 0..maxAttributes;
        columns : integer;
    begin
        writeln('Current database: ', db.title);
        writeln(db.attributes:1, ' attributes');
        writeln(db.entities:1, ' entities');
        writeln;
        writeln('Names of attributes:');
        columns := pageWidth div stringLength;
        for a := 1 to db.attributes do
            begin
                write(db.names[a]);
                if a mod columns = 0 then writeln
            end;
        writeln
    end;  { of describe }


procedure print( var db : baseType;                          { not changed }
                 var x  : indexType );                       { not changed }
    { prints requested attributes for items in db indexed by x }
    const gap       = 3;                          { gap between columns }
          underscore = ' ---------------------------------------- ';
    var howmany : colIndex;                       { how many to print   }
        cols    : colList;                        { list of their columns }
        i       : colIndex;                       { cols subscript      }
        e       : rowIndex;                       { entity subscript    }
    begin
        { find which attributes user wants to print }
        getCols(db, cols, howmany);
        { print names of attributes }
        writeln;
        for i := 1 to howmany do
            write(db.names[cols[i]] : db.widths[cols[i]] + gap);
        writeln;
```

PASCAL SAMPLE 9.29   The program *info* (final version, continued)

```
            { underline attribute names }
            for i := 1 to howmany do
                write(underscore : db.widths[cols[i]], ' ' : gap);
            writeln;

            { print values of attributes for indexed entities }
            for e := 1 to x.size do
                begin
                    for i := 1 to howmany do
                        write(db.items[x.ptrs[e], cols[i]] : db.widths[cols[i]] + gap);
                    writeln
                end
        end;   { of print }


    procedure select( var db : baseType;                          { not changed }
                      var x  : indexType );
        { enables user to thin out the index x }

        var attribute, value : string;
            a                : colIndex;

        begin
            getResponse('Attribute:            ', attribute);
            getResponse('Value to select:      ', value);
            a := att(db, attribute);
            if db.attTypes[a] = intAtt then rightAlign(value, db.widths[a]);
            xselect(db.items, x, a, value);
            writeln(x.size:1, ' entities selected')

        end;   { of select }

                                                                  { not changed }
    procedure sort( var db : baseType;
                    var x  : indexType );
        { enables user to sort indexed entities }

        var attribute : string;

        begin
            getResponse('Attribute to sort: ', attribute);
            xsort(db.items, x, att(db, attribute))
        end;   { of sort }
```

```
procedure commandAnalysis;
    { interpret user's commands }

    var db       : baseType;                              { working database }
        index    : indexType;                          { of selected entities }
        command : string;

    begin

        base(db, index);                              { create working database }

        repeat                                        { interpret user's commands }
            writeln;
            getResponse('Command:                    ', command);
            abbreviate(command);
            if command = 'bas'    then base(db, index)
            else if command = 'des' then describe(db)
            else if command = 'hel' then appendToFile(output, helpinfo)
            else if command = 'pri' then print(db, index)
            else if command = 'res' then xcreate(index, db.entities)
            else if command = 'sel' then select(db, index)
            else if command = 'siz' then
                    writeln(index.size:1, ' entities selected.')
            else if command = 'sor' then sort(db, index)
            else if command = 'sto' then writeln('bye')
            else
                begin
                    writeln('Illegal command. Legal commands are:');
                    writeln('base, describe, help, print, restore');
                    writeln('select, size, sort, stop')
                end
        until command = 'sto'

    end;  { of commandAnalysis }


{ ***** Main Program ***** }

begin
    needInput := true;
    commandAnalysis                                      { interpret commands }
end.  { of info }
```

■ **PASCAL SAMPLE 9.30**   The file *helpinfo*

Command	Action
base filename	retrieves data from named file
describe	describes data in database
help	prints these instructions
print all	prints values of all attributes for the selected entities
print att1 att2 ...	prints values of the named attributes for the selected entities
restore	selects all entities
select att value	selects those entities having the specified value for the named attribute from among the currently selected entities
size	prints the number of selected entities
sort att	sorts the selected entities with the named attribute as key
stop	terminates info

All commands may be abbreviated by their first three letters.
Each command occupies a single line.

Instructions for using *info* are contained in the text file *helpinfo,* displayed as Pascal Sample 9.30, which can be displayed by giving *info* the command `help`. This version of *info* was used to produce the sample interaction displayed in Pascal Sample 9.1. Further improvements in *info* are suggested in the following exercises.

EXERCISES

1. Modify the *select* procedure to ignore a requested selection if it would result in eliminating all entities from the index.

2. Design and implement enhancements to the `restore` command that would allow users to restore the state of the index to a specified previous version.

3. Modify *commandAnalysis* to check for spelling errors in commands if users enter more than three-letter abbreviations.

4. Improve the error handling capability of *info* in the following ways.

   (a) After certain errors, it is safest to discard the remainder of the current line of input and force the user to enter a new command. Decide when this should be done and modify *info* accordingly.

   (b) Users who mistype the name of an attribute should be given a chance to cancel the entire command. Design and implement a method to give them this option.

5. This version of *info* was not designed to allow users to type more than one command on a line, but it does allow this unless one of those commands is a `print` command. Modify *info* to be more consistent in its treatment of multiple commands on a line. (*Hint:* Begin by changing the instructions for *info* to specify the required format for input more clearly.)

6. Design and add commands to *info* that enable it to modify items in the working database and in external data files.

7. Design and add commands to *info* that enable it to add new attributes or entities to, or delete old attributes and entities from, a database.

8. Change the declaration of *baseType* to divide the table in the working database in half, one-half being an array of numbers and the other being an array of strings. Then investigate the following alternative strategies for sorting and selecting.

   (a) Construct two versions of *xsort,* one for numeric arrays and one for string arrays.

   (b) Modify *xsort* to determine the type of comparison it needs to perform during a sort.

   How do these strategies compare with each other and with the strategy we employed in going from *info1* to *info*? What is the extent of the changes that must be made with each strategy?

9. Enhance the `select` command to accept input of the form

   `select` attribute-name relation value

   where the relation is one of $=$, $<>$, $<$, $<=$, $>$, and $>=$.

10. Enhance the `sort` command to give users the option of sorting numbers in decreasing rather than increasing order.

11. Design and add a command or commands that permit the user to compute statistics such as the mean and median for numeric attributes.

12. *The master file update problem*   Many commercial applications of computing rely on and update "master files" of information related to such matters as payroll, inventory, accounts receivable, accounts payable, and the like. Typically these applications process a series of "transactions" by using information in a master file to generate paychecks, purchase orders, invoices, and so on, and by adjusting the master file to reflect the results of the transactions.

   Because of the critical nature of most commercial applications, it is important to have a good design for programs that update master files. In particular, a good design should lead to programs that are

   (a) reliable, so that they process transactions correctly in order to ensure the timeliness and accuracy of information in a master file;

(b) robust, so that they detect (where possible) erroneous transactions in order to protect the integrity of information in a master file;

(c) modifiable, so that they can be adapted economically and reliably to provide new services or to handle new formats for data.

The purpose of this exercise is to design and code an update procedure to a simple master file maintained by the Nuts and Bolts Shipping Company. The master file is a text file with fixed-length lines, each containing a "record" of information for one of the company's customers. Records are divided into fields as follows.

Field	Columns	Format
Account number	1– 5	Letter followed by four digits
Customer name	6–20	Letters, blanks, some punctuation
Account status	21–22	Letter, digit
Phone number	23–35	Digits, hyphen, parentheses
City	36–50	Letters, blanks
State	51–52	Letters, blanks
Zip code	53–57	Digits
Balance	57–68	Blanks, fixed-point number
Filler	69–80	Blanks

All letters in a record are uppercase. The name and city are left-justified in their fields. The fixed-point number representing the balance due is right-justified in its field and contains a decimal point followed by two digits; if the customer has a negative balance, the balance is preceded by a minus sign. Records in the master file are sorted according to the account number.

Changes to the master file are specified in a transaction file, which is also a text file. The first line of that file contains two names separated by a single blank: the name of the master file to update and the name of a new file to hold the results of the update. The remaining lines in the transaction file have the same format as in the master file, although some fields in a record may be blank. Records in the transaction file are also sorted according to the account number, and there is at most one record per account number.

The master file update program should request the name of a transaction file and update the appropriate master file, as follows. If the account numbers in a master and transaction record match, all nonblank fields in the transaction record should be copied into the corresponding field of the master record. An exception is the "balance" field; there, the amount in the transaction record should be added to the amount in the master record. If the account number of a transaction record does not correspond to any master record account number, that transaction should be reported as an error.

For safety's sake, it is a good idea to check the sequence of customer numbers in the transaction file as they are read. Do not preedit or sort the transaction file; this should have been done before the master file update is run. However, detect and report out-of-sequence transaction lines as errors. (Since the old master file is retained, it is not necessary to undo changes already made in the new master file.)

13. *The revised master file update problem* The specifications for commercial programs rarely remain the same for long. However, with a good design for a program, it should

be relatively easy to adapt that program to changing requirements. Assess the design for your solution to Exercise 12 by changing your program to meet the following new requirements.

(a) The account number now contains six characters: a capital letter plus five digits.

(b) The balance field is now located between the phone number and city fields.

(c) A field indicating the customer's credit rating has been added. It consists of three alphanumeric characters, and it uses the first three columns of the filler.

(d) If all fields in a transaction record are blank, the corresponding master record should be deleted from the master file. If there is no matching master record, the transaction record should be reported as an error.

(e) If the account number of a transaction record does not match that of any master record, and if all fields in the transaction record are nonblank, the transaction record should be inserted in the master file in the correct place; if some fields in such a transaction record are blank, that record should be reported as an error.

(f) There can now be multiple transaction records per master record. The transactions should be processed in the order in which they occur in the transaction file. For example, it is possible to delete a master record with a given account number and then add a new one with the same account number, but it is not possible to delete a master record and then change some of its fields.

(g) Finally, more extensive changes are required in the format of the transaction file. The first line of the file is the same as before, indicating the names of the old and new master files. The remainder of the transaction file consists of transaction lines, sorted according to the customer account number, but possibly with several transaction lines per account. A transaction line now consists of the customer account number, followed by four blanks, followed by the new values for the various fields. Since not all fields need to be changed all the time, each field is identified by a two-letter code. Immediately following is the new value for that field, and a semicolon indicates the end of the value. For example,

```
C1234    CTNEW YORK;BL1000;
```

indicates that the city field for customer C1234 should be changed to NEW YORK and that the balance field should be increased by 1000. The two-letter codes for the several fields are

NM	name
AS	account status
PH	phone
CT	city
ST	state
ZI	zip
BL	balance
CR	credit rating

If an error is detected in the transaction lines for a particular customer number, then no changes should be made to that record in the master file. More than one update for any field is an error.

14. Design a set of data to test your solutions to Exercise 12 and 13. Concentrate on making your tests systematic, thorough, and convincing. (Large quantities of random test data generally fail to meet any of these criteria.)

15. Discuss objectively and scientifically which aspects of your solution to Exercise 12 helped in creating a solution to Exercise 13, which aspects hindered creating a solution to Exercise 13, and why.

16. Design and write a program to compute the following statistics concerning a file of text.

    (a) The total number of words in the text.

    (b) The number of different words in the text.

    (c) The length of the longest word in the text.

    (d) The average length of all words in the text.

    Count repeated words when computing the average word length, count contractions as single words, and count apostrophes, but not other punctuation marks, when computing the length of a word. Do not count words as different if they differ only in the use of uppercase and lowercase letters.

17. Enhance the program you wrote for Exercise 16 as follows.

    (a) Print a histogram of the lengths of the words in the text, that is, a bar graph such as

```
1 ***
2 *****
3 *******
    . . .
```

    to indicate that there are three words of length 1, five of length 2, and so on.

    (b) Print a frequency count for each word that appears in the text.

18. Analyze the efficiency of the program you wrote for Exercise 16.

    (a) How many times does your program read the file of text?

    (b) When computing the number of different words in the text, how many times does your program compare one word with another? If there are m different words in a text with n words in all, can you express an upper bound on the number of comparisons performed as a function of m and n?

    (c) How many times does your program move a word in the text from one location to another (for example from the file to a variable or an element of an array, or from one variable or element of an array to another)? Can you express an upper bound on this quantity as a function of m and n?

    (d) Discuss the prospects for devising a more efficient method to solve Exercise 16. How extensively would you have to change your program in order to use a different method?

19. Write a program that enables two players to play a board game such as checkers or chess. Have your program

    (a) accept moves from each player;

    (b) display the current state of the board after each move; and

    (c) reject illegal moves.

    Concentrate on providing a high-quality user interface.

20. How much does the structure of your solution to Exercise 19 depend on the features of the particular computer and computer terminal that you are using? How hard would it be to adapt the program to run on a computer with different features, say, one with or without graphic input and output devices?

SUMMARY

Good programming methodology facilitates the construction of large programs. It structures a large program as an integrated collection of well-designed subprograms, which can be written, tested, and enhanced in an orderly fashion. In a well-designed program,

- each subprogram accomplishes a single, well-defined task,
    1. separate tasks are isolated in separate subprograms, and
    2. each subprogram hides the details of carrying out its task,
- libraries of related subprograms manipulate common data structures; and
- subprograms communicate explicitly through parameters.

The four activities that led to the development of a prototype database management system in this chapter provide guidelines for the development of other large programs.

- Develop and write clear specifications that
    1. describe exactly what the program must do and
    2. serve as a user manual or as comments for the program.
- Write an outline for the program that
    1. designs the division of the program into subprograms,
    2. designs the communication between the subprograms, and
    3. creates a working skeleton program with stubs for subprograms.
- Write a rough draft of the program by
    1. writing rudimentary input–output procedures to facilitate testing,
    2. selecting and designing algorithms and data structures for key subprograms, and
    3. using existing tools, where appropriate.
- Fill in and refine the rough draft:
    1. add or refine one subprogram at a time;
    2. write major subprograms first,
        (a) adding functionality before refining details and
        (b) identifying and correcting design problems as early as possible;
    3. maintain a working program by
        (a) testing, correcting, and retesting each addition or refinement and
        (b) retesting the entire program whenever a problem forces a change in the specification or design; and
    4. save minor enhancements and fine tuning for last.

This sequence of activities

■ makes efficient use of time by minimizing

    1. coding time by providing clear specifications,

    2. testing time by isolating potential sources of errors, and

    3. rewriting time by postponing details until the design stabilizes; and

■ makes efficient use of a constantly improving program by providing a

    1. prototype for evaluating specifications and design,

    2. test environment for additions and enhancements, and

    3. preliminary version for use as deadlines approach.

MERIC METHODS NUMERIC MET
NUMERIC METHODS NUMERIC ME
DS NUMERIC METHODS NUMERIC
HODS NUMERIC METHODS NUMER
ERIC METHODS NUMERIC METHO
NUMERIC METHODS NUMERIC ME
DS NUMERIC METHODS NUMERIC
HODS

NUMERIC METHODS

NUMER

C H A P T E R

10

_M_any of the earliest applications of modern computers involved numeric computations. Computers were used to evaluate mathematical functions, to solve equations, to perform scientific calculations, and to prepare statistical analyses of data. As a result, computer science in its infancy placed considerable emphasis on numeric algorithms. More recently, computer science has shifted its focus from numeric to nonnumeric algorithms, with numeric algorithms being of primary interest now to mathematicians, statisticians, scientists, and engineers.

Still, there are many applications of computing, both within and outside the sciences, that call upon us to manipulate numbers rather than symbols. In Chapters 3 and 4, for example, we considered some typical numeric problems in banking and finance. In at least one case we had to simulate banking transactions, or solve a reasonably complicated equation, to find the answer we desired. Hence it pays to have tools at our disposal for performing standard numeric computations.

In this chapter we develop tools for numeric approximation and for simulation. Some of these tools will enable us to solve problems that are difficult or impossible to solve by mathematical analysis alone; others will enable us to solve problems that ordinarily require more sophisticated mathematical techniques than we possess.

But we should not conclude that computing is a replacement for mathematics. Rather, we will find that computing enables us to put mathematics into practice, and that mathematics helps us find good ways to compute.

Exact answers to questions are the most satisfying, provided we can get them. Often, exact answers are impossible or extremely difficult to obtain, and we may be willing to settle for approximate answers instead. The fact that we cannot write down exact decimal representations for irrational numbers such as π causes us little difficulty; for most purposes it is enough to know that π is approximately 3.14159265. And, in order to win a prize for counting the number of jelly beans in a large jar, we need only to estimate that number more accurately than our competitors.

Approximation, then, helps us obtain answers that are good enough for the need at hand. To illustrate the general nature of approximations, we develop several algorithms in this section for approximating zeroes of functions. We use the exercises at the end of this section to suggest some algorithms for approximating other interesting values.

ZEROES OF FUNCTIONS

We can solve many problems by finding a zero of a function f, that is, by finding a value x such that $f(x) = 0$. In Chapter 4, we found the effective interest rate for a loan by finding a zero of a function f such that $f(r)$ is the final balance of the loan when the interest rate is r. Similarly, in order to find the square root of 2, we can define a function f by letting $f(x) = x^2 - 2$ and then find a zero of f.

More generally, we can reduce the problem of computing the inverse of a one-to-one function to the problem of computing zeroes of related functions. If g is a one-to-one function [that is, if $g(x) = g(y)$ implies $x = y$], then the *inverse* of g is that function g^{-1} such that

$$g^{-1}(y) = x \quad \text{if and only if} \quad g(x) = y.$$

(Note that g must be one-to-one for g^{-1} to be a function.) Now computing $g^{-1}(y)$ is equivalent to finding a zero of the function g_y, where $g_y(x) = g(x) - y$. Since the square-root function is the inverse of the square function, computing square roots is just a special case of computing inverses of functions.

Students who have studied calculus can reduce the problem of finding the maximum or minimum value of a function to the problem of finding the zeroes of the derivative of that function. Thus one technique, namely finding the zeroes of functions, helps solve many seemingly disparate problems.

THE BISECTION ALGORITHM REVISITED

In Chapter 4 we developed a simple method for approximating a zero of a function f. That method, the bisection algorithm, is sure and steady. Given an interval (a, b) such that $f(a)$ and $f(b)$ have opposite signs, it progressively cuts that interval in half, trapping a zero of f between two points that get closer and closer together.

Pascal Sample 10.1 shows the sequences of approximations that are generated by the bisection algorithm to zeroes of $x^2 - 4$ and $\sin x$ in the interval $(1, 10)$. These results were produced by inserting the statement $writeln(x, f(x))$ at the end of the loop in the library *bisect2* used by *zeroDemo2*.

Despite its simplicity and reliability, the bisection algorithm has drawbacks. First, we must supply it with an interval in which f changes sign. This in itself may take some work, and we might prefer an algorithm that requires less information. Second, although the bisection algorithm converges steadily to a zero of f, it does not converge quickly. To approximate $\sqrt{2}$ to within 10^{-6}, it must evaluate $x^2 - 2$ and cut the interval $(1, 10)$ in half 23 times. Hence we might prefer an algorithm that converges more rapidly.

Several possibilities suggest themselves for speeding up the bisection algorithm. In general, we would like to trap a zero of f in an interval that shrinks as rapidly as possible. We could, for example, construct a "trisection" algorithm that cuts an interval in which f changes sign into three pieces and retains the piece in which the change of sign occurs. However, since we must evaluate f twice on each iteration of

---

PASCAL SAMPLE 10.1.   The program *zeroDemo2* (approximations produced by bisection method)

```
5.50000000000000e+00    2.62500000000000e+01
3.25000000000000e+00    6.56250000000000e+00
2.12500000000000e+00    5.15625000000000e-01
1.56250000000000e+00   -1.55859375000000e+00
1.84375000000000e+00   -6.00585937500000e-01
1.98437500000000e+00   -6.22558593750000e-02
2.05468750000000e+00    2.21740722656250e-01
2.01953125000000e+00    7.85064697265625e-02
2.00195312500000e+00    7.81631469726563e-03
1.99316406250000e+00   -2.72970199584961e-02
1.99755859375000e+00   -9.75966453552246e-03
1.99975585937500e+00   -9.76502895355225e-04
2.00085449218750e+00    3.41869890689850e-03
2.00030517578125e+00    1.22079625725746e-03
2.00003051757813e+00    1.22071243822575e-04
1.99989318847656e+00   -4.27234685048461e-04
1.99996185302734e+00   -1.52586435433477e-04
1.99999618530273e+00   -1.52587745105848e-05
2.00001335144043e+00    5.34059399797115e-05
2.00000476837158e+00    1.90735090654925e-05
2.00000047683716e+00    1.90734886018618e-06
1.99999833106995e+00   -6.67571742951623e-06
1.99999940395355e+00   -2.38418543574426e-06
sqr( 1.99999994039536e+00) - 4 = -2.38418575548849e-07
```

```
5.50000000000000e+00  -7.05540325570392e-01
3.25000000000000e+00  -1.08195134530108e-01
2.12500000000000e+00   8.50319789818452e-01
2.68750000000000e+00   4.38647099098633e-01
2.96875000000000e+00   1.71983337815754e-01
3.10937500000000e+00   3.22120803473869e-02
3.17968750000000e+00  -3.80856330952536e-02
3.14453125000000e+00  -2.93859218090776e-03
3.12695312500000e+00   1.46390056816896e-02
3.13574218750000e+00   5.85043271493687e-03
3.14013671875000e+00   1.45593432542455e-03
3.14233398437500e+00  -7.41330717304400e-04
3.14123535156250e+00   3.57302019690784e-04
3.14178466796875e+00  -1.92014377776877e-04
3.14151000976563e+00   8.26438240741599e-05
3.14164733886719e+00  -5.46852773669558e-05
3.14157867431641e+00   1.39792733865351e-05
3.14161300659180e+00  -2.03530020021836e-05
3.14159584045410e+00  -3.18686430827201e-06
3.14158725738525e+00   5.39620453930852e-06
3.14159154891968e+00   1.10467011550663e-06
3.14159369468689e+00  -1.04109709642869e-06
3.14159262180328e+00   3.17865095389888e-08
sin( 3.14159315824509e+00)      = -5.04655293379524e-07
```

this algorithm, such a trisection algorithm actually requires more work than the bisection algorithm. (See Exercise 1 at the end of this section.)

A more promising approach is to cut an interval in which f changes sign into two unequal pieces and hope to trap a zero of f in the smaller of the pieces. This idea leads to the following algorithm.

THE METHOD OF FALSE POSITION

In the *method of false position,* we cut an interval (a, b) in two by constructing the *secant,* or line, joining the point $<a, f(a)>$ to the point $<b, f(b)>$ and letting m_1 be the intersection of this line with the x-axis. (See Fig. 10.1.) The slope s of the secant is given by the formula

$$s = \frac{f(b) - f(a)}{b - a}.$$

Since the point $(m_1, 0)$ lies on the secant, the slope is also given by the formula

$$s = \frac{f(b)}{b - m_1}.$$

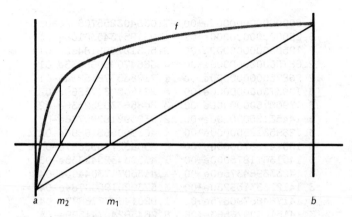

FIGURE 10.1 ■ Fast convergence using method of false position

Hence

$$m_1 = b - \frac{f(b)}{s}$$

$$= b - f(b)\frac{b - a}{f(b) - f(a)}.$$

As in the bisection method, we can evaluate $f(m_1)$ to determine whether f changes sign in the interval (a, m_1) or (m_1, b), and we can subdivide that subinterval further by constructing another secant. Figure 10.1 shows that the method of false position can trap a zero of f much more quickly than bisection.

Unfortunately, as shown in Fig. 10.2, the method of false position can also converge much more slowly than the bisection algorithm. This happens when the zero of f is trapped in the larger of the two pieces rather than in the smaller. Thus, unless we know something special about the function f, the method of false position has little to recommend it over the method of bisection. Consequently, we leave its implementation as an exercise. (See Exercise 2 at the end of this section.)

Still, the method of false position provides some insight into a new approach to approximating zeroes. What it does is to approximate the function f in the interval (a, b) by a straight line—the secant—and to use a zero of this approximate function as an approximation to a zero of f. If the secant is a good approximation to f, then a zero of the secant will be a good approximation to a zero of f. This insight leads us to a third method for approximating zeroes of functions.

THE SECANT METHOD

In the *secant method*, we abandon the strategy of trapping a zero of f in intervals $(a_1, b_1), (a_2, b_2), \ldots, (a_n, b_n)$ that get progressively smaller. Instead, we attempt to

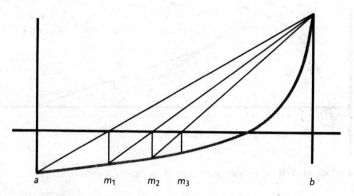

FIGURE 10.2 ■ Slow convergence using method of false position

produce a sequence of approximations $x_1, x_2, \ldots, x_n$ that get progressively closer to a zero of f.

As in the method of false position, we use secants to produce our approximations. Given two approximations x_{n-1} and x_n to a zero of f, we construct the secant connecting $<x_{n-1}, f(x_{n-1})>$ to $<x_n, f(x_n)>$, and we let the next approximation x_{n+1} be the intersection of this secant with the x-axis. Recalling the computation we performed for the method of false position, we see that

$$x_{n+1} = x_n - f(x_n) \frac{x_n - x_{n-1}}{f(x_n) - f(x_{n-1})}.$$

As Fig. 10.3 shows, the intersection of this secant does not need to lie between x_{n-1} and x_n. It usually lies closer to a zero of f, and the construction of further

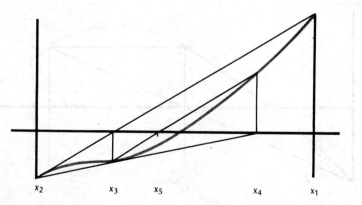

FIGURE 10.3 ■ Approximating a zero of f using the secant method

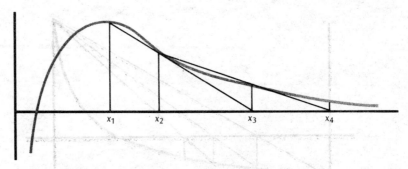

FIGURE 10.4 ■ Divergent approximations using secant method

secants usually produces even better approximations. We say that a new approximation generated by the secant method "usually" lies closer to a zero of f because there are cases in which the secant method does not work. Figure 10.4, for example, shows a case in which the approximations generated by the secant method get farther and farther away from a zero of f. Here, even though the secants are good approximations to f, they lead away from, not toward, a zero of f. Worse yet, as illustrated by Fig. 10.5, the secant method may break down completely by generating a secant that is parallel to the x-axis. Here the secant is not a very good approximation to f.

Such anomalies are the price we pay to construct an algorithm that, most of the time, converges more quickly than the bisection algorithm. In order to determine how much faster the secant method is than bisection, and to discover the precautions that we can take to guard against anomalous 'situations, we construct a new function *zero* to approximate a zero of a given function f by the secant method, and we package this function in a library *secant*, displayed as Pascal Sample 10.2.

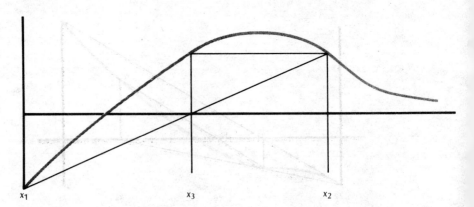

FIGURE 10.5 ■ Horizontal secant generated using secant method

■ **PASCAL SAMPLE 10.2** The library *secant*

{ *secant*: approximates a zero of a function using the secant method }

```
function zero(function f( x : real ) : real;       { function        }
              x1, x2      : real;                   { 1st, 2nd approx }
              epsilon     : real ) : real;          { tolerance       }

    { generates at most maxApprox new approximations x3, x4, ... to a zero of }
    { f, given initial approximations x1 and x2, and returns the first of these }
    { within epsilon of the previous approximation or the last of these if the }
    { approximations do not converge }

const maxApprox = 20;                               { limit on iterations        }
      display   = true;                             { process displayed if true  }

var count : integer;                                { counts iterations          }
    x3    : real;                                   { next approximation         }
    y1, y2 : real;                                  { y1 = f(x1), y2 = f(x2)     }
    done  : boolean;

begin
    count := 0;
    done := false;
    y1 := f(x1);
    repeat
        count := count + 1;
        y2 := f(x2);
        if y1 <> y2 then { use secant approximation }
            x3 := x2 - y2*(x2-x1)/(y2-y1)
        else { move x a small amount }
            x3 := x2 - epsilon*(1 + abs(x2));
        if display then writeln(count, x3);
        if (abs(x3-x2) < epsilon) or (count >= maxApprox) then
            done := true
        else { relabel approximations }
            begin
                x1 := x2;
                y1 := y2;
                x2 := x3
            end
    until done;
    zero := x3
end;  { of zero }
```

The major problem in defining *zero* concerns when to terminate the approximation process. Since we are no longer trapping a zero of f within smaller and smaller intervals, we have no easy way to guarantee that an approximation is within a specified tolerance of an actual zero of f. But we can stop the approximation process when two successive approximations are very close together. Intuitively, if our approximations to a zero of f are getting closer and closer together, then they must be getting closer and closer to a zero of f. Exercises in Section 10.5 provide some mathematical justification for this stopping criterion.

As a precaution against infinite loops, we also stop the approximation process if we reach a fixed limit *maxApprox* on the number of iterations. Since 20 iterations of the bisection algorithm reduce an interval of size 1 to one of size 10^{-6}, and since we hope that the secant method requires fewer iterations than bisection, we may as well give up if the method does not converge in 20 iterations. Finally, we also guard against horizontal secants by taking an alternative corrective action when they arise.

Pascal Sample 10.3 shows that the secant method is faster than the bisection method. We generated the results there using *zeroDemo2* and the version of *zero* contained in *secant*. Whereas the bisection algorithm required 23 iterations to approximate a zero of either $x^2 - 4$ or $\sin x$ to within 10^{-6}, the secant method requires only 7 or 8.

Two anomalies in Pascal Sample 10.3 merit attention. First, since the secant method does not restrict its search for a zero to the interval between the first two approxi-

---

■ PASCAL SAMPLE 10.3. The program *zeroDemo2* (approximations generated by secant method)

```
         1 1.27272727272727e+00
         2 1.48387096774194e+00
         3 2.13617021276596e+00
         4 1.98058546943728e+00
         5 1.99935782422821e+00
         6 2.00000313259266e+00
         7 1.99999999949700e+00
         8 2.00000000000000e+00
sqr( 2.00000000000000e+00 - 4 = -1.55431223447522e-15
         1 6.46610037458189e+00
         2 7.35160680600063e+00
         3 6.23419196742352e+00
         4 6.29332648497374e+00
         5 6.28318208922244e+00
         6 6.28318530723473e+00
         7 6.28318530717959e+00
sin( 6.28318530717959e+00 )     = 0.00000000000000e+00
```

mations, it actually produces a different zero of sine than does the bisection method. Second, although the secant method appears to have found the zero 2 of $f(x) = x^2 - 4$ exactly, it reports a curious value for $f(2)$. We will examine the reason for this in Section 10.5.

NEWTON'S METHOD (OPTIONAL)

We conclude the discussion of techniques for approximating zeroes of functions by using ideas from calculus to produce an algorithm that is even faster than the secant method. Recall that in the secant method we approximate a function f by a secant and use a zero of this secant to approximate a zero of f. If we can find a straight line that is a better approximation to the function f than a secant, the intersection of this line with the x-axis might be a better approximation to a zero of f.

The best linear approximation to a curve at a point is provided by the tangent to that curve. Hence, given an approximation x_n to a zero z of f, we can compute a new approximation x_{n+1} by constructing the tangent to the graph of f at the point $<x_n, f(x_n)>$ and letting x_{n+1} be the point of intersection of this tangent with the x-axis. (See Fig. 10.6.) If the tangent is a good approximation to f at x_n, then x_{n+1} will be a good approximation to a zero of f. If not, we repeat the process to get a new approximation x_{n+2}. This method of approximation is known as *Newton's* method.

As we will see in Section 10.5, Newton's method converges so quickly to a zero of f that in each iteration it can double the number of accurate digits. The price we pay for the increase in speed of Newton's method over the bisection method is in decreased applicability: not only must the function f be continuous, but we must be able to compute the slopes of tangents to its graph. And, as in the secant method, Newton's method may still fail to converge in certain special situations. (See Exercises 5 and 6 at the end of this section.)

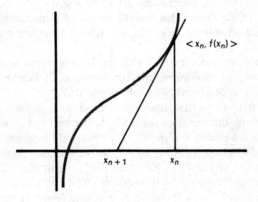

$<x_n, f(x_n)>$

x_{n+1} x_n

FIGURE 10.6 ■   Approximating a zero of f using a tangent

TABLE 10.1 Rules for Computing Derivatives

Function	Derivative
x_n	nx^{n-1}
$\sin x$	$\cos x$
$\cos x$	$\sin x$
$\ln x$	$1/x$
e^x	e^x
$f(x) + g(x)$	$f'(x) + g'(x)$
$cf(x)$	$cf'(x)$
$f(x)g(x)$	$f(x)g'(x) + f'(x)g(x)$
$f(g(x))$	$f'(g(x))g'(x)$

Methods from calculus enable us to compute the slopes of tangents to the graph of a function. The value $f'(x)$ of the *derivative* f' of a function f gives the slope of the tangent to the graph of f at x. Hence, as in the method of false position and the secant method, the point of intersection of the tangent is given by the formula

$$x_{n+1} = x_n - \frac{f(x_n)}{f'(x_n)}$$

But, in order to compute x_{n+1}, we must be able to compute $f'(x)$. Fortunately, calculus enables us to compute f' easily for many functions f. Table 10.1 lists several rules for computing the derivatives of various combinations of simple functions.

The function *zero* in the library *newton*, displayed as Pascal Sample 10.4, uses Newton's method to approximate a zero of a function f given both the function f itself and its derivative g. As in the secant method, we terminate the approximation process when successive approximations get close together or when we reach a maximum number of iterations. This second means of terminating the process is necessary to prevent an infinite loop in cases where Newton's method does not converge.

We can compare Newton's method with the bisection and secant methods by modifying *zeroDemo2* to conform to the requirements of *newton*. The resulting program, *zeroDemo3*, is displayed as Pascal Sample 10.5.

Pascal Sample 10.6 shows that Newton's method does require fewer iterations than the secant method. But this does not necessarily mean that Newton's method is faster than the secant method; it requires us to find two function values on each iteration, whereas the secant method requires us to find only one. When we can compute the derivative of f quickly, Newton's method will outperform the secant method. (See Exercise 3 at the end of this section.) When we can't, we may be better off using the secant method even though it requires more iterations.

PASCAL SAMPLE 10.4. The library *newton*

{ *newton*: approximates a zero of a function using Newton's method }

```
function zero( function f( x : real ) : real;          { function       }
              function g( x : real ) : real;           { its derivative }
                       x       : real;                  { 1st approx     }
                       epsilon : real ) : real;         { tolerance      }
```

{ generates at most *maxApprox* approximations *x1*, *x2*, ... to a zero of *f*, }
{ given the derivative *g* of *f* and an initial approximation *x*, and returns }
{ the first of these within *epsilon* of the previous approximation or the }
{ last of these if the approximations do not converge }

```
  const maxApprox = 20;                    { limit on iterations          }
        display   = true;                  { process displayed if true    }

  var oldx  : real;                        { last approximation           }
      slope : real;                        { g(x) = slope of f at x        }
      count : integer;                     { iteration counter            }

  begin
      count := 0;
      repeat
          count := count + 1;
          oldx := x;
          slope := g(x);
          if slope <> 0 then { use Newton approximation }
              x := x − f(x)/slope
          else { move x a small amount }
              x := x − epsilon*(1+abs(x));
          if display then writeln(count, x)
      until (abs(x − oldx) < epsilon) or (count >= maxApprox);
      zero := x
  end;   { of zero }
```

PASCAL SAMPLE 10.5. The program *zeroDemo3*

{ demonstrates Newton's method for approximating zeros of functions }

```
program zeroDemo3(input, output);

const a         = 1.0;                     { initial approximation }
      tolerance = 1e−6;                    { accuracy desired for zeros }
var z : real;                              { the approximation }

function g( x : real ) : real;             { sample function }
    begin
        g := x*x − 4
    end;   { of g }
```

■ **PASCAL SAMPLE 10.5**   The program *zeroDemo3* (continued)

```
function gprime( x : real ) : real;                          { its derivative }
    begin
        gprime := 2*x
    end;   { of gprime }

function h( x : real ) : real;                          { another sample function }
    begin
        h := sin(x)
    end;   { of h }

function hprime( x : real ) : real;                          { its derivative }
    begin
        hprime := cos(x)
    end;   { of hprime }

#include 'newton';                { subprogram to approximate zeros }

begin

    z := zero( g, gprime, a, tolerance);
    writeln('sqr(', z, ') — 4 = ', g(z));
    z := zero (h, hprime, a, tolerance);
    writeln('sin(', z, ')          = ', h(z))

end.
```

■ **PASCAL SAMPLE 10.6.**   The program *zeroDemo3* (approximations generated by Newton's method)

```
        1 2.50000000000000e+00
        2 2.05000000000000e+00
        3 2.00060975609756e+00
        4 2.00000009292229e+00
        5 2.00000000000000e+00
sqr( 2.00000000000000e+00) — 4 =  8.65973959207622e-15
        1-5.57407724654902e-01
        2 6.59364519248408e-02
        3-9.57219193250848e-05
        4 2.92356625223428e-13
        5 1.89326617253043e-29
sin( 1.89326617253043e-29)       =  1.89326617253043e-29
```

CHOOSING AMONG ALTERNATIVE ALGORITHMS

For most applications, the bisection method is the most reliable algorithm for approximating a zero of a function. It may be slower than the secant method or Newton's method, but it is guaranteed to work. Furthermore, it is not all that slow. So why did we bother to develop two further algorithms?

We did so because special circumstances may warrant the choice of more sophisticated approximation algorithms. In Section 10.2, for example, we will learn how to simulate the motion of various bodies by approximating their positions at successive moments in time. Using these techniques, we can generate video displays of a spacecraft traveling to the moon or of balls colliding on a billiard table. To keep these displays moving at the appropriate speed, we must be able to perform many approximations very quickly—and hence the need for efficient algorithms.

EXERCISES

1. Write a program to approximate a zero of a function by the "trisection" algorithm described in this section. Compare the execution time of this algorithm with that of the bisection algorithm when approximating zeroes of the functions $x^2 - 2$ and $\sin x$.

2. Write a program to approximate a zero of a function by the method of false position. Compare the execution time of this algorithm with that of the bisection algorithm when approximating zeroes of the functions $x^2 - 2$ and $\sin x$.

3. One way to approximate the square root of a real number r is to start with an initial approximation r_0 equal to $r/2$ and then to produce a sequence of better approximations by letting

$$r_{n+1} = \frac{1}{2}\left(r_n + \frac{r}{r_n}\right).$$

   (a) Compare the efficiency of this algorithm with those that approximate zeroes of the function $x^2 - r$ using the procedures in *bisect*, *secant*, and *newton*.

   (b) Show that this algorithm produces the same sequence of approximations as does Newton's method.

4. Newton's method is very powerful if used with care, but it has its pitfalls. Consider the function

$$f(x) = x^3 - 5x + 3.$$

   Use Newton's method to approximate zeroes of this function starting with the following initial approximations, counting the number of iterations required for the method to converge.

$$-2, \, 0, \, 1.2, \, 1.25, \, 1.3, \, 1.4, \, 2$$

   Since f is cubic, you will not be surprised to note that it has three separate zeroes. However, you will also note that initial approximations that are very close together can lead to different zeroes in an apparently haphazard manner, and the number of iterations needed to find a given zero varies considerably.

5. Show that Newton's method diverges when used to approximate a zero of the function $f(x) = e^{-x} \ln(x)$.

6. Find a function f and an initial approximation to a zero of f such that Newton's method oscillates when used to approximate a zero of f starting with that approximation.

*7. Write a program to input the coefficients a, b, c, d of a cubic polynomial

$$p(x) = ax^3 + bx^2 + cx + d$$

and to determine, within an accuracy of 10^{-6} and without any further input, all zeroes of p. Use one of the following methods for $a \neq 0$.

(a) First locate one real zero z of p (which must exist since any polynomial of odd degree has at least one real zero). Then find a quadratic polynomial q such that

$$p(x) = (x - z)q(x)$$

by synthetic division. The remaining zeroes of p are the zeroes of q.

(b) Alternatively, find the relative maxima, minima, and points of inflection of p by finding the zeroes of its derivative. Use this information to determine the number and location of the zeroes of p.

8. Is the bisection method or Newton's method more appropriate for use in the program you wrote for Exercise 7? Why?

*9. Generalize your program for Exercise 7(b) to input the coefficients of an arbitrary polynomial and then determine the number and location of all zeroes of that polynomial. (*Hint:* Use recursion to reduce the problem of finding the zeroes of a polynomial of degree n to the problem of finding the zeroes of the derivative of that polynomial, which itself is a polynomial of degree $n - 1$).

10. Devise an algorithm for approximating the maximum value of a function on an interval.

11. Computers can approximate the values of mathematical functions such as exponential and sine using infinite series. Determine the number of terms in each of the following series that must be summed to produce approximations that are within 10^{-6} of the correct value when $0 \leq x \leq 1$.

(a) $\sin x = x - \dfrac{x^3}{3!} + \dfrac{x^5}{5!} - \dfrac{x^7}{7!} + \cdots$.

(b) $\exp x = 1 + x + \dfrac{x^2}{2!} + \dfrac{x^3}{3!} + \dfrac{x^4}{4!} + \cdots$.

12. To approximate the area under a curve, we can divide that area into a number of strips, approximate the area of each strip, and add the approximations together. Figure 10.7 illustrates three methods for performing such an approximation.

(a) Define three functions beginning with the header

function *area*(**function** $f(x : real)$: *real*;
        a, b : *real*;
        n : *integer*) : *real*;

to approximate the area under the graph of f on the interval (a, b) by dividing it into n strips and using the rectangle, trapezoid, and midpoint methods.

(b) Use these functions to approximate the area under the graphs of x^2, $2x^3 - 3x^2 + 4$, $\sin x$, and e^x in the interval $(0, 2)$.

(c) How many subdivisions do each of the three methods require to approximate the area under the curves in (b) to within 10^{-6}?

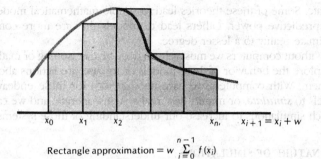

$$\text{Rectangle approximation} = w \sum_{i=0}^{n-1} f(x_i)$$

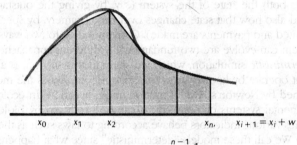

$$\text{Trapezoid approximation} = w \sum_{i=0}^{n-1} \frac{1}{2}(f(x_i) + f(x_{i+1}))$$

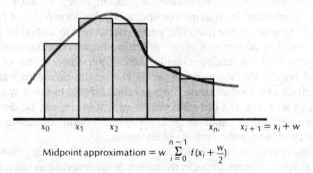

$$\text{Midpoint approximation} = w \sum_{i=0}^{n-1} f(x_i + \frac{w}{2})$$

FIGURE 10.7 ■ Approximations to the area under a curve

10.2   DETERMINISTIC SIMULATION

The world around us is composed of numerous systems, including physical, economic, and political systems. Human beings have long sought to understand such systems and to predict their behavior by formulating various theories about how they operate. Some of these theories lead to simple mathematical models with considerable predictive power. Others lead to models that are more complex or that approximate reality to a lesser degree.

Without computers we must rely on deductive reasoning or mathematical analysis to explore the behavior of these models or to base predictions about the real world on them. With computers we have another tool for these endeavors. We can use models to *simulate*, or mimic, how real systems operate, and we can use the results of such simulations to increase our understanding of those systems.

THE NATURE OF SIMULATIONS

In order to simulate a system, we must first develop a mathematical model that describes both the state of the system (say, by giving the outstanding balance of a loan) and also how that state changes over time (namely, by specifying how interest is computed and payments are made). Corresponding to two ways in which the state of a system can evolve are two fundamentally different approaches to simulation.

Deterministic simulation, which we study in this section, is appropriate for systems that operate by known laws. For example, in physics the motion of a planet is determined by Newton's laws of motion and gravitation. In ecology the changes in environmental systems or populations can be predicted by biological laws. And in economics various indicators behave according to laws such as the law of supply and demand. We call these models "deterministic" since what happens in a given state is determined completely by that state. To simulate a deterministic system, we simply calculate successive changes of state at successive instants in time.

Nondeterministic or *probabilistic* simulation, which we study in Sections 10.3 and 10.4, is appropriate for systems that operate by the occurrence of random events. For example, in genetics the particular genes transmitted to a child by its parents depend on chance. The outcome of games of chance depends on random phenomena such as flipping a coin or dealing a hand of cards. Even the outcome of games of skill can depend on chance (for example, on how well the defensive signal caller and the quarterback in a football game outguess each other). In these systems only the likelihood of an event, not the exact nature of that event, can be determined from the current state of the system. In order to simulate nondeterministic systems, we need some way of simulating random phenomena.

Many systems are nominally deterministic but, in practice, involve measurements and conditions that are imperfectly known. Such systems can often be modeled either deterministically or nondeterministically. For example the behavior of individual molecules of water in the ocean is hard to predict other than nondeterministically. However, in practice, we are concerned with the aggregate behavior of many molecules, and statistical analysis can lead to deterministic models that will help us to predict the behavior of waves.

With the aid of a computer, simulations enable us to conduct experiments that are too time consuming, expensive, or dangerous to conduct in real life. If we want to predict what will happen under certain conditions, we can base this prediction on a simulation; if things go awry, we can adjust our conditions or our model and perform another simulation. By simulating, rather than doing, we minimize the risk of injury, bankruptcy, or some other catastrophe.

The use of simulation as a tool for prediction has two limitations. First, we must develop an accurate model. If we misunderstand or oversimplify the laws governing a system, any simulation based on that model is suspect. Second, our simulation techniques themselves must be accurate. In the same way that numeric errors inherent in finite computations affect the accuracy of approximations, numeric errors affect the degree to which simulations approximate reality. Therefore we must analyze carefully the results of any simulation before we draw conclusions from those results.

SIMULATION OF DETERMINISTIC SYSTEMS

We illustrate the nature of deterministic simulation by writing two programs that simulate moving bodies. The first of these, *pursuit*, simulates one object pursuing another. The second, *orbit*, simulates a satellite in orbit around the earth. Both programs rely on the simple fact that an object traveling at a given speed s for a given time t covers a distance equal to st.

Let us consider the problem of pursuit first. Suppose that two friends, A and B, are out walking in a large field. A is walking leisurely along the edge of a field at 4 feet per second (approximately 2.7 miles per hour). B spots A from the middle of the field and decides to catch up with A by walking briskly toward A at 6 feet per second. We want to write a program *pursuit* to simulate their movement from their initial positions and to determine how long it will take B to catch up with A.

The first step in a deterministic simulation is to choose variables that describe the state of the system at a given instant in time. We choose a coordinate system and variables to describe the positions and velocities of the two friends. Let us assume that the field lies in the first quadrant of the xy-plane, that A starts at the origin $<0, 0>$ and moves along the x-axis at s_A feet per second, and that B moves toward A at s_B feet per second. Let us also denote the positions of the two friends at time t by two points, a and b, with coordinates $<a_x, a_y>$ and $<b_x, b_y>$.

We can easily compute A's position after t seconds have elapsed. In that time, A walks $s_A t$ feet. Hence, at time t, $<a_x, a_y> = <s_A t, 0>$. Since B is constantly changing direction, it is difficult to compute B's position directly. Hence we simulate B's motion to find $<b_x, b_y>$.

At any given time, B is moving directly toward A at a speed of s_B. To compute the effect of this movement on B's position, we must resolve it into a horizontal component (which we use to change b_x) and a vertical component (which we use to change b_y). Figure 10.8 shows how to do this using elementary geometry. The distance between A and B is

$$d = \sqrt{(a_x - b_x)^2 + (a_y - b_y)^2}.$$

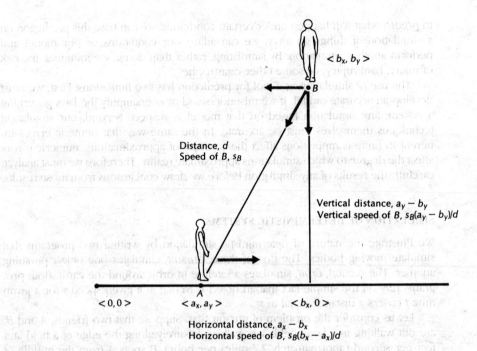

FIGURE 10.8 ■ State of pursuit at time t

Hence B's total speed s_B resolves into a component

$$v_x = s_B \frac{a_x - b_x}{d}$$

in the x direction and a component

$$v_y = s_B \frac{a_y - b_y}{d}$$

in the y direction. We call the vector $<v_x, v_y>$ the *directional velocity* of B at time t.

To simulate B's motion, we divide time into a series of intervals of u seconds apiece and approximate what happens in each of these intervals. If u is small enough, then B will not change direction very much during one interval; hence we can presume that B moves in a straight line toward A during that interval, arriving at a position $<b_x + v_x u, b_y + v_y u>$ at the end of that interval. During successive intervals, B will move in different directions; but during any one interval a straight line will be a reasonable approximation to B's movement. Thus the general plan of our simulation is to

> choose a small value for u;
> determine initial positions and speeds of A and B;
> $t := 0$;
> **repeat**
> > $t := t + u$;
> > compute B's directional velocity;
> > compute A's new position after u seconds;
> > compute B's new position after u seconds
> **until** B catches A

Translating this strategy into Pascal produces the program *pursuit*. (See Pascal Samples 10.7 and 10.8.) In this program, we cannot determine when the pursuit ends simply by checking on whether the distance between the two objects is zero. We observe the positions of the two objects only at discrete intervals of time, so it is unlikely that they will ever be at exactly the same position. Hence we end the simulation when B can cover the remaining distance to A in a single interval of time. If the time unit is small enough, this will be close to the actual time of contact.

PASCAL SAMPLE 10.7   The program *pursuit* (main program)

{ simulates one object pursuing another }

program *pursuit*(*input, output*);

const *unit*   = 0.25;   { time increment for simulation }
       speed1 = 4;   { speeds of objects   }
       speed2 = 6;

type *position* = **record**
                    x, y : *real*   { coordinates of position }
                end;
       velocity = **record**
                    x, y : *real*   { components of velocity }
                end;

var *p1, p2* : *position*;   { positions of objects }
      v1, v2 : *velocity*;   { velocities of objects }
      time   : *real*;   { current time   }

{ declarations of *distance, changePosition, findVelocity* go here }

begin
     p1.x := 0;
     p1.y := 0;
     v1.x := *speed1*;
     v1.y := 0;

```
writeln('Object moves along x-axis at ', speed1:4:2, ' feet per second.');
writeln('Pursuer moves at ', speed2:4:2, ' feet per second.');
write('Initial position of pursuer? ');
read(p2.x, p2.y);

time := 0;
while distance(p1, p2) > (speed2 - speed1)*unit do
    begin
        time := time + unit;
        findVelocity(v2, p2, p1, speed2);
        changePosition(p1, v1, unit);
        changePosition(p2, v2, unit)
    end;

writeln;
write('Pursuit ends in ', time:4:2, ' seconds at position ');
writeln(p1.x:4:2, ', ', p1.y:4:2)
end.
```

PASCAL SAMPLE 10.8   The program *pursuit* (subsidiary procedures)

```
function distance( a, b : position ) : real;
    { returns the distance between the points a, b }

    begin
        distance := sqrt( sqr(a.x - b.x) + sqr(a.y - b.y) )
    end;   { of distance }

procedure changePosition( var a : position; v : velocity; t : real );
    { computes the new position of an object at position a }
    { moving with velocity v for time t                    }

    begin
        a.x := a.x + v.x*t;
        a.y := a.y + v.y*t
    end;   { of changePosition }

procedure findVelocity( var v : velocity; a, b : position; s : real );
    { finds the directional velocity v of an object at position }
    { a moving toward position b with speed s                   }

    var d : real;

    begin
        d := distance(a, b);
        v.x := s*(b.x - a.x)/d;
        v.y := s*(b.y - a.y)/d
    end;   { of findVelocity }
```

PASCAL SAMPLE 10.9   The program *pursuit* (sample use)

```
Object moves along x-axis at 4.00 feet per second.
Pursuer moves at 6.00 feet per second.
Initial position of pursuer? 100 200

Pursuit ends in 47.25 seconds at position 189.00, 0.00
```

Pascal Sample 10.9 shows the results of using *pursuit*. Figure 10.9 presents a better display of the same results, which we obtain by plotting the locations of the two objects at the end of each interval of time. (See Exercise 1 at the end of this section.)

Even though we have simulated all of the movements by a series of straight lines, the pursuer's path in Fig. 10.9 appears to be a smooth curve. When the time increment *unit* is sufficiently small, our eyes cannot distinguish where one straight line ends and the next begins. Figure 10.10 illustrates the effect of choosing a larger time increment, showing quite clearly the approximate nature of the simulation.

Increasing the accuracy of the simulation   Figure 10.10 shows that we must choose a sufficiently small increment of time to achieve an accurate simulation. But the smaller we make the time increment, the longer our simulation will take. Hence we would like to use as large a time increment as accuracy permits.

A simple strategy improves the accuracy of our simulation and permits us to choose a larger time increment. In *pursuit* we compute the pursuer's direction at the beginning of each interval of time; by the end of the interval, that direction is not very accurate. A more accurate approximation heads the pursuer toward where the pursued object will be in the middle of the time interval, rather than where it is at

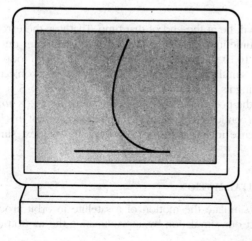

FIGURE 10.9 ■ Paths of objects leading to results in Pascal Sample 10.9

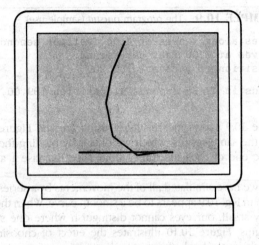

FIGURE 10.10 ■ Simulated motion with large time increment

■ **PASCAL SAMPLE 10.10**   The program *pursuit* (improved simulation strategy)

```
time := unit/2;
changePosition(p1, v1, time);
while distance(p1, p2) > (speed2 − speed1)*unit do
    begin
        findVelocity(v2, p2, p1, speed2);
        time := time + unit/2;
        changePosition(p2, v2, unit);
        time := time + unit/2;
        changePosition(p1, v1, unit)
    end;
```

the beginning or will be at the end of that time. That way the errors in direction at the two ends of a time interval will tend to balance each other out.

Pascal Sample 10.10 shows how we can modify the main loop in *pursuit* to use this more accurate simulation strategy. We give the pursued object a *unit*/2-second head start, computing its position at times *unit*/2, 3 × *unit*/2, 5 × *unit*/2, ... As before, we compute the position of the pursuer at times *unit*, 2 × *unit*, 3 × *unit*, ...

The simulation conducted by *pursuit* is simple enough that this improved strategy makes little difference in the outcome. However, in our next simulation it makes quite a difference.

SIMULATING ORBITAL MOTION

Let us now try to simulate the motion of a satellite in orbit around the earth. As before, we conduct our simulation by approximating the motion of the satellite by straight lines in small intervals of time. But now we must do more work to compute the velocity of the satellite.

Newton's law of gravitation provides the basis for that computation. The earth's gravity causes nearby objects to move toward it (to fall) quickly. It also causes faraway objects to move toward it, but less quickly. With a sufficiently large velocity, a satellite can resist the force of gravity and stay in orbit.

An object dropped near the surface of the earth will accelerate toward the center of the earth, increasing its downward velocity by 32.16 feet per second during each second that it falls. Thus, after t seconds, it is falling at $32.16t$ feet per second. Newton's law of gravitation states that the force of gravity varies inversely with the square of the distance of an object from the center of the earth. Thus, if r is the radius of the earth and h is the height of a satellite above the earth, the force of gravity increases the satellite's downward velocity by $(32.16r^2)/(r + h)^2$ feet per second during each and every second. Since r is approximately 3959 miles and there are 5280 feet per mile, a satellite at a height of h miles above the earth achieves a downward velocity of approximately

$$\frac{32.16 \times 3959^2 \times t}{5280 \times (3959 + h)^2}$$

miles per second in t seconds.

This enables us to rewrite the *findVelocity* procedure from *pursuit* as a new procedure, *changeVelocity*, that approximates the change in velocity of a satellite in a small period of time. (See Pascal Sample 10.11.)

■ **PASCAL SAMPLE 10.11**   The program *orbit* (*changeVelocity* procedure)

procedure *changeVelocity*(**var** *v* : *velocity*; *a* : *position*; *t* : *real*);

{ approximates the velocity after *t* seconds, in miles/second, }
{ of an object with initial velocity *v* under the force of   }
{ gravity at position *a* relative to the center of the earth   }

const *gravity* = −95467;   { = −32.16*3959*3959/5280 }

var *d*   : *real*;   { distance to center of earth }
    dSquared   : *real*;   { square of *d*   }
    acceleration : *real*;   { change in velocity   }

begin
    dSquared := *sqr*(*a.x*) + *sqr*(*a.y*);
    d := *sqrt*(*dSquared*);
    acceleration := *gravity**t/*dSquared*;
    v.x := *v.x* + *acceleration***a.x*/*d*;
    v.y := *v.y* + *acceleration***a.y*/*d*
end;   { of *changeVelocity* }

With this procedure, we can modify *pursuit* to produce the program *orbit* that simulates the motion of a satellite. (See Pascal Sample 10.12.) We choose a coordinate system with the origin at the center of the earth and begin with the satellite on the positive *x*-axis. We end the simulation when the satellite has completed a single orbit,

---

PASCAL SAMPLE 10.12   The program *orbit* (main program)

```
{ simulates orbital motion }
program orbit(input, output);
const earthRadius = 3959;               { radius of earth in miles        }
      unit        = 10;                  { time increment for simulation }
type position = record
                  x, y : real           { coordinates of position }
                end;
     velocity = record
                  x, y : real           { components of velocity }
                end;
var p, prev : position;                 { new, old positions of satellite }
    height  : real;                     { initial height above earth      }
    v       : velocity;                 { velocity of satellite           }
    time    : real;
{ definitions of changePosition and changeVelocity go here }
begin
    write('Initial height (mi), tangential velocity (mi/sec): ');
    read(height, v.y);

    p.x := earthRadius + height;
    p.y := 0;
    v.x := 0;

    prev := p;
    changePosition(prev, v, unit/4);
    changeVelocity(v, prev, unit/2);
    time := unit/2;
    repeat
        prev := p;
        time := time + unit/2;
        changePosition(p, v, unit);
        time := time + unit/2;
        changeVelocity(v, p, unit);
    until (prev.y < 0) and (p.y >= 0);

    writeln;
    writeln('Orbit completed in ', time/60:4:2, ' minutes.');
    writeln('Current position is ', p.x, ', ', p.y);
    writeln('Current velocity is ', v.x, ', ', v.y)
end.
```

■ **PASCAL SAMPLE 10.13**   The program *orbit* (sample use)

```
Initial height (mi), tangential velocity (mi/sec):  312 4.733

Orbit completed in 95.08 minutes.
Current position is  4.27092702379573e+03, 2.49965258607292e+01
Current velocity is -5.38044124748105e-02, 4.73269347363178e+00
```

---

that is, when it next crosses the positive *x*-axis. Since the position of the satellite depends on its velocity, and its velocity depends on its position, we adopted the more accurate simulation strategy of computing the satellite's position at times *unit*, $2 \times unit$, $3 \times unit$, ... and its velocity at times *unit*/2, $3 \times unit/2$, $5 \times unit/2$, ... That way each computation of a position or velocity is based on the average value of the other during an interval of time.

Pascal Sample 10.13 shows that our simulation model is accurate enough to reproduce the results achieved by actual satellites: a satellite in a circular orbit at an altitude of 312 miles takes about an hour and a half to circle the earth.

Figure 10.11 shows that a satellite with the initial altitude and velocity specified in Pascal Sample 10.13 has a circular orbit. That figure was produced by drawing a circle to represent the earth and then by plotting the location of the satellite at the end of each interval of time. (See Exercise 1 at the end of this section.)

The program *orbit* provides convincing evidence of the value of simulation. With it we can estimate the velocities required to keep satellites in orbits of varying altitudes. Even more accurate simulations can take into account other factors, such as atmospheric resistance in orbits close to the earth. But this simple simulation produces surprisingly accurate results and provides the confidence to base actual space flights on simulations that incorporate all our knowledge about gravity, propulsion, air resistance, and the like.

FIGURE 10.11 ■ Path of satellite in orbit around the earth

EXERCISES

1. If your computer system can produce graphic output, modify the programs *pursuit* and *orbit* to plot the paths of the objects in motion. (*Hint:* At the end of each interval of time, draw a line connecting the old position of each object with its new position.)

2. Modify the program *pursuit* as follows.

   (a) *A* is out walking with a dog. When the dog spots *B*, it lopes toward *B* at 5 feet per second. Does the dog reach *B* before *B* reaches *A*? Does it matter when the dog begins moving toward *B*?

   (b) *A* wants to avoid *B*. How long can *A* put off contact by walking at right angles to *B*'s path of approach?

3. Use *orbit* to determine the altitude of a geosynchronous orbit, that is, of a circular orbit that takes exactly one day to complete. A satellite in a geosynchronous orbit above the equator stays above the same spot on the earth. (*Hint:* Use the bisection method.)

4. Modify *orbit* to compute the minimum and maximum altitude of the satellite. Stop the simulation if the satellite crashes into the earth.

5. Modify *orbit* to employ the simpler simulation strategy used in *pursuit* (that is, replace the three statements before the loop by a single statement setting *time* to 0). How much difference does this make in the shape of the simulated orbit?

6. Our priority in writing the programs *pursuit* and *orbit* was clarity, not efficiency. Experiment with optimizing those programs by eliminating redundant calculations, replacing procedure calls by the bodies of the called procedures, and the like. How much difference do such optimizations make in the execution time of the programs? How much difference do they make in plotting speed in Exercise 1? How much difference do they make in the readability of the programs?

7. Simulate the motion of a bouncing rubber ball dropped from a height of 10 feet. When the ball hits the ground, 80 percent of its downward velocity is converted into an upward velocity. How long does it take the ball to stop bouncing (that is, before it bounces less than an inch off the ground)?

*8. Simulate the flight of a spacecraft to the moon. The orbit of the moon is roughly circular, with a radius of 238,857 miles. The radius of the moon is 1080 miles, and the force of gravity at its surface is 1/6 that at the surface of the earth. Try starting with a satellite in a circular orbit 155 miles above the earth. When the satellite is on the opposite side of the earth from the moon, have it accelerate to approximately 6.77 miles per second. How long does it take to reach the moon? What happens after it gets there? What effect does its initial velocity have on its trajectory?

9. Four people start at the corners of a square field with sides 100 feet long. Each person walks counterclockwise toward the person at the next corner of the square. If the people walk at a rate of *x* feet per second, how long does it take them to meet in the center of the square?

10. Repeat Exercise 9 with various numbers of people placed at various starting points (such as at the corners of other regular polygons). What do their paths look like?

11. Simulate unconstrained population growth in which births increase the population *p* by *b* percent each year and deaths decrease it by *d* percent. How long does it take the population to double in size when $b = 10\%$ and $d = 7\%$?

12. Simulate constrained population growth in which births increase the population p by b percent each year and deaths decrease it by $(d + cp)$ percent, the factor cp being attributed to deaths by overcrowding. Plot the size of the population as a function of time. For what values of b, c, and d does the population reach some sort of equilibrium?

10.3 RANDOM NUMBERS AND RANDOM PHENOMENA

Computers are deterministic devices. For a given program, we can predict exactly how a computer will execute that program and what the outcome will be. How, then, can we use a computer to simulate a nondeterministic system, one, for example, in which the outcome of an experiment depends on the toss of a coin or the roll of a pair of dice? In real life, the result—heads or tails—of tossing a coin is completely random; in a computer, the result of every computation is completely determined.

The key to nondeterministic simulations is to employ an algorithm, known as a *random number generator*, that produces a sequence of seemingly random, or *pseudorandom*, numbers. The algorithm will produce the same sequence of numbers each time it is used, but it produces a sequence with no discernible pattern: the numbers in the sequence are spread out uniformly, and any number is just as likely to follow any other in the sequence. It is more accurate to call the entire sequence random than to call its members random: no number is any more random than the next, and only a sequence can exhibit random behavior. However, following common usage, we will refer to a member of a random sequence as a random number.

Most computer systems predefine a function that serves as a random-number generator. Unfortunately, such a function is not part of standard Pascal, so that different systems generate random numbers in different ways. In Berkeley Pascal, the function *random*(0) produces random real numbers between 0 and 1. (The argument 0 plays no role in the evaluation of the function.) In Macintosh Pascal, the function *random*, which has no arguments, produces random integers between −*maxint* and *maxint*.

Our concern in this section is more with the use of random numbers than their generation. Nonetheless, we will begin by ironing out the differences among dialects of Pascal in order to provide a random-number generator that will work in any dialect.

GENERATING RANDOM NUMBERS

We implement our random-number generator as a library *random* of three subprograms. Two of these are functions: *randomReal*, which produces a random real number between 0 and 1, and *randomInt*, which produces a random integer in a specified range.

The third subprogram in *random* is the procedure *randomize*, which initializes the random-number generator, enabling us to choose between a standard sequence of random numbers and a sequence that varies each time a program is run. The standard sequence is most useful when we are writing and debugging a program. If an error occurs, we can reproduce the error by reexecuting the program until we

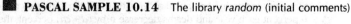

PASCAL SAMPLE 10.14   The library *random* (initial comments)

{ *random*: library of subprograms to generate random numbers }

```
{ Functions:                                                          }
{     randomReal         returns a random real x such that 0 <= x < 1 }
{     randomInt(m, n)    returns a random integer i such that m <= i <= n }
{                                                                     }
{ Procedure:                                                          }
{     randomize(b)       initializes random number generator to a standard }
{                        sequence if b = false and to an arbitrary sequence }
{                        if b = true                                  }
{                                                                     }
{     Any program using random must contain the following declaration: }
{                                                                     }
{         var randomSeed : integer;                                   }
```

can isolate it, correct it, and test the correction. Without a standard sequence of random numbers, errors can be extremely elusive. Varying sequences of random numbers are most useful after we finish writing a program. Without such a variety, our program would produce the same result each time it was run.

Pascal Sample 10.14 contains the comments that appear at the beginning of the library *random*. These comments describe the subprograms in the library. They also require any program using *random* to declare a global variable *randomSeed*, which the library uses to remember where it is in the random sequence. If procedures in Pascal were able to retain the value of a local variable from one invocation to the next, we could dispense with this global variable.

We can produce a sequence of random numbers based on a curious aspect of arithmetic: seemingly haphazard sequences of integers result from repeated applications of a few simple arithmetic operations. Early random-number generators, for example, took an *n*-digit integer, squared it to obtain a 2*n*-digit number, and then extracted the middle *n* digits to produce the next "random" number in a sequence. This new integer bears no discernible relation to the first.

Later investigations have shown that another simple technique produces even better (more random) results. A *linear congruential* random-number generator produces a sequence $r_1, r_2, \ldots, r_n$ of integers by setting

$$r_{n+1} = (multiplier \times r_n + increment) \bmod modulus,$$

where *multiplier*, *increment*, and *modulus* are suitably chosen integer constants. This sequence is not completely random since it repeats itself; there are only a finite number of integers less than *modulus*. But, for proper choices of *modulus*, *multiplier*, and *increment*, it can produce quite a long sequence of seemingly random integers.

For our random-number generator, we let *modulus* be 1,048,576, *multiplier* be 1749, and *increment* be 221,591. Following are the reasons for these choices.

1. Most random-number generators choose *modulus* to be a power of 2. This makes the **mod** operator particularly easy to evaluate on a machine that employs binary arithmetic. (See Exercise 7 at the end of this section.) Our value of *modulus* is 2^{20}

2. With a power of 2 for *modulus*, we can guarantee that $r_1, r_2, \ldots, r_{modulus}$ are distinct integers by choosing *multiplier* so that *multiplier* **mod** $8 = 5$. (See Exercise 8 at the end of this section.) Hence our random-number generator produces more than a million integers before it begins to repeat itself.

3. For the best results, we choose *multiplier* somewhere between

$$\sqrt{modulus} \quad \text{and} \quad modulus - \sqrt{modulus},$$

and we choose *increment* to be an odd number such that *increment*/*modulus* is approximately

$$\frac{1}{2} - \frac{1}{6}\sqrt{3} \quad \text{or} \quad 0.21132\ldots.$$

4. Finally, we choose our "magic constants" small enough to avoid overflows when computing r_{n+1}. With $r_n < modulus = 2^{20}$ and $multiplier < 2^{11}$, $multiplier \times r_n < 2^{31}$ and no overflows will occur when *maxint* is $2^{31} \pm 1$.

To transform the sequence $r_1, r_2, \ldots, r_n$ of random integers produced by this linear congruential generator into a sequence of random reals, we divide each number in the sequence by *modulus*. This leads to the definition of the *randomReal* function, displayed as Pascal Sample 10.15.

Evaluating the *randomReal* function is like throwing a dart at the interval from 0 to 1 and seeing where it lands; the function distributes these darts uniformly and unpredictably in the interval. In order to define the *randomInt* function, we magnify and shift the interval from 0 to 1 so that it becomes the interval from m to $n + 1$, throw a dart at that interval, and see in which subinterval of length 1 it lands. Thus

---

PASCAL SAMPLE 10.15   The library *random* (*randomReal* function)

function *randomReal* : *real*;
    { returns the next real number in the random sequence }
    const *modulus*   = 1048576;   { 2**20 }
            multiplier =   1749;
            increment =   221591;
begin
    randomReal := *randomSeed*/*modulus*;
    randomSeed := (*multiplier***randomSeed* + *increment*) **mod** *modulus*
end; { of *randomReal* }

PASCAL SAMPLE 10.16 The library *random* (*randomInt* function)

function *randomInt*(*m, n* : *integer*) : *integer*;

 { returns a random integer among *m, ..., n* }

 begin

  randomInt := *trunc*(*m* + (*n* − *m* + 1)*randomReal*)

 end; { of *randomInt* }

the expression

$$trunc(m + (n - m + 1)*randomReal)$$

in Pascal Sample 10.16 produces a random integer from among *m, . . . , n*.

Finally, in order to define the *randomize* procedure, we need some way to produce a different initial value for the random-number sequence each time we execute a program. Computer systems typically use a built-in clock for this purpose. In Berkeley Pascal, for example, the *wallclock* function returns the number of seconds that have elapsed since midnight on January 1, 1970. The definition of *randomize* in Pascal Sample 10.17 uses this function.

This completes the development of our random-number generator. When using a system that predefines its own random-number generator, we can choose it or ours. (See Exercise 9 at the end of this section.) Generally it is better to use the one provided by the system; at the very least it performs calculations more quickly.

We turn our attention now to several examples of random phenomena. We will use our random-number generator to simulate those phenomena.

PASCAL SAMPLE 10.17 The library *random* (*randomize* procedure)

procedure *randomize*(*b* : *boolean*);

 { initializes random number generator to standard sequence }
 { if *b* is *false* and to an arbitrary sequence if *b* is *true* }

 const *modulus* = 1048576; { 2**20 }

 begin

  if *b* **then**

   randomSeed := *wallclock* **mod** *modulus*

  else

   randomSeed := 123456

 end; { of *randomize* }

■ **PASCAL SAMPLE 10.18** The procedure *tossCoins*

procedure *tossCoins*(*tosses* : *integer*; **var** *heads* : *integer*);
{ counts the number of heads in a given number of tosses of a fair coin }
var *toss* : *integer*;
begin
    heads := 0;
    for *toss* := 1 **to** *tosses* **do**
        if *randomReal* < 0.5 **then** *heads* := *heads* + 1
end; { of *tossCoins* }

A COIN TOSSING EXPERIMENT

We simulate tossing a coin by using the *randomReal* function to generate random numbers between 0 and 1. One-half of the time these numbers will be less than 0.5, and one-half of the time they will be greater—in the same manner that a fair coin will act when tossed a large number of times. The procedure *tossCoins*, displayed as Pascal Sample 10.18, simulates tossing a coin a specified number of times and counts the number of times it comes up heads.

Since *tossCoins* uses random numbers, we expect its results to vary from invocation to invocation. We embed *tossCoins* in a program *cointoss* that simulates a series of coin-tossing experiments in order to examine the variability of these results. (See Pascal Sample 10.19.) We expect the number of heads that occur in each experiment to be close to one-half the number of tosses, but to vary somewhat from that average. The output of *cointoss* consists of a histogram that shows how many experiments resulted in *h* heads, for *h* from 0 to the number of tosses.

■ **PASCAL SAMPLE 10.19** The program *cointoss*

{ performs a series of coin-tossing experiments, printing a histogram }
{ of the number of heads seen in each experiment   }

program *cointoss*(*input*, *output*);

const *maxTosses* = 100;

var *experiments*, *experiment*   : *integer*;
    tossesPerExperiment, *outcome* : *integer*;
    histogram   : **array** [0..*maxTosses*] **of** *integer*;
    maxEntry   : *integer*;
    randomSeed   : *integer*;   { required by *random* }

#include 'random';   { *randomReal*, *randomize* }

PASCAL SAMPLE 10.19   The program *cointoss* (continued)

```
{ declaration of tossCoins goes here }
begin
    write('Tosses per experiment (at most ', maxTosses:1, ')? ');
    readln(tossesPerExperiment);
    write('Number of experiments? ');
    readln(experiments);
    { initialize histogram }
    maxEntry := 0;
    for outcome := 0 to tossesPerEquipment do histogram[outcome] := 0;
    randomize(true);
    for experiment := 1 to experiments do { perform experiment }
        begin
            tossCoins(tossesPerExperiment, outcome);
            histogram[outcome] := histogram[outcome] + 1;
            if histogram[outcome] > maxEntry then
                maxEntry := histogram[outcome]
        end;
    writeln;
    for outcome := 0 to tossesPerExperiment do
        begin
            write(outcome:5, histogram[outcome]:5);
            writeln('*' : 5 + histogram[outcome]*40 div maxEntry)
        end
end.
```

When the number of experiments is large enough, the histogram produced by *cointoss* exhibits the normal bell-shaped distribution. (See Pascal Sample 10.20.) Close to one-half the tosses in most experiments do indeed turn up heads. But a few experiments produce results that are much farther from the average. Such is the nature of random phenomena.

MONTE CARLO TECHNIQUES

The casino at Monte Carlo is one of the foremost gambling casinos in the world. Although Monte Carlo techniques take their name from this casino, they are not designed to benefit gamblers. Rather they use random or chance phenomena as a tool in approximations.

As an example of a Monte Carlo technique, we approximate the value of π by using our random-number generator to simulate the throwing of darts at a target consisting of a quarter circle inscribed within a square. (See Fig. 10.12.) The fraction

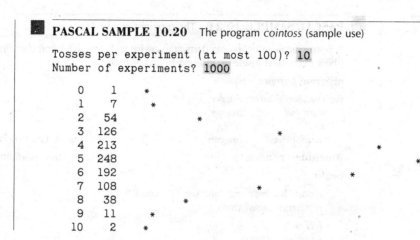

PASCAL SAMPLE 10.20   The program *cointoss* (sample use)

```
Tosses per experiment (at most 100)? 10
Number of experiments? 1000
        0     1    *
        1     7      *
        2    54            *
        3   126                    *
        4   213                              *
        5   248                                   *
        6   192                         *
        7   108                   *
        8    38          *
        9    11      *
       10     2    *
```

of the darts that fall within the circle should be approximately equal to the area of that circle divided by the area of the square, or $\pi/4$. Pascal Sample 10.21, *pi*, uses this technique to approximate π.

The results of Monte Carlo experiments vary considerably: the program *pi* produced approximations of 2.92, 3.068, 3.1152, and 3.13772 for experiments involving 100, 1000, 10,000, and 100,000 darts, respectively. Therefore an extremely large number of darts must be thrown to get even a fair approximation. Monte Carlo techniques are useful when nothing else works, but we must be careful not to place too much faith in the numbers that result.

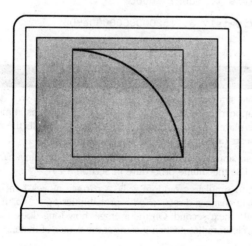

FIGURE 10.12 ■ Target for Monte Carlo approximation of π

■ **PASCAL SAMPLE 10.21**   The program *pi*

{ approximates pi by tossing darts at a square with unit sides and counting }
{ how many land inside an inscribed quarter circle   }

program *pi*(*input*, *output*);

var *numberOfDarts* : *integer*;
    dart, *hits*   : *integer*;
    x, *y*   : *real*;
    randomSeed   : *integer*;   { required by *random* }

#include 'random';   { *randomReal*, *randomize* }

begin
    write('Number of darts to toss? ');
    read(*numberOfDarts*);

    hits := 0;
    randomize(*true*);
    for *dart* := 1 **to** *numberOfDarts* **do**
        begin
            x := *randomReal*;
            y := *randomReal*;
            if *sqr*(*x*) + *sqr*(*y*) < 1 **then** *hits* := *hits* + 1
        end;
    writeln;
    writeln('pi is approximately', 4*hits/*numberOfDarts*)
end.

SAMPLE USE OF *pi*:

Number of darts to toss? 10000

pi is approximately 3.11520000000000e+00

EXERCISES

1. Write a program to simulate a game of craps. A player rolls two six-sided dice. If the total of the numbers appearing on the dice is 7 or 11, the player wins immediately. If the total is 2, 3, or 12, the player loses. In all other cases, the player rolls the dice again until the same total reappears (a win) or the total equals 7 (a loss).

2. Write a program to simulate shuffling a deck of cards and dealing a hand of 13 cards from that deck. (*Hint:* Use the shuffle procedure in Section 8.4.)

3. Write a program to simulate a random walk. A particle moves 1 inch per second. Each second the particle changes direction: with probabilities $p_1, \ldots, p_4$ it goes north, south, east, or west in the next second. On the average, how long does it take the particle to escape from a circle of radius *r* when it starts at the center of that circle? To escape from

a square with sides of r inches? If your computer system can produce graphic output, draw a picture of the path of the particle.

4. Write a program to simulate a game of blackjack. In that game of chance, any number of players bet that they can beat the dealer. The dealer begins each round by dealing two cards to each player, one face up and one face down. Each card has a numeric value: picture cards count ten points each, an ace counts one or eleven points, and the other cards count their face values. The players in turn can request extra cards (called "hits") or "stand pat" with those they have. Their object is to bring the value of their hands as close to 21 as possible without exceeding 21. (A hand with a value greater than 21 is called a "bust.") Finally the dealer takes extra cards until the value of his hand exceeds 16. Those players whose hands are worth more than the dealer's, but are not busts, win their bets; the others lose.

*5. Modify the program you wrote for Exercise 4 to experiment with different strategies for beating the dealer at blackjack. How much does it help to keep track of the number of high and low cards left in the deck and to decide when to take a "hit" on the basis of this information? How effectively can the dealer combat such a strategy by shuffling the deck more often? By using several decks of cards?

6. Write a procedure to generate a sequence of random integers by the middle-square method, that is, by squaring an integer and extracting its middle digits to obtain the next number in the sequence.

7. Why is it easy to compute n **mod** 2^m on a computer that uses binary arithmetic?

*8. Show that the numbers $r_1, \ldots, r_{modulus}$ produced by a linear congruential random-number generator are distinct if *modulus* is a power of 2 and *multiplier* **mod** $8 = 5$.

9. If your computer system predefines a random-number generator, modify *random* to make use of that generator. (*Hint:* In Berkeley Pascal, treat *randomReal* as a synonym for *random*(0).)

10. Find a way to compute (*multiplier* $\times$ *randomSeed* + *increment*) **mod** *modulus* without an overflow when *modulus* is close to *maxint*. (*Hint:* Assume that *modulus* is 2^{2m}. Write each of *multiplier, randomSeed,* and *increment* as a sum $a2^m + b$.)

10.4   NONDETERMINISTIC SIMULATION: WAITING LINES

A *queue* is a waiting line—of customers waiting for service in a bank or for a table in a restaurant, of passengers waiting to board a bus, or of requests waiting to be processed by a computer. The distinguishing feature of a queue is that people or objects are served on a first-come first-served basis. New arrivals are placed at the end of the queue. Service, when it becomes available, is given to the person or object at the beginning of the queue.

In simple situations, a single queue of customers is waiting to be served by a single server. For example, a single queue of customers might be waiting for service by a single teller in a small bank. In more complicated situations, there may be multiple servers and/or multiple queues. For example, a larger bank with several tellers may decide to have a separate queue of customers for each teller, or it may decide to have a single queue served by all the tellers.

We can simulate systems of queues to determine the effects of the number of queues, the number of servers, the rate at which customers arrive, the rate at which they are served, and the *queue discipline* that governs where they wait in line and where they receive service. A typical simulation gathers statistics concerning the total number of customers served, the maximum and average lengths of the queues, the maximum and average waiting time, the variability of the waiting times, and the percentage of time that the servers are busy. We can use the results of such simulations to predict how a bank, restaurant, bus company, or computer system can provide satisfactory service at a reasonable cost.

In this section we examine two strategies for simulating a single queue with a single server, writing two versions of a program *server1* to simulate that queue. In Section 11.5 we will refine these strategies to gather more information about the behavior of the queue. Exercises at the end of these two sections include problems that involve more than one queue or more than one server.

CLOCK-DRIVEN SIMULATIONS

The easiest way to simulate a single-server queue is to use a *clock-driven* simulation strategy. Such a strategy divides time into short intervals (say, of *unit* seconds apiece) and simulates events that occur in each of these intervals. Thus the general form of a clock-driven simulation is as follows:

for interval := first **to** last **do**
     simulate whatever events occur in this time interval

We can refine this recipe for a clock-driven simulation into a procedure *simulate* that simulates a single-server queue if we identify the events that need to be simulated, devise a means of simulating them when they occur, and determine the actions they trigger. We consider each of these tasks in turn.

Identifying events   When faced with a particular simulation, we have some latitude in identifying the number of events to distinguish and the nature of those events. For example, when simulating a single-server queue, we might distinguish from one to three events: the arrival of a new customer, the time at which service begins for that customer, and the time at which service ends. As we will see, the fewer events we distinguish, the more we must do to process each event.

Suppose that the only event we identify is the arrival of a new customer. Then we must simulate everything that will happen to the customer when that event occurs. For a single-server queue, we might do this by keeping track of the next time the server will be free. If we call this time *whenFree*, we can set

whenFree := *whenFree* + time required to serve this customer

whenever a new customer arrives. If we can compute easily the time required to serve a customer, this strategy leads to a particularly simple simulation—one that we can use to estimate the maximum waiting time. But this strategy makes it difficult to record other information such as the maximum length of the queue.

Alternatively, we can identify the arrival and departure of a customer as separate events. With this strategy, customers remain in the queue until they have been served (rather than only until they begin to be served). Hence we can simply increment the length of a queue when customers arrive and decrement the length when they depart. This is the strategy we will adopt. It will enable us to keep track of the maximum length of the queue, but it will make it more difficult to compute the maximum waiting time.

Finally, we can identify the time a customer begins to receive service as a third event. With this strategy, customers remain in the queue only until they can be served. Hence we can serve a new customer immediately upon arrival if the server is not busy or place that customer in the queue if immediate service is not possible. Here the occurrence of one event can trigger another event: an arrival when the server is free triggers the start of service, as does a departure when the queue is nonempty. This strategy provides no advantages over the second, so we proceed with the second.

Having identified the events (arrivals and departures) we want to simulate, we can refine our recipe for a clock-driven simulation as follows:

```
for interval := first to last do
    begin
        if there are any customers then
            if a departure occurs then simulate departure;
        if an arrival occurs then simulate arrival
    end
```

Here we have chosen to simulate departures before arrivals in each interval of time. We do this to prevent a customer from slipping through the simulation unnoticed by arriving, being served immediately, and departing—all within the same interval. By simulating departures first, each customer is forced to wait at least one time interval between the time of arrival and the time service has been concluded.

Simulating when events occur by the clock In order to simulate whether an event occurs during a particular time interval, we use the *randomReal* function from Section 10.3. Suppose, for example, that an arrival occurs every *interarrivalTime* seconds on the average. Then the probability that an arrival occurs in a period of *unit* seconds is *unit/interarrivalTime* (provided that *unit* is small compared to *interarrivalTime*). Thus we can simulate whether an arrival occurs in a given interval of time by evaluating the expression *randomReal* < *unit/interarrivalTime*.

In order to simulate departures, we also use the *randomReal* function. In fact, we can simulate departures in the same way that we simulate arrivals. Suppose that it takes an average of *serviceTime* seconds to serve a customer. If we view service as ending when a messenger arrives to usher a customer out, we see that the average service time is simply the average interarrival time for these messengers. Hence we can simulate whether a departure occurs in a given interval of time by evaluating the expression *randomReal* < *unit/serviceTime* whenever a customer is being served.

With these observations, we can refine our recipe for a clock-driven simulation further:

```
for interval := first to last do
    begin
        if there are any customers then
            if randomReal < unit/serviceTime then simulate departure;
            if randomReal < unit/interarrivalTime then simulate arrival
    end
```

Simulating the actions triggered by an event   Two kinds of actions are triggered by events. The first kind are simply responses to the arrival and departure of customers, incrementing and decrementing the length of the queue. The second kind are concerned with keeping various statistics about the simulation: in the program *server1*, these actions keep track of the total number of customers served and the maximum length of the queue.

Pascal Sample 10.22 displays a procedure *arrival* that the clock-driven variant of *server1* will use to handle arrivals. It increments the length *qLen* of the queue and detects when this length exceeds *maxLen*, the maximum queue length so far. It also displays information about the arrival if the boolean variable *observing* is true. We

---

PASCAL SAMPLE 10.22   The library *server1C* (*arrival* procedure)

procedure *arrival*(*t* : *real*);

{ simulates an arrival at time *t* }

begin

    qLen := *qLen* + 1;

    if *qLen* > *maxLen* **then** *maxLen* := *qLen*;

    if *observing* **then** *writeln*('arrive', *t*:7:1, *qLen*:6)

end;   { of *arrival* }

PASCAL SAMPLE 10.23   The library *server1C* (*departure* procedure)

procedure *departure*(*t* : *real*);

{ simulates a departure at time *t* }

begin

    qLen := *qLen* − 1;

    served := *served* + 1;

    if *observing* **then** *writeln*('depart', *t*:7:1, *qLen*:6)

end;   { of *departure* }

store this procedure in a library *server1C* of procedures suitable for clock-driven simulations.

The procedure *departure* from *server1C* (Pascal Sample 10.23) handles departures similarly, decrementing the length *qLen* of the queue and incrementing the count *served* of the total number of customers served. It also displays information about the departure if the boolean variable *observing* is true.

With these procedures, our recipe for a clock-driven simulation takes a more concrete form:

```
for interval := 0 to last do
    begin
        if there are any customers then
            if randomReal < unit/serviceTime then departure(interval*unit);
            if randomReal < unit/interarrivalTime then arrival(interval*unit)
    end
```

Here we have chosen to number time intervals of *unit* seconds, starting with 0, and to simulate arrivals and departures at the beginning of each interval, that is, at time $interval \times unit$.

Completing the clock-driven simulation   The procedure *simulate* from *server1C* represents the final refinement of our recipe for a clock-driven simulation. (See Pascal Sample 10.24.) It initializes the statistics we want to keep, performs the simulation according to our recipe until a specified finishing time, and computes one additional statistic: the average time customers spend waiting in the queue.

The average waiting time is difficult to compute precisely in *server1C*. In the *arrival* procedure, we do not know when an arriving customer will depart; in the *departure* procedure, we do not know when a departing customer arrived. (We will remedy this defect in the program *server2* in Section 11.5.) Hence we must estimate the average waiting time in the *simulate* procedure itself. We do this by keeping a record of the total time waited by all customers. Rather than increment this record once for each customer served, we increment it once for each time interval: if there are *qLen* customers in the queue at the end of a time interval, then those customers altogether wait a total of $qLen \times unit$ seconds before anything happens in the next time interval. At the end of the simulation, we divide the accumulated waiting time by the number of arrivals to estimate the average waiting time. Since some of the arrivals may still be waiting in the queue, this computation may underestimate the true average waiting time.

We must choose the time increment in a clock-driven simulation carefully. If it is too large, events may not be noticed until after they actually occur, or two arrivals may occur in the same interval of time and we might notice only one of them. At the very least, *unit/interarrivalTime* must be less than one for *prArrive* to make sense. However, if the increment is too small, the simulation will take a long time to run, and nothing will happen in most of the time intervals.

PASCAL SAMPLE 10.24   The library *server1C* (*simulate* procedure)

```
{ server1C: clock-driven simulation procedure for use with server1 }
procedure simulate;
    { simulates queue with specified interarrival and service times   }
    { until a given finishing time, recording the number served, the  }
    { number still in the queue, the maximum queue length, and        }
    { the average waiting time                                        }
    const unit = 0.1;           { time unit for simulation            }
    var prArrive : real;        { probability of arrival in one unit   }
        prDepart : real;        { probability of departure in one unit }
        waitTime : real;        { total time waited by all customers   }
        interval : integer;     { current interval of time            }
    { declarations for arrival, departure procedures go here }
begin
    prArrive := unit/interarrivalTime;
    prDepart := unit/serviceTime;

    served   := 0;              { global: number of customers served }
    qLen     := 0;              { global: current length of queue    }
    maxLen   := 0;              { global: maximum length of queue    }
    waitTime := 0;
    for interval := 0 to trunc(finish/unit) do
        begin
            if qLen > 0 then
                if randomReal < prDepart then departure(interval*unit);
            if randomReal < prArrive then arrival(interval*unit);
            waitTime := waitTime + qLen*unit
        end;
    avWait := waitTime/(served+qLen)
end;   { of simulate }
```

A further complexity in clock-driven simulations is the ordering of events within an interval of time. We must be careful about which of several events that occur in the same interval we simulate first, and we must be careful about when we gather statistics, if we wish the simulation to mirror reality. In *simulate*, we are careful to increment *waitTime* after, and not before, a new arrival is added to the queue; that way we reflect our convention that at least one time interval must transpire between the time a customer arrives and the time service ends for that customer.

Pascal Sample 10.25 displays the main part of the program *server1*. It asks the user to supply the parameters that will drive the simulation, calls *simulate* to perform the simulation, and reports the results.

PASCAL SAMPLE 10.25 The program *server1* (main program)

```
{ simulation of a single-server queue }
program server1(input, output);

var interarrivalTime : real;        { average time between arrivals }
    serviceTime      : real;        { average service time           }
    finish           : real;        { time simulation ends           }
    served           : integer;     { number of customers served     }
    qLen             : integer;     { length of queue                }
    maxLen           : integer;     { maximum length of queue        }
    avWait           : real;        { average time spent in queue    }
    observing        : boolean;     { events displayed if true       }
    answer           : char;        { used to set observing          }
    randomSeed       : integer;     { required by randomReal         }
#include 'random';                  { randomize, randomReal          }
#include 'server1C';                { clock-driven simulate procedure }

begin
    write('Average interarrival, service times? ');
    readln(interarrivalTime, serviceTime);
    write('Length of simulation? ');
    readln(finish);
    write('Do you want to see arrivals and departures [y/n]? ');
    readln(answer);
    if answer = 'y' then
        begin
            observing := true;
            writeln;
            writeln('event ','  time ','  qLen');
            writeln('----- ','  ---- ','  ----');
        end
    else
        observing := false;

    randomize(true);
    simulate;

    writeln;
    writeln('Number served      .    .= ', served:1);
    writeln('Number still waiting  = ', qLen:1);
    writeln('Maximum queue length  = ', maxLen:1);
    writeln('Average waiting time >= ', avWait:1:2)
end.
```

Pascal Sample 10.26 shows a portion of the results of using *server1* to simulate 48 hours in the operation of a queue, with one arrival occurring every 8 minutes on the average and with service taking an average of 6 minutes. As expected, we note that there were approximately 360, or 2880/8, arrivals in the 48-hour period. Somewhat surprisingly, the queue grew to a maximum length of 23 customers during that period before decreasing to a more reasonable length. Yet the average wait was only 32.42 minutes. In the exercises at the end of this section, and in Section 11.5, we will attempt to measure the variability and reliability of the latter two statistics.

■ **PASCAL SAMPLE 10.26**   The program *server1* (results of clock-driven simulation)

```
Average interarrival, service times? 8 6
Length of simulation? 2880
Do you want to see arrivals and departures [y/n]? y

    event     time   qLen
    -----     ----   ----
    arrive    32.4    1
    arrive    46.8    2
    depart    55.5    1
    arrive    55.5    2
    depart    55.7    1
    depart    56.6    0
    arrive    69.8    1
    depart    71.0    0
    arrive    87.8    1
    depart    91.3    0
    arrive    98.4    1
    arrive   101.1    2
    depart   107.6    1
    arrive   108.3    2
    arrive   108.6    3
    depart   126.4    2
    arrive   130.1    3
    depart   131.4    2
    arrive   133.1    3
    depart   136.5    2
    depart   138.1    1
     . . .

Number served       = 357
Number still waiting = 2
Maximum queue length = 23
Average waiting time >= 32.42
```

EVENT-DRIVEN SIMULATIONS

Event-driven simulations circumvent the problem of choosing a suitable time increment for a clock-driven simulation. In event-driven simulations, we do not wait for the next event to occur, but rather we compute the time at which it will occur and proceed directly to simulating the event. The general form for such simulations is as follows.

> **repeat**
>   *time* := time of next event;
>   simulate that event
> **until** *time* >= *finish*

The logic of an event-driven simulation is more straightforward than that of a clock-driven simulation because the sequence of events, rather than the structure of the program, determines the order in which events are simulated. We do not have to worry about when to simulate arrivals and departures during an interval of time; we simply simulate them when they occur.

We will convert *server1* into an event-driven simulation by replacing the clock-driven *simulate* procedure in the library *server1C* by the event-driven procedure *simulate* in a new library *server1E*. In order to write *server1E*, we must find a way to determine which event occurs next and when; and we must review the actions taken by *server1C* in response to each event. We handle the problem of determining which event occurs next by declaring two variables, *arriveTime* and *departTime*, that record respectively the time of the next arrival and the time of the next departure. With these variables we can refine our recipe for an event-driven simulation.

> *arriveTime* := time of first arrival;
> *departTime* := time of first departure;
> **repeat**
>   *time* := *min(min(arriveTime,departTime), finish)*;
>   **if** *time* = *arriveTime* **then**
>   *arrival(time)*
>   **else if** *time* = *departTime* **then**
>   *departure(time)*
> **until** *time* >= *finish*

The major subtlety in an event-driven simulation concerns computing appropriate values for *arriveTime* and *departTime*. We defer the details of these computations by hiding them within a function *when* such that, if *t* is the current time and *averageTime* is the average time to a new event, then *when(t, averageTime)* is a simulated time at which that event will occur. Thus *when(0, interarrivalTime)* is the simulated time of the first arrival; if an arrival occurs at time *t*, then *when(t, interarrivalTime)* is the simulated time of the next arrival.

PASCAL SAMPLE 10.27 The library *server1E* (*arrival* procedure)

```
procedure arrival( t : real );
    { simulates an arrival at time t }
    begin
        qLen := qLen + 1;
        if qLen > maxLen then maxLen := qLen;
        arriveTime := when(t, interarrivalTime);
        if qLen = 1 then departTime := when(t, serviceTime);
        if observing then writeln('arrive', t:7:1, qLen:6)
    end;   { of arrival }
```

These observations prompt us to revise slightly the actions taken by *server1C* in response to arrivals and departures. When an arrival occurs in *server1E*, we must simulate that arrival as in *server1C*. But we must also recompute the time *arriveTime* of the next arrival in order to keep the simulation going. Furthermore, if the new arrival is the only customer in the queue, then we must compute the time *departTime* when service will end for that customer. Pascal Sample 10.27 shows how the *arrival* procedure from *server1E* carries out these actions using the *when* function.

Similarly, when a departure occurs in *server1E*, we must simulate that departure as in *server1C*. But we must also recompute the time *departTime* of the next departure to reflect when the server will be free after serving the next customer, if any, in the queue. If the queue is not empty, this time is simply *when(t, serviceTime)*. However, if the queue is empty, we do not want to simulate any more departures until another arrival occurs. A convenient way to defer simulating departures is to set *departTime* equal to *finish* + 1, that is, to a time beyond the end of the simulation. Pascal Sample 10.28 shows how the *departure* procedure in *server1E* carries out these actions.

PASCAL SAMPLE 10.28 The library *server1E* (*departure* procedure)

```
procedure departure( t : real );
    { simulates a departure at time t }
    begin
        qLen := qLen - 1;
        served := served + 1;
        if qLen > 0 then
            departTime := when(t, serviceTime)
        else
            departTime := finish + 1;
        if observing then writeln('depart', t:7:1, qLen:6)
    end;   { of departure }
```

The convention of setting *departTime* to *finish* + 1 when no customers are being served also provides a way to handle the time of the first departure. Using the *when* function, we can refine our recipe for an event-driven simulation to produce the procedure *simulate* in *server1E*. That procedure, like the corresponding procedure in *server1C*, keeps a record of the total time waited by all customers during the simulation. But now, instead of incrementing that record each time an interval of time passes, we increment the record each time an event occurs by the total time all have waited since the last event. Pascal Sample 10.29 shows how this is accomplished.

■ **PASCAL SAMPLE 10.29**   The library *server1E* (*simulate* procedure)

```
{ server1E: event-driven simulation procedure for use with server1 }

procedure simulate;

    { simulates queue with specified interarrival and service times  }
    { until a given finishing time, recording the number served, the }
    { number still in the queue, the maximum queue length, and       }
    { the average waiting time                                        }

    var arriveTime  : real;     { time of next arrival               }
        departTime  : real;     { time of next departure             }
        waitTime    : real;     { total time waited by all customers }
        lastTime    : real;     { time of last event                 }
        time        : real;     { current time                       }

    #include 'maxmin';

    { declarations for arrival, departure, when procedures go here }

    begin
        served     := 0;     { global: number of customers served }
        qLen       := 0;     { global: current length of queue     }
        maxLen     := 0;     { global: maximum length of queue     }
        waitTime := 0;

        arriveTime := when(0, interarrivalTime);
        departTime := finish + 1;
        time       := 0;

        repeat
            lastTime := time;
            time := min(min(arriveTime, departTime), finish);
            waitTime := waitTime + qLen*(time - lastTime);
            if time = arriveTime then
                arrival(time)
            else if time = departTime then
                departure(time)
        until time > = finish;

        avWait := waitTime/(served + qLen)
    end;   { of simulate }
```

Predicting when events will occur   Finally, we turn our attention to the problem of defining the *when* function, that is, of computing a simulated time for an event to occur. In *server1C* we simply evaluate

$$randomReal < unit/interarrivalTime$$

to determine whether an arrival occurs during a time interval of length *unit*, when one arrival occurs every *interarrivalTime* seconds on the average. This works, of course, only if *unit* is much less than *interarrivalTime*. In *server1E*, we want to generate a sequence of interarrival times t_1, t_2, ..., t_n for which the average is *interarrivalTime*. One way to do this is to find a suitable definition for a function f so that we can generate a random interarrival time by computing $f(randomReal)$. We proceed as follows.

Imagine that a time interval of t seconds is subdivided into $t/unit$ smaller intervals of *unit* seconds each. If *unit* is small, we can estimate the probability Pr[event] of a specified event in a single time interval.

Pr[an arrival within *unit* seconds] = *unit/interarrivalTime*.

Pr[no arrival within *unit* seconds] = 1 − Pr[an arrival within *unit* seconds]

$$= 1 - unit/interarrivalTime.$$

Since the probability of an arrival within any one of these $t/unit$ time intervals is independent of what happened in any other time interval, we conclude that

$$\Pr[\text{ no arrival within } t \text{ seconds }] = \left(1 - \frac{unit}{interarrivalTime}\right)^{t/unit}$$

Letting *unit* tend to 0 to increase the accuracy of this estimate, we observe (using calculus) that

$$\Pr[\text{ no arrival within } t \text{ seconds }] = e^{-t/interarrivalTime}$$

and

$$\Pr[\text{ an arrival within } t \text{ seconds }] = 1 - e^{-t/interarrivalTime}$$

Now we want to define a function f such that $f(randomReal)$ predicts the time of the next arrival. Hence we want

$$\Pr[\ f(randomReal) < t\ ] = \Pr[\text{ an arrival within } t \text{ seconds }]$$

$$= 1 - e^{-t/interarrivalTime}$$

$$= \Pr[\ randomReal > e^{-t/interarrivalTime}\ ]$$

$$\text{(since } 1 - x = \Pr[\ randomReal > x\ ] \text{ when } 0 \leq x \leq 1)$$

$$= \Pr[\ \ln(randomReal) > -t/interarrivalTime\ ]$$

$$\text{(since } x > y \text{ precisely when } \ln x > \ln y)$$

$$= \Pr[\ -interarrivalTime \times \ln(randomReal) < t\ ].$$

PASCAL SAMPLE 10.30   The library *server1E* (*when* function)

function *when*(*currentTime*, *averageTime* : *real*) : *real*;
  { generates the time of the next event, when the average time }
  { between events is *averageTime*   }
  begin
      when := *currentTime* − *averageTime* * *ln*(*randomReal*)
  end; { of *when* }

Thus we define *f* so that

$$f(x) = -interarrivalTime \times \ln x$$

and evaluate *f*(*randomReal*) to obtain a series of interarrival times for which the average is *interarrivalTime*.

With this formula for computing a simulated time until the next arrival, we can define the *when* function, as in Pascal Sample 10.30, and thereby complete the construction of *server1E*.

Pascal Sample 10.31 displays the results of using *server1E* instead of *server1C* with *server1* to simulate 48 hours in the operation of a queue with one arrival

---

PASCAL SAMPLE 10.31   The program *server1* (results of event-driven simulation)

```
Average interarrival, service times? 8 6
Length of simulation? 2880
Do you want to see arrivals and departures [y/n]? y

event    time   qLen
-----    ----   ----
arrive    5.3      1
arrive    7.3      2
depart    7.4      1
depart    8.0      0
arrive    9.6      1
depart   11.7      0
arrive   28.0      1
depart   28.9      0
arrive   29.5      1
depart   30.4      0
arrive   44.8      1
arrive   47.4      2
depart   50.6      1
arrive   51.3      2
arrive   56.0      3
depart   64.8      2
```

■ **PASCAL SAMPLE 10.31**   The program *server1* (event-driven results, continued)

```
depart   77.1    1
arrive   77.9    2
depart   85.7    1
arrive   89.5    2
 . . .

Number served       = 373
Number still waiting = 4
Maximum queue length = 17
Average waiting time >= 24.17
```

---

occurring every 8 minutes on the average and with service taking an average of 6 minutes.

The results of this simulation are roughly comparable to those produced by *server1C*. Although there are more arrivals this time, the maximum queue length and the average waiting time are somewhat less than before. The most significant difference between the two simulations is that the second required considerably less computer time. (See Exercise 2 at the end of this section.)

EXERCISES

1. Experiment with *server1C* to find out how the results of the simulation are affected by
   (a) the length of the simulation; and
   (b) the size of the time interval.

2. Compare the execution time of *server1C* with that of *server1E*. How big must *unit* be to achieve comparable execution times? How reliable is *server1C* when *unit* is this big?

3. The *utilization* of a queue is defined to be the fraction of the time that the server is busy.
   (a) Modify *server1C* to compute the utilization of the queue.
   (b) Modify *server1E* to compute the utilization of the queue.
   (c) Intuitively, the utilization of the queue should equal *serviceTime/interarrivalTime*. Experiment with the programs you wrote for (a) and (b) to determine how well this intuition is borne out for various arrival rates and service times.
   (d) Intuitively, the average waiting time should increase as the utilization of the queue increases, that is, as the service time approaches the interarrival time. Experiment with your programs to see how quickly this happens.
   (e) What happens to the average serving time when the utilization of the queue equals 1? What happens when it exceeds 1?

4. The *average queue length L* is the average of the queue lengths witnessed at regular intervals of time.
   (a) Modify *server1C* to compute the average length of the queue.
   (b) Modify *server1E* to compute the average length of the queue. Be careful about how you sample the length of the queue.

(c) In theory, $L = u/(1 - u)$, where L is the average length and u is the utilization of the queue. How well do the results of using your program compare with this theoretical value for L?

*(d) Verify mathematically the theoretical value for L. (*Hint:* Show by induction that $\Pr[\, L = n \,] = u^n(1 - u)$; then sum the series $\sum_{n=0}^{\infty} n\Pr[\, L = n \,]$.)

(e) In theory, the average waiting time W equals the average length L of the queue times the average interarrival time A. (Intuitively, the length of the queue is L just after the average customer arrives and again just after that customer departs. In the intervening time W, L customers must depart, and an average of W/A new customers arrive. Hence $L = W/A$.) How well do the results of using your program compare with this theoretical value for W?

5. Suppose that the service time for a queue is constant.

(a) Write a clock-driven simulation of a queue with a constant service time. Keep track of the maximum and average waiting times. (*Hint:* As suggested in this section, define a variable *whenFree* to indicate when the server will be free.)

(b) Write an event-driven simulation of a queue with a constant service time.

(c) Was it easier to modify *server1C* or *server1E* to simulate a queue with a constant service time? Why?

(d) In theory, the average waiting time for a queue with constant service times is half that for a queue with variable service times. How well is this relationship borne out by the results of your simulations?

6. Suppose that two servers are available.

(a) Modify *server1C* to simulate a queue discipline in which there is a separate queue for each server, with arrivals going into the shortest queue. (*Hint:* Two types of departures must be simulated.)

(b) Modify *server1C* to simulate a single queue for two servers, with the first person in the queue going to whichever server becomes free.

(c) Is (a) or (b) easier to accomplish with a clock-driven strategy? Why?

(d) Repeat (a)–(c) using an event-driven simulation.

(e) Was it easier to modify *server1C* or *server1E* to simulate systems with more than one queue or more than one server? Why?

(f) Which of the two queue disciplines provides better service? How much better?

7. Modify *server1C* or *server1E* to graph the length of the queue as a function of time.

(a) What is the average duration of a busy spell for the server?

(b) What is the average duration of an idle spell for the server?

10.5   **ANALYSIS OF NUMERIC ALGORITHMS**

As for algorithms in general, we are concerned with the correctness and efficiency of numeric methods. Yet, because of the special nature of numeric computations, we now phrase questions about correctness and efficiency in somewhat different terms.

To illustrate the difference, let us consider a simple numeric problem. Suppose that we drop a ball from a height of h feet. How long will it take the ball to reach the ground? Newton's law of gravity says that the ball will fall $gt^2/2$ feet in t seconds, where g is a constant measuring the force of gravity. Hence there are several ways in which we can proceed: we can approximate a zero of the function f defined by $f(t) = h - gt^2/2$; we can evaluate $\sqrt{2h/g}$; or we can simulate the motion of the ball. However we proceed, we cannot escape errors that arise from the finite nature of computation. We can keep these errors under control by proceeding carefully and by analyzing what we are doing. But we must recognize the following limits on our ability to obtain an exact answer to our question.

■ **Limitations of finite measurement:** We know the initial height h of the ball only to within the accuracy of some measuring device, and we know the gravitational constant g only approximately (that is, $32.16\ldots$). If we base computations on approximate data, we can expect only approximate results. But the more accurate our data, the more accurate our results.

■ **Limitations of finite precision:** Computers manipulate finite representations of real numbers, and they round the results of all arithmetic operations to fit these representations. If we attempt to compute even simple quantities such as $1/3$, we can expect only approximate results such as 0.333333. But, as we will see, we can take steps to limit the extent of such *roundoff error*.

■ **Limitations of finite time:** Algorithms must stop. If we use the bisection method to find a zero of a function, or Newton's method to evaluate a square root, we do not continue forever; instead, we stop when some small error still remains. But, by analyzing the algorithm, we can measure the extent of such *algorithmic error*.

■ **Limitations of finite models:** When we use a computer to simulate continuous systems, we generally utilize a model that divides time into a sequence of discrete intervals. By approximating what happens in each of these intervals, we attempt to mimic the system's evolution. But each such approximation introduces a tiny algorithmic error, which we try to minimize by choosing small intervals and accurate approximations.

Thus numeric algorithms are approximate in nature. Whether we use them explicitly for approximation, as in Section 10.1, or to approximate reality, as in Sections 10.2–10.4, we must accept the numbers they produce with caution. As the mathematician Richard Hamming noted, "The purpose of computing is insight, not numbers."

The approximate nature of numeric computation largely transforms our concern for correctness into a concern for accuracy. Since exact results may be out of reach, we do not ask whether an algorithm is correct but whether its results are "correct enough." And our concern for efficiency largely becomes one for how quickly numeric algorithms produce sufficiently accurate results.

NUMERIC ACCURACY

How correct is correct enough? It seems natural to ask that an approximation a to a real number x be "correct to n digits." But if x is 2.00000000001 and a is 1.99999999998, then a is a good approximation to x even though none of its digits is "correct." Furthermore, a good approximation a to x may not agree exactly even after rounding: if x is 1.7171717 . . . , then x or anything close to it, when rounded to an odd number of digits, is off by one in the last digit. Exercises 1–3 at the end of this section explore this phenomenon in more detail, showing how hard it is to guarantee that all digits in an approximation are correct.

We can provide a more realistic measure of correctness simply by requiring that an approximation a to a real number x be "close to" x. In the bisection algorithm, for example, we sought an approximation a to a zero x of the function f such that $|a - x| < 10^{-6}$. The quantity $|a - x|$ is known as the *absolute error* of the approximation.

The absolute error is not the only measure of the accuracy of an approximation. It works well for approximating numbers of moderate size. But it works less well for approximating numbers that are very small or very large. If x is 0.000000123 and its approximation a is 0.000000246, the absolute error of the approximation is small, but a is wrong by a factor of two. If x is approximately 10^{10}, then asking for an absolute error of 10^{-6} may be asking for more than the finite precision of a computer can provide.

For many applications it makes more sense to require that the *relative error* $|(a - x)/x|$ of an approximation be small. By dividing the absolute error by x, we measure how close we are to x relative to x itself. For other applications, it may make sense to measure the quality of an approximation in entirely different terms. For example, when seeking a zero of a function f, we may be content with a value of x such that $|f(x)|$ is very small. Such an x need not be a good approximation to a zero of f (for example, when the graph of f is flat near x). But it is an actual zero of a function that approximates f [that is, of a function g such that $g(x) = f(x) - c$ for some small number c]. Particularly when the definition of f depends on experimental measurements, an exact zero of an approximation to f may be just as good as an approximation to a zero of f itself. Let us now consider how two types of numeric errors—roundoff and algorithmic—affect the accuracy of an approximation.

Roundoff errors   Roundoff errors result from the finite precision of computer arithmetic. We can illustrate how they arise by considering a hypothetical computer that represents real numbers in floating-point decimal notation $s \times 10^e$ with a 3-digit integer significand s and a 1-digit integer exponent e. This computer can manipulate the number 0 and numbers with absolute values in the range 1×10^{-9} to 999×10^9. It can represent 123,000 exactly as 123×10^3, but it is forced to represent 122,501 through 123,499 as well by 123×10^3, because there are no closer 3-digit representations for these numbers. Furthermore, it is forced to round the results of calculations such as $123 \times 10^3 + 1$ to three significant digits, thereby introducing roundoff errors into these calculations.

Pascal Sample 10.32, *roundoff*, illustrates some effects caused by rounding. The most curious of these is the fact that counting up and counting down by a fixed increment produce dissimilar results: we would expect both loops in *roundoff* to display the same number of values, but the second displays one less value.

What happened to the value 0 on the way down? On our hypothetical computer, it disappears. That computer represents $1/6$ as 167×10^{-3}, producing the values 1, 0.833, 0.666, 0.499, 0.332, 0.165, and -0.002 when counting down. Since this last

---

PASCAL SAMPLE 10.32   The program *roundoff*

```
{ illustrates effects of rounding }
program roundoff(input, output);

var x : real;
    n : integer;

begin
    { illustrate rounding of large numbers }
    x := 1;
    while x < x+1 do x := 10*x;
    writeln(x:3:1, ' + 1 rounds to ', x+1:3:1);

    { illustrate rounding of small numbers }
    writeln;
    write('Enter number of steps to take from 0 to 1: ');
    read(n);
    writeln;
    writeln('Going from 0 to 1 in steps of 1/', n:1, ':');
    x := 0;
    while x <= 1 do
        begin
            writeln(x);
            x := x + 1/n
        end;

    writeln;
    writeln('Going from 1 to 0 in steps of -1/', n:1, ':');
    x := 1;
    while x >= 0 do
        begin
            writeln(x);
            x := x - 1/n
        end
end.
```

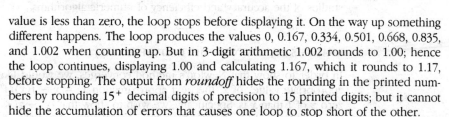

```
SAMPLE USE OF roundoff:
1000000000000000000.0 + 1 rounds to 1000000000000000000.0

Enter number of steps to take from 0 to 1: 6
Going from 0 to 1 in steps of 1/6:
  0.00000000000000e+00
  1.66666666666667e-01
  3.33333333333333e-01
  5.00000000000000e-01
  6.66666666666667e-01
  8.33333333333333e-01
  1.00000000000000e+00

Going from 1 to 0 in steps of -1/6:
  1.00000000000000e+00
  8.33333333333333e-01
  6.66666666666667e-01
  5.00000000000000e-01
  3.33333333333333e-01
  1.66666666666667e-01
```

value is less than zero, the loop stops before displaying it. On the way up something different happens. The loop produces the values 0, 0.167, 0.334, 0.501, 0.668, 0.835, and 1.002 when counting up. But in 3-digit arithmetic 1.002 rounds to 1.00; hence the loop continues, displaying 1.00 and calculating 1.167, which it rounds to 1.17, before stopping. The output from *roundoff* hides the rounding in the printed numbers by rounding 15^{+} decimal digits of precision to 15 printed digits; but it cannot hide the accumulation of errors that causes one loop to stop short of the other.

In most simple calculations, we do not need to worry about the effects of rounding. If we perform these calculations with more digits of precision than we really need, we can circumvent roundoff errors by rounding the final result to fewer digits. But for more extensive calculations we must prevent an accumulation of roundoff errors from affecting the correctness of the final result.

When necessary, we can minimize the effects of rounding by carefully ordering a computation. For example, to add a long list of positive numbers, we can add the smaller numbers in the list first, saving the larger numbers until last. That way we can avoid the rounding that would result from adding small numbers to a large sum. Exercises 6 and 7 at the end of this section explore this and other sources of roundoff errors, together with ways to keep them under control.

Algorithmic errors   Algorithmic errors result from the approximate nature of numeric algorithms. In order to measure the extent of these errors, we must analyze specific algorithms.

The bisection algorithm stops when an interval (x_1, x_2) containing a zero of a function f is sufficiently small. By choosing x to be the midpoint of this interval, we guarantee that the absolute error between x and a zero of f is at most $|x_2 - x_1|/2$. Hence, by bisecting an interval containing a zero of f enough times, we can get as much accuracy out of the bisection algorithm as the precision of our computer system will allow. When an approximation algorithm gets progressively closer to the correct result, we say that the algorithm *converges*; when it gets farther away, or when it oscillates without converging, we say that it *diverges*.

Newton's method stops when two successive approximations x_n and x_{n+1} to a zero of f are close together. However, we must know something about the nature of the function f to conclude that the final approximation is close to a zero of f. More importantly, we must know something about the nature of f to conclude that Newton's method converges: Exercises 5 and 6 in Section 10.1 show that Newton's method can fail in certain special situations.

We can use mathematical analysis to find conditions on the function f that guarantee convergence of Newton's method. This analysis also helps us to assess the speed with which Newton's method converges. Similar techniques, which are beyond the scope of this book, can be used to assess the accuracy of the algorithms that we used in Section 10.2 to simulate motion. The field of *numerical analysis*, which lies on the border between computer science and mathematics, concerns itself with such studies of the accuracy and efficiency of numeric algorithms.

ANALYSIS OF NEWTON'S METHOD (OPTIONAL)

In order to show that Newton's method converges, we would like to show that for appropriate values of x, the next approximation $x' = x - f(x)/f'(x)$ is closer to a zero z of f than x is. Specifically, we wish to show that $|x' - z| < |x - z|$.

Calculus enables us to find conditions on the function f for which this inequality is true. Taylor's theorem relates the error in approximating a function f by the tangent to its graph at a point $<a, f(a)>$ to values of the second derivative f'' of f (the second derivative of a function is the derivative of the derivative).

Taylor's Theorem. If f'' is defined on the closed interval $[a, b]$, then

$$f(b) = f(a) + (b - a)f'(a) + (b - a)^2 f''(c)/2$$

for some c between a and b.

Using Taylor's theorem with $a = x$ and $b = z$, we obtain

$$f(z) = f(x) + (z - x)f'(x) + (z - x)^2 f''(c)/2$$

for some c between x and z. But $f(z) = 0$, so

$$0 = \frac{f(x)}{f'(x)} + z - x + (z - x)^2 \frac{f''(c)}{2f'(x)}$$

provided $f'(x) \neq 0$. Now $x' = x - f(x)/f'(x)$, so

$$z - x' = -(z - x)^2 \frac{f''(c)}{2f'(x)}$$

Hence x' and all successive approximations are closer to z than x, and Newton's method will converge, whenever

1. $f''(c)$ exists for all c such that $|c - z| < |x - z|$;

2. $f'(x'') \neq 0$ for all x'' such that $|x'' - z| \leq |x - z|$; and

3. $\left| (z - x'') \dfrac{f''(c)}{2f'(x'')} \right| < 1$ for all such c and x''.

The graphic intuition behind condition (3) is as follows: convergence occurs if $|z - x''|$ is small (that is, x was a good guess), $f'(x'')$ is large (that is, the slope of the graph is steep between x and z), and $f''(c)$ is small (that is, the slope is not changing rapidly). This analysis helps to explain the behavior of Newton's method in the program *zeroDemo3*. First let us see what our analysis shows about the convergence of Newton's method.

If $f(x) = x^2 - 4$, then $|(z - x)f''(c)/2f'(x)| = |(2 - x)/2x|$, which is less than 1 if $x > 2$. Hence Newton's method will converge to $\sqrt{4}$ if we start with any larger approximation to x. In fact, Newton's method will converge if we start with any nonzero approximation.

If $f(x) = \sin x$, then $|f''(c)/2f'(x)| = |(\sin c)/(\cos^2 x)|$, which is less than 1 if x is close to a zero of the sine function. If x is close to a zero of the cosine function, then Newton's method behaves randomly until it produces an approximation close to a zero of the sine function, whereupon it converges on that zero.

Finally, let us see what our analysis shows about how quickly Newton's method converges. Suppose that $|f''(c)/2f'(x)| < 1$, which it must be for Newton's method to converge. Now if $|x - z|$ is less than 10^{-n}, then $|x' - z|$ will be less than 10^{-2n}. Hence one iteration of Newton's method doubles the number of accurate decimal places in the approximation. With the bisection method, three to four iterations are necessary to gain just one more decimal place of accuracy.

We characterize these differences in speed by saying that Newton's method converges *quadratically*, whereas the bisection method converges only *linearly*. The error after each iteration of Newton's method is a quadratic function of the previous error, whereas the error after each iteration of the bisection method is a linear function of the previous error. When we studied algorithms for searching and sorting, we preferred linear algorithms to quadratic algorithms: linear functions increase execution time less rapidly than do quadratic functions. Now, by contrast, we prefer quadratic convergence to linear convergence: quadratic functions decrease errors more rapidly than do linear functions.

EXERCISES

1. Suppose that a is an approximation to a real number x such that $|a - x| \leqslant 1/2$.

    (a) Show that $|trunc(a) - trunc(x)| \leqslant 1$. [*Hint:* $|trunc(a) - trunc(x)|$ is an integer bounded by $|trunc(a) - a| + |a - x| + |x - trunc(x)|$.]

    (b) Show that $|round(a) - round(x)| \leqslant 1$.

    (c) Show that $|round(a) - trunc(x)| \leqslant 1$.

    (d) Show that the inequalities in (a), (b), and (c) are the best possible.

2. Show that if $|a - x| \leqslant 10^{-n}/2$, then a and x differ by at most one in the nth digit beyond the decimal point. (*Hint:* Use the results of Exercise 1.)

3. Show that if $|(a - x)/x| \leqslant 10^{-n}/2$, then a and x differ in their nth significant digit by at most one. (*Hint:* First apply Exercise 2 to the case that $0.1 \leqslant x < 1.0$.)

4. Modify the algorithms in *bisect*, *secant*, and *newton* to stop when the relative error is small. [*Hint:* Define a function *relDiff*, to compute the relative difference between x and y, namely, $|x - y|/max(|x|, |y|)$. Be careful when both numbers are zero.]

5. With a hypothetical computer that has a 3-digit decimal integer significand and a 1-digit exponent, which of the following calculations produce the correct result?

    (a) $(10^3 + 1) - 1$

    (b) $(10^3 - 1) + 1$

    (c) $(10^4 - 1) + 1$

    (d) $(1 + 10^3) - 10^3$

    (e) $(10^3 + 1) + (10^3 - 1)$

    (f) $(10^3 - 1) - (10^3 - 1)$

6. Suppose that the absolute errors in the approximations a_1 and a_2 to two positive real numbers x_1 and x_2 are both less than e. How large can the absolute error be in the following approximations?

    (a) approximating $x_1 + x_2$ by $a_1 + a_2$

    (b) approximating $x_1 - x_2$ by $a_1 - a_2$

    (c) approximating $x_1 x_2$ by $a_1 a_2$

    (d) approximating x_1/x_2 by a_1/a_2

7. Repeat Exercise 6 for relative errors instead of absolute errors.

8. Suggest accurate ways to evaluate

    (a) $\displaystyle\sum_{n=1}^{100} \frac{1}{n} = 1 + \frac{1}{2} + \frac{1}{3} + \cdots + \frac{1}{100}$

    (b) $\displaystyle\sum_{n=1}^{100} \frac{(-1)^{n+1}}{n} = 1 - \frac{1}{2} + \frac{1}{3} - \cdots - \frac{1}{100}$

(c) $\sum_{n=1}^{100} cx_n$, where $|c|$ is small

9. Describe two ways in which rounding can affect the operation of the bisection algorithm. How serious are these effects?

10. Show that Newton's method converges linearly, rather than quadratically, to a zero of the function $f(x) = x^{1/n}$.

SUMMARY

Computers manipulate finite approximations to real numbers. Hence numeric algorithms (which accept real numbers as input and produce real numbers as output) are approximate in nature. Errors in numeric computations arise from

- finite measurements (data errors),
- finite-precision arithmetic (roundoff errors), and
- finite computations (algorithmic errors).

Good numeric algorithms converge quickly to accurate approximations.

Numeric algorithms can approximate quantities such as the value of a mathematical function, a zero of a function, or the area under a curve. Among the approaches to approximating zeroes of functions are

- the bisection method, which

    1. approximates a zero of a continuous function in an interval,
    2. requires the function to have opposite signs at the ends of the interval, and
    3. halves the error in the approximation with each iteration, adding one decimal digit of accuracy with every $\log_2 10$ or 3.32 iterations;

- Newton's method, which

    1. approximates a zero of a function by constructing tangents to its graph,
    2. requires the function to have a derivative,
    3. doubles the number of decimal digits of accuracy in a good approximation with each iteration, and
    4. can fail to converge;

- the secant method, which

    1. approximates a zero of a function by constructing secants to its graph,
    2. does not require evaluation of a derivative,
    3. requires somewhat more iterations than Newton's method, and
    4. can also fail to converge.

Simulation algorithms approximate the operation of real systems. They are based on mathematical models that describe the state of a system and the ways in which that state can change.

■ Deterministic simulations

 1. are appropriate for systems that change state predictably;

 2. are typified by simulation of motion; and

 3. divide time into discrete intervals and simulate the predicted change of state in each interval.

■ Nondeterministic simulations

 1. are appropriate for systems that change state under the influence of random phenomena;

 2. are typified by simulation of waiting lines;

 3. with a clock-driven strategy, divide time into small intervals and simulate the changes of state that occur in each interval;

 4. with an event-driven strategy, predict the time at which a system next changes state and simulate that change of state; and

 5. generate pseudorandom numbers to mimic random phenomena.

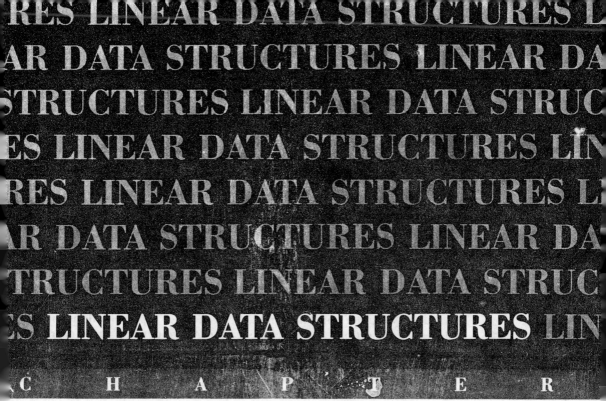

11

A *linear data structure* or *list* is a sequence of items of data. So far we have used two representations for lists: vectors (one-dimensional arrays) and files. Each of these representations has certain advantages. Since we can access items in a vector directly through their subscripts, we can search lists represented as vectors with efficient algorithms such as the binary search. And since files are dynamic rather than static data structures, we can allow lists that are represented as files to grow beyond the bounds imposed by particular programs.

However, our previous representations for lists share a major disadvantage: it can be costly to insert an item into, or to delete an item from, a list represented as a vector or a file. Unless that item is the last in the list, we must copy other items to make room or to close up a gap.

In this chapter and Chapter 12, we seek other representations for lists that make insertions and deletions easier. As we develop these representations, we will focus our attention on the operations needed to maintain different kinds of lists. The frequency with which various operations are performed usually determines the most appropriate representation for a list.

Many applications of computing use various representations for lists to economize on both time and storage. Typical examples of such applications are systems that allocate resources: an airline reservation system (which maintains a list of flights and lists of passengers holding reservations for those flights) or a multiprogrammed computer system (which maintains lists of active and inactive programs currently in and out of memory).

Vector and file representations for lists share a common handicap: it can be costly to reorganize a list if the reorganization involves moving many items of data. In programming languages such as Pascal, vectors have another handicap in that they are *static* data structures. The size of a static data structure is fixed when we write a program, not when we use it; such a structure always occupies the same amount of space in memory. Hence, if we represent a list as a vector, we must anticipate the maximum length of that list when we write a program; it is impossible to expand the list later to utilize whatever memory space is available. Furthermore, we may find it difficult to balance the space required by several static data structures: if we need to manipulate 100 lists, each of which may contain up to 1000 items, it may be too expensive to allocate 100 vectors with 1000 items apiece; yet, if most of the lists are short most of the time, we may need to keep far fewer than 100×1000 items at any given time.

File representations for lists overcome the disadvantages of static data structures. Files are *dynamic* data structures in that they can change in size while a program is running. But reorganizing a file stored on secondary storage is even more costly than reorganizing a vector. Furthermore, files in Pascal are sequential and do not support direct access. Hence we cannot use efficient algorithms such as the binary search with sequential files, and we must resort to less efficient algorithms such as the linear search.

Therefore we need to develop representations for lists as dynamic data structures in which insertions and deletions are relatively inexpensive. But less costly insertions and deletions do not come without cost: our new representations consume more storage per item than do vectors and files. And linear data structures, like files in Pascal, permit sequential access only. Hence we must search them linearly, rather than with a binary search. Nonlinear data structures, which we will study in Chapter 12, can support efficient searches in addition to insertions and deletions, but sometimes at the expense of consuming even more storage per item. Yet this extra storage per item is often a small price to pay for increased efficiency; many times, this price is more than offset by substantial savings in the total storage needed to maintain several lists.

POINTERS

We can reorganize a list more efficiently by using pointers to items in the list. To insert or remove an item from a list, we will manipulate pointers and avoid the expense of moving data. Twice in earlier chapters we used an index of pointers to arrange and rearrange data without having to move the data. In Section 8.5, we constructed a procedure *xsort* to sort an index *x* of pointers to rows in a table *a*. And in Chapter 9, such an index played a key role in a prototype database management system.

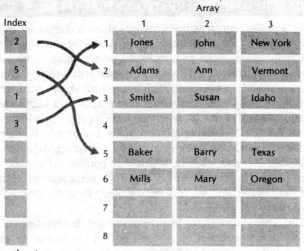

Figure 11.1 ■ Index of pointers to rows in an array

In those applications, a pointer $x[i]$ in an index x was simply a subscript that helped us locate an item $a[x[i], j]$ in a particular row and column of a table stored in an array a. Figure 11.1 illustrates one such indexed table. Here the index references some, but not all, the rows in the array. Both the index and the array contain unused space to allow for expansion. Reserving such extra space is the price we pay when we use static data structures to represent lists that can grow or shrink in size.

In the approach illustrated by Figure 11.1, there is no need for the data in the table to occupy consecutive rows in the array. So long as we always access data in the table indirectly through the index rather than directly, by referring to $a[x[i], j]$ rather than to $a[i, j]$, we do not care where the data actually reside in the array. Furthermore, we can rearrange the table by rearranging the index, delete an entry from the table by deleting a pointer from the index, or maintain an additional table in the same array simply by utilizing a second index.

In programming languages such as Pascal, we can do even better by dispensing with the array entirely. As we will see, we can store data in a dynamic data structure, rather than a static one such as an array, allocating exactly as much space as we need. Figure 11.2 illustrates how this might appear.

To declare a dynamic table such as this in Pascal, we proceed as follows. First, we declare the type

type *rowType* = **array** [1..*maxCols*] **of** *string*;

of a row in the table to be a vector with room for a single row. Now, instead of allocating a table as a static data structure

var *a* : **array** [1..*maxRows*] **of** *rowType*;

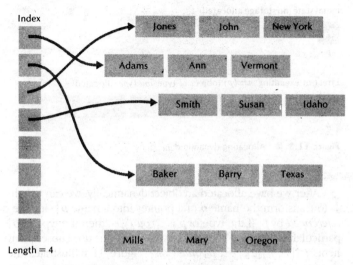

Figure 11.2 ■ Index of pointers to dynamic data

with a predetermined number *maxRows* of rows, we allocate rows dynamically as we need them, using the pointer data type in Pascal. Whereas the type of a pointer in Fig. 11.1 was a scalar subrange type

type *rowPtr* = 1..*maxRows*;

with values that served as subscripts in an array, the type of a pointer in Fig. 11.2 is a special *pointer type*

type *rowPtr* = ↑*rowType*;

in Pascal with values that point directly to, or *reference*, objects of type *rowType*. (The ↑ symbol suggests a pointer, and we read ↑*rowType* as "pointer to an object of type *rowType*.") For the approach shown in either figure, we declare the type

type *indexType* = **array** [1..*maxRows*] **of** *rowPtr*;

of the index to be a vector of pointers. Thus an index is a static data structure with exactly *maxRows* entries. But in Fig. 11.2, as opposed to Fig. 11.1, there is no array declaration that allocates space for the table itself.

To allocate space in a dynamic table, we use the procedure *new*, which is predefined by Pascal. If we declare a variable *p* using

var *p* : *rowPtr*;

then *p* takes pointers to rows as values, and the procedure invocation

new(*p*)

allocates space for an object of type *rowType*, assigning a pointer to this new object to *p*. Figure 11.3 illustrates the effect of allocating storage dynamically in this fashion.

Initial state (no storage allocated)

p

Effect of executing *new(p)* (object of type *rowType* allocated)

p

Figure 11.3 ■ Allocating dynamic data

After we have allocated an object dynamically, we can use the "points to" symbol ↑ to transform the name p of a pointer into a name p↑ for the object *pointed to* or *referenced* by p. If the type of p is ↑*rowType*, then the type of p↑ is *rowType*. In this particular example, p↑ is an array, and we can use subscripts to denote its components p↑[1], p↑[2], . . . , p↑[*maxCols*]. Figure 11.4 illustrates the effect of accessing dynamically allocated storage in this manner.

Note that Pascal utilizes similar notations for pointers and files. In both cases the symbol ↑ distinguishes the pointer or file itself from the item of data referenced by the pointer or included in the file. But there are important differences between the two uses of the symbol ↑. Hence, before proceeding further with our example involving an index of pointers, we need to summarize the treatment of pointers in Pascal.

Pointer declarations   The syntax diagram in Fig. 11.5 gives the precise syntax for specifying pointer types in type and variable declarations. Here the type identifier names any previously defined type (or, as we will see in Section 11.2, any type declared in the same declaration section). Hence

> **type** *stringType* = **packed array** [1..20] **of** *char*;
>   *stringPtr*   = ↑*stringType*;
>
> **var** *p* : ↑*real*;
>   *q* : *stringPtr*;
>   *r* : ↑*stringPtr*;

Effect of executing p↑[2] := 'John'

p↑

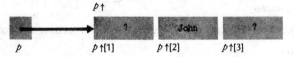

p p↑[1] p↑[2] p↑[3]

Figure 11.4 ■ Manipulating dynamic data

pointer type

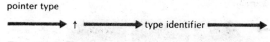

Figure 11.5 ■   Syntax diagram, pointer type

are legal declarations, whereas

>**var** *q* : ↑**packed array** [1..20] **of** *char*;

is not (since what follows the ↑ is not a type identifier). We can use pointers as
components of arrays and records; thus

>**type** *newStringType* = **record**
>>>*length*   : *integer*;
>>>*theString* : *stringPtr*
>>**end**;
>**var** *index* : **array** [1..*maxRows*] **of** *newStringType*;

are legal declarations. Pascal also allows pointers to occur as components of files, so
that

>**type** *stringFile* = **file of** *newStringType*;

is legal. Yet reading pointers previously written to files rarely has the expected result.
(See Exercise 4 at the end of this section.) Hence it is wisest to avoid mixing pointers
and files.

An important feature of Pascal is that it allows functions to return pointers as
values. Thus

>**function** *makeDynamic*(*s* : *stringType*) : *stringPtr*;

is a legal header for a function declaration in Pascal. In this respect, the pointer type
in Pascal is closer to the simple types than to the composite types.

Manipulating pointers   We can manipulate variables having values that are pointers just as we manipulate other variables in Pascal. Recall that we can assign a value
to a pointer by invoking the *new* procedure. We can also assign the value of one
pointer to another of the same type by using an assignment statement. Figure 11.6
illustrates the effect of such an assignment when *p* and *q* are both declared to be of
type *rowPtr*.

As Fig. 11.6 shows, assigning a pointer is similar to passing a variable by reference:
both actions create a new name for an existing object, and neither copies the object
itself. Furthermore, unless we keep a copy of the original value of a pointer *p*, we
will not be able to access the object that *p* referenced after we assign a new value
to *p*.

Pascal requires that the two pointers in an assignment statement have the same
type. (See Section 5.6.) For an assignment *p* := *q* to be valid when *p* and *q* are

Previous state of variables

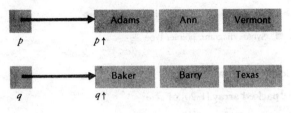

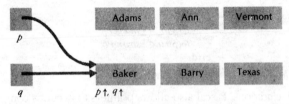

Figure 11.6 ■ Assignment of pointers

pointers, both p and q must be declared with the same type identifier, as in

> **var** p : *stringPtr*;
> q : *stringPtr*;

or with synonymous type identifiers, as in

> **type** *stringPtr1* = *stringPtr*;
> **var** p : *stringPtr*;
> q : *stringPtr1*;

or in the same variable declaration, as in

> **var** p, q : ↑*stringType*;

Pascal will disallow the assignment if p and q are simply equivalent types, as in

> **var** p : ↑*stringType*;
> q : ↑*stringType*;

We cannot read pointers from the file *input*, write them to the file *output*, or read or write them from or to any other text file. However we can read and write the objects they reference.

Pointers of the same type can appear in relational expressions such as $p = q$ and $p <> q$. As Fig. 11.7 shows, two pointers p and q can point to identical objects without $p = q$ being true. Hence $p = q$ is a sufficient, but not necessary, condition for $p\uparrow = q\uparrow$.

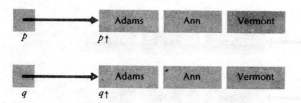

Figure 11.7 ■ Unequal pointers pointing to equal objects

Pascal provides a constant **nil** that belongs to every pointer data type. (See Fig. 11.8.) A pointer that has the value **nil** is said to point "nowhere." We can assign the value **nil** to a pointer by an assignment $p := $ **nil**, and we can test whether a pointer has this value using the expressions $p = $ **nil** and $p <> $ **nil**.

On many systems, all pointers receive an initial value of **nil**. When we are finished with the object referenced by a pointer p, we can set p to **nil** again. However, it is better to invoke the predefined procedure *dispose* by *dispose*(p) before setting p to **nil**. The *dispose* procedure releases the storage formerly occupied by $p\uparrow$, making it available for reuse later in the program.†

Figure 11.9 contrasts what happens when we use the *dispose* procedure to release storage with what happens when we do not. If we do not invoke *dispose*, any storage allocated by the *new* procedure remains allocated for the duration of the program, even though it may be inaccessible. Even exiting from a procedure in which storage was allocated by *new* does not release that storage because some value returned by the procedure may contain a pointer to the storage. Thus, to ensure that programs do not needlessly run out of dynamic storage, we should take care to release such storage when it is no longer needed.

---

†On some systems, *dispose*(p) will also set p to **nil**.

constant

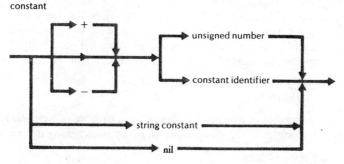

Figure 11.8 ■ Syntax diagram, constant (final version)

Initial state of variables

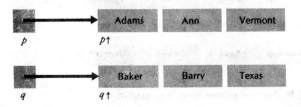

p $p\uparrow$

q $q\uparrow$

Effect of executing $p := q$ on initial state

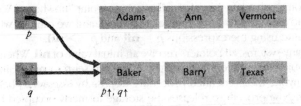

p

q $p\uparrow, q\uparrow$

Effect of executing $dispose(p)$; $p := q$ on initial state

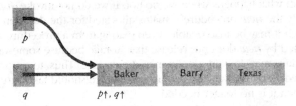

p

q $p\uparrow, q\uparrow$

Figure 11.9 ▓ Disposing of dynamic storage

Manipulating objects referenced by pointers If p is a variable with a value that is a pointer, then $p\uparrow$ is the object referenced by that pointer. The precise syntax for naming the object referenced by a pointer—called *dereferencing* that pointer—is the same as for naming the object referenced by a file buffer variable. (See Section 6.6.) In fact, a file buffer variable is nothing more than a pointer to an object in a file.

Suppose, for example, that we have declared *rowType* and *rowPtr* as before:

type *rowType* = **array** [1..*maxCols*] **of** *string*;
       rowPtr = ↑*rowType*;

If p is a variable of type *rowPtr*, then $p\uparrow$ is a variable of type *rowType*. Furthermore, we can manipulate the components of $p\uparrow$ by subscripting this variable, as in

    $p\uparrow[1]$:= 'Adams'

or in

   $write(p\uparrow[2])$

Since functions in Pascal can return pointers as values, we can even declare a function

   function $findRow(\ s : string\ ) : rowPtr;$

to search for a row containing a particular string, perform an assignment such as

   $p := findRow(\text{'Adams'})$

and afterwards reference $p\uparrow[3]$. But we cannot use a notation such as $findRow(\text{'Adams'})\uparrow[3]$ since Pascal uses the symbol $\uparrow$ to construct variables, not expressions, and variables must begin with a variable or field identifier, not with a function identifier.

Finally, there is an important difference between manipulating pointers and the objects they reference. It is instructive to contrast Fig. 11.6, in which we copied a pointer and did not move data, with Fig. 11.10, in which we copy an object referenced by a pointer and move data as a result. Whereas the assignment $p := q$ in Fig. 11.6 makes p the same as q (makes it point to the same place), the assignment $p\uparrow := q\uparrow$ in Fig. 11.10 makes the object that p references the same as that which q references (copies data from place to place).

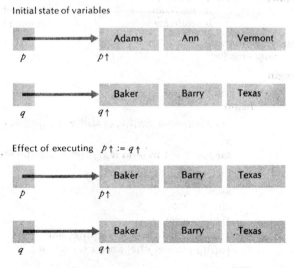

Figure 11.10 ■ Assignment of data indicated by pointers

Manipulating an index of pointers   Let us return now to the task of constructing and manipulating an index of pointers to rows in a table. Recapitulating our earlier development, we have declared an index x to a dynamic table.

type *rowType*   = **array** [1..*maxCols*] **of** *string*;
   rowPtr   = ↑*rowType*;
   indexType = **array** [1..*maxRows*] **of** *rowPtr*;
var x : *indexType*;

Thus x is a static data structure with **maxRows** entries. But the table referenced by x is a dynamic data structure. Initially, this table does not contain any entries. When we need to allocate a new row in a table, we can do so by a statement such as *new*(x[3]). Later we can manipulate the components of that row using subscripted variables such as x[3] ↑ [j].

In Section 8.5 we constructed a library *xsort1* that contained the procedure *xsort* to sort the rows in a table by rearranging an index of row subscripts rather than by rearranging the table itself. We now modify that procedure to create a new library *xsort2*, displayed as Pascal Sample 11.1, which uses an index of pointers and which

---

■ **PASCAL SAMPLE 11.1**   The procedure *xsort2*

{ *xsort2*: sorts index x of pointers to vectors a using $a[k]$ as key }
{ returns x rearranged so that $x[1]↑[k] <= x[2]↑[k] <= ... <= x[n]↑[k]$ }
procedure *xsort* (**var** x : *indexType*;   { index to table   }
              n : *rowIndex*;   { length of index }
              k : *colIndex*);   { column for key   }
   var i, j, p : *rowIndex*;
      temp : *rowPtr*;
   begin
      for $i := 1$ **to** $n - 1$ **do**
         begin
            { find minimum $x[p]↑[k]$ of $x[i]↑[k]$, ..., $x[n]↑[k]$ }

            $p := i$;
            for $j := i + 1$ **to** n **do if** $x[j]↑[k] < x[p]↑[k]$ **then** $p := j$;
            { interchange $x[i]$ and $x[p]$ }

            temp := $x[i]$;
            $x[i]$:= $x[p]$;
            $x[p]$:= *temp*
            { now $x[1]↑[k] <= ... <= x[i]↑[k]$ and   }
            { $x[i]↑[k] <= x[j]↑[k]$ when $i < j <= n$ }
         end
   end;   { of *xsort* }

represents the table as a dynamic data structure rather than a static data structure. As a result, the table no longer appears as a parameter to the procedure *xsort*; the pointers in the index x suffice to locate the rows in that table.

EXERCISES

1. Suppose that p, q, and r are declared to be pointers to integers. What are the effects of the following sequences of statements? (Draw diagrams to justify your conclusions.)

    (a) *new(p)*;
    $p\uparrow := 1$;
    $q := p$;
    $p\uparrow := 2$;
    write(p↑, q↑);

    (b) *new(p)*;
    $p\uparrow := 1$;
    $q\uparrow := p\uparrow$;
    $p\uparrow := 2$;
    write(p↑, q↑);

    (c) *new(p)*;
    $p\uparrow := 1$;
    $q := p$;
    dispose(p);
    write(q↑);

    (d) *new(p)*;
    $p\uparrow := 1$;
    $q\uparrow := p\uparrow$;
    dispose(p);
    write(q↑);

2. Write a program to test and time the index sort procedure in *xsort2*.

3. Rewrite *indexSubs* and *info* from Chapter 9 using a dynamic data structure for the working database instead of a static one.

4. Experiment with files of pointers on your system. Create a long string and a pointer to it. Then write that pointer to a file. If you later read the pointer from the file, does it point to the same string? What happens if you dispose of the pointer to the string before rereading it? What happens if the file is an external file and you use a separate program to reread the pointer?

11.2   LINKED LISTS

Indices of pointers help us conserve space when maintaining lists that change in size. But they help us only slightly when we need to insert an item into, or remove one from, the middle of a list. Indices are lists, and in order to insert a pointer into the

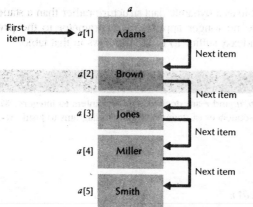

Figure 11.11 ■ Vector a with implicit pointers indicating order of items

middle of an index, or to remove such a pointer, we must move all subsequent pointers in the index to make room or to close a gap. We save some effort by not moving the data referenced by these pointers, but we must still move the pointers.

A more imaginative use of pointers can help much more with insertions and deletions. To see how, let us first visualize a list represented as a vector as having implicit pointers from each item in the list to the next. (See Fig. 11.11.) These pointers indicate the order in which we examine items during a linear search.

Now let us make these implicit pointers explicit and, simultaneously, use them to distinguish the physical order of items in a vector from the logical order in which

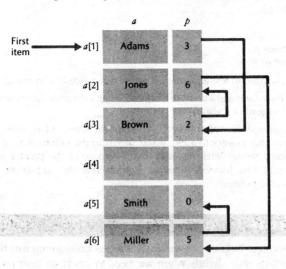

Figure 11.12 ■ Vector p of explicit pointers indicating order of items in a

we want to access them. By following explicit pointers, we can access the items in a list in an order independent of where they are stored in memory, and we can skip over potential gaps in a list. Furthermore, by changing pointers, it will be easy to insert items into or remove them from a list. Figure 11.12 illustrates how we can access items in a list in a predetermined order by creating a vector of subscripts to serve as explicit pointers into a vector representing the list; there an illegal subscript, 0, marks the end of the list.

Better yet, we can represent a list as a dynamic data structure by using actual pointers in Pascal rather than as a static data structure with subscripts as pointers. Figure 11.13 illustrates how we can depict a list not as a sequence of contiguous entries but as a sequence of entries in an order that is determined solely by pointers leading from one entry to another; there the end of the list is marked by a **nil** pointer. We call such a representation a *linked list*.

To declare a linked list in Pascal, we use the record and pointer data types. A *node* in a linked list is a record containing an *item* of data and a *link* to another node; a linked list is simply a pointer to the first node in the list.

```
{ declaration for linked list }
type itemType  = . . . ;
     linkedList = ↑node;
     node       = record
                    item : itemType;
                    link : linkedList
                  end;

var p : linkedList;
```

The last node in a linked list, by convention, contains a pointer with a value of **nil**, since there is nowhere else for that pointer to point. An empty linked list is likewise represented by a **nil** pointer. Figure 11.14 illustrates these conventions.

Two technicalities in our declaration of a linked list deserve attention. First, we have declared a link to have type *linkedList* rather than ↑*node* to give that type an

First item

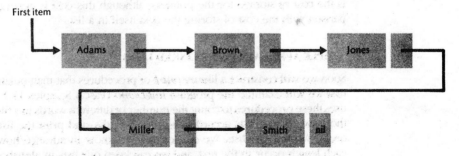

Figure 11.13 ■ Linked list with pointers indicating order of items

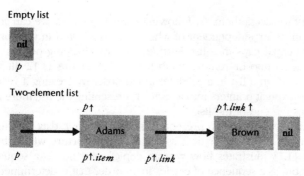

Figure 11.14 ■ Pascal representation of linked lists

explicit name and to make a pointer to the first node in a linked list have the "same" type as pointers to subsequent nodes. If we had not done this, the Pascal rules governing the assignment of pointers would make it awkward to manipulate pointers in a linked list. By doing this, we can manipulate pointers easily. Furthermore, we have a useful alternative conception of a linked list: any nonempty linked list is composed of a first item, called the *head* of the list, and another linked list, called the *tail* of the list, that contains all items other than the first. The first conception of linked lists—as sequences of nodes connected by pointers—leads naturally to iterative algorithms for processing lists. The second conception leads naturally to recursive algorithms.

Second, as is natural in a recursive setting, the declarations of *linkedList* and *node* refer to one another. To get around the chicken-and-egg problem of which to declare first, we make use of the convention (noted in Section 11.1) that allows the declaration of a pointer type to precede the declaration of the type referenced by that pointer.

The linked representation for lists makes it easy to insert items in and delete them from lists. By manipulating pointers we can avoid moving data. The principal price we pay for this is that the only way to find the *n*th item in a linked list is to start at the first item and follow the pointers until the *n*th item is reached. Also, there is the cost of storage for the pointers, although this cost is generally small in comparison with the cost of storing the data itself in a list.

SAMPLE APPLICATIONS OF LINKED LISTS

Soon we will construct a library *link1* of procedures that manipulate linked lists. But first we will examine the program *linkDemo* (Pascal Samples 11.2 and 11.3), which uses these procedures to count the number of different words in a file of text, separate those words into lists according to their lengths, and print the lists in alphabetical order. With linked lists, we do not need to know in advance how many words of each length occur in the text, and we can keep our lists in alphabetical order as we construct them without moving large amounts of data.

When given a possibly familiar file of text, *linkDemo* produces the output displayed in Pascal Sample 11.4.

Although *linkDemo* contains three type declarations (for *itemType, linkedList,* and *node*) that will be used by the procedures in *link1*, the way in which lists of words are represented makes no difference to *linkDemo*. We declare lists *lists*[1], ..., *lists*[*nCats*] to be of type *linkedList* and invoke four procedures in *link1* to maintain and manipulate these lists: the *startList* procedure to initialize a list to the empty list, the *inList* function to determine whether a particular word is already entered in a list, the *insert* procedure to enter a word in alphabetical order in a list, and the *print* procedure to print the words contained in a list. Thus the program *linkDemo* treats a list as an abstract data type maintained by the procedures in *link1*.

■ **PASCAL SAMPLE 11.2**   The program *linkDemo* (declarations)

```
{ demonstrates use of linked lists by extracting words from a file }
{ and placing them in linked lists according to their category     }
{ (here category = length)                                         }

program linkDemo(input, output, source);

const nCats        = 26;              { number of categories }
      stringLength = 16;

type string    = packed array [1..stringLength] of char;
     itemType  = string;
     linkedList = ↑node;
     node      = record
                       item : itemType;
                       link : linkedList
                 end;

var filename : string;
    source   : text;
    word     : string;
    nWords   : integer;
    nDiff    : integer;
    lists    : array [1..nCats] of linkedList;
    count    : array [1..nCats] of integer;
    distinct : array [1..nCats] of integer;
    c        : 1..nCats;

#include 'stringSubs2';          { readString, skipBlanks }
#include 'link1';                { linked list procedures }

function category( s : string ) : integer;
    { returns the category in which s falls }
    begin
        category := length(s)
    end;   { of category }
```

PASCAL SAMPLE 11.3   The program *linkDemo* (main program)

```
begin
    write('File name:  ');
    readString(input, filename);
    reset(source, filename);
    for c := 1 to nCats do { initialize lists and counts }
        begin
            startList(lists[c]);
            count[c] := 0;
            distinct[c] := 0
        end;
    nWords := 0;
    nDiff   := 0;
    skipBlanks(source);
    while not eof(source) do { extract words from file }
        begin
            readString(source, word);
            nWords := nWords + 1;
            c := category(word);
            count[c] := count[c] + 1;
            if not inList(lists[c], word) then
                begin
                    nDiff := nDiff + 1;
                    insert(lists[c], word);
                    distinct[c] := distinct[c] + 1
                end;
            skipBlanks(source)
        end;
    writeln;
    write('There are ', nWords:1, ' in all, ');
    writeln(nDiff:1, ' of which are distinct.');
    for c := 1 to nCats do { display lists }
        if count[c] > 0 then
            begin
                writeln;
                write('List ', c:1, ' contains ', count[c]:1, ' words, ');
                write(distinct[c]:1, ' of which are distinct.  ');
                writeln('They are:');
                print(lists[c]);
                writeln
            end
end.   { of linkDemo }
```

■ **PASCAL SAMPLE 11.4**   The program *linkDemo* (sample use)

```
File name: words
There are 25 words in all, 21 of which are distinct.

List 1 contains 1 words, 1 of which are distinct.  They are:
a

List 2 contains 3 words, 3 of which are distinct.  They are:
of              to              up

List 3 contains 5 words, 3 of which are distinct.  They are:
and             his             the

List 4 contains 10 words, 8 of which are distinct.  They are:
came            down            fell            hill
jack            jill            pail            went

List 5 contains 5 words, 5 of which are distinct.  They are:
after           broke           crown           fetch
water

List 8 contains 1 words, 1 of which are distinct.  They are:
tumbling
```

We can easily change the criterion used by *linkDemo* to place a word in a list by changing the definition of the *category* function. For example, to place a word in one of 26 lists according to its first letter (which is assumed to be lowercase), we can use the following definition of the *category* function:

```
function category( s : string ) : integer;
    begin
        category := ord(s[1]) − ord('a') + 1
    end;   { of category }
```

Thus *linkDemo* is actually a general purpose program for sorting words from a text into categories.

In another application of linked lists, we exhibit the sorting procedure *sort* in a library *sort6* that sorts an array by inserting its elements one by one in the proper order into an initially empty linked list and then by copying the linked list back into the array. (See Pascal Sample 11.5.) The execution times of this variant of the insertion sort on a VAX 750 running Berkeley Pascal are less than those of the procedures in *sort1* through *sort4* that we developed in Chapter 8: even though *sort6* still performs between $n - 1$ and $n(n - 1)/2$ comparisons when sorting a list of length n, it moves each item of data only twice, once from the array into the linked list and once back into the array. Thus it is quicker than the selection sort in *sort1*, which always

■ **PASCAL SAMPLE 11.5**   The library *sort6* (insertion sort using linked list)

{ *sort6*: insertion sort of $a[1]$, ..., $a[n]$ using a linked list }

procedure *sort*(**var** *a* : *itemList*;   { list to sort   }
                    n : *index*);   { length of list }

 type *linkedList* = ↑*node*;
    node   = **record**
         item : *itemType*;
         link : *linkedList*
       end;

 var *i* : *index*;
    p : *linkedList*;

#include 'link1';

 begin
   { create linked list containing $a[1]$, ..., $a[n]$ in order }
   startList(*p*);
   for *i* := 1 **to** *n* **do** *insert*(*p*, *a*[*i*]);
   { copy linked list back into $a[1]$, ..., $a[n]$ }
   for *i* := 1 **to** *n* **do** *pop*(*p*, *a*[*i*])
 end;   { of *sort* }

performs $n(n - 1)/2$ comparisons, and it is quicker than the insertion sort in *sort4*, which can move up to $n(n - 1)/2$ items of data.

 Like *linkDemo*, *sort6* invokes the *startList* procedure from *link1* to create an empty list *p*, and it uses the *insert* procedure to insert new items in order in that list. To copy the linked list *p* back into the array *a* in order, *sort6* invokes the *pop* procedure from *link1* to remove items one at a time from the beginning of the list *p*.

PROCEDURES TO MAINTAIN A LINKED LIST

Let us now build the library *link1* of procedures to maintain linked lists. To guide our intuition, we will keep Fig. 11.15 in mind. It depicts a typical linked list consisting of a sequence of nodes linked by pointers. Each node contains an item of data and a link to the next node in the list. A separate pointer points to the first node in a list, and a pointer of **nil** indicates the end of the list. Comments at the beginning of *link1*

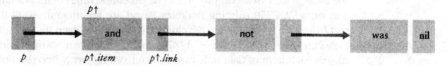

Figure 11.15 ■ Typical linked list

PASCAL SAMPLE 11.6 The library *link1* (description)

```
{ link1: iterative procedures to manipulate a linked list }

{     The following procedures and functions are available for }
{ manipulating a linked list p:                                 }
{                                                               }
{ Procedures:                                                   }
{                                                               }
{ delete(p, x)      deletes all entries containing x from p     }
{ insert(p, x)      inserts an entry containing x in order in p }
{ pop(p, x)         removes the first entry from p and assigns  }
{                   its contents to x                           }
{ print(p)          prints the contents of all entries in p     }
{ push(p, x)        inserts an entry containing x in front of p }
{ startList(p)      initializes p to be an empty list           }
{                                                               }
{ Functions:                                                    }
{                                                               }
{ emptyList(p)      returns true if p is an empty list          }
{ inList(p, x)      returns true if an entry in p contains x     }
{                                                               }
{     Any program calling one of these procedures or            }
{ functions must contain the following declarations:            }
{ (Here itemType is a real, ordinal, or string type.)           }
{                                                               }
{ type itemType  = ...;                                         }
{      linkedList = ↑node;                                      }
{      node       = record                                      }
{                       item : itemType;                        }
{                       link : linkedList                       }
{                   end;                                        }
```

describe the procedures that manipulate linked lists together with the declarations required to use those procedures. (See Pascal Sample 11.6.)

We define the procedures in *link1* using iteration to move along the sequence of nodes in a list. The *print* procedure in *link1* is typical of iterative list-processing procedures, accessing each item in a linked list in succession. This procedure is similar to the usual procedure for printing the items in a list represented as a vector $item[1], \ldots, item[n]$. In the abstract, both procedures follow the same recipe:

```
locate the first item in the list;
while items remain in the list do
    begin
        display the current item;
        locate the next item
    end
```

In order to print the first n items in a vector, we generally refine this recipe in a fashion equivalent to the following.

```
next := 1;
while next <= n do
    begin
        write(item[next]);
        next := next + 1
    end
```

Here we use the variable *next* to indicate the next item in the list. Initially this variable points to the first item in the list. So long as it points within the list, we print the indicated item and advance *next* to point to the next item in the list.

Since *link1* represents lists as linked lists and not as vectors, we must refine the recipe somewhat differently for use in the *print* procedure. However, the refinement proceeds almost exactly as before: we simply replace the mechanisms for locating the first item in a list, extracting an item from the list, locating the next item, and detecting the end of a list by mechanisms appropriate for linked lists. Thus, if p points to the first item in a linked list,

$next := 1$	becomes	$next := p,$
$item[next]$	becomes	$next\uparrow.item,$
$next := next + 1$	becomes	$next := next\uparrow.link,$ and
$next <= n$	becomes	$next <> nil.$

The effect of these replacements is illustrated in Pascal Sample 11.7, which exhibits the declaration of the procedure *print*.

As an alternative to this iterative definition of *print*, we could have constructed a recursive definition. In the case of *print*, recursion presents no real advantages over iteration. But for several other procedures, recursive definitions can be much clearer and more compact. Hence it is worthwhile to examine recursive alternatives even to

---

■ PASCAL SAMPLE 11.7   The library *link1* (*print* procedure)

procedure *print* (*p* : *linkedList*);

   { prints the contents of all entries in the list *p* }

   var *next* : *linkedList*;

   begin

      next := *p*;

      while *next* <> **nil do**

         begin

            write(*next*↑.*item*);

            next := *next*↑.*link*

         end

   end;   { of *print* }

■ **PASCAL SAMPLE 11.8** The library *link1r* (recursive *print* procedure)

procedure *print*(*p* : *linkedList*);

  { prints all entries in the list *p* }

  begin

    if *p* <> **nil then**

      begin

        write(*p*↑.*item*);

        print(*p* ↑ .*link*)

      end

  end; { of *print* }

simple procedures such as *print*. At the very least, such an examination increases our understanding of recursion.

As we have noted, the declaration of linked lists in Pascal makes it natural for us to employ recursion. According to that definition, a nonempty linked list consists of an item at the head of the list and another linked list, called the tail, that contains the remaining items. Hence we can display the contents of a linked list using the following recursive recipe.

    if the list is not empty **then**

      begin

        display the item at the head of the list;

        display the tail of the list

      end

Pascal Sample 11.8, taken from a library *link1r* of recursive procedures that perform the same tasks as the iterative procedures in *link1*, refines this recipe into an alternative declaration for the *print* procedure.

Similar to the *print* procedure is the *inList* function (Pascal Sample 11.9), which conducts a linear search of a linked list. The iterative definition of this function also utilizes a loop; it searches for the desired item *x*, starting at the first item in the list and advancing the pointer *next* until either *x* is found or the end of the list is reached.

Just as *print* can be written either iteratively or recursively, so can *inList*. Pascal Sample 11.10 shows the recursive version: *x* cannot be in an empty linked list, and it is in a nonempty list if it is either at the head of the list or in the tail (a fact that can be checked recursively).

If Pascal evaluated logical expressions from left to right, we could define the *inList* procedure much more compactly as

$$inList := (p <> \textbf{nil}) \textbf{ and } ((x = p{\uparrow}.item) \textbf{ or } inList(p{\uparrow}.link, x))$$

However, Pascal specifies full evaluation of logical expressions, so such a definition has serious flaws: *inList* invokes itself endlessly until *p* = **nil**, at which time evaluation

---

■ **PASCAL SAMPLE 11.9**   The library *link1* (*inList* procedure)

function *inList*(*p* : *linkedList*; *x* : *itemType*) : *boolean*;
  { returns *true* if *x* is in linked list *p* }
  var *found* : *boolean*;
    next   : *linkedList*;
  begin
    found := *false*;
    next   := *p*;
    while not *found* **and** (*next* <> **nil**) **do**
      if *x* = *next*↑.*item* **then**
        found := *true*
      else
        next := *next*↑.*link*;
    inList := *found*
  end;   { of *inList* }

of *p*↑.*item* results in an error because *p*↑ is undefined. Hence we must use the less compact definition shown in Pascal Sample 11.10.

Let us now turn our attention to the construction of lists that can be processed by the *print* and *inList* procedures. The *startList* procedure creates an empty list and is the same in *link1* and *link1r*. (See Pascal Sample 11.11.)

Why do we bother declaring a procedure for something so simple? We do so to separate the operations that maintain a list from the representation for that list. If a program sets *p* to **nil** directly, without invoking *startList*, it is dependent on the particular representation we have chosen for linked lists. Since we are more likely to change the representation for a linked list (say, to make it easier to find the last item in the list) than the operations we perform on the list, it pays not to make our programs overly dependent on the representation. If a program manipulates lists

---

■ **PASCAL SAMPLE 11.10**   The library *link1r* (recursive *inList* procedure)

function *inList*(*p* : *linkedList*; *x* : *itemType*) : *boolean*;
  { returns *true* if *x* is in linked list *p* }
  begin
    if *p* = **nil then**
      inList := *false*
    else if *x* = *p*↑.*item* **then**
      inList := *true*
    else
      inList := *inList*(*p*↑.*link*, *x*)
  end;   { of *inList* }

PASCAL SAMPLE 11.11   The library *link1* (*startList* procedure)

procedure *startList*(**var** *p* : *linkedList*);
   { initializes *p* to the empty list }
   begin
      p := **nil**
   end;   { of *startList* }

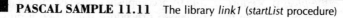

PASCAL SAMPLE 11.12   The library *link1* (*emptyList* function)

function *emptyList*(*p* : *linkedList*) : *boolean*;
   { returns *true* if list *p* is empty }
   begin
      emptyList := (*p* = **nil**)
   end;   { of *emptyList* }

---

only through the procedures in *link1*, we can change the representation of those lists by minor, rather than major, surgery. So that programs can determine whether a list is empty without depending on the representation for the list, we also define the function *emptyList*, shown as Pascal Sample 11.12.

If we want to add items to lists created by *startList*, we need additional procedures that correspond to where we want those items: at the beginning of a list, in the middle, or at the end. Of these locations, the first is the easiest to achieve (though not always the most useful). In order to add an item at the end or in the middle of a list, we must find the end or the appropriate place in the middle; in order to add an item at the beginning of a list, we need look only at the pointer to its first item.

We consider first the simplest operation of adding an item at the beginning of a linked list. The *push* procedure in *link1* (Pascal Sample 11.13), which is identical to

---

PASCAL SAMPLE 11.13   The library *link1* (*push* procedure)

procedure *push*(**var** *p* : *linkedList*; *x* : *itemType*);
   { puts an entry containing *x* at the beginning of list *p* }
   var *q* : *linkedList*;
   begin
      new(*q*);   { allocate entry   }
      q↑.*item* := *x*;   { store *x* there   }
      q↑.*link* := *p*;   { link to rest of list }
      p := *q*   { make it first in list }
   end;   { of *push* }

the *push* procedure in *link1r*, accomplishes this task. It obtains a node to hold the item by invoking the predefined procedure *new*. Then it puts this node at the beginning of a linked list *p* by changing two pointers: the pointer in the new node must point to the item formerly first in the list, and *p* itself must point to the new first node. The order in which we change these pointers, as shown in Pascal Sample 11.13, is crucial to prevent destruction of a link.

Figure 11.16 illustrates the sequence of changes that occur when we invoke the *push* procedure to add an entry containing the word too at the beginning of a linked list *p*. Note that the same sequence of changes also works when the list *p* is empty initially. In that case, the value **nil** assigned to *p* is copied into the link in the node containing too, making that node the only one in the new list.

State of variables upon entry to *push*

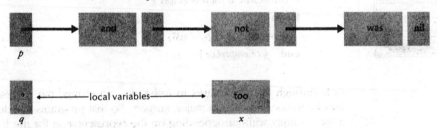

State after executing *new(q)*; *q↑.item := x*; *q↑.link := p*

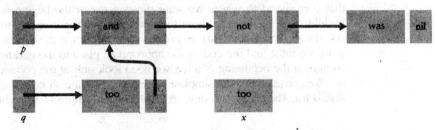

State of variables after exit from *push*

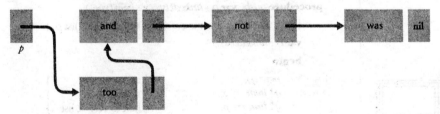

Figure 11.16 ■ Pushing an item onto the head of a list

PASCAL SAMPLE 11.14 The library *link1* (*pop* procedure)

procedure *pop*(**var** *p* : *linkedList*; **var** *x* : *itemType*);
    { removes first entry from list *p*, assigns contents to *x* }
    var *q* : *linkedList*;
    begin
        if *p* <> **nil then**
            begin
                x := *p*↑.*item*;   { extract item   }
                q := *p*;   { remember entry }
                p := *p*↑.*link*;   { remove it   }
                dispose(*q*)   { release storage }
            end
        else
            writeln('Attempt to pop empty list ignored.')
    end; { of *pop* }

Just as it is easiest to add an item at the beginning of a linked list, so too is it easiest to delete the first item. The procedure *pop* in *link1* and *link1r* sets its second argument equal to the first item in a linked list and removes that item from the linked list, calling the *dispose* procedure to release the node that contained the item. As in the definition of *push*, the sequence of steps in the definition of *pop* displayed as Pascal Sample 11.14 is crucial. Figure 11.17 illustrates the sequence of changes that occur when we invoke the *pop* procedure.

Linked lists maintained by using the *push* and *pop* procedures alone are known as *stacks* or *last-in first-out* (*LIFO*) lists. Such lists are analogous to stacks of plates in spring-loaded receptacles found in many cafeterias. Only the plate on top of a stack is readily accessible. When that plate is removed, the rest of the stack pops up to provide access to the next plate. When a plate is added to a stack, its weight pushes

State of variables upon entry to *pop*

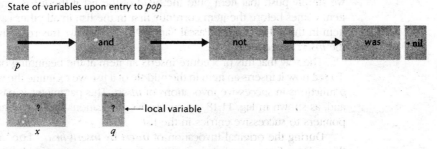

Figure 11.17 ■ Popping an item off the head of a list

(continued)

State after $x := p\uparrow.item; q := p; p := p\uparrow.link;$

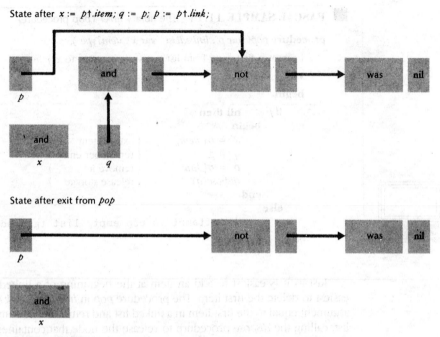

State after exit from *pop*

Figure 11.17 ■ Popping an item off the head of a list

the stack down. And the plate added last to a stack is the first to be removed. Stacks are important data structures in their own right. As we will see in Section 11.4, they can be applied to implement procedure calls and to convert recursive procedures into iterative ones.

The remaining two procedures in *link1* and *link1r* enable us to insert and delete items other than at the head of a linked list. Here recursion leads to simpler definitions than does iteration. For example, to insert an item in order in a linked list, we simply push that item onto the head of the list if the list is empty or if the new item comes before the item currently first in the list; in all other cases, we insert the item in the tail of the list. Pascal Sample 11.15 displays this recursive formulation of the *insert* procedure.

The way that this procedure inserts an item at the beginning of a list is obvious. To see how it inserts an item in the middle of a list, we examine the way the parameter *p* functions in successive invocations of *insert*. This parameter is passed by reference and, as shown in Fig. 11.18, on successive invocations of *insert* it acts as an alias for pointers to successive entries in the list.

During the original invocation of *insert* by *insert(first,* 'too'), *p* is an alias for the pointer *first* to the first item in the list. Since *x* is greater than $p\uparrow.item$ (which is

---

PASCAL SAMPLE 11.15 The library *link1r* (recursive *insert* procedure)

procedure *insert*(**var** *p* : *linkedList*; *x* : *itemType*);
  { inserts a new entry containing *x* in an ordered list *p* }
  begin
    if *p* = **nil then**
      push(*p*, *x*)   { new entry is only one }
    else if *x* < *p*↑.*item* **then**
      push(*p*, *x*)   { new entry is first   }
    else
      insert(*p*↑.*link*, *x*)   { new entry is in middle }
  end; { of *insert* }

---

an alias for *first*↑.*item*), *insert* invokes itself recursively by *insert*(*p*↑.*link*, *x*). The formal parameter *p* in this second invocation of *insert* is an alias for the actual parameter *p*↑.*link* supplied by the first invocation, which itself is an alias for *first*↑.*link*. Hence the formal parameter *p* in the second invocation of *insert* is an alias for the link to the second item in the list. Likewise, the formal parameter *p* in the third invocation of *insert* is an alias for the link to the third item in the list. Since *x* is now less than *p*↑.*item*, the third invocation of *insert* calls the *push* procedure by *push*(*p*, *x*). The effect of this call is as follows: *push* creates a new node for the list, puts 'too' in this node, sets the link in this node equal to *p* (which is an alias for the link to the third item in the list), and finally makes *p* point to this new node; but

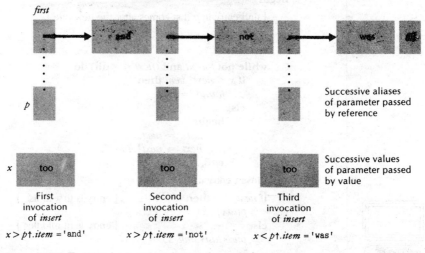

Figure 11.18 ■ Formal parameters of *insert* after *insert*(*first*, 'too')

since p is an alias for the link to the third item in the list, this link now points to the new node and the insertion is complete.

What makes the recursive definition of the *insert* procedure particularly short is the fact that all this bookkeeping goes on behind the scenes. If, instead, we want to provide an iterative definition of *insert*, we must do this bookkeeping ourselves, and we must exercise considerable care in doing so. First of all, we must search the list for an item y that is larger than the new item x; only then do we know where x belongs in the list. Then we must insert a node containing x immediately before the node containing y or at the end of the list if there is no such y. But to do this, we must back up to the last node we examined in order to link that node to x. It is precisely here that recursion helps us with the bookkeeping: the parameter p in the call of *insert* is an alias for the link that must be changed.

Backing up in a list using iteration would be easier if the list were *doubly linked* with *backward pointers* to help traverse the list in reverse. [See Exercise 9(a) at the end of this section.] With single links, we must keep track of the last node examined as well as the next one to be examined, looping until we find the place to insert x or until we reach the end of the list. When we find where x belongs, we invoke the

---

■ PASCAL SAMPLE 11.16   The library *link1* (*insert* procedure)

procedure *insert*(**var** p : *linkedList*; x : *itemType*);
    { inserts a new entry containing x in an ordered list p }
    var *last, next* : *linkedList*;
        found   : *boolean*;
begin
    { find entry in p that comes after the new one }
    found := *false*;
    next   := p;
    while not *found* **and** (*next* <> **nil**) **do**
        if x < *next*↑.*item* **then**
            found := *true*
        else
            begin
                last   := *next*;
                next := *next*↑.*link*
            end;
    { insert entry in list }
    if *next* = p **then**   { entry is first in list }
        push(p, x)
    else   { entry is in middle }
        push(*last*↑.*link*, x)
end; { of *insert* }

push procedure to put it there, being careful to note whether we are putting x at the beginning of the list or later in the list. Pascal Sample 11.16 displays an iterative definition for *insert* based on this strategy. The state of *insert* just before it invokes the *push* procedure to insert the new item is illustrated in Fig. 11.19.

To delete all entries containing a particular item from a linked list, it is again easier to proceed by recursion. We simply pop the first node off the list if it contains that item and use recursion to remove further entries from the tail of the list. Pascal Sample 11.17 presents such a definition of the *delete* procedure.

If we choose to delete entries from a linked list iteratively, rather than recursively, we not only need to find those entries, but we must also remember the preceding nodes in order to change the pointers there. The iterative definition of the *delete*

State prior to inserting too via *push*(*last*↑*.link*, x)

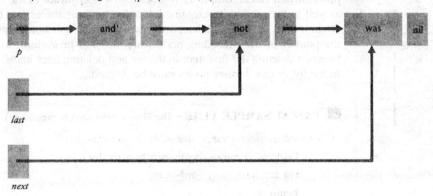

State prior to inserting act via *push*(*p*, x)

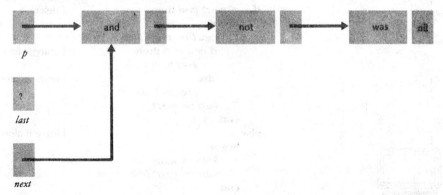

Figure 11.19 ■ Locating where to insert new entries in a list

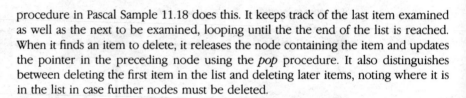

PASCAL SAMPLE 11.17   The library *link1r* (*delete* procedure)

procedure *delete*(**var** *p* : *linkedList*; *x* : *itemType*);
   { deletes all entries containing *x* from the list *p* }
   begin
      if *p* <> **nil then**
         begin
            delete(*p*↑.*link*, *x*);
            if *x* = *p*↑.*item* **then** *pop*(*p*, *x*)   { delete entry }
         end
   end;   { of *delete* }

procedure in Pascal Sample 11.18 does this. It keeps track of the last item examined as well as the next to be examined, looping until the the end of the list is reached. When it finds an item to delete, it releases the node containing the item and updates the pointer in the preceding node using the *pop* procedure. It also distinguishes between deleting the first item in the list and deleting later items, noting where it is in the list in case further nodes must be deleted.

PASCAL SAMPLE 11.18   The library *link1* (*delete* procedure)

procedure *delete*(**var** *p* : *linkedList*; *x* : *itemType*);
   { deletes all entries containing *x* from the list *p* }
   var *last*, *next*, *next1* : *linkedList*;
   begin
      next := *p*;
      while *next* <> **nil do**   { examine next entry }
         if *x* = *next*↑.*item* **then**   { delete it   }
            begin
               next1 := *next*↑.*link*;
               if *next* = *p* **then**   { entry is first in list   }
                  pop(*p*, *x*)
               else   { entry is later in list }
                  pop(*last*↑.*link*, *x*);
               next := *next1*
            end
         else   { leave it alone   }
            begin
               last := *next*;
               next := *next*↑.*link*
            end
   end;   { of *delete* }

Our library of procedures that manipulate linked lists is now complete. In the process of constructing this library, we have gained further practice in using the important tool of recursion. This tool, although dispensable, has enabled us to create more succinct definitions than those based on iteration. We will exploit this benefit of recursion in the last two chapters as we attack much more ambitious problems.

EXERCISES

1. Write procedures suitable for inclusion in the library *link1* to
   (a) add a new item to the end of a list;
   (b) append one list to the end of another;
   (c) copy a list;
   (d) test whether two lists contain identical sequences of items; and
   (e) reverse the order of the items in a list.

   These procedures should perform their tasks by manipulating pointers only; no data should be moved.

2. Repeat Exercise 1, but define procedures for inclusion in *link1r* by recursion rather than by iteration. In which cases does recursion lead to substantially simpler definitions than iteration?

3. Modify *linkDemo* so that
   (a) all words in the text are entered in some list, even if they duplicate words already there; and
   (b) the words in the lists are arranged in the order in which they occur in the text, not in alphabetical order.

4. Create a streamlined version of the library *link1*, as follows. Include the *startList* and *print* procedures. Create a procedure *insertIfNew* that begins with the header

   > **procedure** *insertIfNew*(*p*   : *linkedList*;
   >   *x*   : *itemType*;
   >   **var** *new* : *boolean*);

   and that combines the functions of the *inList* and *insert* procedures. Specifically, this procedure should insert a node containing x in order in the linked list p if x does not occur in that list already, and it should leave the list unchanged otherwise. Upon exit from *insertIfNew*, the parameter *new* should have the value *true* if a new node containing x was inserted and the value *false* if an item containing x was already in the list.

5. Write a program to analyze a file of text by counting the total number of words in that file as well as the number of distinct words. (See Exercises 16 and 18, Section 9.4.) Compare the time required by programs that read one word at a time from the file and that use
   (a) a linear search of a single vector that contains a list of the distinct words read so far, with new words added to the end of the list;

(b) a binary search of a single vector that contains a list of the distinct words read so far, with new words inserted in alphabetical order;

(c) the *insertIfNew* procedure developed in Exercise 4 to create a single linked list that contains the distinct words read so far; and

(d) the *category* function from *linkDemo* together with the *insertIfNew* procedure to create several linked lists, each of which contains some of the distinct words read so far.

6. Estimate the number of comparisons and data movements required by the alternatives in Exercise 5 to process a text with n words, m of which are distinct. Can you explain the running times you observed using these estimates?

7. Devise an algorithm to sort the items in a linked list into alphabetical order by manipulating pointers. Is it easy to modify the various techniques we used to sort vectors in order to sort linked lists? Explain.

8. Devise an algorithm to merge two sorted linked lists into a single sorted linked list. Use this algorithm together with your solution to Exercise 5(d) to generate an alphabetical list of the distinct words in the text. How efficient is this method of producing an alphabetical list compared to other methods based on Exercise 5(a)–(c)?

9. Modify the procedures in *link1* to handle lists with the following representations.

(a) Doubly linked lists in which each node contains two links, one to the previous node and one to the next node. [See Fig. 11.20(a).]

(b) Circular lists, in which the link in the last node points to the first node. [See Fig. 11.20(b).]

(c) Doubly linked circular lists.

(d) Lists in which the pointer to the first node is located in a dummy *header* node. [See Fig. 11.20(c).]

(e) Doubly linked lists with header nodes.

(f) Circular lists with header nodes.

(g) Doubly linked circular lists with header nodes.

Discuss which operations on linked lists are simpler, and which are more difficult, with each of these representations.

10. The pointer data type helps us implement linked lists, but it is not essential. Write a library *link2* of procedures with the same specifications as those in *link1*, but which stores items for linked lists in a vector using the following declarations.

```
const maxItems = . . .;
      endOfList = 0;
type itemType = . . .;
     linkedList = 0..maxItems;
     node      = record
                     item : itemType;
                     link : linkedList
                 end;
var storage : array [0..maxItems] of node;
```

(a) Doubly linked list

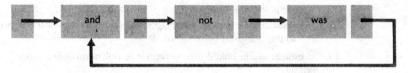

(b) Circular list

(c) List with header node

Figure 11.20 ■ Alternative representations for lists

Here we represent a linked list by a subscript telling where to find its first item in the vector *storage*. Links to subsequent items are also subscripts, with a link of zero marking the end of a list. The list beginning with *storage*[0] plays a special role: it contains all nodes not in any other list, serving as a source of new nodes for the *push* and *insert* procedures and as a repository for nodes discarded by the *pop* and *delete* procedures.

11. *The Josephus problem* The Roman general Josephus, once faced with certain defeat, proposed the following scheme for the remnants of his army to die honorably by their own hands. He arranged himself and his soldiers in a circle. Then, beginning with a particular soldier, they kept counting around the circle and killing every fourth soldier until only one remained. Josephus proposed that this last soldier then commit suicide. But he cleverly arranged to be that last soldier himself and slipped away under cover of darkness.

If Josephus had possessed a computer, he might have determined where to stand in the circle by writing a program that sets up a circular linked list representing n people arranged in a circle and then runs along the list, deleting every mth person. Write such a program that prints the order in which deletions occur and announces who is the last person left. When n is 8 and m is 4, the order of departure should be 48521376. (To visualize this, draw a diagram showing eight people in a circle, numbered from 1 to 8; then start counting with number one, crossing off each fourth person.) Run your program with $n = 24$ and $m = 11$.

12. Write a program to find the smallest positive integer that can be expressed as a sum of two cubes in two different ways. (*Hint:* Systematically generate all pairs of integers, adding them to a list ordered by the sum of the cubes of the integers and removing them from the list when you determine that no other pair of integers can produce the same sum of cubes. To find the smallest integer with two representations, make sure that any pair of integers not yet considered must have a sum of cubes larger than that of the first pair in the list. Stop when the first two pairs in the list have the same sum of cubes.)

13. Investigate using linked lists to represent variable-length strings, as follows.

   (a) Design a representation for variable-length strings that uses a linked list to hold the characters in a string.

   (b) Rewrite the library *stringSubs3* of procedures that manipulate variable-length strings using this representation.

   (c) What are the relative advantages and disadvantages of this representation compared to the one used by *stringSubs3*?

14. Investigate using linked lists to represent polynomials such as $x^{12} - 3x^8 + 2x^3 - 1$, as follows.

   (a) Design a representation for a polynomial in a single variable x using a linked list to hold the exponents and coefficients of all terms in the polynomial with nonzero coefficients.

   (b) Write a library of procedures to add, subtract, multiply, and evaluate polynomials.

   (c) Does it help to maintain any particular order for the terms in a polynomial?

   (d) Write a procedure to differentiate a polynomial.

   (e) What are the advantages and disadvantages of this representation for polynomials compared to one that simply stores the coefficients of a polynomial in a vector c, with the coefficient of x^n going in $c[n]$?

HASH TABLES

The binary search provides us with one means for reducing the time required to search a list. But there are others as well. We study now one that does not require a sorted list, but uses extra storage to organize the search.

Our strategy is to divide a long list L systematically into shorter sublists L_1, L_2, ..., L_n so that, whenever we need to determine whether an item is in L, we have to search just one of these sublists. Then the time required to search L will be no more than the time required to search the longest sublist. The program *linkDemo* in Section 11.2, for example, counts the number of different words that occur in a file of text by maintaining linked lists of words having the same length. Since *linkDemo* needs only to compare a new word from the file with previous words of the same length, it is considerably faster than programs that simply put all distinct words into a single list. (See Exercise 5, Section 11.2.)

To get the most out of our strategy, we should divide a long list of items into many sublists and apportion the items as evenly as possible among those sublists. Then, by further reducing the length of the longest sublist, we can further reduce the time required by a search. For example, if we apportion a list of 500 distinct items evenly among 100 sublists, we can determine whether an item is in the list by making at most 5 comparisons rather than the 500 required by a linear search or the 9 required by a binary search.

We can achieve this maximum gain in efficiency by defining a function that tells us in which sublist an item belongs. Simply categorizing words by their lengths neither creates enough sublists nor creates sublists of approximately the same size. A better way to assign a word to a sublist is to *hash code* it by scrambling its characters together to produce the number of the list in which it belongs, somewhat akin to the way in which we generated random numbers in Section 10.3. A good hash-coding scheme will distribute items evenly among all sublists. A bad one will put all items in a single sublist. A reasonably good one will distribute items fairly evenly.

In Pascal, we can use the *ord* function to construct such a hash code. This function transforms a character into a numeric code, and we need only to devise a way to scramble these codes together. We could simply add the codes, but then words such as `mate`, `meat` and `tame`, which contain the same letters in different orders, would be placed in the same list. To distribute the words as evenly as possible, we want to destroy any such accidental correlations between words and lists. One way to do this is shown in Pascal Sample 11.19. There we add character codes one at at time to a number h, scrambling h beforehand by multiplying it by a large prime and reducing the result afterwards to serve as a number for a sublist.

Using *hash*, we can divide a long list into several linked sublists by hash coding items to determine in which sublist they belong. Such a representation for a list is known as a *bucketed hash table*, with each of the sublists acting as a bucket that contains some of the items in the list.

We leave the programming details associated with hash tables to the exercises at the end of this section. Exercise 1 calls for using a bucketed hash table as the underlying representation for an unordered list treated as an abstract data type. Exercises 2 and 3 contrast the efficiency of this representation with that in the last section.

Exercises 4 and 5 explore other ways to represent hash tables—ways that do not require linked allocation. An *unbucketed hash table* keeps items in a vector, but not

---

■ PASCAL SAMPLE 11.19 The procedure *hash*

function *hash*(*s* : *string*; *n* : *integer*) : *integer*;

    { hash codes a string *s* as an integer between 1 and *n* }

    var *i* : 1..*stringLength*;

        h : *integer*;

begin

    h := 0;

    for *i* := 1 **to** *stringLength* **do** *h* := (5179*h + *ord*(*s*[*i*])) **mod** *n*;

    hash := *h* + 1

end; { of *hash* }

necessarily in consecutive locations in that vector (that is, locations in the vector may be occupied or unoccupied). To insert an item or to look for an item, we hash code the item to determine where it belongs in the table. If that location in the table is unoccupied, we know the item is not in the table. If the location is occupied, then two things can happen: the item we are seeking can be in that location, in which case we have found it; or it may have *collided* with another item inhabiting that location, in which case we need to search further.

Linear probing (Exercise 4) reacts to collisions by starting a linear search for an item at the location indicated by its hash code. The search stops when it finds the item or when it reaches an unoccupied location in the hash table; if it reaches the end of the table before either of these events occurs, then it continues from the beginning of the table. A new item is inserted in the first unoccupied location found by such a search.

A disadvantage of linear probing is that items tend to cluster in the table well before it becomes full. Hence it can take a long time to find some items. Other strategies for handling collisions reduce the amount of clustering that occurs (see Exercise 5).

EXERCISES

1. Write a library of procedures to maintain a list as an abstract data type, using a bucketed hash table as the underlying representation for the list. Provide definitions for the following procedures and functions:

addIfNew(L, x, new)	adds *x* to the list *L* if it is not already there, setting *new* true if *x* was new
addToList(L, x)	adds *x* to the list *L*
delete(L, x)	deletes all occurrences of *x* from *L*
startList(L)	initializes *L* to the empty list
inList(L, x)	returns *true* if *x* is in the list *L*
emptyList(L)	returns *true* if the list *L* is empty

2. Modify *linkDemo*, or the program you wrote for Exercise 5, Section 11.2, to construct hash table containing the distinct words in a file of text. Contrast the time required this program to count the number of distinct words with the time required by *linkDemo* or your earlier program.

3. Experiment with other definitions for a hash function, comparing how evenly these definitions distribute words into sublists.

4. Investigate maintaining an unbucketed hash table using linear probing, as follows.

   (a) Write a library of procedures to maintain a list as an abstract data type, using unbucketed hash table with linear probing as the underlying representation. Provide definitions for all procedures and functions described in Exercise 1 except *delete*. [*Hint:* Mark the locations in the table that are occupied, either by using a special item (such as the null string) to indicate an unoccupied location or by having each location contain a record with a boolean component that indicates whether the location occupied.]

(b) Devise a procedure to delete an item from a hash table. Make sure that you can still find the remaining items in the table. (*Hint:* Mark locations in the table as occupied, unoccupied, or deleted; revise your search and insertion procedures to handle deleted locations properly.)

(c) Determine experimentally how the average time required to find an item in a hash table varies according to how full that table is.

(d) Determine experimentally how evenly entries are distributed in a hash table when it is 75%, 85%, and 95% full.

5. A *rehash* function tells us where to look next in an unbucketed hash table in case a collision has occurred. If we have just examined the entry in *table*(i), then we look next at the entry in *table*(*rehash*(i)). The rehash function for linear probing is particularly simple: *rehash*(i) = (i **mod** n) + 1, where n is the length of the table. Investigate maintaining an unbucketed hash table using the following rehash functions.

(a) *rehash*(i) = ($i + k$) **mod** n + 1, where k is some positive integer. Are some values for k and n better than others?

(b) *rehash*(i) = (i^2 **mod** n) + 1. Are some values for n better than others?

(c) *rehash*(i) = *newhash*(i, n), where *newhash* is another hash function that scrambles an integer, as opposed to a string, to produce a code between 1 and n.

11.4 STACKS

A *stack* is a list for which there are rigidly prescribed rules for insertions and deletions. We can add an item to a stack by pushing it onto the top of the stack, and we can remove an item from a stack by "popping" it off the top. Thus we remove items from a stack in an order opposite to that in which we added them.

As we saw in Section 4.8, computer systems use a stack to keep track of nested procedure invocations while executing a program: the last procedure added to the stack (the one invoked most recently) will be the first to disappear (the first to terminate). In this section we explore how we can use a stack to order the tasks performed by a program. In so doing, we will learn how to transform any recursive task into an iterative task that uses a stack.

Let us first consider the problem of printing the binary representation of an integer. Using the **mod** and **div** operations in Pascal, we can peel off and print the digits in the binary representation of a positive integer n from right to left.

```
{ print binary representation of n in reverse order }
repeat
    write( n mod 2 );     { print last digit of n      }
    n := n div 2          { trim n to leading digits }
until n = 0
```

But we really want to print the digits in the opposite order, from left to right. The easiest way to do this uses recursion. In the program *binary*, displayed as Pascal Sample 11.20, we reduce the problem of printing the binary representation of an

PASCAL SAMPLE 11.20   The program *binary*

{ prints the binary representation of an integer }

program *binary*(*input*, *output*);

var *number* : *integer*;

procedure *print*(*n* : *integer*);

    { recursive procedure to print binary representation of *n* }

    begin

       if *n* < 0 **then** *write*('−');

       n := *abs*(*n*);

       if *n* > 1 **then** *print*(*n* **div** 2);   { print leading digits }

       write(*n* **mod** 2 : 1)   { print last digit   }

    end; { of *print* }

begin

    write('Enter an integer: ');

    read(*number*);

    writeln;

    write('Its binary representation is ');

    print(*number*);

    writeln

end.

SAMPLE USE OF *binary*:

Enter an integer: 45

Its binary representation is 101101

integer *n* to the problem of printing the leading digits in that representation followe
by the last digit.

    In this solution to our problem, we rely on a computer system's mechanism fc
recursion to keep track of the digits we need to print. But suppose that we want t
proceed without recursion. Then we must keep track of these digits ourselves. W
could keep a list of digits in an array, as in the procedure *convert* (Section 7.1
which found the multiple-precision representation for an integer. But since we wa
only to put digits into a list and take them out again in the reverse order, we can u
a stack in place of an array.

    Pascal Sample 11.21 provides an alternative definition of the *print* procedu
from *binary*, storing digits in a stack represented as a linked list. It uses the proc
dures *push*, *pop*, *emptyList*, and *startList* from the library *link1* to manipulate t
stack. This definition is lengthier than that in Pascal Sample 11.20, but it is just

---

PASCAL SAMPLE 11.21 The program *binary* (iterative *print* procedure)

```
procedure print( n : integer );
    { iterative procedure to print binary representation of n }
    type itemType  = integer;                      { declarations for link1 }
         linkedList = ↑node;
         node       = record
                          item : itemType;
                          link : linkedList
                      end;
    var digitStack : linkedList;
        digit      : integer;
    #include 'linkl';                              { procedures to maintain stack }
    begin
        if n < 0 then write('-');
        n := abs(n);
        startList(digitStack);
        repeat                                     { stack digits }
            digit := n mod 2;
            push(digitStack, digit);
            n := n div 2
        until n = 0;
        repeat                                     { print digits }
            pop(digitStack, digit);
            write(digit:1)
        until emptyList(digitStack)
    end;   { of print }
```

simple: it peels the digits off the binary representation of *n* from right to left, stacking them as it goes; then it pops the digits off the stack in reverse order, printing them as it goes.

In general, we can use a stack to eliminate recursion from any computer program. We illustrate how this is done by writing iterative versions of the two recursive sorting procedures, *quicksort* and *msort*, that we developed in Section 8.6.

A NONRECURSIVE VERSION OF QUICKSORT

Let us tackle *quicksort* first. The recursive version of that procedure sorts a sublist $a[first], \ldots, a[last]$ of a list $a[1], \ldots, a[n]$ by invoking a procedure *split* to rearrange the sublist, if necessary, and find an index *middle* so that $a[i] \leq a[middle] \leq a[j]$ when $first \leq i < middle < j \leq last$; then it invokes itself recursively to sort the two halves $a[first], \ldots, a[middle-1]$ and $a[middle+1], \ldots, a[last]$ of the sublist. Thus *quicksort* reduces the task of sorting a long list to the simpler tasks of sorting shorter sublists, each of which can be accomplished by *quicksort* itself.

We can implement *quicksort* iteratively instead of recursively by maintaining a stack of tasks that will finish the job of sorting $a[1], \ldots, a[n]$. Each task on the stack corresponds to an invocation of the recursive version of *quicksort* and consists of a pair *<first, last>* of indices bounding an unsorted portion of the list a. Initially the stack contains the single entry *<1, n>*. On each pass through a loop, we take a task off the stack and check whether *first* < *last*; if it is, then we use *split* to divide the sublist $a[first], \ldots, a[last]$ in half and stack two tasks to sort these two pieces; if it is not, then the task requires no further action. The entire list has been sorted when no tasks remain on the stack.

In Pascal Samples 11.22 and 11.23, we use this strategy to convert the recursive version of *quicksort* in the library *sort5* into an iterative version in the library *sort5i*.

▇ PASCAL SAMPLE 11.22   The library *sort5i* (iterative *quicksort*)

{ *sort5i*: quicksort of $a[1], ..., a[n]$ (iterative version) }

```
procedure sort( var a : itemList;                       { list to sort    }
                    n : index );                        { length of list }
        type entryType  = record                        { declarations for stack }
                              first, last : index
                          end;
             stack       = ↑node;
             node        = record
                              entry : entryType;
                              link  : stack
                          end;
        var first, middle, last : index;
            activities          : stack;
#include 'stack';                                       { procedures to maintain a stack }
        { declarations for split, stackTask, unstackTask go here }
        begin
            startStack(activities);
            stackTask(activities, 1, n);
            repeat
                unstackTask(activities, first, last);
                if first < last then
                    begin
                        split(a, first, last, middle);
                        stackTask(activities, first, middle − 1);
                        stackTask(activities, middle + 1, last)
                    end
            until emptyStack(activities)
        end;  { of sort }
```

PASCAL SAMPLE 11.23   The library *sort5i* (*stackTask*, *unstackTask* procedures)

procedure *stackTask*(**var** *s* : *stack*; *first*, *last* : *index*);

{ stacks a task to sort *a*[*first*], ..., *a*[*last*] on *s* }

var *task* : *entryType*;

begin

    task.first := *first*;
    task.last := *last*;
    push(*s*, *task*)

end;   { of *stackTask* }

procedure *unstackTask*(**var** *s* : *stack*; **var** *first*, *last* : *index*);

{ retrieves sorting task from *s* }

var *task* : *entryType*;

begin

    pop(*s*, *task*);
    first := *task.first*;
    last := *task.last*

end;   { of *unstackTask* }

Since entries on its stack are records, *sort5i* cannot use *link1* to maintain that stack: the *insert* procedure there requires that *itemType* be a real or ordinal type. Hence *sort5i* uses a new library *stack* containing the four procedures *startStack*, *emptyStack*, *push*, and *pop* defined as in *link1*, but with the entries on the stack coming from an arbitrary type *entryType* rather than an ordinal type *itemType*. It also uses two procedures, *stackTask* and *unstackTask*, tailor-made to its definition of *entryType*. The first of these procedures constructs an entry and places it on the stack; the second pops an entry off the stack and retrieves its components. Pascal Sample 11.24 contains the descriptive comments at the beginning of the library *stack*; the rest of the library is left to the exercises at the end of this section.

A NONRECURSIVE VERSION OF MERGE SORT

Removing recursion from procedures such as *quicksort* is relatively easy. These procedures reduce a complicated task to a succession of smaller tasks, which we can push onto a stack and later process iteratively. Removing recursion from procedures such as the recursive merge sort *msort* is somewhat harder. These procedures also reduce a complicated task to a succession of smaller tasks, but must then assemble the outcomes of these smaller tasks to finish the original task. For example, *msort* sorts a list *a*[*first*], . . . , *a*[*last*] by letting *middle* be the average of *first* and *last*, invoking itself recursively to sort the two halves *a*[*first*], . . . , *a*[*middle*] and *a*[*middle* + 1], . . . , *a*[*last*] of the list, and then invoking the procedure *merge* to combine these sorted halves.

■ **PASCAL SAMPLE 11.24**   The library *stack* (initial comments)

```
{ stack: procedures to maintain a stack }
{      The following procedures and functions are available }
{ for maintaining a stack s:                               }
{                                                          }
{ Procedures:                                              }
{                                                          }
{ pop(s, x)          pops stack s into x                   }
{ push(s, x)         pushes x onto stack s                 }
{ startStack(s)      initializes s to be an empty stack    }
{                                                          }
{ Function:                                                }
{                                                          }
{ emptyStack(s)      returns true if s is an empty stack   }
{                                                          }
{      Any program calling one of these procedures or      }
{ functions must contain the following declarations:       }
{                                                          }
{ type entryType = ...;                                    }
{      stack    = ↑node;                                   }
{      node     = record                                   }
{                    entry : entryType;                    }
{                    link  : stack                         }
{                  end;                                    }
```

Fortunately, it is not much more difficult to remove recursion from arbitrary procedures than to remove it from *quicksort*. The key lies in generalizing the notion of a task. In *sort5i*, a task corresponds to an entire invocation of the recursive version of *quicksort*. In a more general setting, a task corresponds to a sequence of actions in an invocation of some procedure. By keeping enough information to undertake these tasks (that is, the current values of all variables and parameters) on a stack, we can eliminate recursion from any procedure.

For example, each invocation of the recursive merge-sort procedure consists of two sequences of actions. The first sequence divides a list in half and sorts the two halves; the second sequence merges the sorted halves. To eliminate recursion, we proceed as we did for *quicksort*. But now each recursive invocation causes us to push three tasks onto the stack: two to handle the recursive invocations, and one to resume the current invocation when the others finish. Since we wish to resume the current task only after finishing the others, we must push the other tasks onto the stack first. Pascal Sample 11.25 shows how this is done. The procedures *stackTask* and *unstackTask* are similar to those in *sort5i*. Hence we leave their definition to the exercises at the end of this section.

Using a stack to eliminate recursion may not always be the most efficient way to proceed. For example, the version of the merge-sort procedure that we developed

---

■ **PASCAL SAMPLE 11.25**   The library *sort7* (iterative merge sort)

{ *sort7*: merge sort of *a*[1], ..., *a*[*n*] (iterative version) }

```
procedure sort( var a : itemList;                              { list to sort   }
                    n : index );                               { length of list }
    const undefined = 0;                              { initial value for variables }
    type action    = (sortHalves, mergeHalves);         { declarations for stack }
         entryType = record
                         first, middle, last : index;
                         whatToDo          : action
                     end;
         stack     = ↑node;
         node      = record
                         entry : entryType;
                         link  : stack
                     end;
    var first, middle, last : index;
        whatToDo          : action;
        activities        : stack;
#include 'stack';                              { procedures to maintain a stack }
    { declarations for merge, stackTask, unstackTask go here }

    begin
        startStack(activities);
        stackTask(activities, 1, undefined, n, sortHalves);
        repeat
            unstackTask(activities, first, middle, last whatToDo);
            case whatToDo of
                sortHalves :
                    if first < last then
                        begin
                            middle := ( first + last ) div 2;
                            stackTask(activities, first, middle, last, mergeHalves);
                            stackTask(activities, first, undefined, middle, sortHalves);
                            stackTask(activities, middle + 1, undefined, last, sortHalves)
                        end;
                mergeHalves :
                    merge(a, first, middle, last)
            end
        until emptyStack(activities)
    end;   { of sort }
```

in Section 8.7 for use with external files makes do without a stack and involves much less overhead than our current version. Therefore what we have done is to show that we can, if necessary, replace recursion by iteration—not that we should replace recursion by iteration in this case. Sometimes, as with *quicksort*, a stack provides a good way to proceed. At other times a different approach may yield better results.

EXERCISES

1. Provide definitions for the four procedures in the library *stack*.

2. Write a program to input a list of numbers and print them out in the opposite order.

3. Write a program to determine whether a line of input contains a balanced string of parentheses and brackets, as defined by the following syntax diagram.

balanced string

(*Hint:* Place unmatched left parentheses and brackets on a stack.)

4. Provide definitions for the *stackTask* and *unstackTask* procedures used by *sort7*.

5. Another representation for a stack uses a vector s instead of a linked list. A variable *top* records the subscript of the entry on top of the stack. New entries are added to the stack by increasing *top* by one and placing the new entry in $s[top]$.

    (a) Rewrite the library *stack* using this new representation for a stack.

    (b) Revise the iterative version of *quicksort* in *sort5i* to use the new version of *stack*.

    (c) Compare the execution times of the original version of *quicksort* in *sort5*, the iterative version in *sort5i*, and the version you wrote for (b). Which is the most efficient? How would you go about making *quicksort* even more efficient?

6. Devise a scheme for representing two stacks using a single vector.

7. Show that the maximum height of the stack in *sort7* when sorting a list with n items is approximately $\log_2(n)$.

8. Investigate the size of the stack created by the iterative version of *quicksort*.

    (a) How large can the stack grow in the worst case?

    (b) How large can it grow in the average case?

    (c) When stacking tasks to sort the two portions of a list, why and how much does it help to stack the larger portion first?

11.5 QUEUES

In Chapter 10 we wrote the program *server1* to simulate the operation of a single-server queue, keeping such statistics as the maximum queue length and the total waiting time (from which the average waiting time is approximated). However, that program does not keep enough information to compute the maximum waiting time or to determine the variation in the waiting time. It would be interesting to know the maximum waiting time, and it would be useful to know the variance of the waiting times in order to determine the reliability of the simulation.

To compute the maximum waiting time, we need to keep track of the time that each customer arrives; then when a customer departs we can compute the time waited and compare it with the previous maximum waiting time. Fortunately we do not need to retain the arrival times for all customers during the simulation; we need to retain only the arrival times of customers who have not yet departed.

By retaining these arrival times, we can also measure the variability inherent in the operation of the queue. The *variance* of the waiting times is a statistic that can be computed from the individual waiting times $w_1, \ldots, w_n$ by the formula

$$variance = \frac{1}{n} \sum_{i=1}^{n} (w_i - w)^2,$$

where w is the average waiting time. The *standard deviation* is defined to be $\sqrt{variance}$. Both the standard deviation and the variance are measures of the variability of the waiting times. The advantage of this particular definition of variance (as opposed to one that sums $|w_i - w|$) is that it simplifies to the formula

$$variance = \frac{1}{n} \sum_{i=1}^{n} w_i^2 - w^2.$$

Thus we can compute the variance by accumulating the sum, and the sum of the squares, of the individual waiting times. Again, this can be done if we keep track of the arrival time for each customer until that customer departs.

The program *server2* is based on the event-driven simulation conducted by *server1* in conjunction with *server1E*. In order to compute the maximum waiting time and the variance of the waiting times, *server2* keeps a list of the arrival times of customers still in the queue. In a sense, the operation of this program is a much more faithful simulation of the operation of a queue. By placing arrival times in a list, and later removing them, we mimic the actual arrivals and departures. For this reason, the type of list we need in *server2* is known as a *queue*.

More formally, a queue is a linear data structure maintained on a *first-in first-out* (*FIFO*) basis. Only two operations are needed to maintain a queue: one called *enqueue,* which places a new entry at the end of the queue; and one called *dequeue,* which removes the first entry from the queue. Shortly we will construct a library *queue* of procedures to maintain a queue. But first we will use the procedures *enqueue* and *dequeue* from that library to construct *server2*.

■ PASCAL SAMPLE 11.26   The program *server2* (*arrival* procedure)

```
procedure arrival( t : real );
    { simulates an arrival at time t }
    begin
        enqueue(q, t);
        qLen := qLen + 1;
        if qLen > maxLen then maxLen := qLen;
        arriveTime := when(t, interrarivalTime);
        if qLen = 1 then departTime := when(t, serviceTime);
        if observing then writeln('arrive', t:7:1, qLen:6)
    end;   { of arrival }
```

The *arrival* procedure from *server2* (Pascal Sample 11.26) is practically identical
to the *arrival* procedure in *server1E*. The only difference is that the new version of
this procedure calls the *enqueue* procedure to record the time that the arrival occurred in a queue *q* of arrival times.

The *departure* procedure from *server2* (Pascal Sample 11.27) is somewhat lengthier than before. It computes the exact waiting time for a departing customer by
invoking the *dequeue* function to find out when that customer arrived. Then it updates
various statistics: the maximum time waited, the total waiting time (which will be
used to compute the average waiting time), and the sum of the squares of the waiting

---

■ PASCAL SAMPLE 11.27   The program *server2* (*departure* procedure)

```
procedure departure( t : real );
    { simulates a departure at time t }
    var aTime : real;       { time this departure arrived   }
        wait  : real;       { time waited by this departure }
    begin
        dequeue(q, aTime);
        wait     := time − aTime;
        waitTime := waitTime + wait;
        waitTime2 := waitTime2 + sqr(wait);
        if wait > maxWait then maxWait := wait;
        qLen := qLen − 1;
        served := served + 1;
        if qLen > 0 then
            departTime := when(t, serviceTime)
        else
            departTime := finish + 1;
        if observing then writeln('depart', t:7:1, qLen:6)
    end;   { of departure }
```

times (which will be used to compute the standard deviation of the waiting times). Thus the computation of the average waiting time and related statistics is much more straightforward in *server2* than before.

The *simulate* procedure from *server2* (Pascal Sample 11.28) is somewhat simpler than that in *server1E*. Since the *departure* procedure now keeps track of the total waiting time, the main simulation loop no longer needs to update this total each time a new event occurs. Furthermore, since this total no longer contains the time waited by customers still in the queue, it is easier to compute the average waiting time when

---

PASCAL SAMPLE 11.28   The program *server2* (*simulate* procedure)

procedure *simulate*;

```
{ simulates queue with specified interarrival and service times    }
{ until a given finishing time, recording the number served, the   }
{ number still in the queue, the maximum queue length, and         }
{ the average waiting time                                         }

var arriveTime  : real;      { time of next arrival                }
    departTime  : real;      { time of next departure             }
    waitTime    : real;      { total time waited by all customers }
    waitTime2   : real;      { sum of squares of wait times       }
    time        : real;      { current time                       }
    q           : queue;     { queue of arrival times             }
```

#include '**m**axmin';

```
{ declarations for arrival, departure, when procedures go here }

begin
    served    := 0;      { global: number of customers served }
    qLen      := 0;      { global: current length of queue    }
    maxLen    := 0;      { global: maximum length of queue    }
    maxWait   := 0;      { global: maximum waiting time       }
    waitTime  := 0;
    waitTime2 := 0;

    arriveTime := when(0, interarrivalTime);
    departTime := finish + 1;
    startQueue(q);

    repeat
        time := min(min(arriveTime, departTime), finish);
        if time = arriveTime then
            arrival(time)
        else if time = departTime then
            departure(time)
    until time >= finish;
    avWait := waitTime/served;
    sdWait := sqrt(waitTime2/served − sqr(avWait))
end;   { of simulate }
```

PASCAL SAMPLE 11.29   The program *server2* (main program)

{ improved event-driven simulation of a single-server queue }

program *server2*(*input, output*);

type *itemType* = *real*;   { type declarations for *queue* }
           nodePtr = ↑*node*;
           node   = **record**
                             item : *itemType*;
                             link : *nodePtr*
                       end;
           queue   = **record**
                             first, last : *nodePtr*
                       end;

var *interarrivalTime* : *real*;   { average time between arrivals   }
        serviceTime   : *real*;   { average service time   }
        finish   : *real*;   { time simulation ends   }
        served   : *integer*;   { number of customers served   }
        qLen, maxLen   : *integer*;   { length of queue, maximum   }
        avWait, maxWait   : *real*;   { average, maximum waiting time   }
        sdWait   : *real*;   { standard deviation of *avWait*   }
        observing   : *boolean*;   { events displayed if *true*   }
        answer   : *char*;   { used to set *observing*   }
        first, last   : *nodePtr*;   { pointers for *enqueue, dequeue*   }
        randomSeed   : *integer*;   { required by *randomReal*   }

#include 'random';   { *randomize, randomReal* procedures   }
#include 'queue';   { procedures to maintain a queue   }

{ declaration for *simulate* goes here }

begin

    { initialization, as in *server1*, goes here }

    randomize(*true*);
    simulate;

    writeln;
    writeln('Number served   = ', *served*:1);
    writeln('Number still waiting = ', *qLen*:1);
    writeln('Maximum queue length = ', *maxLen*:1);
    writeln('Maximum waiting time = ', *maxWait*:1:2);
    writeln('Average waiting time = ', *avWait*:1:2);
    writeln('Standard deviation   = ', *sdWait*:1:2)

end.   { of *server2* }

---

the simulation ends. The *simulate* procedure also computes the standard deviation
of the waiting times when the simulation ends.

Finally, the main program from *server2* (Pascal Sample 11.29) contains the necessary additions to keep and report the new statistics. Several of these additions are

---

■ **PASCAL SAMPLE 11.30**   The program *server2* (sample use)

```
Average interarrival, service times? 8 6
Length of simulation? 2880
Do you want to see arrivals and departures [y/n]? n

Number served       = 373
Number still waiting = 4
Maximum queue length = 17
Maximum waiting time = 97.66
Average waiting time = 24.31
Standard deviation   = 22.65
```

---

used solely by the library *queue* of procedures that maintain a queue; in fact, the representation of that queue does not affect the main program.

Pascal Sample 11.30 shows the results of using *server2* rather than *server1* with *server1E* to simulate 48 hours of operation of our standard queue. The number of customers served, the number remaining in the queue, and the maximum length of the queue are the same as before; we have changed nothing in the simulation that would affect these quantities. The average waiting time is now slightly higher and more accurate than before. And we can finally display the maximum waiting time together with the standard deviation of the waiting times.

The standard deviation displayed in Pascal Sample 11.30 is of particular interest. General results in statistics tell us that about two-thirds of a set of measurements should fall within one standard deviation of the average measurement. Hence, when the standard deviation is close to the average, nearly one-third of the measurements will exceed twice the average. In terms of our simulation, this means that one-third of the customers experience a wait of more than twice the average! Though many customers get served quickly, some customers must wait a long time.

PROCEDURES TO MANIPULATE QUEUES

The library *queue* of procedures to maintain a queue is similar to the library *link1* of procedures to maintain a linked list. But since additions to a queue always go to the end of the queue, it pays to represent a queue by using two pointers rather than one: a pointer to the first entry in the queue (to make removals efficient) and a pointer to the last entry (to make additions efficient).

We will represent queues as a linked collection of nodes together with two pointers, *first* and *last,* pointing to the first and last nodes in the queue. As in the case of linked lists, a link of **nil** marks the last node in a queue, and an empty queue is indicated by having *first* equal **nil**. Comments at the beginning of the library *queue* establish these conventions. (See Pascal Sample 11.31.)

The *startQueue* procedure is the easiest to define. (See Pascal Sample 11.32.) The major purpose in defining this procedure is to hide the representation of a queue from programs using the library.

PASCAL SAMPLE 11.31   The library *queue* (initial comments)

```
{ queue: library of procedures to maintain a queue }

{ Procedures:   enqueue(q, x)      adds x to the end of the queue q          }
{               dequeue(q, x)      sets x equal to the first entry in the queue q }
{                                  and removes this entry from the queue       }
{               startQueue(q)      sets q to an empty queue                    }
{ Function:      queueEmpty(q)     returns true if the queue q is empty        }

{      Any program invoking one of these procedures or functions must contain  }
{ the following declarations:                                                   }
{                                                                               }
{ type itemType =  . . .;                                                       }
{      nodePtr  = ↑node;                                                        }
{      node     = record                                                        }
{                      item : itemType;                                         }
{                      link : nodePtr                                           }
{                 end;                                                          }
{      queue    = record                                                        }
{                      first, last : nodePtr                                    }
{                 end;                                                          }
```

PASCAL SAMPLE 11.32   The library *queue* (*startQueue* procedure)

```
procedure startQueue( var q : queue );
      { sets q to an empty queue }
      begin
          q.first := nil
      end;   { of startQueue }
```

The *emptyQueue* function is similarly easy to define. (See Pascal Sample 11.33.) It too hides the representation of a queue from programs that need to determine whether that queue is empty.

PASCAL SAMPLE 11.33   The library *queue* (*emptyQueue* function)

```
function queueEmpty( q : queue ) : boolean;
      { returns true if the queue q is empty }
      begin
          queueEmpty := (q.first = nil)
      end;   { of queueEmpty }
```

PASCAL SAMPLE 11.34 The library *queue* (*enqueue* procedure)

procedure *enqueue*(**var** *q* : *queue*; *x* : *itemType*);
{ puts an entry containing *x* at the end of the queue *q* }
var *p* : *nodePtr*;
begin

```
    new(p);                    { create entry                  }
    p↑.item := x;              { place x in it                 }
    if q.first = nil then      { if queue is empty             }
        q.first := p           {    new entry is first         }
    else                       { else                          }
        q.last↑.link := p;     {    old last entry points to it }
    p↑.link := nil;            { mark new entry as last        }
    q.last := p
end;  { of enqueue }
```

The *enqueue* procedure appends a new entry to the end of the queue. Comments in Pascal Sample 11.34 describe how this is done.

The *dequeue* procedure removes the first entry from the queue and returns the item of data in that entry. Comments in Pascal Sample 11.35 describe how this is done.

PASCAL SAMPLE 11.35 The library *queue* (*dequeue* procedure)

procedure *dequeue*(**var** *q* : *queue*; **var** *x* : *itemType*);
{ removes the first entry from the queue *q*, setting *x* equal to the item }
{ in that entry }
var *p* : *nodePtr*;
begin

```
    p := q.first;              { point to entry                }
    if p <> nil then           { if entry exists then          }
        begin
            x := p↑.item;      { remove value                  }
            q.first := p↑.link; { remove entry from queue      }
            dispose(p)         { release storage               }
        end
    else
        begin
            writeln('Queue empty for dequeue');
            halt
        end
end;  { of dequeue }
```

Note that the last entry in the queue can be found either by looking at the pointer *last* or by following links down the list until a link of **nil** is encountered. This redundancy simplifies queue manipulations: having *q.last* makes the *enqueue* procedure easy to code; having a final link of **nil** makes it easy to display the contents of a queue in the same way that we display the contents of a linked list, that is, by a routine such as

```
p := q.first;
while p <> nil do
    begin
        write(p↑.item);
        p := p↑.link
    end
```

If we try to rewrite this routine by testing whether $p = q.last$ to determine when the end of the list is reached, the code becomes much more complicated. It then becomes more difficult to handle the last entry in the queue properly, or to handle queues with zero or one entry in them.

EXERCISES

1. Enhance the library *queue* of procedures to manipulate a queue by writing
   (a) a function *queueLength* that returns the length of the queue; and
   (b) a procedure *printQueue* that prints the contents of the queue.

2. Another representation for queues is based on a *circular array*. Entries in a queue are kept in a vector *q*. Two variables, *first* and *last,* record the subscripts of the first and last entries in the queue. Ordinarily, new entries are added to the queue by increasing *last* by one and placing the new entry in *q*[*last*]; however, if *last* already has the maximum legal value for a subscript in *q*, then *last* is set equal to 1 and the new entry is placed in *q*[1]. In this way, we can reuse storage in the array. But note that *last* may be less than *first* with this strategy. Hence we need a special conventi. n to determine when the queue is empty; one such convention is to set *last* = *first* − 1 when the queue is empty.
   (a) Refine the details of the circular array representation for a queue. Construct a library of procedures to maintain a queue using a circular array.
   (b) Modify *server2* to use this new library of procedures.

3. Write a program to simulate the operation of a supermarket checkout system with lines for regular and express service. Input the following parameters for the simulation.
   (a) The average interarrival time for customers.
   (b) The fraction of customers qualifying for express service.
   (c) The numbers of express lines and regular lines.
   (d) The average service rates for express and regular service.
   (e) The length of the simulation.

Regular customers always choose the shortest regular checkout line. Express customers choose an empty line if one is available; otherwise they choose the shortest express line. If no express line is open, they choose the shortest open line. Keep track of the following statistics.

(a) The number of express and regular customers served.

(b) The average waiting time for express and regular customers.

(c) The maximum waiting times for express and regular customers.

At a hypothetical supermarket customers arrive to check out at a rate of one a minute, with 30 percent requiring express service and 70 percent regular service. The average express service time is 2 minutes and the average regular service time is 5 minutes. The management of the supermarket has decided to keep as many lines open as are necessary to ensure that express customers never wait more than 5 minutes to check out and that regular customers wait no more than an average of 15 minutes.

When you are sure your program is working, use it to answer the following questions. What is the smallest number of lines that must be kept open to achieve the manager's goal? How many of the lines should be express lines? With this many lines, how much faster can customers arrive without the waiting times becoming longer than the manager desires? (*Hint:* You will have to keep track of the type of service required for each customer so that you can keep statistics properly. Be sure that your program can handle the case in which there are no express lines.)

4. Write a program to simulate the use of a runway by airplanes arriving at and departing from an airport. Input the following parameters for the simulation.

(a) The average number of planes that arrive per hour (which equals the average number of planes that depart each hour).

(c) The number of minutes required for a plane to take off.

(d) The number of minutes required for a plane to land.

Assume that planes needing to land have priority for the use of the runway over planes needing to take off (that is, there are two queues served by a single server—the runway—and one of these queues has priority over the other). Keep track of, and print, the following statistics for an 8-hour period of operation of the airport.

(a) The number of planes that take off and land.

(b) The percentage of the time the runway is idle.

(c) The maximum lengths of the take-off and landing queues, together with the earliest times when these occurred.

(d) The average lengths of the take-off and landing queues.

(e) The maximum time waited by planes to land and to take off.

(f) The average time waited by planes to land and to take off.

Try your program for arrival rates of 5, 7, and 10 planes per hour. For each of these arrival rates, try landing times equal to 1, 3, 5, and 6 minutes. Assume that take-offs take one minute more than landings. (Thus there will be 12 trials in all.)

To gauge the accuracy of your results, note that with 5 planes per hour and a landing time of 3 minutes, we expect the runway to be occupied about 5×3 minutes per hour by planes landing and 5×4 minutes per hour by planes taking off, or about 35 minutes per hour in all. An arrival rate of 5 planes per hour and a landing time of 5 minutes yields a predicted 55 minutes per hour of demand for the runway, while 10 arrivals per hour with a landing time of 5 minutes yields an expected demand for 110 minutes per hour (and clearly overloads the runway).

Summarize your results and comment on what they show. In particular, comment on the heaviest load that the airport can handle without continually increasing delays.

5. Enhance your airport simulation to simulate an airport with two runways. Would it be better to use one runway for arrivals and another for departures, or would it be better to use both runways for both arrivals and departures?

6. Verify mathematically that the formula that defines the variance of the waiting times simplifies to the formula used in *server2*.

SUMMARY

Static data structures are fixed in size when a program is written. Dynamic data structures vary in size during program execution. They

- consume only as much storage as needed,
- consume storage only when needed, and
- can be reconfigured efficiently.

In Pascal, pointers help to keep track of the dynamic storage currently in use.

Linear data structures, or lists, are sequences of items of data. The efficiency of operations that manipulate a list depends on the static or dynamic representation chosen for the list. For

- sorted arrays,
  1. binary searches take logarithmic time, and
  2. insertions and deletions take linear time;
- unsorted arrays or sequential files,
  1. linear searches take linear time,
  2. insertions (at end of list) take constant time, and
  3. deletions take linear time;
- linked lists,
  1. linear searches take linear time,
  2. insertions and deletions take constant time, and
  3. extra storage is required for pointers; and
- hash tables,
  1. hash-coded searches take constant time,
  2. insertions and deletions take constant time, and
  3. extra storage is required to divide the list into small buckets.

Two linear data structures play particularly important roles in computer systems and programs.

■   A stack is

1. a last-in first-out list, wherein

    (a) additions and deletions occur at the same end of the list, and

    (b) representation is provided by a linked list or an array;

2. used by compilers and interpreters to process procedure calls and recursion; and

3. used as a data structure to provide an alternative to recursion.

■   A queue is

1. a first-in first-out list, wherein

    (a) additions and deletions occur at opposite ends of a list, and

    (b) representation is provided by a linked list or a circular array;

2. used by operating systems to record information about events; and

3. used as a data structure in simulations of waiting lines.

UCTURES NONLINEAR DATA STRU

AR DATA STRUCTURES NONLINEA

NONLINEAR DATA STRUCTURES N

UCTURES NONLINEAR DATA STRU

AR DATA STRUCTURES NONLINEA

NONLINEAR DATA STRUCTURES N

UCTURES NONLINEAR DATA STRU

NONLINEAR DATA STRUCTURES N

C   H   A   P   T   E   R

12

At times linear data structures provide either more or less structure than we need. Neither they nor rectilinear data structures such as multidimensional arrays provide enough structure for hierarchies (such as business organizations) or for networks (such as railroad connections between cities in the United States). And they provide too much structure for unordered collections of objects (such as the different geometric shapes in a picture).

In this chapter we examine two nonlinear data structures, one of which provides more structure than a list and the other less structure. The first of these, known as a *tree*, is appropriate for applications involving hierarchical relationships such as those among the members of a family, the workers in an organization, the categories in a classification scheme, or the components of a computer program. The second of these, known as a *set*, is familiar from its uses in mathematics and is appropriate for applications involving unordered collections of objects.

Trees in particular have many important applications in computing. We can develop efficient searching algorithms by representing the sequence of probes in a binary search as a tree. We can locate files in a computer system by using a tree of directories: a master directory contains information about various subdirectories (say, one for system software, one for user directories, and so on), and each of these in turn contains files or further directories. We can evaluate arithmetic expressions and execute Pascal programs by representing the syntax of those expressions and programs as a tree. And we can search for a winning move in a game of strategy by representing the legal positions in that game as a tree. In this chapter and Chapter 13 we explore some of these applications of trees.

We begin our study of trees by developing a new representation for an ordered list. This representation will combine the advantages of our previous representations using arrays and linked lists. As for sorted arrays, we will be able to search ordered trees efficiently by using a variant of the binary search. As for linked lists, we will be able to insert items in or delete them from a tree without moving any other items.

THE BINARY SEARCH REVISITED

First, let us consider how we might build a linked data structure that allows us to conduct a binary search of a list. Linked lists, as developed in Chapter 11 and depicted in Fig. 12.1, are unsatisfactory; we do not have any way to access the item that is exactly halfway through the list without accessing the items that come before (nor is there any way to determine the length of the list without accessing all items).

So, let us discard the links between the items in a linked list and replace them with pointers that help us conduct a binary search. We start by creating a pointer to the item halfway through the list so that we know where to make the first probe into the list. (See Fig. 12.2.) Next we attach pointers to this item, identifying the items to examine next if the first probe does not find the desired item. Here we need two pointers: one giving the location of the second probe if the item in the middle of the list is too large, and one giving the location of the second probe if the item in the middle is too small. (See Fig. 12.3.)

Continuing in this fashion, we attach two pointers to each of the remaining items in the list, the first indicating where to probe next when searching for a smaller item, and the second indicating where to probe next when searching for a larger item.

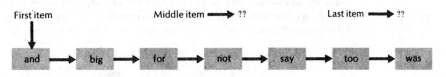

First item   Middle item ⟶ ??   Last item ⟶ ??

and ⟶ big ⟶ for ⟶ not ⟶ say ⟶ too ⟶ was

Figure 12.1 ■   Inadequacy of a linked list for a binary search

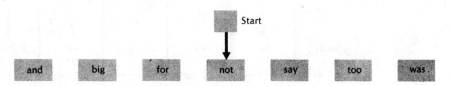

Start

and   big   for   not   say   too   was

Figure 12.2 ■   Pointer to location of first probe in a binary search

583

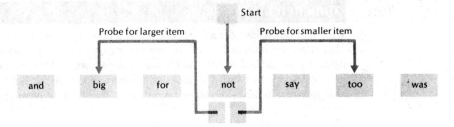

Figure 12.3 ■ Pointers to locations of first two probes in binary search

When no further probes can be made, a **nil** pointer stops the search. (See Fig. 12.4.) Finally, we pull up the middle item and let the others dangle below. Figure 12.5 depicts the result.

TREES

The data structure in Fig. 12.5 is an example of an *ordered binary tree*. A *tree* is a collection of items that satisfy three properties:

1. each item is related to zero or more other items that are called its *children*;

2. if the tree is not empty, then exactly one item, called the *root* of the tree, has no *parent* (that is, is not the child of any other item); and

3. every other item in the tree has exactly one parent and is a descendant (a child or a child of a child, and so on) of the root.

In Fig. 12.5, the root of the tree contains the item we examine first in a binary search, and the children of any item are those we can examine next. If we view trees recursively, we see that any nonempty tree consists of a root and zero or more subtrees; the roots of those subtrees are the children of the root in the parent tree.

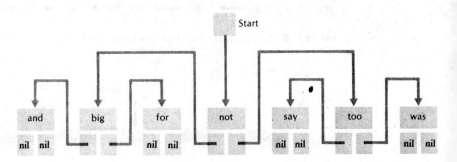

Figure 12.4 ■ Pointers indicating succession of probes in binary search

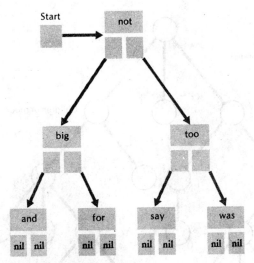

Figure 12.5 ■ Data structure associated with binary search

The terminology concerning trees mixes metaphors, combining genealogical terms (such as parent and child) that are appropriate for family trees with agricultural terms (such as root) that are appropriate for ordinary trees. Pictorially, we represent trees by diagrams such as those in Figs. 12.5 and 12.6. Lines extending downward from an item connect that item to its children. The root appears at the top of a tree, not at the bottom. While ordinary trees grow up (not down), trees that represent hierarchies grow downward, with the root sitting at the top of the hierarchy.

The tree in Fig. 12.5 is a *binary* tree since each item in the tree has at most two children. The first of these is its *left* child and the second its *right* child. Furthermore, it is an *ordered* tree since each item in the tree is greater than (in numeric or alphabetic order) the items in the subtree rooted at its left child and is less than or equal to the items in the subtree rooted at its right child.

A simple variant of the binary search hunts for a specified item in an ordered binary tree. We compare that item with those in the tree, starting at the root of the tree. If the item is smaller than the one at the root, we look for it in the left subtree; if it is larger, we look for it in the right subtree. We stop looking when we find the item or when we encounter a **nil** pointer.

We will code this procedure as a boolean-valued function *inList* in Pascal. In fact, we will create a library *tree1* of procedures, analogous to *link1*, that maintains lists represented as ordered binary trees. As before, the tasks performed by this library are more important than the particular representation chosen for a binary tree. These tasks include creating an empty tree, adding items to a tree, removing them from a tree, searching a tree, and displaying its contents.

First, however, we need to introduce some additional terminology concerning trees. An item in a tree with no children is called a *leaf* of the tree. A *path* in a tree

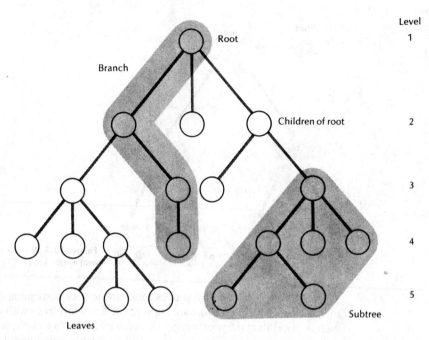

Figure 12.6 ■ Components of a tree of height 5

is a linear sequence of items, each of which (other than the last) is the parent of the next item in the sequence. A *branch* in a tree is a path extending from the root of the tree to a leaf. A *subtree* of a tree consists of some item in that tree together with its children, its children's children, and so on. The *level* of an item in a tree is the number of items on the unique path in the tree extending from the root to that item. Finally, the *height* of a tree is the maximum level attained by items in that tree. Figure 12.6 illustrates these conventions.

REPRESENTATIONS FOR TREES

Pointers help to provide a natural representation for binary trees in Pascal. The declaration

```
{ declaration for binary tree }
type itemType   = . . .;
     binaryTree = ↑node;
     node       = record
                      item        : itemType;
                      left, right : binaryTree
                  end;
var t : binaryTree;
```

bears a strong resemblance to that for linked lists, the principal difference being that each node in a binary tree contains two pointers as opposed to one in a linked list. As before, the dynamic nature of the data structure will enable us to insert items into and remove them from a tree, without having to move other items in the tree.

SAMPLE APPLICATION OF ORDERED BINARY TREES

Before we construct the library *tree1*, we use it to write a program *treeDemo* (Pascal Samples 12.1 and 12.2) that counts the number of distinct words in a file of text and prints an alphabetical list of those words. As with *linkDemo*, we treat a list as an abstract data type to be manipulated by a library of procedures. In *treeDemo* itself, we pay little attention to the data structure used by the procedures in the library *tree1* and no attention to the algorithms used to add words to the list or to display the contents of the list in order. Yet, when provided with *tree1* to maintain a list efficiently as an ordered binary tree, *treeDemo* counts the words in a text much more quickly than does *linkDemo*.

When we give *treeDemo* the same file of text that we gave *linkDemo*, it produces the output displayed in Pascal Sample 12.3, counting the words in that text in about 70 percent of the time required by *linkDemo*. Later in this section we analyze the procedures in the library *tree1* to explain the increased efficiency of *treeDemo*.

■ **PASCAL SAMPLE 12.1**   The program *treeDemo* (declarations)

{ demonstrates the use of an ordered binary tree by counting the total }
{ number of words and the number of distinct words in a file of text   }

program *treeDemo*(*input*, *output*, *source*);

const *stringLength* = 16;

type *string*   = **packed array** [1..*stringLength*] **of** *char*;
     itemType   = *string*;
     binaryTree = ↑*node*;
     node   = **record**
                 item   : *itemType*;
                 left, *right* : *binaryTree*
            end;

var *filename* : *string*;
     source : *text*;
     word   : *string*;
     nWords : *integer*;   { counts all words   }
     nDiff   : *integer*;   { counts different words }
     t   : *binaryTree*;

#include 'stringSubs2';   { *readString*, *skipBlanks* }
#include 'treel';   { tree handling procedures }

PASCAL SAMPLE 12.2   The program *treeDemo* (main program)

```
begin
    write('File name: ');
    readString(input, filename);
    reset(source, filename);

    nWords := 0;
    nDiff := 0;
    startList(t);

    skipBlanks(source);
    while not eof(source) do
        begin                                    { extract words from file }
            readString(source, word);
            nWords := nWords + 1;
            if not inList(t, word) then
                begin
                    insert(t, word);
                    nDiff := nDiff + 1
                end;
            skipBlanks(source)
        end;

    writeln;
    write('There are ', nWords:1, ' words in all, ');
    writeln(nDiff:1, ' of which are distinct.');
    writeln('They are:');
    print(t);
    writeln
end.   { of treeDemo }
```

PASCAL SAMPLE 12.3   The program *treeDemo* (sample use)

```
File name: words

There are 25 words in all, 21 of which are distinct.
They are:
a               after           and             broke
came            crown           down            fell
fetch           hill            his             jack
jill            of              pail            the
to              tumbling        up              water
went
```

LIBRARIES TO MAINTAIN ORDERED BINARY TREES

As for linked lists, we can use iteration or recursion to maintain an ordered binary tree. Now, however, the use of recursion makes our work substantially easier. To illustrate the power of recursion, we construct two libraries of procedures that maintain an ordered binary tree: *tree1* for iterative procedures and *tree1r* for recursive procedures.

Comments at the beginning of *tree1* describe the procedures in that library and the declarations they require. (See Pascal Sample 12.4.) Identical comments (except for the first line) occur at the beginning of *tree1r*. The *startList* procedure and the *emptyList* function are practically identical to those in *link1*, differing only in that their parameter is now a *binaryTree* rather than a *linkedList*. (See Pascal Sample 12.5.)

■ **PASCAL SAMPLE 12.4** The library *tree1* (initial comments)

```
{ tree1: iterative procedures to maintain an ordered binary tree }

{    The following procedures and functions are available to  }
{ maintain a list represented as an ordered binary tree t:    }
{                                                             }
{ Procedures:                                                 }
{                                                             }
{ delete(t, x)      deletes all entries containing x from t   }
{ insert(t, x)      inserts an entry containing x in t        }
{ print(t)          prints the contents of all entries in t in order }
{ startList(t)      initializes t to be an empty list         }
{                                                             }
{ Functions:                                                  }
{                                                             }
{ emptyList(t)      returns true if t is an empty list        }
{ inList(t, x)      returns true if an entry in t contains x   }
{                                                             }
{                                                             }
{    Any program calling one of these procedures or functions }
{ must contain the following declarations. (Here itemType is a }
{ real, ordinal, or string type.)                             }
{                                                             }
{ type itemType    = . . .;                                   }
{      binaryTree  = ↑node;                                   }
{      node        = record                                   }
{                       item       : itemType;                }
{                       left, right : binaryTree              }
{                    end;                                     }
```

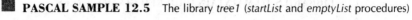

PASCAL SAMPLE 12.5   The library *tree1* (*startList* and *emptyList* procedures)

procedure *startList*(**var** *t* : *binaryTree*);
    { initializes *t* to an empty tree }
    begin
        t := **nil**
    end;   { of *startList* }

function *emptyList*(*t* : *binaryTree*) : *boolean*;
    { returns *true* if the tree *t* is empty }
    begin
        emptyList := (*t* = **nil**)
    end;   { of *emptyList* }

SEARCHING AN ORDERED BINARY TREE

To determine whether an ordered binary tree contains a specified item, we use the underlying order of the tree to direct our search toward the desired item. Using recursion, we arrive immediately at the definition of the *inList* function from *tree1r*, displayed as Pascal Sample 12.6. There we search for an item x by looking first at the root of the tree. If the item at the root is larger than x, we search for x in the left subtree; if it is smaller, we search for x in the right subtree. We stop when we find x or reach an empty subtree.

To use iteration instead of recursion, we must proceed down a branch of the tree looking for x. Starting at the root of the tree, we compare x with items in the tree, stopping the search when we find the item or when we encounter a **nil** pointer at the end of a branch. If an item in the tree is too big, we examine its left child

PASCAL SAMPLE 12.6   The library *tree1r* (recursive *inList* function)

function *inList*(*t* : *binaryTree*; *x* : *itemType*) : *boolean*;
    { returns *true* if *x* is in the tree *t* }
    begin
        if *t* = **nil then**
            inList := *false*
        else if *x* = *t↑.item* **then**
            inList := *true*
        else if *x* < *t↑.item* **then**
            inList := *inList*(*t↑.left*, *x*)
        else
            inList := *inList*(*t↑.right*, *x*)
    end;   { of *inList* }

PASCAL SAMPLE 12.7 The library *tree1* (iterative *inList* function)

function *inList*(*t* : *binaryTree*; *x* : *itemType*) : *boolean*;

> { returns *true* if *x* is in the tree *t* }
>
> **var** *found* : *boolean*;   { true if *x* is found   }
>   *next*   : *binaryTree*;   { next node to examine }
>
> **begin**
>   *found* := *false*;
>   *next* := *t*;
>   **while not** *found* **and** (*next* <> **nil**) **do**
>   **if** *x* = *next*↑.*item* **then**
>   *found* := *true*
>   **else if** *x* < *next*↑.*item* **then**
>   *next* := *next*↑.*left*
>   **else**
>   *next* := *next*↑.*right*;
>   *inList* := *found*
> **end**; { of *inList* }

---

next; if it is too small, we examine its right child. A variable *next* keeps track of the item to be examined next. (See Pascal Sample 12.7.)

Searching an ordered binary tree with *inList* is generally faster than searching a vector or a linked list with a linear search. This is because the maximum number of items examined by *inList* equals the height of the tree, not the number of items in the tree. The height of an *n*-item tree can be as small as $\lceil \log_2(n+1) \rceil$, so that *inList* makes the same number of probes as a binary search when all branches in the tree have approximately the same length. (See Exercises 4 and 5 at the end of this section.) However, if an *n*-item tree consists of a single branch, then its height is *n* and *inList* degenerates into a linear search of that branch. Thus we may want to take extra care when inserting items in a tree to ensure that it does not become too tall. (See Exercise 7 at the end of this section.)

INSERTING ITEMS IN AN ORDERED BINARY TREE

The *insert* procedures from *tree1* and *tree1r* do as little as possible when they insert items in a tree. They preserve the order in a binary tree, but do not keep the height of the tree to a minimum. They insert a new item in an ordered binary tree by making it a leaf of the tree—to add a leaf requires changing but a single pointer. Figure 12.7 shows the effects of adding the words in the phrases look before you leap and before you leap, look as leaves of an initially empty ordered binary tree. The two phrases contain the same words, but the different order of insertion results in different trees.

Order of insertion: look before you leap

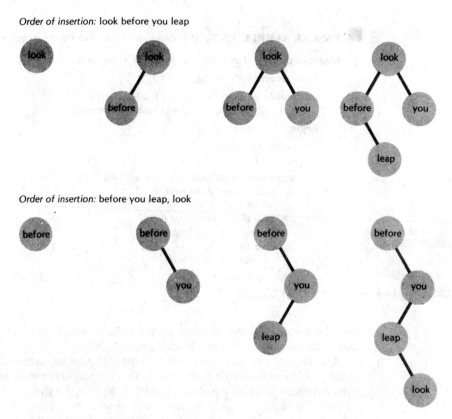

Order of insertion: before you leap, look

Figure 12.7 ■ Inserting words in an ordered binary tree

A procedure to insert items in a tree is similar to the *inList* procedure in that it must search for the place to add a new leaf. The recursive version of the procedure *insert*, displayed as Pascal Sample 12.8, is somewhat simpler than the iterative version. It adds a leaf to an empty tree by making that leaf the root of the tree. It adds a leaf to a nonempty tree by adding it to the left subtree if it is less than the item at the root and to the right subtree otherwise. As did the recursive version of *insert* in *link1*, the recursive version of *insert* in *tree1* relies on a **var** parameter in Pascal to keep track of which pointer must change when a new leaf is added to the tree.

Note that *insert*, unlike *inList*, does not distinguish the case in which $x = t\uparrow.item$. As it did in *link1*, *insert* duplicates an item that is already in the tree, the duplicate going into the right subtree below that item.

To construct an iterative version of *insert*, we modify the iterative version of *inList*. Now we must remember the last node that we examined on the way to the point of insertion, and we must remember whether the new leaf is to be the left or

---

PASCAL SAMPLE 12.8   The library *tree1r* (recursive *insert* procedure)

procedure *insert*(**var** *t* : *binaryTree*; *x* : *itemType*);
    { inserts a new node containing *x* in the *tree t* }
    begin
        if *t* = **nil then**
            begin
                new(*t*);
                t↑.*item* := *x*;
                t↑.*left* := **nil**;
                t↑.*right* := **nil**
            end
        else if *x* < *t*↑.*item* **then**
            insert(*t*↑.*left*, *x*)
        else
            insert(*t*↑.*right*, *x*)
    end; { of *insert* }

right child of that node. The variable *last* in Pascal Sample 12.9 keeps track of where a pointer to the new leaf belongs, and the variable *goLeft* keeps track of whether that leaf should be added to the left or to the right. As in the iterative *insert* procedure from *list1*, we treat adding an item to an empty tree as a special case.

PASCAL SAMPLE 12.9   The library *tree1* (iterative *insert* procedure)

procedure *insert*(**var** *t* : *binaryTree*; *x* : *itemType*);
    { inserts a new node containing *x* in the tree *t* }
    var *last*, *next* : *binaryTree*;
        goLeft   : *boolean*;
    begin
        { find node that will be *x*'s parent }
        last := **nil**;
        next := *t*;
        while *next* <> **nil do**
            begin
                last := *next*;
                goLeft := (*x* < *next*↑.*item*);
                if *goLeft* **then**
                    next := *next*↑.*left*
                else
                    next := *next*↑.*right*
            end;

PASCAL SAMPLE 12.9   The library *tree1* (iterative *insert* procedure, continued)

```
{ insert new node containing x under last node visited }
new(next);
next↑.item := x;
next↑.left  := nil;
next↑.right := nil;
if last = nil then
    t := next
else if goLeft then
    last↑.left := next
else
    last↑.right := next
end;   { of insert }
```

DISPLAYING THE CONTENTS OF AN ORDERED BINARY TREE

Just as we can insert items efficiently in an ordered binary tree, so can we display in order the entire contents of that tree. Here recursion makes an even more striking difference than it did for the *insert* procedure. The recursive version of the *print* procedure is short and straightforward. The iterative version is considerably longer and more subtle.

To generate an ordered list of the items in an ordered binary tree, we must list the items in its left subtree first, then the item at the root of the tree (which, by definition, comes after the items in the left subtree), and then the items in its right subtree (which, by definition, come after the item at the root). Recursion helps us to list in order the items in a subtree: we simply apply our listing procedure to that subtree instead of to the entire tree. Pascal Sample 12.10 displays the recursive version

---

PASCAL SAMPLE 12.10   The library *tree1r* (recursive *print* procedure)

```
procedure print( t : binaryTree );
    { prints in order the contents of all nodes in t }
    begin
        if t <> nil then
            begin
                print(t↑.left);
                write(t↑.item);
                print(t↑.right)
            end
    end;   { of print }
```

of *print* from *tree1r* that operates in this manner. We defer presenting the iterative version of *print* momentarily while we analyze the efficiency of the *treeDemo*.

EFFICIENCY OF ALGORITHMS USING ORDERED BINARY TREES

The *insert* and *print* procedures together enable us to sort and print a list of n items in time proportional to $n \log_2 n$. For such a list, we invoke the *insert* procedure n times to insert each of the items in an ordered binary tree. If the resulting tree is not too bare, each of these insertions requires examining approximately $\lceil \log_2(n + 1) \rceil$ nodes in the tree. Then we invoke the *print* procedure to display the items in order. Regardless of the shape of the tree, the *print* procedure examines each node only once. Hence the time required by this sorting algorithm is proportional to $n \lceil \log_2(n + 1) \rceil + n$, which grows like $n \log_2 n$, if the shape of the tree remains reasonable.

Is the shape of the tree likely to remain reasonable if we use this algorithm to sort a list? Analyses such as those in Exercise 5 at the end of this section show that if a list of n items is arranged randomly to begin with, we can expect the height of the ordered binary tree generated from that list to be about $1.39 \log_2 n$. Hence, on the average, this sorting algorithm works in time proportional to $n \log_2 n$. Of course, nonrandom lists can lead to much taller trees and much longer sorting times. In Section 12.3, we will construct a variation *heapsort* of this algorithm that always works in time proportional to $n \log_2 n$.

These calculations explain why *treeDemo* takes less time to count the number d of distinct words in a file of text than does *linkDemo*. Roughly speaking, *linkDemo* must compare each of the n words in the file with the d distinct words, for a total of nd comparisons. By using a binary tree, *treeDemo* makes only on the order of $n \log_2 d$ comparisons.

DISPLAYING THE CONTENTS OF AN ORDERED BINARY TREE, REVISITED

Let us return now to the *print* procedure and consider how to code it iteratively rather than recursively. Our task now is much more difficult than before. In order to find and print the smallest item in a tree, we must follow the left pointers from the root of the tree as far as possible, remembering the nodes we pass along the way, and printing the first item we encounter that has no left child; this item is indeed the smallest in the tree. Then we must back up to the nodes we passed over, printing the items in those nodes followed by the items in the right subtrees below them. A stack is the appropriate data structure for remembering passed-over nodes, because we want to return to them in the opposite order of our original examinations. Pascal Sample 12.11 displays an iterative version of *print*. The comment at the beginning of the main loop in that procedure describes exactly how the stack keeps track of the items that remain to be printed. The complexity and subtlety of this iterative procedure clearly show the power of recursion.

■ **PASCAL SAMPLE 12.11**   The library *tree1* (iterative *print* procedure)

procedure *print*(*t* : *binaryTree*);
    { prints in order the contents of all nodes in *t* }
    const *maxHeight* = 100;   { maximum height of tree }
    var *stack* : **array** [1..*maxHeight*] **of** *binaryTree*;
        n   : 0..*maxHeight*;
        s   : *binaryTree*;
    begin
        n := 0;
        s := *t*;
        while (*s* <> **nil**) **or** (*n* > 0) **do**
            begin
                { need to print items in the subtree *s* followed by   }
                { the items at the roots of the trees in the stack and }
                { in the right subtrees of those trees   }
                while *s* <> **nil do**   { find smallest item   }
                    begin
                        n := *n* + 1;   { remember larger item   }
                        stack[*n*] := *s*;
                        s := *s*↑.*left*
                    end;
                s := *stack*[*n*];   { unstack smallest item   }
                n := *n* − 1;
                write(*s*↑.*item*);   { print it   }
                s := *s*↑.*right*   { process its right subtree }
            end;
    end;   { of *print* }

DELETING ITEMS FROM AN ORDERED BINARY TREE

Finally, let us turn our attention to the problem of deleting items from an ordered binary tree. This task requires that we exercise some care if the tree is to remain ordered. Certain items are easy to remove. A leaf, for example, can be removed or *pruned* from the tree by changing a single pointer to **nil**. Furthermore, if a node has a single child, we can simply delete that node and move its child up into its place. Figure 12.8 illustrates how easy it is to remove these types of nodes from a tree.

If a node has two children, more work is required to delete that node. For a first approach, we could delete that node, move its left child up into its place, and move its right child to the appropriate place below the left child. As shown by Figs. 12.9 and 12.10, the difficulty with this approach is that it can increase the height of the tree—something that should happen only when we insert nodes in the tree, not when we delete them.

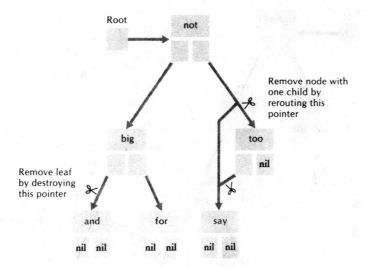

Figure 12.8 ■ Removing nodes with few children from a tree

A better approach to deleting a node with two children is to proceed as follows. First we locate the largest item in the left subtree below the node we want to delete. (In Fig. 12.9, this would be `for`.) Next we extract this item from the tree, which is easy since it has at most one child. Then we replace the node we want to delete with

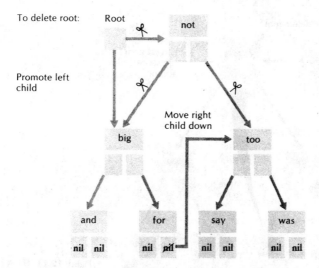

Figure 12.9 ■ Simple, but poor, method for removing node with two children

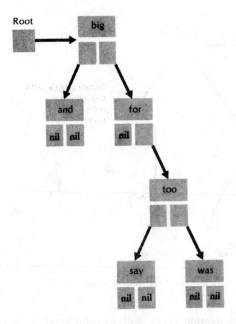

Figure 12.10 ■ Taller tree that results from poor deletion

this largest of its left descendents. Figure 12.11 illustrates the effect of deleting the root of the tree in Fig. 12.9 when we use this more sophisticated procedure, which does not increase the height of the tree.

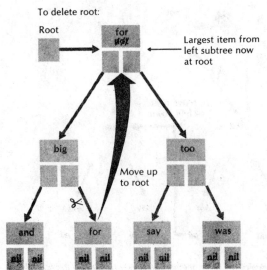

Figure 12.11 ■ A better way to delete a node with two children

PASCAL SAMPLE 12.12   The library *tree1r* (recursive *delete* procedure)

```
procedure delete( var t : binaryTree; x : itemType );
    { deletes all nodes containing x from the tree t }
    var oldNode : binaryTree;                        { node to delete from tree }

    procedure changeRoot( var p : binaryTree );
        { replaces the node at the root of the tree t by the node }
        { containing the largest item in the subtree p           }
        var q : binaryTree;                          { node with largest item    }
        begin
            if p↑.right = nil then                   { p↑.item is largest        }
                begin
                    q := p;                          { node to move              }
                    p := p↑.left;                    { remove it from subtree    }
                    q↑.right := t↑.right;            { attach branches of tree   }
                    q↑.left := t↑.left;
                    t := q                           { make it the root          }
                end
            else
                changeRoot( p↑.right )               { find larger item          }
        end;   { of changeRoot }

    begin
        if t <> nil then
            if x = t↑.item then                      { delete this node          }
                begin
                    oldNode := t;                    { remember node             }
                    if t↑.left = nil then            { prune null left branch    }
                        t := t↑.right
                    else if t↑.right = nil then      { prune null right branch   }
                        t := t↑.left
                    else
                        changeRoot( t↑.left );       { find new root             }
                        dispose( oldNode );          { release old root          }
                        delete( t, x )               { look for another x        }
                end
            else if x < t↑.item then
                delete( t↑.left, x )
            else
                delete( t↑.right, x )
    end;   { of delete }
```

The *delete* procedure from *tree1r*, displayed as Pascal Sample 12.12, deletes all nodes containing a specified item from a tree using the procedure just described. When it must delete a node with two children, it invokes a subsidiary procedure to move the largest of the items in the left subtree up into its place. Implementation of an iterative version of this procedure is left to the exercises that follow.

EXERCISES

1. Define functions suitable for inclusion in *tree1r* that return

   (a) the height of a binary tree;

   (b) the number of nodes in a binary tree;

   (c) the average level of a node in a binary tree;

   (d) the smallest item in an ordered binary tree;

   (e) the largest item in an ordered binary tree;

   *(f) the median item in an ordered binary tree (that is, the item that occurs halfway through the ordered list of all items in the tree).

2. There are five ordered binary trees that contain the three distinct words in the phrase see spot run! run spot run!.

   (a) Draw diagrams of these five ordered binary trees.

   (b) Which of these trees requires, in the worst case, the fewest probes to locate a word from the phrase in the tree? How many probes are required in this worst case?

   (c) Which of these trees requires, in the average case, the fewest probes to locate a word from the phrase in the tree? More precisely, if we locate the word see in the tree once, the word spot twice, and the word run three times, which tree requires the fewest probes altogether? How many probes are required in the average case for this tree?

3. Write the following procedures.

   (a) An iterative version of the *delete* procedure suitable for inclusion in *tree1*.

   (b) A procedure *insertIfNew*, as described in Exercise 4, Section 11.2, that inserts an item into an ordered binary tree only if that item does not occur already in the tree.

4. Suppose that a binary tree contains n items.

   (a) How long can its longest branch be?

   (b) How short can its longest branch be?

5. Estimate the average height of an ordered binary tree with n items as follows.

   (a) Write a program to estimate this average empirically by creating ordered binary trees from randomly ordered lists of the integers from 1 to n and using the function defined in Exercise 1(a) to compute the height of those trees.

   *(b) Show mathematically that the average height of an ordered binary tree with n items is $2 \ln 2 \log_2 n$.

   (c) How much higher is this average height than the height of the shortest ordered binary tree with n items?

6. A binary tree is *perfectly balanced* if, for any node in the tree, the two subtrees below that node differ in size by at most one. Show that the maximum time required to insert an item in a perfectly balanced ordered binary tree increases linearly with the size of the tree. (*Hint:* Show that adding a new item may require changing every node in the tree.)

•7. A binary tree is *balanced* if, for any node in the tree, the two subtrees below that node differ in height by at most one.

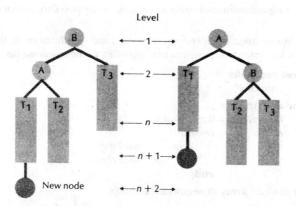

Figure 12.12 ■ Rebalancing a tree when exterior subtree grows in height

(a) Devise an algorithm for inserting an item in a balanced ordered binary tree. (*Hint:* Modify the representation for a binary tree to keep track of a balance factor at each node, where this factor equals the height of the right subtree minus that of the left. When inserting a new item in the tree, update the balance factors of its ancestors and correct any imbalance of ± 2 by one of the strategies illustrated in Figs. 12.12 and 12.13.)

(b) Show that the time required to insert an item in a balanced ordered binary tree increases linearly with the height of the tree.

(c) Show that the maximum height of a balanced ordered binary tree increases logarithmically with the size of the tree.

(d) Devise an algorithm for deleting an item from a balanced ordered binary tree.

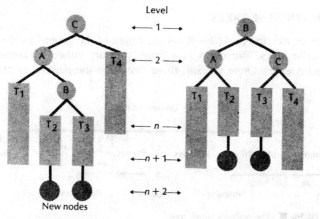

Figure 12.13 ■ Rebalancing a tree when interior subtree grows in height

8. Devise an algorithm for converting an ordered binary tree into an ordered doubly linked list.

9. Write a library *tree2* of procedures with the same specifications as those in *tree1*, but which uses a vector to represent a tree according to the following declarations.

```
const maxNodes = . . .;
      nullLink  = 0;

type itemType   = . . .;
     binaryTree = 0..maxNodes;
     node       = record
                    item       : itemType;
                    left, right : binaryTree
                  end;

var storage : array [0..maxNodes] of node;
```

Here we represent a binary tree by a subscript that indicates where to find its root in the vector *storage*. Links to the children of a node are also subscripts, with a subscript of zero representing a null link. The node in *storage*[0] plays a special role: its left child is the first node in a linked list extending to the left of nodes not currently in any tree; this list serves as a source of new nodes for the *insert* procedure and as a repository of nodes discarded by the *delete* procedure.

12.2   OTHER TREE STRUCTURES

Ordered binary trees are but one of many kinds of trees. Just as they provide a convenient data structure for applications involving searching and sorting, so do other trees provide convenient data structures for other applications. This section introduces us to some of those applications and to some common methods for manipulating trees.

APPLICATIONS OF TREES

The *family tree* in Fig. 12.14 shows the origin of the genealogical terminology used to describe trees. The items in a family tree are either unmarried individuals or married couples. Quite literally, these items are the parents of their children. The

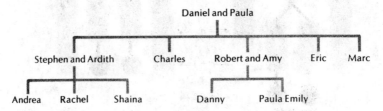

Figure 12.14 ■ The author's family tree

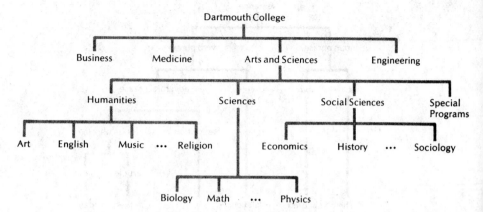

Figure 12.15 ■ Simplified organization chart for the Faculty of Dartmouth College

head of the family is the root of the tree. And since a couple is a single item in the tree, every item other than the root does have exactly one parent.

Similarly, trees provide natural representations for many other hierarchical structures. Figure 12.15, for example, displays a typical organization chart. The items in the tree are administrative units, and the children of any unit are its administrative subunits.

Classification schemes provide other examples of hierarchical structures. Figure 12.16 illustrates a familiar classification scheme from biology. Similar hierarchical schemes occur in the classification of rocks and minerals, in the Library of Congress cataloging system, in the table of contents for a book, and in the system of file directories maintained by typical computer systems.

Applications involving such hierarchies require us to create, search, or otherwise manipulate trees. For example, in order to find an item in a hierarchy, we must search a tree. To display the entire hierarchy, we must examine the items in a tree in an appropriate order. And to change a hierarchy, we must move items or subtrees from one location in a tree to another.

Somewhat less obviously, hierarchical classification schemes also arise in linguistics. Figure 12.17 shows how we can use a tree to clarify the syntactic structure

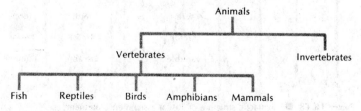

Figure 12.16 ■ Zoological classification of animals

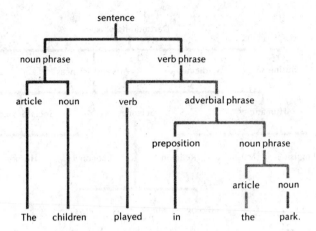

Figure 12.17 ■ Syntactic structure of an English sentence

of a sentence in the English language. The ancestors of an item describe the syntactic role that the item plays in a sentence. An algorithm that creates such a tree, thereby revealing the syntactic structure of a sentence, is said to *parse* that sentence.

Trees also help us to clarify the syntactic structure of phrases in artificial languages such as Pascal. For example, the tree in Fig. 12.18 shows how to derive an

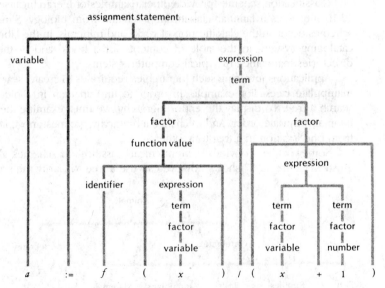

Figure 12.18 ■ Syntactic structure of Pascal assignment statement

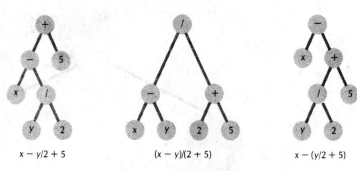

$x - y/2 + 5$ $(x - y)/(2 + 5)$ $x - (y/2 + 5)$

Figure 12.19 ■ Syntax trees for arithmetic expressions

assignment statement from the syntax diagrams in this book. The children of an item correspond, from left to right, to the objects encountered by tracing a path through the relevant syntax diagram.

We can describe the syntactic structure of an arithmetic expression or a Pascal program somewhat more compactly by means of a *syntax tree*. For example, let us consider arithmetic expressions such as $x - y/2 + 5$ that are built up from numbers and variables using the binary operators $+$, $-$, $*$, and $/$. Figure 12.19 contrasts the syntactic structure of this expression with two others, showing that we evaluate it as $(x - (y/2)) + 5$ and not as $(x - y)/(2 + 5)$ or $x - (y/2 + 5)$.

The items in these syntax trees are numbers, variables, and operators. Each operator in a syntax tree has two children corresponding to its left and right operands. Numbers and variables in a syntax tree have no children. To evaluate an expression represented by a syntax tree, we use recursion or we work our way up from the bottom of the tree toward the root, evaluating operators by applying them to the values of their children. The operator at the root is evaluated last.

Nonlinear representations as trees for expressions such as $x - y/2 + 5$ have decided advantages over linear representations of these expressions as strings of characters. All the information required to evaluate an expression is contained in its syntax tree, and we do not need to know anything about operator precedence or parentheses to find its value. In Chapter 13, we will write a program that builds a syntax tree by parsing an expression and then uses the tree to evaluate the expression.

REPRESENTATIONS FOR TREES

There is a clear representation for a binary tree as a linked data structure with two pointers per node. But there is no clear representation for a tree with a branching factor greater than two. When the branching factor in a tree is low, or when all its items have approximately the same number of children, we can use a vector of pointers to locate those children. (See Fig. 12.20.)

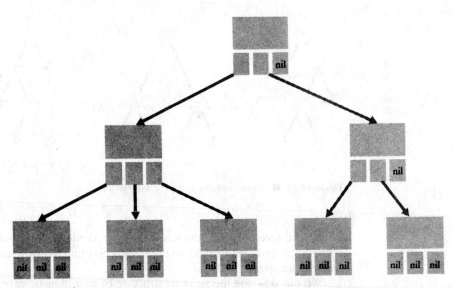

Figures 12.20 ■ Locating children in a tree with a vector of pointers

However, this representation is less than satisfactory when some items have many children and others have few. In these situations, we can avoid allocating space for many large vectors by placing the children of an item in a linked list. As Fig. 12.21 illustrates, such a representation requires only two pointers per item: one to the left-most child of that item and one to its next sibling.

Some applications warrant more elaborate structures. For example, each item in a tree could carry a pointer to its parent. However, for the remainder of this chapter we will restrict our attention to binary trees. Despite their simplicity, they provide enough generality for use with many interesting applications.

TREE TRAVERSALS

The manner in which we create a tree generally depends on what that tree represents. For example, in Section 12.1 we learned how to create an ordered binary tree, which represents an ordered list, by inserting items in that tree. And in Chapter 13 we will learn how to create a syntax tree by parsing an arithmetic expression. Similarly, what we want to do with a tree often depends on what that tree represents. However, many applications require us to process all the items in a tree in some particular order, and so it pays to develop some general strategies for *traversing* a tree, that is, for examining or *visiting* all the nodes in a tree.

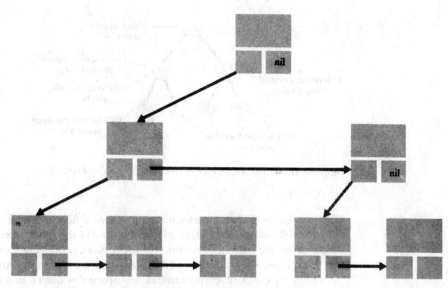

Figure 12.21 ■ Locating children in a tree with a linked list

We have already used one such strategy in Section 12.1, where the procedure *print* in the library *tree1r* displayed the items from an ordered binary tree in increasing numeric or alphabetic order. That procedure uses the following recursive strategy, known as an *inorder* traversal, to visit all nodes in a tree.

```
{ inorder traversal of a tree }
if tree is nonempty then
    begin
        traverse left subtree;
        process root;
        traverse right subtree
    end
```

The term "inorder traversal" relates not so much to printing the contents of an ordered binary tree in the appropriate order as it does to reconstructing an arithmetic expression from its syntax tree using the normal *infix* notation for binary operators. Infix notation places binary operators between their operands, as in the expression $b*b - 4*a*c$. Figure 12.22 illustrates how we can use an inorder traversal to reconstruct this expression from its syntax tree.

In general, we must exercise a bit more care than shown in Fig. 12.22 when we reconstruct an arithmetic expression from its syntax tree using an inorder traversal.

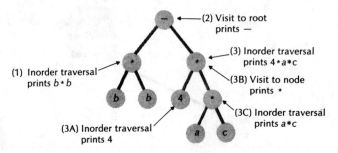

Figure 12.22 ■ Inorder traversal of syntax tree for $b*b - 4*a*c$

The problem is that an inorder traversal of two different syntax trees can produce the same results. For example, an inorder traversal of the syntax tree for $(b*b - 4)*a*c$ simply drops the parentheses from that expression, producing the same results as in Fig. 12.22. Exercise 7 at the end of this section suggests ways to remedy this problem.

Other traversals of a syntax tree do not share this defect. In a *preorder* traversal, we visit the root first by using the following recursive strategy.

{ preorder traversal of a tree }

if tree is nonempty **then**
    begin
        process root;
        traverse left subtree;
        traverse right subtree
    end

A preorder traversal of the syntax tree in Fig. 12.22 produces the expression $-*bb*4*ac$, written in *prefix* notation, in which each operator appears before its operands. Prefix notation looks more familiar if we regard operators such as $-$ and $*$ as functions and insert a few parentheses and commas. Then $-*bb*4*ac$ becomes $-(*(b, b), *(4, *(a, c)))$, which is the way we normally write expressions using functional notation. While parentheses and commas increase the readability of prefix notation, we can get by without them: preorder traversals of different syntax trees produce different prefix expressions. (See Exercise 5 at the end of this section.) The advantages of prefix notation were noticed first by Polish mathematicians; hence many call it *Polish* notation.

A preorder traversal of a binary tree is also known as a *depth-first* traversal. It visits nodes in a tree starting with the root and always proceeds as far as possible down the left-most branch of any subtree before heading off to the right. When it reaches the end of a branch, it backs up to the nearest untraveled route to the right. By contrast, a *breadth-first* traversal visits the nodes in a tree a level at a time starting

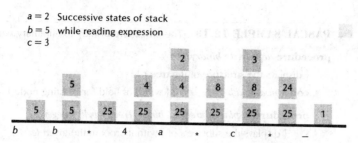

$a = 2$ Successive states of stack
$b = 5$ while reading expression
$c = 3$

Figure 12.23 ■ Evaluation of postfix expression using a stack

at the root and proceeding to levels 2, 3, 4, ..., n in that order. (See Exercise 4 at the end of this section.)

Finally, in a *postorder* traversal of a binary tree, we visit the root last by using the following recursive strategy.

{ postorder traversal of a tree }

if tree is nonempty **then**
    begin
        traverse left subtree;
        traverse right subtree;
        process root
    end

A postorder traversal of the syntax tree in Fig. 12.22 yields the expression $bb*4ac**-$, written in *postfix* notation, in which each operator appears after its operands. Like prefix notation, postfix is unambiguous: postorder traversals of different syntax trees produce different postfix expressions. Several commercial pocket calculators exploit another advantage of postfix notation, which is also known as *reverse Polish* notation. As Fig. 12.23 shows, it is particularly easy to evaluate a postfix expression by using a stack of intermediate values: we simply read an expression from left to right, stacking the values of numbers and variables; whenever we reach an operator, we pop the last two values off the stack, apply the operator to them, and push the result back onto the stack; when we reach the end of the expression, its value resides on the stack. (See Exercise 9 at the end of this section.)

DISPLAYING THE STRUCTURE OF A TREE

We conclude this section by using an inorder traversal of a binary tree, similar to that performed by the *print* procedure in *tree1*, to display the structure of that tree. We begin by having an inorder traversal display each item in the tree on a separate

---

PASCAL SAMPLE 12.13   The procedure *display* (preliminary version)

procedure *display*(*t* : *binaryTree*);
   { displays the structure of the tree *t* }
   const *nodeWidth* = 5;   { width of field for printing node }

   procedure *displaySubtree*(*s* : *binaryTree*; *level* : *integer*);
      { displays the subtree *s* of *t* with its root at the given *level* }
   begin
     if *s* <> **nil then**
       begin
         displaySubtree(*s*↑.*left*, *level* + 1);
         writeln(' ' : *nodeWidth*∗(*level* − 1) + 1, *s*↑.*item*);
         displaySubtree(*s*↑.*right*, *level* + 1)
       end
   end; { of *displaySubtree* }

   begin
     displaySubtree(*t*, 1)
   end; { of *display* }

---

line, indented a distance proportional to its level in the tree. When applied to the tree that we created in the sample use of *treeDemo*, the version of the *display* procedure in Pascal Sample 12.13 produces the results shown in Pascal Sample 12.14.

PASCAL SAMPLE 12.14   The procedure *display* (preliminary version's output)

```
          a
     and
               fetch
          hill
jack
     jill
                              of
                    pail
               the
                    to
          up
               water
          went
```

Here the structure of the tree is just beginning to emerge. The root is printed left-most in the display, the right subtree at the bottom of the display, and the left subtree at the top. Words occur in alphabetical order as we read down the display. If we change Pascal Sample 12.13 to print the items in the right subtree before those in the left, we can improve the picture somewhat. As Pascal Sample 12.15 shows, we can now turn the display a quarter turn to have the root appear at the top and the left and right subtrees in the proper locations in the tree.

Better yet, we can have *display* remember how it got to each node and use this information to draw lines showing the branches in the tree. We modify *display* by passing the recursive *displaySubtree* procedure an additional parameter *d* that indi-

■ **PASCAL SAMPLE 12.15**   The procedure *display* (printing right subtree first)

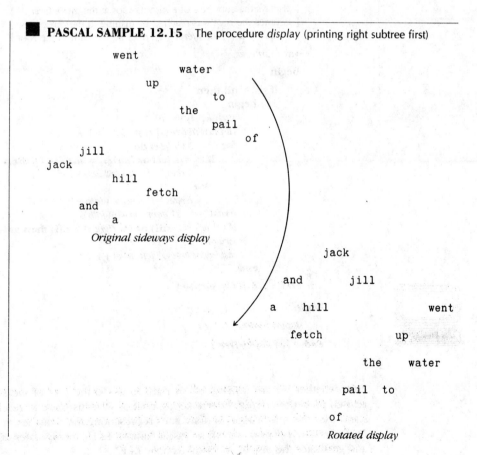

Original sideways display

Rotated display

PASCAL SAMPLE 12.16   The procedure *display* (final version)

```
procedure displayTree( t : binaryTree );
    { displays the structure of the tree t }
    const maxHeight = 10;                            { maximum height of tree        }
          nodeWidth = 5;                             { width of field for printing node }
    type direction = (L, R);
    var turn : array [1..maxHeight] of direction;
    procedure displaySubtree( s     : binaryTree;    { subtree to display }
                              level : integer;       { level of its root }
                              d     : direction );   { how we got there }
    { displays the subtree s of t with its root at the given level   }
    { assumes the root was reached by turning in the directions      }
    { turn[1] = L, ..., turn[level − 1], d along the path to the root }
    var i : integer;
    begin
        if s <> nil then
            begin
                turn[level] := d;
                displaySubtree(s↑.right, level + 1, R);
                for i := 2 to level do
                    if (i = level) or (turn[i] = turn[i + 1]) then
                        write(' ' : nodeWidth + 1, '   ');
                    else
                        write(' ' : nodeWidth + 1, ' | ');
                write('−', s↑.item : nodeWidth);
                if (s↑.left <> nil) or (s↑.right <> nil) then write ('−| ');
                writeln;
                displaySubtree(s↑.left, level + 1, L)
            end
    end;  { of displaySubtree }
begin
    displaySubtree( t, 1, L)
end;  { of displayTree }
```

cates whether we are turning left or right to get to the root of the subtree *s*. The revised procedure *displaySubtree* keeps track of all turns made to reach the subtree *s* and uses this information to draw lines representing the branches in the tree. The final version of *display*, shown as Pascal Sample 12.16, incorporates these revisions and generates the display in Pascal Sample 12.17.

◼ **PASCAL SAMPLE 12.17**   The procedure *display* (output from final version)

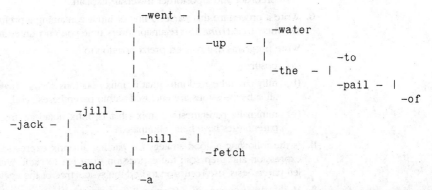

```
                        -went -  |  |
                        |        |           -water
                        |        -up   -  |
                        |                 |            -to
                        |                 -the   - |
                        |                          -pail -  |
                        |                                       -of
            -jill -     |
 -jack -  |
          |             -hill -  |
          |             |           -fetch
          |  -and  -  |
             -a
```

EXERCISES

1. Contrast the efficiency of searching an arbitrary binary tree with that of searching an ordered binary tree, as follows.

   (a) Define a function that returns the smallest item in an arbitrary binary tree.

   (b) How many comparisons does this function make when searching an *n*-item binary tree?

   (c) How many comparisons does your solution to Exercise 1(d) in Section 12.1 make when searching an *n*-item ordered binary tree?

2. Define boolean-valued functions suitable for inclusion in *tree1r* that take two trees *s* and *t* as parameters and return the value *true* if

   (a) *s* is identical to *t* (that is, *s* has the same items in the same locations as *t*);

   (b) *s* is the mirror image of *t*; and

   (c) *s* is a subtree of *t*.

3. Write a program to compute the number of binary trees that have height at most *n*. (*Hint:* Use recursion, noting that a tree has height at most *n* if its two subtrees have height at most *n* − 1.)

4. Write a procedure to print the items in a binary tree using a breadth-first traversal. (*Hint:* As you visit each node, enter its children into a queue.)

5. Investigate the information a traversal provides about the structure of a tree, as follows.

   (a) Prove that two syntax trees must be identical if they produce the same results under a preorder traversal.

   (b) Find two different binary trees that produce the same sequence of items under a preorder traversal.

   (c) Find two different binary trees that produce the same sequence of items under a postorder traversal.

    (d) Can two different binary trees produce the same sequences of items under both a preorder and a postorder traversal? Explain.

6. Write a procedure that parses a line of input containing a prefix expression and creates its syntax tree. (*Hint:* Use recursion every time you encounter an operator.)

7. Write programs that convert prefix notation to

    (a) postfix;

    (b) fully parenthesized infix [that is, infix notations such as $((b*b)-(4*(a*c)))$ in which all subexpressions are enclosed within parentheses]; and

  *(c) minimally parenthesized infix (that is, infix notations from which all superfluous parentheses have been eliminated).

8. Is the following a good strategy for parsing an infix expression? Fully parenthesize an expression and then scan the expression from left to right. Whenever you encounter a left parenthesis, use recursion to find the syntax tree of the enclosed subexpression.

9. Modify the program *calc3* (Section 7.4) so that it evaluates expressions in postfix notation.

10. Write a program to maintain a directory structured as a tree. Nodes in the tree correspond to directories, and the children of a node correspond to its subdirectories. Each directory has a name distinct from the names of its sibling directories, but not necessarily distinct from the names of other directories. Your program should respond to the following commands, enabling you to move around in, inspect, and change the tree.

    (a) c(hange directory) name

    Move to the subdirectory of the current directory with the given name. If no name is given, move to the directory at the root of the tree. If the name . . is given, then move to the parent of the current directory.

    (b) m(ake directory) name

    Create a new subdirectory with the given name in the current directory.

    (c) r(emove directory) name

    Remove the named directory from the current directory.

    (d) l(ist directory)

    List the contents of the current directory in alphabetical order.

    (e) l(ist directory) r(ecursively)

    Provide a recursive listing of the contents of the current directory, the contents of its subdirectories, and so on, in the following format.

```
subdirectory 1
    subdirectory 1.1
    subdirectory 1.2
        subdirectory 1.2.1
        subdirectory 1.2.2
    subdirectory 1.3
subdirectory 2
    subdirectory 2.1
        ⋮
```

11. Medical diagnostic procedures, chemical analyses, and games such as Twenty Questions involve a sequence of questions in which the answer to each question determines what will be asked next. The sequence of questions asked in such procedures can be represented by a tree. In the simplest case, each question can be answered either yes or no, and the tree is a binary tree. At each node of the tree is a question. A yes answer directs us to the left child for the next question, and a no answer directs us to the right child. The various possibilities that the sequence of questions can distinguish among form the leaves of the tree.

Write a program that plays the following guessing game. The program asks its user to think of an animal and then attempts to guess that animal by asking questions. During each play of the game, the program begins at the root of a tree of yes-no questions and asks the questions along the branch determined by the user's responses until a leaf is reached. The questions at the leaves have the form Is it a ...? (for example, Is it a mongoose?). If the user responds yes to this last question, the program is in luck and gloats appropriately. If the user responds no, the program capitulates gracefully and asks the user what the animal was. Then it asks the user to supply a question that would distinguish between this animal (say, a tarantula) and its last guess (say, a mongoose); that is, it requests a question that would be answered yes for a tarantula and no for a mongoose. Finally, the program adjusts the tree so that the branch it had just followed now ends in two leaves, Is it a mongoose? and Is it a tarantula?, with the parent node for these leaves containing the question supplied by the user. In this way the program learns to play better!

Initially, the tree of questions consists of a single node with a question such as Is it a monkey? After each play of the game, the program asks whether the user wants to play again and, if so, plays another game with its current tree of questions, which may be larger than in the previous game.

12. Enhance the program you wrote for Exercise 11 to initialize its tree of questions from a file containing the final state of the tree from the last play of the game.

*13. Devise an algorithm for producing an upright display of a binary tree rather than the sideways display produced by *display*. (*Hint:* Modify the representation for a binary tree to keep track of the width of the subtree below each node. Use a preorder traversal of the tree to compute these widths. Then display the tree using a breadth first traversal.)

12.3 HEAPSORT

In Section 12.1 we learned how to sort a list of items by inserting them into an ordered binary tree. This sorting algorithm has many characteristics in common with *quicksort*: on the average, it takes time proportional to $n \log_2 n$ to sort a list with n items; in the worst case, it takes time proportional to n; and it requires extra storage to organize the search (binary trees consume extra storage for pointers and *quicksort* consumes extra storage by invoking itself recursively). The merge sort is faster than either in the worst case, always taking time proportional to $n \log_2 n$; but it too requires extra storage for merging lists. Hence we may well wonder whether there is a sorting algorithm that takes time $n \log_2 n$ in the worst case, but does not consume any storage beyond that required for the list.

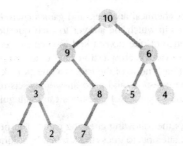

Figure 12.24 ■ A heap

As it happens, we can answer this question with a yes by using a special kind of binary tree known as a *heap*. Specifically, a heap is a binary tree satisfying the following three conditions.

1. Every item in a heap is larger than its children.

2. Every item in a heap either has exactly two children or occurs on the bottom two levels of the heap.

3. The leaves on the bottom level of the heap occur as far to the left as possible.

Figures 12.24 and 12.25 contrast a heap with some binary trees that fail to satisfy these three conditions.

Condition (1) guarantees that the largest item in a heap sits at the top of the heap. But it says nothing about which of its two children is larger. Thus a heap imposes less of an order than does an ordered binary tree.

Conditions (2) and (3) permit us to represent a heap using a nonlinked data structure. Namely, we can store the items in a heap of size n in a vector $a[1], \ldots, a[n]$ without wasting any space and without using any extra storage for pointers. We

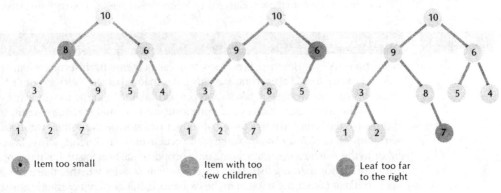

Figure 12.25 ■ Some nonheaps

put the item at the top of the heap in $a[1]$, and we put the children of $a[i]$ in $a[2i]$ and $a[2i+1]$. Thus the first level of the heap occupies the first element of a, the second level occupies the next two elements, the third the next four, and so on. In general, we store the mth level of the heap in $a[2^{m-1}]$ through $a[2^m - 1]$, and the height of the heap is $\lceil \log_2(n+1) \rceil$.

The *heapsort* algorithm sorts a list $a[1], \ldots, a[n]$ by first transforming it into a heap. This has the strange effect of moving big items to the beginning of the list—a seemingly poor way to start. But, once we have a heap, we can finish sorting the list in $n - 1$ steps, each of which requires at most $2\lceil \log_2(n+1) \rceil$ comparisons. To do this, we first interchange $a[1]$ with $a[n]$. This puts the largest item in the list in the proper location, but it causes condition (1) to fail at the root of the tree. Fortunately, we can repair the damage by moving quickly down a single branch in the tree and transform $a[1], \ldots, a[n-1]$ once again into a heap. As Fig. 12.26 illustrates, we interchange the small item at the root of the tree with the larger of its two children and continue such interchanges until condition (1) is satisfied throughout the new, but smaller heap.

Repeating this process, we sort the list by interchanging $a[n-1]$, $a[n-2]$, and so on, in succession with $a[1]$ and repairing the damage to the heap after each step. Thus we extract successively smaller items from the heap and place them in their proper positions toward the end of the list.

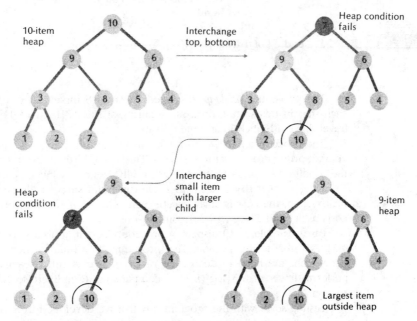

Figure 12.26 ■ Extracting the largest item from a heap

PASCAL SAMPLE 12.18   The procedure *fixHeap*

procedure *fixHeap*(**var** *a* : *itemList*; *top*, *bottom* : *index*);
    { assumes: *heap*(*top* + 1, *bottom*) }
    { returns: *heap*(*top*, *bottom*) }
    { where   *heap*(*m*, *n*) means that $a[i \ \textbf{div} \ 2] >= a[i]$ }
    {   whenever $m <= i \ \textbf{div} \ 2 < i <= n$ }
    var *i* : *index*;
      x : *itemType*;
    begin
      i := 2*top;
      if $i <= bottom$ **then**
          begin
            if $i < bottom$ **then if** $a[i] < a[i + 1]$ **then** *i* := *i* + 1;
            { $a[i]$ is the largest child of $a[top]$ }
            if $a[top] < a[i]$ **then**
                begin
                  x   := *a*[*top*];
                  a[*top*] := *a*[*i*];
                  a[*i*]   := *x*;
                  { heap is ok except possibly at *i* }
                  fixHeap(*a*, *i*, *bottom*)
                end
          end
    end;   { of *fixHeap* }

The procedure *fixHeap*, displayed as Pascal Sample 12.18, repairs the heap at each step in this sorting process, requiring at most $2\lceil \log_2(n + 1)\rceil$ comparisons to travel down a branch in an *n*-item heap.

The procedure *fixHeap* also helps us to transform $a[1], \ldots, a[n]$ into a heap to get the sorting process started. Since $a[i]$ has no children in the tree when $i > n \ \textbf{div} \ 2$, the condition *heap*(*i*, *n*) is true automatically. Hence, by invoking *fixHeap*(*a*, *i*, *n*) for *i* ranging from *n* **div** 2 down to 1, we can build successively larger portions of a heap. Again, the cost is fairly cheap: each of these *n* **div** 2 invocations of *fixHeap* costs us at most $2\lceil \log_2(n + 1)\rceil$ comparisons.

Pascal Sample 12.19 displays a procedure *sort* in a library *sort8* that sorts a list $a[1], \ldots, a[n]$ in this fashion. That procedure first builds a heap; then it removes items from the heap in decreasing order of size. A rough estimate shows that it performs fewer than $3\lceil \log_2(n + 1)\rceil$ comparisons. (See Exercise 2 at the end of this section.)

Testing *sort8* with the program *sort* that we developed in Section 8.4 confirms our expectations. Like the recursive sort merge, *heapsort* avoids the quadratic worst

---

■ **PASCAL SAMPLE 12.19**   The library *sort8* (heapsort)

{ *sort8*: heapsort of $a[1], ..., a[n]$ }

procedure *sort*(**var** a : *itemList*; n : *index*);

 var i : *index*;

  x : *itemType*;

 { declaration for *fixHeap* goes here }

 begin

  for $i := n$ **div** 2 **downto** 1 **do** *fixHeap*(a, i, n);

  { now $a[1], .., a[n]$ is a heap }

  for $i := n$ **downto** 2 **do**

   begin

    x := $a[1]$;

    $a[1] := a[i]$;

    $a[i] := x$;

    fixHeap$(a, 1, i-1)$

    { now $a[i] <= a[i+1] <= ... <= a[n]$ and }

    { $a[j] <= a[i]$ when $j < i$; furthermore, }

    { $a[1], ..., a[i-1]$ is a heap   }

   end

 end;   { of *sort* }

case of *quicksort*. It turns out to be somewhat faster than the recursive merge sort in all cases, but somewhat slower than *quicksort* in sorting a randomly ordered list. Hence it is a good algorithm to use when we are concerned about worst cases. When we care only about average time requirements, *quicksort* remains the algorithm of choice.

EXERCISES

1. Rewrite the *fixHeap* procedure to use iteration instead of recursion.

2. Analyze the number of comparisons performed by *heapsort*, as follows.

 (a) Verify the rough estimate of $3\lceil \log_2(n+1) \rceil$ comparisons given this section. (*Hint:* Assume that each invocation of *fixHeap* results in $2\lceil \log_2(n+1) \rceil$ comparisons.)

 *(b) By using a more careful estimate, show that *heapsort* performs at most $1.5\lceil \log_2(n+1) \rceil$ comparisons. (*Hint:* Count the number of comparisons that *fixHeap* actually makes.)

3. A *priority queue* is an abstract data type that provides two operations for manipulating an ordered list: the *insert* operation inserts an item in the list; the *removeTop* operation removes the largest item (that with the highest priority) from the list. Write a library of procedures to maintain a priority queue using a heap, as follows.

   (a) Have the *removeTop* procedure remove the largest item from the top of the heap, fill the hole with the item at the bottom of the heap, and invoke *fixHeap* to repair the damage.

   (b) Define the *insert* procedure in a fashion similar to *fixHeap*. Have it insert the new item at the bottom of the heap and then repair the damage by moving it up along a path toward the root.

4. Contrast the time requirements of the *insert* and *removeTop* operations in a priority queue when the queue is represented as

   (a) an unordered list of items, with new items going at the end of the list;

   (b) an ordered list of items, with new items inserted in the proper order; and

   (c) a heap, as in Exercise 2.

5. Redo Exercise 12, Section 11.2, using a priority queue. Is the new program significantly faster than the old?

12.4   SETS

The notion of a set is one of the most fundamental, simple, and powerful in all of mathematics. Somewhat surprisingly, this notion receives much less attention in computing than do the less fundamental notions of arrays and records.

A *set* is a collection of objects. The objects in that collection are called the *members* of the set. The language of mathematics provides both symbols and terminology to describe sets and their members. We can define a set by listing or describing its members; thus

$$\{\, 1, 3, 5, 7, 9 \,\} \quad \text{and} \quad \{\, n : 0 \leq n \leq 10 \textbf{ and } n \text{ is odd} \,\}$$

are two descriptions of the set of odd integers between 0 and 10. We write $x \in s$ to indicate that x is a member of the set s. Thus

$$3 \in \{\, n : 0 \leq n \leq 10 \textbf{ and } n \text{ is odd} \,\}.$$

Two sets are equal if they have exactly the same members, that is, $s = t$ if $x \in s$ precisely when $x \in t$. The *empty set* $\varnothing$ is the unique set without any members at all. A set s is a *subset* of a set t if every member of s is also a member of t; we write $s \subseteq t$ to indicate that s is a subset of t. The *union* $s \cup t$ of s and t is the set of all elements that are members of either s or t; that is

$$s \cup t = \{\, x : x \in s \textbf{ or } x \in t \,\}.$$

The *intersection* $s \cap t$ of s and t is the set of all elements that are members of both s and t; that is

$$s \cap t = \{\, x : x \in s \textbf{ and } x \in t \,\}.$$

The *difference* $s \sim t$ of s and t is the set of all elements that are members of s, but not of t; that is

$$s \sim t = \{\, x : x \in s \textbf{ and not } x \in t \,\}.$$

THE SET DATA TYPE

Pascal provides a limited capability for treating sets as a composite data type. Specifically, Pascal allows us to construct sets of members that all have the same ordinal type. For example, we can use the declarations

type *colors*   = (*red, white, blue, orange, green, yellow, purple*);
      colorSet   = **set of** *colors*;
      letterSet   = **set of** 'a'..'z';
      numberSet = **set of** 0..100;

   var *hues, tints*   : *colorSet*;
      vowels, used   : *letterSet*;
      primes, evens, s : *numberSet*;

to create variables ranging over sets of colors, letters, or numbers. However, Pascal stops short of allowing us to declare sets of real numbers, sets of strings, or sets of other structures. If we want to manipulate such sets, we must provide our own representation. (See Exercise 10 at the end of this section.)

The ordinal type of the elements in a set is known as the *base type* of that set. Most systems restrict the size of the base type for a set, making it impossible to have **set of** *integer* as a type. Unfortunately, some systems are overly restrictive, making it impossible to have the very useful **set of** *char* as a type. Figure 12.27 specifies the syntax for declarations involving sets.

SET EXPRESSIONS

The real power of sets in Pascal stems from our ability to construct set-valued expressions using symbols denoting the operations of set formation, union, intersection, and difference. Without set-valued expressions, we might just as well represent sets as boolean arrays. Declaring

   var *tints* : **array** [*colors*] **of** *boolean*;

allows us to keep track of which colors belong to the set *tints*, but declaring *tints* as a **set of** *colors* allows us to manipulate that set much more easily.

As we saw in Section 5.5, we can form descriptions of sets by enclosing a list of their elements by brackets; thus

   vowels := ['a', 'e', 'i', 'o', 'u']

makes *vowels* into the set of vowels and

   used := [ ]

set type

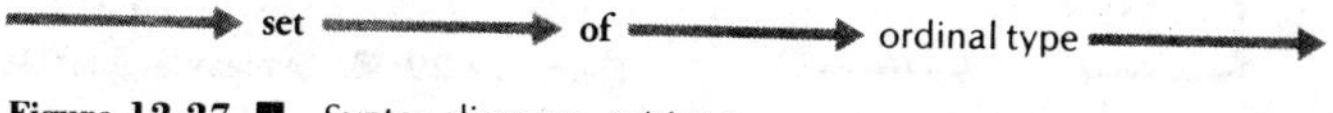

$$\longrightarrow \text{set} \Longrightarrow \text{of} \longrightarrow \text{ordinal type} \longrightarrow$$

Figure 12.27 ■ Syntax diagram, set type

assigns the empty set to *used*. We can also use the subrange notation to describe the members of a set; thus

$s := [1..n, 2*n]$

assigns to s the set consisting of the integers from 1 to n and the integer $2n$. Figure 5.12 (Section 5.5) specifies the syntax for describing sets in this fashion.

Since the ordinary typewriter keyboard does not have keys for the symbols ∪, ∩, and ~, Pascal instead uses the symbols +, *, and − for the operations of union, intersection, and difference. Thus set-valued expressions in Pascal look very much like numeric expressions. For example, the statements

```
used := [ ];
while not eoln do
    begin
        read(c);
        used := used + [c]
    end
```

assign to *used* the set of lowercase letters appearing in a line of input; the statement

$used := used - vowels$

discards the vowels from this set, leaving a set of consonants.

The operators +, *, and − have the same precedence for sets as they do for numbers. The syntax diagrams in Figs. 12.28–12.30 govern the formation of set-valued expressions and reflect this precedence.

We must be careful when assigning the value of an expression to a set. In the preceding example, the expression *used* + [c] always has a set of characters as its value, but an error results if we try assigning this set to *used* when the character c does not belong to the base type 'a'..'z' of *setOfLetters*. To avoid errors of this sort, we should verify that c is a lowercase letter before attempting the assignment.

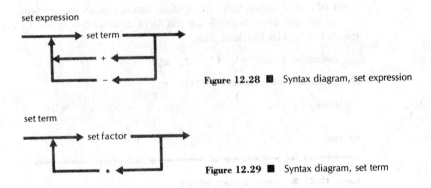

set expression

set term

+

−

Figure 12.28 ■ Syntax diagram, set expression

set term

set factor

*

Figure 12.29 ■ Syntax diagram, set term

set factor

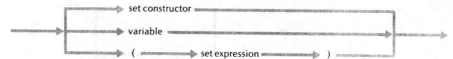

Figure 12.30 ■ Syntax diagram, set factor

RELATIONAL EXPRESSIONS INVOLVING SETS

We can test whether an object belongs to a set by using the keyword **in**, which corresponds to the membership relation denoted by ϵ in the language of mathematics. As we saw in Section 5.5, the expression

   c **in** $[\,'A'..'Z'\,]$

has the same value as the expression

   $('A' <= c)$ **and** $(c <= 'Z')$;

namely, it has the value *true* if c is an uppercase letter and the value *false* otherwise.

   Just as some of the usual arithmetic operators have a natural meaning when applied to sets, so do some of the usual relational operators. Table 12.1, which summarizes the treatment of sets in Pascal, describes the meanings of these operators.

   The operator **in** completes the list of relational operators available in Pascal. With it, we can give the final version of the syntax diagram governing the formation of relational expressions. (See Fig. 12.31.) Section 5.6 contains a list of restrictions on the types of the constituent expressions in a relational expression. The only restriction that must be added to that list applies to the operator **in**: the value of the variable x in the expression x **in** s must belong to the base type of the set s.

TABLE 12.1 Notations for Sets in Pascal and Mathematics

Pascal notation	Mathematical notation	Meaning
[ ]	$\varnothing$	empty set
[...]	{...}	the set containing ...
$s + t$	$s \cup t$	the union of s and t
$s * t$	$s \cap t$	the intersection of s and t
$s - t$	$s \sim t$	the difference of s and t
$s = t$	$s = t$	*true* if s equals t
$s <> t$	$s \neq t$	*true* if s does not equal t
$s <= t$	$s \subseteq t$	*true* if s is a subset of t
$s >= t$	$s \supseteq t$	*true* if t is a subset of s
x **in** s	$x \in s$	*true* if x is a member of s

relational expression

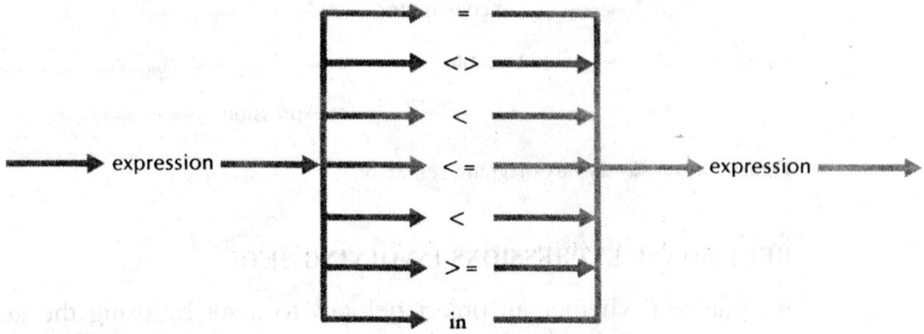

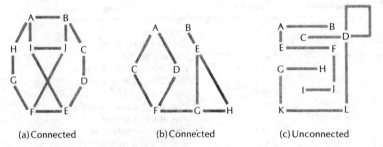

Figure 12.31 ■ Syntax diagram, relational expression (final version)

REPRESENTING GRAPHS

We conclude this section with an application that illustrates the power of sets in Pascal. Suppose that certain roads in a northern state have been blocked by a recent heavy snowfall. How can we tell whether all the cities in that state can still be reached by road from the capital, or whether some cities are completely cut off? We can get in a car and try driving from one city to another, or we can study a map on which we have marked the blocked-off roads. But, if there are many cities in the state, either of these two methods may take a long time; we may well want to enlist the aid of a computer in solving our problem.

To help describe our problem to a computer, we introduce some mathematical terminology. A network of cities and connecting roads is an example of a mathematical structure known as a *graph*. A graph consists of a set of *vertices* (the cities in this example) and a set of *edges* (the unblocked roads in this example); each edge connects two of the vertices. Two vertices are *adjacent* if there is an edge connecting them. A *path* in a graph is a sequence $v_1, v_2, \ldots, v_n$ of vertices such that v_i and v_{i+1} are adjacent for $i = 1, \ldots, n - 1$. A graph is *connected* if, for any two vertices, there is a path from one to the other. Figure 12.32 displays some examples of connected

(a) Connected   (b) Connected   (c) Unconnected

Figure 12.32 ■ Examples of graphs

and unconnected graphs; in that figure, letters represent vertices and lines represent edges.

To ask whether every city in the state is reachable from the capital is to ask whether the graph with cities as vertices and unblocked roads as edges is connected. Hence we seek to design an algorithm for testing whether a graph is connected.

The first problem that faces us is how to represent a graph as a data structure. We can easily represent the vertices of the graph as an ordinal type. But how can we represent the edges? One solution is to use a boolean array A, called an *adjacency matrix*, such that $A[i, j]$ is *true* if vertex i is adjacent to vertex j. Another solution is to use a vector of edges, that is, a list of pairs of vertices. And a third solution is to use a vector N of sets such that $N[i]$ is the set of *neighbors* of vertex i, that is, the set of vertices adjacent to i. Which of these solutions is best depends on the computations we intend to perform. For our present purpose, the third solution works well; it also gives us an opportunity to illustrate how we manipulate sets in Pascal.

To determine whether a graph is connected, we form the set *reachable* of all vertices connected by a path to a fixed vertex in the graph. If this set contains all the vertices in the graph, the graph is connected; otherwise it is not. Initially, *reachable* contains a single vertex. We enlarge *reachable* progressively until we can enlarge it no more, adding at each stage in the enlargement all neighbors of vertices currently in the set. To keep track of when no further enlargement is possible, we form a second set *visited* of vertices the neighbors of which we have already added to *reachable*. When *visited* equals *reachable*, we have found all the vertices that are connected to the original vertex.

In Pascal Sample 12.20, *connect*, we use this algorithm to solve our problem concerning snowbound cities. The first loop in that program interacts with the user to determine the neighbors (via unblocked roads) of each city. The second loop computes the set of cities reachable from city A. What makes this program particularly succinct in Pascal is its use of the set constructor [ ] and the union operator $+$, which allow us to express ourselves in Pascal just as we do in English. Pascal Sample 12.21 shows the results of using *connect* to establish the connectedness of the graph in Fig. 12.32(b).

■ PASCAL SAMPLE 12.20   The program *connect*

{ determines whether a set of cities is connected (illustrates sets) }

program *connect*(*input*, *output*);

const *firstCity* = 'A';

type *cities*   = 'A'..'Z';
       citySet = **set of** *cities*;

var *city*, *lastCity*, *neighbor* : *cities*;
      neighbors   : **array** [*cities*] **of** *citySet*;
      reachable, *visited*   : *citySet*;

PASCAL SAMPLE 12.20 The program *connect* (continued)

```
begin
    write('Enter letter [A to Z] representing last city: ');
    readln(lastCity);
    for city := firstCity to lastCity do
        begin
            write('Enter letters for neighbors of ', city, ': ');
            while not eoln do
                begin
                    read(neighbor);
                    neighbors[city] := neighbors[city] + [neighbor];
                    neighbors[neighbor] := neighbors[neighbor] + [city]
                end;
            readln
        end;
    reachable := [firstCity];
    visited := [ ];
    while reachable - visited <> [ ] do
        for city := firstCity to lastCity do
            if city in reachable - visited then { visit city }
                begin
                    reachable := reachable + neighbors[city];
                    visited := visited + [city]
                end;
    writeln;
    if reachable = [firstCity..lastCity] then
        writeln('All cities are connected')
    else
        writeln('Not all cities are connected')
end.  { of connect }
```

PASCAL SAMPLE 12.21 The program *connect* (sample use)

```
Enter letter [A to Z] representing last city: H
Enter letters for neighbors of A: CD
Enter letters for neighbors of B: E
Enter letters for neighbors of C: ADF
Enter letters for neighbors of D: ACF
Enter letters for neighbors of E: BH
Enter letters for neighbors of F: CDG
Enter letters for neighbors of G: EFH
Enter letters for neighbors of H: DG

All cities are connected
```

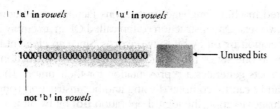

Figure 12.33 ■ Representation of the set *vowels* of lowercase letters

SYSTEMS: REPRESENTATION OF SETS

The most common representation for a set is as a sequence of bits, a single bit for each potential element of the set. A bit that equals one designates a member of the set, and a bit that equals zero designates a nonmember. Thus the representation for a set is the same as for a packed boolean array indexed by an ordinal type. But even though their representations are the same, Pascal allows us to do more with sets than with boolean arrays.

Suppose that we declare *vowels* to be a **set of** 'a'..'z' and assign the set ['a', 'e', 'i', 'o', 'u'] to *vowels*. Then, on a computer with 32 bits per word, a single word is sufficient to represent this set. (See Fig. 12.33.)

What makes this representation particularly efficient on most computers is the existence of machine-language instructions corresponding to operations and relations involving sets. Consider, for example, the set intersection operation. If *letters* is the set of letters in the string haste makes waste, we can compute the set of vowels in this string by computing the intersection *letters* * *vowels* of two sets. As shown in Fig. 12.34, this can be accomplished by applying the logical operation **and** bit by bit to the representations of these two sets. Since most computers provide an instruction (often called AND in assembly language) that computes the bit-by-bit **and** of two words, it takes very little time to compute the intersection of two sets.

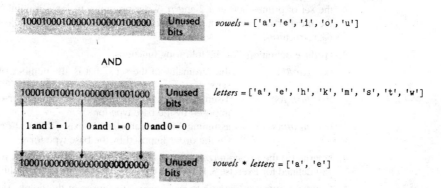

Figure 12.34 ■ Computing the intersection of two sets

Two related machine-language instructions facilitate computing the union and difference of two sets. One instruction (often called OR in assembly language) applies the logical operation **or** bit by bit to two words. Since an element is in the union of two sets if it is in one set or the other, applying the OR instruction to the representations for two sets generates a representation for their union. The difference $s - t$ of two sets s and t can be computed using another instruction (often called NOT in assembly language) to apply the logical operation **not** bit by bit to the representation for t, thereby generating a representation for the set of elements not in t, and then intersecting this set with s.

A final instruction makes it easy to determine whether two sets are identical or one is a subset of the other. The exclusive-or instruction (often called XOR in assembly language) applies the boolean operation $<>$ bit by bit to two words. If two sets are equal, the exclusive-or of their representations generates a boolean array that contains only zero bits; if the sets are not equal, this operation generates at least one nonzero bit. Hence it is easy to detect when two sets are equal. Finally, a set s is a subset of a set t if the intersection $s * t$ of s and t equals s. Hence the relation $s <= t$ is true if the logical **and** of the representations for s and t equals the representation for s.

EXERCISES

1. Suppose that the base type for a set variable s is an ordinal type with n different values (say, the type *colors* with seven different values *red, white, blue, orange, green, yellow,* and *purple*). How many different values can s have?

2. The *sieve of Eratosthenes* is a fast method for determining all primes less than some integer n. Starting with the set of all integers from 2 to n, it eliminates first all multiples of 2 other than 2 itself, then all multiples of 3 other than 3 itself, then all multiples of 5 other than 5 itself (the multiples of 4 already having been eliminated), ..., until it has eliminated all nontrivial multiples of every integer not exceeding $\sqrt{n}$. What remains is the set of primes between 2 and n. Write programs to input a number n and to count the number of primes not exceeding n using (a) sets and (b) boolean arrays for your data structures.

3. Produce definitions for the following functions.

    (a) *card(s)*   the cardinality of the set s, that is, the number of members in the set s.

    (b) *firstIn(s)*   assuming that s is nonempty, the first member of s (in the order imposed by the base type for s).

    (c) *nextIn(s, x)*   assuming that such an element exists, the next member of s after x (in the order imposed by the base type for s).

4. Rewrite (a) the program *connect* and (b) your solution to Exercise 2 using the functions you defined for Exercise 3. How does the use of these functions simplify those programs?

5. Rewrite *connect* using an adjacency matrix to represent the graph. How does this representation affect the program?

6. A *connected component* in a graph is a set of vertices such that (a) there is a path connecting any two vertices in the set and (b) any vertex adjacent to a vertex in the set is itself in the set. Write a program to determine the connected components of a graph.

7. A *bipartite* graph is a graph with vertices that can be partitioned into two sets, A and B, such that any vertex adjacent to a vertex in A is itself in B and vice versa. Write a program to determine whether a graph is bipartite.

8. A graph is *Eulerian* if there is a path leading from some vertex back to itself that traverses every edge in the graph once and only once.

   (a) Write a program to determine whether a graph is Eulerian.

   (b) Enhance your program to display an Eulerian path if one exists.

   (c) Eulerian graphs take their name from Leopold Euler, who showed in 1736 that an Eulerian path exists if and only if every vertex in the graph has an even number of neighbors. Does this information help in constructing a solution to either (a) or (b)?

*9. The problem of coloring a map can be expressed as a problem regarding graphs: given a set of *k* colors, can we color the vertices of a graph (which correspond to the countries on a map) in such a way that adjacent vertices receive different colors?

   (a) Write a program that colors a graph using the fewest possible colors. (*Hint:* Try recursion.)

   (b) Use your program to color a map of the United States or Europe. (*Hint:* Four colors are enough.)

   (c) Construct a graph that cannot be colored with four colors. In what way does this graph differ from those corresponding to ordinary maps?

10. Develop a library of procedures for maintaining sets of reals or strings as abstract data types, as follows.

   (a) Decide whether to use a boolean array, an unordered list of elements, an ordered list of elements, a tree, a heap, or some other data structure to represent a set. What factors influenced your decision?

   (b) Write procedures that find the union, intersection, and difference of two sets.

   (c) Write a procedure that constructs a set containing a single specified element.

   (d) Write a procedure that determines whether an element belongs to a set.

   (e) Write procedures that determine whether two sets are equal or whether one is a subset of the other.

   (f) Write definitions for the functions described in Exercise 3.

   (g) Relate the time required by each of your definitions to the number of elements in a set.

SUMMARY

Sets and trees are nonlinear data structures. A set is an unordered, unindexed collection of items. A tree is a hierarchical collection of items such that

□   each item is the parent of some number (possibly zero) of other items (its children);

■ if the tree is nonempty, exactly one item (the root) has no parent; and

■ every other item has exactly one parent and is a descendant of the root.

A leaf in a tree is an item with no children.

Pascal recognizes sets of items from an ordinal type as a composite data type. For such sets, it recognizes the operation of set membership and the operations of set union, intersection, and difference. Trees and sets of other objects must be represented as abstract data types.

Trees have many important applications in computing. Special types of trees occurring in these applications include

■ ordered binary trees, which

    1. provide efficient representations for dynamic ordered lists wherein each item

        (a) has at most two children (its left and right children) and

        (b) is ordered between those in the subtree rooted at its left child and those in the subtree rooted at its right child;

    2. combine the advantages of sorted arrays and linked lists in that

        (a) searches take logarithmic time on the average, and

        (b) insertions and deletions take constant time;

■ syntax trees, which

    1. are descriptions of linguistic objects such as English sentences or arithmetic expressions and

    2. resolve syntactic ambiguities (for example, associativity of operators);

■ heaps, which

    1. are compact binary trees wherein each item is larger than its children,

    2. are a basis for heapsort, an $n \log n$ worst-case sorting algorithm, and

    3. provide a representation for priority queues;

■ directory and classification structures, which

    1. provide hierarchical classifications of items that occur as leaves and

    2. establish the primary classification at the root.

Many algorithms must traverse a tree (visit all its items) in a particular order. Normally, tree traversals use recursion or a stack to control the order in which they visit items in a tree.

■ An inorder traversal

    1. visits the left subtree first, then the root and right subtree;

    2. produces an infix notation from a syntax tree; and

    3. lists in order the items in an ordered binary tree.

■ A preorder or depth-first traversal

    1. visits the root first, then the left and right subtrees;

    2. produces a prefix notation from a syntax tree; and

    3. produces a table of contents from the directory structure.

■ A postorder traversal

    1. visits the left subtree first, then the right subtree and root;

    2. produces a postfix notation from a syntax tree; and

    3. evaluates syntax trees for arithmetic expressions.

■ A breadth-first traversal

    1. visits the root first, then the other items level by level;

    2. is nonrecursive; and

    3. keeps nodes to be visited in a queue.

THMS AND DATA STRUCTURES APP
D ALGORITHMS AND DATA STRUC
ES APPLIED ALGORITHMS AND DA
IS AND DATA STRUCTURES APPLI
THMS AND DATA STRUCTURES APP
D ALGORITHMS AND DATA STRUC

APPLIED ALGORITHMS AND DATA STRUCTURES

13

As we approach the end of our introduction to computer science, we find ourselves in command of a wide variety of algorithms and data structures. This knowledge, together with the experience we have acquired in programming methodology, puts us in a position to undertake significant applications of computing. In this final chapter, we consider several such applications.

The first application extends the techniques that we developed for multiple-precision arithmetic in Section 7.1. Since many of us learned the same algorithms for arithmetic in elementary school, this application shows how appropriate data structures help us to implement familiar algorithms.

The next two applications shed light on how computer systems process computer programs. We enhance the simple calculator *calc3* written in Section 7.4 so that it can recognize and evaluate arbitrary arithmetic expressions, thereby learning how interpreters understand computer programs. Then we enhance *calc3* further so that it can remember and invoke simple function definitions, thereby learning how compilers translate programs from one language into another.

Finally, we learn how to write programs that can solve problems ordinarily thought to require some degree of human intelligence. Such programs show that we have come a long way from our simple beginnings. What we have learned really does enable us to tackle ambitious problems.

In Section 7.1 we wrote a library *arith1* of procedures to perform multiple-precision arithmetic with positive integers. However, that library uses a fairly primitive representation for integers with many digits, wasting both space and processing time by storing and manipulating superfluous leading zeroes. In this section, we will reconsider and improve the library *arith1*, using what we have learned about linked data structures. Our goals are to

- represent each integer with exactly as many digits as needed, thereby economizing on the space required to store integers and the time required to process them;

- remove the *a priori* limit on the number of digits in integer representations, thereby enabling us to manipulate integers with an arbitrarily large number of digits; and

- construct procedures for other operations such as subtraction and division, thereby increasing the utility of our library.

As before, we will base our algorithms on those taught in elementary school. But now we will use recursion to express those algorithms more succinctly. Furthermore, we will accomplish our first two goals by using linked lists, rather than fixed-length vectors, to hold the digits for the decimal representation of an integer.

It will be a simple matter to convert any program, such as *power1*, that uses the library *arith1* to use the new library *arith2* instead. All we have to do is replace the declarations

```
const base     = 10;          { base for arithmetic   }
      lastDigit = 19;          { number of digits − 1 }
var posInt  = 0..maxint;
    longInt = array [0..lastDigit] of posInt;
```

that *arith1* uses to represent integers as arrays with the declarations

```
const base = 10;                    { base for arithmetic }

var posInt  = 0..maxint;
    longInt = ↑node;
    node    = record
                  head : longInt;       { leading digits }
                  tail : posInt;         { last digit      }
              end;
```

that *arith2* will use to represent integers as linked lists. Figure 13.1 shows that *arith2*, like *arith1*, stores integers backward, with the least significant digit first and the most significant digit last. A measure of how well *arith2* achieves our first goal is the fact that *power1* computes 2^{60} more than eight times faster when we replace *arith1* by *arith2* (using Berkeley Pascal on a VAX 780).

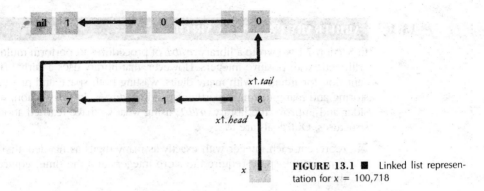

FIGURE 13.1 ■ Linked list representation for x = 100,718

It is tempting to make yet another change as we convert *arith1* to *arith2*. Since functions in Pascal can return pointers as values, we could actually recast the procedures in *arith1* as functions, thereby enabling us to perform a computation such as

$$x := y*y + z*z$$

with a single statement

$$x := add(multiply(y, y), multiply(z, z))$$

rather than with a sequence of procedure invocations.

multiply(*y, y, x1*);	{ *x1* = *y*y* }
multiply(*z, z, x2*);	{ *x2* = *z*z* }
add(*x1, x2, x*)	{ *x* = *x1* + *x2* }

However, such a change would have an unfortunate side-effect. Pascal does not dispose of any storage allocated by the procedure *new* unless we explicitly ask it to do so by calling the procedure *dispose*. Hence the only way to dispose of linked lists that represent intermediate values such as $y*y$ and $z*z$ is to retain pointers to those lists and to dispose of them ourselves. If we fail to do this, and our program computes many such intermediate values inside a loop, it may run out of storage needlessly before finishing its computation. Consequently it is safest to leave the procedures in *arith1* as procedures, which force us to keep pointers to intermediate values, rather than convert them into functions, which tempt us to lose those pointers.

PROCEDURES FOR ARBITRARY-PRECISION ARITHMETIC

We now turn our attention to constructing the library *arith2*. As usual, we begin by writing comments that describe the procedures in the library and the conventions required for their use. (See Pascal Sample 13.1.) These comments indicate that we intend to treat arbitrary-precision integers as an abstract data type; we will even provide our own procedures to assign one integer to another, and to test two integers

---

■ **PASCAL SAMPLE 13.1** The library *arith2* (initial comments)

{ *arith2*: procedures for arbitrary-precision integer arithmetic }

```
{       The following procedures manipulate arbitrary-precision  }
{ integers x, y, z whose type longInt is described below. The    }
{ variables m, n represent single-precision positive integers.   }

{ Procedure                    Action or value                   }
{ --------------               ---------- --- --------            }
{ add(y, z, x)                 x := y + z                         }
{ assign(y, x)                 x := y                             }
{ convert(n, x)                x := n                             }
{ divide(y, z, x)              x := trunc(y/z) unless z = 0       }
{ equals(x, y)                 true if x = y                      }
{ lessOrEqual(x, y)            true if x <= y                     }
{ multiply(y, z, x)            x := y*z                           }
{ print(x)                     display x                          }
{ scale(m, n, x)              x := m*x + n                        }
{ subtract(y, z, x)            x := max(y - z, 0)                 }

{       All references to arbitrary-precision integers must be   }
{ made through procedures in this library. In particular, to     }
{ assign the value of y to x, use assign(y, x) and not x := y.    }
{ And to test whether x and y have the same integer value, use   }
{ equals(x, y) and not x = y.                                     }

{       Any program using these procedures must contain the      }
{ following declarations:                                         }
{                                                                 }
{     const base = 10;                      (base for arithmetic) }
{                                                                 }
{     type posInt  = 0..maxint;                                   }
{          longInt = ↑node;                                       }
{          node    = record                                       }
{                      head  : longInt;                           }
{                      tail  : posInt;                            }
{                    end;                                         }
{                                                                 }
{ These declarations represent arbitrary-precision integers as   }
{ linked lists. The least significant digit occurs first in the list }
{ and the most significant digit occurs last. The declaration for }
{ the base of the number system may be changed, e.g., to 2 for   }
{ binary arithmetic or to 1000 to store three decimal digits in  }
{ each node of the linked list.                                   }
```

for equality, rather than fall back on the assignment operator := and equality symbol = in Pascal. As we will see, we do this in order to manipulate variables of type *longInt* safely, without causing unexpected results or side-effects.

PASCAL SAMPLE 13.2 The library *arith2* (further comments)

{   Those procedures that assign a new value to *x* dispose of   }
{ the storage associated with the former value of *x* just before   }
{ making the assignment. Thus programs using these procedures }
{ need not dispose of this storage themselves. Furthermore,   }
{ procedure calls such as *add*(*x*, *x*, *x*) will work.   }

{   Several procedures in *arith2* rely upon there being no   }
{ leading zeroes in the representation of an integer, including   }
{ the integer zero itself. Thus zero is represented by the empty }
{ list, not by the list containing the single digit 0. Every   }
{ procedure in *arith2* guarantees that this is the case.   }

These comments are followed by those in Pascal Sample 13.2, which summarize two other aspects of *arith2*: (1) storage is managed intelligently; and (2) one particular representation for zero is maintained out of the several that are possible. This latter fact discloses something about the inner workings of *arith2* that we should not rely upon when writing other programs. Yet its truth will be important for the correctness of several procedures in *arith2*, and hence it is worth emphasizing at the outset.

PRINTING INTEGER REPRESENTATIONS

Let us construct the ***print*** procedure first. That procedure would be easy to write if we had stored the digits representing an integer forward, rather than backward, in a linked list: then we could simply run along the list, printing digits as we encounter them. But storing digits backward helps us to carry out arithmetic operations more easily, and so we are willing to work slightly harder to print the results of those operations. Fortunately, recursion helps us to display the entries in a linked list in reverse order, and so we do not have to work very much harder.

In general, we exploit the declaration of the type *longInt* to construct the ***print*** procedure and the remaining procedures in *arith2* as well. That declaration decomposes an integer *x* as a sum $10x_1 + x_2$, where x_2 is the last digit in the decimal representation of *x* ($0 \leq x_2 < 10$) and x_1 is an integer with a representation that contains the leading digits in the representation of *x*. Hence we can print the value of *x*, as follows.

to print the value of *x*:

decompose *x* as $10x_1 + x_2$ with $0 \leq x_2 < 10$
if $x_1 > 0$ **then** print the digits representing x_1 (using recursion)
print the digit x_2 immediately following these digits

The *print* procedure in Pascal Sample 13.3 does just this, printing a single 0 as the value of an empty list. For *print* to work properly, we must be careful to keep the other procedures in *arith2* from generating leading zeroes in any representation for an integer.

PASCAL SAMPLE 13.3   The library *arith2* (*print* procedure)

procedure *print*(*x* : *longInt*);
{ displays the integer represented by *x* }
{ assumes *base* <= 10   }
begin
    if *x* = **nil then**
        write(0:1)
    else
        begin
            if *x*↑.*head* <> **nil then** *print*(*x*↑.*head*);
            write(*x*↑.*tail* : 1)
        end
end;   { of *print* }

COMPARING INTEGER REPRESENTATIONS

Recursion likewise provides simple definitions for the functions *equals* and *less-OrEqual*. Let us consider *equals* first. To test whether y and z represent the same value, we must test whether they point to identical lists of digits. We cannot simply test whether $y = z$ since, as Fig. 11.7 shows, distinct pointers may still point to identical objects. We can compare two lists iteratively, running along the lists and comparing digits. But it is easier to do it recursively: for two lists to be identical, their first entries must be the same (which we can test directly) and the remainder of the lists must be identical (which we can test by recursion). Putting it mathematically, if $y = 10y_1 + y_2$ and $z = 10z_1 + z_2$, with $0 \le y_2, z_2 < 10$, then $y = z$ precisely when $y_1 = z_1$ and $y_2 = z_2$. In Pascal Sample 13.4, we convert these observations into a recursive definition for *equals*.

PASCAL SAMPLE 13.4   The library *arith2* (*equals* function)

function *equals*(*y*, *z* : *longInt*) : *boolean*;
{ returns *true* if $y = z$ (i.e., if y and z represent the same integer) }
begin
    if *y* = **nil then**
        equals := (*z* = **nil**)
    else if *z* = **nil then**
        equals := *false*
    else if *y*↑.*tail* = *z*↑.*tail* **then**
        equals := *equals*(*y*↑.*head*, *z*↑.*head*)
    else
        equals := *false*
end;   { of *equals* }

PASCAL SAMPLE 13.5   The library *arith2* (*lessOrEqual* procedure)

```
function lessOrEqual( y, z : longInt ) : boolean;
    { returns true if y <= z }
    begin
        if y = nil then
            lessOrEqual := true
        else if z = nil then
            lessOrEqual := false
        else if y↑.tail <= z↑.tail then
            lessOrEqual := lessOrEqual( y↑.head, z↑.head )
        else
            lessOrEqual := not lessOrEqual(z↑.head, y↑.head )
    end;   { of lessOrEqual }
```

The definition of *lessOrEqual* is similar to that of *equals*. If we represent y and z as before, then $y \leq z$ will be true in two cases: either $y_1 \leq z_1$ and $y_2 \leq z_2$ (for example, 596 < 599), or $y_1 < z_1$ (for example, 596 < 612). In order to recast this observation as a recursive definition of *lessOrEqual* (Pascal Sample 13.5), we convert the condition $y_1 < z_1$ into the equivalent condition **not** $z_1 \leq y_1$.

ASSIGNMENT

The procedures in *arith2* that assign a new value to a variable x of type *longInt* involve several other issues, which we will address by considering the *assign* procedure. That procedure would be easy to write if we could assign y to x simply by executing the assignment $x := y$. But this approach can have undesirable side-effects. Suppose, for example, that we want to change the last digit of y after executing *assign*(y, x); if x and y point to the same list of digits, we are in danger of changing the last digit of x as well! If we want x and y to function as numeric variables and not as pointers, it is safest to have *assign* make a copy of the value represented by y when assigning it to x. That way the representation for one arbitrary-precision integer will not get tangled up with the representation of another.

To have *assign* copy a list of digits, we proceed recursively rather than iteratively, copying the leading digits in the list and then appending the last digit to the copy, as in the following fragment of code.

```
{ preliminary plan for making a copy x of a list y }
if y = nil then                                  { nothing to copy      }
    x := nil
else
    begin
        new(x);
        assign( y↑.head, x↑.head );       { copy leading digits }
        x↑.tail := y↑.tail                     { copy last digit        }
    end
```

But we should exercise some care with the variable x to turn this fragment into a good definition for *append*. Specifically, we should not ignore the old value of x, that is, the linked list of digits x pointed to when *assign* was invoked. Rather, we should have *assign* and the other procedures in *arith2* dispose of this storage themselves; that way a statement such as

> **for** $i := 1$ **to** n **do** *multiply*(y, x, y)

in *power1* will not leave behind $n - 1$ inaccessible linked lists that represent previous values of y. The comments we wrote at the beginning of *arith2* in fact commit us to doing just this.

But we must dispose of storage carefully. Someone might invoke *assign* by the statement *assign*(w, w). Why anyone would do this is beside the point; *assign* should work correctly whatever it is asked to do. Care is required in this case since the variables x and y in the preceding fragment of code will point to the same linked list of digits; hence we must not dispose of this list before attempting to copy it. One strategy is to have *assign* do nothing if $x = y$; if $x \neq y$, it can dispose of the list referenced by x and then execute the above fragment of code.

A better strategy reduces the number of times that we invoke *new* and *dispose*. Instead of disposing of the old list referenced by x and then allocating a new list, we reuse the old list to hold a copy of the list referenced by y. If the old list is too long or short for this purpose, we dispose of unnecessary nodes or allocate new ones as needed. The version of the *assign* procedure displayed as Pascal Sample 13.6 reuses the old list in this way, invoking a (still-to-be-written) procedure *release* when it needs to dispose of superfluous nodes.

ADDITION

Let us now turn our attention to arithmetic operations, namely, to adding, subtracting, multiplying, and dividing two arbitrary-precision integers y and z. The algorithms we

PASCAL SAMPLE 13.6 The library *arith2* (*assign* procedure)

```
procedure assign( y : longInt; var x : longInt );
    { returns x = y (i.e., makes x into a copy of y) }
    begin
        if y = nil then
            release(x)
        else
            begin
                if x = nil then new(x);
                assign( y↑.head, x↑.head );
                x↑.tail := y↑.tail
            end
    end;   { of assign }
```

$$\begin{array}{r} {\scriptstyle 1 \quad 1 \; 1} \\ 7\,1\,4\,8 \\ +6\,3\,5\,9 \\ \hline 1\,3\,5\,0\,7 \end{array}$$ Add corresponding digits right to left.
Carry to the left.

FIGURE 13.2 ■ School algorithm for adding 7148 and 6359

$$\begin{array}{r} 7\,1\,4\,8 \\ +6\,3\,5 \\ \hline 1\,3\,4\,9\,8 \\ +9 \\ \hline 1\,3\,5\,0\,7 \end{array}$$ Add leading digits (using recursion).

Then add last digit (using *scale*).

FIGURE 13.3 ■ Recursive algorithm for adding 7148 and 6359

learned in elementary school for these operations all involved working with the decimal representations of the integers y and z. Figure 13.2, for example, illustrates how we were taught to add two integers.

We can, in fact, convert this algorithm into an iterative definition of *add*. (See Exercise 7 at the end of this section.) However, it is easier to employ recursion, as illustrated in Fig. 13.3. We can reduce the problem of adding two long integers to the simpler problem of adding two shorter integers, consisting of their leading digits, and eventually to the problem of adding a single digit to an arbitrary precision integer. We can farm out this last problem to the procedure *scale* in *arith2*: invoking $scale(1, n, x)$ adds the single-precision integer n to x. The definition of *add* displayed as Pascal Sample 13.7 carries out this recursive algorithm, handling directly the simple cases when $y = 0$ or $z = 0$. Like *assign*, *add* reuses the nodes in the linked list x to hold the digits in the sum, calling *release* to dispose of extra nodes and calling *new* to generate new ones as needed.

SUBTRACTION

The usual algorithm for subtraction is similar to that for addition, except that we subtract corresponding digits instead of adding them, and we borrow from preceding digits when necessary instead of carrying. Hence the definition of *subtract*, displayed as Pascal Sample 13.8, is similar to that of *add*. The major difference relates to a decision that we must make about the meaning of subtraction. We have made no provision for dealing with negative integers, so we have to decide what should happen if we try to subtract z from y when $y < z$. By convention, we let the result of such a subtraction be zero.

■ **PASCAL SAMPLE 13.7** The library *arith2* (*add* procedure)

procedure *add*(*y, z* : *longInt*; **var** *x* : *longInt*);
    { returns $x = y + z$ }
    var *zLast* : *posInt*;   { last digit of *z* }
    begin
        if *y* = **nil then**
            assign(*z, x*)
        else if *z* = **nil then**
            assign(*y, x*)
        else
            begin
                if *x* = **nil then** *new*(*x*);
                add(*y*↑.*head, z*↑.*head, x*↑.*head*);
                zLast := *z*↑.*tail*;
                x↑.*tail* := *y*↑.*tail*;
                scale(1, *zLast, x*)
            end
    end; { of *add* }

■ **PASCAL SAMPLE 13.8** The library *arith2* (*subtract* procedure)

procedure *subtract*(*y, z* : *longInt*; **var** *x* : *longInt*);
    { returns $x = y - z$ if $y > z$, 0 if $y <= z$ }
    var *zLast* : *posInt*;   { last digit of *z* }
    begin
        if *lessOrEqual*(*y, z*) **then**
            release(*x*)
        else if *z* = **nil then**
            assign(*y, x*)
        else
            begin
                if *x* = **nil then** *new*(*x*);
                subtract(*y*↑.*head, z*↑.*head, x*↑.*head*);
                zLast := *z*↑.*tail*;
                x↑.*tail* := *y*↑.*tail*;
                scale(1, − *zLast, x*)
            end
    end; { of *subtract* }

MULTIPLICATION

When it comes to multiplying or dividing integers, recursion helps even more in cutting down on the bookkeeping required by the algorithms that we learned in school. Figure 13.4 illustrates the effort that goes into multiplying two four-digit numbers by hand. There we must align columns of digits properly, and we must add whole columns of digits, not just two digits at a time.

The recursive algorithm described in Fig. 13.5 simplifies the process of multiplication by breaking it into several parts: multiply 7148 by the leading digits 635 in 6359 and then by 10; multiply 7148 by the last digit 9 in 6359; then add these two numbers to obtain the final product.

The *multiply* procedure in Pascal Sample 13.9 carries out this recursive algorithm, using two variables *v* and *w* to hold the intermediate results and disposing of those results when no longer needed. Since this algorithm is more subtle than that for addition, comments at the beginning of *multiply* remind us of its mathematical basis.

MIXED SINGLE AND ARBITRARY PRECISION OPERATIONS

We have invoked *scale* three times—in *add*, *subtract*, and *multiply*—so it is time to construct that procedure. We could have avoided the need for *scale* by developing special-purpose procedures for carrying in *add*, borrowing in *subtract*, or multiplying by a single digit in *multiply* (Exercises 7, 9, and 11, respectively, at the end of this section). But these procedures have so much in common that we can combine them into a single procedure that adjusts the value of an arbitrary-precision integer x to equal $mx + n$, where m and n are single-precision integers. Recursion again comes

```
        7 1 4 8
      × 6 3 5 9
      ─────────
        6 4 3 3 2      Multiply 7148 by 9.
      3 5 7 4 0        Multiply 7148 by 5.
    2 1 4 4 4          Multiply 7148 by 3.
  4 2 8 8 8            Multiply 7148 by 6.
  ─────────────
  4 5 4 5 4 1 3 2      Add the results.
```

FIGURE 13.4 ■ School algorithm for multiplying 7148 by 6359

```
          7 1 4 8      Multiply 7148 by leading digits
        ×   6 3 5      635 of 6359 (using recursion).
        ───────────
        4 5 3 8 9 8 0
              ×   1 0  Multiply product by 10.
      ─────────────────
      4 5 3 8 9 8 0 0
      +     6 4 3 3 2  Add 7148 × 9.
      ─────────────────
      4 5 4 5 4 1 3 2
```

```
        7 1 4 8        Multiply 7148 by last digit
          ×   9        9 of 6539 (using scale).
        ───────
        6 4 3 3 2
```

FIGURE 13.5 ■ Recursive algorithm for multiplying 7148 by 6359

PASCAL SAMPLE 13.9   The library *arith2* (*multiply* procedure)

procedure *multiply*(*y, z* : *longInt*; **var** *x* : *longInt*);

    { returns $x = y*z$ }

    { Note that if $z =$ $z1*base +$ $z2,$ }
    { then $y*z = y*z1*base + y*z2.$ }

    var *v* : *longInt*;   { $v = y*z1*base$ }
          w : *longInt*;   { $w = y*z2$ }

    begin

        if (*y* = **nil**) **or** (*z* = **nil**) **then**
            release(*x*)
        else
            begin
                new(*v*);
                multiply(*y, z*↑.*head, v*↑.*head*);
                v↑.*tail* := 0;
                new(*w*);
                assign(*y, w*);
                scale(*z*↑.*tail*, 0, *w*);
                add(*v, w, x*);
                release(*v*);
                release(*w*)
            end

    end;   { of *multiply* }

to our aid in performing the adjustment:

    to scale *x* as $mx + n$:

    decompose *x* as $10x_1 + x_2$ with $0 \leq x_2 < 10$
    change x_2 to $mx_2 + n$
    adjust x_2 by subtracting $10k$ so that $0 \leq x_2 < 10$
    if $k <> 0$ **or** $m <> 1$ **then** scale x_1 as $mx_1 + k$

The definition of *scale* in Pascal Sample 13.10 is based on this sequence of steps. Like *assign* and *add*, *scale* allocates new nodes as needed for *x*, and it disposes of superfluous nodes. Furthermore, *scale* involves particular precautions when $n < 0$. Comments at the beginning of *scale* state clearly the assumptions required for it to function correctly when supplied with negative values for *n*. And *scale* eliminates leading zeroes created by borrowing, as when we subtract 9 from 15 to get 6 and not 06.

This general approach to the *scale* procedure provides an easy way to produce the arbitrary precision representation *x* for a single-precision integer *n*: we simply scale *x* as $0x + n$ by invoking *scale*(0, *n, x*). Thus the *convert* procedure in Pascal Sample 13.11 is particularly succinct.

PASCAL SAMPLE 13.10   The library *arith2* (*scale* procedure)

procedure *scale*(*m* : *posInt*; *n* : *integer*; **var** *x* : *longInt*);
{ assumes: $-base < n, m*x + n >= 0$ }
{ returns: $x = m*(\text{old } x) + n$ }

    var *digit* : *integer*;   { last digit in new value of *x* }
    begin
        if ($n = 0$) **and** (($m = 0$) **or** ($x = $ **nil**)) **then**   { make *x* zero }
            release(*x*)
        else
            begin
                if *x* = **nil then**   { allocate node for digit }
                    begin
                        new(*x*);
                        x↑.*head* := **nil**;
                        x↑.*tail* := 0
                    end;
                digit := *m**x↑.*tail* + *n*;   { scale last digit of *x* }
                if *digit* < 0 **then**
                    begin { set last digit and borrow from preceding digit }
                        x↑.*tail* := *digit* + *base*;
                        scale(*m*, −1, *x*↑.*head*)
                    end
                else if (*digit* > 0) **or** (*x*↑.*head* <> **nil**) **then**
                    begin { set last digit and propagate carry if necessary }
                        x↑.*tail* := *digit* **mod** *base*;
                        if (*digit* >= *base*) **or** (*m* <> 1) **then**
                            scale(*m*, *digit* **div** *base*, *x*↑.*head*)
                    end
                else { remove leading zero }
                  release(*x*)
            end
    end;   { of *scale* }

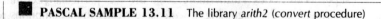

PASCAL SAMPLE 13.11   The library *arith2* (*convert* procedure)

procedure *convert*(*n* : *posInt*; **var** *x* : *longInt*);
    { returns $x = n$ (i.e., converts *n* to arbitrary-precision *x*) }
    begin
        scale(0, *n*, *x*)
    end;   { of *convert* }

DIVISION

Finally, we tackle the problem of division. The algorithm for division, illustrated in Fig. 13.6, is arguably the most difficult algorithm taught in elementary school. For a dividend y and a divisor z, we obtain a quotient q and a remainder r such that $y = qz + r$ and $0 \leq r < z$. We do this by guessing successive digits in the quotient, multiplying them by the divisor, and subtracting the carefully aligned products from the results of previous operations.

The long division algorithm may be the best available for working with pencil and paper. But when we have powerful tools such as recursion at our disposal, we can try to develop a simpler algorithm. Figure 13.7 illustrates one such algorithm. Given y and z, we use this algorithm to find the desired quotient and remainder by first decomposing y as $10y_1 + y_2$ with $0 \leq y_2 < 10$. Then, using recursion, we divide y_1 by z to obtain a quotient q_1 and a remainder r_1 such that $y_1 = q_1z + r_1$ and $0 \leq r_1 < z$. Now $y = 10q_1z + 10r_1 + y_2$, and we would be done if $10r_1 + y_2 < z$, for then we could simply set $q = 10q_1$ and $r = 10r_1 + y_2$. However, if this value for r is

```
      2 7 4      Quotient
2 6)7 1 4 8
    5 2          2 × 26
  ─────
    1 9 4        (71 − 52) × 10 + 4
    1 8 2        7 × 26
    ─────
      1 2 8      (194 − 182) × 10 + 8
      1 0 4      4 × 26
      ─────
        2 4      128 − 104 (remainder)
```

FIGURE 13.6 ■ School algorithm for dividing 7148 by 26

```
        2 7
  2 6)7 1 4      Divide leading digits 714 of 7148 by 26
      7 0 2      (using recursion).
      ─────
        1 2
```

$714 = 26 \times 27 +$	12	Write 714 as 26 × quotient + remainder.
$7140 = 26 \times 270 +$	120	Multiply through by 10.
$7148 = 26 \times 270 +$	128	Add last digit 8 to 7148 and to remainder.
$7148 = 26 \times 271 +$	102	Reduce remainder by 26, adding 1 to quotient.
$7148 = 26 \times 272 +$	76	Repeat this step
$7148 = 26 \times 273 +$	50	until
$7148 = 26 \times 274 +$	24	remainder < 26.

FIGURE 13.7 ■ Recursive algorithm for dividing 7148 by 26

greater than z, we subtract z from r repeatedly, adding 1 to q each time, until $r < z$. How many times must we do this before arriving at the final quotient and remainder? Since $10r_1 + y_2 \leq 10(z - 1) + 9 = 10z - 1$, we must subtract z at most 9 times from r to find the last digit of the quotient. Hence repeated subtraction is not too expensive a procedure for finding successive digits in the quotient.

The definition of the *divide* function in *arith2* uses the algorithm we have just described. That definition comes in two parts: (1) a recursive procedure *findQuotient* (Pascal Sample 13.12), which computes both the quotient and remainder; and (2) the

---

PASCAL SAMPLE 13.12   The library *arith2* (*findQuotient* procedure)

```
procedure findQuotient(      dividend, divisor    : longInt;
                        var quotient, remainder : longInt );
  { assumes: divisor <> 0                                     }
  {          quotient, remainder reference variables distinct }
  {          from each other and from dividend, divisor       }
  { returns: quotient, remainder so that                      }
  {              dividend = divisor*quotient + remainder      }
  {              0 <= remainder < divisor                     }
  begin
    if dividend = nil then
      begin
        quotient  := nil;
        remainder := nil
      end
    else
      begin
        new(quotient);
        new(remainder);
        findQuotient(dividend↑.head, divisor, quotient↑.head, remainder↑.head);
        remainder↑.tail := dividend↑.tail;
        if (remainder↑.tail = 0) and (remainder↑.head = nil) then
          release(remainder);
        quotient↑.tail := 0;
        while lessOrEqual(divisor, remainder) do
          begin
            quotient↑.tail := quotient↑.tail + 1;
            subtract(remainder, divisor, remainder)
          end;
        if (quotient↑.tail = 0) and (quotient↑.head = nil) then
          release(quotient)
      end
  end;  { of findQuotient }
```

PASCAL SAMPLE 13.13   The library *arith2* (*divide* procedure)

procedure *divide*(*y, z* : *longInt*;   **var** *x* : *longInt*);
  { returns $x = trunc(y/z)$ if $z <> 0$ }
  { leaves *x* unchanged if $z = 0$ }
  var *q, r* : *longInt*;
  begin
    if $z =$ **nil then**
        writeln('Division by zero ignored')
    else
        begin
            findQuotient(*y, z, q, r*);
            release(*x*);
            release(*r*);
            x := *q*
        end
  end;   { of *divide* }

procedure *divide* (Pascal Sample 13.13), which invokes *findQuotient* and then throws away the remainder.

STORAGE MANAGEMENT

One last detail must be added in order to complete the construction of *arith2*: the *release* procedure that disposes of storage no longer needed for integer representations. Pascal Sample 13.14 displays a recursive definition of that procedure.

With the library *arith2* in hand, we can carry out a large number of interesting computations that require many digits of precision. The following exercises suggest some of these possibilities.

PASCAL SAMPLE 13.14   The library *arith2* (*release* procedure)

procedure *release*(**var** *x* : *longInt*);
  { returns $x =$ **nil**, disposing of the storage used to represent *x* }
  begin
    if $x <>$ **nil then**
        begin
            release(*x*↑.*head*);
            dispose(*x*);
            x := **nil**
        end
  end;   { of *release* }

EXERCISES

1. Write a program that uses the procedures in *arith2* to compute arbitrary-precision factorials of integers supplied as input to the program. Compare the efficiency of this program with that of a similar program using *arith1*. (See Exercise 1, Section 7.1.)

2. Compare the efficiency of raising a number to a power using the program *power1*

    (a) as developed in Section 7.1;

    (b) modified to use *arith2* instead of *arith1*;

    (c) modified to use *arith2* instead of *arith1* and to use *scale* instead of *multiply* to perform multiplications;

    (d) modified as suggested in Exercise 9, Section 7.1, to use the more efficient recursive algorithm for raising a number to an integral power; and

    (e) modified as in (b) and (d).

3. Write procedures to approximate the square root of a positive integer n to d decimal places using the following methods.

    (a) Use the bisection algorithm to compute the square root of $n10^{2d}$ to the nearest integer.

    (b) Use Newton's algorithm to generate a sequence of approximations to the square root of $n10^{2d}$, stopping when two successive approximations differ by at most one.

4. Write a procedure suitable for inclusion in *arith2* that reads an arbitrary-precision integer from a text file.

5. Write a program that determines whether an arbitrary-precision integer has any small prime factors. Is it reasonable to use such a program to determine whether an arbitrary-precision integer is prime?

6. What would be the effect of replacing the body of the function definition for *equals* in *arith2* by the following statements?

    (a) *equals* := ($y = z$)

    (b) *equals* := ($y{\uparrow}.tail = z{\uparrow}.tail$) **and** ($y{\uparrow}.head = z{\uparrow}.head$)

    (c) **if** ($y = $ **nil**) **or** ($z = $ **nil**) **then**
        equals := ($y = z$)
    else
        equals := ($y{\uparrow}.tail = z{\uparrow}.tail$) **and** ($y{\uparrow}.head = z{\uparrow}.head$)

7. Rewrite the *add* procedure in *arith2* to employ a subsidiary procedure *addWithCarry* instead of *scale*. The new subsidiary procedure should add two arbitrary-precision integers y and z together with a single-precision carry c to form an arbitrary-precision sum x.

8. What is the purpose of the variable *zLast* in *add*? [*Hint:* Consider the effect of the procedure invocation *add(a, b, b)*.]

9. Rewrite the *subtract* procedure in *arith2* to employ a subsidiary procedure *subtractAndBorrow* instead of *scale*. The new subsidiary procedure should subtract an arbitrary-precision integer z and a single-precision borrow b from an arbitrary-precision integer y to produce an arbitrary-precision result x.

10. What is the purpose of the variable *zLast* in *subtract*? (*Hint:* What happens if the last digit in *y* is less than the last digit in *z*?)

11. Rewrite the *multiply* procedure in *arith2* to use a subsidiary procedure *singleMultiply* instead of *scale*. This new subsidiary procedure should multiply an arbitrary-precision integer *y* by a single-precision integer *n*.

12. Rewrite the *divide* procedure in *arith2* to estimate the last digit in the quotient rather than to compute it by repeated subtraction. (*Hint:* Compare the first digit of the divisor to the first digit of the remainder obtained by the recursive invocation of *findQuotient*.)

13. Rewrite the *convert* procedure in *arith2* to convert a single-precision integer directly to its arbitrary-precision representation without invoking *scale*.

14. Rewrite the procedures in *arith2* to use iteration rather than recursion. What effects does the rewrite have on the comprehensibility and efficiency of the procedures?

15. Develop a definition for the *divide* procedure based on the ordinary algorithm for long division.

16. Prove that the following procedure invocations work correctly.
    - (a) *assign*(*x, x*)
    - (b) *add*(*x, x, x*)
    - (c) *subtract*(*x, x, x*)
    - (d) *multiply*(*x, x, x*)
    - (e) *divide*(*x, x, x*)

17. Prove that the procedures *add, subtract, multiply, divide,* and *scale* in *arith2* generate no overflows, provided that $base^2 + base < maxint$.

18. Prove that the procedures in *arith2* generate no superfluous leading zeroes.

19. Prove that the storage used to represent an arbitrary-precision integer *x* is disposed of properly when a procedure in *arith2* is invoked to assign a new value to *x*.

20. Rewrite the procedures in *arith2* using doubly linked lists with header nodes as representations for arbitrary-precision integers. Record the number of digits in an arbitrary-precision representation in its header node. Which operations does this representation make more efficient?

21. Redo Exercises 15 and 16, Section 7.1, using linked data structures.

13.2 SYNTAX DIAGRAMS AND PARSING

The program *calc3* in Chapter 7 simulates a simple pocket calculator with memory. It can perform a series of calculations, printing the result of each calculation or assigning it to a variable for use in later calculations. However, it proceeds strictly from left to right, recognizing neither parentheses nor the usual precedence of arithmetic operations. In particular, it interprets 1 + 2*3 as (1+2)*3, producing the value 9 instead of the value 7. In this section we improve *calc3* by writing a program *calc4* that recognizes parentheses and follows the usual rules of precedence for arithmetic operations.

On the surface, we will convert *calc3* into *calc4* by redefining the principal procedure *calculate* in *calc3*. But to do this, we will find it necessary to use a more abstract approach than before. In *calc3*, we used the *scan* procedure in the library *scanner* to decompose the input as a sequence of tokens, that is, as a sequence of numbers, variables, and symbols designating operations. We read those tokens one at a time and decided what to do with each token as we read it, performing the necessary calculations as we went. If we are to cope with precedence and parentheses in *calc4*, we must view an arithmetic expression as something more than a simple sequence of tokens to be evaluated from left to right.

SYNTAX DIAGRAMS

Syntax diagrams provide just the view we need. Indeed, syntax diagrams provide a means for defining a legal arithmetic expression. In Chapter 2 we used syntax diagrams to describe the arithmetic expressions that could occur in Pascal programs. And in Section 7.4, we saw how syntax diagrams provided a basis for writing the token scanner used by *calc3*.

We can also use syntax diagrams to describe the expressions that our improved program *calc4* will recognize. The diagrams in Fig. 13.8 describe expressions that

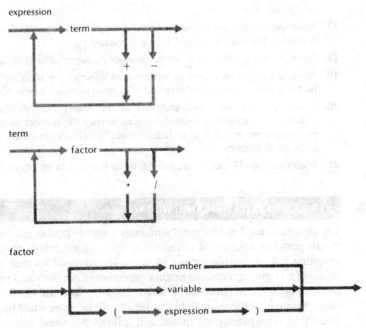

FIGURE 13.8 ■ Syntax of arithmetic expressions recognized by *calc4*

are somewhat simpler than those allowed in Pascal programs: they cannot contain leading plus or minus signs, the **div** or **mod** operators, constant identifiers, or function values. Yet they are general enough to make *calc4* a useful calculator and to illustrate how we can process even more general expressions.

PARSING

In order to write *calc4*, we must devise an algorithm that recognizes arithmetic expressions and relates them to their constituent parts. Such an algorithm is said to *parse*, or analyze the syntax of, a sequence of symbols. When studying English syntax, we parse a sentence to identify its subject, verb, and object. When studying the syntax of arithmetic expressions, we parse an expression to identify its primary operation and operands.

There are two general types of parsers: (1) bottom-up parsers, which attempt to piece together a syntactic object by piecing together its parts, and (2) top-down parsers, which attempt to recognize a syntactic object by recognizing its parts. A bottom-up parser for English sentences would attempt to piece words together to form phrases and then piece phrases together to form sentences; by contrast, a top-down parser would attempt to recognize a sentence by recognizing its subject, verb, and object. We pursue the top-down approach here, leaving the other to the exercises at the end of this section.

RECOGNIZING EXPRESSIONS

Let us consider how to recognize an arithmetic expression using a top-down approach. According to Fig. 13.8, an expression is a sequence of terms separated by the operators + and −. Hence, in order to recognize an expression, we should look for such a sequence of terms, that is, we should reduce the problem of recognizing expressions to the "simpler" problem of recognizing terms.

The syntax diagram for an expression in Fig. 13.8 leads directly to the following strategy for recognizing and evaluating the next expression supplied as input to *calc4*.

{ strategy for recognizing and evaluating an expression }
initialize *result* to the value of the next term supplied as input
while the next token supplied as input is + or − **do**
    adjust *result* by the value of the next term supplied as input
assign *result* as the value of the expression

We refine this strategy by turning it into a definition for a function *valueOfNextExpression* in Pascal that detects and evaluates an expression supplied as input to *calc4*. To obtain the next token supplied as input, we will rely on the procedure *scan* in the library *scanner*. And to obtain the value of the next term supplied as input, we will rely on a yet-to-be-written function, *valueOfNextTerm*, which is similar to *valueOfNextExpression*. Pascal Sample 13.15 exhibits a preliminary definition for

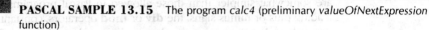

PASCAL SAMPLE 13.15   The program *calc4* (preliminary *valueOfNextExpression* function)

function *valueOfNextExpression* : *real*;

   { parses an arithmetic expression, returns its value   }
   { scans one token beyond the end of the expression }

   var *nextToken* : *token*;
      result   : *real*;

   { declaration for *valueOfNextTerm* goes here }

begin
      result := *valueOfNextTerm*;
      scan(*nextToken*);
      while *nextToken.sym* **in** [*plus*, *minus*] **do**
         begin
               if *nextToken.sym* = *plus* **then**
                     result := *result* + *valueOfNextTerm*
               else
                     result := *result* − *valueOfNextTerm*;
               scan(*nextToken*)
         end;
      valueOfNextExpression := *result*
   end;   { of *valueOfNextExpression* }

valueOfNextExpression. (See the discussion of the library *scanner* in Section 7.4 for a declaration of the type *token*.)

The treatment of *nextToken* in Pascal Sample 13.15 leaves something to be desired. Since *valueOfNextExpression* recognizes the end of an expression only when it has scanned one token too many, it should pass this extra token on to another procedure for further processing. Instead, *valueOfNextExpression* does nothing with this extra token. Let us try to remedy this defect by considering the definition of the subsidiary function *valueOfNextTerm*.

RECOGNIZING TERMS

The syntax diagram for a term in Fig. 13.8 is remarkably similar to that for an expression. Whereas an expression is a sequence of terms separated by the operators + and −, a term is a sequence of factors separated by the operators * and /. Hence we can pattern a preliminary definition of *valueOfNextTerm*, displayed as Pascal Sample 13.16, on that of *valueOfNextExpression*.

Here again the treatment of *nextToken* leaves something to be desired: like *valueOfNextExpression*, *valueOfNextTerm* detects the end of a term only by reading one token too many. But now we can see what should happen to this extra token.

PASCAL SAMPLE 13.16   The program *calc4* (preliminary *valueOfNextTerm* function)

```
function valueOfNextTerm : real;
      { parses an arithmetic term, returns its value   }
      { scans one token beyond the end of the term }
   var nextToken : token;
       result    : real;
   { declaration for valueOfNextFactor goes here }
   begin
         result := valueOfNextFactor;
         scan(nextToken);
         while nextToken.sym in [times, divides] do
            begin
               if nextToken.sym = times then
                  result := result * valueOfNextFactor
               else
                  result := result / valueOfNextFactor;
               scan(nextToken)
            end;
         valuesOfNextTerm := result
   end;   { of valueOfNextTerm }
```

Since this token is not part of the current term, *valueOfNextTerm* should pass it back to *valueOfNextExpression*. There we can detect whether it is a + or −, in which case it is part of the current expression and will be followed by another term, or whether it is some other symbol, in which case it must be the token following the end of an expression. In this latter case, *valueOfNextExpression* should pass the extra token back to the procedure that invoked it for further processing.

The simplest way to pass extra tokens back to other procedures is to make *nextToken* a global variable. That may seem a rather drastic step, but it enables us to define *valueOfNextTerm* and *valueOfNextExpression* as functions rather than as procedures with two parameters, *result* and *nextToken*, passed by reference. For consistency, we will use uniform conventions regarding the global variable *nextToken*: on exit from any procedure, *nextToken* will be the next symbol to process. And for symmetry, on entry to any procedure *nextToken* will also be the next symbol to process. For example, on entry to *valueOfNextTerm* and *valueOfNextExpression*, *nextToken* will be the first token in a term or an expression.

With these conventions, we can present a final definition for *valueOfNextExpression*. (See Pascal Sample 13.17.) Here *nextToken* has become a global variable, and the two calls to *scan* have become one that sets *nextToken* to the first token in the term following a + or − operator.

■ PASCAL SAMPLE 13.17   The program *calc4* (*valueOfNextExpression* function)

function *valueOfNextExpression* : *real*;
    { parses an arithmetic expression, returns its value }
    var *result*   : *real*;
       operator : *token*;
    { declaration for *valueOfNextTerm* goes here }
    begin
       result := *valueOfNextTerm*;
       while *nextToken.sym* **in** [*plus*, *minus*] **do**
          begin
             operator := *nextToken*;
             scan(*nextToken*);
             if *operator.sym* = *plus* **then**
                result := *result* + *valueOfNextTerm*
             else
                result := *result* − *valueOfNextTerm*
         end;
       valueOfNextExpression := *result*
    end;   { of *valueOfNextExpression* }

Similarly, we can present a final definition for *valueOfNextTerm*. (See Pascal Sample 13.18.) Here we have chosen to embellish the preliminary definition by detecting division by zero as an error and by assigning the task of recovering from this error to a procedure named *error*, as in Section 7.4. We pass two parameters to *error*: (1) a member *zeroDiv* of an enumerated type describing the nature of the error; and (2) the token being evaluated when the error occurred. Later we will write a definition for *error* that produces an appropriate error message and resumes processing.

RECOGNIZING FACTORS

In order to finish the job of recognizing arithmetic expressions, we must devise a way to recognize factors. According to Fig. 13.8, there are three types of factors: numbers, variables, and parenthesized subexpressions. Fortunately, we can recognize which is which by examining the first (and possibly only) token in the factor: if it is a number or a variable, then we have found the entire factor; if it is a left parenthesis, then we must look for an expression and a matching right parenthesis.

The major subtlety in the design of *calc4* occurs at this point. How do we keep track of where we are when, in the course of trying to recognize one expression, we are forced to look for another expression that occurs within parentheses as a factor of the first? The answer is surprisingly simple: we resort to recursion and use the previously written function *valueOfNextExpression*.

■ **PASCAL SAMPLE 13.18** The program *calc4* (*valueOfNextTerm* function)

function *valueOfNextTerm* : *real*;
   { parses an arithmetic term, returns its value }
   var *result, operand* : *real*;
      operator   : *token*;
   { declaration for *valueOfNextFactor* goes here }
   begin
      result := *valueOfNextFactor*;
      while *nextToken.sym* **in** [*times, divides*] **do**
         begin
            operator := *nextToken*;
            scan(*nextToken*);
            operand := *valueOfNextFactor*;
            if *operator.sym* = *times* **then**
               result := *result* ∗ *operand*
            else
               if *operand* = 0 **then**
                  error(*zeroDiv, operator*)
               else
                  result := *result* / *operand*
         end;
      valueOfNextTerm := *result*
   end;   { of *valueOfNextTerm* }

Pascal Sample 13.19 presents a definition for the function *valueOfNextFactor* based on these observations. It evaluates numbers and variables in the same way that the *value* function did in *calc3*, and it invokes *valueOfNextExpression* recursively to evaluate a parenthesized subexpression. In addition, it exits with *nextToken* set to the token following the factor, and it calls *error* if it detects either of two syntactic errors when looking for a factor: *needVal* (for "need a value") if the factor does not begin with one of the expected tokens, and *needPar* (for "need parenthesis") if a parenthesized subexpression is missing a right parenthesis.

The three functions, *valueOfNextExpression*, *valueOfNextTerm*, and *valueOf-NextFactor*, work together to recognize arithmetic expressions. Now that we can recognize such expressions, we are in a position to write the program *calc4*.

RECOGNIZING STATEMENTS

We could plunge right in and, with some luck, complete *calc4*. However, our approach to expressions using syntax diagrams has served us so well that it pays to continue with this approach.

As we did for *calc3*, we want to give *calc4* the ability both to display the value of an expression and to assign a value to a variable. We will use the same conventions

---

PASCAL SAMPLE 13.19   The program *calc4* (*valueOfNextFactor* function)

function *valueOfNextFactor* : *real*;
   { parses an arithmetic factor, returns its value }
  begin
      if not (*nextToken.sym* **in** [*number, identifier, lparen*]) **then**
        error(*needVal, nextToken*);
      case *nextToken.sym* **of**
        number   : *valueOfNextFactor* := *nextToken.val*;
        identifier : *valueOfNextFactor* := *memory*[*nextToken.id*];
        lparen   : **begin**
              scan(*nextToken*);
              valueOfNextFactor := *valueOfNextExpression*;
              if *nextToken.sym* <> *rparen* **then**
                error(*needPar, nextToken*)
        end
      end;
     scan(*nextToken*)
  end; { of *valueOfNextFactor* }

regarding input for *calc4* as we did for *calc3*: if an expression is followed by the symbol @ and a variable, we will assign the value of the expression to that variable; otherwise, we will print the value. The syntax diagram in Fig. 13.9 reflects these conventions by defining a statement to consist of an expression alone or of an expression followed by the symbol @ and a variable.

As before, we can easily convert this syntax diagram into a procedure that recognizes and executes a statement supplied as input to *calc4*. As shown by Pascal Sample 13.20, the procedure *executeStatement* invokes *valueOfNextExpression* to find the value of an expression. Then it checks the next token to see if it is @ (which is called *assignTo* by *scan*); if it is, then *executeStatement* assigns the value of the expression to the following variable; otherwise it prints the value. Also as before, *executeStatement* exits with *nextToken* set to the token following the statement, and

statement

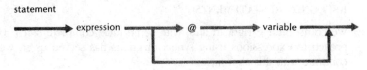

FIGURE 13.9 ■ Syntax of statements recognized by *calc4*

■ **PASCAL SAMPLE 13.20** The program *calc4* (*executeStatement* procedure)

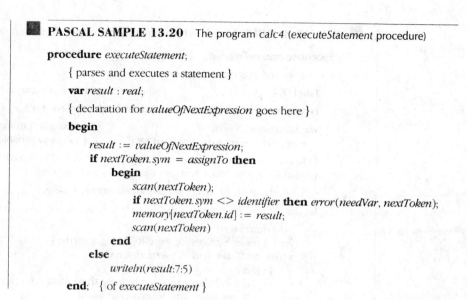

```
procedure executeStatement;
    { parses and executes a statement }
    var result : real;
    { declaration for valueOfNextExpression goes here }
begin
        result := valueOfNextExpression;
        if nextToken.sym = assignTo then
            begin
                scan(nextToken);
                if nextToken.sym <> identifier then error(needVar, nextToken);
                memory[nextToken.id] := result;
                scan(nextToken)
            end
        else
            writeln(result:7:5)
end;  { of executeStatement }
```

it calls *error* if it detects anything other than a variable following the @ operator (*needVar* stands for "need a variable").

RECOGNIZING PROGRAMS

Finally, we carry our approach to *calc4* using syntax diagrams to its ultimate conclusion by designing a replacement for the *calculate* procedure in *calc3*. As for *calc3*, input for *calc4* consists of a sequence of lines containing statements. The syntax diagram in Fig. 13.10 reflects this conception of the program of action executed by *calc4*. The arrow at the top of the diagram allows null statements in the input to *calc4*; that is, it allows blank lines in the input. That way we do not need to include any special error detection in *calc4* for missing statements or programs; given nothing, *calc4* will do nothing.

program

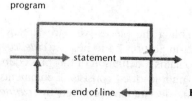

FIGURE 13.10 ■ Syntax of programs recognized by *calc4*

PASCAL SAMPLE 13.21   The program *calc4* (*executeProgram* procedure)

procedure *executeProgram*;
    { parses and executes a program }
    label 9999;   { where to resume following an error }
    type *errors* = (*needPar*, *needSep*, *needVal*, *needVar*, *zeroDiv*);
    var *nextToken* : *token*;   { next token in input }
       memory   : **array** [*variable*] **of** *real*; { values of variables }
    { On entry to and exit from *executeStatement* and each of its subsidiary }
    { procedures, *nextToken* is always the next token to process.   }
    { The declarations for *error* and *executeStatement* go here. }
    begin
        scan(*nextToken*);
        9999: { resume processing here following an error }
        while *nextToken.sym* <> *terminator* **do**
            begin
                if *nextToken.sym* <> *separator* **then** *executeStatement*;
                if *nextToken.sym* = *separator* **then**
                    scan(*nextToken*)
                else if *nextToken.sym* <> *terminator* **then**
                    error(*needSep*, *nextToken*)
            end;
        writeln;
        writeln('Done.')
    end; { of *executeProgram* }

We can easily translate the syntax diagram for a program into a procedure *executeProgram* that recognizes and processes a program. Pascal Sample 13.21 presents a definition of this procedure, which initiates the scanning process by setting *nextToken* to the first token in the input and then invokes *executeStatement* repeatedly until it reaches the terminating token (the end of the input file). If a statement appears to end before the end of a line of input, then *executeProgram* calls the *error* procedure (*needSep* stands for "need a separator").

THE FINISHED CALCULATOR

We complete *calc4* by assembling the pieces we have already written, adding a procedure *error* similar to that in Section 7.4 to help *executeProgram* recover from errors. Pascal Sample 13.22 contains a definition of this procedure.

As in *calc3*, the main program in *calc4* consists of comments that describe the operation of the calculator, the declarations required by *scanner*, and one major

■ **PASCAL SAMPLE 13.22**   The program *calc4* (error procedure)

procedure *error*(*trouble* : *errors*; *t* : *token*);

{ prints a message indicating location and nature of trouble }
{ detected upon processing the token *t*; then skips to the   }
{ end of the current statement and resumes processing   }

const *promptLength* = 2;   { length of '> ' }

begin

   writeln('↑' : *promptLength* + *t.pos*);
   case *trouble* **of**
      needPar : *writeln*('`Expected a right parenthesis here`');
      needSep : *writeln*('`Expected end of statement here`');
      needVal : *writeln*('`Expected a value here`');
      needVar : *writeln*('`Expected variable here`');
      zeroDiv : *writeln*('`Division by zero`')
   end;

   while not ⟨*nextToken.sym* **in** [*separator, terminator*]) **do**
      scan(*nextToken*);
   goto 9999

end;   { of *error* }

procedure that interprets the input and performs the requested computations. In fact, little other than the initial comments have changed. (See Pascal Sample 13.23.)

As Pascal Sample 13.24 shows, *calc4* does indeed interpret arbitrary arithmetic expressions. It prints their values or saves them in its memory for use in later calculations.

■ **PASCAL SAMPLE 13.23**   The program *calc4* (main program)

{ simulates a calculator that evaluates a series of arithmetic expressions }
{   The calculator interprets its input according to the following rules of syntax: }
{   }
{ -- a program is a sequence of lines containing statements   }
{ -- a statement is an expression optionally followed by the assignment   }
{   operator @ and a variable (if @ is present, the value of the expression }
{   is assigned to the variable; otherwise the value is printed)   }
{ -- an expression is a sequence of terms separated by the operators + or − }
{ -- a term is a sequence of factors separated by the operators * or /   }
{ -- a factor is a number, variable, or expression enclosed in parentheses }
{ -- a number is a sequence of digits optionally followed by a decimal point }
{   and zero or more digits   }
{ -- a variable is a lowercase letter   }

■ **PASCAL SAMPLE 13.23**   The program *calc4* (main program, continued)

program *calc4*(*input, output*);

{ The following declarations are those required by *scanner.* }

type *symbol* = (*identifier, number, plus, minus, times, divides, lparen,*
                 rparen, assignTo, separator, terminator, unknown);

   variable = 'a' .. 'z';

   token   = **record**

                   sym : *symbol*;   { type of token   }
                   val : *real*;   { value of numeric token }
                   id   : *variable*;   { identifier for variable }
                   pos : *integer*;   { position on input line }

              end;

var *scanState*   : (*needLine, haveLine, allDone*);
   scanPosition : *integer*;

#include 'scanner';   { *startScan* and *scan* procedures }

{ The declaration for *executeProgram* goes here. }

begin

   startScan;
   executeProgram

end.

■ **PASCAL SAMPLE 13.24**   The program *calc4* (sample use)

> 5@n

> n*(n+1)/2
15.00000

> 2@a

> 3@b

> 1@c

> b*b-4*a*c
1.00000

> ■
Done.

EXERCISES

1. Enhance the program *calc4* so that it recognizes unary + and − signs, as in the expression
   (−x)*(−y) + 2. (*Hint:* First modify the syntax diagrams defining what constitutes a
   legal expression.)

2. Enhance *calc4* so that it recognizes ** as the exponentiation operator, as follows.

(a) Modify *scanner* to recognize ** as a token.

(b) Modify the syntax diagrams for an expression to treat exponentiation as a right-associative operation with higher precedence than multiplication or division [that is, interpret 2*x**y**z as $2x^{y^z}$, not as $2(x^y)^z$ or $(2x)^{y^z}$].

(c) Modify *calc4* in accordance with your new syntax diagrams.

3. Modify *scanner* and *calc4* to recognize

(a) the *sqrt* function;

(b) the *max* and *min* functions, which take an arbitrary number of arguments; and

(c) the **mod** and **div** operators.

4. Write a program to evaluate logical expressions built up from boolean variables and constants, using the operators **and**, **or**, and **not**.

5. For the parsing strategy in this section to succeed, we must use syntax diagrams that satisfy the following two requirements.

▪ We must always be able to tell which arrow to follow in a syntax diagram by looking at the next token in the input.

▪ After entering any syntax diagram, we must always read at least one token from the input before entering that diagram again.

(a) Suppose that we change the syntax of an assignment statement to bring it more into line with that of Pascal, as shown by Fig. 13.11. Why does this violate one of our requirements, and how does it cause trouble for *calc4*?

(b) How would you change the parsing strategy employed by *calc4* to handle this change in syntax? (*Hint:* Look farther ahead.)

(c) Show that the syntax diagram in Fig. 13.12 provides an equivalent definition of the expressions recognized by *calc4*.

(d) Why does this diagram violate one of our requirements, and what trouble would it cause if we were to use it as a basis for writing *parseExpression*?

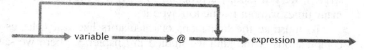

FIGURE 13.11 ▪ Alternative syntax for assignments in *calc4*

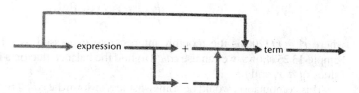

FIGURE 13.12 ▪ Alternative description of syntax for expressions

6. Write a program to parse and evaluate an arithmetic expression by using the following bottom-up technique. Read a line of input from left to right, pushing numbers, the values of variables, and left parentheses onto a stack as you encounter them. Whenever you encounter an operator or a right parenthesis, the item on top of the stack should be a number. Examine the item underneath it on the stack and take one of the following actions.

(a) If the new token is a right parenthesis and the item underneath the top of the stack is an operator, then pop the top three items off the stack, apply the stacked operator to the other two (which should be numbers), push the result back onto the stack, and repeat the appropriate action.

(b) If the new token is a right parenthesis and the item underneath the top of the stack is a left parenthesis, then pop the top two items off the stack, push the number that was on top of the stack back onto the stack, and scan the next token.

(c) If the new token is an operator and the item underneath the top of the stack is an operator with a precedence at least as high, proceed as in (a).

(d) If the new token is an operator and the item underneath the top of the stack is a left parenthesis or an operator with lower precedence, or if the stack contains a single number, then stack the new operator and scan the next token.

When you reach the end of the expression, its value will be the only item on the stack.

7. Enhance the program you wrote for Exercise 6 to detect, report, and recover from typing mistakes.

13.3 SYNTAX TREES AND PARSING

As is an ordinary pocket calculator, the program *calc4* is most useful for simple, one-time calculations. It is less useful for calculations with many steps or for calculations that we need to repeat many times. A computer is more appropriate than a calculator for these applications, letting us separate the task of constructing a program to perform a calculation from the actual performance of that program. After it has been written, we can modify a program to correct a mistake, or we can use a program many times without having to retype it.

To illustrate the limitations of calculators like *calc4*, let us consider financial computations of the kind we studied in Chapter 3. There we saw that the balance due on a loan of a dollars at r percent annual interest after 6 monthly payments of p dollars each is

$$(a - \frac{p}{r'})(1 + r')^6 + \frac{p}{r'},$$

where $r' = r/1200$ is the monthly interest rate expressed as a fraction. As Pascal Sample 13.25 shows, we can use *calc4* to find the balance due on a loan for particular values of a, r, and p.

This computation would be somewhat less awkward if *calc4* recognized a symbol for exponentiation. But even if it did, we would still have to type a lot if we wanted

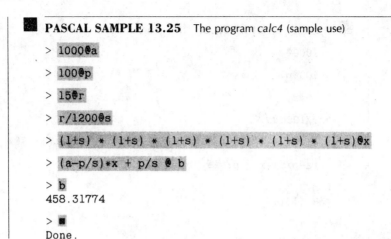

PASCAL SAMPLE 13.25   The program *calc4* (sample use)

```
> 1000@a

> 100@p

> 15@r

> r/1200@s

> (1+s) * (1+s) * (1+s) * (1+s) * (1+s) * (1+s)@x

> (a-p/s)*x + p/s @ b

> b
458.31774

> ■
Done.
```

to compute the balance of the loan for several values of *r*. Since *calc4* evaluates an expression immediately, we would have to retype the formula for *b* each time we changed the value of *r*.

Clearly, our work would be easier with a calculator that remembered the formula defining the final balance *b* in terms of *a*, *p*, and *r*. Then we could ask this calculator to reevaluate that formula each time we changed the value of *r*. In this section we modify *calc4* to create one last calculator, *calc5*, that functions in this way. The primary difference between *calc5* and *calc4* is that *calc5* regards lines of input that contain the symbol @ as defining a functional relationship between the expression to the left and the variable to the right, and it uses these relationships when evaluating expressions on lines that do not contain the symbol @. Thus *calc5* separates preparing a program, which involves defining several functions, from executing that program, which involves evaluating expressions.

Pascal Sample 13.26 illustrates the operation of *calc5*, showing how it can recompute the value of *b* when we change the value of *r*. Commercial microcomputer software packages known as *spreadsheets* function in this manner, allowing the user to define dependencies among many variables and displaying updated values for all variables whenever the user changes one of them.

STORED PROGRAMS AND SYNTAX TREES

In order to write *calc5*, we must enable it to remember the defining expressions for certain variables. We could do this by having *calc5* store these expressions as strings of characters, interpreting them only when it needs their values. But such a strategy would require *calc5* to parse the same expression many times. A more economical strategy separates the task of parsing an expression from the task of evaluating that expression.

PASCAL SAMPLE 13.26   The program *calc5* (sample use)

```
> 1000@a

> 100@p

> 15@r

> r/1200@s

> (1+s) * (1+s) * (1+s) * (1+s) * (1+s) * (1+s)@x

> (a-p/s)*x + p/s @ b

> b
458.31774

> 18@r

> b
470.48817

> ■
Done
```

What *calc5* really needs to remember is the syntactic structure of an expression, not the actual sequence of characters we typed. Syntax trees, such as those we described in Section 12.2, provide a convenient means for remembering this structure. As we will see, after we parse an expression to create its syntax tree, we can easily evaluate that expression. Furthermore, we can discover and report typing mistakes when we parse the expression, not when we evaluate it.

Figure 13.13 displays the syntax tree for $(a - p/s) * x + p/s$, the expression that we supplied to *calc5* as a definition for the variable b. The nodes in this tree contain tokens: the leaves contain variables and numbers; the other nodes contain

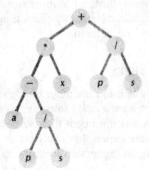

FIGURE 13.13 ■   Syntax tree for $(a - p/s)x + p/s$

operators. We produce the value of such a tree by applying the operator at its root to the values of the left and right subtrees below the root.

CALCULATOR DESIGN

We can keep the design of a sophisticated program like *calc5* under control by apportioning its duties among independent libraries of procedures. One library, *parser*, will parse statements supplied by the user. The other, *evaluator*, will evaluate these statements and take the appropriate action. The first library produces a syntax tree, the second does something with it. Both libraries handle the errors they recognize: *parser* reports typing mistakes; *evaluator* reports execution errors such as division by zero.

Pascal Sample 13.27 displays the entirety of the program *calc5*, showing how it relies on subsidiary libraries to perform the bulk of its work. Declarations at the

---

■ **PASCAL SAMPLE 13.27**   The program *calc5* (main program)

```
{ simulates a spreadsheet calculator that allows the user to define the }
{ values of variables in terms of expressions involving other variables }
program calc5(input, output);

type symbol    = (identifier, number, plus, minus, times, divides, lparen,
                  rparen, assignTo, separator, terminator, unknown);
     variable  = 'a' .. 'z';
     token     = record
                    sym : symbol;        { type of token           }
                    val : real;          { value of numeric token  }
                    id  : variable;      { identifier for variable }
                    pos : integer;       { position on input line  }
                 end;
     syntaxTree = ↑node;                 { syntax of expression    }
     node       = record
                    op    : token;       {    primary operation    }
                    left  : syntaxTree;  {    left operand          }
                    right : syntaxTree;  {    right operand         }
                 end;
     memoryType = array [variable] of syntaxTree;

var scanState    : (needLine, haveLine, allDone);
    scanPosition : integer;
    memory       : memoryType;
    statement    : syntaxTree;

#include 'scanner';        { used by parser          }
#include 'parser';         { parseStatement procedure }
#include 'evaluator';      { execute and mainOp procedures }
```

■ **PASCAL SAMPLE 13.27**   The program *calc5* (main program, continued)

begin
    startScan;
    repeat
        statement := *parseStatement*;
        execute(*statement*, *memory*)
    until *mainOp*(*statement*) = *terminator*;
    writeln;
    writeln('Done.')
end.

---

beginning of the program define the syntax trees that will serve as the means of communication between the two libraries.

AN EXPRESSION PARSER

The procedures in the library *parser* are similar to the parsing procedures in *calc4*. Now, however, the procedures are somewhat simpler. They do not need to evaluate an expression, but only to produce a syntax tree.

The new definition of *parseExpression*, displayed as Pascal Sample 13.28, is typical of the definitions in *parser*. It is practically the same as that for *parseExpression* in *calc4*, the primary difference being that the type of *result* is now *syntaxTree* rather

---

■ **PASCAL SAMPLE 13.28**   The library *parser* (*parseExpression* function)

function *parseExpression* : *syntaxTree*;
    { parses an arithmetic expression, returns its syntax tree }
    var *result*   : *syntaxTree*;
       operator : *token*;
    { declaration for *parseTerm* goes here }
    begin
        result := *parseTerm*;
        while *nextToken.sym* **in** [*plus*, *minus*] **do**
            begin
                operator := *nextToken*;
                scan(*nextToken*);
                result := *makeTree*(*operator*, *result*, *parseTerm*)
            end;
        parseExpression := *result*
    end;   { of *parseExpression* }

■ **PASCAL SAMPLE 13.29**   The library *parser* (*makeTree* procedure)

function *makeTree*(*operator* : *token*; *arg1, arg2* : *syntaxTree*) : *syntaxTree*;

    { returns a syntax tree with a specified operator and operands }

    var *t* : *syntaxTree*;

    begin

```
    new(t);
    t↑.op      := operator;
    t↑.left    := arg1;
    t↑.right   := arg2;
    makeTree := t
```

    end; { of *makeTree* }

---

than *real*. The *parseExpression* procedure invokes a procedure *makeTree* that is defined elsewhere in *parser* to build a syntax tree with a specified operator at the root and specified subtrees representing operands for that operator.

The *makeTree* procedure, displayed as Pascal Sample 13.29, is straightforward. We will need it several times in the library *parser*, so it pays to package it as a separate procedure.

As in *calc4*, the *parseExpression* function in *parser* invokes a subsidiary function *parseTerm*, which in turn invokes a subsidiary function *parseFactor*. Pascal Samples 13.30 and 13.31 display the definitions for these functions, which again bear a close resemblance to those in *calc4*.

■ **PASCAL SAMPLE 13.30**   The library *parser* (*parseTerm* function)

function *parseTerm* : *syntaxTree*;

    { parses an arithmetic term, returns its syntax tree }

    var *result*   : *syntaxTree*;
           operator : *token*;

    { declaration for *parseFactor* goes here }

    begin

```
    result := parseFactor;
    while nextToken.sym in [times, divides] do
        begin
            operator := nextToken;
            scan(nextToken);
            result := makeTree(operator, result, parseFactor)
        end;
    parseTerm := result
```

    end; { of *parseTerm* }

■ **PASCAL SAMPLE 13.31**   The library *parser* (*parseFactor* function)

function *parseFactor* : *syntaxTree*;
    { parses an arithmetic factor, returns its syntax tree }
    begin
        if not (*nextToken.sym* **in** [*number*, *identifier*, *lparen*]) **then**
            error(*needVal*, *nextToken*);
        case *nextToken.sym* **of**
            number   : *parseFactor* := *makeTree*(*nextToken*, **nil**, **nil**);
            identifier : *parseFactor* := *makeTree*(*nextToken*, **nil**, **nil**);
            lparen   : **begin**
                    scan(*nextToken*);
                    parseFactor := *parseExpression*;
                    if *nextToken.sym* <> *rparen* **then**
                        error(*needPar*, *nextToken*)
            end
        end;
        scan (*nextToken*)
    end;   { of *parseFactor* }

Finally, to tie these function definitions together, we create a definition for the primary function *parseStatement* in the library *parser*. (See Pascal Samples 13.32 and 13.33.) This definition is similar to that for *executeStatement* in *calc4*, but once again

■ **PASCAL SAMPLE 13.32**   The library *parser* (initial comments)

{ *parser*: library for parsing arithmetic expressions }
{   The function *parseStatement* returns a syntax tree for the statement on   }
{ the current line of input. The syntax of this statement is as follows: }
{   }
{ -- a statement is an expression optionally followed by the assignment   }
{   operator @ and a variable; a statement ends with an end-of-line   }
{ -- an expression is a sequence of terms separated by the operators + or − }
{ -- a term is a sequence of factors separated by the operators * or /   }
{ -- a factor is a number, variable, or expression enclosed in parentheses   }
{ -- a number is a sequence of digits optionally followed by a decimal point }
{   and zero or more digits   }
{ -- a variable is a lowercase letter   }
{   The function definition detects and reports typing mistakes. It returns   }
{ an empty syntax tree when it detects an error or a null statement. It   }
{ returns a syntax tree with the symbol *terminator* at the root upon   }
{ detecting the end of the input.   }

PASCAL SAMPLE 13.33   The library *parser* (*parserStatement* function)

```
function parseStatement : syntaxTree;
    label 9999;                          { where to resume following an error }
    type errors = (needPar, needSep, needVal, needVar);
    var expTree    : syntaxTree;
        operator   : token;
        target     : syntaxTree;
        nextToken : token;
    { The declarations for error, makeTree, and parseExpression go here.   }
    { On entry to and exit from parseExpression and each of its subsidiary }
    { procedures, nextToken is always the next token to process.           }
    begin
        scan(nextToken);
        if nextToken.sym = separator then { null statement }
            expTree := nil
        else if nextToken.sym = terminator then { all done }
            expTree := makeTree(nextToken, nil, nil)
        else
            begin
                expTree := parseExpression;
                if nextToken.sym = assignTo then
                    begin
                        operator := nextToken;
                        scan(nextToken);
                        if nextToken.sym <> identifier then
                            error(needVar, nextToken);
                        target := makeTree(nextToken, nil, nil);
                        expTree := makeTree(operator, target, expTree);
                        scan(nextToken)
                    end;
                if nextToken.sym <> separator then error(needSep, nextToken)
            end;
    9999:  { resume here following an error }
        parseStatement := expTree
    end;  { of parseStatement }
```

it simply produces a syntax tree and does not evaluate an expression. Furthermore, it does not rely on any external procedures to help it handle errors; it calls its own error-reporting procedure, the definition for which is displayed as Pascal Sample 13.34, and exits cleanly with an empty syntax tree as its value.

■ **PASCAL SAMPLE 13.34** The library *parser* (*error* procedure)

procedure *error*(*trouble* : *errors*; *t* : *token*);

> { prints a message indicating location and nature of trouble }
> { detected upon processing the token *t*; then skips to the   }
> { end of the current statement, sets *expTree* to **nil**, and   }
> { exits to the label 9999 in *parseStatement*   }

const *promptLength* = 2;   { length of ' > ' }

begin

> *writeln*(' ↑ ' : *promptLength* + *t.pos*);
> **case** *trouble* **of**
>> *needPar* : *writeln*('Expected a right parenthesis here');
>> *needSep* : *writeln*('Expected end of statement here');
>> *needVal* : *writeln*('Expected a value here');
>> *needVar* : *writeln*('Expected a variable here')
> **end**;
> **while not** (*nextToken.sym* **in** [*separator*, *terminator*]) **do**
>> *scan*(*nextToken*);
> **goto** 9999

end;   { of *error* }

AN EXPRESSION EVALUATOR

We conclude our development of *calc5* by writing a library *evaluator* of procedures to evaluate the syntax trees produced by *parseStatement*. The main part of that library, displayed as Pascal Sample 13.35, is fairly straightforward. It leaves most of the work to a function *eval*, which produces the value of an expression from its syntax tree. The procedure *execute* decides whether to display the value of an expression or to save the syntax tree for that expression in the memory of *calc5*.

The *eval* function computes the value of an expression by taking an action determined by the token at the root of the syntax tree for that expression. (See Pascal Sample 13.36.) If this token is a number, the value of the expression is that number. If this token is an operator, *eval* invokes itself recursively to find the values of the two operands for that operator before computing the value of the expression. If the token is a variable, *eval* looks up the definition of that variable in the memory of *calc5* and invokes itself recursively to evaluate that definition. With the power of recursion at our disposal, the definition of *eval* contains nothing more than a single **case** statement.

As we did for *parser*, we have *evaluator* handle its own errors. Since the line of input responsible for an execution error may be long since gone, *evaluator* simply reports the nature of the error and not its specific location.

Exercises at the end of this section illustrate the generality of the techniques used to construct *calc5*. Extensions of these techniques form the basis for interpreters, which parse and execute programs written in languages like Pascal, and for compilers, which translate those programs into machine language.

PASCAL SAMPLE 13.35   The library *evaluator* (execute procedure)

{ *evaluator*: library to evaluate syntax trees for *calc5* }

function *mainOp*(*t* : *syntaxTree*) : *symbol*;
    { returns the symbol at the root of *t* }
    begin
        if *t* = **nil then**
            mainOp := *unknown*
        else
            mainOp := *t↑.op.sym*
    end;   { of *mainOp* }

procedure *execute*(*t* : *syntaxTree*; **var** *memory* : *memoryType*);
    { executes the statement with syntax tree *t* }
    label 9999;   { error exit }
    { declaration of *eval* goes here }
    begin
        if *t* = **nil then**
            { do nothing }
        else if *mainOp*(*t*) = *assignTo* **then**
            memory[*t↑.left↑.op.id*] := *t↑.right*
        else
            writeln(*eval*(*t*):7:5);
        9999;   { error exit }
    end;   { of *execute* }

PASCAL SAMPLE 13.36   The library *evaluator* (eval function)

function *eval*(*t* : *syntaxTree*) : *real*;

   { returns the value of a tree *t* representing an expression }
   { exits to the label 9999 in *execute* in case of an error   }

   var *divisor* : *real*;

   begin
      case *t↑.op.sym* **of**
         plus   : *eval* := *eval*(*t↑.left*) + *eval*(*t↑.right*);
         minus   : *eval* := *eval*(*t↑.left*) − *eval*(*t↑.right*);
         times   : *eval* := *eval*(*t↑.left*) * *eval*(*t↑.right*);
         divides : **begin**
                 divisor := *eval*(*t↑.right*);
                 if *divisor* = 0 **then**
                    begin
                       writeln('Division by zero');
                       goto 9999
                    end
                 else
                    eval := *eval*(*t↑.left*) / *divisor*
                end;
         number : *eval* := *t↑.op.val*;
         identifier : **if** *memory*[*t↑.op.id*] = **nil then**
                    begin
                       writeln('Variable ', *t↑.op.id*, ' undefined');
                       goto 9999
                    end
                 else
                    eval := *eval*(*memory*[*t↑.op.id*])
      end
    end; { of *eval* }

EXERCISES

1. What modifications to *calc5* will cause it to function the same way as *calc4*? (*Hint:* It is sufficient to change only a single declaration in *calc5* and two assignment statements in *evaluator*.)

2. The program *calc5* runs into trouble if its user defines a variable in terms of itself.

   (a) What is the nature of this trouble?

   (b) Define a procedure that finds the set of variables the values of which are needed to evaluate an expression.

   (c) Have the *execute* procedure recognize circular definitions by invoking this procedure before storing a definition in the memory of *calc5*.

(d) Alternatively, have the *eval* function detect and report circular definitions.

3. Write a program that enables its user to enter the definition of a function f of a single variable x and then approximates a zero of that function on a specified interval.

4. Write a procedure to simplify the syntax tree for an expression by evaluating subexpressions that involve constants, recognizing multiplication by 0 and 1, and so on.

5. Write a procedure that finds the syntax tree for the derivative of an expression in a single variable x. (*Hint:* Apply the rules for computing derivatives given in Section 10.1.)

*6. Write a procedure to determine whether two expressions in the single variable x are equivalent, that is, whether they have the same values whatever the value of x. (*Hint:* Find out whether the difference of the two expressions simplifies to zero.)

*7. Design an interpreter for a simple programming language that includes compound, **if**, and **while** statements in addition to the statements recognized by *calc4*. (*Hint:* Use syntax diagrams to define your language. Enhance *parser* to create a syntax tree that represents a program in your language. Enhance *evaluator* to execute that program.)

*8. Suppose that we wish to evaluate an expression many times using the hypothetical computer described in Sections 2.9 and 3.9. We can speed up this evaluation by producing a sequence of machine-language instructions that evaluate the expression, thereby saving the time required to traverse a syntax tree many times. Write a procedure that produces such a machine-language program from the syntax tree for an expression. (Such a procedure is the basis for the code generation phase in a compiler.)

13.4 ARTIFICIAL INTELLIGENCE: GAMES OF STRATEGY

The field of artificial intelligence concerns itself with the solution of problems ordinarily thought to require some degree of human intelligence. The name of the field is somewhat problematic because no one really knows how to define intelligence, let alone artificial intelligence. To some, the notion of artificial intelligence is a contradiction in terms: if a machine can do it, then it must not require intelligence. To others, the notion of artificial intelligence is one of the most exciting in computer science, as its study forces us to come to grips with what constitutes human intelligence and the degree to which we can mimic it in a computer program.

In this section we will study one particular aspect of artificial intelligence, namely, the application of computing to games of strategy. Such an application, while enjoyable, is far from frivolous. Deciding what constitutes a good move in a game is just one instance of deciding how to approach a complicated problem. Hence techniques for playing particular games extend to techniques for solving general problems.

GAMES

Programs that referee a game with two or more participants are nothing more than bookkeeping routines. Simple games such as tic-tac-toe require relatively simple bookkeeping; more complicated games such as checkers, chess, and Monopoly require extensive bookkeeping. Although such bookkeeping may call for some cleverness in keeping detail under control and in choosing data structures, it can hardly be said to require intelligence.

Programs that take an active part in a game are more sophisticated because they must use some strategy for playing the game. Some simple games possess relatively routine strategies. More complicated games are generally thought to require some intelligence to be played well.

In order to illustrate the problems we face in developing automatic strategies for playing games, we will consider a family of four simple games. In each of these games, two players alternately remove some number of stones, up to a prescribed maximum number, from a pile of stones. In the game *lastWins*, the player to remove the last stone wins. In the game *lastLoses*, the player to remove the last stone loses. In the game *evenWins*, the pile contains an odd number of stones initially and the player who removes an even number wins. In the game *evenLoses*, the pile contains an odd number of stones initially and the player who removes an even number loses.

Some games possess relatively simple winning strategies. As we will see, *lastWins* and *lastLoses* are two such games. The winner of either game is determined by the number of stones in the pile and the maximum that can be removed; that player can compute exactly how many stones to remove per turn to guarantee a win. Other games possess more complicated strategies. Sometimes we can base a winning strategy on an exhaustive or selective search for a good move. At other times we can develop a winning strategy by writing a program that learns from experience what constitutes a good move.

GAME TREES

It is easiest to talk about strategies for playing a game in terms of a *game tree* with nodes that represent positions in a game. For example, in chess or checkers a position consists of a particular state of the board and an indication of who moves next. The children of any node in a game tree are those positions that can be reached in a single move from that node. The root of a game tree is the initial position of the game. The leaves of a game tree are the final positions in the game, that is, the positions at which the game is won or lost or ends in a draw.

Figure 13.14 displays a portion of the game tree for *evenWins*, where there are five stones in the pile at the beginning of the game and each player can remove at most three stones per turn. The positions in the game show the number of stones left in the pile and the number each player has removed. Markings at the leaves of the tree show whether Player I or Player II has won at those positions.

We will focus our attention on games that have trees like the one in Fig. 13.14. Four properties distinguish these games from others.

1. They are *two-person* games of *strategy*. Both players have complete control over their choice of moves. Nothing depends on random phenomena, such as rolling dice or dealing cards.

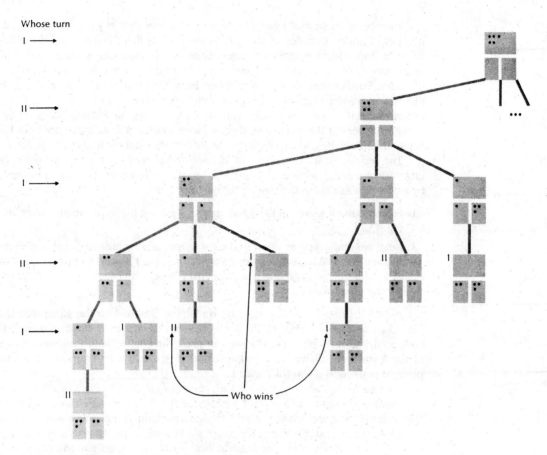

FIGURE 13.14 ■ Portion of game tree for *evenWins*

2. They are games of *perfect information*. Both players have exactly the same information about the current position. There is no concealed information, such as hidden cards.

3. They are *finite* games. Only a finite number of moves are possible in any position, and all plays of the game must end after a finite number of moves (that is, all branches in the game tree are finite in length). Special rules about repeated positions in games such as chess generally ensure that they are finite games.

4. They are *determined* games. At the end of any game, one player or the other has won. There are no draws. Chess and checkers are not determined games in this sense, but our sample games are. We can turn games with draws into determined games by arbitrarily defining a draw to be a win for the second player.

The requirement that a game be finite guarantees that its game tree has a finite number of nodes. In order to see this, let us suppose that the game tree for a finite game had an infinite number of nodes. Then one of the finite number of children of the root of the tree must itself be the root of a subtree that has an infinite number of nodes. Furthermore, one of its children must be the root of yet another subtree that has an infinite number of nodes. Continuing in this manner, there must be an infinite branch in the game tree, with all nodes along that branch being roots of infinite subtrees of the game tree. But the game tree for a finite game does not have any infinite branches, so there cannot be an infinite number of nodes in the tree.

The requirement that a game be determined guarantees that one player or the other has a winning strategy. When the game tree is finite, we can find this strategy by marking positions in the tree, as follows.

1. First, we mark leaves in the game tree as wins for the appropriate player, as in Fig. 13.14.

2. Next, we mark each position in the game tree all of whose children are already marked. We mark a position as a win for the player who is to move next if one of its children is marked as a win for that player. Otherwise we mark it as a win for the other player.

Applying these rules, we mark the remaining positions in the game tree from Fig. 13.14, as shown in Fig. 13.15. We work from the leaves of the tree toward the root, applying our rules. Note that we can mark the root without looking at the rest of the game tree: all we need to know is that one of Player I's moves leads to a position marked as a win for Player I.

This marking procedure shows which player can force wins from which positions. If a position is marked as a win for a player, and it is that player's turn, a move to a child marked as a win leads to a new winning position. If a position is marked as a win for a player, and it is the other player's turn, any move leads to a new winning position for the first player. The mark at the root of the game tree indicates who has a winning strategy for the entire game.

Such a simple method for constructing a winning strategy is not practical for most interesting games. If it were, few people would still play checkers or chess. The problem lies in the fact that a game tree is generally much too large for us to mark all of its nodes. In chess, for example, we can estimate the size of the game tree as follows. An average game of chess involves 40 turns for each player, or 80 moves in all. Each player has a choice of about 20 possible moves per turn. Hence a conservative estimate gives us 20^{80} positions in the game tree for chess. Since $20^{80} = 10^{80}2^{80}$ and $2^{80} = (2^{10})^8 > (10^3)^8 = 10^{24}$, there are more than 10^{100} nodes in the game tree for chess. How long would it take us to mark all of these nodes? If we had started marking nodes at the rate of one billion a second when the universe was created several billions of years ago, we would have marked only 10^{25} or so nodes. Hence we would still have a very long way to go!

Whose turn

I ⟶

II ⟶

I ⟶

II ⟶

I ⟶

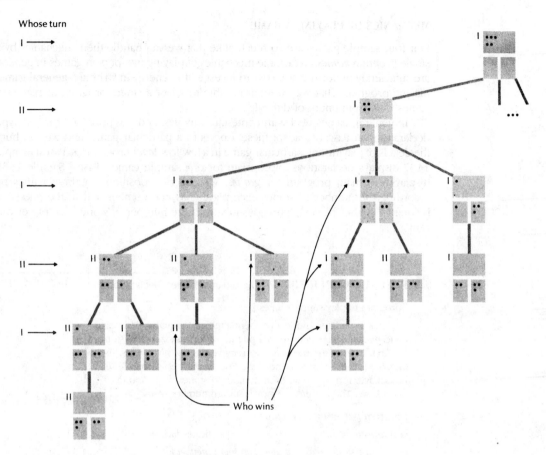

Who wins

FIGURE 13.15 ■ Winning positions for Players I and II

Despite the impracticality of marking all nodes in the game tree for chess, we can use game trees to develop winning strategies for many games. First, certain simple games such as *evenWins* have no obvious winning strategy but have small enough game trees for us to mark. Thus we can use a game tree to find a winning strategy in such games. Second, in more complicated games, we can often search for a good move in a game tree even if we cannot mark it entirely.

We will illustrate the first of these possibilities by writing a program to play our four sample games. However, before we can address ourselves to the interesting question of computing a winning move, we must handle the routine mechanics of playing the game.

MECHANICS OF PLAYING A GAME

Our four sample games are so much alike that we can handle their mechanics by a single program *games*. In fact, the mechanics of playing two-person games in general are sufficiently uniform that it pays to invest a little energy in writing a general game-playing program. That way we will be able to adapt a single program to play new games with a minimum of difficulty.

In general, games deal with contestants, moves, and positions. We can use type declarations in Pascal to adapt these aspects to a particular game, and we can bury the details of playing any particular game in a few low-level procedures. Pascal Sample 13.37 displays declarations appropriate for our sample games. Pascal Sample 13.38 displays the main program for *games*. We describe positions in these games by recording the number of stones each player has, the number still in the pile (that belong to neither player), who goes next, and the number of stones that player can remove.

PASCAL SAMPLE 13.37   The program *games* (declarations)

```
{ program to play simple games }

{      The computer and its opponent alternately remove between 1  }
{ and maxToTake stones from a pile that contains sizeOfPile stones  }
{ at first. In lastWins, the player to remove the last stone wins. In  }
{ lastLoses, the player to remove the last stone loses. In evenWins,  }
{ the player to remove an even number of stones wins. And in  }
{ evenLoses, The player to remove an even number loses.  }

program games(input, output);

const none = 0;                       { indicates lack of good move }

type contestant = (computer, opponent, neither);
     move       = integer;
     state      = record
                      stones  : array [contestant] of integer;
                      maxMove : integer;
                      player  : contestant
                  end;

var sizeOfPile   : 1..maxint;
    maxToTake   : 1..maxint;
    stateOfGame : state;
    randomSeed : integer;                    { required by random }

{ declarations for general procedures such as makeMove go here }
{ game-specific procedures like winner are in separate libraries  }

#include 'lastLoses';    { game specific procedures       }
#include 'random';       { used when no good move exists }
```

■ **PASCAL SAMPLE 13.38** The program *games* (main program)

```
begin
    write('Number of stones in pile: ');
    readln(sizeOfPile);
    write('Maximum number that can be taken: ');
    readln(maxToTake);
    if maxToTake > sizeOfPile then
        maxToTake := sizeOfPile;

    randomize(true );
    initialize(stateofGame);
    while not gameOver(stateOfGame) do
        makeMove(nextMove(stateOfGame), stateOfGame);
    writeln;
    case winner(stateOfGame) of
        computer : writeln('I win.');
        opponent : writeln('You win.');
        neither   : writeln('It!''s a draw.')
    end
end.
```

The main program shows that a game consists of a series of moves, starting in some initial state, with the winner being determined from the final state of the game. Subsidiary procedures carry out all the details.

The *initialize* and *gameOver* procedures, displayed as Pascal Sample 13.39, are the same for each of our four sample games. If we want to play some other game, we must modify these procedures accordingly.

■ **PASCAL SAMPLE 13.39** The program *games* (*initialize, gameOver* procedures)

```
procedure initialize( var s : state );
    { initializes state to beginning of game }
    var response : char;
    begin
        s.stones[computer] := 0;
        s.stones[opponent] := 0;
        s.stones[neither] := sizeOfPile;
        s.maxMove := maxToTake;
        s.player := neither;
```

PASCAL SAMPLE 13.39   The program *games* (*initialize*, *gameOver*, continued)

> *writeln*;
> *write*('Will you go first? ');
> **repeat**
>> *readln*(*response*);
>> **if** *response* **in** ['Y', 'y'] **then**
>>> *s.player* := *opponent*
>> **else if** *response* **in** ['N', 'n'] **then**
>>> *s.player* := *computer*
>> **else**
>>> *writeln*('Please answer ''yes'' or ''no''.')
>
> **until** *s.player* <> *neither*
>
> **end**;   { of *initialize* }

function *gameOver*(*s* : *state*) : *boolean*;
> { returns *true* if game is over in state *s* }
> **begin**
>> *gameOver* := (*s.stones*[*neither*] = 0)
>
> **end**;   { of *gameOver* }

The *makeMove* procedure is also the same for each of our four games. It simply moves stones from one pile to another and sets who goes next. (See Pascal Sample 13.40.) This procedure and the two previous ones are the principal bookkeeping procedures required for any game.

PASCAL SAMPLE 13.40   The program *games* (*makeMove* procedure)

procedure *makeMove*(*m* : *move*; **var** *s* : *state*);
> { makes a legal move *m* in state *s* }
> **begin**
>> *s.stones*[*s.player*] := *s.stones*[*s.player*] + *m*;
>> *s.stones*[*neither*] := *s.stones*[*neither*] − *m*;
>> **if** *s.stones*[*neither*] < *s.maxMove* **then**
>>> *s.maxMove* := *s.stones*[*neither*];
>> **if** *s.player* = *computer* **then**
>>> *s.player* := *opponent*
>> **else**
>>> *s.player* := *computer*
>
> **end**;   { of *makeMove* }

PASCAL SAMPLE 13.41   The program *games* (*nextMove* function)

function *nextMove*(*s* : *state*) : *move*;
   { returns the next move from the computer or its opponent }
   var *n* : *integer*;
   begin
      writeln;
      n := *s*.*stones*[*neither*];
      if *n* = 1 **then**
         writeln('There is one stone left.')
      else
         writeln('There are ', *n* : 1,' stones left.');
      write('I have ', *s*.*stones*[*computer*] : 1);
      writeln(' and you have ', *s*.*stones*[*opponent*] : 1, '.');
      if *s*.*player* = *opponent* **then**
         nextMove := *suppliedMove*(*s*)
      else
         nextMove := *pickedMove*(*s*)
   end;   { of *nextMove* }

We complete the main program in *games* by providing a definition of the *nextMove* function. In Pascal Sample 13.41, this function decides whether to interact with the opponent to get the next move (by a function *suppliedMove*) or to pick a move for the computer (by a function *pickedMove*). Prior to getting the next move, it displays the state of the game for all to see. A more general version of this function would give the opponent the option of entering a command instead of a move (for example, to retract a move), to have the computer suggest a good move, or to force the computer to make a particular move.

The *suppliedMove* function simply asks the opponent for a move, checking to make sure that it is legal. (See Pascal Sample 13.42.) A more general version of this function would enable *nextMove* to invoke it when the opponent wants to supply a move for the computer. To achieve this generality, we need to change only the message printed by *suppliedMove*. The rest of the function definition is not affected.

Finally, the *pickedMove* function invokes a game-specific function, *bestMove*, to try to find a winning move for the computer. (See Pascal Sample 13.43.) If *bestMove* returns the value *none*, indicating that it could not find a winning move, then *pickedMove* simply picks a move at random from among the legal moves. Here again we could enable *pickedMove* to pick a move for either player simply by changing the message it prints.

■ **PASCAL SAMPLE 13.42**   The program *games* (*suppliedMove* function)

function *suppliedMove*(*s* : *state*) : *move*;
   { returns a legal move supplied by the opponent }
   var *legal* : *boolean*;
      m   : *move*;
   begin
      repeat
         write('How many do you take? ');
         readln(*m*);
         legal := (*m* > 0) **and** (*m* <= *s.maxMove*);
         if not *legal* **then** *writeln*('Illegal move.')
      until *legal*;
      suppliedMove := *m*
   end;   { of *suppliedMove* }

■ **PASCAL SAMPLE 13.43**   The program *games* (*pickedMove* function)

function *pickedMove*(*s* : *state*) : *move*;
   { returns a move picked by the computer }
   var *m* : *move*;
   begin
      m := *bestMove*(*s*);
      if *m* = *none* **then** { pick random legal move }
         m := *randomInt*(1, *s.maxMove*);
      write('I take ', *m* : 1, ' stone');
      if *m* = 1 **then** *writeln*('.') **else** *writeln*('s. ');
      pickedMove := *m*
   end;   { of *pickedMove* }

PICKING GOOD MOVES IN A GAME

At this point, we have taken care of all the details common to our four sample games. What remains to be done is to define the functions *winner* and *bestMove* for each of these games; the function *bestMove* is by far the most interesting.

   The functions *winner* and *bestMove* for the game *lastLoses* are particularly simple. The winner is simply the player to move next when the game ends. The player who is able to leave (*maxMove* + 1)*n* + 1 stones in the pile, for any value of *n*, can force a win in the game. No matter how many stones *m* the other player removes next,

---

■ **PASCAL SAMPLE 13.44**   The library *lastLoses*

{ *lastLoses*: functions to use with *games* to play *lastLoses* }

function *winner*(*s* : *state*) : *contestant*;
   { returns the winner of a game that ends in state *s* }
   begin
      winner := *s.player*
   end;   { of *winner* }

function *bestMove*(*s* : *state*) : *move*;
   { returns a winning move for the player to move in state *s* }
   { returns the value *none* = 0 if no winning move exists   }
   begin
      bestMove := (*s.stones*[*neither*] − 1) **mod** (*s.maxMove* + 1)
   end;   { of *bestMove* }

---

the player in control can remove $maxMove + 1 - m$ stones to leave $(maxMove + 1)(n - 1) + 1$ in the pile. Eventually the other player is forced to move when one stone remains in the pile, thereby losing the game. The library *lastLoses*, displayed as Pascal Sample 13.44, contains the definitions of the functions required for playing that game.

The game *evenWins* does not possess such a simple winning strategy; consequently, it is harder to play well. But we can find good moves in *evenWins* by evaluating the positions in its game tree, using the marking procedure described above. The simplest way to do this is by recursion. The *bestMove* function in the library *evenWins* examines all moves available in a given position, looking for one that leads to a win. It recognizes such a move by invoking itself recursively to see if that move leaves the other player without a winning response. If such a move exists, *bestMove* returns it as its value. If not, it returns the value *none* to indicate that the other player, with careful play, can force a win. (In this latter case, the procedure *pickedMove* picks a random legal move for the computer, hoping that the opponent will subsequently make a mistake.) Definitions for the *winner* and *bestMove* functions in *evenWins* are displayed as Pascal Sample 13.45.

The simplicity of the *bestMove* function results directly from taking a sophisticated view of two-person games. By using an appropriate data structure to represent a game, we were able to devise an algorithm that found a winning move. And by using an appropriate program structure, recursion, to implement this algorithm, we were able to write a simple program that plays a subtle game.

PASCAL SAMPLE 13.45   The library *evenWins*

{ *evenWins*: functions to use with *games* to play *evenWins* }

function *winner*(*s* : *state*) : *contestant*;

    { returns the winner of a game that ends in state *s* }

  begin

    if *s.stones*[*opponent*] **mod** 2 = 0 **then**

        winner := *opponent*

    else

        winner := *computer*

  end;   { of *winner* }

function *bestMove*(*s* : *state*) : *move*;

    { returns a winning move for the player to move in state *s* }

    { returns the value *none* if no winning move exists   }

    { assumes *s.maxMove* > 0   }

  var *foundMove* : boolean;   { *true* when win is found }

      m   : *move*;   { candidate move   }

      newState : *state*;   { state after that move }

  begin

    m := *s.maxMove*;   { try largest move first }

    repeat

      newState := *s*;

      makeMove(*m*, *newState*);

      if *gameOver*(*newState*) **then**

        foundMove := (*winner*(*newState*) = *s.player*)

      else

        foundMove := (*bestMove*(*newState*) = *none*);

      if not *foundMove* **then** *m* := *m* − 1

    until *foundMove* **or** (*m* = *none*);

    bestMove := *m*

  end;   { of *bestMove* }

EXERCISES

1. Use *games* to play *evenWins* for *n* = 9 and *m* = 3. Determine which positions are wins for which player.

2. Devise a strategy for playing *evenWins* that does not involve searching a game tree or recursion. (*Hint:* The Fibonacci numbers are involved.)

3. Write libraries of functions to play the games *lastWins* and *evenLoses*.

4. Modify *games* to play the following variant of the game *lastWins*. The first player must leave at least one stone in the pile after his or her first turn. On subsequent turns, each player may remove up to twice the number of stones just removed by the other player. The player to remove the last stone wins.

5. The recursive strategy for marking the nodes in the game tree for *evenWins* is easy to describe but is not very efficient. It can examine a single position many times, duplicating its efforts instead of remembering what it discovered before. Modify the function *bestMove* to eliminate this inefficiency. (*Hint:* Create a table of winning moves.)

6. Modify the program *games* to enable a user to enter one of the following commands in place of any move.

   (a) `auto n`

   Have the computer make the next *n* moves for the user.

   (b) `force n`

   Allow the user to supply the next *n* moves for the computer.

   (c) `retract n`

   Retract the last *n* moves the user has made.

   (d) `quit`

   Stop playing the game.

   (e) `skip`

   Skip the user's turn, making the computer move next.

   (f) `position p p1 p2`

   Reset the position of the game to have *p* stones in the pile, with the two players having removed *p1* and *p2* already.

   If no value for *n* is supplied in one of these commands, assume that $n = 1$.

SUMMARY

The applications in this chapter illustrate the ways in which sophisticated algorithms and data structures simplify ambitious programming projects. Each application uses recursion to reduce complicated problems to simpler problems. And each application uses a dynamic data structure, either explicitly or implicitly, to organize the information it must process.

The library *arith2* contains procedures for arbitrary-precision integer arithmetic. It uses linked lists rather than vectors to provide a more efficient representation for an abstract data type (first introduced in Chapter 7). The new representation

- conserves storage by eliminating leading zeroes,

- avoids an explicit limit on the precision of integers, and

- helps circumvent superfluous operations on digits.

In *arith2*, recursion provides a clear formulation of the familiar algorithms for addition, subtraction, multiplication, and long division.

The programs *calc4* and *calc5* enhance the pocket calculator programs developed in Chapter 7. Both interpret arithmetic expressions that contain parentheses and that presume the usual precedence for arithmetic operators. And both store information about variables in a memory: *calc4* stores values for variables; *calc5* stores expressions that provide values for variables. These programs illustrate the techniques used by more elaborate interpreters and compilers, in which

- syntax diagrams describe expressions,
- recursive descent parsers recognize expressions,
- syntax trees record the structure of expressions, and
- recursive evaluators find the values of expressions.

Finally, the program *games* illustrates problem-solving techniques in the field of artificial intelligence. It plays a simple game of strategy by searching recursively for a winning move in a game tree that represents all possible states in a game. Similar searches through other trees of states aid in solving many problems ordinarily thought to require some degree of human intelligence.

SUMMARY OF
STANDARD PASCAL

A

This appendix summarizes the features of Standard Pascal used in this book. Foot-notes call attention to features of Pascal not addressed in the text.

PROGRAMS AND IDENTIFIERS

program

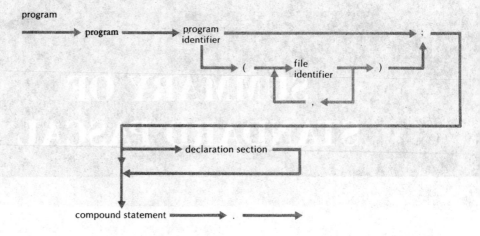

comment

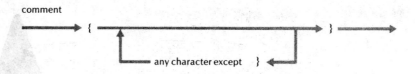

identifier

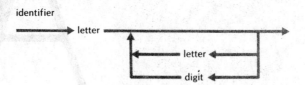

DECLARATIONS

declaration section

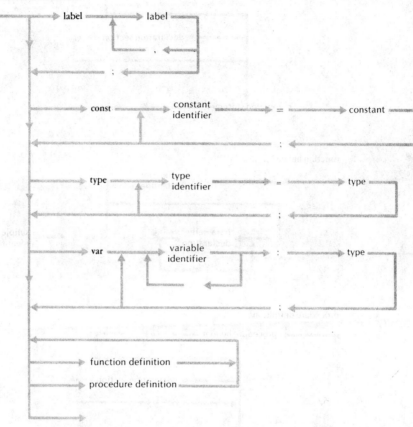

function definition[†]

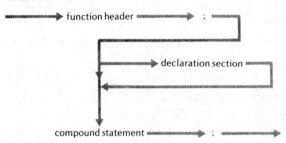

function header

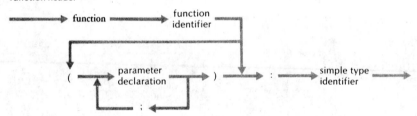

procedure definition[†]

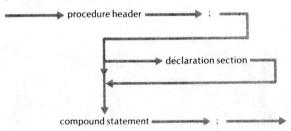

[†]In standard Pascal, we can postpone giving the declarations and compound statement in a function or procedure definition if we replace them by the directive **forward**, as in

function $f(n : integer) : integer;$ **forward**;

Later in the same declaration section, we complete the definition by providing an abbreviated header followed by the deferred declarations and compound statement, as in

function $f;$ { declarations and body of definition }

This feature allows two subprograms to invoke each other.

procedure header

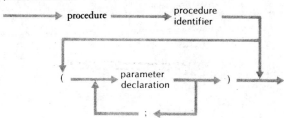

parameter declaration

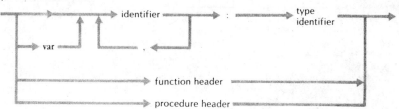

type

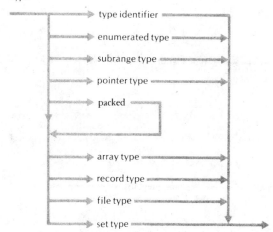

array type

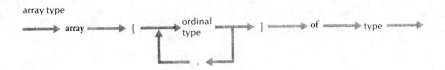

enumerated type

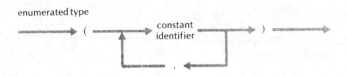

file type

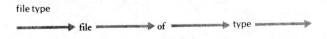

pointer type

record type

component list

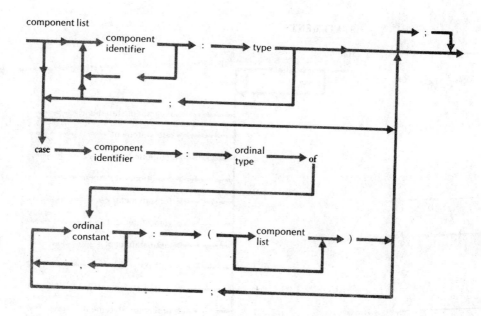

set type

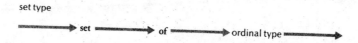

subrange type

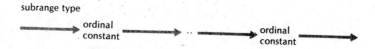

STATEMENTS

statement[†]

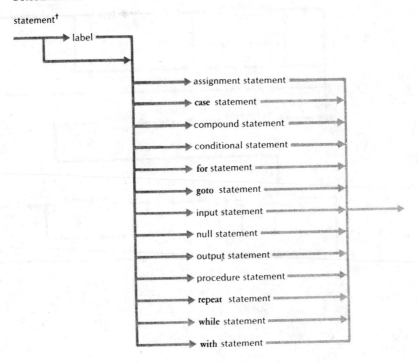

label

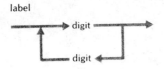

assignment statement

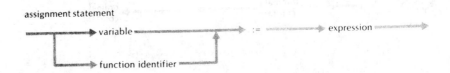

[†]In standard Pascal, a label can precede any statement, not just those in the body of a compound statement.

case statement

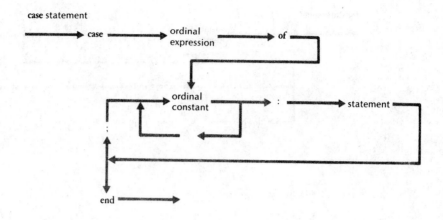

compound statement

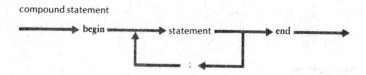

conditional statement

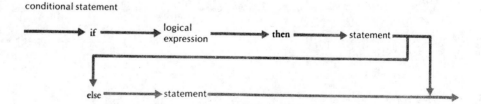

for statement

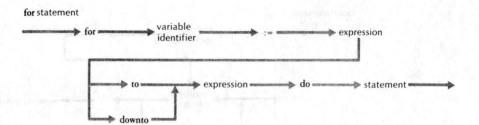

goto statement

➤ goto ➤ label ➤

input statement

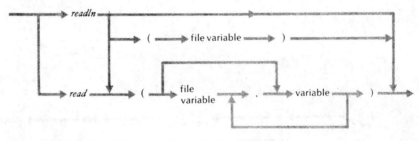

null statement

➤

output statement

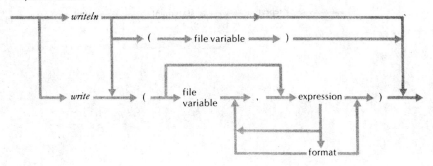

format

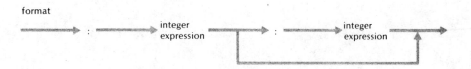

procedure statement

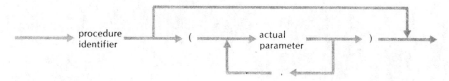

repeat statement

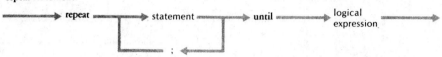

while statement

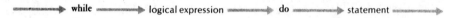

with statement

EXPRESSIONS

expression

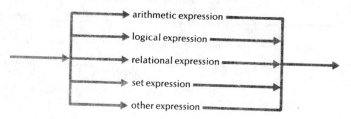

arithmetic.expression

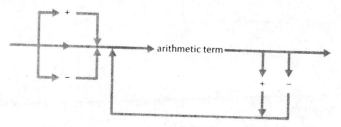

arithmetic term

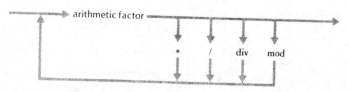

arithmetic factor

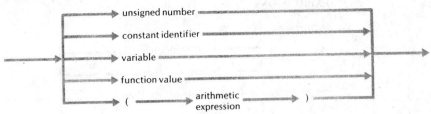

logical expression

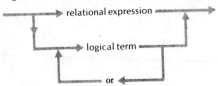

logical term

logical factor

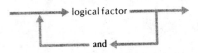

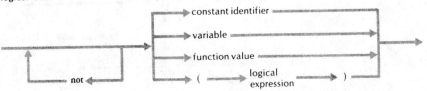

relational expression

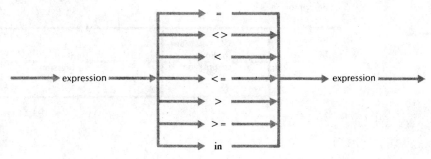

set expression

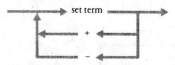

set term

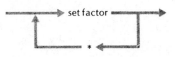

set factor

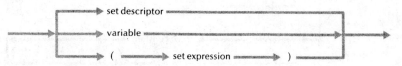

set descriptor

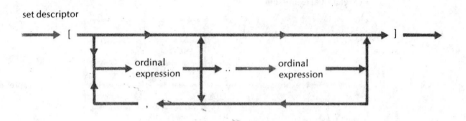

CONSTANTS

other expression

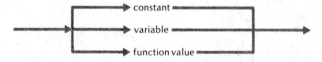

constant

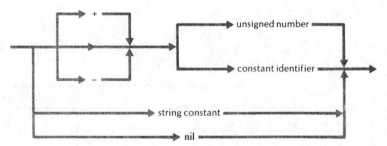

unsigned number

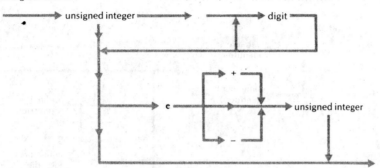

unsigned integer

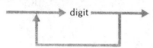

digit

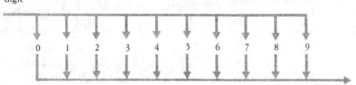

string constant

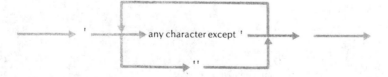

VARIABLES AND FUNCTION VALUES

variable

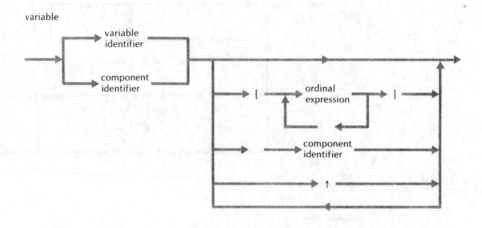

function value

function value

actual parameter

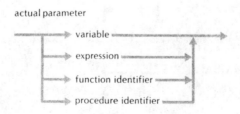

RESERVED WORDS

The following words may not be used as identifiers.

and	array	begin	case	const	div
do	downto	else	end	file	for
function	goto	if	in	label	mod
nil	not	of	or	packed	procedure
program	record	repeat	set	then	to
type	until	var	while	with	

PREDEFINED IDENTIFIERS

The following tables describe the predefined identifiers supplied by Pascal. There an ordinal type is an enumerated type, a subrange type, or one of the types *boolean*, *char*, or *integer*. A simple type is an ordinal type or the type *real*. A string type is a packed array of characters. And a text file is a file of characters.

Predefined constants: *true, false, maxint*
Predefined types: *boolean, char, integer, real, text*
Predefined files: *input, output*

Predefined Functions

Function	Parameter type	Result type	Description
abs(x)	*integer* or *real*	same as parameter	absolute value of *x*
arctan(x)	*integer* or *real*	*real*	arctangent of *x*
chr(n)	*integer*	*char*	character with code *n*
cos(x)	*integer* or *real*	*real*	cosine of *x*
eof(f)	file	*boolean*	*true* at end of file *f*
eoln(f)	text file	*boolean*	*true* at end of line in *f*
exp(x)	*integer* or *real*	*real*	e^x
ln(x)	*integer* or *real*	*real*	natural logarithm of *x* (*x* must be positive)
odd(n)	*integer*	*boolean*	*true* if *n* is odd
ord(x)	ordinal type	*integer*	position of *x* in ordinal type
pred(x)	ordinal type	same as parameter	predecessor of *x*
round(x)	*integer* or *real*	*integer*	*x* rounded
sin(x)	*integer* or *real*	*real*	sine of *x*
sqr(x)	*integer* or *real*	same as parameter	square of *x*
sqrt(x)	*integer* or *real*	*real*	square root of *x*
succ(x)	ordinal type	same as parameter	successor of *x*
trunc(x)	*integer* or *real*	*integer*	*x* truncated

Predefined Procedures

Procedure	Description
dispose(*p*)	disposes of storage referenced by the pointer *p*
get(*f*)	assigns the next value in the file *f* to *f*↑
new(*p*)	allocates storage for variable referenced by the pointer *p*
pack(*a, i, b*)	copies items beginning with *a*[*i*] into packed array *b*
page(*f*)	advances output to next page of text file
put(*f*)	appends *f*↑ to the end of *f*, making *f*↑ undefined
read(*f, a, b, ...*)	reads *a, b, ...* from file *f* (reads *input* if *f* omitted) (for text file, parameter types must be *char, integer,* or *real*)
readln(*f, a, b, ...*)	reads *a, b, ...* from text file *f*; advances to next line in file (reads *input* if *f* omitted)
reset(*f*)	prepares file *f* for reading
rewrite(*f*)	erases file *f* and prepares it for writing
unpack(*b, i, a*)	copies packed array *b* into *a*[*i*], ...
write(*f, a, b, ...*)	writes *a, b, ...* into file *f* (writes *output* if *f* omitted) (for text file, parameter types must be *boolean, char, integer, real* or string)
writeln(*f, a, b, ...*)	writes *a, b, ...* followed by end-of-line into text file *f* (writes *output* if *f* omitted)

OPERATORS

Operator	Operand types	Result type	Description
+	*integer* or *real* set	*integer* or *real* set	addition set union
−	*integer* or *real* set	*integer* or *real* set	subtraction set difference
*	*integer* or *real* set	*integer* or *real* set	multiplication set intersection
/	*integer* or *real*	*real*	division
div	*integer*	*integer*	integer division
mod	*integer*	*integer*	integer modulus
=	simple, string, or pointer	*boolean*	equal to
<>	simple, string, or pointer	*boolean*	not equal to
<	simple or string	*boolean*	less than
<=	simple or string set	*boolean* *boolean*	less than or equal to subset
>	simple or string	*boolean*	greater than
>=	simple or string set	*boolean* *boolean*	greater than or equal to superset
in	ordinal type and set	*boolean*	set membership
[...]	ordinal type	set	set constructor
:=	any nonfile type	none	assignment

OTHER SYMBOLS

Symbol	Alternate	Usage
,		separates parameters, subscripts, other items in a list
;		separates statements, declarations
:		separates identifier from type in declaration
		separates **case** constants from statements
		separates parameter for *write* from format
		separates labels from statements
'		delimits character and string constants
.		decimal point
		selects component of record variable
		terminates program
..		separates bounds for subrange
↑	^, @	designates variable referenced by pointer
		designates next item in a file
(		starts nested expression, parameter list, or enumerated type
)		ends nested expression, parameter list, or enumerated type
[	(.	starts subscript list or set descriptor
]	.)	ends subscript list or set descriptor
{	(*	starts a comment
}	*)	ends a comment

CHARACTER SETS CHARACTER S
TER SETS CHARACTER SETS CHA
CHARACTER SETS CHARACTER S
TER SETS CHARACTER SETS CHA
CHARACTER SETS CHARACTER S
R SETS CHARACTER SETS CHARAC
CHARACTER SETS CHARACTER S
R SETS **CHARACTER SETS** CHARAC

B

ASCII (American Standard Code for Information Interchange)

The ASCII codes 0 to 31 and 127 represent nonprintable control characters.

ord	chr	Description	ord	chr	Description
0		Null	45	–	Hyphen (minus sign)
1		Start of heading	46	.	Period
2		Start of text	47	/	Slant
3		End of text	48	0	Zero
4		End of transmission	49	1	One
5		Enquiry	50	2	Two
6		Acknowledgment	51	3	Three
7		Bell	52	4	Four
8		Backspace	53	5	Five
9		Horizontal tab	54	6	Six
10		Line feed	55	7	Seven
11		Vertical tab	56	8	Eight
12		Form feed	57	9	Nine
13		Carriage return	58	:	Colon
14		Shift out	59	;	Semicolon
15		Shift in	60	<	Less than
16		Data link escape	61	=	Equals
17		Device control 1	62	>	Greater than
18		Device control 2	63	?	Question mark
19		Device control 3	64	@	Commercial at
20		Device control 4	65	A	Uppercase A
21		Negative acknowledgment	66	B	Uppercase B
22		Synchronous idle	67	C	Uppercase C
23		End of transmission block	68	D	Uppercase D
24		Cancel	69	E	Uppercase E
25		End of medium	70	F	Uppercase F
26		Substitute	71	G	Uppercase G
27		Escape	72	H	Uppercase H
28		File separator	73	I	Uppercase I
29		Group separator	74	J	Uppercase J
30		Record separator	75	K	Uppercase K
31		Unit separator	76	L	Uppercase L
32		Space	77	M	Uppercase M
33	!	Exclamation point	78	N	Uppercase N
34	"	Quotation mark	79	O	Uppercase O
35	#	Number sign	80	P	Uppercase P
36	$	Dollar sign	81	Q	Uppercase Q
37	%	Percent sign	82	R	Uppercase R
38	&	Ampersand	83	S	Uppercase S
39	'	Apostrophe	84	T	Uppercase T
40	(	Opening parenthesis	85	U	Uppercase U
41	)	Closing parenthesis	86	V	Uppercase V
42	*	Asterisk	87	W	Uppercase W
43	+	Plus sign	88	X	Uppercase X
44	,	Comma			*(Continued)*

ord	chr	Description	ord	chr	Description
89	Y	Uppercase Y	109	m	Lowercase m
90	Z	Uppercase Z	110	n	Lowercase n
91	[	Opening bracket	111	o	Lowercase o
92	\	Reverse slant	112	p	Lowercase p
93	]	Closing bracket	113	q	Lowercase q
94	^	Circumflex	114	r	Lowercase r
95	_	Underscore	115	s	Lowercase s
96	`	Grave accent	116	t	Lowercase t
97	a	Lowercase a	117	u	Lowercase u
98	b	Lowercase b	118	v	Lowercase v
99	c	Lowercase c	119	w	Lowercase w
100	d	Lowercase d	120	x	Lowercase x
101	e	Lowercase e	121	y	Lowercase y
102	f	Lowercase f	122	z	Lowercase z
103	g	Lowercase g	123	{	Opening brace
104	h	Lowercase h	124			Vertical line
105	i	Lowercase i	125	}	Closing brace
106	j	Lowercase j	126	~	Tilde
107	k	Lowercase k	127		Delete
108	l	Lowercase l			

EBCDIC (Extended Binary Coded Decimal Interchange Code)

The EBCDIC codes 0 to 63 and 250 to 255 represent nonprintable control characters.

ord	chr	Description	ord	chr	Description
64		Space	129	a	Lowercase a
.			130	b	Lowercase b
.			131	c	Lowercase c
.			132	d	Lowercase d
74	[	Opening bracket	133	e	Lowercase e
75	.	Period	134	f	Lowercase f
76	<	Less than	135	g	Lowercase g
77	(	Opening parenthesis	136	h	Lowercase h
78	+	Plus sign	137	i	Lowercase i
79	!	Exclamation point	.		
80	&	Ampersand	.		
.			.		
.			145	j	Lowercase j
.			146	k	Lowercase k
90	]	Closing bracket	147	l	Lowercase l
91	$	Dollar sign	148	m	Lowercase m
92	*	Asterisk	149	n	Lowercase n
93	)	Closing parenthesis	150	o	Lowercase o
94	;	Semicolon	151	p	Lowercase p
95	^	Circumflex	152	q	Lowercase q
96	–	Hyphen (minus sign)	153	r	Lowercase r
97	/	Slant	.		
.			.		
.			161	~	Tilde
106	|	Vertical line	162	s	Lowercase s
107	,	Comma	163	t	Lowercase t
108	%	Percent sign	164	u	Lowercase u
109	_	Underscore	165	v	Lowercase v
110	>	Greater than	166	w	Lowercase w
111	?	Question mark	167	x	Lowercase x
.			168	y	Lowercase y
.			169	z	Lowercase z
121	`	Grave accent	.		
122	:	Colon	.		
123	#	Number sign	*(Continued)*		
124	@	Commercial at			
125	'	Apostrophe			
126	=	Equals			
127	"	Quotation mark			

ord	chr	Description	ord	chr	Description
192	{	Opening brace	224	\	Reverse slant
193	A	Uppercase A	.		
194	B	Uppercase B	.		
195	C	Uppercase C	.		
196	D	Uppercase D	226	S	Uppercase S
197	E	Uppercase E	227	T	Uppercase T
198	F	Uppercase F	228	U	Uppercase U
199	G	Uppercase G	229	V	Uppercase V
200	H	Uppercase H	230	W	Uppercase W
201	I	Uppercase I	231	X	Uppercase X
.			232	Y	Uppercase Y
.			233	Z	Uppercase Z
.			.		
208	}	Closing brace	.		
209	J	Uppercase J	.		
210	K	Uppercase K	240	0	Zero
211	L	Uppercase L	241	1	One
212	M	Uppercase M	242	2	Two
213	N	Uppercase N	243	3	Three
214	O	Uppercase O	244	4	Four
215	P	Uppercase P	245	5	Five
216	Q	Uppercase Q	246	6	Six
217	R	Uppercase R	247	7	Seven
.			248	8	Eight
.			249	9	Nine
.			.		
			.		

REFERENCES FOR FURTHER STUDY

ALGORITHMS AND DATA STRUCTURES

Alfred Aho, John Hopcroft, and Jeffrey Ullman, *Data Structures and Algorithms*. Reading, Mass.: Addison-Wesley, 1983.
> Emphasizes the analysis of algorithms; sample programs in Pascal.

Donald Knuth, *The Art of Computer Programming, vol. 1 (Fundamental Algorithms)*, 2d ed. Reading, Mass.: Addison-Wesley, 1973.
> Thorough treatment of linked lists, stacks, queues, and trees in Chapter 2; sample programs in assembly language hard to read, but not essential to an understanding of the text.

· Donald Knuth, *The Art of Computer Programming, vol. 3 (Searching and Sorting)*. Reading, Mass.: Addison-Wesley, 1973.
> Classic reference on searching and sorting; thorough analysis of algorithms; sample programs in assembly language.

Robert Sedgewick, *Algorithms*. Reading, Mass.: Addison-Wesley, 1983.
> Wide ranging survey of algorithms for many applications: multiple-precision arithmetic, random-number generation, numeric methods, searching, sorting, string processing, geometry, and graphs; sample programs in Pascal.

Niklaus Wirth, *Algorithms + Data Structures = Programs*. Englewood Cliffs, N.J.: Prentice-Hall, 1976.
> Terser treatment of searching, sorting, linked data structures than in Knuth; sample programs in Pascal; also covers parsing.

NUMERIC METHODS

Samuel D. Conte and Carl deBoor, *Elementary Numerical Analysis: An Algorithmic Approach*, 3d ed. New York: McGraw-Hill, 1980.
> Mathematical coverage of number systems and errors, solutions of equations, matrices, approximation, differentiation, and integration. Presents algorithms coded in Fortran.

Richard W. Hamming, *Numerical Methods for Scientists and Engineers,* 2d ed. New York: McGraw-Hill, 1973.
> Treats sources of numeric error, approximations, other mathematical algorithms.

Donald Knuth, *The Art of Computer Programming, vol. 2 (Seminumerical Algorithms),* 2d ed. Reading, Mass.: Addison-Wesley, 1980.
> Thorough coverage of random-number generation, floating-point arithmetic, and multiple-precision arithmetic.

ARTIFICIAL INTELLIGENCE

Eugene Charniak and Drew McDermott, *Introduction to Artificial Intelligence.* Reading, Mass.: Addison-Wesley, 1985.
> Uses machine vision and natural language processing to motivate basic problems and concepts concerning the representation of information, reasoning, search, logic, expert systems, and learning. Sample programs in Lisp.

Patrick Henry Winston, *Artificial Intelligence,* 2d ed. Reading, Mass.: Addison-Wesley, 1984.
> Written for readers with little background in programming or mathematics. Explains the basic theoretical concepts of artificial intelligence, but in less detail than Charniak and McDermott.

Patrick Henry Winston and Berthold Klaus Paul Hoor, *LISP,* 2d ed. Reading, Mass.: Addison-Wesley, 1984.
> Companion text for Winston's *Artificial Intelligence.* Introduces Lisp, an influential programming language based on recursion. Covers the programming aspects of artificial intelligence as well as abstraction and object-oriented programming.

DATABASE MANAGEMENT SYSTEMS

C. J. Date, *An Introduction to Database Systems, Volume 1,* 4th ed. Reading, Mass.: Addison-Wesley, 1986.
> Comprehensive treatment of database systems. Covers database models, queries, integrity, security, etc.

Jeffrey D. Ullman, *Principles of Database Systems,* 2d ed. Rockville, Md.: Computer Science Press, 1982.
> Similar in scope to Date's book, but somewhat more theoretical.

PROGRAMMING METHODOLOGY

Frederick Brooks, Jr., *The Mythical Man Month.* Reading, Mass.: Addison-Wesley, 1975.
> Entertaining and insightful essays on software engineering by the manager of one of the largest software projects ever.

Ole-Johan Dahl, Edsger Dijkstra, and C. A. R. Hoare, *Structured Programming.* New York: Academic Press, 1972.
> Important early statement of the principles of program structure and correctness.

David Gries, *The Science of Programming*. New York: Springer-Verlag, 1981.
  Rigorous treatment of how to write correct programs and prove them correct as you write them.

John Guttag and Barbara Liskov, *Abstraction and Specification in Program Development*. Cambridge, Mass.: MIT Press. New York: McGraw-Hill, 1986.
  Practical and substantive treatment of procedural and data abstraction, informal and formal specifications, program design, testing, debugging, and verification. Introduces the programming language CLU; also contains advice for structuring programs in Pascal.

Gerald M. Weinberg, *The Psychology of Computer Programming*. New York: Van Nostrand Reinhold, 1971.
  Cogent observations on what makes programmers tick.

Edward Yourdon, *Classics in Software Engineering*. New York: Yourdon Press, 1979.
  Reprints of many well-known articles on programming methodology, including several seminal articles by Edsger Dijkstra.

PROGRAMMING

Brian W. Kernighan and P. J. Plauger, *Software Tools in Pascal*. Reading, Mass.: Addison-Wesley, 1981.
  Carefully developed programs for applications such as string handling and text formatting; contains sage advice on program development.

Charles Wetherell, *Etudes for Programmers*. Englewood Cliffs, N.J.: Prentice-Hall, 1978.
  Collection of interesting programming projects.

PROGRAMMING LANGUAGES

Alfred V. Aho, Ravi Sethi, and Jeffrey D. Ullman, *Compilers: Principles, Techniques, and Tools*. Reading, Mass.: Addison-Wesley, 1986.
  Covers grammars for defining the syntax of programming languages as well as methods of scanning for tokens, top-down and bottom-up parsing, type checking, run-time environments, code generation, and optimization.

Terrence W. Pratt, *Programming Languages: Design and Implementation,* 2d ed. Englewood Cliffs, N.J.: Prentice Hall, 1984.
  Discusses the concepts underlying the operation of language processors. Compares the features and implementation requirements of a variety of typical programming languages.

PASCAL

Kenneth Bowles, *UCSD Pascal*. New York: Springer-Verlag, 1979.
  Description of a popular dialect of Pascal, written by its designer.

Doug Cooper, *Standard Pascal User Reference Manual*. New York: W. W. Norton, 1983.
  Readable paraphrase of the international standard for Pascal.

Kathleen Jensen and Niklaus Wirth, *Pascal User Manual and Report,* 3d ed. New York: Springer-Verlag, 1985.
> The original definition of Pascal by its designer, Niklaus Wirth, brought up to date.

Robert Moll and Rachel Folsom, *Macintosh Pascal.* Boston: Houghton-Mifflin, 1985.
> Elementary introduction to Pascal on the Macintosh. Also covers system use, graphics, problem solving, and top-down design.

COMPUTER SYSTEMS

Andrew S. Tanenbaum, *Structured Computer Organization,* 2d ed. Englewood Cliffs, N.J.: Prentice-Hall, 1984.
> Presents levels of computer system organization from digital logic through machine language to operating systems.

John F. Wakerly, *Microcomputer Architecture and Programming.* New York: John Wiley, 1981.
> Introduction to machine and assembly language. Good coverage of number representations, addressing, input-output, and subroutine implementation.

GENERAL REFERENCE

Anthony Ralston (Ed.), *Encyclopedia of Computer Science and Engineering*, 2d ed. New York: Van Nostrand Reinhold, 1982.

GLOSSARY

abstract data type   A data type defined in terms of operations that manipulate abstract objects. The representation of the objects themselves is hidden by procedures performing these operations.

accuracy   The exactness of an approximation.

actual parameter   An expression or variable supplied when invoking a function or procedure that gives meaning to a formal parameter in the definition of that function or procedure.

address   A number indicating a location in the memory of a computer.

algorithm   An explicit method for carrying out a computation.

approximation   A number within a specified tolerance of a desired value; the process of producing such a number.

argument   See *actual parameter*.

array   A collection of objects indexed by subscripts.

ASCII   American Standard Code for Information Interchange. An assignment of numeric codes to characters.

assembly language   A low-level language providing a shorthand notation for machine-language instructions.

assertion   A statement about the current state of affairs during the execution of a program.

batch processing   A noninteractive mode of operating a computer that requires users to submit data along with programs for execution and only later returns the results.

binary search   An algorithm for searching an ordered list that repeatedly divides the list in half.

binary tree   A tree in which each node has at most two children.

bisection algorithm   An algorithm for approximating a zero of a function that repeatedly divides an interval containing the zero in half.

bit   A single binary digit, which can have the value zero or one.

boolean   A data type consisting of the two logical values *true* and *false*.

bottom-up   A method that performs simple tasks first and then assembles the results to perform more ambitious tasks.

buffer   A location that holds information in transit from one place (say, a file) to another.

bug   A mistake.

byte   A unit of information, typically eight bits, that holds the representation for a character.

call   To invoke a procedure or function.

CPU   Central processing unit. The part of a computer that interprets machine-language instructions residing in memory and carries out the indicated actions.

character   A letter, digit, punctuation mark, or other symbol.

children   The immediate descendants of an item in a tree.

compiler   A program that translates other programs written in some high-level language into machine language.

computer   A device, generally electrical in nature, for carrying out the computations specified by a program.

correct   Producing the desired result. Said of a program that performs in accordance with its specification.

data   Information available as input to a computer program.

data structure   A way of organizing related pieces of information; for example, an array, record, set, or file.

data type   A collection of similar objects such as integers, real numbers, or strings of characters.

debugging   The process of correcting mistakes in a program.

declaration   A specification of the data type for a variable or of a definition for a procedure or function.

disk   A physical medium for storing data. *Hard disks* have larger capacities and higher transfer rates than *flexible* or *floppy* disks. But floppy disks are more transportable.

dynamic data structure   A data structure that can change in size.

editor   A program that enables users to inspect and modify programs or files of text.

efficiency   A measure of the resources, such as time and memory, consumed by an algorithm or program.

error   A mistake. Compilers and interpreters detect *syntax errors*, which violate the rules of a programming language. Computer systems detect *execution* or *runtime errors*, which occur when a syntactically correct program malfunctions. Programmers themselves must detect *logical errors*, which result from incorrect algorithms or incorrect translations of algorithms into programs.

file   A named collection of information residing in secondary storage. A particular data type in Pascal that reflects the sequential nature of many files.

floating-point notation   A scientific notation for real numbers, such as that used for real constants in Pascal.

formal parameter   A dummy variable appearing in the definition of a function or procedure that receives a value from an actual parameter when the function or procedure is invoked.

full evaluation   A method of evaluating logical expressions that evaluates all subexpressions, whether or not they affect the value of the entire expression.

global identifier   An identifier having an existence and identity outside a specific function or procedure definition.

hardware   The physical components of a computer system.

heap   A linked data structure used for sorting and for maintaining priority queues. Also the portion of memory used to allocate storage for dynamic data structures.

high-level language   A programming language with a vocabulary directed more toward applications than toward a particular computer system. A compiler or interpreter is required to execute programs written in such languages.

identifier   A name for a variable, function, procedure, and the like.

implement   To write a program that carries out a particular task.

increment   To add one to.

initialize   To prepare for use, say by assigning an initial value.

interactive system   A computer system that enables users at terminals to converse with programs.

interpreter   A program that executes other programs written in some programming language without first translating them into machine language.

invariant   An assertion in a loop that is true on each pass through the loop.

invocation   An activation of a procedure or function definition.

iterate   To repeat, as for the body of a loop.

K   A factor of 1024 in storage capacity; for example, 64K bytes, or 64 *kilobytes*, is approximately 64,000 bytes.

keyword   A word with a special meaning in a programming language, generally not available for use as an identifier.

linear search   An algorithm for searching an unordered list, which proceeds sequentially through the list.

linear time   A growth rate for the time required by an algorithm that increases in direct proportion to the size of a problem.

linked list   A list that uses pointers rather than sequential allocation to indicate the succession of items.

list   A sequence of items.

local identifier   An identifier having an existence and identity only within a specific function or procedure definition.

logarithmic time   A growth rate for the time required by an algorithm that increases in direct proportion to the logarithm of the size of a problem.

loop   A programming construct for repeated execution of a sequence of instructions.

low-level language   A programming language with a vocabulary directed more toward a particular computer system than toward an application.

machine language   A programming language that can be understood directly by the hardware in a computer system.

memory   The component of a computer that holds instructions and data during execution of a program.

operand   A value used by an operator.

operating system   Software that manages the resources provided by the hardware in a computer system.

operator   A symbol such as − or ∗ denoting an operation that produces a new value from the value of one or two operands.

overflow   An execution error that arises when a computation produces a value too large to represent within the limits of machine arithmetic.

parameter   An identifier serving to transmit information to or from a function or procedure. See *formal parameter* and *actual parameter*.

parse   To analyze the syntax of an expression in some language.

partial evaluation   A method of evaluating logical expressions that evaluates only those subexpressions that affect the final value.

pointer   A reference to dynamic data.

precedence   The order of evaluation of operators in an expression.

precision   The exactness of a representation for real numbers.

procedure   A subprogram that carries out specified actions, but does not produce a single value as its result.

program   A set of instructions for a computer.

pseudocode   An informal mixture of English and a programming language used to describe an algorithm or the design of a program.

quadratic time   A growth rate for the time required by an algorithm that increases in direct proportion to the square of the size of a problem.

queue   An abstract data type that maintains a list by adding new entries to the end of the list and removing old entries from the beginning.

random access   The ability to access items in a file or another data structure directly, as opposed to sequentially.

random number   A member of a uniformly distributed, patternless sequence of numbers.

recursion   A programming technique that allows subprograms to invoke themselves.

scope   The extent to which an identifier has an existence and an identity in a computer program.

searching   The process of finding a specified item in a data structure such as a list.

secondary storage   A storage medium in a computer with a higher capacity, but slower speed of access, than primary memory. See *disk*.

sequential access   A method of accessing data in a list or file that requires items to be accessed in sequence, starting at the beginning of the list or file.

set   A collection of objects.

side effect   A change in the value of a global variable caused by the action of a subprogram.

software   A collection of computer programs that enable a computer system to perform useful work; more generally, a synonym for *program*.

sorting   The process of arranging a list in order.

specification   A precise statement of the actions to be performed by a program.

stack   An abstract data type that maintains a list by adding and removing items at a single end of the list; also, the data structure used by most computer systems to handle invocations of procedures and functions.

static data structure   A data structure with a fixed size.

string   A sequence of characters.

subprogram   A procedure or function defined within a program.

subscript   An index used to access an item in an array.

syntax   The grammatical rules of a natural or programming language.

testing   The act of determining whether a program meets its specifications by executing that program.

token   A sequence of characters treated as a single symbol; for example, an identifier or operator in a program, or a word or punctuation mark in an English text.

top-down   A method that approaches a complex task by breaking it down into simpler tasks.

tree   A data structure used to represent hierarchical relationships or collections of information. Each item in a tree, other than the *root*, has a unique *parent*, and all items can trace their lineage back to the root of the tree.

type   See *data type*.

underflow   An execution error that arises when a computation produces a nonzero value that is too close to zero to represent within the limits of machine arithmetic.

value parameter   A formal parameter that receives a value from an actual parameter when a subprogram is invoked, but which is local to that subprogram and does not change the value of the actual parameter when the subprogram terminates.

variable   An identifier denoting a value that can change during the execution of a program.

variable parameter   A formal parameter, designated by the keyword **var** in Pascal, that serves as a synonym for an actual parameter when a subprogram is invoked. Changes in the value of a variable parameter result in changes in the value of the corresponding actual parameter.

verification   The act of demonstrating that a program meets its specifications, for example, by testing or proving the program correct.

word   A unit of information in a computer system. A location in the memory of a computer system.

worst case   The circumstances that cause an algorithm or program to consume the greatest amount of a resource such as time or space.

INDEX